E-Learning Methodologies and Computer Applications in Archaeology

Dionysios Politis
Aristotle University, Greece

Information Science REFERENCE

INFORMATION SCIENCE REFERENCE

Hershey · New York

Acquisitions Editor: Kristin Klinger
Development Editor: Kristin Roth
Senior Managing Editor: Jennifer Neidig
Managing Editor: Jamie Snavely
Assistant Managing Editor: Carole Coulson
Copy Editor: Lanette Ehrhardt
Typesetter: Sean Woznicki
Cover Design: Lisa Tosheff
Printed at: Yurchak Printing Inc.

Published in the United States of America by
Information Science Reference (an imprint of IGI Global)
701 E. Chocolate Avenue, Suite 200
Hershey PA 17033
Tel: 717-533-8845
Fax: 717-533-8661
E-mail: cust@igi-global.com
Web site: http://www.igi-global.com

and in the United Kingdom by
Information Science Reference (an imprint of IGI Global)
3 Henrietta Street
Covent Garden
London WC2E 8LU
Tel: 44 20 7240 0856
Fax: 44 20 7379 0609
Web site: http://www.eurospanonline.com

Library of Congress Cataloging-in-Publication Data

Politis, Dionysios.

E-learning methodologies and computer applications in archaeology / Dionysios Politis, editor.
p. cm.

Summary: "This book presents innovative instructional approaches for archaeological e-learning based on networked technologies, providing researchers, scholars, and professionals a comprehensive global perspective on the resources, development, application, and implications of information communication technology in multimedia-based educational products and services in archaeology"--Provided by publisher.

Includes bibliographical references and index.
ISBN-13: 978-1-59904-759-1 (hardcover)
ISBN-13: 978-1-59904-761-4 (e-book)

1. Archaeology--Computer network resources. 2. Archaeology--Computer-assisted instruction. 3. Archaeology--Information technology. 4. Archaeology--Study and teaching. 5. Internet in education. 6. Virtual reality in education 7. Multimedia systems. 8. Virtual computer systems. I. Title.

CC82.9.P65 2008
930.1'0285--dc22

2007037721

British Cataloguing in Publication Data
A Cataloguing in Publication record for this book is available from the British Library.

To Alexia, Cleopatra, Basil, Anastasia, Georgia and George.

Table of Contents

Foreword xiv

Preface xvi

Acknowledgment xxii

Section I
E-Learning Technologies, Strategies, and Methodologies

Chapter I
Educational Technologies and the Emergence of E-Learning 2.0 1
Panagiotis D. Siozos, Aristotle University of Thessaloniki, Greece
George E. Palaigeorgiou, Aristotle University of Thessaloniki, Greece

Chapter II
Basic Aspects of VLEs and Guidelines for Supporting Learning Communities
and E-Collaboration 18
Thrasyvoulos Tsiatsos, Aristotle University of Thessaloniki, Greece
Eleftheria Giannaka, University of Patras, Greece

Chapter III
Open and Distance Learning Tools and Strategies 34
Cristina Girona, Universitat Oberta de Catalunya, Spain

Chapter IV
Teaching and Learning in Virtual Environments 48
Joan Campas, Universitat Oberta de Catalunya, Spain

Chapter V
Evaluation Models for E-Learning: Experiences in Teaching Archaeology 64
Cèsar Carreras, Universitat Oberta de Catalunya, Spain

Section II
Spatial-Computational Technologies and Virtual Reality Reconstructions in Archaeology

Chapter VI
From Observation to Interpretation 79
Cynthia Jaulneau, Archaeologist, France

Chapter VII
Databases for Multiple Archaeological Excavations and Internet Applications 104
Athanasios Karamalis, Computer Scientist and Researcher, Germany

Chapter VIII
Geographical Information Systems (GIS) and Learning Applications in Archaeology 128
Dimitrios Margounakis, Computer Scientist and Researcher, Greece

Chapter IX
Virtual Reconstructions in Archaeology 146
Dimitrios Margounakis, Computer Scientist and Researcher, Greece

Chapter X
The Use of Virtual Museums, Simulations, and Recreations as Educational Tools 157
Dionysios Politis, Aristotle University of Thessaloniki, Greece
Ioannis Marras, Aristotle University of Thessaloniki, Greece

Chapter XI
Social Modeler: The Use of Expert Systems in Archaeology 199
Panagiotis Linardis, Aristotle University of Thessaloniki, Greece

Chapter XII
Machine Translation Systems 211
Athanasios Tryferidis, Electrical and Computer Engineer, MLS SA, Greece
Theofanis Korlos, Aristotle Univerity of Thessaloniki, Greece

Section III
Electronic Publishing and Copyright Protection over Archaeological Computer Networks

Chapter XIII
Legal Issues of Electronic Publishing in Virtual Environments 221
Ioannis Iglezakis, Aristotle University of Thessaloniki, Greece

Chapter XIV
Drama-Merdžumekja: A Southeast Bulgarian Monument of the European Culture Heritage and Its Publication 229
Rudolf Echt, University of Saarland, Germany

Chapter XV
Posting Articles about Excavations in Electronic Forums 254
Charilaos Thomos, Computer Scientist and Researcher, Greece
Alexandros Gouniotis, Computer Scientist and Researcher, Greece
Konstantinos Kechagias, School of Second Chance, Greece

Section IV
Selected Readings

Chapter XVI
Communication Barriers and Conflicts in Cross-Cultural E-Learning 276
Rita Zaltsman, International Center of Modern Education - Prague, Czech Republic

Chapter XVII
Multimedia, Cognitive Load and Pedagogy 289
Peter E. Doolittle, Virginia Polytechnic Institute & State University, USA
Andrea L. McNeill, Virginia Polytechnic Institute & State University, USA
Krista P. Terry, Radford University, USA
Stephanie B. Scheer, University of Virginia, USA

Chapter XVIII
Knowledge Through Evolution 311
Russell Beale, University of Birmingham, UK
Andy Pryke, University of Birmingham, UK

Chapter XIX
Collaborative Geographic Information Systems: Origins, Boundaries, and Structures 325
Shivanand Balram, Simon Fraser University, Canada
Suzana Dragicevic, Simon Fraser University, Canada

Chapter XX
Towards an Ontology for Information Systems Development: A Contextual Approach 342
Mauri Leppänen, University of Jyväskylä, Finland

Chapter XXI
Personalization Issues for Science Museum Web Sites and E-Learning 371
Silvia Filippini-Fantoni, The University of Paris I Sorbonne University, France
Jonathan P. Bowen, London South Bank University, UK
Teresa Numerico, London South Bank University, UK

Chapter XXII
A Virtual Museum Where Students can Learn 388
Nicoletta Di Blas, Politecnico di Milano, Italy
Paolo Paolini, Politecnico di Milano, Italy
Caterina Poggi, Politecnico di Milano, Italy

Chapter XXIII
Enhancing Learning Through 3-D Virtual Environments 407
Erik Champion, School of ITEE, University of Queensland, Australia

Compilation of References 423

About the Contributors 459

Index 463

Detailed Table of Contents

Foreword xiv

Preface xvi

Acknowledgment xxii

Section I
E-Learning Technologies, Strategies, and Methodologies

Chapter I
Educational Technologies and the Emergence of E-Learning 2.0 1
Panagiotis D. Siozos, Aristotle University of Thessaloniki, Greece
George E. Palaigeorgiou, Aristotle University of Thessaloniki, Greece

Addressing the learner of the 21st century, this chapter explains how learning and relearning implement a widespread culture of life-long education. The new teaching model is presented, which, enhanced by state-of-the art technological achievements, reshapes the way users may access and use content. Mobile computational devices, smart learning environments and other utilities facilitate the creation and sharing of digital resources within the Internet community, leading the way to a new version of e-learning, e-learning 2.0.

Chapter II
Basic Aspects of VLEs and Guidelines for Supporting Learning Communities
and E-Collaboration 18
Thrasyvoulos Tsiatsos, Aristotle University of Thessaloniki, Greece
Eleftheria Giannaka, University of Patras, Greece

The design principles for virtual spaces focused on e-learning and e-collaboration are presented in this chapter. Technologies like virtual reality (VR), 2D or 3D-centered multiuser tools, and microscopic or macroscopic visualization, offer high levels of interaction along with a sense of immersion. Accordingly, virtual learning environments (VLEs) are designed, enhancing the student's learning experience.

Chapter III
Open and Distance Learning Tools and Strategies 34
Cristina Girona, Universitat Oberta de Catalunya, Spain

The role of information and communication technologies (ICTs) and their impact on open and distance learning (ODL) are encountered in this chapter. The learning process, the instructional design, the use of study plans, the design and editing process of multimedia learning materials and resources, and author and teacher training, are some of the processes influenced by the new educational paradigm emerging with e-learning.

Chapter IV
Teaching and Learning in Virtual Environments 48
Joan Campas, Universitat Oberta de Catalunya, Spainn

The establishment of Virtual Learning Communities alters the way instruction is offered. Education, knowledge work, metacognitive skills, and learning are offered via hypertext-hypermedia, telematics, and rich multimedia content. Ideas that may alter traditional formation are presented, aiming to reinvent education and learning offered in a Web page-based environment.

Chapter V
Evaluation Models for E-Learning: Experiences in Teaching Archaeology 64
Cèsar Carreras, Universitat Oberta de Catalunya, Spain

Evaluation methods and techniques are vital elements of the e-learning process. By evaluating the learning processes, the teaching materials and the learning, along with the students' reactions and performance, we may form an image of how successful the pedagogic model and the methodologies we have used are.

Section II
Spatial-Computational Technologies and Virtual Reality Reconstructions in Archaeology

Chapter VI
From Observation to Interpretation 79
Cynthia Jaulneau, Archaeologist, France

This chapter presents the ontologies and the domain specific vocabulary used for knowledge representation and reasoning in archaeology. Taking into account a specific archaeological site, it explains how the retrieval of ground data leads by proper analysis and reconstitution to a meaningful interpretation.

Chapter VII
Databases for Multiple Archaeological Excavations and Internet Applications 104
Athanasios Karamalis, Computer Scientist and Researcher, Germany

The problems when handling multiple archaeological excavations using one database are presented in this chapter. The design, realization, and the linking with Internet applications is examined along with the challenges for using the database interface for visualizations and other complex applications, like expert tools and geographical information systems.

Chapter VIII
Geographical Information Systems (GIS) and Learning Applications in Archaeology 128
Dimitrios Margounakis, Computer Scientist and Researcher, Greece

The rapidly growing technological field that incorporates graphical features with tabular data in order to assess real-world problems is presented in this chapter. Geographical information systems have the capacity to integrate spatial information with higher end statistical and analytical processes, transforming the simplicity of a single map to the interactivity of GIS information, linking spatial with descriptive data.

Chapter IX
Virtual Reconstructions in Archaeology 146
Dimitrios Margounakis, Computer Scientist and Researcher, Greece

Methods and techniques for archaeological reconstructions are presented in this chapter. By explaining what virtual reality (VR) is and its potential for reconstructions, an introduction to the techniques that may present artifacts in high-level graphics systems with photorealism is attempted.

Chapter X
The Use of Virtual Museums, Simulations, and Recreations as Educational Tools 157
Dionysios Politis, Aristotle University of Thessaloniki, Greece
Ioannis Marras, Aristotle University of Thessaloniki, Greece

This chapter describes in depth two vertical applications that demonstrate the simulation fidelity of computer-made virtual worlds. The first application is a dynamic virtual museum that can be used for cognitive walkthroughs, while the second application is comprised of virtual environments that reproduce ancient greek music. Both applications have a clear pedagogical dimension.

Chapter XI
Social Modeler: The Use of Expert Systems in Archaeology 199
Panagiotis Linardis, Aristotle University of Thessaloniki, Greece

This chapter links computational intelligence, expert systems and archaeology. A rule-based system is presented, using a relatively simple model that can be adapted to solving a number of problems in archeology linked with social scenarios.

Chapter XII
Machine Translation Systems 211
Athanasios Tryferidis, Electrical and Computer Engineer, MLS SA, Greece
Theofanis Korlos, Aristotle Univerity of Thessaloniki, Greece

Machine translation (MT) is a subfield of computational linguistics that investigates the use of computer software to translate text or speech from one natural language to another. MT is changing and broadening its scope of interest to encompass all branches of computational linguistics and language engineering. For archaeology, MT is performed as a simple substitution of atomic words in one natural language for words in another. Using corpus techniques, specific dictionaries for use in Archaeology can be made, promoting better handling of differences in linguistic typology.

Section III
Electronic Publishing and Copyright Protection over Archaeological Computer Networks

Chapter XIII
Legal Issues of Electronic Publishing in Virtual Environments 221
Ioannis Iglezakis, Aristotle University of Thessaloniki, Greece

Electronic publishing is a new concept, aiming at replacing traditional publishing media and making available the electronic delivery of digital content. However, authors are sceptical about the copyright protection of their intellectual property. This chapter gives insight on how protection may be given to authors by the grant of exclusive rights. The same time it points out the loopholes of protection as well as the limitations that exclusive right may have.

Chapter XIV
Drama-Merdžumekja: A Southeast Bulgarian Monument of the European Culture Heritage
and Its Publication 229
Rudolf Echt, University of Saarland, Germany

Twenty years of excavation at Drama-Merdžumekja are concisely presented in this chapter. This article briefly reviews the exercise of electronic publishing in archaeology and introduces some major attempts for its development. By examining the challenges and opportunities for the digital presentation of the archaeological procedures and excavation findings, the article attempts to pinpoint potential directions of development.

Chapter XV
Posting Articles about Excavations in Electronic Forums 254
Charilaos Thomos, Computer Scientist and Researcher, Greece
Alexandros Gouniotis, Computer Scientist and Researcher, Greece
Konstantinos Kechagias, School of Second Chance, Greece

This chapter presents methods that promote the sustainability of electronic publishing in archaeology. Electronic publications are not merely an alternative that allows some savings because we do not require the physical distribution and reproduction of printouts; they are a pertinent way to promote articles on archaeology to vast audiences that use the Internet as their primary communication medium.

Section IV
Selected Readings

Chapter XVI
Communication Barriers and Conflicts in Cross-Cultural E-Learning 276
Rita Zaltsman, International Center of Modern Education - Prague, Czech Republic

A chapter devoted to the globalization of e-learning cultural changes. Important for archeological studies where different languages and cognitive styles are still used.

Chapter XVII
Multimedia, Cognitive Load and Pedagogy 289
Peter E. Doolittle, Virginia Polytechnic Institute & State University, USA
Andrea L. McNeill, Virginia Polytechnic Institute & State University, USA
Krista P. Terry, Radford University, USA
Stephanie B. Scheer, University of Virginia, USA

The role of interactive multimedia in education and training is examined.

Chapter XVIII
Knowledge Through Evolution 311
Russell Beale, University of Birmingham, UK
Andy Pryke, University of Birmingham, UK

The advances in applied artificial intelligence and their prospect for archaeological implementations are presented in this chapter.

Chapter XIX
Collaborative Geographic Information Systems: Origins, Boundaries, and Structures 325
Shivanand Balram, Simon Fraser University, Canada
Suzana Dragicevic, Simon Fraser University, Canada

A further insight on geographical information systems, as a supplement to chapter 8, promoting the idea of collaborative work.

Chapter XX
Towards an Ontology for Information Systems Development: A Contextual Approach 342
Mauri Leppänen, University of Jyväskylä, Finland

The role of databases in archaeology is revisited in this chapter. Contemporary issues in database design and the development of information systems (IS) are concisely presented.

Chapter XXI
Personalization Issues for Science Museum Web Sites and E-Learning 371
Silvia Filippini-Fantoni, The University of Paris I Sorbonne University, France
Jonathan P. Bowen, London South Bank University, UK
Teresa Numerico, London South Bank University, UK

In this chapter, e-learning is linked with the visualization sciences and techniques.

Chapter XXII
A Virtual Museum Where Students can Learn 388
Nicoletta Di Blas, Politecnico di Milano, Italy
Paolo Paolini, Politecnico di Milano, Italy
Caterina Poggi, Politecnico di Milano, Italy

The role of a virtual museum as a learning tool is examined in this chapter. Emphasis is given on the new experiences that technological innovation offers over traditional learning techniques and methodologies.

Chapter XXIII
Enhancing Learning Through 3-D Virtual Environments 407
Erik Champion, School of ITEE, University of Queensland, Australia

This chapter examines the new experiences that 3D learning environments may offer to students, learners and the general public in general.

Compilation of References 423

About the Contributors 459

Index 463

Foreword

Using the opportunity given under the SOCRATES-MINERVA EU funded project "SEEArchWeb - South Eastern Europe Archaeology Web: An Interactive Web-based Presentation of Southeastern European Archaeology," managed by the multimedia lab, Department of Informatics, Aristotle University of Thessaloniki, a consortium of prestigious European institutes focused on the implementation of state-of-the art e-learning strategies for the subject domain of archaeology.

The last few decades have witnessed the rapid growth and development of information and communication technology (ICT). Due to the application of the new technologies in learning and teaching, e-learning has emerged as a highly effective teaching tool. E-learning is not simply about transfer of know-how to a particular field of studies, such as archaeology. It is about enhancing the teaching-learning process, and therefore requires an in-depth understanding of it.

Archaeology is a multifaceted discipline. Its learning curriculum encompasses a wide range of subject/period themes and methodological and theoretical approaches, as well as practical experience in the field. A map of core competencies is needed to transform these perspectives into a well-geared carrier of instructional events using educational technology. These include, among others, the usage of virtual reality environments, databases acting as excavation repositories, geographical information systems, and animated reconstructions.

How can an archaeologist use these diverse tools in a constructive manner? How can an instructor in archaeology use integrated packages that deliver teaching without becoming a computer scientist? How can a junior archaeologist take advantage of computer-based training and alter his cognitive paradigm? All these and other relevant issues are addressed in the chapters that follow, with the aim of enhancing the existing learning styles.

The motivation for preparing this concise handbook with introductory and interrelated subjects was given by the 1st SEEArchWeb Conference, "*E-learning and Computer Applications in Archaeology,*" that was organised in Thessaloniki on September 29-30, 2006. The new ideas presented in the conference appear in this collective volume, an opus from the SEEArchWeb experience.

I offer my congratulations to the scholars involved in this consortium, and I hope that this is only the beginning of a fruitful scientific process that will promote the practice and the teaching of archaeology.

Professor Ioannis A. Tsoukalas
Secretary General for Research and Technology
Ministry of Development, Greece

Ioannis Tsoukalas *is currently the secretary general for research and technology of the Greek government. He was born in Thessaloniki in 1941. He has studied physics in the Aristotle University of Thessaloniki. He has received his PhD in solid state physics from the same university. He has committed post graduate studies in the UK (Liverpool University), Germany (Braunschweig Polytechnic University), France (Grenoble) and USA (MIT). He has published more than 100 papers and articles in books, highly ranked journals, newspapers and international conferences. He has lectured in various universities as visiting professor (England, France, Germany, USA, and Japan), and was head of the Department of Physics (1984-1989) and of the Department of Informatics (1990-1997). He has directed or participated as a member in various committees, boards and research projects, which include, among others, the EU funded project VALUE (1990-1993), "Information Society SA" (2001-2004), the Data Protection Authority in Greece (2003-2004), and the Senate of the Aristotle University in Thessaloniki (1984-1997, 2003-2004). He has served as first coordinator of the EU funded multinational project "SEEArchWeb – South Eastern Europe Archaeology Web" (2003-2004).*

Preface

TEACHING, LEARNING AND RELEARNING WITH TECHNOLOGY IN ARCHAEOLOGY

One of the most obvious events of the last decade has been the explosion of the World Wide Web and its effect on learning with multimedia. In parallel, this decade has witnessed a fundamental shift on paradigms for learning and instruction that have altered our learning culture and learning styles. Learners are not passive beings, waiting to be taught basic skills by adults; these skills, rather, emerge as a function of adaptation to the real world (either present or past), where they pick up the ability to communicate with peers and solve problems. As such, learners gradually become natural speakers, scientists, writers, and problem solvers, utilising information that is offered via various technological means.

Therefore, within the context of the current technological status-quo, e-learning methodologies and techniques have been developed. E-learning is a very promising way of delivering training and is broadly used in tertiary education. In this introductory chapter, the benefits that e-learning offers over traditional methods of education are concisely presented, and its imperative for archaeology is rationalized. For this reason, special focus is given on the progress of information and communication technology (ICT) in shaping our information society, and on the degree to which e-learning has been incorporated in the citizens' everyday routines.

The rapid growth of ICT over the last few decades has opened up new possibilities for governments and individuals. Governments are increasingly using Wide Area Networks, the Internet, and mobile computing in their daily interactions with citizens and businesses. E-government applications are improving interactions with businesses by centralizing information sources into topical gateways, using Web-based expert tools to help businesses access rules and regulations, and developing applications to allow electronic tax filings. For citizens, they are attempting to make transactions, such as renewing licenses and certifications, paying taxes, and applying for benefits, less time consuming and easier to carry out.

Apart from government services, ICT has been also utilized in other sectors such as health, commerce, and of course, education. The increased use of ICT has actually been the motivation force for e-learning. By its name, e-learning can be understood as any type of learning delivered electronically. Clark and Mayer (2002) define e-learning as training delivered on a computer (including CD-ROM, Internet, or Intranet) that is designed to support individual learning or organizational performance goals.

E-learning can be synchronous or asynchronous, depending on the extent to which it is bound by place or time. E-learning is synchronous when two or more events occur at the same time. For example, when attending live training simulating a class or a workshop, e-learning is synchronous, because the event and the learning occur at the same time. In the opposite case, learning is asynchronous, for example when attending an online course and completing events at different times (Codone, 2001).

There are a number of other terms also used to describe this mode of teaching and learning, such as online learning, virtual learning, network, and Web-based learning. They all refer to educational processes that utilize ICTs to mediate asynchronous, as well as synchronous learning and teaching activities. However, e-learning comprises a lot more than any of these terms. As the letter "e" in e-learning stands for the word "electronic," e-learning would incorporate all educational activities that are carried out by individuals or groups working online or off-line, and synchronously or asynchronously via networked or standalone computers and other electronic devices (Naidu, 2005).

E-LEARNING AND EFFECTIVE TECHNOLOGY INTEGRATION

E-learning, among others, is a tool for expanding and widening access to tertiary education. A key attribute of ICT is its ability to enable flexible access to information and resources. Flexible access refers to access and use of information and resources at a time, place, and pace that are suitable and convenient to individual learners rather than the teacher or the educational organization. Using ICTs, e-learning allows more people to participate in tertiary education: working students and adults, people living in remote areas, nonmobile students, and even foreign students can now access education. In a few words, e-learning has the ability to provide information to anyone, anytime, anywhere (Roblyer, 2003).

E-learning also promises to improve the quality of tertiary education and the effectiveness of learning. Due to the use of ICTs, e-learning gives easier and almost instant access to data and information in a digital form that allows manipulations that are sometimes not possible otherwise. E-learning can lead to innovative pedagogic methods, and new ways of learning and interacting, because of the easy sharing of these new practices among learners and teachers, as well as by easier comparisons between teaching materials and methods. E-learning can also be seen as a promising way to reduce the cost of tertiary education, which is critical for expanding and widening its access worldwide.

E-learning in its nature is rather autonomous, allowing learners to select the topics they want, control the pace at which they progress, and decide whether to bypass some lesson elements such as examples or practice exercises. The opposite takes place in traditional education, where the learning process is highly dependent on the reactions of the student-instructor relationship. Although more reliable, in turmoil the classic way of studying may lead to abrupt, chaotic and misleading professionally trajectories.

Figure 1. Differences between learning in the 20th and 21st century

Learning in the 20th century (Instructor oriented)	Learning in the 21st century (Student/group oriented)
Lecture	Support for autonomous learning
Autonomous learning and self-study	Group oriented learning
Taking classes / attending lectures	Collaborative study
Information transmission	Strengthening the learning potential
Instructor = hub of information	Instructor has a supportive role
Static content	Dynamic content
Homogeneity of learning sources	Variety of learning sources
Tests and exams	Applications and upgraded task performance

In Figure 1, the differences between learning in the 20th century (instructor-oriented) and learning in the 21st century (student/group-oriented) are presented, as encoded by Chute, Thompson, and Hancock (1999).

Depending on the use of ICTs and the level of reform, learning can be separated in four categories, as shown in Figure 2. Successful e-learning requires both the use of ICT and reform. Therefore, successful e-learning does not imply merely that the tools of the trade have to be used; it also means the Web-based training provider should analyze needs and carefully select the delivery methods (Driscoll, 2002).

THE RANGE OF E-LEARNING IMPLEMENTATION IN THE KNOWLEDGE SOCIETY

The growing interest for e-learning seems to be coming from several directions. Organizations that have traditionally offered distance education programs see the incorporation of online learning in their repertoire as a logical extension of their distance education activities. The corporate sector, on the other hand, is interested in e-learning as a way of rationalizing the costs of their in-house staff training activities. For instance, multinational companies need to train their employees in new technologies. E-learning is of interest to residential campus-based educational organizations that see e-learning as a way of improving access to their programs. More rigorously, educational institutions see advantages in making their programs accessible via a range of distributed locations, including on campus, home, and other community learning or resource centers.

The increasing significance of ICTs has become a factor defining contemporary influence. We are experiencing a transformation in the nature of economic activity, with associated implications for the shape of society.

The generation and exploitation of knowledge is now the predominant factor in the creation of wealth. Knowledge has always been a factor of production, and a driver of economic and social development. However, technology-related developments have fundamentally transformed the degree to which knowledge is being integrated into economic activity, to the extent that we are witnessing a shift in the very basis of competitive advantage. Unlike capital and labour, information and knowledge have many of the characteristics of what economists call public goods. Once discovered and made public, knowledge

Figure 2. Types of learning depending on the level of reform and the use of ICTs

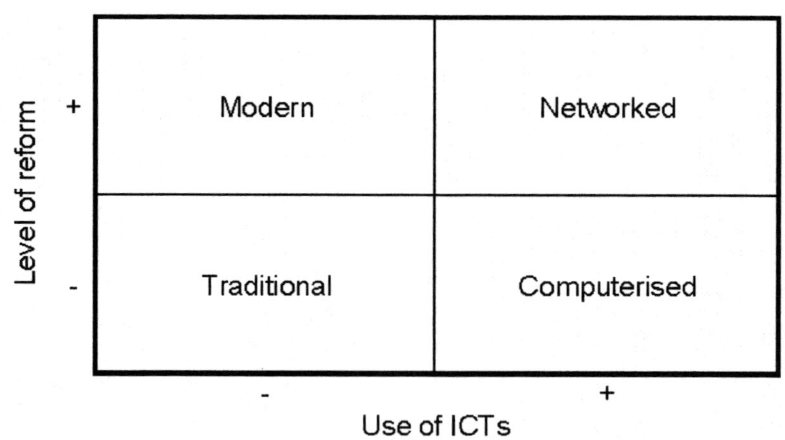

can be shared at zero marginal cost and its value is not depleted in consumption: it is nonrival. Indeed, the economic and social value of information and knowledge actually increases as it is shared with and used by others (Means, Haertel, & Moses, 2003).

The next society, the one that will succeed the current information society, will be a knowledge society. Knowledge will be its key resource, and knowledge workers will be the dominant group in its workforce. There will be an increased demand for a well-educated and skilled workforce across the whole economy. As access to information becomes easier and less expensive, it becomes more crucial that we have the skills and competencies relating to the selection and use of that information. There is a clear imperative for continuous education and training, and the establishment of incentives for firms and individuals to make the critical adjustment to a culture of lifelong learning. Workers at all levels in the 21st century knowledge society will need to be lifelong learners, adapting continuously to changed opportunities, work practices, business models and forms of economic and social organization. E-learning can offer lifelong, better, faster, and less expensive education for citizens and organizations.

A special interest group of e-learning is the one that enhances relearning. Because many competencies of the working force are technology-related, it is obvious that scientists need to revamp their outpaced knowledge base and potential. This is especially true in Archaeology. That archaeologists "collect data" and "feed them into a computer" are almost taken as givens within everyday conversation (Lock, 2003). However, the use of computer technology is not deteriorated to creating archaeological data repositories and warehouses. A new scientific field has emerged referred to as computer applications in archaeology (CAA).

Computer Applications in Archaeology, using as updated as possible ICTs, support archaeologists in managing, presenting, and utilizing the results of their work with the help of new technology. With such tools, observations from practical work are transformed to virtual reality (VR) reconstructions in such a photorealistic manner that sometimes it is hard to say where reality ends and virtual dreams begin. Clearly, with CAA the procedures of modeling the past perform a cognitive walk in new dimensions.

Amid this canopy studio, the e-learning potential in Archaeology emerges, promoting the increase and the dissemination of archaeological knowledge. Also, it becomes manifested as a cross domain activity, disseminating learning or relearning about technological factors that have changed significantly within the recent years. For example, it is rather unlikely for mid-aged archaeologist to be proficient on encoding mark-up languages like VRML or handling geographical information systems (GIS) for the very simple reason that these technologies were practically nonexistent some 10-15 years ago, when he was studying archaeology. Therefore, e-learning in archaeology does not involve only knowledge dissemination using ICTs for the subject domain only, but also computer aided instruction about the new technologies in focus.

ORGANIZATION OF THE BOOK

This book is organized in 23 chapters clustered in four sections. The last section is comprised of eight chapters, coming from IGI's InfoSci-Online database; these are selected readings, already published, that enhance and promote understanding for the amalgam of computers applications in archaeology and e-learning tools. A brief description of each of the 23 chapters follows:

Section I, titled "E-learning Technologies, Strategies and Methodologies," is comprised of four chapters.

Chapter I describes the impact of technology on education, providing definitions on what e-learning is about, and mostly, what e-learning is *not* about, separating facts from speculation and the likely from the unlikely. Also, it describes how e-learning has evolved along with the World Wide Web and its changing to a degree significant enough to warrant the recent neologism "E-learning 2.0."

Chapter II digs in the computer aspects of virtual worlds used for e-learning. It explains how a computer system can generate a 3-D virtual environment, with which the user can interact and receive real time feedback. Then it describes what virtual learning environments (VLEs) are, and explains how enhanced educational functionality can be achieved when the learner uses virtual worlds.

Chapter III expands the e-learning paradigm from a mere immersion to a virtual reality system to a complete open and distance learning (ODL) strategy. It also explains the format of the multimedia materials and the structure of teaching when instruction is delivered within a VLE.

Chapter IV continues even further, explaining how virtual learning communities may be created when education and learning are offered through a Web site. It also explains how cognitive walkthrough may be achieved by using elements and features of online education.

The concluding chapter for section I, **Chapter V**, it illuminates the process of evaluating e-learning outcomes. Evaluation is conducted on the pedagogic paradigm, on the learning process and on the teaching materials and learning tools. Some case studies present in practice how evaluation should be conducted.

Section II, titled "Spatial-Computational Technologies and Virtual Reality Reconstructions in Archaeology," describes spearhead technologies that form the main context of CAA.

Chapter VI is the link between traditional archaeology and CAA. It deciphers how from observation we may have a fruitful interpretation of archaeological data that lead the way for computer animated reconstructions.

Chapter VII describes how archaeological data, coming from multiple excavations, can be stored in a relational database management system and accessed via the Internet.

Chapter VIII is a primer to geographical information systems. Adopting a user-oriented approach (rather than a programmer's approach) it describes how geographic data and elements, like spatial queries, may be used within an e-learning context.

Chapter IX presents the rapid evolution of virtual reality technologies and expands the digitization process of archaeological data to reconstruction techniques and methodologies using high level deductive reasoning.

In **Chapter X**, two vertical applications are analyzed in depth. They refer to simulations and virtual reality reconstructions, using high-level programming tools. The first focuses on the emerging sector of on-the-fly creation of virtual museums, mining data from linked archaeological databases. The second is an avant-garde application is presented conveying the acoustic reproduction of ancient Greek singing in a parameterized composing environment.

Chapter XI describes the implementation of an expert system's architecture on predicates of archaeological content. By using a network of rules, associated with a confidence factor that is derived from the interpretation of archaeological data, the system may deduce some propositions that perform a modeling of archaeological excavations in terms of "social"-like predicates.

Chapter XII demonstrates the tools that help us cope with the inherent multilingualism of archaeological publications. Namely, machine translation systems promote a subfiled of computational linguistics that helps translate the bulk volume of texts that are kept in archaeological repositories. Of course, the system does not have 100% success and post-processing human intervention is needed, but it is encouraging that archaeologists have started using and developing such tools, boosting their productivity.

Section III is titled "Electronic Publishing and Copyright Protection over Archaeological Computer Networks."

The first chapter in this section, **Chapter XIII**, gives concisely the legal framework within which authoring in virtual environments is protected. It does not go into an in depth analysis, because jurisdictional segregation implies that each county's legal system has its own rules and particularities.

Chapter XIV presents in a systematic manner the electronic publication of a monument of the European cultural heritage. Methods of electronic data processing that fit in for medium to long lasting excavations are presented so that archaeologists can take them into account.

The last chapter of this section, **Chapter XV**, is devoted to clarifying how *blogs* and *forums* may host electronic publications in a manner that copyright protection is safeguarded. Emphasis is given on how automated multilingualism may be sustained, using machine translation tools.

The last section, section IV, is titled "Selected Readings." It is virtually an annex for the cross-border concepts that have been presented in the first three sections. It aims to enhance the scientific background of those seeking more insight on the technological and pedagogical aspects of CAA.

More specific, **Chapter XVI** examines cross-cultural e-learning problems and conflicts. In **Chapter XVII**, the pedagogical impact of multimedia is presented. The next chapter, **Chapter XVIII**, digs into artificial intelligence (AI) evolutionary techniques that may be used within the context of CAA. **Chapter XIX** focuses on the collaborative aspects of GIS, while **Chapter XX** examines contemporary issues on database design and the development of information systems (IS). Finally, **Chapters XXI**, **XXII**, and **XXIII** are devoted to 3D visualizations and their profound learning dimension. The last two chapters especially emphasize the role of virtual museums in offering new learning experiences to the general public.

REFERENCES

Chute, A., Thompson, M.M., & Hancock, B.W. (1999). *Handbook of distance learning*. New York: McGraw-Hill.

Clark, R., & Mayer, R. (2002). *E-learning and the science of instruction: Proven guidelines for consumers and designers of multimedia learning*. San Francisco: Pfeifer.

Codone, S. (2001). An e-learning primer. Retrieved October 24, 2007, from http://faculty.mercer.edu/codone_s/elearningprimer.pdf

Driscoll, M. (2002). *Web-based training. Creating e-learning experiences.* San Francisco: Jossey-Bass/Pfeiffer.

Lock, G. (2003). *Using computers in archaeology – towards virtual pasts.* New York: Routlege.

Means, B., Haertel, G., & Moses, L. (2003). Evaluating the effects of learning technologies. In G. Haertel & B. Means (Eds.), *Evaluating educational technology.* New York: Teacher's College Press.

Naidu, S. (2005). *Learning and teaching with technology: Principles and practice*. New York: Routlege Falmer.

Roblyer, M.D. (2003). *Integrating educational technology into teaching.* New Jersey: Pearson Education.

Dionysios Politis
Thessaloniki, Greece
August 2007

Acknowledgment

This book would not be possible if I did not enjoy the entire support of the publisher, IGI Global. A chain of helpful consultants, whose last link was Ms. Jessica Thompson, walked with me the bumpy way of forming the unstructured incoming material of interrelated articles to a reasonable thematic concatenation. For the history of the book, the first link was Dr. Mehdi Khosrow-Pour, whose enthusiasm motivated me to initially accept his invitation for taking on this project.

In academic terms, the incentive and the know-how has been tapped from the EU funded SOCRATES-MINERVA project "SEEArchWeb-South Eastern Europe Archaeology Web," that has provided the knowledge pool on the e-learning dimension of computer applications in archaeology.

The first coordinator of this project, professor I.A. Tsoukalas, then head of the Department of Informatics, Aristotle University of Thessaloniki, and currently secretary general for research and technology in the Hellenic Ministry of Development, has kindly accepted to foreword this volume. I feel grateful for his willingness to support novelty.

Special thanks go to two world renowned archaeologists, professor emeritus of *Université Paris 1, Panthéon - Sorbonne* Marion Lichardus-Itten and professor Rudolf Echt of the *Universität des Saarlandes,* that have contributed in chapters 6 and 14 by projecting in the e-learning dimension their long expertise in supervising the excavation works of the Kovačevo and Drama-Merdžumekja sites, respectively, in Bulgaria.

Some of the authors of chapters included in this book also served as referees for articles written by other authors. I would like to express my gratitude to the pool of reviewers, who have helped in evaluating and homogenizing research outcomes originating from different authors and expressed in variant styles. They are:

- Thrasyvoulos Tsiatsos
- Cèsar Carreras
- Konstantinos Kechagias
- Panagiotis Linardis

Last, but not least, I would like to thank all the contributors of this book, who have lined up in transferring further knowledge on how e-learning methodologies could benefit and reshape the subject domain of archaeology.

In closing, I wish to express my deep appreciation to my wife and children, to whom this book is devoted to, for providing me the needed inspirational resources to balance my career and family trajectories.

Dionysios Politis
Thessaloniki, Greece
August 2007

Section I
E-Learning Technologies, Strategies and Methodologies

Chapter I
Educational Technologies and the Emergence of E-Learning 2.0

Panagiotis D. Siozos
Aristotle University of Thessaloniki, Greece

George E. Palaigeorgiou
Aristotle University of Thessaloniki, Greece

INTRODUCTION

The creative and productive incorporation of new technologies across all frames and levels of education constitutes a promising frontier; however, up to now, it has not fulfilled the initial high expectations. Although corporate training and informal learning have, to a certain degree, utilized those technologies, the progress achieved in the field of formal education is clearly less evident: a teacher of the beginning of the previous century would have found his way around a modern classroom rather easily. There are two major reasons for this lag. The first reason is that social institutions (educational, political, etc.) do not always possess the necessary flexibility to adapt to the rapid rhythms of digital cosmogony. The second reason is that, in most cases, technologies were thought of as tools solving problems of quantity ("faster, cheaper, more," etc.), not of quality. More often than not, technological innovations take researchers, educational specialists and teachers by surprise.

A range of novel, much promising, information and communication technologies (ICTs) emerge and transform the current landscape of e-learning. Though long established as part of everyday life, the personal computer now sheds its familiar cloak (PC box-monitor-keyboard) and is introduced to our direct environment in many new forms (personal digital assistants [PDAs], intelligent mobile telephones, multimedia devices, gaming machines), extremely usable software, the effect of Internet connectivity and the social trends arising on the World Wide Web (WWW) complete the picture.

In this chapter, we attempt a comprehensive presentation of how new technologies are brought into the realm of education and we explore the potential and implications of e-learning. We also present the latest technological developments that may transform the look, feel and nature of e-learning. Our major objective is to create fruitful reflection on how to achieve creative learning synergies between information technology and the humanities.

THE IMPACT OF TECHNOLOGY ON EDUCATION

One of the basic assumptions of a sociocultural approach on human learning is that "learning" actually means "learning to do something using cultural tools" (Såljo, 1999 as cited in Sutherland, 2004). The concept of "tool" includes a wide range of artefacts and semiotic systems - both material and symbolic or mental - that control the interactions of subjects with their environment. A "tool," in a wider sense, can even denote another subject supporting a human action.

Every human action is mediated by tools, while every historical period is determined as much by the available tools (artefacts), as by the ways they are used. Using a tool does not merely facilitate an action (which would be realised no matter what), but induces essential qualitative changes in the flow and structure of the action itself. Therefore, tools can either strengthen or deter an action. This characteristic of utilizing artefacts is of exceptional importance when it comes to exploring the role of technology in human learning.

However, the acceptance of a cultural tool is not always a linear process and should not be taken for granted. A characteristic example is found in the Platonic dialogue "Phaedrus" (Plato, 1986), where Socrates is presented as one of the first critics of new media and technologies, expressing his scepticism about the usefulness of the "new technology" of writing and the effect it would have on human learning abilities. Socrates recounts a parable about how god Theuth presents to the king of Egypt, Thamus, his last inventions, such as arithmetic, geometry, astronomy and writing, and asks to be given to all Egyptians. Writing, in particular, Theuth argues, would "make the Egyptians wiser and improve their memory." Yet, the king appears sceptical; he believes that the inventor is not always the most suitable person to judge his creation and that writing might also have negative repercussions (Plato, 1986):

> *For your invention will produce forgetfulness in the souls of those who have learned it, through lack of practice at using their memory, as through reliance on writing they are reminded from outside by alien marks, not from inside, themselves by themselves: you have discovered an elixir not of memory but of reminding. To your students, you give an appearance of wisdom, not the reality of it; having heard much, in the absence of teaching, they will appear to know much when for the most part they know nothing, and they will be difficult to get along with, because they have acquired the appearance of wisdom instead of wisdom itself.* (p. 123)

Further down the dialogue, Socrates recognizes certain advantages of writing (for writing down and recording poetry or laws), but insists that it does not necessarily constitute a suitable mean for teaching, due to its stability: the written text is fixed and tells the same story to all of its readers. According to Socrates, the most suitable path to learning comes through interactive and dynamic dialogue, as his "Maieutics" teaching method asserts (Klass, 2000). The fact that Socrates' opinion survived via the writings of Plato is certainly paradoxical, but it should not cancel the meaning of this parable. Similar arguments regarding the forgetfulness which the computers and the Internet would bring upon people are rather frequent.

Information and communication technologies constitute very powerful cultural tools and have much transformative potential. From a learning point of view, we may claim that, following language and writing, the computer is the third most important cultural tool. The use of computer and other information and communication technologies for facilitating teaching and learning gave rise to the field of e-learning and birth to many hopes and expectations.

WHAT E-LEARNING IS

One of the most challenging tasks regarding e-learning is the definition of what the field comprises. The often thoughtless use of the term "e-learning" for describing heterogeneous and highly diverse technologies, processes and methodologies, and its extensive use as a marketing slogan—especially during the era of the "dotcom boom"—has not helped formulating a common comprehension about this field. E-learning is constantly evolving: the rate by which the various definitions of e-learning become obsolete almost equals the rate by which new technologies are incorporated to it. In order to avoid this obstacle, we shall try to formulate a modular definition for e-learning.

- **E-learning** (known also as elearning or eLearning) is learning facilitated, supported and enhanced through the use of digital tools and content:
  - E-learning refers to education, training or self-improvement
  - E-learning is mediated, exclusively or complementarily, through computers or other electronic devices (mobile phones, PDAs, digital television, etc.)
  - The digital content is delivered either through physical storage media (audio and videotape, CD-ROM/DVD, etc.) or through communication technologies (radio, satellite, intranet, Internet, etc.)

E-learning constitutes an umbrella term that encompasses a heterogeneous set of technological tools, resources, applications, processes and methods, which are used for the creation, storage, dissemination, management and evaluation of knowledge—all those actions that constitute the core of every learning process. The various utilized technologies can be categorized according to the delivery media (e.g., web based training (WBT), online learning, distributed learning, etc.) or the applied interaction tools (e.g., computer based training (CBT), mobile learning, etc.). E-learning can be synchronous, asynchronous, instructor-led or computer-based, or a combination of the above.

In our effort to comprehend the nature of e-learning, as well as to predict its development, we will be assisted by the ascertainment that e-learning is the result of the convergence of two evolutionary paths: first, the correspondence/distance education movement and second, the technological means (digital or not) used for educational purposes, namely, for the storage, management and transmission of information.

Distance/correspondence education has its roots in the 1830s, while early signs can be traced further back. According to Holmberg (1995):

Correspondence education is taken to denote teaching in writing by means of so-called self-instructional texts, combined with communication in writing, that is, correspondence between students and tutors. (p. 3)

The term "distance education" is more contemporary (dating around 1970) and coincides with the adoption of the correspondence educational model by established academic institutions (e.g., Open University in the United Kingdom), a development that brings along recognition and prestige, but also osmosis with other research fields that will eventually shape its future.

Distance education has initially been through a phase of intense growth. It was thought of as a much promising solution to the need of supplying education and training to people who could not or did not want to participate in classroom teaching. Policy makers, teachers and academics recognized the potential benefits of distance education for educating various social groups (working, unemployed, minorities, underprivileged, etc.) and tackling sociopolitical, geographical and other inequalities and constraints. At the same time, distance education promised educational services of high quality at a very low cost for all stakeholders.

During this early phase several questions arose regarding the effectiveness of the distance educational model (slow learning rates, great numbers of individuals abandoning training programs, low motivation and lack of academic socialization). The most important objection, though, was that learning comprises much more than the simple acquisition of knowledge.

The second path involves the tools used for the enhancement of teaching and learning. It is not the first time—and certainly will not be the last—that a certain technological innovation is presented as a panacea and promises to solve all the problems of educational practice. Since the introduction of gramophone records for school use over a century ago, numerous technologies have been enthusiastically introduced to education, revealing a clear pattern.

The pattern is as follows: a technology (i.e., television, radio, film, PC, Internet) is introduced into educational practice aiming at the improvement of some (and sometimes all) facets of learning. This phase is followed by a period of research, in order to obtain empirical and reliable data that would support the effectiveness of the particular technology. When the technology fails to achieve its goals and fulfil its promises, there follows a period of reflection, scepticism, and blame (Cuban, 1986).

This process hardly produced any major changes. One of the reasons for this inadequacy is the limited usability, flexibility and durability that each one of the novel technologies brings along. Usually, these issues are not anticipated at the beginning, under the pressure to present the impressive possibilities of the new medium or tool.

Although teachers, who have to cope with the limitations of the new technologies, are the first to blame, the main reason for this failure lies elsewhere, in the attempt to fit the various educational technologies into the existing educational paradigm and configurations. The applied technological resources and tools were not created through "parthenogenesis;" on the contrary, they already possess certain political and social characteristics. Quite a few times, innovations were used for the sake of technology (as is the case with the various consumer appliances that were not designed—or even adapted—according to the training needs of learners and teachers). And, more often than not, before any in-depth assessment and re-evaluation of technology and its learning potential is carried out, some new technology emerges and the cycle begins again. Such a background of false expectations renders a lot of educationalists hesitant to invest time and effort in each new technology.

WHAT E-LEARNING IS NOT

Even though e-learning appears to provide some satisfactory answers to quite a few problems faced by the educational systems (access barrier removal, cost effectiveness, increased quality of learning experiences), and its ability to enhance many aspects of the learning process is widely recognized, until now it has not fulfilled the expectations. The academic and the wider educational community often regard the advocates of technological innovations with scepticism, thus avoiding the pitfalls of an overoptimistic and technologically deterministic approach to education, but also paying the price of the resulting delays. Other educators among these ranks doubt the role of technology as a powerful pedagogical tool and confine it to that of a rich information source.

But how effective is e-learning, really? In a recent report by the Organisation for Economic Cooperation and Development (2005) it is asserted that "e-learning has not really revolutionized learning and teaching to date. Far-reaching, novel ways of teaching and learning, facilitated by ICT, remain nascent or still to be invented," while it is noted that its real impact can be found mainly in all kinds of administrative services (e.g., admissions, registration, fee payment) rather than in pedagogic processes.

Quite a few researchers are sceptical about the technocentric character of the emerging educational model and its possible repercussions, like dependence from technology, pedagogic uniformity, depreciation of the role of text and discourse, deepening of the digital divide and so forth. Moreover, at an academic level there is much worry about the potential consequences of e-learning, such as the massification and commercialisation of teaching, the depreciation of the role of the academic teacher, or the restrictions to academic freedom.

Considering the critical mass reached by e-learning, in terms of acceptance, usage and investments, we should by now be able to assess its effectiveness using empirical and research findings. However, any such effort owes to consider the protean character of e-learning and to take into account that research in this field is still in formative stage. No single study could prove sufficiently the effectiveness of e-learning as a whole. We are in need of an overall framework for the evaluation of e-learning—across all educational levels and all kinds of learning—in order to be able to come to safe conclusions.

So far, research findings demonstrate that, before any attempt to introduce technology for enhancing a learning process is made, it is of eminent importance to carry out thorough analysis, explore the interactions between the proposed tools and the pedagogical strategies we plan to support and study the cultural, social and learning environment. The use of technology for supporting learning is not a technical issue and should not be limited to the characteristics of educational equipment and software. Besides, no technology is pedagogically neutral. Educational technological resources (like instructional books or any other cultural artefact), are employed within set social environments and mediated by the learning interactions between learners and teachers.

ADDRESSING THE LEARNER OF THE 21ST CENTURY

The form of modern educational systems was established at the end of the 19th century, during an era where almost 90% of students were dropping school after primary education. At that time the agricultural and rural economic model was already replaced by the industrial revolution. During that period, literacy comprised of three basic skills, "reading, 'riting, 'rithmetic," also known as the 3 R's. These skills were sufficient for anyone wishing to sustain a family and take a role as an active citizen. Since the establishment of the industrial model of production a demand for workers has arisen, workers who could man lines of mass production and execute precise and repeated movements, following strict industrial standards. The primary qualities of learning were memorization and repetition.

The industrial model of production left indelible marks on the pedagogical structures, causing the formation of what is described as the "factory model of education." The basic features of this model were standardization of curriculum, mass teaching in large groups of students, and teacher-centred teaching, with the teacher occupying the centre of the room and broadcasting his lectures. Raw material (students) passes through assembly lines (classrooms), where workers (teachers) add parts (knowledge), and comes out as brand new products (graduates). These characteristics constitute common experience for most people and continue to direct—even to this day—the bulk of educational practices. On the other hand, we should recognize that the traditional school and university model was highly effective, achieving its objectives: it allowed the efficient schooling of large population groups with heterogeneous backgrounds.

The advent of personal computers and the Internet generated yet another fundamental shift of economy, from factories and industrial production toward the dominance of trade, services and information, and preluded the educational model of the knowledge age. The socioeconomic repercussions of this transition cross over the narrow limits of workplace, home or community: they are universal and extensive, connecting individuals on a planetary scale. The speed of changes has become the trade-mark of the information age. In the postindustrial age, knowledge is a factor of distinction, within a society more and more literate, knowledgeable and always in need for more education, training and lifelong learning.

In order to comply with these requirements the "3 R's" are not sufficient and new learning expectations emerge. Modern economy, which will shape the structure of future educational systems to a great extent, is in need of employees able to solve problems, to communicate effectively and to make decisions based on critical thinking skills and on the comprehension of complex organizational and technical systems.

Several initiatives were established for identifying new learning outcomes and expectations. Wolff (2002) summarizes the learning objectives for 21st century learners as identified by the League for Innovation in the Community College (1999):

... achievement of strong (a) communication and persuasive expression skills; (b) computation skills that included the capability of reasoning, analyzing, and using numerical data; (c) community skills (citizenship, tolerance, diversity and pluralism; (d) local, global, and environmental awareness; (e) critical thinking and problem solving skills; (f) information management skills; (g) interpersonal skills including teamwork, relationship management, conflict resolution, and workplace skills; and (h) personal skills that included management of change, learning to learn, and personal responsibility. (p. 3-4)

The emerging qualities of learning are skills for navigating through organized information repositories and producing solutions to novel problems.

Alongside these changes, pedagogical research made several steps forward regarding the evolution of learning theory, primary, and practice, secondary. The most significant change we note is the emergence of a constructivist theory of learning and the transition from a transmission model of teaching to a constructivist one. In complete contradistinction to the notion of the learner as an empty vessel that should be filled with knowledge, the constructivist approach asserts that students create their own knowledge through assimilating new information on top of existing information. Learning is regarded as an active process that depends considerably on the current knowledge, comprehension and mental condition of the learner.

A direct consequence of the above is the shifting of the teaching model from a teacher-centred to a learner-centred one. In many cases, therefore, learners are given control over their own learning: they are empowered and held partly accountable. The learner is allowed to adapt several characteristics of the learning process according to his or her needs and preferences (such as setting his or her own objectives and defining the content knowledge and pace of learning). Learners may guide themselves, having the teacher standing by as a helper (according to the common saying being the "guide on the side" instead of the "sage on the stage"). They are given more hands-on training opportunities, while at the same time they can adapt their learning strategies, exchange common practices with peers and seek help from external resources or individuals. The main objective of the novel pedagogical approach is the connection of knowledge to the context, the environment and the actual needs of the subject, so that she is able to solve authentic problems. Also, less emphasis is being put on facts memorization.

Naturally, today's youth is the primary targets of novel educational policies, methodologies and technologies. Early in their childhood they are accustomed with computers and other sophisticated technical devices, usually with greater success than their parents or teachers. Having developed new behaviours, they are collectively identified as the "net generation." They prefer to learn through practice, exploration and "trial and error." They prefer acting to listening, fast and multimodal interactions and communications to text and reading and frequent changes to stability; just like the movies and computer games they fancy. Young learners show a preference for socializing with peers, participating in group activities and working in groups. On the other hand, several researchers claim that these particular characteristics of the "net generation" may also be their disadvantages. The development of certain cognitive skills requires review, reflection and patience, which are not always the strong points of the net generation.

The sweeping reference to the "net generation," however, partially conceals the differentiations among users regarding their possibilities, roles and needs. This oversimplified assumption on the natural propensity of youngsters toward technology may function as an alibi for the introduction of technology in education, for reasons other than purely scientific. It also leads to the overlooking of affective, psychological and pedagogical factors that determine the successful introduction of technology in education (Selwyn, 1999).

WHAT E-LEARNING DOES

E-learning comes at the right time to fulfil the contemporary learning needs and expectations. As Patel and Patel (2006) stated "there seems to be a coincidence between e-learning as a tool and the necessity to modify the traditional model of education." E-learning comes to support and enhance learning processes and teachers and not to replace them. Traditional educational structures and practices should not be replaced altogether, but rather blended with the new technologies, through a process of technological syncretism.

E-learning offers a multitude of opportunities for the development of pedagogical practices and the enhancement of learning. In traditional classroom training, mass teaching is directed toward the average student and the time that can be devoted to each student's needs is limited. E-learning, on the other hand, opens bright prospects for the differentiation and adaptation of teaching and learning to individual needs. It is compatible with various pedagogical methods, such as self-paced or directed learning, individual or collaborating learning, individual or group teaching, synchronous or asynchronous collaboration, and so forth. Paraphrasing and updating Holmberg's (1995) statement about the potential of distance education, we may claim that:

[e-learning] has vast application potentials not only for independent study attractive to adults but also for mass education through what has been described as industrial methods, and for the highly individualized study and personal approaches with a great deal of rapport between the teaching and learning parties. (p. 17)

E-learning enhances the flexibility and accessibility at all levels of education and training. Learners are able to take courses and use learning material whenever they have the time and the mood for it. This characteristic is particularly valued by the growing number of adult learners—who have to find a balance between study, work and social commitments—as well as by full-time students.

The educational use of new technologies may also increase the attention, concentration and motivation of learners. The presentation of the learning material through various media enhances retention, while the use of novel tools that technology places at our disposal facilitates communication and collaboration among learners. E-learning technologies allow the creation of active learning environments, by providing learners with opportunities to assess their knowledge, to reflect upon their progress and to make decisions regarding the learning strategies they deploy.

Various e-learning configurations provide significant opportunities for learner control. Learners may be allowed to adjust the selection, sequence, pace and presentation of the learning material according to their needs. This may have positive effects on learner engagement, creativity, autonomy and self-efficacy. Learner control, however, should be exercised with caution, as learners do not always have the metacognitive abilities, the will or the time to direct their own learning, and they may get easily "lost in learning space."

Increased costs for the production of high quality learning objects require that they are extensively reused. E-learning material should be used, reused and rearranged. Digital repositories serve this purpose, allowing the search and composition of learning objects into customized lectures and courses. Reuse of learning objects is facilitated through the development of educational metadata standards and compatible educational software. One widely known repository is the Multimedia Educational Resource for Learning and Online Teaching (MERLOT, http://www.merlot.org). MERLOT stores over 400 learning objects on history alone, ranging from stand-alone lectures and online history archives to entire courses.

Possibly the most important contribution of e-learning is its enormous capabilities for mass, free access to ideas, information, and knowledge. The "World Open Material" project at the Massachusetts Institute of Technology (MIT) provides free access to over 1400 courses from 34 different academic departments (http://mitworld.mit.edu/). The educational material for each course is identical to that used by the registered students of the university and ranges from syllabi and lecture notes to video lectures and whole exams. Another example of high quality free learning material is that of the Canada-led project "Professeurs Pour la Liberté" (PPL). PPL intends to offer online education, free of charge, to more than 100,000 African students each year. It will utilize reusable computers, reusable books, volunteers and courses donated by academic institutions coming from the G8, European and Scandinavian countries (http://www.myppl.org/report/). Various public institutions, such as libraries, archives, and museums, possess vast knowledge, and they should be supported in order to ensure public access to that material.

Another, rather dull but equally important, part of e-learning concerns organizational and administrative operations, attempting to save precious teacher time for supporting learning and teaching. Such operations include grade-keeping, digital student records (along with student profile and learning portfolios), computer-assisted assessment, and so forth.

WHAT E-LEARNING WILL DO

As various new information and communication technologies become more widespread, the cycle of their educational implementation begins again. Mobile computational devices, ubiquitous computing, social software, and virtual worlds are the most promising and capable of transforming the landscape of educational technology. New services and routines reshape the way the Internet is perceived. Putting these advancements into practice as educational and learning tools makes way for the new generation of e-learning, known as e-learning 2.0.

Mobile Computational Devices

E-learning has prophesized "anywhere, anytime" access to learning, thus overlooking the precondition of a personal computer that confines the learner in a house, workplace or computer lab. Throughout the following years, however, it is expected that more and more learners will carry with them some kind of mobile computational device. The cost of these devices has decreased dramatically and henceforth the supply of each learner with the necessary equipment is feasible. M-learning (i.e., e-learning through the use of portable appliances and wireless networking) can transform the way we learn, providing continuous access to learning material, learning activities and communication tools and facilitating collaborative interaction.

Mobile computational devices may take a variety of forms and have several capabilities, ranging from specialized devices, like response pads, graphical calculators and electronic dictionaries, to more generic devices, such as mobile telephones, PDAs, portable computers and Tablet PCs. These days, even some entertainment devices (mp3 players, ipods, portable video game consoles, etc.) have capabilities matching those of personal computers (e.g., Internet connectivity, high quality graphics, etc.) and are able to support communicative and multimedia operations.

The case of the mobile phone is typical. Their evolution during the last few years was extreme and by now more and more mobile phones can capture and handle multimedia, connect to the Internet, and even locate their position through geographical positioning system (GPS) Mobile phones constitute the most widespread portable computational device, with nearly one billion phones sold during 2006 worldwide. Even though their presence in the classroom is not yet allowed, soon they could be treated as essential educational tools (much like pens, notebooks and calculators).

But how can mobile computational devices be used for supporting learning? Even though they do not appear capable of substituting the computers, their complementary use for supporting learning activities opens up various prospects. Recent empirical research has uncovered certain advantages of the use of portable, networked computational devices within learning environments, such as the enhancement of availability and accessibility of informational sources, the engagement of students in learning activities while located in different physical spaces, the support of group and collaborative activities, and the enhancement of communicative actions.

Their portability allows learners and teachers to make use of their spare time, while travelling or commuting, in order to finish homework or to get prepared for a course. Mobile computational devices constitute ideal companions for field working and learning. A student walking around in a museum or participating in an excavation can have direct access to supporting material through the Internet. She can take pictures or video and store the material for future use, for example, on a paper that she has been working, upload it on the course's Web site or dispatch it to the teacher. The capabilities of geolocation allow the recording of geographical information and its combination with satellite photos and digital maps.

Mobile computational devices enable the design and implementation of mobile collaborative learning activities (mobile computer supported collaborative learning—mCSCL). During a mobile collaborative activity learners use their own device, which is connected to those of their peers. The device is the only resource they will need for the completion of the activity, because wireless networking allows access to learning objects and instructions necessary to support collaboration. The small size of these devices does not impede the natural social interaction and learners can move freely in space, cooperating and interacting with team members. While learners communicate and interact face to face, they participate simultaneously in artificial collaborative networks that support electronic communication with other team members or the teachers sitting in their office.

However, the educational implementation of mobile computational devices is not without problems. Critics claim that many educational institutions, following consumer trends, hasten to equip their students with such devices without having first any suitable teaching programs. More often than not, such premature efforts led to applications that were very different from what was planned, such as chatting during lectures or cheating during tests. In most cases mobile devices were not designed with educational uses in mind. The most attractive features of mobile devices (small size, portability, special interfaces) can also prove to be their disadvantages. They usually have small screen sizes, rendering the reading of large texts difficult, and limited processing power, while the interoperability between various technologies is actually hard to achieve.

Ubiquitous Computing: Smart Environments

The term "ubiquitous computing" refers to invisible or transparent computer systems, which are part of everyday settings and available to their users at any time. The technological developments that realize applications of that kind are the ever-shrinking size and cost of computational devices and the almost ubiquitous presence of the Internet, through wired and wireless broadband high-speed connections. Beside our computers and mobile phones, even our automobiles and refrigerators are capable of accessing the Internet, at speeds unimaginable a few years ago.

"Smart environments" are a reflection of this tendency. According to a broad definition, a "smart environment" is an area in which various interconnected devices operate and cooperate in order to facilitate the life of its inhabitants. A smart environment can, on its own, collect, evaluate and handle information regarding the state of the space and its objects and adapt to the preferences and intentions of its inhabitants, so as to enhance their interactions and living experiences.

The various technologies that may constitute smart environments include: computational devices (such as sensors, embedded computer systems, wearable computers, etc.), networking infrastructures (local area networks, personal area networks, sensorial networks, the Internet, etc.), as well as the necessary software (such as autonomous systems, artificial intelligence applications, etc.)

The development of ubiquitous computing and smart environments may bring multiple benefits to e-learning. Design principals and technologies of ubiquitous computing can be applied to technological classrooms and labs; besides, learning is a ubiquitous endeavour and state of mind. The physical learning space can be equipped with intelligent computational devices, which interact with learners, learning resources and with each other, offering rich multisensorial learning experiences. The incorporation of technological tools is transparent and their use is freed from the usual interactional barriers (making it ideal for teaching people with special learning and physical abilities). One could envisage learning environments (real instead of virtual) imitating archaeological sites; they are filled with "findings" which students can "excavate." The "findings" guide students on how they should be unearthed, and the "site" records their moves, while other students watch and participate through remote connections.

Web 2.0

The new trend on the Internet invites users not as passive receivers of information, but as creators, or at least as gatherers and redistributors. User-created content is the core means of development for this new era and is expressed through blogs, wikis and photocollections. Small, interconnected tools allow anyone to have their own place on the Web, through which they can display their creative skills in writing, photography, film making and much more. Creating and sharing digital resources is becoming easier. A shared culture emerges throughout the Internet, based on co-ownership and co-management of collective knowledge, or at least of collective "taste."

Blogs (short for Web logs) are Web sites used for the recording and chronological presentation of journal-type entries. They can combine text, images and hyperlinks—just like in any other Web site, while posting an entry is extremely easy. Although their topics can be strictly personal, "bloggers" usually comment on social, cultural, political and technical matters. In March 2007, Technorati (http://technorati.com), a blog search engine, reported over 70 million blogs.

While blogs facilitate expression of a single person, wikis, on the other hand, facilitate collaboration and common understanding. Wikis are Web applications that allow many authors to make changes on a Web page, enabling collaborative content authoring. Users of a wiki are able to review and undo changes to the text, and also access its older versions. The most well-known wiki application is the online collaborative encyclopedia Wikipedia (http://www.wikipedia.org).

These novel Internet applications have the additional advantage of extreme usability and accessibility. On most cases they are free of charge, they are operated through a simple Web browser and do not require special technical skills, which contributes to their appeal to people of all ages and social classes.

This emerging form of the Internet and the WWW is known by the term "Web 2.0." While the former structure—now known as "Web 1.0"—was based primarily on passive access to content, which someone else, usually a professional, created and published ("push technology"), the current trend facilitates the creation, assimilation and distribution of information and knowledge. At a technical level, Web 2.0 is based on small chunks of information (ideas, knowledge, artefacts), loosely interconnected through a range of standards and Web services. Web 2.0 is blurring the boundaries, allowing consumers to be themselves the producers.

Web sites like Flickr (http://www.flickr.com) and YouTube (http://www.youtube.com/) attract millions of users, who, even though they are not necessarily the content creators (of pictures and video, respectively), they can search, filter, evaluate, and comment on the available user-provided material, and assimilate it to their personal collections. The Web site del.icio.us (http://del.icio.us) is an archive of collective knowledge, allowing its users to create and share lists of Web bookmarks. Bookmarks are rated and categorized by the users according to their own knowledge, objectives or plain preferences. The popularity of this service suggests that, on many occasions, collective human knowledge may produce better search results than massive, automated search engines.

Several academic institutions (e.g., Warwick University, Brighton University) are experimenting with the application of Web 2.0 technologies. Students are encouraged to keep their own blogs, not necessarily linked to courses and studies, but rather as tools of personal communication, expression and idea sharing (Attwell, 2007). Teachers and learners are beginning to use blogs and wikis to create libraries of learning resources (such as lecture notes, photographs, instructional videos, papers, etc.), in order to support lectures and projects. They are able to publish lists of bibliography, articles, Web bookmarks, and so forth, and can cowrite and coreview papers and publications. Dispersed learning resources are compiled into personal learning spaces, compatible with individual learning objectives, but also taking part into wider learning communities.

Social Networking

More and more Web sites and blogs allow users to create lists of personal contacts of their choice (friends, family, colleagues or even strangers), with whom they share some common feature, value or interest, thus creating extensive social networks and communities. Members of these networks are able to present their interests and views, communicate and collaborate, and share content and services with other member of the community. "Social software" is software that supports the creation and support of social networks.

Social networking constitutes the essence of Web 2.0 and is probably its most pervasive feature. Web sites like myspace.com (http://www.myspace.com) were the motivation for thousands of young people to access the Internet for the first time; they created their personal "Internet corners," they shared music and photos and they formed their Internet identity through participation in formal or informal Web communities. Members of social networks develop a sense of belonging, trust and safety that supports their socialization. Social networking sites are by now among the most popular sites on the Internet, and they are studied extensively for their wider social role.

As soon as the dynamics of social networks is realized, it is reasonable to explore how they could be utilized as learning tools. After all, youngsters spend a lot of time "surfing," contributing to or socializing within social networks, whereas they scarcely visit the Web sites of the lectures they attend and barely answer their teachers' messages in forums. Although the objectives are obviously different, e-learning has much to gain if it succeeds "to harness the power of social networking to build rich, interactive, robust learning communities" (New Media Consortium, 2007).

On several occasions, universities are already trying to add social networking sites to their arsenal, both for supporting learning processes and enhancing student socialization and self-expression. Social networks of classmates and peers can support learning and can function as personal support networks or as knowledge management tools. At the University of Pennsylvania, freshmen students are encouraged to use the campus-based social networking site "Pennster," in order to get to know their classmates (New Media Consortium, 2007). Other social networking sites, with a more educational orientation, allow students to create Web pages to organize and share their classroom schedules (http://www.collegeruled.com) or to evaluate their teachers (http://www.ratemyprofessors.com).

Virtual Worlds

"Virtual worlds" are digital simulated environments that depict real or imaginary spaces with the use of 3D computer graphics. Users of virtual worlds may simply explore them or even "inhabit" them, by operating digital entities known as "avatars." Users guide avatars through the topography of the virtual world and interact with the environment and its objects. Depending on the nature of the virtual world and the physics that has been programmed into it, users are able to "walk," "fly" or "swim" through their embodied avatars. Users are also able to communicate and interact with other avatars, either exchanging messages or talking in real-time.

Virtual worlds are the most eloquent expression of cyberspace. They create strong senses of presence and immersion, thus facilitating highly effective and enjoyable digital interactions. Virtual worlds may be of immense size—as they can be expanded at will—and assemble great number of users. The most well known virtual world is "Second Life" (http://www.secondlife.com/), which has over 7,500,000 inhabitants-digital citizens. Corporations, organizations, university branches and even state embassies are being created within this world in order to serve its inhabitants. Virtual worlds should not be confused with various computer games, though they have many characteristics in common. They are able to support computer games (and some virtual worlds are created especially for that purpose), but their features primarily facilitate social interaction, role-playing, exploration, and collaboration.

Virtual worlds are established, by their various features, as particularly attractive and promising learning tools. On one hand, high-analysis 3D graphics offers great possibilities for realistic representations of spaces and objects. We are able to recreate and depict, with high accuracy, any environment we desire: real or imaginary, coming from the past, present or future, microscopic or macroscopic. On the other hand, facilitated by the interaction with the virtual environment, hands-on operation of objects and real-time communication with other participants makes virtual worlds an entirely active and interactive learning experience.

Virtual classrooms can be created within virtual worlds, in which avatar-learners can attend lectures given by avatar-teachers through the use of multimedia and real-time communications. Commuting to and from campus requires only a few mouse clicks. Detailed copies of actual spaces can be recreated and used as simulation spaces, allowing learners to explore and practice. Students can resume any role and experiment with their skills without risking harming themselves or their environment.

A range of virtual worlds of archaeological interest has already emerged. In June 2007 the "Rome Reborn" project was unveiled. This project resulted in the creation of an exact digital replica of ancient Rome, with a notional date of June 21, 321 A.D. (http://www.romereborn.virginia.edu/). The exploration of this model provides researchers, teachers and the public with accurate historical, architectural and topographical information, while at the same time it creates an amazing feeling of "time travel." Around the same period a recreation of the Chichen-Itza, on the Yucatan Peninsula, was presented on Second Life. Commissioned by the Mexico Tourism Board, this virtual archaeological site initially targeted tourists, but its realistic and accurate representation enables its use as a learning resource.

CONSIDERATIONS REGARDING E-LEARNING

All evidence indicates that in the foreseeable future, technology and e-learning will play an even greater role as part of education, both as primary and supportive tools. The adequate use of computers and the new literacy skills will soon constitute prerequisites for participating in learning processes, for both learners and teachers. Learner and teacher e-learning readiness is essential, if we really aim at its function as a balancing and enabling innovation, instead of another barrier to learning and potential source of new economic, social and political segregations. The most vulnerable groups of the population in particular, who are the most in need of learning support and guidance, should be helped to get on the train of e-learning.

As noted above, the common reference to the "net generation" should not mislead to consider it a homogeneous population; rather, it is of great importance to acknowledge that youngsters' relationships with computers and technology are characterized by a significant lack of uniformity. The computer is a versatile, multimodal interaction object and is being used in many ways, for diverse purposes and with different expectations. Furthermore, the personal characteristics, attitudes, previous knowledge, and experience of the subject form a complex cognitive and affective canvas, upon which learning must take place (Palaigeorgiou, Siozos, & Konstantakis, 2006). According to contemporary approaches to individualized learning, through creating, updating and using learner models, we are able to draw optimal learning paths for each individual. Learner diversity can be used as a starting point for learning.

The various intentional models of human behavior identify attitudes toward a behavior or an object as an important indicator of prospective behavior. Therefore, the successful integration of new technologies in education depends significantly upon positive teacher and learner attitudes (Selwyn, 1999). As Liaw (2002) points out "...no matter how sophisticated and how capable the technology, its effective implementation depends upon users having positive attitude towards it." Positive, anxiety-free attitudes toward computers and technology are regarded as a fundamental prerequisite for participating in activities that utilize

ICT and as a principal component of computer literacy. Positive attitudes are correlated with acceptance and use of computers; they moderate the result of related training programs (Torkzadeh & Van Dyke, 2002) and may support or hinder academic success (Mizrachi & Shoham, 2004).

Special reference should be made to the differentiation in computer relationships between genders. In research bibliography we come across many empirical studies which conclude that female students of all ages participate less than their male counterparts to various computer-related activities (such as computer use at school, Internet use, video games, etc.), have more anxiety, less confidence, and less favorable dispositions toward computers and technologies (e.g., Liaw, 2002). Though more recent results show that differences are gradually diminishing or even vanishing, it seems that the gender gap is still existent, even in first-world countries, and may undermine the effective use of e-learning.

The technology skills and attitudes of teachers, which will plan, implement and support e-learning, is of equal importance. Several teachers regard technology as an extra burden on their overloaded schedules, even as a threat to their teaching practices and their established academic freedom. Depending on their field, their teaching expertise and their relationship with technology, they use various facets of e-learning to express and cover different needs. The teacher, as the natural introducer of new educational technologies, must be allowed to decide which role technology will have in his teaching agenda, if any, and also be in a position to support it. He should be trained on new technologies (possibly through e-learning) in order to grasp their capabilities and restrictions and to broaden his options.

Teachers that use technology as part of their everyday and teaching activities often note the difficulties equipment and software failures can cause, interrupting the flow of the learning activities and causing frustrations. Even minor technical glitches can take precious teacher time away from the learning activities. Students and teachers should be able to cope with common technical problems, as well as have access to sufficient technical support staff and resources. Before any e-learning program is applied, users should pass through an orientation phase, which will ensure self-confidence and an adequate level of participation to all teaching and learning interactions.

The ever-increasing use of e-learning brings along a range of ethical issues that we should study with care. One of these is plagiarism. The growth of digital libraries and the access to e-books, electronic texts and ready-made papers, increases the risk and the temptation of improper copyright use, and is already considered a major problem within the academic community. Another issue that digital environments bring on is the privacy of user data and actions. All learners using a learning environment (either Web site or virtual world) leave behind digital traces that may reveal much about their behaviors, habits, and even their thoughts. E-learning, even more than learning, is a process that above all presupposes trust among all stakeholders.

FINAL REMARKS

The debate about the impact of new technologies on learning is far from being over, while the current educational model faces a constant shift. Research results point to the need to achieve a dynamic balance between the introduction of new educational technologies, their application on novel teaching and learning methods and the thorough evaluation of the resulting changes.

Previous experiences in e-learning create some justified scepticism, but they still leave much room for great expectations. Novel technological advancements, combined with approaches on learning that are firmly grounded on theory, can transform the ways we learn and study. No one can underestimate the fact that a low-tech, black and white, paper book can constitute a powerful, sometimes life-changing learning experience. On the other hand, anyone that has had the experience of a virtual world can appreciate the enormous learning potential new technologies bring about.

FUTURE RESEARCH DIRECTIONS

There are many future directions for e-learning. As previously mentioned, new e-learning modalities, such as ubiquitous computing, mobile learning, blogging, podcasting, social networking, educational and collaborative virtual environments, are emerging. This field needs more experiences and evaluation in order to judge their usefulness as well as to create evidence of a relationship between the use of these modalities and learning outcomes.

The e-Learning Guild Research (2006) report refers that the main focus on e-learning research will be on content quality and rapid development, as well as development of the resources that make better, faster e-learning possible. This fact implies two different research directions. The first one concerns both the creation and re-usability of the e-learning content. As referred to in Weller (2007) "research will need to further develop tools that facilitate searching across distributed collections, and pulling resources into the virtual learning environment, while recording rights and permissions for usage." The second direction concerns the development of a fully service-oriented approach for supporting virtual learning environments and lies not only on the technical part but also in the effectiveness of such an approach.

Another research direction is the investigation of the integration of the e-learning environments in the business cycle of an organization. In other words there is a need for the creation of business models for the licensing and usage of e-learning content, e-learning services, e-learning platforms and in general e-learning technologies.

REFERENCES

Attwell, G. (2007). The personal learning environments - the future of eLearning? *eLearning Papers, 2(1)*. Retrieved October, 24, 2007, from http://www.elearningpapers.eu/index.php?page=doc&doc_id=8553&doclng=6

Cuban, L. (1986). *Teachers and machines: The classroom use of technology since 1920*. New York: Teachers College Press.

Holmberg, B. (1995). *Theory and practice of distance education*. London and New York: Routledge.

Klass, G. (2000). Plato as distance education pioneer: Status and quality threats of Internet education. *First Monday, 5*(7). Retrieved October, 24, 2007, from http://www.firstmonday.org/issues/issue5_7/klass/index.html

Liaw, S. S. (2002). An Internet survey for perceptions of computers and the World Wide Web: Relationship, prediction and difference. *Computers in Human Behavior, 18*, 17-35.

League for Innovation in the Community College. (1999). *League connections and leadership abstracts*.

Mizrachi, D., & Shoham, S. (2004). Computer attitudes and library anxiety among undergraduates: A study of Israeli B.Ed students. *The International Information & Library Review, 36*(1), 29-38.

New Media Consortium. (2007). The Horizon Report: 2007 Edition. Retrieved October 24, 2007, from http://www.nmc.org/horizon/2007/report

Organisation for Economic Co-operation and Development. (2005). *E-learning in tertiary education. Where do we stand*? OECD: OECD Publishing.

Palaigeorgiou, G. E., Siozos, P. D., & Konstantakis, N. I. (2006). CEAF: A measure for deconstructing students' prior computer experience. *Journal of Information Systems Education, 17*(4), 459-468.

Patel, C., & Patel, T. (2006). Exploring a joint model of conventional and online learning systems. *e-Service Journal, 4*(2), 27-46.

Plato. (1986). *Phaedrus* (C. J. Rowe, Trans.). Warminster, UK: Aries & Phillips.

Selwyn, N. (1999). Students' attitudes towards computers in sixteen to nineteen education. *Education and Information Technologies, 4*(2), 129-141.

Sutherland, R. (2004). Designs for learning: ICT and knowledge in the classroom. *Computers and Education, 43*(1-2), 5-16.

The eLearning Guild Research. (2006). Future Directions in e-Learning Research Report 2006. Retrieved June, 10, 2007 from http://www.elearningguild.com/pdf/1/apr06-futuredirections.pdf

Torkzadeh G., & Van Dyke T.P. (2002). Effects of training on Internet self-efficacy and computer user attitudes. *Computers in Human Behavior, 18*, 479-494.

Weller, M. (2007). *Virtual Leaning Environments: Using, choosing and developing your VLE.* Routledge; 1st edition (April 12, 2007). ISBN-10: 0415414318.

Wolff, S. J. (2003). *Design features of the physical learning environment for collaborative, project-based learning at the community college level.* St. Paul, MN: National Research Center for Career and Technical Education. (http://www.nccte.org)

ADDITIONAL READING

Abowd, G. (1999). Classroom 2000: An experiment with the instrumentation of a living educational environment. *IBM Systems Journal, 38*(4), 508-530.

Anderson, T., & Elloumi, F. (Eds.) (2004). *Theory and practice of online learning.* Athabasca, Canada: Athabasca University.

Collis, B. (1998). New didactics for university instruction: Why and how? *Computers & Education, 31*, 373-393.

DeRouin, R. E., Fritzsche, B. A., & Salas, E. (2004). Optimizing e-learning: Research-based guidelines for learner-controlled training, *Human Resource Management, 43*, 147-162.

Kwok, C.N. (2007). Replacing face-to-face tutorials by synchronous online technologies: Challenges and pedagogical implications. *The International Review of Research in Open and Distance Learning, 8*(1).

Motiwalla, L. F. (2007). Mobile learning: A framework and evaluation. *Computers & Education, 49*, 581-596.

New Media Consortium. (2007). The Horizon Report: 2007 Edition. Retrieved October 24, 2007, from http://www.nmc.org/horizon/2007/report

O'Neill, K., Singh, G., & O'Donoghue, J. (2004). Implementing e-learning programmes for higher education: A review of the literature. *Journal of Information Technology Education, 3*, 313-323.

Palaigeorgiou, G. E., Siozos, P. D., & Konstantakis, N. I. (2006). CEAF: A measure for deconstructing students' prior computer experience. *Journal of Information Systems Education, 17*(4), 459-468.

Patel, C., & Patel, T. (2006). Exploring a joint model of conventional and online learning systems. *E-service Journal, 4*(2), 27-46.

Pelgrum, W. (2001). Obstacles to the integration of ICT in education: Results from a worldwide educational assessment. *Computers & Education, 37*(2), 163-178.

Politis, D. (2006). Introduction: E-learning trends in Archaeology. In C. Carreras (Ed.), *Open and distance learning (ODL) strategies*. Athens: Klidarithmos Publications.

Politis, D. (Ed.). (2006). *The e-learning dimension of computer applications in archaeology*. Athens: Klidarithmos Publications.

Roffe, I. (2002). E-learning: Engagement, enhancement and execution. *Quality assurance in education*, *10*(1), 40-50.

Zurita, G., & Nussbaum, M. (2004). Computer supported collaborative learning using wirelessly interconnected handheld computers. *Computers & Education, 42*(3), 215-317.

KEY TERMS

Blogs: Also known as Web logs. Blogs are Web sites that are used for the recording and chronological presentation of journal-type entries. They can combine text, images and hyperlinks, just like in any other Web site, and make posting an entry extremely easy.

E-Learning: (known also as elearning, e-Learning or eLearning) Learning facilitated, supported and enhanced through the use of digital tools and content.

Mobile Computational Devices: Portable electronic devices that can be used for input, storage and processing of data or communications. May be able to capture, store and show multimedia formats and connect to networks (e.g., mobile telephones, personal digital assistants (PDAs), portable computers, Tablet PCs).

Smart Environments: Physical areas and spaces in which various interconnected digital devices and sensors operate and cooperate in order to facilitate the life of their inhabitants.

Social Software: Software that supports the creation and support of social networks. Social networks are virtual communities of personal contacts (friends, family, colleagues, etc.) who share some common feature, value or interest. Members of these networks are able to present their interests and views, communicate and collaborate, and share content and services with other members of the community.

Virtual Worlds: Digital simulated environments that depict real or imaginary spaces with the use of 3D computer graphics. Users of virtual worlds may simply explore them or even "inhabit" them, by operating digital entities known as "avatars."

Web 2.0: The emerging form of the Internet and the WWW. While the former structure – now known as "Web 1.0" – was based primarily on passive access to content, which someone else, usually a professional, created and published ("push technology"), the current trend facilitates the creation, assimilation and distribution of information and knowledge by any user. Web 2.0 is based on small chunks of information loosely interconnected through a range of standards and Web services.

Wikis: Web applications that allow many authors to make changes on a Web page, enabling collaborative content authoring.

Chapter II
Basic Aspects of VLEs and Guidelines for Supporting Learning Communities and E-Collaboration

Thrasyvoulos Tsiatsos
Aristotle University of Thessaloniki, Greece

Eleftheria Giannaka
University of Patras, Greece

INTRODUCTION

This chapter aims to present the basic design principles for virtual spaces for facilitating educational designers and developers by providing a point of reference for making decisions about whether or not to incorporate 3D environments into the resources they develop as well as for extending their capabilities by integrating more functionality.

A variety of tools and technologies have been developed and used for supporting learning communities and e-collaboration. The current components, tools and systems available can be divided into three different basic concepts (Bouras & Tsiatsos, 2005; Spellmann, Mosier, Deus, & Carlson, 1997): (a) document-focused Web-based training tools, (b) meeting-focused tools, and (c) 3D-centered multiuser tools.

In particular, the document-focused Web-based training tools (e.g., WebCT, www.webct.com) focus on the management of documents and on individual learning. As far as it concerns the meeting-focused tools, they focalize on the support of synchronous communication of a user group, which is independent of place. These tools that can be separated into video conferencing tools (e.g., Microsoft's NetMeeting, www.microsoft.com) and synchronous training tools (e.g., Centra Symposium, www.centra.com), offer Web-based communication support, where participants are represented by their name and live video picture. Some of the video conferencing tools were designed especially for the purpose of training situations. The approach of these tools is to virtually represent the concept of frontal learning. A general problem of these tools is the reduced social presence of the participants that are represented in windows, by means of live pictures. Finally, regarding the 3D-centered multiuser tools, they focus on letting each participant experience the existence of other participants as well as the interaction between them. In 3D-centered tools the participants of a virtual session are represented by avatars, which can navigate through 3D environments, and all other participants can view the actions of all other participants as well. 3D-centered multiuser tools, used as communication media, can offer the advantage of creating proximity and social presence, thereby making participants aware of the communication and interaction processes with others.

It seems that 3D-centered multiuser tools, as well as meeting-focused tools configured for e-collaboration, could be used for supporting learning communities and e-collaboration. However, current e-learning applications have many limitations that should be overcome. Some of the limitations mainly involve the lack of peer contact and interaction of learners/users working alone and the need for flexible, available tutorial support. Furthermore, the main effort is focused on designing environments that could be characterized as "places" of interaction and not simple, plain spaces. Current user interfaces have been proven insufficient to enable the user to be fully creative. In the case of 3D-centered tools, the theoretical advantages of multiuser VR technology are not exploited in an extended manner as they mainly offer text chat communication and users' representation through avatars. For example, advanced communication features, as voice or user gestures, are not commonly utilized.

For facilitating educational designers and developers on making decisions on whether to incorporate 3D environments into the resources they develop, this chapter presents two different tools as solutions for supporting e-collaboration and multiuser communication in Web-based learning communities. The first solution, called Virtual Conference, is a two-dimensional space where participants represented by their photos can use various e-collaboration tools. The second solution, called EVE Training Area, is a three-dimensional space where participants, represented by 3D humanoid avatars, can use a variety of e-collaboration tools. To this direction, the chapter describes the functionality provided by both tools, compares them, and proposes cases for exploiting each solution.

VR IN EDUCATION, TRAINING AND COLLABORATION

This section presents an overview of existing work on the usage of VR technology in distance education, learning and collaboration.

According to Kalawsky, there are many areas where VR could be used to support education:

- **Simulation of complex systems:** The benefit compared to traditional methods is the ability to observe system operation from a number of perspectives aided by high quality visualisation and interaction.
- **Macroscopic and microscopic visualisation:** The benefit compared to traditional methods is the observation of system features that would be either too small or too large to be seen on a normal scale system.
- **Fast and slow time simulation:** The benefit compared to traditional methods is the ability to control timescale in a dynamic event. This feature could operate like a fast forward or rewind preview of a modern video recorder.

Other significant characteristics of VR that could be exploited to support education are the following:

- **High levels of interactivity that VR allows:** The benefit compared to traditional methods is that most people learn faster by "doing" and the VR system provides significantly greater levels of interactivity than other computer-based systems. Given the fact that the interfaces are intuitive and easy to use, the degree of interactivity can be very beneficial.
- **Sense of immersion:** Sense of immersion is a powerful characteristic. In some applications the sense of scale is extremely important. For example, architecture is an area where a sense of scale is required to visualise the impact of a building design on the external environment and the inhabitants.
- **Inherent flexibility/adaptability:** The inherent flexibility of a VR system comes from the underlying software nature of the virtual environment. A VR system can be put to many uses by loading different application environments. This means that it is feasible to use a VR system for a range of teaching applications. This means that if the system is properly applied it will soon generate cost savings.

VR has been exploited in various projects for supporting education, training or collaboration. Concerning education, much research has been done on the exploration of the unique features of VR and their interaction with cognition and learning in high-end, laboratory-based projects. A very good overview of relative projects is presented in Hay et al (2002). These projects aimed to create learning environments based on the exploration of various scientific concepts. Examples are the following: (a) exploration of scientific concepts where 3D models were important to conceptual development; (b) exploitation of VR's ability to shrink or expand 3D distances to make the models easy to manipulate; and (c) usage of the simulation mode of integrating models into learning environments and capitalization VR's ability to more accurately present the phenomena to the learner, thus building superior understandings.

Furthermore, VR technology has been used in other areas such as military training and medical education and training. Examples are: NPSNET-IV (Macedonia et al, 1995), Gorman's Gambit (Weil, Hussain, Brunye, Sidman, & Spahr, 2005), VirRAD (Virtual Radiopharmacy, http://www.virrad.eu.org/) European project; Medical Readiness Trainer project (http://www-vrl.umich.edu/mrt/index.html), and CeNTIE project (Matthew, Hutchins, Duncan, Stevenson, Gunn, Krumpholz et al., 2005). In addition, multiuser virtual reality technology (also referred as collaborative virtual environments – CVEs,) which allows collaboration among users, integrates networking technology with immersive virtual environments and supports synchronous interaction of multiple users at various locations (Singhal & Zyda, 1999). Multiuser virtual reality technology is being used for cooperative work (Dumas, Saugis, Degrande, Plenacost, Chaillou, & Viaud, 1999), for education and training, for engineering and design, for commerce and entertainment, and is being studied extensively in 3D and time dependent representations of scientific and technical models (Singhal & Zyda, 1999).

VR applications, which are specifically designed to support learning, come in many different forms, from desktop virtual worlds to fully immersive virtual environments (Jackson & Winn, 1999). Collaborative e-learning VR applications draw on ideas of distributed constructionism to allow multiple users to work together in the same virtual space and to provide them with the power to construct shared representations of the topic they investigate.

As it becomes possible to learn by interacting with other students in virtual environments as well as virtual objects similar to how they would interact with real people and objects, it becomes important to investigate the design principles that should be adopted by the educational designers for effectively designing virtual spaces for e-learning and e-collaboration. As described above little research has been done on these principles and guidelines.

DESIGN PRINCIPLES FOR VIRTUAL SPACES FOCUSED ON E-LEARNING AND E-COLLABORATION

This section presents the design principles that should be taken into account by designers and developers when designing a virtual space for learning communities and e-collaboration.

In order to implement a functional and effective e-learning collaborative virtual environment, the first step is to investigate its main functional features. These functional features should differentiate an e-learning and collaborative environment from other virtual environments (3D or not), which are designed and implemented for general use. The virtual spaces should be designed according to the concepts introduced by Dourish and Harrison (1996) about space and place: "A space is always what it is, but a place is how it's used." In addition, we have to deal with some aspects of the "real world" which can be exploited by virtual spaces for collaboration and learning. The real-world value of the features listed below is that they provide critical cues, which allow individuals to organize their behaviour accordingly (such as moving toward people to talk to them, or referring to objects so that others can find them). Every tool designed for supporting e-collaboration should exploit aspects of space and spatial mechanisms, such as providing identity, orientation, a locus for activity and a mode of control, which can be considered as powerful tools for the design. These aspects are:

- **Relational orientation and reciprocity:** The spatial organization of the tools should be the same for all participants. Because people know that the world is physically structured for others in just the same way as it is for them, they can use this understanding to orient their own behaviour for other people's use.
- **Proximity and activity:** People act, more or less, where they are. They pick up objects that are near, not at a distance; they carry things with them; and they get closer to things to view them clearly. An understanding of proximity helps when relating people to activities and to each other. The learners/collaborators in the environment should not be passive but active and able to interact.
- **Partitioning:** Following on from the notion of proximity and activity is a notion of partitioning. Because actions and interactions fall off with distance, this distance can be used to partition activities and the extent of interaction.
- **Presence, awareness and support of users' representation:** The sense of other people's presence and the ongoing awareness of activity allow them to structure their own activity, integrating communication and collaboration seamlessly, progressively and easily. The environment could be populated by concurrent users, who could be represented in the environment. The use of avatars (3D or 2D) for user representation in virtual environment is a key feature for supporting e-collaboration and collaborative e-learning. Therefore, it might be useful to represent the users by avatars that can support mimics and gestures, in order to support virtual and social presence as well as to enhance the ways of communication among the users with nonverbal communication.

Additional design elements of a virtual space, which is focused on e-collaboration and e-learning, could be extracted by a generalization of the design elements presented by Bouras and Tsiatsos (2005) (that are targeted on collaborative e-learning using only 3D virtual environments) and based on Dillenbourg's (1999) interpretation of collaborative learning, and Moshman's (1982) interpretation of dialectical constructivism. These design elements are the following:

- Situated remote communication by supporting multiple communication channels such as avatar gestures, voice chat and text chat.
- *Remote task collaboration*: Distributed environments allow users to collaborate on tasks. This design element could be realized by:
  - Tools such as: Manipulation of shared objects, brainstorming board tool, locking/unlocking shared objects, user handling, as well as slide presentation and creation.
  - Supporting users who have different roles and rights when visiting the environment.
- *Remote task support*: Remote support by other learners, teachers, moderators and participants. This design element could be realized by uploading material in the virtual space and data sharing.
- *Scaffolding tools*: Tools that can support collaborative scenarios as well as support the learners to undertake tasks in the virtual space. This design element could be formed by whiteboard, brainstorming and slide creation tools. For example, the whiteboard tool could support the learner in making a presentation of a task that he or she has been undertaken. Similarly, both the brainstorming tool and slide creation could support the learners to exchange and collect ideas for a task that has been assigned to them by the tutor.
- Representation of the environment by various representation forms, which can range from simple text to 3D worlds.

2D OR 3D E-LEARNING AND E-COLLABORATION TOOLS?

This section presents and compares two different tools as solutions for supporting e-collaboration and multiuser communication in Web-based learning communities. The first solution, called Virtual conference is designed and implemented in the framework of the VirRAD European project. It is a two-dimensional space where participants represented by their photos can use various e-collaboration tools. The second solution, called EVE training area, is a three-dimensional space where participants, represented by 3D humanoid avatars, can use a variety of e-collaboration tools. The comparison between the above tools is based on the design principles presented in the previous section.

VirRAD Virtual Conference Tool

This section presents the Virtual Conference (VC) tool, which has been designed and implemented in the framework of VirRAD European project. VirRAD is related to section III.2 of the IST 2001 work program "Education and Training."

The general aim of the VirRAD environment is to provide a sustainable, user-driven Web-based interface, which supports communication between all members of the worldwide Radiopharmaceutical community. The final prototype of the VirRAD system is available at http://community.virrad.eu.org. The Virtual Conference tool, as a collaboration component of the VirRAD environment, has been designed and implemented in order to support virtual collaborative sessions supported by audio and text chat. The interface of the virtual conference tool is divided into six (6) areas, as it is shown in Figure 1. These areas are:

- *Collaborative area* (Figure 1f), where users can share applications such as Shared Whiteboard, Slide Show and Prepare Slides with other participants. The "shared whiteboard" tool supports the user in making various actions such as: write text, draw lines/arrows, draw a rectangle, erase an object in the whiteboard, resize an object in the whiteboard and change colours. The "slide show" tool could be used for making shared Macromedia flash presentations. The "prepare slides" tool supports the users to collaboratively create an online presentation by using various features such as: viewing of ready slides, shared navigation, creation and deletion of a slide.

- *Text chat area* (Figure 1d), which provides to the user the opportunity to send and receive short messages to and from other members of the community, respectively.
- *Voice chat area* (Figure 1c), where the user has the ability to talk with other members of the community.
- *Gestures area* (Figure 1b), where the user can select an icon gesture (i.e., agree, disagree, bye, etc.) so as to make the conversation with other members more efficient and realistic. The gestures appear next to the member's avatar image (Figure 1c).
- *User representation area* (Figure 1a), where each user is represented by a photo. Further features in this area inform other participants about the shared tool that the user currently uses (Figure 2a and Figure 2b) as well as about her or his feeling represented by an icon-gesture (Figure 2c).

Figure 1.

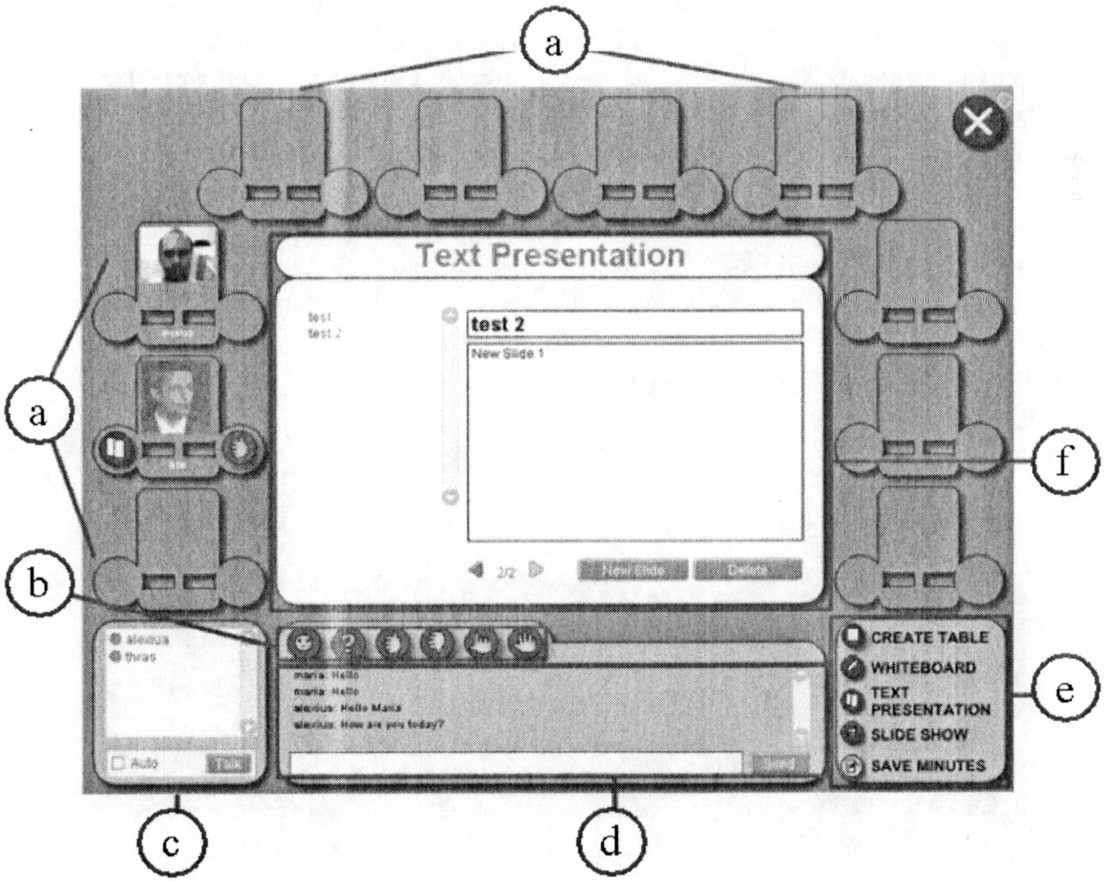

- *Sharing applications area* (Figure 1e), where the user can select an application (white-board, slide show and prepare slides) he or she wants to share with other participants. In addition the last user who has remained in the virtual conference room has the ability to save the log files/minutes of the chat for the conference session.

EVE Training Area

EVE Training Area (http://ouranos.ceid.upatras.gr/vr) is designed and implemented for hosting synchronous e-learning and e-collaboration sessions. It combines 2D and 3D features in order to provide the users with the necessary communication and collaboration capabilities. The main feature of EVE training area is the 3D representation of a multiuser virtual classroom. The user interface of the training area is depicted in Figure 3. The participants in the virtual classroom could have two different roles: tutor (only one participant) and students.

The users that participate in the virtual classroom are represented by humanoid articulated avatars, which can support animations (such as walking and sit down) and gestures for nonverbal interaction among the users. EVE's avatars support functions not only for representing a user but also for visualizing his or her actions to other participants in the virtual space. Available functions in EVE Training Area are: Perception (the ability of a participant to see if anyone is around); localization (the ability of a participant to see where the other person is located); gestures (representation and visualization of others' actions and feelings. Examples are: "Hi," "Bye," "Agree," "Disagree," and "Applause"); bubble chat (when a user sends a text message, a bubble containing the message appears over his or her avatar).

The virtual classroom is supported by various communication channels such as (a) audio chat, which is the main interaction channel, (b) 3D text/bubble chat, (c) nonverbal communication using avatar gestures in order to provide a more realistic interaction among users, expressing, when needed, the emotion of each one to the others. Furthermore, EVE Training Area supports manipulation of users and shared objects by integrating two specific tools: (a) expel learner/participant and (b) lock/unlock objects. EVE Training Area integrates a "presentation table," which is the central point in the virtual space, in order to provide specific collaboration tools. Using the functionality of this table the users can present their slides and ideas, can comment on slides, and upload and view learning material, as well as view streaming video. The avatars of all participants in the virtual space can sit next to this table, viewing not only what is presented on the table but also the other participants. Furthermore,

Figure 2. User representation area

a b c

Figure 3. User interface of the training area

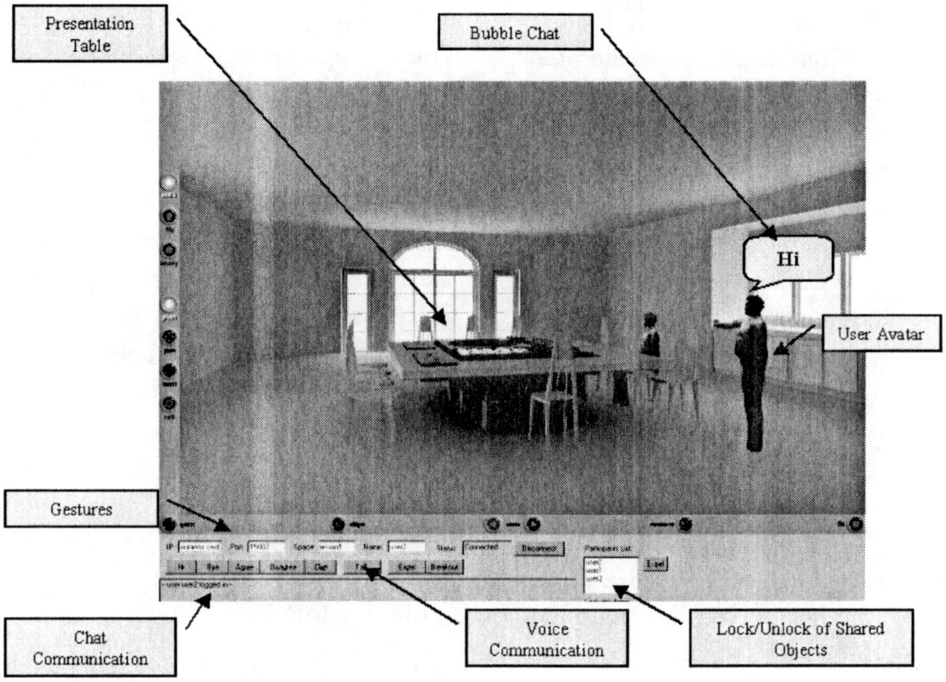

the user can change his or her viewpoint in order to zoom in and out on the presented material.

The presentation table has the following functionality:

- **3D whiteboard:** The 3D whiteboard supports slide projection, line, circle and ellipsis drawing in a wide range of colours and text input in many sizes and colours. It also offers "undo last action" capability, as well as the erasure of all previous actions on the whiteboard.
- **Brainstorming board:** The brainstorming board can be used in a range of collaborative learning techniques for learners to present their ideas in a structured way. The users can create cards in three shapes (rectangle, circle and hexagon) and five colours attaching text on them. It should be mentioned that the shape and colour of the cards is attached to a defined argument. They can also move and delete a card.
- **Video presenter:** Video presenter is used so that the user can attend streaming video presentation/movies inside the 3D environment. The users have the capability to start and stop the movie. Supported formats are rm mpeg, and avi.
- **Library with drag and drop support:** The users have the capability to drag and drop learning material on the table. This material is represented as a small icon on the backside of the table. When the user clicks on the icon the corresponding file is opened either on the whiteboard (if the corresponding file is picture or VRML object), on the video presenter (if the corresponding file is a rm, mpeg or avi) or on a new pop-up window (if the corresponding file is not supported by the VRML format).

Comparison

In this section a comparison between Virtual Conference and EVE Training Area is elaborated taking into account the main principles presented previously. According to Table 1, where the comparison is summarized, it is clear that on the one hand, EVE Training Area supports almost all the previous defined design elements, and on the other hand the Virtual Collaboration application provides the necessary tools for collaboration and interaction but offers limited support for spatial metaphors in a virtual collaboration space. These limitations arise from the two dimensional substance of the Virtual Collaboration tool. Therefore, the main result of this comparison is that even if the use of virtual reality technology is not a required feature a priori, it seems that the use of collaborative 3D virtual environments and humanoid avatars along with supportive communication channels fit well as a solution for virtual collaboration spaces.

Humanoid avatars are a unique solution that 3D-centered tools offer to group communication and learning. It is a fact that persons participating in the virtual learning experience with human like full-body avatars feel more comfortable than in chat or audio-communication (Bouras & Tsiatsos, 2006). The main benefit of the avatars is the psychological feeling of a sense of "presence." The sense of "presence" results in a suspension of disbelief and an increase in motivation and productivity (Bouras & Tsiatsos, 2006). There are a number of important attributes to this experience. The ability to make basic gestures along with a voice or text message strengthens the understanding of the communication context (Redfern & Galway, 2002). This feature is partially supported by the Virtual Collaboration tool but it is limited due to the fact that there is no support of relational orientation and reciprocity. Therefore, due to the fact that the user's awareness of the spatial proximity and orientation of others has a strong impact on the dynamics of group communication (Redfern & Galway, 2002), we could say that 3D multiuser virtual spaces are more suitable for supporting learning communities and e-collaboration. In such an environment users feel as though they are working together as a group and tend to forget they are working independently.

A general problem of meeting focused tools, such as the Virtual Conference tool, is the reduced social presence of the participants that are

Table 1. Comparison of Virtual Conference and EVE Training Area

Designing principle	EVE	VirRAD Virtual Community
Relational orientation and reciprocity	Yes	No
Proximity and activity	Yes	Partially
Partitioning	Partially	No
Presence, awareness, users representation	Yes	Partially
Situated remote communication	Yes	Yes
Remote task collaboration	Yes	Yes
Different roles & rights	Yes	No
Remote task support	Yes	Yes
Scaffolding tools	Yes	Yes
Various representation forms	Yes	Partially

represented in windows by means of live pictures or photos. Thus, participants are rather given a feeling of distance than a feeling of proximity and group awareness

The main advantage, of Virtual Conference tool is the limited requirements in terms of network bandwidth needed for participating in a collaborative session. Furthermore, the development of the Virtual Conference tool is not so time consuming as EVE three-dimensional space. Finally, the Virtual Conference tool is usually more user-friendly, especially for users with a weak background on 3D technology and 3D navigation and object manipulation.

FURTHER CONSIDERATIONS CONCERNING CVES EXTENSIONS FOR SUPPORTING LEARNING COMMUNITIES AND E-COLLABORATION

Taking into account the design principles described in a previous section, as well as the CVEs substance, we can realize that CVEs should be extended in order to support e-learning services. Several extensions should be made for supporting a virtual e-learning community using CVEs. First of all, an e-learning community should have members with different roles, such as tutors and learners. Furthermore, more media should be integrated in the collaborative virtual environments in order to satisfy the user needs, to realise the collaborative e-learning scenarios and to offer advanced awareness of other people and objects.

Many People with Different Roles

An e-learning system should be able to be used concurrently by many users. Furthermore, these users should create an e-learning community. The users will have different roles and rights in this community. This raised the following two issues.

The first one is that many concurrent users and concurrent courses should be supported by the system. The second issue is that the users should have different access rights on both the learning content and the levels of functionality. For example, only the tutor can assign the learners in breakout session rooms. This problem can be solved using customisable interfaces and virtual places according to the e-learning scenario, supported by a database which handles the users' profiles.

More Media-Learning Centric View

There are three approaches regarding CVEs. The first one (VR-centric view) characterises CVEs as systems based only on virtual reality and nothing else. The second approach, which is a step-up of the VR-centric view, is the mixed reality systems. In these systems the main user interface is VR and the users can interact with the system navigating only in the 3D world and accessing the rest of media only within the 3D area. The third approach (media centric view, described by Robinson et al, 2001) tends to integrate more media in a CVE system. Audio, text, documents, video, and so forth, are such media. However, in this approach VR is not the access point for the rest of media, and is regarded as one medium among the others.

Regarding e-learning, the most suitable approach is the media centric view. However, this approach needs to be extended in order to realise the e-learning scenarios and to satisfy the users' needs. For supporting a learning centric view, we need to take into account the necessary media derived from the above-referred scenarios. Main features and media are the content (learning content), Web, virtual reality, video, audio, application sharing and text chat. These media should be integrated in a way that assists the user to learn and to use the system effectively.

According to Figure 4, e-learning systems supported by collaborative virtual environments should be based on three main categories: Content, learning context and communication media. Both Web and virtual environments are the media to support the community and the e-learning context giving the users the feeling that they are in the same place, in an easy way. Communication media (text and audio chat, application sharing, message board, etc.) can support the communication and interaction between the users. Content is the core media for learning and supporting learners to learn and tutors to teach.

However, for supporting collaborative e-learning effectively, more tools for sharing information should be investigated and implemented, such as a presentation table, where all users can present their own content and can open it, view it and collaborate on it.

Added Awareness

Not only the current e-learning systems, but also collaborative virtual environments, lack of awareness. There are two types of awareness: the awareness of other people and the awareness of objects. The suitable combination of these two types of awareness is very critical in e-learning environments in order for the users to be aware, not only of the others and the content but also of the e-learning procedure.

The target for satisfying the need for awareness is to concentrate on both the visualization of other users and the representation of their actions on the objects they are communicating about. The collaborative virtual environments support the awareness of other people and their activity effectively. The avatars along with gestures and mimics represent not only the users but they also make their activity shared to the rest of participants.

In the case of awareness of objects, collaborative virtual environments can support shared virtual objects and generally media that can be integrated in a virtual world such as pictures, audio and video. Furthermore, documents or learning content that cannot be displayed in the virtual world should be supported in an e-learning platform. In addition, the participants should be aware of the number and the identity of the users who view the document at this time. Also, the actions on the objects and the documents should

Figure 4. Learning centric view

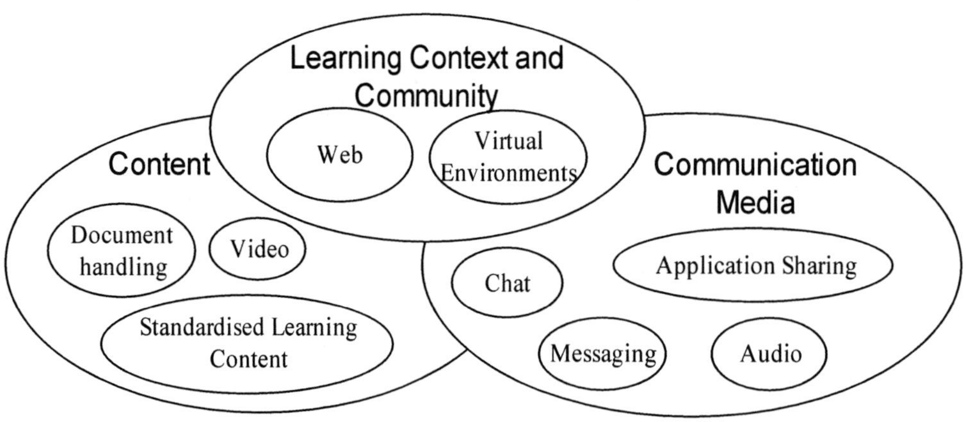

be visible from the other users. This could be achieved, for example, by application sharing.

Combining gestures, mimics, user representation, audio and text chat communication, as well as application sharing, provides to the users the ability to share their views, to show the object that they are talking about and for other users to be aware who is talking and what they are talking about.

COLLABORATIVE E-LEARNING USAGE SCENARIOS EXPLOITING MULTIUSER VIRTUAL REALITY ENVIRONMENTS

The aforementioned e-learning and collaboration tools could be used for supporting collaborative e-learning scenarios. As the comparison has shown in the previous section, EVE Training Area could be a more suitable solution for supporting these services.

Main collaborative learning techniques used today are: brainstorming/roundtable (Millis & Cottell, 1998; Osborne, 1963), think pair share (Lymna, 1981), jigsaw (Aronson, Blaney, Stephan, Sikes, & Snapp, 1978), quickwrites/microthemes (Young, 1997), and structured academic controversies (Johnson, Johnson, & Smith, 1998). Here, the processes for realizing these techniques using multiuser virtual reality environments (and more specifically, collaborative virtual environments-CVEs) are presented. Before describing these processes, we describe specific functionality, which is derived from the collaborative learning techniques.

First of all, we propose the tutors and learners to use a 3D virtual classroom (with functionality similar to EVE's Training Area) and supportive break-out session rooms for dividing the users in subgroups (in case required by the scenario). Both the specific functionality and the access rights on it depend on the e-learning scenario. The transformation and the basic processes are described in the following paragraphs.

Brainstorming/Roundtable

The tutor and learners enter the classroom represented by avatars. The tutor asks a question using audio collaboration functionality (or alternatively text chat). Furthermore, the tutor can write the question and upload it to the presentation table as a document. The learners can answer to the questions using the audio collaboration functionality (or alternatively, text chat). Furthermore, the learners can use the brainstorming tool for writing and attach their ideas to it. When the brainstorming phase is completed, the learners can review and clarify their ideas in the text chat area or in the brainstorming tool.

Think Pair Share

The tutor poses a question (or a problem) as a file on the presentation table or using audio/text chat and introduces the collaboration technique. After a short pause for reflecting, the learners turn into the whisper-mode with their neighbour and discuss privately the problem. The preferable way for whispering would be a private audio-channel within the classroom (audio-whisper function). Alternatively, a private text chat can be used. When the assigned discussion time is finished, the tutor gathers the attention of the learners by "ringing the bell" (sending a text message to all of the participants). Then, the learners exit the whispering mode and return to a group for discussion.

For discussing in a larger group, the groups split up into separate corners of the learning environment (breakout session rooms). Each group should have a brainstorming tool available, though the equipment should be in the breakout room available only on demand and not by default. The default situation is a group with high visibility of all avatars, gestures and facial expressions. Again the tutor can send a text chat message to all learners in the different breakout areas ("ringing the bell"). Then the avatars physically gather back in the virtual classroom place.

Jigsaw

The whole Jigsaw procedure can be handled within the virtual classroom, which has also four breakout session rooms. The tutor first introduces shortly the procedure and then asks for the number of learners (good numbers are any multiple of four). For 16 learners, the tutor suggests study groups of four and four sections.

Then the tutor needs to formulate the sections: he or she divides the users in the sections and attached the necessary learning content to each section. The tutor then assigns the learners to their role (group number and section number). The learners will then receive an automated message about the room they need to go to: there they find the section description on the presentation table and any study material the tutor might have assigned to the focus group. After that, the learners of each section participate all together in a section-shared place. The places can be virtual small classes (breakout session rooms) with audio collaboration, application, sharing, and text-chat functionality. Also, the tutor can assign documents to this section. These documents will be available to the learners in the breakout room. The learners can take material from the presentation table to their other session, by saving the materials into his or her local PC and upload it again.

Quickwrites / Microthemes

The whole procedure for this technique can be handled within a 3D classroom, which has also four breakout session rooms. In the virtual classroom and the breakout out session rooms the users can use audio collaboration, application sharing and text chat functionality. The tutor presents to the learners the microthemes in the presentation table space. Also, he or she uploads and presents supporting documents on the shared space.

The learners can open for themselves a notepad or other text editor; focus on the proposed documents and after completion of the assignment, easily save their result on their local PC and upload it into the shared space. The tutor assigns groups to the themes that should be discussed (2-4 persons).

The learners move to the breakout-rooms, pull their documents onto the presentation area in those rooms and discuss the outcomes. One person writes a protocol of the group discussion and saves the result back to his or her local PC and then upload it into the classrooms' shared space. The tutor can visit the breakoutout session rooms groups and discuss the status of the work. Furthermore, the tutor has the capability to call the learners group to return back to the main classroom area, using text chat or by visiting the breakout session rooms. In the main classroom area the groups present their results using application sharing and audio chat.

Structured Academic Controversies

The whole procedure for this technique can be handled within a 3D classroom, which has also 4 breakout session rooms in case of 16 learners. In the virtual classroom and the breakout out session rooms the users can use audio collaboration, application sharing and text chat functionality.

The tutor selects and uploads a topic with two different viewpoints on the presentation table. The learners form groups of 4 and divide into two pairs. Each pair goes to a breakout session room and the tutor uploads supportive documentation. Furthermore, the learners can upload their own content that think it could be supportive for formulating their assigned advocacy position. The pairs of learners have the possibility to visit breakout session rooms of the other pairs with the same positions. Each learner pair can prepare a short presentation using application sharing and collaboration on documents and to upload this presentation in the original groups of four learners. Each pair presents its position to the other pair in their group using application sharing and audio chat. In this case, no debate allowed and the tutor restricts the audio, application sharing, text chat, and gestures functionality from the opposite pair. Afterward, the other pair presents its position, and then the learners debate and provide more evidence. Finally, learners drop their advocacy role and generate a consensus report addressing the original question posed using application sharing, collaboration on documents, and audio chat.

CONCLUSION

Virtual reality technology could be used to support education in many areas, such as simulation of complex systems, macroscopic and microscopic visualisation as well as fast and slow time simulation. Significant characteristics of VR that could be exploited to support education are the high levels of interactivity, the sense of immersion and the inherent flexibility/adaptability. For that reason, VR has been exploited in various projects in order to support education, training or collaboration. However, little research has been done on the investigation or definition of the design principles that the educational designers should follow for designing effective virtual spaces for e-learning and e-collaboration.

This chapter presented the design principles for virtual spaces and two different tools as solutions for supporting e-collaboration and multiuser communication in Web-based learning communities. The comparison of these tools verifies that 3D multiuser virtual spaces are more suitable for supporting learning communities and e-collaboration. Concerning two-dimensional virtual places, we propose to use them for supporting virtual communities where the spatial metaphors and virtual presence is not a major requirement and also when there are budget and network bandwidth limitations.

Furthermore, this chapter presented further considerations concerning CVEs extensions for supporting learning communities and e-collaboration. Such extensions are the integration of supportive communication and collaboration tools and services in CVEs, as well as the integration of tools for effective manipulation of both the learning content and the users' roles and rights. If such an extended and integrated CVE will be developed, we can say that collaborative virtual environments have many possibilities to support e-learning communities and especially to realize effectively collaborative e-learning scenarios, as presented in this chapter.

FUTURE RESEARCH DIRECTIONS

We believe that future generations will spend a substantial portion of their life in electronically mediated spaces complementing today's environments and marketplaces. A perception of being "virtually present" in CVEs will emerge. An essential ingredient of this virtual lifestyle is a sophisticated communication infrastructure, high-quality rendering equipment and virtual "things" and "beings." Virtual environments do provide different levels of human communication and collaboration such as video, audio and gestures. Distributed communities will develop and provide a consistent set of rules for social behaviour. These rules go beyond mere human to human (i.e., avatar to avatar) interaction. Human to agent interaction also has to be considered. Agents can represent humans or computers. Embodied conversational agents are specifically conversational in their behaviours, and specifically humanlike in the way they use their bodies in conversation (Cassell, Bickmore, Campbell, Vilhjalmsson, & Yan, 2000). Therefore, the investigation of human agent interaction that is relative to e-collaboration and e-learning processes is among future research directions. In particular, the development of interaction strategies where the best agent (whether human or computer) is chosen for each specific task on a continual basis is one major research direction.

REFERENCES

Aronson, E., Blaney, N., Stephan, C., Sikes, J., & Snapp, M. (1978). *The jigsaw classroom.* Sage Publications.

Bouras, C., & Tsiatsos, T. (2005). *Educational virtual environments: Design rationale and architecture multimedia tools and applications journal.* Kluwer Academic Publishers (to appear).

Cassell, J., Bickmore, T., Campbell, L., Vilhjálmsson, H., & Yan, H. (2000). Human conversation as a system framework: Designing embodied conversational agents. In J. Cassell, J. W. Sullivan, S. Prevost, & E. F. Churchill (Eds.), *Embodied conversational agents* (pp. 29-63). Cambridge, MA: MIT Press.

Dillenbourg, P. (1999). What do you mean by collaborative learning?. In Dillenbourg, P., (Ed.), *Collaborative-learning: Cognitive and computational approaches* (pp. 1-16). Amsterdam: Pergamon.

Dourish, P., & Harrison, S. (1996). Re-placing space: The roles of place and space in collaborative systems. In *Proceedings of the ACM CSCW'96 Conference on Computer Supported Cooperative Work*, (pp. 68-85).

Dumas, C., Saugis, G., Degrande, S., Plénacoste, P., Chaillou, C., & Viaud, M. (1999). Spin: A 3D interface for cooperative work. *Virtual reality.* London: Springer-Verlag. ISSN: 1359-4338 (Paper) 1434-9957 (Online).

Hay, K. E., Elliot, D., & Kim, B. (2002). Collaborative network-based virtual reality: The past, the present, and the future of the virtual solar system. In *Paper presented at the CSCL Conference*, Boulder, CO. Retrieved October 24, 2007, from http://newmedia.colorado.edu/cscl/151.pdf

Jackson, R. L., & Winn, W. (1999). Collaboration and learning in immersive virtual environments. In C. Hoadley & J. Roschelle (Eds.), *Proceedings of the Computer Support for Collaborative Learning (CSCL)* Conference. Mahwah, NJ: Lawrence Erlbaum.

Johnson, D. W., Johnson, R. T., & Smith, K. A. (1998). *Active learning: Cooperation in the college classroom.* Edina, MN: Interaction Book Company.

Kalawsky, R. S. *Exploiting virtual reality techniques in education and training: Technological issues.* A report prepared for AGOCG. Retrieved October 24, 2007, from http://www.agocg.ac.uk/reports/virtual/vrtech/title.htm

Lymna, F. (1981). The responsive classroom discussion. In A. S. Anderson (Ed.), *Mainstreaming digest.* College Park, MD: University of Maryland College of Education.

Macedonia, M. R., Zyda, M. J., Pratt, D., Brutzman, R., Donald, P., & Barham, P.T. (1995). Exploiting reality with multicast groups: A network architecture for large-scale virtual environments. In *Proceedings of the IEEE Virtual Reality Annual International Symposium (VRAIS'95),* North Carolina.

Matthew, A., Hutchins, L., Duncan, R., Stevenson, Gunn, C., Krumpholz, A., et al. (2005). Communication in a networked haptic virtual environment for temporal bone surgery training. *Virtual reality.* London: Springer-Verlag. ISSN: 1359-4338 (Paper) 1434-9957 (Online).

Millis, B. J., & Cottell, P. G. (1998). Cooperative learning for higher education faculty. *American Council on Education: Series on higher education.* Phoenix: The Oryx Press.

Moshman, D. (1982). Exogenous, endogenous and dialectical constructivism. *Developmental Review, 2*, 371-384.

Osborne, A. (1963). *Applied imagination.* New York: Scribner's.

Redfern, S., & Galway, N. (2002). Collaborative virtual environments to support communication and community in Internet-based distance education. *Journal of Information Technology Education (JITE), 1*(3), 201-211.

Robinson, M., Pekkola, S., Korhonen, J., Hujala, S., Toivonen, T., & Saarinen, M-J. (2001). Extending the limits of collaborative virtual environments. In E. Churchill, D. Snowdon, & A. Munro (Eds.), *Collaborative virtual environments: Digital places and spaces for interaction*, (10), London Berlin Heidelberg, Germany: Springer-Verlag.

Singhal, S., & Zyda, M. (1999). *Networked virtual environments: Design and implementation.* ACM Press.

Spellmann, P., Mosier, P., Deus, L., & Carlson, J. (1997). Collaborative virtual workspace. In *Proceedings of GROUP'97,* Phoenix, AZ, (pp. 197-203). ACM.

Weil, S., Hussain, T., Brunye, T., Sidman, J., & Spahn, L. (2005). The use of massive multiplayer gaming technology for military training: A preliminary evaluation. In *Proceedings of the 49th Annual Meeting of the Human Factors and Ergonomics Society*, Orlando, FL.

Young, A. (1997). Mentoring, modeling, monitoring, motivating: Response to students' ungraded writing as academic conversation. In M. D. Sorcinelli & P. Elbow (Eds.), *Writing to learn: Strategies for assigning and responding to writing across the disciplines.* New Directions for Teaching and Learning, No. 69.

KEY TERMS

E-Collaboration: Defined as "collaboration which is conducted without face-to-face interaction among individuals or members of virtual teams engaged in a common task using information and communication technologies (ICT)."

E-Learning: (known also as eLearning or e-Learning) Learning facilitated, supported and enhanced through the use of digital tools and content

Virtual Worlds: Digital simulated environments that depict real or imaginary spaces with the use of 3D computer graphics. Users of virtual worlds may simply explore them or even "inhabit" them, by operating digital entities known as "avatars."

Virtual Learning Environments (VLEs): Systems designed to enhance a student's learning experience by supporting a range of learning contexts, ranging from conventional, classroom implementations to off-line, distance learning and online learning, implemented using Virtual Worlds.

Chapter III
Open and Distance Learning Tools and Strategies

Cristina Girona
Universitat Oberta de Catalunya, Spain

INTRODUCTION

There exists nowadays an enormous variety of models of e-leaning, from the technological, methodological and management perspective. At the university level, but also in company-training, in schools and formal education institutions, the different educational models appear, moving in a continuum from those who use technology as a complement or support to traditional attended sessions, to those that base the teaching and learning process in completely online environments. They try a variety of teaching methods while using differing degrees of virtualisation in the organisation (Bates, 2005).

Years ago, when ICT in education started to be widely used, the success of the e-learning experience and the institutions themselves depended on their technological means; the platform was the most important of the model adopted by e-learning institutions. Initial efforts were put in market analysis aiming at finding out which was the best platform developed by ICT providers. Major investments in economical terms were dedicated to the acquisition of what was considered "the best" platform.

Some years later, it was seen that institutions were different from the rest, and that not all educational platforms could cover all their needs. They realised that the success of their educational offer could not only be based on technology but in the learning materials provided. At that moment, the industry of online resources and hypermedia materials for educational uses grew up quickly. For some years, the success of e-learning mainly depended on the quality of the online materials provided, and that distinguish one institution from others.

However, it came out soon that users did not value an online experience only by the quality of the materials provided, but by the closeness of a tutor, his or her capacity to guide the learning process according to a teaching and learning plan, the competence to provide feedback as subject matter expert and the flexibility facilitated when needed along the course.

Nowadays, quality in e-learning focuses on an intelligent combination of the perceived coherence among technology, Web materials and teaching action, together with the facilities and services offered by the e-learning provider, from a client perspective. In that sense, quality e-learning universities and educational institutions should guarantee personal attention and commitment to the task of taking care of adult learner with specific characteristics and lifelong learning needs.

These become the key factors of all those who challenge getting into the e-learning market. Nowadays, evaluation of e-learning models, in general terms, incorporate them as indicators (C. Carreras, Chapter V).

The present chapter attempts to show how some of the agents in e-learning (students and tutors) interact in the virtual environment of UOC (Open University of Catalonia), and how some of the most important elements (online materials and resources) are designed and developed according to quality criteria.

AGENTS AND ELEMENTS IN OPEN AND DISTANCE LEARNING

Beyond the ideas about the curriculum (teacher-centered vs. student-centered) from the point of view of the role of the teacher and the use of resources, there exist significant differences between face-to-face and distance education by

Table 1. Differences in face-to-face and in open and distance learning

Traditional Education	Open and Distance Learning
Agents of the teaching and learning process sharing time and physical space. Immediateness of relationship.	Agents of the teaching and learning process relate independently of time and space
Contents to transmit are structured and organised in the way the trainer plans and decides.	Contents must be structured previously to the starting of the course.
Rhythm of work and sequence of the course are distributed in sessions.	Rhythm of work and sequence of the course might be more flexible.
Voice and body language are the main communication means.	Voice and body language are replaced by other non face-to-face means, or are registered to be displayed and transmitted under a different time and space coordinates.
Conversation is the mean to control and drive the training action.	Differed conversation is needed.
The use of new technologies puts up the cost of training (more equipment and maintenance needed).	The use of new technologies might be more cost-effective.
The use of new technologies has been always perceived as a long term challenge.	The evolution of new technologies facilitates communication among agents and subjects, so that they are incorporated very quickly.
Apparently, to work collaboratively is easier and of a higher immediateness.	To work collaboratively requires planning and establishment of working procedures.
The level of reflection and contributions in class are highly improvised.	Participating at a distance makes necessary a previous reflection.

means of technology. This differentiation must be taken into account when defining the role of the educator in a VLE (virtual learning environment) and the function of the learning resources to be used by the students.

The most important agents involved in the teaching and learning process are obviously the teacher and the learner. The elements that play a significant role are the learning materials and resources and the virtual learning environment itself, its tools and functionalities.

Let's see, then, who and what changes by the use of technology in education, from the perspective of the student, the trainer and the learning resources:

- **The student:**
  - Increases his/her autonomy in the learning process
  - Generates new learning strategies and study habits
  - May put into practice cooperative learning

- **The trainer:**
  - As a coordinator, is the responsible of organizing and planning the course
  - Plays the role of a facilitator
  - Suggest a study plan
  - Supports the student in the process of learning
  - Fosters cooperative work
  - Recommends resources

- **The learning resources:**
  - Are the basic tool for the student
  - Facilitate and stimulate the learning process
  - Are interactive and very practical
  - Allow the generation of new knowledge
  - Are easy to use and consult and allow for more efficient work
  - Content self-paced materials
  - Integrate all the needed study and consultation elements

Apart from the trainer or tutor and the student, there is another professional who must be taken into account, playing an active role in the design of an online course: the subject matter expert (SME). That is, the author of the contents and the developer of learning materials and resources.

Figure 1. Roles and responsibilities of teachers and authors in traditional and online environments

The role of the teacher

Face-to-face models

	Teac.
Transmits knowledge	X
Develops content	X
Organizes learning	X
Assigns time to the training activity	X
Conducts the learning activity	X
Facilitates learning	X
Motivates students	X
Evaluates learning	X

Online models

	SME	Teac.
Transmits knowledge	X	
Develops content	X	
Organizes learning	X	
Assigns time to the training activity	X	X
Conducts the learning activity		X
Facilitates learning		X
Motivates students	X	X
Evaluates learning		X

When this new professional—"new" in distance education models, because his role is not that evident in traditional education environments—takes part in the process, the role of the teacher changes in parallel, and their functions are distributed differently.

Figure 1 shows the responsibilities of both agents (the teacher and the subject matter expert) especially in distance teaching and learning environments: Being an author is much more than transmitting content, but they also give advice and suggest innovative teaching strategies.

LEARNING RESOURCES, ACTIVITIES AND MATERIALS IN ODL

When playing the role of a teacher, a course designer or a subject matter expert in a virtual environment, the idea of having to start from scratch and the feeling that the previous teaching experience has nothing to do with the new situation is extended. This has often persuaded many professionals from even trying it.

But, in fact, what really changes is the environment, which may not be face-to-face anymore or may be blended, incorporating face-to-face and online teaching in different percentages. The agents and the elements of the teaching and learning process are the same, but they just play a different role.

What kind of resources for learning online can a teacher or a subject matter expert develop? As we may see in Figure 2, the type of resources might not differ from face-to-face or traditional educational situations.

Debates can be conducted online, as well as conferences, seminars and role-playings; tutorials may help the students play an active role when learning; the use of glossaries may help them comprehend concepts in a particular context; simulations allow to bring near to real situations, as well as animations and case-studies; self-assessment activities facilitate to control and follow their own learning process; conceptual maps and

Figure 2. Learning resources for online learning environments

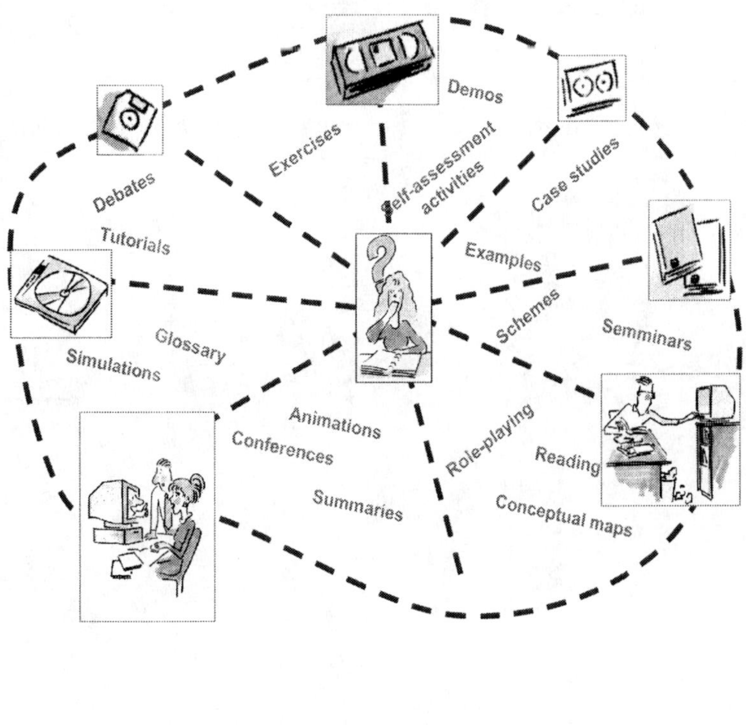

summaries make it possible to approach content in a synthetic way; and so forth.

Format and Structure of Teaching and Learning Materials for VLEs

For years, distance education through VLEs and technological means has been linked to the use of Web-based materials. Although it is true to a certain extent that multimedia materials allow for higher levels of interactivity from the point of view of the users and their autonomous relation with them, we should not forget that paper-based resources, available online, may play its function as well as Web-based multimedia materials (Alessi & Trolip, 2001). One of the clues for a significant learning lies in the planning of the whole course and the organisation of the resources, allowing for independent, autonomy and self-paced learning.

According to this and independently of the type of the support the material is presented (paper or Web-based), it is considered that it should be structured containing, at least, the following elements:

- An introduction
- Learning objectives to achieve
- Activities of different types (self-assessment, graded and not graded activities)
- Properly structured contents and resources
- A summary
- Related bibliography
- A learning plan as a dynamic tool

Students at a distance have a specific profile which differs from those attending traditional education: adult learners, with little time and with personal and professional responsibilities of all types, are willing to stay on the track of life-long learning. Self-explanatory materials (allowing self-learning), motivational activities (encouraging learning) and assorted study proposals (adapted to students different learning styles), are needed.

In online courses, a coherent combination of the mentioned elements and a consistent study plan will ensure covering the needs of these kinds of students.

Traditionally, when the use of the Web was not so extended in distance education, digital resources were used as a complement for more paper-based materials. In that sense, audio and video files, for instance, were implemented in a course Web site provided to students. In the case

Figure 3. Paper-based learning materials

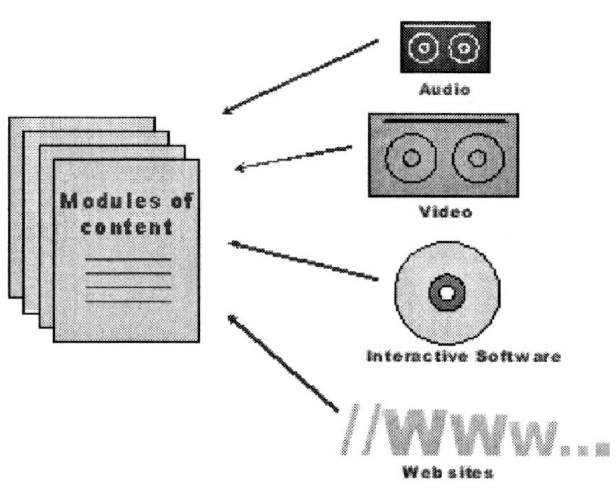

Figure 4. Web based learning materials

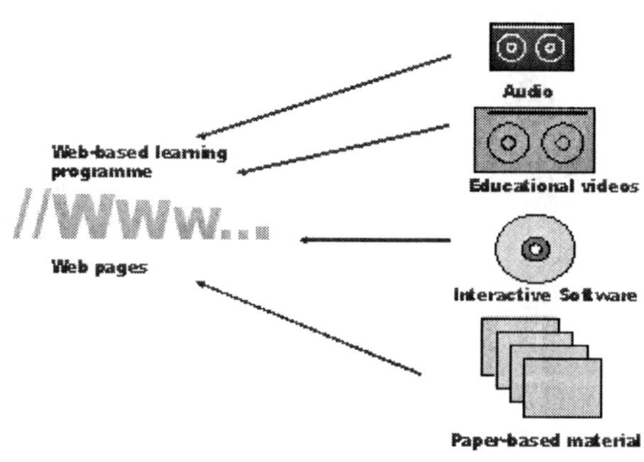

Figure 5. Web based learning materials

media	What do they bring to . . .
Text	text sequential, easy to transport, access and emphasize
Illustrations	examples, emphasis, creativity, accessability, lessen amount of text
Animations	motivation, interactivity, simulation of reality, exemplification, creativity, lessens amount of text
Audio	keep attention, reinforces interaction, helps identification, motivation, contextualization and control
Video	realism, contextualization, creativity, motivation, emphatic, controllable, lessens amount of text
Software	access at random, dynamic, interactivity, modularity, creativity, integration
Hypermedia	access at random, dynamism, interactivity, linking, modularity, creativity, open-up, update, integration

they could not be easily downloaded, audio and video sequences had been often presented in a CD format. However, in most of these cases, paper-based course modules, books and other resources were the main resource in which contents were presented and delivered.

Once the use of the Web could be generalised, when Internet services increased wideband and communication technologies improved, the world of education made a step forward. In terms of content delivery, printed materials gave way to digital resources. The Web site became the main delivery system for the teaching and learning online. The graphics below express the idea.

Digital-based resources and Web-based learning materials are built as a whole and combine the different technologies available in order to obtain the maximum of pedagogical benefits. Audio and video elements and paper-based materials are not complementary elements, but part of the materials. They are designed so that each student can move ahead at his own pace.

Apart from audio and video files, the graphic below shows what the different *media* contribute to learning in distance education.

Hypermedia appears to be one of the media with more possibilities from an educational perspective. It allows information and resources to be connected, so that they are organized and facilitates and encourage students' work.

Principles of VLEs Learning Materials

As mentioned previously, because of distance learners' profile, format and structure of educational materials for online teaching and learning, and also because our experience in virtual higher education, we can consider that VLEs learning materials should accomplish the following principles:

- **Principle of Necessity:** Learning goals allow the understanding of the need for the expected learning.
- **Principle of Multiple Entries:** The user is able to get to content from different "entry doors": text, simulations, conceptual maps . . .
- **Principle of Interconnectivity:** The student must perceive a global vision of the training activity or course and all the elements must be put in context.
- ***Principle of Interactivity:*** The training action must require and active role by the students and provide them with enough feed-back.
- **Principle of Autonomy:** Although the structure of the material is predetermined, the user should be able to freely navigate.
- **Principle of Vitality:** The students must perceive the screen as a dynamic environment.
- **Principle of Consistency:** Coherence of style, reliability, clearness and validity of criteria.
- **Principle of Integration:** The material is something systemic as a whole, not an isolated sum of its parts.

- **Principle of Construction:** Learning implies a personal structure of knowledge to be acquired.
- **Principle of Significance:** The possibility to relate learning to background, experience and personal interests allows for meaningful quality learning experiences.

INSTRUCTIONAL DESIGN: A BASIC TOOL

Traditionally, the term Instructional Design has been used to describe the process in which:

- The learning needs and the environment where they will manifest are analysed
- Training needs are defined
- The most appropriate resources regarding the learning process are chosen
- Evaluation is designed

The Applied Research Laboratory at Pennsylvania State University defines instructional design as a "systematic development of instructional specifications using learning and instructional theory to ensure the quality of instruction. It is the entire process of analysis of learning needs and goals and the development of a delivery system to meet those needs. It includes development of instructional materials and activities; and tryout and evaluation of all instruction and learner activities" (http://www.umich.edu/~ed626/define.html).

However, the role of multimedia instructional design applied to the new information and communication technologies substantially changes in those teaching and learning models based on open and distance learning.

Instructional design is understood as an iterative process in which pedagogical conceptualisation of the learning material comes together with the process of Web design for online delivery. We are nowadays facing the challenge of making good use of the possibilities of multimedia technologies in order to offer much more significant learning than those which traditional educational materials would facilitate; so, it is necessary to take into account all the elements intervening in the instructional design of a concrete training action for ODL. In that sense, the coherence of the materials and the teaching strategy, together with the functionalities of the virtual environment and the relations that will be developed will be fundamental. Thus, it seems evident instructional designers, teachers, subject matter experts or even more editors and technologists cannot work independently. Instructional design is, overall, a team work.

See in Figure 6 the work team for efficiency instructional design, together with the phases of the process of designing and developing materials for online learning, course content or a whole training action.

Planning the learning process: the use of the study plan

To affirm that a particular educational model, (in face-to-face or in ODL) is a student-centred model is easy to say but hard to put into practice efficiently. Unfortunately, too often the autonomy of the students, their active role and supposed capacity to lead their own learning process successfully, and the supposed flexibility that a course may offer, have been understood and translated as "putting the student in front of study modules and resources, expecting him to manage the entire course completely on his own." A certain amount of guidance and support is needed, even in those courses or distance education processes which are defined as completely self-training.

It is not only the tutor who gives this guidance and support to students. He gives it according to a comprehensive work plan developed by a team of professionals, including:

- Full time professors and teachers responsible for each of the subjects or courses
- Subject matter experts and content developers

Figure 6. Instructional design process

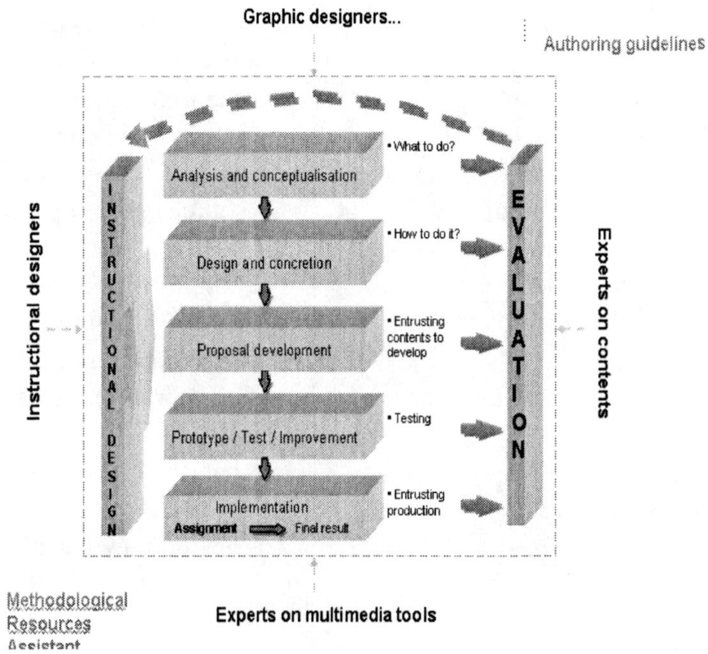

Figure 7. Instructional design process

	Objectives	Content	Activities	Duration
.../...	.../...	.../...	.../...	.../...
Unit 2 Clinical consequences of interactions between medicines	Evaluate the clinical importance of interactions between medicines.	- Factors limiting the observation of the interaction. - Reasons of pharmacological interaction. - Algorithmic method for the search of interactions.	**Activity 3.** Study and discussion of clinical cases. D.: 3 h **Activity 4.** Algorithmic application starting form the proposed cases. D.: 2 h 30 min	6 h 30 min
.../...	.../...	.../...	.../...	.../...

- Instructional designers and methodologists
- Technical experts

This work plan (also called teaching, learning or study plan) is designed according to the following major issues:

- The stated learning objectives and competencies to be accomplished by the students
- The proposed learning activities and resources
- The students' workload

Just like multimedia materials for online learning, the study plan is composed by the following methodological elements:

- *Specific objectives* of the learning process, which give sense to the units of content and learning sequences. They should be defined clearly and express the expected activity from the students perspective.
- *Resources aimed to show content*, which can be readings, instructional units of knowledge, videos, conceptual maps, and so forth. They are aimed at showing the content necessary for the student to fulfil the activities and to achieve the objectives of the unit.
- *Learning activities*, which may be case studies, open questions, surveys, synthesis activities, exercises, problem-solving, and so forth. Their function is to make the students work through the content and introduce different strategies that will help them to integrate their learning process.
- *Allotted time*, the expected time for the student to complete the unit. It includes the total time necessary to fulfil the activities as well as the reading and the work with the resources showing content.

The design of educational activities, courses or instructional programmes requires instructional designers, teachers and subject matter experts to give an answer to the following questions:

- What do we wish the students learn?
- How do they learn it?
- When do they learn?

Table 2. Section of the study plan, Asian geography course

Thematic unit	Course learning objectives	Activities and assessment	Contents and resources	Allotted time
East Asian physical geography	To get familiar with the geography of East Asia, identifying its main physic and human regions.	Learning activity 1. The physic regions of East Asia. Answering questions with respect to the physic regions of East Asia	Module 1 (paper-based): "Geography of East Asia: China, Japan and Korea"	20 hours
	To analyse the complex geographical diversity of East Asia together with its main characteristics.	GRADED LEARNING ACTIVITY 1: Identification of physic regions. To recognize and identify physic regions of East Asia through different maps (part 1), solve questions on the basis of different texts (part 2) and compare a rainfall map with a map of vegetation (part 3).	China: CRESSEY, G. B.(1934), China's geographic Foundations. A Survey of the Land and its People. Nova York: McGraw-Hill. Japan: KARAN, P. (2005), Japan in the 21st century. Chapter 4, "Japanese Landscapes", The University Press of Kentucky Corea: GENTELLE, P i PELLETIER, P. (1994), Chine, Japon, Corée. Article:	
	To get familiar with and identify place names and homonyms of the region. To interpret maps.	GRADED LEARNING ACTIVITY 5 (cross activity): Development of a comparative table or graphic showing the main physic, human, economic, urban and politic indicators applied to 4 of the cities of East Asia. To complete the part of the table corresponding to module 1.	Links: - University of Washington: Chronology and Maps of China - Japan Guide: Geography of Japan - Korean Geography	

A study plan must be the response of these questions to students. The first of the questions above should identify learning objectives; the second should define a certain teaching and learning methodology; and the third should organise learning.

It appears to be hard to attempt designing a course by the use of these or other types of learning plans, when a teacher or an educator faces it for the first time. As a teacher, there is a lot to consider, information to have in mind from scratch and the challenge to encourage students to have a meaningful learning experience. However, the exercise itself allows trainers controlling the workload of each part of the learning material to make adjustments to objectives and contents before its definitive development. The invested time is, thus, worthwhile at all levels.

For the students, the plan is the tool allowing them to have available all elements linked to each learning objective, in order to facilitate the organisation and follow-up of their learning process.

The tool is also valuable for editors, who have available a complete guide with the indication of the correct position of each element that has to be edited.

AUTHORS AND TEACHER TRAINING

"It's necessary to invest more in design than in technology...the learning outcomes are related also to design of the course and the tutor's support," Michael Moore stated during a conference at UOC, Barcelona (Moore, 2001).

This implies teacher and authors training in how to elaborate teaching material for distance learning. In only a few years the growth of services offered by our university and its associated institutions has created the need to contact a high number of these collaborators, who could be authors of our learning materials or have developed specific training tasks.

At UOC, experts on methodology work together with professors and tutors and give guidance and support to the design of subjects, courses and whole programmes of study. Guidelines, tutorials and tools of different types have been developed in this direction.

The so-called methodological resources assistant (MRA) is one of these tools. Many other distance learning institutions have had to plan the creation of such tools to allow continuous training and tutoring of online tutors.

At the light of this institutional need, and from our experience, authors trained realise that they can count on most of the resources that they use in their traditional classrooms and in face-to-face educational situations. To develop new material and resources for VLEs is perceived as a challenge by many of them. In fact, a content developer in a VLE plays the role of a teacher at the same time. It is probably an indirect task, which makes them become conscious of their new responsibility. In our case, training the trainers for ODL becomes not only a need but an institutional compromise.

THE DESIGN AND EDITING PROCESS OF MULTIMEDIA LEARNING MATERIALS AND RESOURCES

Instructional design applied to online education is a complex task where the contribution, teamwork and perspectives of professionals from different fields of expertise turn out to be a fundamental need (Khan, 2005).

Thus, conceptualisation involves three diverse design processes:

- Pedagogical design
- Graphic design
- Functional design

Figure 8. The creation and design of multimedia materials

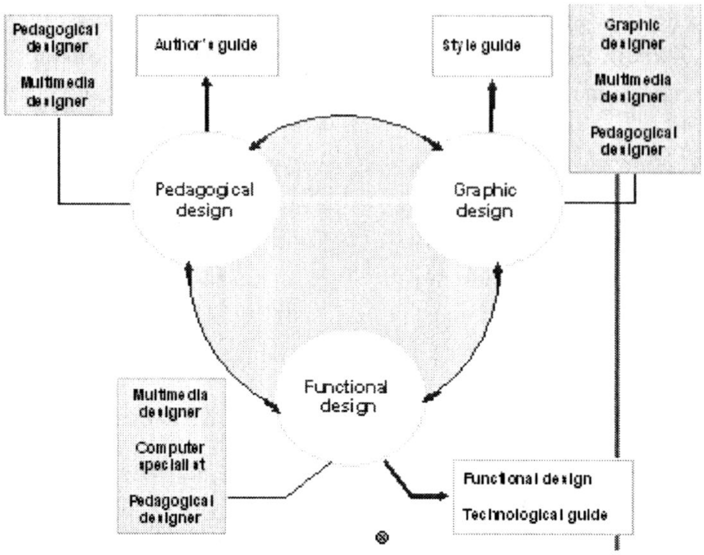

Figure 9. The editing process of multimedia materials

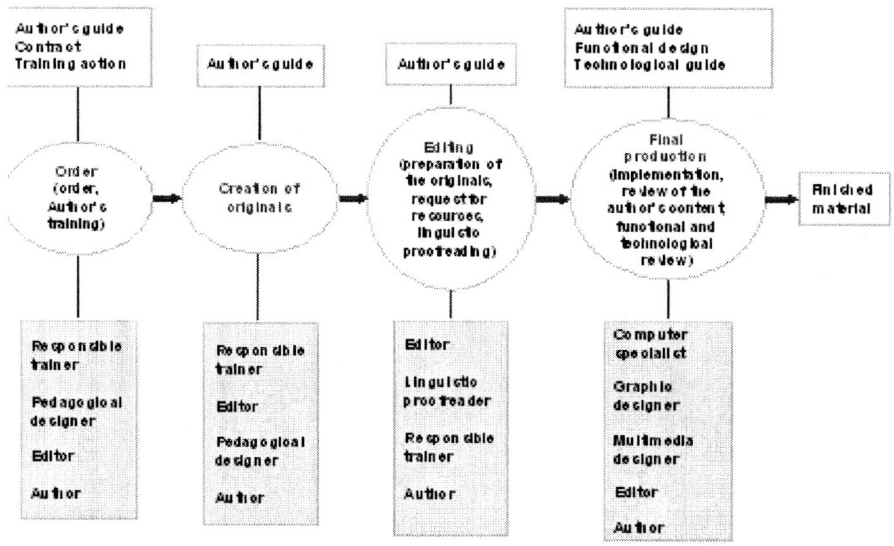

Figure 8 shows the relationship between the three processes, together with the professional involved in each of them and the resources provided to them as tools and support.

The development of the material, from the early conception to the final product ready to deliver to students or users, follows several steps. In some of these steps, "new" professionals intervene, such as editors and linguistic proofreaders.

FINAL REMARKS

The present section has attempted to show how the learning resources and materials play a different role when using them in VLEs and online education in general terms. Furthermore, our wish was to highlight the importance of conceptualising them for virtual environments from the very beginning, considering that the role of the rest of the elements and educational agents in these scenarios are also different than in traditional teaching and learning situations.

Many experiences exist aiming at redesigning traditional materials for online scenarios. Blended models of teaching and learning usually adopt this strategy to create courses which combine face-to-face and online resources. Significant bibliography could be provided about it, showing successful practices.

However, though the UOC model is not a blended one but totally virtual, our experience has showed us that not only materials but the whole of the courses and programmes must be "thought" for online delivery from the very beginning. It is the teamwork among professors, tutors, instructional designers, subject matter experts, computer experts, editors, and so forth, which make the existence of this virtual university possible.

Further research must be done in the field. Our experience and those best practices of many other distance higher education institutions worldwide should positively contribute to the improvement of online teaching and learning at all levels.

FUTURE RESEARCH DIRECTIONS

European universities are adapting their offerings to the requirements of the new scenario in higher education. This adaptation is taking place at many levels. From a pedagogical perspective, the so-called Bologna process has turned out to be the chance to rethink university teaching and learning in Europe: the design based on professional competences to acquire and a student-centered methodology are at the base of the challenge that the European Higher Education Area represents.

The implications of the mentioned adaptation are enormous. In the following years, the main actions and research in higher education will be focused on the assessment of competencies and skills, the accreditation of these competencies, the measurement of the effort and time invested in learning by the student, quality assurance of e-learning, or teacher training.

But this "revolution" in higher education is not only taking place in Europe. Beyond the Bologna process and its political, economical and educational grounds, universities all over the world are facing up to new challenges together with new responsibilities: assuring personal and professional growth of society by offering quality education.

My field of research is instructional design in e-learning. With this reality at the background, my research interests in the next years focus on:

- *Specific didactics:* Effective online teaching and learning methodologies, practices, activities and resources for the different fields of knowledge or disciplines students must learn.
- The design by competencies, as a methodology to develop graded and master courses
- *Typologies of learning activities:* E-learning resources to make learning meaningful to students according to competencies and learning objectives in each case.
- *Teacher training:* Methodologies, processes and resources to improve their competencies in teaching online.
- Online assessment of attitudinal skills and values

REFERENCES

Alessi, S., & Trollip, S. (2001). *Multimedia for learning – methods and development.* Massachusetts: Allyn & Bacon.

Bates, A. W. (1995). *Technology, open learning and distance education.* London: Routledge.

Khan, B. H. (2005). *Managing e-learning strategies: Design, delivery, implementation and evaluation.* Hershey, PA: Information Science Publishing.

Moore, M. G. (2001, June 6). *Distance education in the United States.* In *Proceedings of the Conference given at UOC*. Retrieved October 25, 2007, from http://www.uoc.es/web/esp/art/uoc/moore/moore.html

ADDITIONAL READING

Applied Research Laboratory, the Pennsylvania State University (1996). Definitions of instructional design. Adapted from *Training and instructional design* at http://www.umich.edu/~ed626/define.html. University of Michigan. Retrieved October 25, 2007, from http://www.arl.psu.edu/

Bates, A. W. (1999). *Managing technological change: Strategies for academic leaders.* San Francisco: Jossey Bass.

Busquets, A., & Girona, C. (2006). Instructional design and quality: The two walk together. In *Paper presented at the ICDE Conference: The key factor of distance and ICT-based education: Quality*, Tianjin, China.

Guardia, L. (1999). El disseny formatiu: un nou enfocament del disseny perdagògic dels materials didàctics en suport digital. In Sangrà, A. Et al. *Aprenentatge i virtualitat.* Disseny pedagògic de materials didàctics per al www. Editorial UOC i Pòrtic. Barcelona.

Harton, L., & Ingram, A. (2002). Cooperation and collaboration using computer mediated communication. *Journal of Educational Computing Research, 26*(3), 325-347.

Holmberg, B. (1995). *Theory and practice of distance education.* New York: Routledge.

Kearsley, G. (2000). *Online education: Learning and teaching in cyberspace.* Belmont, CA: Wadsworth.

Keegan, D. (1996). *Foundations of distance education* (3rd ed.). New York: Routledge

Laurillard, D. (1993). *Rethinking university teaching.* London: Routledge

Macdonald, J. (2003). Assessing online collaborative learning: Process and product. *Computers & Education, 40*(4), 377-391.

Moore, M. G., & Anderson, W. G. (2003). *Handbook of distance education.* Lawrence Erlbaum & Associates.

Politis, D. (2006). Introduction: E-learning trends in archaeology. In C. Carreras (Ed.), *Open and distance learning (ODL) strategies.* Athens: Klidarithmos Publications.

Politis, D. (Ed.) (2006). *The e-learning dimension of computer applications in archaeology.* Athens: Klidarithmos Publications.

Ragan, L. C., & Terheggen, S. L. (2003). Effective workload management strategies for the online environment. Report*: Findings of a research.* The Alfred P. Sloan Foundation. Pennsylvania State University U.Ed. OCE 03–1818. Retrieved October 25, 2007, from http://www.worldcampus.psu.edu/pdf/fac/workload_strat.pdf

Resnick, M. (2002). Rethinking learning in the digital age. In G. Kirkman (Ed.), *The Global Information Technology Report: Readiness for the networked world.* Oxford University Press.

Rowntree, D. (1997). *Making materials-based learning work.* London: Routledge

Ryan, S., Scott, B., Freeman, H., & Patel, D. (2000). *The virtual university: The Internet and resource based learning.* London: Kogan Page.

Salmon, G. (2000). *E-moderating: The key to teaching and learning online.* London: Kogan Page.

Salmon, G. (2001). *E-tivities: The key to active online learning.* London: Kogan Page.

Sangra, A., Guardia, L., Gonzalez Sanmamed, M. (2007). Educational design as a key issue in planning for quality improvement. *Making the transition to e-learning: Strategies and issues.* Hershey, PA: Idea Group.

Stephenson, J. (2001). *Teaching and learning online: Pedagogies for new technologies.* London: Kogan Page.

Wilson, B. G. (2005). Broadening our foundation for instructional design: Four pillars of practice. In E. Rose (Ed.), *Educational Technology, 45*(2), 10-15. Special issue on cultural studies.

KEY TERMS

ICT: Information and communication technology.

Open and Distance Learning: Used synonymously with "open education" to emphasize systems of education which allow entry into the system without consideration of prior educational experiences. Also, describes a model of distance education developed by Kember, which considers the influences of social and academic factors on learning outcomes (See Moore & Kearsley, 1996, p. 209-210).

Subject Matter Expert: It refers to an expert in a specific field of knowledge who is authoring the material.

Instructional Design: A system of developing well-structured instructional materials using objectives, related teaching strategies, systematic feedback and evaluation (See Moore & Kearsley, 1996, p. 102).

Work Plan: methodological element of online courses. It allows the setting of learning objectives, choosing media applications, planning evaluation and preparing instructional strategies in advance of student recruitment and development of course materials.

Methodological Resources Assistant: It is an authoring tool for the design and elaboration of methodological resources adapted to different objectives and training needs, in a virtual learning environment. Its aim is to provide a wide range of distance learning methodological resources, as well as tools to facilitate material creation, for professors and authors.

Chapter IV
Teaching and Learning in Virtual Environments

Joan Campas
Universitat Oberta de Catalunya, Spain

INTRODUCTION

The paradigm shift that education experiments now, it does not stem neither from the existence of Internet and telematic networks nor applications of new technologies in teleformation. It comes from a lost value underwent in the 60s, one of the basis of education, that it was in continuous crisis since the 16th century: the perennial knowledge.

Since then, it was thought that people's knowledge did not change much during their whole life. Anything learned in their youth at primary and secondary school would be useful and applicable all their life. Knowledge always suffered changes and evolutions, however, at a rhythm that did not affect much individual formation.

Therefore, people learned a job after childhood and they spent the rest of their lives—in general terms—developing, improving and acquiring experience with regards to this job. In the last decades, the situation has shifted radically:

- The fast evolution of many disciplines make that any specialist should require further education, updating courses, learning new modules, and so forth.
- Most people change jobs and adopt diverse roles in their professional lives, so they require new capacities and competences.
- Professional posts do not respond to straight professional profiles, which are homologated by suitable diplomas.

GOING UPRIVER, OR SEA NAVIGATION

We will use a hydric parable to illustrate the shift of basic paradigm that experiments education: traditional education was based on "river courses," where students went upriver with effort, going up in different stages in which they could obtain some kind of degree (diploma, degree, PhD, etc.). But nowadays, the way of knowledge cannot be considered like an upward path that goes from the plain of a simple life to the altitudes of Gnosis.

In the same way, the shift from industrial to information society paradigm implies a move

Table 1. A hydric parable

River courses	Sea navigation
Knowledge is static and orderly	Knowledge is dynamic and shaking
Upward vertical structure of learning	Navigation in the sea of knowledge
Teachers teach, learners learn	Cooperative learning and collective intelligence
University homogenizes students	Individuals design their own multiversality
Learning a profession and starting a job	Assimilating new capabilities constantly
Learning knowledge and skills	Learning how to learn what interest us
Value of diplomas and degrees	Value of capacities and experiences
Learning based on objectives	Learning based on competences

from a vertical and pyramidal organisation to a network structure. The shift in the education paradigm moves us from a river of turbulent waters, but unchangeable in its course, to a sea of information. In this sea of information, courses are infinites and routes are sailed not only with effort in displacement, but also with the effort of cutting through waves, in which we ourselves fix destinations.

The paradigm of education in the information society passes through adapting studies to the requirements of each individual, and not the other way around, as happened in the past. Our social reality makes possible that anyone could be interested in physics of particles, biology of viruses, fractal mathematics and sociological theory. And all this knowledge may have an effect in its quality of current activities. Less bizarre combinations are produced by millions of individuals.

Key points of the new paradigm of education:

- Fostering of learning
- Training how to search information, how to process it, how to organise it, and how to distribute it
- Training how to work in teams and how to organise groups

Teaching how to learn cooperatively is a learning process in which teachers also acquire new knowledge thanks to the synergies created. A great part of the work in many industrial professions consists of executing repetitive and predictable tasks. In the information society, most tasks are automated, and our present occupations involve every day more problems resolution, team coordination and knowledge transfer.

VIRTUAL LEARNING COMMUNITIES

A common metaphor is considering Internet as a meeting point for any virtual community, even the virtual learning communities. According to Rheingold (1996): "the communities are social aggregations that emerge in the net when enough number of people sustains public discussions over a certain period of time, with enough human components to shape networks of social relationships in the cyberspace." Rheingold (1996) explains that:

People of virtual communities use words in screens to exchange jokes and to argue, to take part in intellectual discussions, to manage commercial operations, to exchange knowledge, to share emotional support, to make brainstormings, chat flat, to quarrel, to fall in love, to make new friends and lose them, to play, to flirt, to create art and many insubstantial conversation. The components of virtual communities make all that it is done

Figure 1. The Virtual Campus of the UOC (Open University of Catalonia), the first asynchronous University with telematic means. It was created in 1995 by the government of the Generalitat de Catalunya with the aim to provide higher education to people who due to work, residence, age or personal reasons prefer a system of non-presential education

in real life, but without physical presence. We can not kiss anyone and none can beat us, but between both extremes many things may happen. Wealth and live of cultures related to computers is attractive, and even addictive for millions who have tasted it.

However, can a virtual community of teaching-learning be created? Schrage (1991) offers a model that remarks the importance of collaboration. According to him, the final aim should be the creation of a shared experience instead of an experience that is shared. An experience that is shared is passive, while a shared experience is participative. For Schrage (1991), Internet and the groupware offer an immense potential as a context for the support of collaboration: "a good collaborative environment integrates the intellectual virtues of printing, the visual appeal of television and the potential in information manipulation of personal computers. Well calibrated, the means of collaboration are independents, but they can work in a productive way in a larger network."

The concept of collaboration is, then, fundamental, because it is the premise of a virtual learning community. Schrage (1991) says:

Collaboration is the process of shared creation: two or more subjects with complementary skills interact to create a shared understanding that nobody had ever possessed before or at which nobody would have ever arrived by itself. Collaboration could be done by mail, by telephone or in person. But the authentic mean of collaboration is the other people.

Figure 2. The UOC has promoted interaction and connectivity amongst its members. Forums that can be freely created by any member (teachers, students, and administrative staff), associations of any kind, activities (virtual presentations of books, sessions on line...), Campus for Peace, adverts... These are some of the options implemented to create virtual communities, to share ideas and experiences, and to create network of common interests and activities

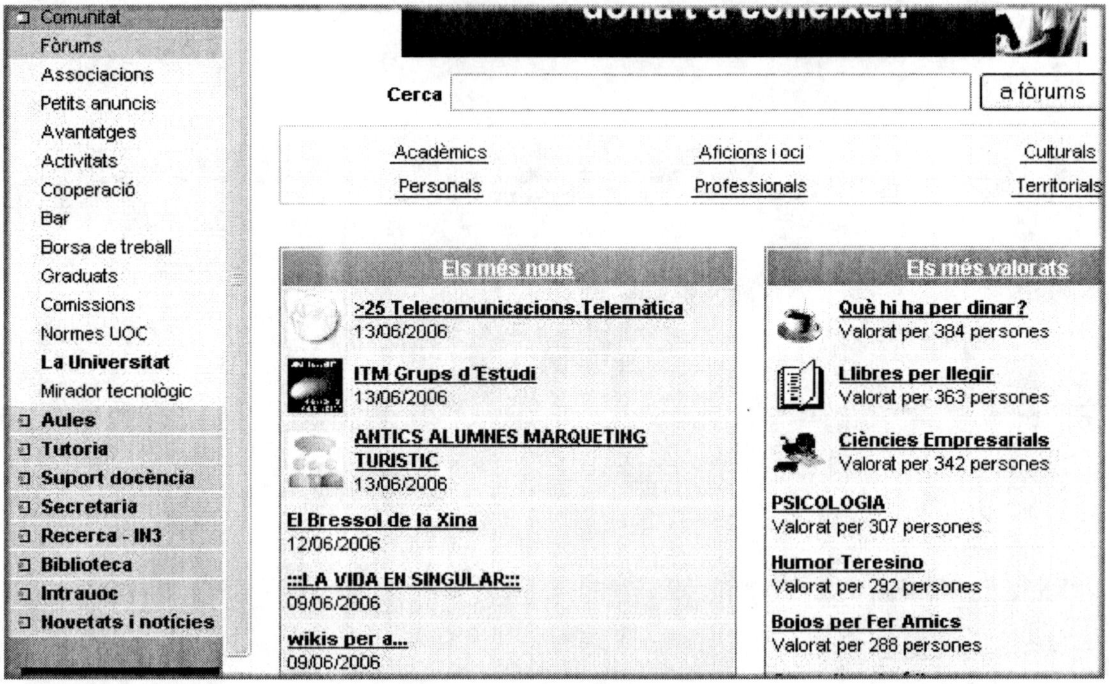

Collaboration is an intentional relationship based on the desire or need to solve some problem, to create or discover something in a particular frame. Schrage (1991) remarks that: "the essence is not the communication or work in group; the one that is really important is the creation of value."

EDUCATION AND LEARNING THROUGH THE WEB SITE

According to Romiszowski (1997), the educational system has to prepare people for the type of predominant work for the 21st century society: "knowledge work." The worker of knowledge will get its earnings using its own knowledge in order to create new knowledge. Therefore, it should have:

- Capacities of critical analysis well-developed in order to select information
- High degree of creativity in order to develop new knowledge that can become a competitive advantage for its organization

Tasks of such workers will consist of renewing constantly the process of knowledge creation and always to keep as leaders in their career. Because computer programs will substitute routine tasks, knowledge creation will become the only area of employment where human beings will be able to stand out.

The aim of formation will be, then, acquiring the required skills to be able to become a good knowledge employee. If such scenario comes true, how would processes, systems and supports in which education takes place be affected?

Figure 3. Also, the classrooms structure that is articulated around an educational plan and activities, is designed to foster interactions amongst students (forum, debate) or work in groups

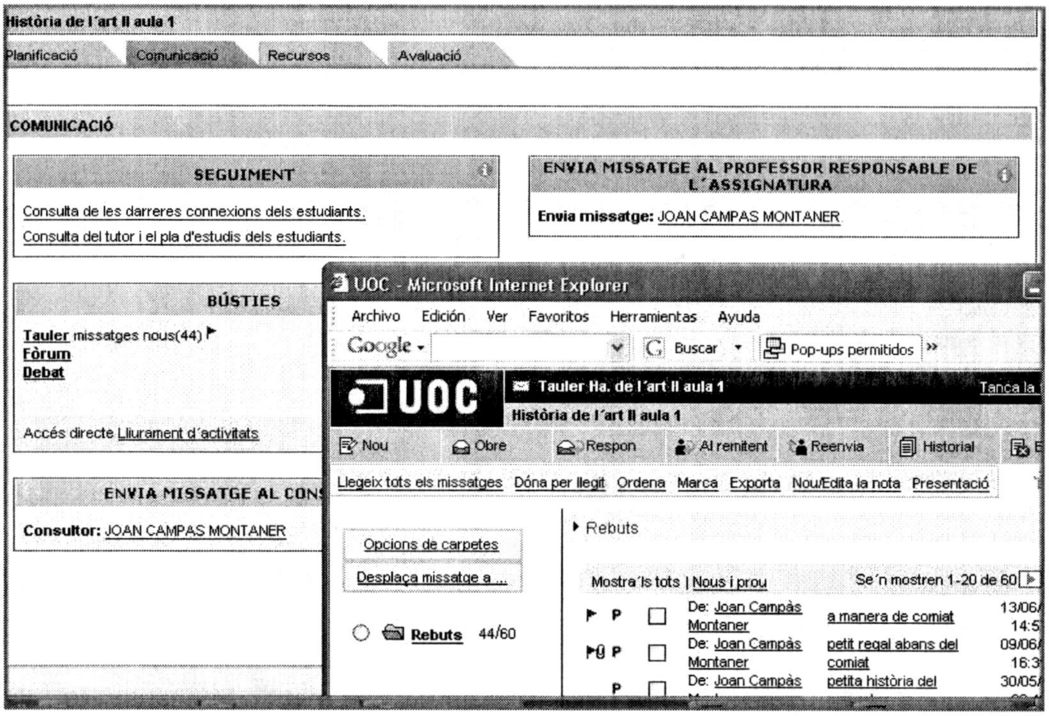

It should be taken into account that every few years the amount of information is doubled in the world. And the more information is generated the more difficult it becomes to find the specific one. We suffer, therefore, a paradox situation:

- It is needed to act quickly in order to be continuously up-to-date.
- But everyday it becomes more difficult and slow to generate new knowledge

On the one hand, we are pushed to adapt ourselves sooner and more creatively as possible to an environment of constant evolution. On the other hand, such activity of change forces us to readapt ourselves constantly to knowledge generation, and fast implementation contributes to accelerate the process. So, digital technologies,

- Offer us tools to face new challenges in the information society
- Are real responsibilities of changes that generate new challenges that shift everyday

In this context, which are the skills and competences that this future knowledge employee will require? And which methodologies, processes of learning and contents typologies will be taken into account to describe the new educational curriculum?

A way to design the curriculum is to conceptualize key competences for an employee in effective knowledge. And these competences include some related to performance, not only in terms of fast and effective learning of use of new tools and techniques that keep on turning in the professional world. That is why the focus is on learning "just-in-time." Besides, they include competences related to skills of access, location, analysis and evaluation of information, as well as the ones related to processes that transform existing knowledge into new knowledge. And here lies the importance of learning for experience and reflexive learning. We list the basic aspects to these key competences:

a. **Self-directed learning:** It is a matter of "learning how to learn" as an answer to confirm that learning will be an activity that will go on during the whole life. Most of such learning will take place in formal educational institutions. One of the areas of further education is the need to learn how to use new tools for accessing, processing and transforming information into new knowledge. It is a formation "just-in-time" that implies that everyone who needs a new skill has to be formed in the moment, in which it requires it. It is then a matter of bringing up a distributed formation at work that can be used, under students' control, at any place and time, thanks to the use of systems of formation based on digital technologies.

b. **Hypermedia learning:** It is necessary that anyone has access to information available and relevant in order to become a creative employee. Therefore, information should be available in a well-organized way. Solutions offered us by digital technologies (to organize great amounts of information in clear and logical structures) are "universes of information" formed by documents interwoven electronically, which is called the hypertext format. The WWW is the last creation of hypertext environments, which allow practical implementation and the use of hypertext environments from relatively small autonomous systems.

c. **Learning of metacognitive skills of information analysis:** They are skills required to locate and evaluate information value. They

Figure 4. Web pages are powerful when associated to databases. This image show a model of analysis of a Net.art work. It is part of the material of the subject Digital Art (UOC) to which students can access through an index or a browser. Students have more than 500 commented works-of-art that can be updated by tutors in the future

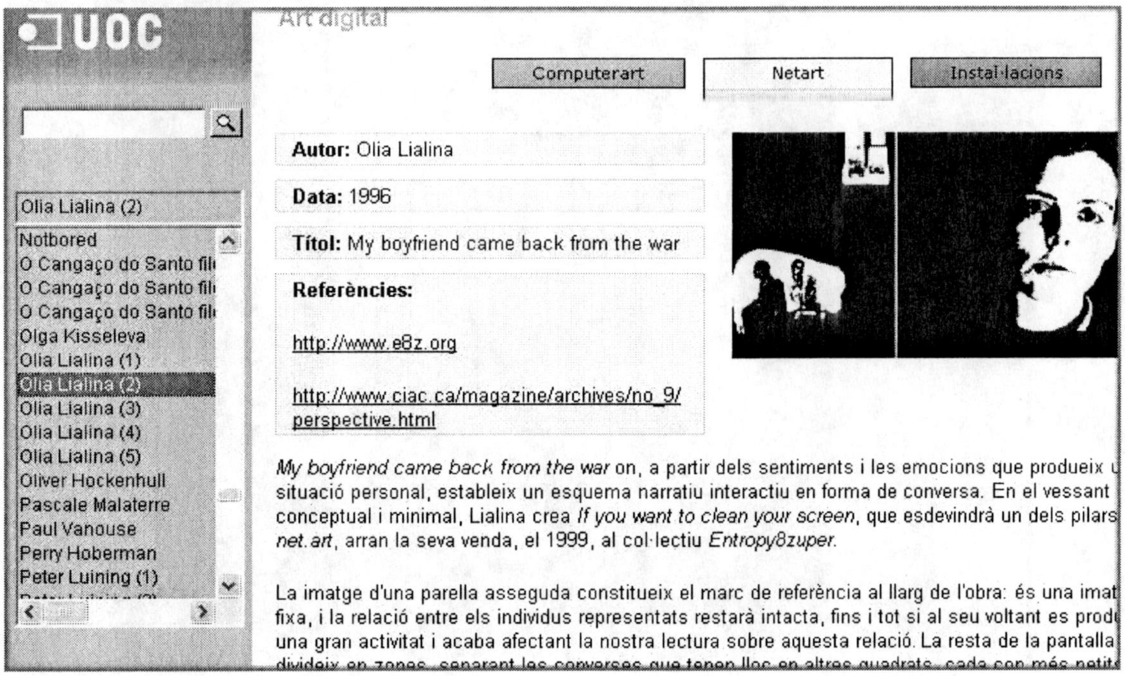

are in the "skills of critical thought," area of research in which many cognitive scientists have focused. An approach to the problem refers to making sense of the information available: the one who will give meaning to information sources will be the final user.

d. **Learning of creative skills for problem resolution:** Activities of the knowledge employee when uses important available knowledge in order to generate new useful one. It consists of adding value to existing knowledge, and transforming it to more specific knowledge for applications. Moreover, it consists of skills in analysis to identify important knowledge and skills in evaluation to judge practical application of such knowledge. Knowledge employees will require synthesis skills in order to generate new ideas from a combination of previous ones:

The global computer network, fit out by Internet and well-incorporated into the World Wide Web at the present, it is a revolutionary force that it is changing the educational and formative framework. However, we also observe that computer network is so much a technological device that clusters human beings in conversation or participative networks, where they can exchange ideas and share material. Such materials are often stored as information networks of hypertext

Figure 5. This hypertextual study of the painting Las Meninas by Velázquez (http://www.uoc.edu/humfil/digithum/digithum1/jcampas/menines.html) is designed following constructivist purposes in order to generate a cognitive conflict in students' mind

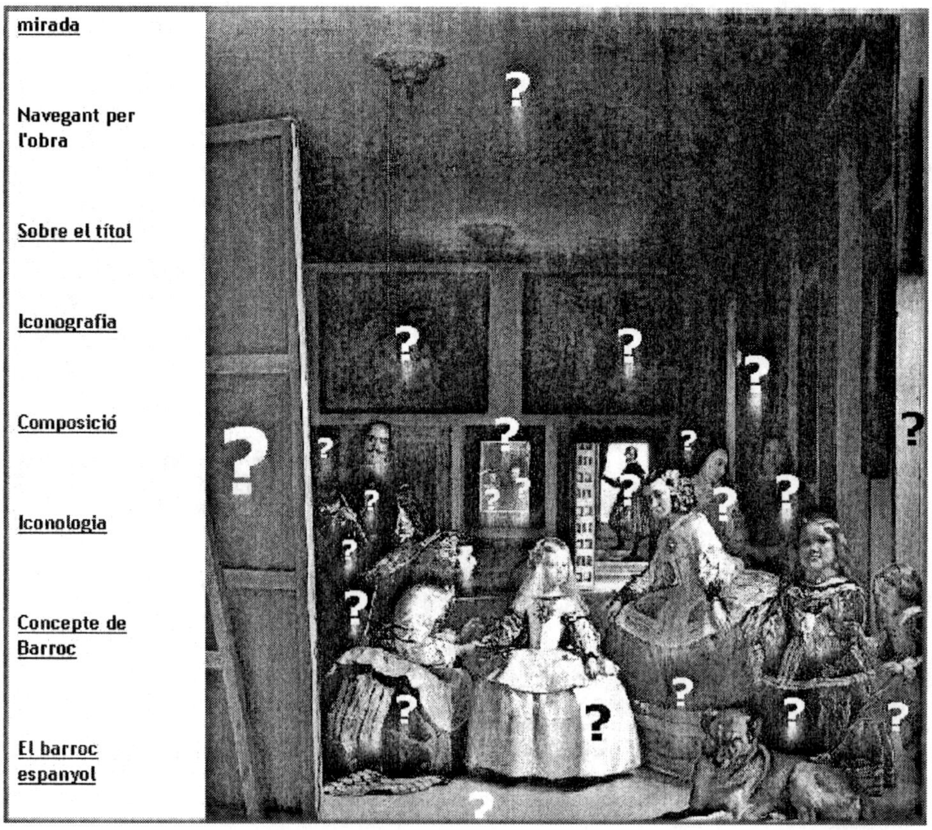

or hypermedia. But the final aim of all the exercise is to help individuals to create (and, in turn, to enable them so that they can help other people to create) their own conceptual networks of interrelated ideas, strategies and theories. These networks are fundamental for processes of critical analyses, evaluation of existing knowledge and creative synthesis of new knowledge: the essential components of the knowledge work, the key to find work and have a professional satisfaction in the future interconnected society. (Romiszowski, 1997)

TRADITIONAL FORMATION AND FORMATION IN A WEB PAGE-BASED ENVIRONMENT

Cuban (1993) in a study and analysis of systematic practices undertaken in the classroom during a century, portrays formation in the classroom like a model which goes from a curriculum centered in teacher's role to one centered on the student.

Cuban (1997) concludes that "yet there has not been any compilation of results in research or written observations that allow to the image of permanent domination of a curriculum centered in teachers." Relan and Gillani (1997) add more criteria to interpret traditional formation:

- Spatial and temporary structures, in which students should adapt, are very specific. Learning is boxed off geographically (classrooms, laboratories, courtyards, outings…) and disciplines are taught in some predetermined moments and in a preestablished order (temporary and sequential structure).
- Physical presence of student and teacher in the same classroom is an indispensable requirement so that learning can be produced.

Goodlad (1984) explains what we consider "traditional formation:"

What predominates was not the how, but the what. Teachers as well as students were busy working what was explained in the textbooks. Girls and boys, as individuals or groups, did not search solutions to problems that they had identified as important and significant. They were occupied in predetermined assignments by teachers. In general, subjects turned up like something remote or driven away from problems and daily interests of students... Despite the fact that they did not

Table 2. Comparison between curriculum centered on the teacher and on the student

Curriculum centered on the teacher	Curriculum centered on the student
Teacher speaks more than students do	Students speak as much as teacher or even more
Formation is usually carried out with all classmates. Formation in small groups or individuals is less frequent	Most formation takes place in small groups
Timetables are determined by teacher	Students define partially rules, rhythms
Teachers are based on textbooks to guide curriculum and instructional decision making	Students help choose contents, which should be organized by them as well as how to learn them. Several types of educational materials are employed, individually and in small groups, determined by individuals or groups
Furniture in classrooms is organized in rows of tables and chairs facing the blackboard	Furniture is put in such way that students can work in small groups or individually

Source: Adapted from Relan and Gillani (1997)

reveal any great interest and excitement, they did not get bored either.

How is it that the "traditional formation" has been to a large extent devoid of powerful educational strategies from the cognitive point of view? Cuban (1997) affirms that many effective practices in classrooms are difficult to integrate and to implement in infrastructural structures in which the "traditional formation" is produced. That is the reason why there is a stability of traditional practices in the classroom model (availability of space in schools, organization of contents in different levels, periods of fifty minutes, large classrooms.)

What Brings the Formation in Web Page Support?

The WBI (Web-based instruction) is the application of a series of educational strategies in a cognitive plan, implemented in a constructivist environment and learning in groups, using attributes and resources of the World Wide Web (Wilson, 1996).

In Which Way Can Educational Strategies be Designed Through the Web Site?

- As resource for identification, evaluation and integration of several information
- As means of collaboration, conversation, discussion, exchange and communication of ideas
- As international platform for expression and contribution of meaning and artistic and cognitive interpretation

Which is the Context that Reconfigures the WBI?

- Permanent access to the Web site and possibility of navigation and interaction with their contents
- Constructivist environment
- Reconfiguration of teacher: disseminator of information, facilitator to search, evaluate and give meaning to information
- Interdisciplinary learning

WBI broadens the limits of learning, so it can take place in the classroom, at home or in the job. The permanent access to a mass of learning resources independently of the geographical location where we are, allow us continuous learning and promotes uninterrupted reflection on the subject.

It fosters learning through experience or learning "on-site," because it allows integrating the process of learning into the real world. For example, through students' participation in a scientific expedition or in an excavation, in real time (the experience of the expedition MayaQuest can be consulted at http://www.mayaquest.mecc.com).

It broadens cooperative learning, because it offers several means for social interaction generated when learning. While traditional education tends to de-encourage social interaction, the WBI is designed for collaboration and interaction. Therefore, it favors a different perception of sense of responsibility among students. It moves the main source of contents from the textbooks and teachers to more diverse information sources.

The nature of contents becomes dynamic as a contrast to static one from the textbooks. Besides, research and students' assignments provide new contents, so individual learning is socialized and metacognitive skills are developed (to collect, revise, evaluate, select and integrate significantly).

Presentation of contents in hypertextual format allows users to follow a sequence of contents being based on their own criteria, so they have control of learning, something that does not exist in the traditional formation (to see some hypertextual students' assignments of art history, visit http://www.uoc.edu/humfil).

It facilitates personalization of learning processes, feed-back, and elaboration of assignments. Students can select their own contents, timing, sources and feedback, as well as a variety of means to express what they learn. As Damarin (1993) says: "...knowledge is not only an individual acquisition, but it also lies on in groups and communities who share it." And, the World Wide Web is, for the time being, the only environment in which "communities of learning" can be created.

RECONFIGURATIONS IN VIRTUAL ENVIRONMENTS

Reconfiguring Teachers

One of the main effects of hypertextual materials online is the way in which it questions the conventional figures of teachers, students and educational institutions. The evaluation of the Perseus project (http://www.perseus.tufts.edu) refers to: "every time that a new technology applies to education and learning, questions on principles and fundamental methods arise." Multimedia materials considered as didactic tools include:

- The central element is the user as an active participant in an interaction with information
- Students who use hypermedia act as readers-authors choosing individual routes among connected information and adding links to hyperdocuments
- Emphasis in active students because "learning systems with hypermedia will leave more responsibility to students regarding information access and its sequence"
- Hypermedia users should be mentally active when retrieving information
- Hypermedia systems do not have to be considered mainly as educational tools but learning tools
- Such systems represent an environment in which learning by discovery or research is developed

Multimedia materials online like dynamic hypertexts redefine the teachers' role, transferring part of their authority toward students. Teachers become a coach more than a lecturer. Teachers face two problems:

- Subjects, even brilliant and innovative ones, seldom survive more than a course
- Materials of one subject can hardly be used in another

Such problems come from the hierarchical structure of information in rigid structures of courses and subjects, and formats like paperwork. However, Web site materials can be modified, be accumulated, be put away, be broadened, be updated, be integrated, establish several itineraries, incorporate students' assignments, solve questions, and so forth. Tools make available interdisciplinarity, contextualization, research and interaction in forums or blogs.

Reconfiguring Students

How do multimedia materials online reconfigure students behavior?

- Experience of hypertexts as a network of navigation relations means a much faster and easy access to a wide information and documentation (availability is not the same as accessibility)
- If nodes are information, links provide knowledge. Links are a good way to get students used to establishing relationships among contents. A fundamental component of critical thought consist of the habit of looking for several causes that bring about any particular phenomenon and evaluate their relative weight afterward.

- Contributes to acquiring a habit of reading in a nonsequential way, typical of science or humanistic writings
- Provides means to integrate contents of a course with contents of another ones
- Creates a learning environment in which the support documentation of each subject exists in a relationship more direct than the one achieved with conventional didactic technologies
- Allows to see how an expert in a given field establishes relationships and formulates lines of research
- Hypertextual materials work as a electronic library in the measure in which they provide contents when required, not when the program says
- Allows the use of a wide range of contents at several degrees of difficulty, because their authors do not have to adapt them to a particular level
- Readers-students can control much part of what they read. They can configure what they read depending on their needs. They can explore contents at their own rhythm and following particular interests
- Supposes a new way of participating in discussions, contributing to debates and creating knowledge

Reconfiguring Time of Study

One of the most thrilling and tested uses of hypertextual didactic systems is the way in which limits of time are modified:

Two suppositions of Newtonian origin dominate our present culture and organizations: (a) the atomic supposition that time can divided infinitely, (b) the supposition of homogeneity in which all the time atoms are equivalent, so every moment can be exchanged by any other. But such supposi-

Figure 6. One of the most powerful tools of any e-learning system is the virtual library. It is a centered service not only to offer usual functions of loan, obtaining documents... but catering student with powerful databases of journals, bibliographical searches, Ph theses as well as filtering information

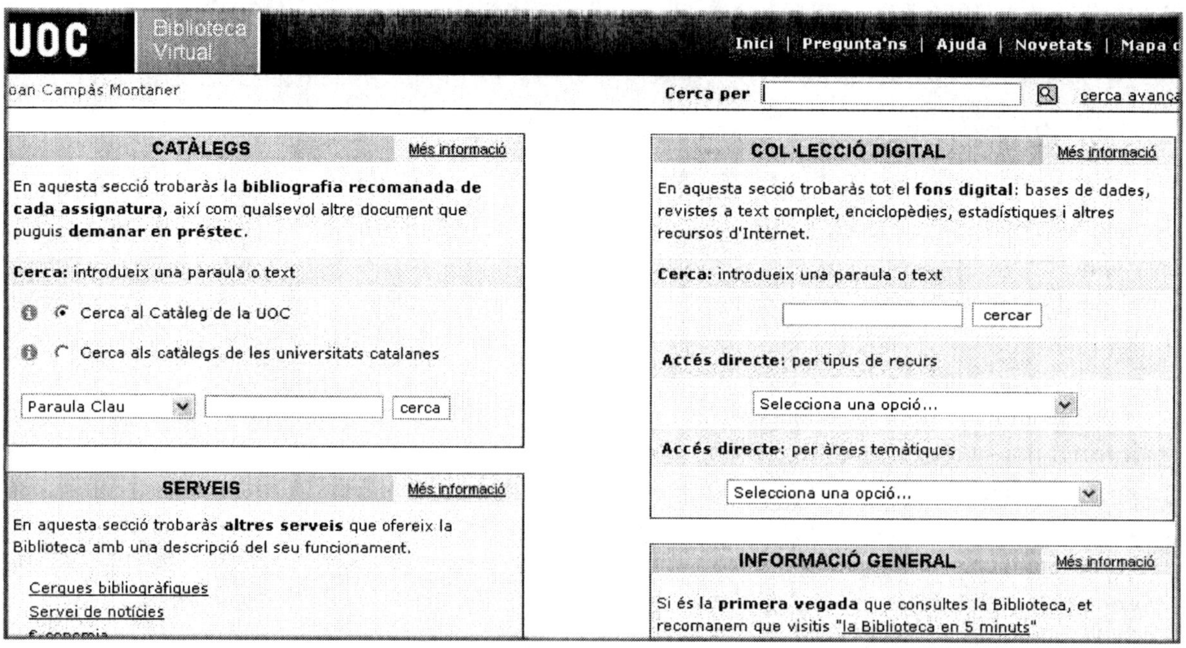

tions do not match our experience... Ten sessions of one minute work during the whole day are not the same as one session from quarter past nine to twenty-five past nine. (McGarth, 1990)

Division in weeks or separate units makes students consider texts and subjects isolated in units. However, using hypermedia or materials in a Web page:

- Improves productivity of students
- Establishes relationships among subjects developed along the course or those that will be treated further on
- Integrates materials of other subjects
- Allows "asynchronous communication" among students and materials
- Frees students from any limitations in planning without destroying structure and coherence of courses
- Reorganizes and integrates subjects previously studied
- Contributions and students' assignments convert hypermedia into a cooperative pedagogic environment

Besides, not everyone has the same way of learning. One of the main features of e-learning should be to help everyone decide their own way of learning, so they can continue their further education in the future.

Reconfiguring Evaluation

The current mechanisms of evaluation take into account more what one does not know than what one does. When sitting an exam, a question is asked and one fails if one does not know the answer. Never is it asked what one knows, about what one may show knowledge and competences. In order to use all the advantages of hypermedia, teachers will have to decide the role of online materials and use them in a conscious way. It is required to make clear the course objectives and the role of hypermedia in achieving such goals.

It is a matter of developing most complex capacities and not only transferring content through a new technology. Working with hypermedia does not mean to click and browse screens or print texts. Uses of hypertext make assignments designed so that they provide an experience to students in its more significant advantage, the links.

- Teachers should reconsider exams and other methods of evaluation. If links are the most useful didactic tool of a hypertext, exams should evaluate results of how these links are used in the development of relationships.
- Teachers should reconsider goals and methods of education. If the main aim is to develop capability of critical thought in students, it requires a process of knowledge construction and methodological approach, and not quantitative answers.

Hypertext, with a great level of control by users, is more a training technology than a managing technology. Students can elaborate their own knowledge browsing hyperdocuments according to associations in their own cognitive structures. However, as happens in the case of access, control also requires responsibility and capability of taking decisions. (Manchionini, 1990)

CONCLUSION: SIX IDEAS TO REINVENT EDUCATION-LEARNING

a. Technologies are useful, but not enough. They are a required condition for education renewal, but they are not "a unique condition." Even more important than infrastructure (virtual campus, telematic connections, e-mail, debates, wikis, blogs, e-portfolios, Web quest, etc.) it is infostructure (contents and capabilities of people using them). We remember the words of Einsenstein, the famous cinema director: "A good film may come out from a good script." Machines do not work when teachers do not feel comfortable with them or when there are not adapted contents in the network. Reconfiguring teachers and creating multimedia material online are two critical aspects in the e-learning development. The main aim is to covert both into the virtual learning community at the start of a course.

b. Teachers will neither use digital technologies nor multimedia materials (not even create them), if its use is not evaluated in the general evaluation system. In other words, what is evaluated is to which extent the previous educative program has been covered (compulsory contents of the course) and how students pass or fail a series of exams or tests. Only a few teachers will employ digital tools for something else than doing the same with "modern" means. E-learning cannot be reduced to make easier contact between teachers and students through computers. E-learning is not distance learning education with digital technologies. It is chiefly a way to construct knowledge in the information society. Therefore, it is a process of reinvention of the virtual learning communities.

c. Such reinvention entails, among other things, that teaching concrete knowledge in a sequential way is no longer relevant. Now it is a matter of situating students in contexts, situations and interactions that will force them to think in a polyhedral way, using paradigms of complexity in the perception of phenomena and problems resolution, and use their autonomy to manage information.

d. It is necessary to stimulate creative thought together with a critical, innovative and searching spirit. Otherwise, e-learning will be reduced to a mere application of ruled contents (in the form of books, modules in paper, and Web sites that substitute books) to proposed activities. We do not need to forget that learning should be carried in a social context, as otherwise it will fall down to sterile individualism. We are social beings, and this implies using the network to create interconnected nodes and to construct a great hypertext. Node and network, and autonomy and social group are the two poles connected to e-learning. One does not exist without the other.

e. Teachers-students-materials interaction is the central axis of the e-learning system. According to students, a good teacher is the one who exposes clearly what he or she will do and replies quickly to any students' requirements (replies in less than 24 hours). Besides, teachers should keep the course rhythm, stimulate and achieve through debate exchange of information, and create a learning community. Other tasks are clarifying doubts and ideas, implicating themselves in contents, adoring it, bringing complementary material, transmitting interest, suggesting, fixing key issues, clarifying difficulties, stimulating critical reflection about contents, giving voice to everyone and promoting participation and opening doors to invention. Teachers should transmit especially the conviction that they devote time to "that," because it is important for them. If there is intellectual implication (engagement) between teachers and students, it will bring about "education" (and not only intelligent transmission). Work in the network is, at the present, the most powerful process to put in common tools to put forward problems, locate information and solve them.

FUTURE RESEARCH DIRECTIONS

It becomes difficult to foresee future trends in e-learning. This is due in part to technological developments in computer science and telecommunications, convergence or not of the different platforms, evolution of the systems of edition online, success of open-contents, capacity of 3D in construction of simulations, solution to derivative problems of author's copyright, costs and benefits of the institutions that dedicate themselves to it, and so forth.

Apart from a prospective study of lines that the future can offer us, if the information society wants to be inclusive, digital technologies should present themselves united social values. They should be understood as social instruments capable of improving democratic participation and people's quality of life. From this principle, one can talk about the new future paradigm: social e-learning.

Before, social problems such as digital exclusion ought to be faced, and not only focusing on problems derived from absence of infrastructure. There is an important qualitative difference between one who is completely excluded, and requires understanding and using ICT, and someone who only needs formal knowledge to access.

The e-learning communities are now a very popular subject. However, they are usually analyzed like simple instrumental concepts toward the improvement of learning. ICT offer us a software that can be used in original ways to help expand the cultural, social and political horizons of such communities. It would be necessary to have all the power of Internet communication present for describing and struggling against social exclusion. This is a key strategy when we take into consideration isolated or immigrant communities that work far from their homes, and it can also be an important measure to struggle against sexism in the computer world and to help women to work with and to transform the ICT.

The personal computers, the software show and new characteristics every year and with this are made every time more difficult to use. This is not problematic for the users that are familiarized with the TIC. However, makes that they are the things much more complex for the ones excluded digital, especially when we speak about persons of age advanced or with disabilities. It would be necessary to work in strategies and technologies that make the programs much easier and intuitive of using.

We should aim for a design and implementation of e-learning materials that are useful, practical and motivating. This implies having the specific social and cultural contexts present. In a few years time, knowing a word processor or being an e-mail customer will not be relevant for any job demand. This is another reason to search a methodology based on the resolution of problems. A general course of how to use several programs of graphic edition can be useful, but a course is much better to solve problems. It should be advanced in a model of the participative e-learning, constructed "among equals" and "mixed."

- **Participative:** It is important that the user implicates himself in the process of system creation from the beginning, so that we can see what works and what does not, and not simply to be mere passive consumers of "interactive tools."
- **Learning "among equals" (peer to peer):** E-learning cannot consist of spreading or transmitting the same contents by different ways than books. People have to advance in the elaboration of strategies that allow the collective construction of knowledge, breaking the structure of the rigid classroom, if required, and allowing exchange and contact among students of several areas and levels. There is not anything more motivating than knowing that what one is making can be useful to other colleagues. Everyone should bear in mind the social dimension of learning.
- **"Mixture" (Blended):** Digital revolution has carried us new concepts like that of hybridization, immersion, hypertextuality, interactiveness, and so forth. We cannot

continue thinking of terms gutenbergians (text, image, music, image in motion, etc.) not even in the parameters derived from the Cartesian rationality (nature-culture, form-content, natural-artificial). We are cyborgs, as Donna Haraway has formulated it. And what should be promoted is mixture, this crossbreeding of contexts, the e-learning, and not the standardization, the atomization, the homogenization. Talking of inclusion is to speak about mixture, not of integration. It is to speak about diversity and multiplicity, and it is to believe Internet and the hypertextual paradigm: connected nodes from which a more radically democratic and creative society can be built.

The ICT are social instruments, with values embedded in them. It should be one of the main tasks of e-learning to assure that these values bring us to a more inclusive and egalitarian society, where we can use ourselves to improve the democratic participation and give power to the ones excluded socially.

Or, also, e-learning will be able to be reduced to incorporate segments of market into the business of asynchronous education, and bring up the future in terms of management of processes, of learning-objects, of platforms or professional e-portfolios. The market will depend, and of the political will...

REFERENCES

Cuban, Larry. (1993). *How teachers taught: Constancy and change in american classrooms 1890-1990.* 2nd ed. New York: Teachers College Press.

Damarin, S. (1993). Schooling and situated knowledge: Travel or tourism?. *Educational Technology, 33*(10).

Goodlad, John I. (2004). *A place called school: Twentieth anniversary edition.* 2nd ed. New York: McGraw-Hill.

Marchionini, G. (1990). Evaluating hypermedia-based learning. In Jonassen, D. H., & Mandl, H. (Eds.). (1990). *Designing Hypermedia for Learning* (pp. 355-376). London. Springer-Verlag.

McGrath, J.E. (1990). Time matters in groups. In J. Galegher, R. E. Kraut, & C. Egido (Eds.), *Intellectual team work: Social and technological foundations of cooperative work.* Mahwah, NJ: Lawrence Erlbaum Associates, Inc.

Relan, T.I., & Gillani, B.B. (1997). Web page-based instruction and the traditional classroom: Similarities and differences. In B. H. Khan (Ed.), *Web page-based instruction.* New Jersey: Educational Technology Publications.

Rheingold, H. (1996*). La comunidad virtual. Una sociedad sin fronteras.* Barcelona.

Romiszowski, A. (1997). Web-page based distance learning and teaching: Revolutionary invention or reaction to necessity. In B. H. Khan (Ed.), *Web page-based instruction.* New Jersey: Educational Technology Publications.

Schrage, M. (1991). *Shared minds: The new technologies of collaboration.* Random House.

Wilson, B.G. (Ed.). (1996). *Constructivist learning environments: Case studies in instructional design.* Englewood Cliffs, NJ: Educational Technology Publications.

ADDITIONAL READING

Aldrich, C. (2004). *Simulations and the future of learning: An innovative (and perhaps revolutionary) approach to e-learning.* San Francisco: Pfeiffer.

Aldrich, C. (2005). *Learning by doing: A comprehensive guide to simulations, computer games, and pedagogy in e-learning and other educational experiences*. San Francisco: Pfeiffer.

Babot, I. (2003). *E-learning, corporate learning.* Barcelona: Gestión 2000.

Bates, T. (2005). *Technology, e-learning and distance education*. London: Routledge.

Bernard, M. (dir.) (2005). *Le E-learning: la distance en question dans la formation*. París: CIEF – L'Harmattan.

Catherall, P. (2005). *Delivering e-learning for information services in higher education.* Oxford: Chandos Publishing.

Clark, R. C. (2003). *E-learning and the science of instruction: Proven guidelines for consumers and designers of multimedia learning.* San Francisco: Jossey-Bass/Pfeiffer.

Conole, G., & Oliver, M. (Eds.). (2007). *Contemporary perspectives in e-learning research: Themes, methods and impact on practice*. New York: Routledge.

Gardner, J. (2006). *E-learning: Concepts and practice*. Thousand Oaks, CA: Sage Publications.

Garrison, R. (2003). *E-learning in the 21st century: A framework for research and practice.* New York: Routledge-Falmer.

Khan, B.H. (2005). *E-learning QUICK checklist.* Hershey, PA: Information Science Publishing.

Maragliano, R. (2004). *Pedagogie dell'e-learning.* Roma: Laterza.

McConnell, D. (2006). *E-learning groups and communities*. The Society for Research into Higher Education. Berkshire: Open University Press.

Politis, D. (2006). Introduction: E-learning trends in archaeology. In C. Carreras (Ed.), *Open and distance learning (ODL) strategies*. Athens: Klidarithmos Publications.

Politis, D. (Ed.). (2006). *The e-learning dimension of computer applications in archaeology.* Athens: Klidarithmos Publications.

Watkins, R. (2005). *75 e-learning activities: Making online learning interactive*. San Francisco: Pfeiffer.

Zongmin, M. (Ed.). (2006). *Web-based intelligent e-learning systems: Technologies and applications.* Hershey, PA: Information Science Publishing.

KEY TERMS

Pedagogic Model: Model on which is based the tuition or process of learning.

Virtual Platform: Virtual space in which the process of e-learning takes place. It is a social space for communication among students and lecturers.

Course Coordinators: Teaching staff responsible of managing subjects, tutors, counselor and materials.

Learning Materials: Contents in any format that are supposed to be learned by students.

Student Profile: Typologies of students according to their academic background, professional duties and personal conditions.

Learning Objects: Modular digital resources, uniquely identified and metatagged, that can be used to support learning.

Chapter V
Evaluation Models for E-Learning: Experiences in Teaching Archaeology

Cèsar Carreras
Universitat Oberta de Catalunya, Spain

INTRODUCTION

E-learning is still a quite young discipline that undergoes a continuous process of change due to new potentials that technology brings every day. After hardly 10 years of experience, it is difficult to envisage what is the degree of success of such new approaches to learning. Of course, the number of virtual students is increasing day by day because of the flexibility of such new environments that overcome constraints of time and space (Salmon, 2000; Palloff & Pratt, 2003). However, no such effort has been put into evaluating how the process of learning is taking place and comparing e-learning results with traditional distance learning studies, or even presential courses.

The present chapter attempts to show some evaluation models for e-learning and how their results may contribute to define future research agenda and new technological implementations. Our experience of coordinating and teaching courses in archaeology and ancient history in the UOC (Open University of Catalonia) may shed some light into such a complex issue.

EVALUATING THE PEDAGOGIC MODEL: THE CASE OF UOC

As it was discussed before (see chapters by J. Campas and C. Girona), virtual learning environments rely on students' effort and commitment to the process of learning (Palloff & Pratt, 2003). Therefore, the whole pedagogical model is focused on students, creating suitable tools and conditions to keep such effort and commitment spirited all over the learning period.

Most e-learning models are based on three main elements: a *virtual platform* where communication takes place, *learning materials* that contained the knowledge to be learned and *learning processes,* together with tutors (consultant professor) who are responsible for guidance in such learning processes of any particular content. Apart from such basic elements, there are other complementary factors that may enhance the virtual learning environment, such as counsellors (tutorial professors), virtual libraries, teaching curriculum and continual evaluation. The UOC pedagogical model includes all those basic and complementary elements which appear in Figure 1. From the UOC foundation in 1994, a significant effort has been put on evaluating all those elements of the pedagogical model in order to improve its learning environment, as well as keeping track of technological developments. Such evaluations and later evolution can be clearly seen from the history of UOC technological model[1], one of the key elements in the whole educational system.

Initial evaluations were basically online satisfaction questionnaires to be answered by students, tutors and counsellors in order to know whether the learning environment and their components were suitable for e-learning processes. They were standard quantified questionnaires mixing enquires going from general questions about the virtual campus or the figure of counsellors to related to every particular subject and tutor. They kept the same questionnaire every term; so after few terms, student and tutor participation decreased by around 20%.

Together with satisfaction questionnaires, another way to acquire information about how the pedagogical model worked was simple indicators of students' success. In other words, percentages of students obtained particular marks or passing subjects. Besides, some particular evaluations such as the figures of tutors and counsellors required a different methodology, which included interviews.

However, in the early 2000s, the UOC decided to develop the technological model and revise the virtual platform. Such specific development involved a more systematic way to evaluate only the technological part with the support of an external firm such as Gartner Group. First of all, a comparative analysis of other educational virtual platforms according to some critical factors provided by Brandon-Hall report[2], Gartner Group analysis and the UOC own evaluation. Then, a second stage of the evaluation involved interviews with focus groups of a stratified sample of the UOC educational community. Such interviews attempted to acquire information on technical requirements of each particular university group. Concepts such as *utility*, *usability* and *accessibility* were key in the future technical developments of the virtual environment.

This specific analysis of only one of the key elements of the UOC e-learning model, *the virtual platform*, showed that evaluations should be focused on each of the elements in order to adjust methodologies and obtain accurate results. Therefore, evaluations since then have been focused more on separate element such as *learning processes* or *materials* than overall views.

EVALUATION OF LEARNING PROCESSES

The success of the whole e-learning model lies in the degree of accomplishment of students' expectations in terms of acquiring knowledge and if this knowledge is valued by the rest of society. Thereby, it is important to take into account the students results, their opinion (satisfaction) and the opinion of our own society.

Students Results

Every term, results obtained by students are quantified and analyzed according to subject. In the Department of Humanities of the UOC, normally between 65-70% of students pass our subjects[3], though there is certain variability according to typology of subjects and whether it is attended when students start their university life. Any variation from the normal pattern expected, calculated with the help of statistical indicators (i.e., means, medians, standard deviation) and

Figure 1. The UOC pedagogical model

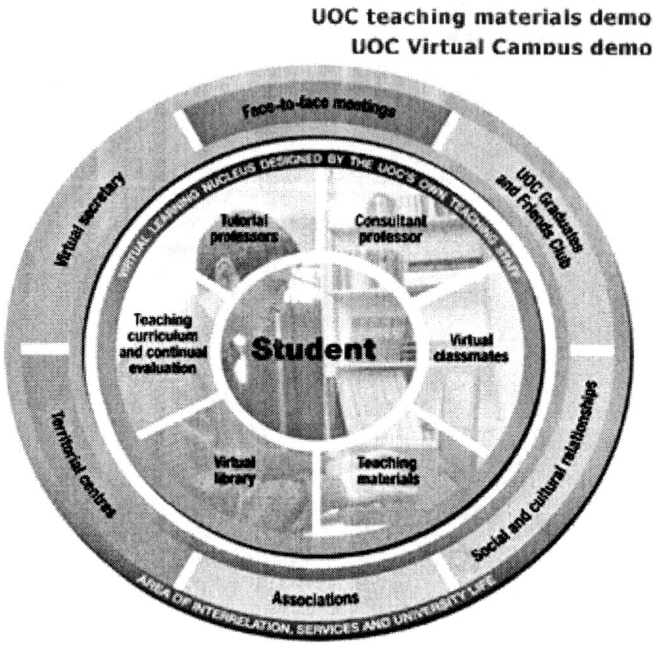

compared to historical data, will require a further examination after conversations with the subject tutor and coordinator. Historical data of each subject is kept as a way to control a normal evolution of students' results.

Because our e-learning method involves a "continuous evaluation" of students' progress all over the term with short practices, another good indicator of results is the attendance to this continuous evaluation. Nowadays, between 65-60% of students in humanities in the UOC follow the "continuous evaluation." Almost 98% of students that follow this "continuous evaluation" will pass the subject at the end. Therefore, increasing participation in the "continuous evaluation" is a key of students' success. Again, this second indicator is analyzed every term with reference to normal distribution and standard deviation.

Students' Satisfaction

From the beginning, the UOC was interested in gathering students' opinion on how the whole educational model worked. Therefore, a short virtual questionnaire was sent by e-mail to any student every term, asking questions about teaching, communication, learning sources, assessment and the virtual learning environment (i.e., virtual campus). The quantified results of such questionnaires (rated from 1-5) provided us with an indicator of each individual *subject*, *tutor* and *counsellor* (Sangrà, Cabrera, & Girona, 2005).

A normal distribution curve centred on the average value of every student's questionnaire should give a quantified image of the student's satisfaction regarding a *subject*, *tutor* or *counsellor*. Nevertheless, it has been detected that sometimes two curves appear which identify the two extreme groups: students very satisfied and the critics' ones to the model. Average values and distributions are then compared by subjects, degrees (programs and courses) and as a whole in the university.

Despite that this information is quite valuable, questionnaires do not allow an open answer, and

Figure 2. Results from the satisfaction questionnaire

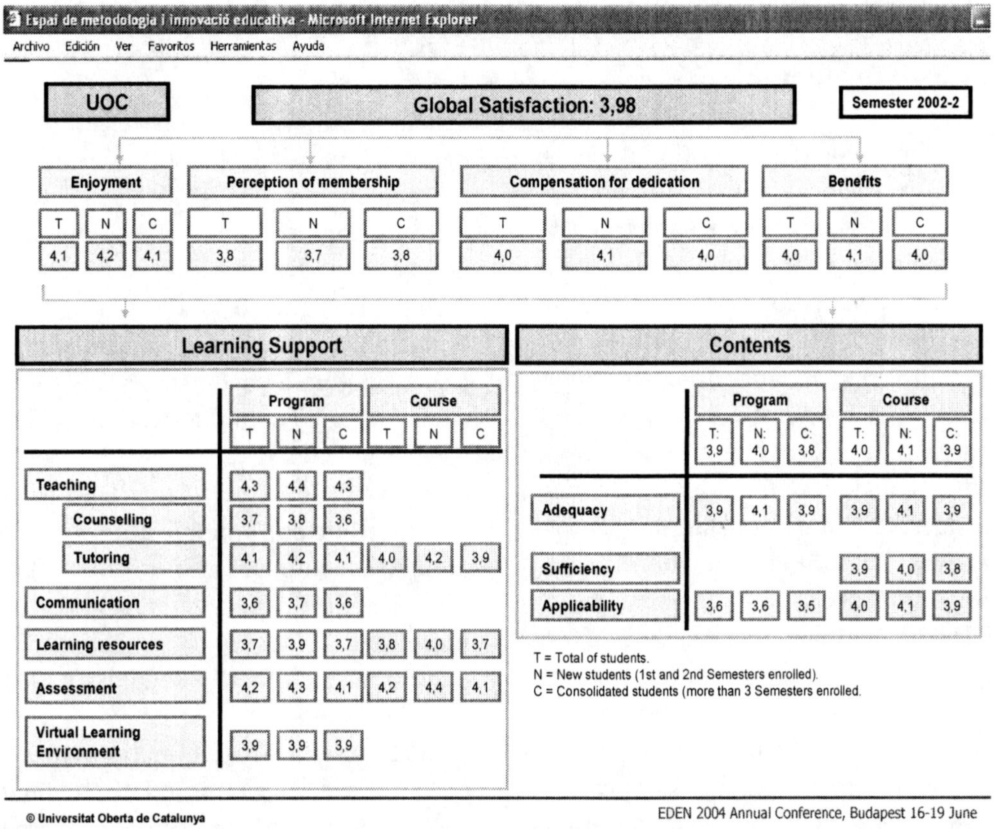

therefore they do not provide qualitative information easy to interpret.

But, of course, that is not enough. Therefore, presential interviews with some selected students were used from the early start in order to get qualitative information on *tutors*, *subjects* and *materials*. Such interviews have increased in recent years in order to address some special problems of learning processes.

Panfilhum is a research project coordinated by J. Campas (UOC)[4] which aims to understand how students in virtual universities learned. So far, more than 40 interviews of students of Humanities have been carried out covering subjects such as use of materials, assessments, continuous evaluation, expectations, level of difficulty, and so forth. Panfilhum has detected:

- Wide variety of opinions
- Virtual students focus their effort on assessments, either continuous evaluation or exam.
- Contents not included in assessments are left aside
- Virtual campus is highly rated
- Materials are used only to consult in order to solve questions of the assessments
- They appreciate quick reply of tutors and their involvement in the course (more materials, debates, humour, etc.)
- ...

Most of this data is making us change our viewpoint on virtual learning and the value of materials and tutors. In the future, we will have to redesign our courses taking into account such straight comments of our students.

Coordinators' Analysis

Quantitative information from questionnaires is analyzed for *course coordinators* with the help of tutors and counsellors. However, sometimes it is not enough to have a clear picture of the whole learning process. *Course coordinators* are full time lecturers in the UOC responsible of working together with a team of tutors from particular subjects related to their own speciality.

Coordinators have access to virtual classrooms, so they can follow the whole learning process. Besides, coordinators design materials together with authors and can be directly approached by students for any question about courses. Therefore, they may access only a part of qualitative information, which will help in order to interpret quantitative data from questionnaires. Besides, coordinators are the main leaders of all the initiatives of presential interviews, which are providing an excellent complement of information to the quantitative data.

As mentioned before, one of the possible indicators of the learning model success was how society rates graduates coming from the university. That is something that no one has paid much attention to in the UOC so far. There has been some questionnaires and follow up of graduates from the UOC, but little information has been gathered from employers or the public in general in order to compare UOC graduates' achievements to other graduates from other local universities. Perhaps, such kind of evaluation should be undertaken by public institutions such as AQU or DURSI[5], which are responsible for university quality.

EVALUATION OF TEACHING MATERIALS AND LEARNING TOOLS

Teaching materials are one of the key issues of the UOC learning model, because they include the contents, which students are supposed to learn during the course. Teaching materials are prepared in advance of the course, and normally order to recognized scholars from different national universities. Therefore, teaching materials are not created by tutors who will teach a particular subject in the UOC, which may create some problems.

It has been detected that learning materials developed by presential lecturers are sometimes thought as complements to presential courses and not as self-sufficient documents for virtual learning. Besides, tutors in UOC using such materials may not agree with their contents, which generate some problems.

The institutional questionnaire normally encompasses questions related to materials of each subject. Sometimes materials are low rated by students and tutors, and therefore coordinators are obliged to mend or complement them in following terms. Learning materials are critical points in the model, and that is why a special pedagogical unit in the UOC took responsibility of generating a document of how to evaluate learning materials.

This document is known in the UOC as PAM and is based on other similar documents such as Scienter (Delphi project), MIME (Georgia University), Multimedia Rubic project (Central Florida University) and CIDOC (Multimedia Working group).

The PAM defines a series of criteria for any learning material according to:

Figure 3. Learning materials of Roman law in the UOC

a. **Technology:** Multimedia materials should be used in different platforms and easily adapted to further technical developments
b. **Aesthetics:** Design is also an important part for the final result
c. **Usability:** How users employ materials
d. **Pedagogy:** Pedagogical treatment of contents
e. **Contents:** How knowledge is recorded in a multimedia format (text, audio, video, image, etc.)

Thereby, learning materials should be evaluated by coordinators (chiefly for contents) and experts (tutors, editors, etc.) before they are edited in any format. Evaluation should take place by a formal report or by a questionnaire, which combine inquiries that cover the criteria defined in the PAM. Figure 4 shows an example of a Web-based questionnaire developed for the SEEARCH-Web project that allows users to give a value between 1 and 5.

Together with standard learning materials, tutors have the chance to include contents from papers supplied by the virtual library, images and other multimedia material. Such complements allow tutors to update subject contents, adjust learning to different users' profiles and modify educational aims. This issue is relevant because different courses (i.e., further education, summer courses, and degrees) are offered to different public containing basically the same standard material or part of it, but complement other materials offered by tutors.

Adjustment of learning contents to a myriad of potential e-learning students goes along with a change in learning tools such as a learning guide, set of activities for continuous evaluation, final evaluation and teaching support to every student's profile. For instance, it was detected that learning material from the course "Olympic Games" developed by the SEEARH-Web consortium could aimed to six target groups with different level and expectation toward a course of this particular content. Table 1 summarizes such categories according to the level of studies and knowledge of the subject, which varies according to whether students are Greeks or from other nationalities.

Figure 4. Web-based questionnaire for learning materials

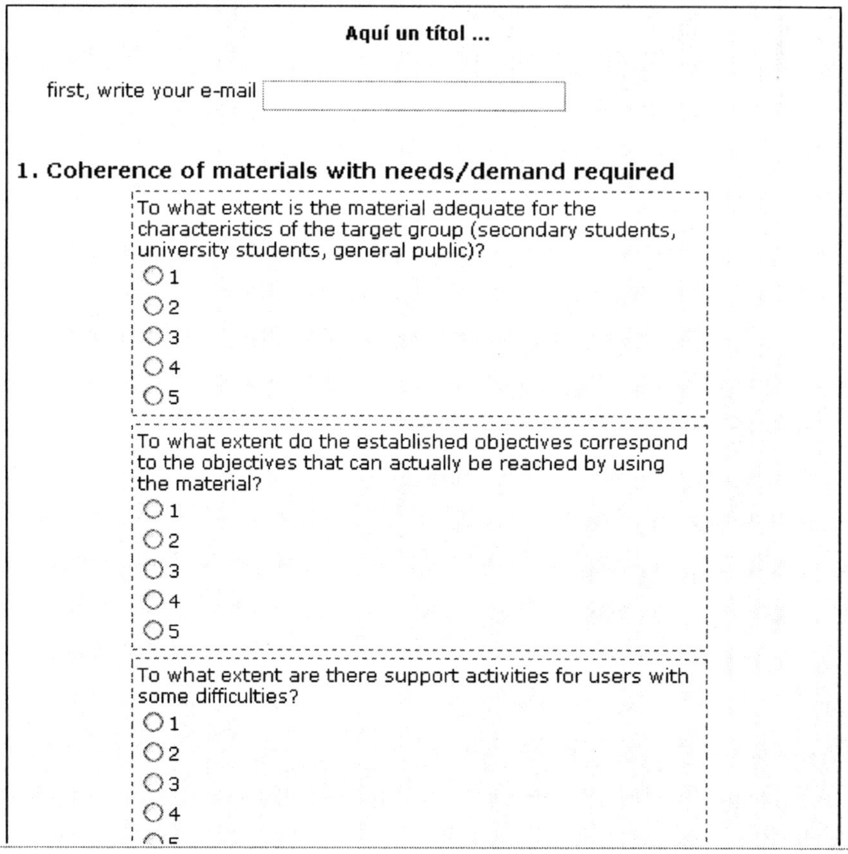

Aquí un títol ...

first, write your e-mail

1. Coherence of materials with needs/demand required

To what extent is the material adequate for the characteristics of the target group (secondary students, university students, general public)?

1
2
3
4
5

To what extent do the established objectives correspond to the objectives that can actually be reached by using the material?

1
2
3
4
5

To what extent are there support activities for users with some difficulties?

1
2
3
4

Coordinators, tutors and other experts in universities should recognize the existence of such distinctive profiles and then, adjust materials with learning tools to every profile. As can be observed, use of standard learning materials for different purposes and profiles lays on the basis of the "learning objects" (LOs) philosophy. However, "learning objects" are not enough for the purpose of learning; they require some kind of "narrative" provided by learning tools, teaching skills, guidelines and complementary information.

LEARNING AND TEACHING ANCIENT HISTORY AND ARCHAEOLOGY IN THE UOC: SOME CASE STUDIES

Prehistory and Ancient History (Degree of Humanities)

Prehistory and Ancient History is offered as a subject of the degree of Humanities in the UOC. It is a compulsory subject in the degree, normally

Table 1. Profiles of students of the "Olympic Games" course

	Greeks	Other nationalities
Secondary schools	Non-specialized background	Common knowledge
University graduates	Specialized background	Specialized background
General public	Common knowledge	Common knowledge

followed during the first term in Humanities. Therefore, first year students, apart from getting used to the virtual campus and a new way of learning, should acquire knowledge of the most ancient cultures in the world. Prehistory and Ancient History is one of the highest rated subjects by students in questionnaires in Humanities since the start. It receives very high scores in all the questions related to learning processes (i.e., tutors, continuous evaluation, exams), except learning materials that initially were rated quite low.

The reason was quite simple. Learning materials were written by well-known Spanish professors from presential universities specialized in Archaeology, but with no experience in e-learning or students from Humanities. Therefore, tutors did not find such materials suitable to the profile of Humanities students. They sorted it out by adding new documents (i.e., papers, images, and summaries), adjusting guidelines and generating a series of activities (i.e., debates, presential visits) that overcome such problems.

A few years ago, part of the learning materials were revised by the tutors of the UOC complementing initial contents. Such new materials were part of a hypertext, which included explanatory texts, images, articles and other complements. Nowadays, learning materials of Prehistory and Ancient History are also highly rated by students in questionnaires.

Nevertheless, some deficiencies such as historical maps or quick content update are still unsolved. Future developments of learning materials would require a solution to these aspects. So, what are the keys of such success in this subject? Well, as coordinator in Prehistory and Ancient History in the UOC, I believe that there are a myriad of reasons of this success:

- There are four tutors teaching this subject for around 225 students of the first term. They work as a team because each of them is specialized in a different period and culture (i.e., Hominids, Egypt, Roman Archaeology), but they prepare together course guidelines, activities for continuous evaluation and exams. They combine their own expertise in the course working as a team.
- Despite the fact that the subject covers a wide period and a huge number of diverse cultures, there is a common thread: a comparison between manners with which each culture understands the world. Actually, tutors compare two epistemological discourses, mythic and logical, which are used to explain any natural and human phenomena. In other words, opposition between logical and mythical arguments can be found at the heart of every society. Such debate goes on with students in the virtual forums and allows making comparison with present societies. This virtual debate with a high participation generates a social interaction in the course and incorporates "real life" into the subject.
- There are a wide variety of short activities for continuous evaluation, some compulsory

and others optional. Therefore, students can organize their own process of learning.

- There are optional presential meetings to visit museums, archaeological sites and urban remains that allow students to get a real contact with Archaeology and with their tutors. Such gatherings are also highly valued by students, who normally work on their own at home (Salmon, 2000).

As can be observed, part of the success in *Prehistory and Ancient History* comes from the way tutors "teach" the subject (Draves, 2002). It is not a self-sufficient course in which learning materials are a key issue in the learning process, but a subject in which the social dimension of teaching and learning acquires an overwhelming importance.

Prehistory and Ancient History in Catalonia (Degree of Humanities)

This subject covers the same period but only deals with local history; in other words, all the prehistoric and ancient cultures that lived in the present territory of Catalonia. It is also part of the degree in Humanities in the UOC, but it is an optional subject. Prehistory and Ancient History in Catalonia is also a highly rated subject in the students' questionnaires. Only one group of around 50 students attends it every term, which involves a unique tutor for this subject. Learning materials are valued by students despite the fact that initially they were also created by presential lecturers. However, they have been updated by the tutor in order to be suitable for our virtual students.

Some hypertexts were created to reproduce some of the most relevant sites in Catalonia such as Emporion (a Greek colony) and Tarraco (the Roman capital). In both cases, information is organized on the basis of a site map from which every outstanding feature can be accessed by clicking on it. Such hypertexts provided a more detailed insight into the local Archaeology and colour images were an important complementary resource for tuition. Besides, tutors normally offer the possibility to meet together once a term to visit an archaeological site, normally the Emporion and Tarraco. Perhaps, one of the most original aspects of this subject is an activity in which students are invited to collect archaeological press news in Catalonia and refer to it in the forum. This activity is quite successful and allows students to be aware of current problems of rescue excavation in Catalonia. Furthermore, this new information provides an update of whatever is happening in local Archaeology.

Summing up, this subject enjoys a good student's opinion, because of its combination of good learning materials and good tutoring with complementary materials and activities, as well as an easy way to update contents through students' participation.

Archaeological Heritage Management (Further Education)

This is a postgraduate course that attempts to give a professional perspective of the archaeological world. Potential students are not only Archaeology undergraduates, but also other students or professionals who are involved in archaeological work and management. It is even suitable for tourism students who use Archaeology as an attraction in cultural projects or destinations. Course contents cover aspects such as archaeological methodology, present law, dissemination and archaeological tourism. It aims to illustrate the best way to manage archaeological heritage in this global world.

Two of the tutors of Prehistory and Ancient History were also authors of this course learning material, as well as direct tutors when it was first offered in 2000. Apart from the standard materials, the course includes archaeological legislation at the regional, national and international level together with some freeware software that could

Figure 5. Hypertext of cases studies on current archaeology

help teach some methodological aspects (i.e., StratiGraf, BASP). Apart from this, there are numerous resources online that could complement content such as the well-known "Introduction to Archaeology" by Kevin Greene (2002) (http://www.staff.ncl.ac.uk/kevin.greene/wintro/).

Besides, it was attempted to adapt a learning simulation archaeological model called Windig created for Windows 95/NT (http://www.gla.ac.uk/Inter/Computerpast/archtltp/content.html), which reproduces the kind of decisions taken by an archaeologist (i.e., analysis of aerial photography, excavation strategy, statistics, bone identification, forensic Archaeology, scientific dating, geophysical surveying, excavation simulation[6]). Unfortunately, numerous flaws in the software customization made its regular use impossible, despite its potential for virtual teaching.

Perhaps, one original application regarding the learning material was a hypertext that collects more than 30 national and international case studies on field archaeology. They show good and bad practices in rescue excavations at the urban level, in infrastructure works (i.e., railway, motorways, and pipelines) and dissemination combined with cultural tourism. Every case includes at least two-three pages of text and four-five pictures, although there are extensive cases.

Students appreciate such case studies because they help them learn from particular examples. Some of the students' assignments that cover other case studies may in the future become part of the same materials. The hypertext has been updated at least once, but in the future could be organized as a database in order to be more easily updated.

Case studies hypertext is a type of resource that has been used later in different kind of materials and normally helps to explain the most particular details of an applied field of knowledge.

Iberian Culture (3-Week Summer Courses)

Summer courses are a completely different kind of courses with a more general public than specialized one. Archaeology is one of the subjects that fit quite well in this format, because there is a public interest in such exotic and past cultures. Therefore, university learning materials of Archaeology adapted with activities and complementary information to a general public with common knowledge is normally successful. Our first experience was a summer course on Iberian culture (Spanish iron age) because an important exhibition on this culture was held at the same time in Barcelona.

Students attending this summer course were not only students from Humanities, but also from other degrees in the university (Law, Psychology, Documentation, Economics, etc.), other universities and teachers of secondary school. Material used for this course was a CD-ROM created by a lecturer from the University of Barcelona, who employed it as a complement in his presential courses in his own university (Gracia, 2001). Besides, it was complemented with a Web site with numerous images and a presential visit to an Iberian site, Ullastret. This three-week course was offered during three summers (1998-2000) with a great success.

Later on, the same material was used by the University of Barcelona for one complete virtual subject as part of the degree in History, and some of our students in the UOC also attended the course. Comparisons between how students of both universities behaved in the same virtual classroom deserved an article by Gracia (2001).

He demonstrated that UOC students were better suited to a virtual environment because they already had practice, but the UB students were having serious problems getting used to the environment and how to organize their time with the continuous evaluation. At the end of the course, 50% of the UB students showed their preferences for presential courses and having learning materials only as complements for the tuition. Besides, results were also different because UOC students revealed a higher quality in their works, because of their average age (35 years old) and commitment to their study.

Introduction to Egyptology: The World of Death (3-Week Summer Courses)

One of the tutors of Prehistory and Ancient History thought about the possibility of offering a short course on his own speciality, Egyptology. The course was first offered in 2001, and still continues to be one of the most successful in Humanities. Again students of this course are quite heterogeneous; some come from Humanities and others from different studies and specialities.

Learning materials were designed as hypertext that can be easily updated every year with new documents. Illustrations, maps and texts are basic contents of such materials, which allow students to be fully aware of the context in which the Egyptian culture took place. Exotic aspects of the Egyptian culture have been the key of this course success, apart from the quality of material and learning processes. Furthermore, the course may be complemented with a trip to Egypt organized by the course tutor. Again, summer courses have a special treatment that combines academic tuition with leisure activities (i.e., visits to sites or travels).[7]

Introduction to Archaeology (3-Week Summer Courses)

This summer course includes part of the materials used in Archaeological Heritage Management, but with a different treatment for a more general public. Instead of attempting to give a professional perspective, the course is a simple introduction to this "romantic" profession.

Learning materials have been adapted and complemented with new resources, learning guidelines and activities in order to satisfy a different type of potential students. Again, similar learning materials are used for different purposes with a change in the learning tools and treatment by tutors.

FINAL REMARKS

The present section has attempted to underline the importance of proper evaluation of virtual learning environments. We still do not know much about why an e-learning course becomes successful and why students who attend it feel satisfied. A great amount of data has been collected in the past years from our experience in the UOC, which shows that every single part of the teaching model should be evaluated and analyzed separately.

At least three key parts of the model were detected in the UOC: virtual campus, learning processes and teaching materials-tools. Great effort has been put on developing virtual campus and learning processes in the UOC, and nowadays major improvements have been introduced in these aspects. However, there is still a lot to do regarding learning materials and how to update it and customize according to different students needs and profiles. More standardized evaluation is required to recognize key issues in how to design a suitable learning material and tailor it to a potentially diverse uses. Such an approach is currently related to research in learning-objects (LOs) (McNaught, 2006) that are expected to provide breakthroughs in this field.

In Archaeology, the UOC experience shows that use of real case studies is highly valued by students, together with a fast update of this current information. Maps are also quite useful requirement, and not always sorted out by present materials. Apart from these features, little is known about how students employ interactive materials, prepare their essays or select what is important to learn. Studies such as the one undertaken in Panfilhum by J. Campàs on how students behave in virtual learning environments will probably shed some light into the learning model perception from the students' point of view.

REFERENCES

Bates, A.W., & Escamilla, J.G. (1997). Crossing boundaries: Making global distance education a reality. *Journal of Distance Education, XII*(1/2), 49-66.

Draves, W.A. (2002). *Teaching online*. River Falls: LERN Books.

Gracia, F. (2001). Docència presencial v. docència virtual (UOC-UB). El ejemplo de la asignatura de Cultura Ibérica. In *Jornades d'Arqueologia I Tecnologies de la Informació i la Comunicació: Recerca, docència i difusió*. (pp 135-142). Barcelona.

McNaught, C. (2006). *Are learning repositories likely to become mainstream in education?* WEBIST 2006, Sétubal.

Palloff, R.M., & Pratt, K. (2003). *The virtual student: A profile and guide to working with online learners*. San Francisco: Jossey-Bass.

Price, T.D., & Gebauer, A.B. (2002). *Adventures in Fugawiland. A computerized simulation in Archaeology*. London: McGraw-Hill.

Salmon, G. (2000). *E-moderating. The key to teaching and learning online*. Londres.

Sangrà, A., Cabrera, N., & Girona, C. (2005). *El Quadre de comandament: una eina per a la millora metodològica en l'àmbit de l'ensenyament universitar* (http://www.upf.edu/bolonya/butlletins/200/marc1/quadre.pdf).

ADDITIONAL READING

Antonnen, S., Onnela, T., & Terho, H. (2006). *E-learning history. Evaluating European experiences.* Turku.

Barberà, E. (2004). *La educación en la red. Actividades de enseñanza y aprendizaje.* Barcelona: Paidós.

Bates, A.W. (2004). *Technology, e-learning and distance education.* San Francisco: Jossey-Bass.

Bates, A.W., & Pool, G. (2003). *Effective teaching with technology in higher education: Foundations for success.* San Francisco: Jossey-Bass.

Bautista, G., Borges, F., & Forés, A. (2006). *Didáctica universitaria en entornos virtuales de Enseñanza-Aprendizaje.* Madrid: Narcea.

Brace-Govan, J. (2003). *A method to track discusión forum activity: The moderator's assessment matrix.* The Internet and Higher Education 6.

Conrad, D.L. (2002). Engagement, excitement, anxiety, and fear: Learners' experiences of starting an online course. *The American Journal of Distance Education, 16*(4), 205-226.

Coomey, M., & Stephenson, J. (2001). Online learning: It's all about dialogue, involvement, support and control according to research. In J. Stephenson (Ed.), *Teaching and learning online: Pedagogies for new technologies.* London: Bogan Page.

Dezhi, W., & Hiltx, R. (2004, April). Predicting learning from asynchronous online discussions. *Journal of Asynchronous Learning Networks, 8*(2).

Eder, F.X., & Fuchs, E. (2004). Lernmodelle und neuen medien: Historisches lernen und lernen am beispiel Geschichte Online (GO). *Histoire et Informatique 15*, 263-181.

Epple, A., & Haber, P. (Eds.). (2004). *Geschichte und Informatik. Histoire et Informatique* 15. Bern.

Flores, J. (2005). *How to become a proficient online learner.* EEUU: 1stBooks.

Garrison, D., & Anderson, T. (2003). *E-learning in the 21 Century. A framework for research and practice.* London: Routledge.

Goodyear, P., Salmon, G., Spector, J.M., & Tickner, S. (2001). Competentes for online teaching: A special report. *Educational Technology, Research and Development, 49*(1), 65-72.

Guilbert, L., & Ouellet, L. (2002). *Étude de cas. Apprentissage par problèmes.* Québec:PUQ.

Kerres, M. (2001). *Multimediale und telemediale Lernunggebungen. Konzeption und Entwicklung.* Viena.

Kleimann, B., & Wannemacher, K. (2005). E-learning-strategien deutscher Universitäten. *Fallbeispiele aus der Hochschulpraxis.* Hannoer (http://his.de/Service/Publikationen/Kib/pdf/kib200504.pdf)

Kleimann, B., & Wannemacher, K. (2006). Es geht nicho mehr ohne: E-Learning als element der Hochschulentwicklung. *Forschung & Lehre,* 7, 372-374.

Kirkpatrick, D.L. (1998). *Another look at evaluating training programs.* Alexandria, VA: American Society for Training & Development.

McVay Linch, M. (2002). *The online educator. A guide to creating the virtual classroom.* London: Routledge.

Meyer, K.A. (2004, April). Evaluating online discussions: Four different frames of analysis. *Journal of Asynchronous Learning Networks, 8*(2).

Morgan, C., & O'Reilly, M. (1999). *Assessing open and distance learners.* London: Bogan Page.

Reeves, T.C., & Hedberg, J.G. (2003). *Interactive learning systems evaluation.* Englewood Cliffs, NJ: Educational Technology Publications.

Salmon, G. (2000). *E-moderating: The key of teaching and learning online.* London: Kogan Page.

Weller, M. (2002). *Delivering learning on the net. The why, what and how of online education.* London: Routledge.

KEY TERMS

Pedagogic Model: Model on which is based the tuition or process of learning.

Virtual Platform: Virtual space in which the process of e-learning takes place. It is a social space for communication among students and lecturers.

Course Coordinators: Teaching staff responsible of managing subjects, tutors, counselor and materials.

Learning Materials: Contents in any format that are supposed to be learned by students.

Student Profile: Typologies of students according to their academic background, professional duties and personal conditions.

Learning Objects: Modular digital resources, uniquely identified and metatagged, which can be used to support learning.

ENDNOTES

1 A technological history of the UOC is summarized in http://www.uoc.edu/mirador/mmt_mirador/mmt_contingut/mmt_general/mmt_angles/historia.htm?eng-1-1-2-0-n-

2 The report on Learning Systems can be accessed at http://www.brandonhall.com/

3 Similar percentages of success were obtained in the e-learning courses of the Monterrey Institute of Technology (ITESM) (Bates & Escamilla, 1997).

4 The project is under way and the final report will probably finish in the next year.

5 AQU (http://www.aqucatalunya.org) is a public agency that evaluates the quality of Catalan Universities and DURSI (http://www10.gencat.net/dursi) is the Department of Universities in our autonomous government in Catalonia.

6 Other simulation software that recreates the kind of decision taken by archaeologist is "Adventures in Fugawiland" (Price & Gebauer, 2002).

7 This summer we are offering another three-week course on the Maya culture, which follows the same pattern.

Section II
Spatial–Computational Technologies and Virtual Reality Reconstructions in Archaeology

Chapter VI
From Observation to Interpretation

Cynthia Jaulneau
Archaeologist, France

INTRODUCTION

From the excavation to the data analysis and interpretation…which method should be used to manage, extract, analyze and interpret data? Where, when and how do archaeologists use computers? What part do they play in the interpretation of archaeological problems?

This chapter underlines the necessity of establishing a carefully thought-out method to answer precise questions. We will also use this opportunity to discuss the possibilities and difficulties generated by the use of computers to record and process data from archaeological excavations. Which reflections lead the archaeologist to use a particular tool? The amount of data-processing software for the treatment of various types of information (word processing, spreadcards, CAD, data bases, GIS, etc.) is continuously growing and developing. While it is obvious that the use of certain software facilitates the analysis of archaeological data (up to the point where it becomes essential to the archaeologist), is it also necessary to constantly adapt archaeological data processing methods to the use of new software?

For example, the last 15 years have seen an increase in research projects involving the use of geographical information systems (GIS) software. This type of software is employed to answer questions about the concept of **space**. It is frequently used today in studies broadly concerned with **spatial analysis** (at all scales: regional, microregional and intrasite). Indeed, GIS is "a set of procedures used to store and process information with geographical reference," or "a powerful set of tools to input, preserve, extract, transmit and display spatial data describing the real world." Although this tool has indeed made it possible to answer questions which combine spatial information (geography, environment, geology, sedimentology,, etc.) and archaeological data, unfortunately it is not always used with the necessary preliminary reflection. Thus, motivation for the study is not the resolution of a specific archaeological problem, but simply the desire of the researcher to use GIS. This is why it seemed interesting to us to examine the necessity of using GIS software through the example of a recent intrasite spatial study. It is above all the archaeologist's approach and thinking that are highlighted, whatever the method. We want to show that it is the reflection and the reasoning of the researcher which should determine the interpretation of a site and not the use of software. The reflection is founded on observation of the field data and finds, as well as use of reliable recording systems.

The spatial analysis of a settlement is the study of "spatial distributions of material remains [...]. The methods of spatial analysis highlight spatial patterns" (Djindjian, 1997). This spatial analysis of architectural remains is undertaken with data from the site of Kovačevo (southwest Bulgaria). Campaigns of excavation and study have been carried out here since 1986 under a convention signed by the French Ministry of Foreign Affairs, the French *Centre National de la Recherche Scientifique*, the Bulgarian Academy of Science and the Bulgarian Ministry of Culture. The project is directed by Jean-Paul Demoule and Marion Lichardus-Itten on the French side and by Vasil Nikolov, Lilijana Perničeva, Malgoržata Grębska-Kulova and Ilija Kulov on the Bulgarian side. Kovačevo is a settlement site intensely occupied during the early Neolithic period. Remains also indicate occupation during the middle Neolithic and the early Bronze age. One of the interests of this settlement, the earliest Bulgarian Neolithic site, lies in its geographical situation: located in the Struma valley, it is one of the rare communication points between the Aegean Sea and the interior of the Balkans (Lichardus-Itten, Demoule, Perniceva, Grebska-Kulova, & Kulov, 2002). The site has improved our understanding of the neolithisation of the Balkan Peninsula. No sites of this period are known within a radius of 100 to 200 kilometres, not even in northern Greece (Eastern Macedonia and Thrace) (Demoule & Lichardus-Itten, 1994). The site covers a surface area of 6 to 7 hectares. The systematic and extensive excavation (1,5 hectares) uncovered a 2,5 metre stratigraphy. A flat site rather than a tell, it provides data of exceptional quality and quantity, whether finds (almost 39 tons of finds have been recorded, including ceramics, lithics, animal bone, daub) or features (888 plans and section drawings at 1/20° scale, approximately 4000 photographs, nearly 3500 identified features, approximately 160 metres of recorded profiles...). All these characteristics led us to undertake a spatial analysis of the architectural remains to understand village organization. This was initially approached along strict spatial and functional lines before dealing with chronology (the periods and the settlement phases). This analysis is based especially on the raw field data (plans, recording of the finds and features) but also on certain aspects such as the distribution of ceramics (through refitting). The ultimate aim is to be able to understand the organization of features (buildings and annexes). While a geographical information system was initially envisaged, we will explain how and why it was eventually decided not to use it in this study. The undertaking of this work is, however, not possible without various other kinds of software (data bases, spreadcards, computer-assisted drawing, etc.). The creation of a data base combining all the available information (the excavation records and the specialist studies) became necessary and the most frequently used software for this study is a data base programme (FileMaker Pro). Fortunately, the excavation methods and techniques used since the first campaign, with all data systematically recorded on computer, made the creation of the data base relatively easy.

The principal aim of this chapter is to present the method which was adapted to the data from the excavation and developed to address specific research issues.

Before describing the method of spatial analysis of architectural remains at Kovačevo, precise definition of archaeological excavation and certain concepts like stratigraphy (vertical and horizontal) is required to understand the approach chosen to solve problems of spatial analysis. The work involves three distinct phases:

- **Observation** via the description of the excavation method applied on this site and the method of recording remains.
- **Analysis** and **reconstitution** via the description of the database and presentation of the extraction and treatment methods.
- **Interpretation** of the excavated, recorded, organized, sorted, extracted and analyzed data to solve particular research problems.

GENERAL INFORMATION ON ARCHAEOLOGY

The aim of archaeology (a discipline of the human sciences) is to study all remains left by man (buildings, finds, diverse features, in particular of the landscape, etc.) covering all the periods from Prehistory until the present day. This enables us to understand the links that man maintained with his natural environment and to reconstruct his way of life. Archaeologists have a variety of procedures at their disposal, from fieldwork to publication (survey, sondage, excavation, data analysis, finds and sample analysis, dating, etc.).

The Archaeological Excavation

Excavation is one of the procedures archaeologist can use to solve research problems. In the majority of cases, the data used during a study are obtained from archaeological excavations. The goal of excavation is to uncover traces of human occupations and remains buried below the ground. These traces are characterized by the nature of the sediment (granulometry, colour, texture, etc.) and by the form and thickness of the layer or the feature. All the resulting data are then processed for study by researchers for the site publication or as part of work on their own research topics.

There are three types of archaeological excavation: preventive excavations, rescue excavations and research excavations.

Preventive excavation is carried out *before* major construction work: roads, railways, car parks, housing, factories, and so forth. Trial trenches are initially opened to detect possible remains (the diagnostic phase), and then (in case of a discovery) a preventive excavation is carried out before construction work starts. The data from these excavations are seldom studied in an exhaustive way. They constitute obligatorily the subject of a report, but are rarely published due to lack of means and time.

Rescue excavation is also carried out during construction work, but happens when remains are *fortuitously* discovered. Only the signatory countries of the European convention for the protection of the archaeological heritage (revised), signed in Malta in 1992, are obliged to implement this. While preventive excavation and rescue excavation share the same principle (preservation of the archaeological heritage), research excavation is different.

Research excavation can be distinguished from the other types of excavation because it deals with solving problems related to clearly defined research objectives. The project has initially to be approved by a committee of experts. It is generally carried out over several annual field seasons. French archaeologists can set up projects outside France. The research is often designed to solve problems of typological (type of burial, settlement, enclosure, etc.) or chronological nature. The excavation is then studied in order to address site, microregional, or regional (or even broader scale) issues. At Kovačevo, both the regional and the site level are involved. At the first level, questions concern the neolithisation of the Balkan Peninsula. This requires work on a regional scale, with an inventory of all sites of the period, enabling study of their spatial distribution and comparison of finds with Kovačevo. The second level involves analysis of data specifically at the scale of the site. Here, archaeologists try to understand and reconstruct the site's history. They can examine many aspects like the function of the features, their relationships, their organization, their internal chronology, the occupation phases, and so forth. Thus, researchers try to go back in time by identifying the layers and the features within the site stratigraphy. They establish and highlight the links that exist between them. The issues under investigation and the type of the site have a direct influence on the methods and techniques of excavation chosen by the archaeologists.

Stratigraphy

A large part of the work presented below is based on stratigraphy. It is therefore important that the definition of this term and the issues related to it should be made clear, in order to understand the site of Kovačevo and the method used for the study of the spatial organization of remains.

The term "stratigraphy" was borrowed by archaeologists from geology in the 19th century. A stratigraphy is a superposition of layers (natural layers in geology), which are deposited one over the other following the chronology of the events that took place. Thus, in theory, the latest layers are at the top, while the oldest are the deepest. On an archaeological excavation, stratigraphy appears as layers resulting from human actions and superposed one over the other throughout the occupation of the site. Human actions (construction of a wall, digging or filling of a pit, backfill, etc.) leave traces on the ground (characterized by a layer or features included in a layer). An archaeological site does not present a stratigraphy if erosion has destroyed the layers. In this case only the features dug into the natural subsoil are preserved (the natural ground on which the first occupation of the site was established). Thus, the archaeologist quite logically starts by excavating the most recent layers and features (on top) and finishes by the earliest layers (at the bottom). Analysis of the arrangement of layers and features within the stratigraphy enables the site history to be reconstructed through relative chronology. Relative chronology consists of the recognition of the relationships of anteriority, posteriority or contemporaneity of the layers or features within them. We can then define a stratigraphic sequence, providing a vertical vision of the site.

A stratigraphy can have a depth of several meters and can vary according to the type of site, which can either be a "tell" (or magoula, toumba) or an "extensive site."

The term "tell" is employed to indicate an artificial mound or hill formed by the accumulation of the remains of successive settlements on one particular area. The features identified on these sites are mostly remains of buildings made from earth. The best preserved remains have undergone burning. The preservation of archaeological layers on tells is due to their own nature: the mounds have been protected from agricultural activity, severely damaging and even destroying many sites, which is normally carried out on flat surfaces (Lichardus & Lichardus-Itten, 1986, p. 220). The stratigraphy of a tell can reach up to 20 meters. Tells occur in the Near and Middle East and in southeastern Europe. For the Neolithic and the Chalcolithic periods (and occasionally later), tell stratigraphy provides a means to establish major chronological sequences (Lichardus & Lichardus-Itten, 1985, p. 219). Most tell excavations are old because these sites were easily identifiable in the landscape. Consequently, the majority of the tells present an old documentation resulting from excavations carried out on a limited surface area, thus restricting the possibilities of interpretation of the sites' spatial organization. Even today, tells present a considerable disadvantage as far as excavation method is concerned: the stratigraphic height of a tell does not facilitate large-area excavation, as this becomes extremely costly. However, some tells have been completely excavated in recent years.

An extensive site can also present a stratigraphy of several meters. It differs from a tell in the duration of occupation and also in the manner in which space was used: the occupied surface area is much larger. In this case, the successive occupations were not all concentrated in the same area, as with tells, but are more widely dispersed, sometimes over several hectares. Thus, even if several periods of occupation are represented, they will not all appear in the same stratigraphic section. This is why the term horizontal stratigraphy is used. Kovačevo is an extensive site with a stratigraphy 2,5 meters thick. Due to the site's formation history, the area initially excavated provided direct access to the early Neolithic layers situated just beneath the ploughsoil (with some features and layers of the middle Neolithic and the early Bronze Age). As the thickness of the stratigraphy was much less than on a tell, it was possible to excavate a large area, enabling us to carry out a spatial study.

However, the successive occupations, the various human activities and dynamic natural processes (taphonomic conditions) very often disturbed the stratigraphy. The duration of the occupation, the process of sedimentation of remains and the site taphonomy all affect the clarity of the stratigraphy and thus the possibilities of interpretation.

Structures and Their Conservation in Kovačevo

Every archaeological site represents an entity and is defined by its own characteristics. We will now define the term "feature" (*structure* in French) as it is used in this study, and then go on to describe the taphonomic conditions on the site, as these determine the excavation method and data interpretation.

The Structure: Definitions

The remains identified during the excavation were systematically called "features," with a number of variants. At Kovačevo, as in almost all sites, a significant number of features were defined. In the spatial analysis of the architectural remains, the features that are defined during the excavation are the first elements to be exploited. This is why it is important to define this term to understand the way in which the data resulting from the excavation are apprehended, recorded, and processed.

The term "feature" actually covers a large variety of remains. A feature can be seen as *significant grouping* of evidence, the relevance of which is based on the *repetition of similar situations*. Let us retain here the definitions suggested by André Leroi-Gourhan (Leroi-Gourhan & Brezillon, 1972) by integrating the concepts of *obvious features* and *latent features*.

Features vary according to the state and mode of preservation of the sites (sites with settlement layers, in primary or secondary deposits, preserved with or without a soil level, without settlement layers and with only negative features (*structures en creux* in French) such as pits (Brochier, 1999, p. 19). Preservation conditions at Kovačevo have produced a wide range of features corresponding to these definitions: the obvious features are represented by fragments of floors, burials, gravel patches, concentrations of stones, and negative features. Latent features include wall effects, the traces revealed by the *ethnofaciès* recorded by the sedimentologists in the field (Jacques-Léopold Brochier, UMR 5594 of CNRS, Prehistoric Archeology Centre of Valence, and Jean-François Berger, UMR 6130 of CNRS, Sophia-Antipolis, Valbonne).

Taphonomy

To treat the structures and furniture resulting from Kovačevo, it is essential to understand the taphonomy of the site. The taphonomic state of the structures influences directly the degree of reliability of the built vestiges (primary, secondary, tertiary deposit, or even more). We should never forget that the vestiges we discover at the time of the excavation are structures post abandonment, having undergone multiple disturbances as much anthropic as natural, not excluding the sedimentary processes of covering, which are generally slow, during or after the occupation.

The taphonomy and sedimentary processes at Kovačevo are conditioned by the presence of earth-built architecture. Thus, most of the sediment results from their destruction (Brochier, 1994, p. 626). Originally, the material comes from the silty subsoil, on which the first occupation was established, but the building soil used afterward is already anthropized because it comes from the archaeological layers underlying the new construction. Unlike the majority of well-known Neolithic sites of Bulgaria, the structural remains at Kovačevo had not been burned and are therefore difficult to detect. Even if we identify the obvious features quite easily, there are still poorly understood areas, which often correspond to the remains of badly preserved architectural elements made from unfired earth. So, the definition of *ethnofaciès* made it possible to reveal patterns in the anthropized sediments, thus providing another form of archaeological documentation (Brochier, 1988). Moreover, many disturbances (various human actions) come to upset the archaeological layers that are already in place. Thus, features dug into in the lower layers, pits back-filled with earlier sediments, collapse of earth walls made up of earlier archaeological sediments, as well as anthropic accumulations in heaps or overlapping lenses, all complicate the reading of the built remains and considerably mix the finds. Thus, the identification of a feature on the excavation does not ensure the chronological homogeneity of the associated finds (Beeching & Brochier, 2003, p. 24). The house floors are often not preserved because of this mixing, due primarily to reusing earth for the construction of buildings (Brochier, 1994, p. 624). This also shows that obvious features located at the same level are not necessarily contemporary (Beeching & Brochier, 2003, p. 24). In addition to human disturbances, the site of Kovačevo has been subjected to strong erosion since the beginning of the occupation, due to its location at the edge of a terrace and to the nature of its sediment. Certain layers have disappeared. We also observe "compressing" of archaeological layers which may also influence the form of the

Figure 1. Possible heterogeneity of the times fossilized in the middle of the construction in raw ground (Brochier, 1994)

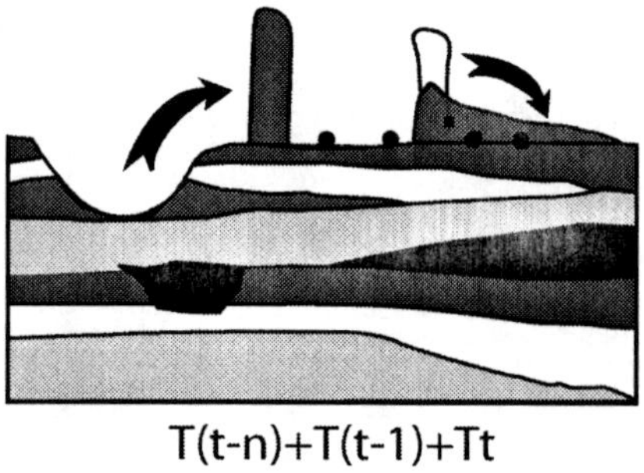

T(t-n)+T(t-1)+Tt

Figure 2. Possible heterogeneity of the times fossilized at the time of the digging and then the filling of a pit (Brochier, 1994)

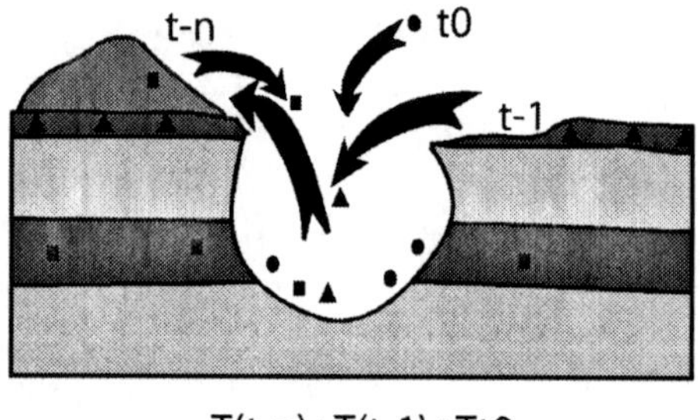

T(t-n)+T(t-1)+Tt0

obvious features a fortiori, in particular those of the negative features.

METHODS AND TECHNIQUES OF EXCAVATION AND RECORDING IN KOVAČEVO: OBSERVATION

"Observation," as we intend to define it, is carried out primarily on site and thus remains a very significant part of the archaeologist's work. The directors of the excavations, before beginning fieldwork, must imperatively set up an excavation "protocol": an excavation method adapted to a type of site and its taphonomic conditions. The adopted excavation method directly influences the possibilities of finds analysis and the broader interpretation of the site. The observation here obviously includes the work carried out directly on site, but also the work known as post-excavation, like the washing, recording and conditioning of the finds collected on site. All

Figure 3. Topographic plan of the site of Kovačevo, with the situation of the principal building site and the surveys as well as the squaring of the archeomagnetic prospection

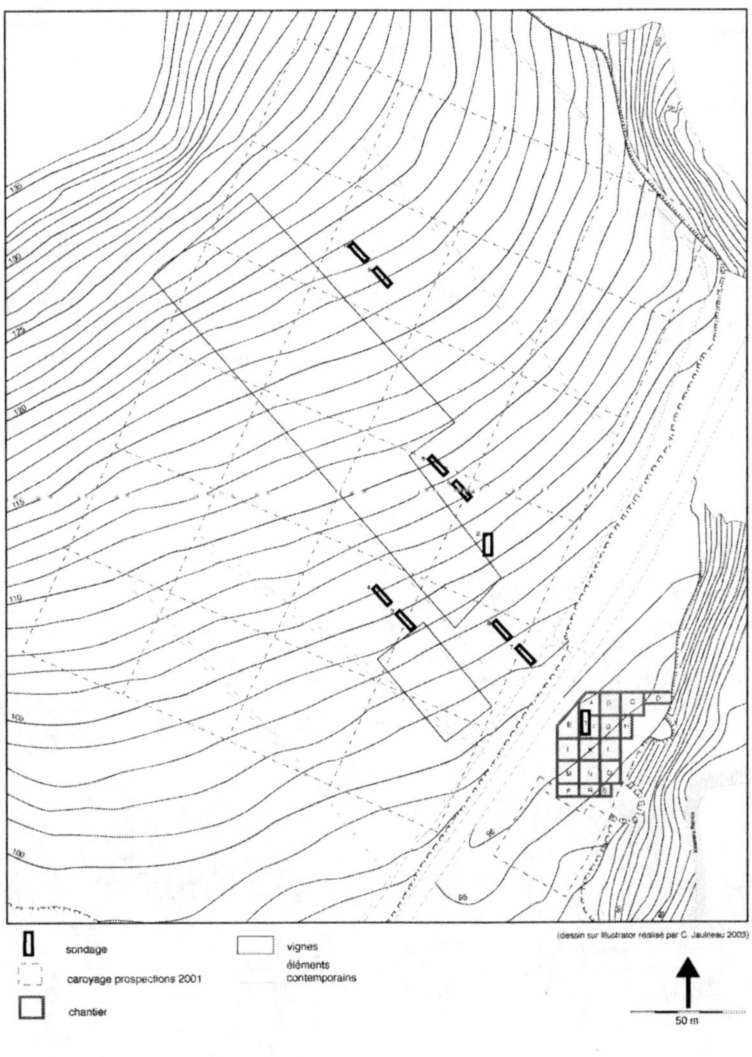

these stages form a study process for which we will give an example.

Methods and Techniques of Excavation in Kovačevo

Kovačevo presents a considerable stratigraphy (evaluated before the beginning of the project through a survey carried out in 1981 [Perničeva, 1990]) and the occupation extends over a large area estimated at approximately 6,5 hectares, known thanks to fieldwalking, trial trenches and archeomagnetic survey (undertaken in 2001 by Ján Tirpák, geophysicist at the Archaeological Institute of the Slovak Academy of Sciences in Nitra). Thus, from the first year, the decision was made to open an excavation of approximately 1500 m2. The extension and the organization of the remains became clearer during the analysis. It is an open-area excavation, orientated north/south to facilitate on-site recording.

The excavation was divided into 17 sectors, including 1 of 106 m^2, 11 of 100 m^2, 5 of 50 m^2 and 1 of 25 m^2. This grid split the excavation into areas separated by baulks 1-2 meters wide. Each sector is cut out in 4 squares of 5x5 m with square meters numbered from 1 to 100. The classification of the squares is carried out from the east to the west by Roman numerals and from the north to the south by Arabic numerals. This grid enables all the remains to be positioned in space (in X and Y). The daily use of a theodolite with a reference altitude provides the third dimension (Z). Thus, the sector is the largest element of the squaring, while the square meter is smallest.

The placing of baulks was decided from the very beginning to facilitate the vertical recording of the site. The baulk known as "principal" (a large baulk of 40 x 2 meters orientated north/south) was placed between the sectors E, I, M, P and the sectors A, F, K, N, R to obtain a near total coverage of the excavation. This baulk was removed in 2002, after complete excavation of all the sectors. All the other baulks between sectors were 1 meter wide. Baulks known as "controls" were placed from time to time within the sectors as work progressed. Their position, their dimensions and their orientation varied according to the features that they cut. They were all drawn at 1/20° to obtain stratigraphic sections. Thus, we have a vertical and horizontal view of the feature at the same time. They make it possible to understand

Figure 4. Squaring of the building site of Kovačevo

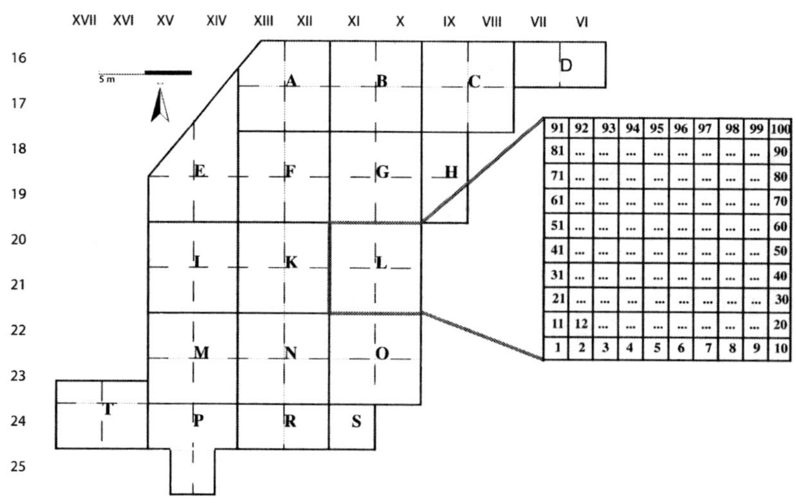

the excavated feature (orientation, construction, etc.) and to establish, as soon as the observation was made on site, a relative chronology thanks to relationships with various other features.

The excavation was carried out without machines. The systematic sieving of the sediment, with a mesh of 0,5 cm, lends a particular interest to the finds from Kovačevo because, for the first time, researchers can examine all the finds of an excavated Bulgarian early Neolithic site.

All the sectors were excavated by levels, numbered from 1 to N, in a top-down manner. These levels mostly correspond to annual spits and, due to the fact that sectors were excavated at different rates and with different teams, the levels of the various sectors do not have the same chronological significance. The features were numbered from 1 to N for the whole excavation. The features (under the previously defined meaning) and the *excavation units* (U.F.) are indicated here. The U.F. correspond more or less to artificial spits. They are created when no feature is clearly identifiable. In general, they are defined on the scale of the square. Their thickness is never decided in advance because it depends entirely on the possible presence of subjacent remains. The excavation of a U.F. finishes when "comprehensible" remains are discovered and defined as *feature*_(s). A *spit* corresponds to the state of a sector at a given moment of the excavation. On site, features and U.F. are recorded in a book (common for all the excavation): "the book of features."

Planimetric and stratigraphic drawings are made as the excavation progresses. The drawings are all at 1/20° (and 1/10° for details). Most refer to a whole sector with all the features uncovered in a spit. As well as the drawings, photographs are taken (3 color slides, 1 black and white, and since 2002, 1 digital).

The description of the features defined in the "book of features" is made on preprinted cards (one card = one feature). Each card contains the creation date of the feature, its number (number given in the book of features), its "address" (sector, square, level, m^2), a diagram of the sector (with grid) to indicate its precise position in space, its altitudes (high and low), a "description" zone in which the excavator can note all its characteristics (width, nature, sediment, etc.), its relative stratigraphic position (by noting the overlying and underlying features), the finds it contains and finally the name of the excavator. The excavators also have an excavation notebook for each sector in which they can note all the information that seems useful and interesting.

Figure 5. Sheet resulting from the file File Maker Pro "furniture recording"

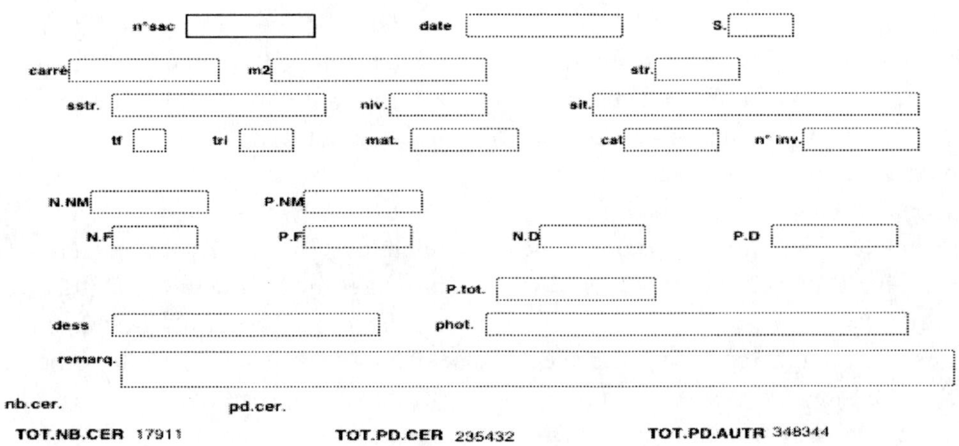

Table 6.1. Coding of the headings of the file "furniture recording"

Headings	Codes	Significances
ET (excavation technique)	1	Pick without sifting
	2	Trowel without sifting
	3	Pick with sifting
	4	Trowel with sifting
Sorting	YES	Part of the material was not recorded
	NO	All the material was recorded
Mat. (material)	CER	Ceramics
	TOR	Building material
	P-L	Small lithic industry (of quartz and flint)
	P-L RO	Object formed on rock (marble, hard stone…)
	G-L	Big lithic industry (grinding material…)
	OS	Fauna
	O-O	Animal hard matter industry
	COQ	Object formed on shell
	PREL	Various samples (coals, seeds, shells…)
Cat. (category)	D	Decorated ceramic element
	F	Ceramic element of edge, melts, gripping…
	NM	Ceramic element of paunch
	VASE	Archaeologically complete ceramic element
	FUS	Fusaïole
	FIG	Figurine
	S	Flint
	S LAM	Flint blade
	Q	Quartz
	MEUL	Grind
	MOL	Serrated roller
	HA	Chop
	POIN	Punch
	SPA	Spatula
	TRAN	Cutter
	PAR	Ornament
	BRA	Bracelet
	CHAR	Coal
	COQ	Shell
	BOT	Sampling intended for the botanical analysis

Once the feature is defined, its "high" altitude is taken, and then the basins (for the sediment to be sieved and the finds from the feature) are labelled (sector, level, n°, square, m^2, excavation date). When a feature is entirely uncovered, it is described, recorded and photographed. Finally, it is removed and the "low" altitude is taken. The sediment is gradually sieved during excavation of the feature.

The basins are brought back to the project base daily and the finds are washed, sorted, recorded and stored. Washed finds are laid out with the label of the corresponding basin, and then sorted, counted, weighed and put in bags. All the information noted on the bags is then recorded in a computer file (data base on File Maker Pro). Certain headings of the card are filled in according to a very simplified code allowing fast and reliable recording. The material is sorted and put into bags according to the feature number, then the heading "material" (mat.), and finally the heading "category" (cat.). It is then recorded in the computer by n° of bag (one bag = one card of the file "inds recording"). The bags are numbered from 1 to N for the whole excavation (65267 bags recorded since 1986). The number or the weight are entered (various headings N [number] and P [weight]). An automatic calculation is made after each card is recorded. In certain cases, the altitude and the m^2 are specified in the headings "situation" (sit.) and "m^2". Otherwise, the necessary information for finds location is available in the file "feature." The file "finds recording" belongs to a data base which gradually builds up as work progresses.

After each recording, the finds contained in the bags are marked in Indian ink. The sector followed by the bag number is noted on each item.

Data Recording Methods

The quantity of the information that is generated by this excavation led the directors to use computers to record the data as work progressed. The project, which started in 1986, has seen a number of successive software and operating systems: data recording was carried out on Macintosh with its operating systems Mac OS (currently Mac OS X). The data base software passed from File II to File Maker Pro (4 to 7). Files of various recordings were created by the excavation directors.

At the beginning data recording "files" were created, while an actual "data base" made of several interlinked files was applied from then on. The multiplication of files and studies required simplification of the data layout. Thus, this data base was created to allow and facilitate the access to the data, the information management and navigation between each file. The data bases created for various studies were then joined to the principal data base. Specialists created each file in accordance with the specific questions of their studies.

The principal data base, (called "excavation"), consists of 6 files. They all have a direct link with the file "features." It is made up on the one hand of files relating to finds (finds recording, "small-finds" (objects recorded at the museum of Blagoevgrad), and drawings) and on the other hand of two files relating only to the site data (site drawings and photographs). It is not necessary to describe each of these files here.

On the other hand, (as with the file "finds recording" described previously), we will observe here the file "features," which remains the most significant file because it is a reference for all the other files. All the specialists use it because it contains the site information which locates the finds in space. The file "features" is composed of 19 headings. They allow a precise description of the feature. The information noted by the excavators in the book of features and the preprinted cards is recorded there. We can note the addition of four headings which do not appear on the preprinted card: the headings "str. princ." (principal features), "qual. obs" (observation quality), "code" and "prof./ép" (depth/thickness). These headings enable the entry of information that is essential to various studies. Their function and their interest are described later on because they are fully part of the method that is applied for the spatial analysis of the architectural remains. We can also note the presence of two "buttons" which give access to the files "principal features" and "finds recording" thanks to a link created with these two other files.

Eleven more sets of files are grafted to the "excavation" files. They belong to the "post-excavation" study. Each study makes it possible to approach a particular aspect of the site. These data bases are to some extent a "secondary" use of the "excavation" data base files to allow the exploitation of their raw data. These bases consist of files in which new data resulting from the study of the vestiges, whether they are movable or built, are recorded.

The data base "space analysis," suitable for the issues of the organization of the architectural vestiges is presented to you only briefly for the moment because it is detailed more thoroughly in the part devoted to the method. It is made up of 4 files. The "main" file of this base is the file

Figure 6. Databases of Kovačevo

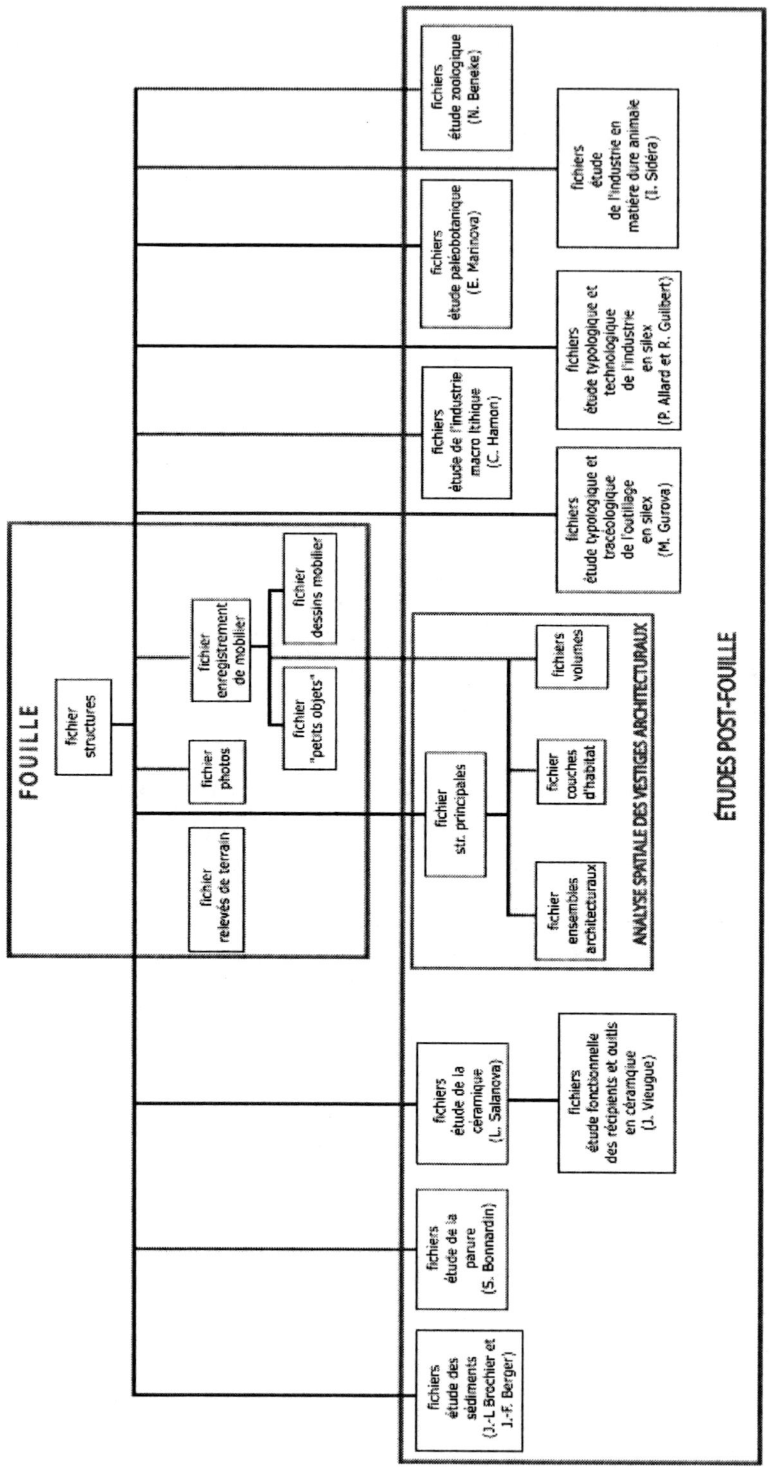

Figure 7. Sheet resulting from the File Maker Pro file "structures"

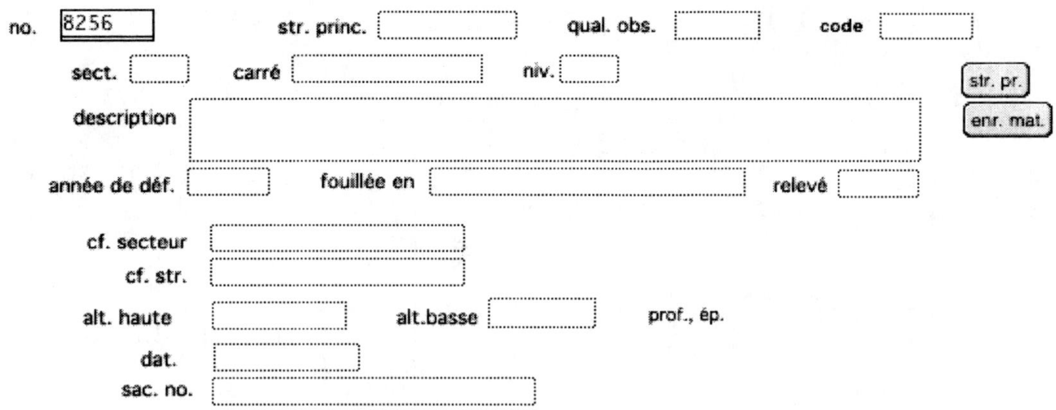
no. 8256
str. princ.
qual. obs.
code
sect.
carré
niv.
str. pr.
description
enr. mat.
année de déf.
fouillée en
relevé
cf. secteur
cf. str.
alt. haute
alt.basse
prof., ép.
dat.
sac. no.

"principal structures" (itself linked to the file "structures"). The files "architectural units," "layers of habitat" and "volumes" are linked to it.

RETRIEVAL OF THE GROUND DATA: ANALYSIS AND RECONSTITUTION

The spatial analysis of the architectural remains is carried out in three main stages. The number of excavators (due to the duration of the project) generates a certain heterogeneity which has to be processed before integrating the data into the geographical information system, in spite of use of files with carefully chosen headings. Aiming at homogenisation, the first stage of this study was therefore the definition of the "principal features" and creation of a "coding" of a "typology" of the features, based on the features such as they were defined on site. This time-consuming stage is the base of the study. It is the first interpretative phase carried out, based on the archaeologist's reflections. After examining the qualitative aspect of the data through features, work related to the quantitative aspect was started. It was therefore decided to calculate the volumes of the negative features and the excavation units, as well as the density of certain finds categories associated (selected according to the criteria of finds recording). This purely quantitative aspect also enables study of other qualitative aspects of the feature. Finally, the third stage fully approaches the distribution of the remains (principal features) within space. This work is completed in three dimensions thanks to stratigraphic and planimetric diagrams of the data already interpreted.

Principal Structures and Structure Coding

The first goal here is to identify the various units making up the settlement. By unit, we mean a set of remains (buildings, combustion features, channels, etc.). The 3544 features required a great deal of sorting. The features defined on the site mostly correspond to a type of remain (a floor, a post hole, a pit, a trench, a wall fragment, etc.). The principal feature is thus the union of elements (features) in a functional or coherent chronological unit. A principal feature can unite features of different sectors if the stratigraphy is coherent and identifiable. Thanks to this work, the various units of the settlement gradually take shape. The categories of principal features thus include: the architectural units (union of elements comprising

Figure 8. Principal structures of the principal building site of Kovačevo (E.A: architectural unit, V.A: isolated architectural vestige, t.d.p : pole hole)

secteur	nombre de structures définies					nombre de structures principales définies												
	UF	str. en creux		VAS	total	couches d'habitat	E.A.	V.A.	str. de comb.	pav./caill	sép	str. en creux					autres	total
		fosse	t.d.p.									fosse	tranchée	t.d.p.	dépr.	str. stoc.		
A	58	38	108	71	**275**	9	8	0	2	3	0	6	1	1	0	0	2	**32**
B	42	52	103	103	**300**	11	7	1	3	1	1	6	1	1	0	0	2	**34**
C	2	2	8	3	**15**	1	0	0	0	2	0	0	0	0	0	0	1	**4**
D	1	0	1	4	**6**	1	0	0	0	0	0	0	0	0	0	0	0	**1**
E	83	57	299	206	**645**	16	13	12	3	15	3	30	2	0	1	0	0	**95**
F	17	38	61	53	**169**	11	4	1	0	1	0	8	1	1	0	3	1	**31**
G	31	40	77	68	**216**	8	5	4	1	1	0	4	1	1	0	1	1	**27**
H	0	0	0	0	**0**	0	0	0	0	0	0	0	0	0	0	0	0	**0**
I	89	52	147	220	**508**	16	7	6	2	0	1	17	0	0	0	2	1	**52**
K	45	56	68	94	**263**	6	4	2	0	3	1	1	3	1	1	0	4	**26**
L	30	29	47	43	**149**	6	2	4	1	2	0	9	1	2	0	0	1	**28**
M	171	59	142	110	**482**	14	4	5	0	2	0	5	1	0	0	1	1	**33**
N	107	30	27	79	**243**	10	3	2	1	4	1	4	3	0	0	0	1	**29**
O	32	19	9	31	**91**	4	0	1	0	1	0	7	4	0	1	2	1	**21**
P	46	9	72	29	**156**	6	0	5	1	1	0	5	7	2	1	1	0	**29**
R	2	1	0	4	**7**	1	0	0	0	0	0	0	2	0	0	0	0	**3**
S	0	0	0	3	**3**	1	0	0	0	0	0	0	0	0	0	0	0	**1**
T	6	3	0	5	**16**	1	0	3	1	0	0	3	0	0	0	0	1	**9**
TOTAL	**762**	**485**	**1169**	**1126**	**3544**	**122**	**57**	**46**	**15**	**36**	**7**	**105**	**27**	**9**	**4**	**10**	**17**	**455**

Figure 9. Number of structures per principal structure per sector

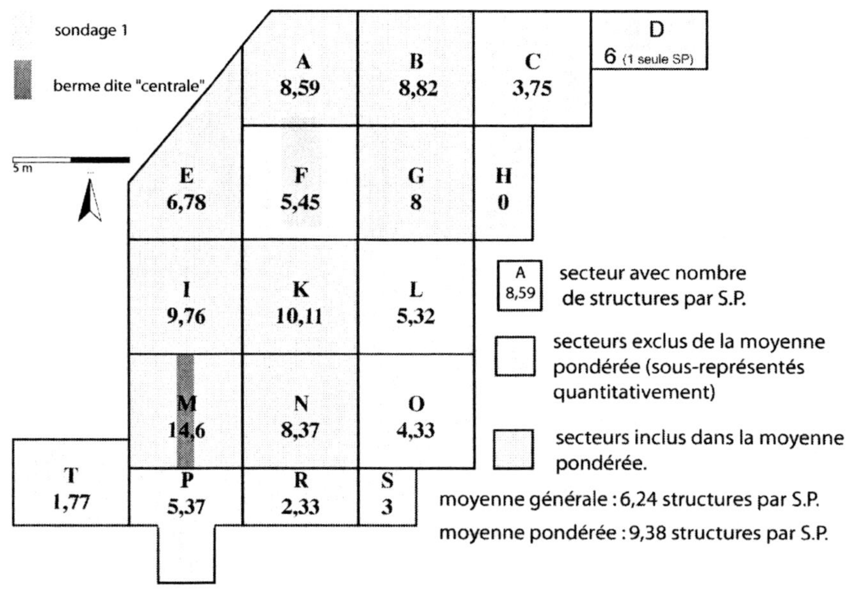

the architecture of a building), pits (with variable and often multiple functions), settlement layers (made up of excavation units and scattered features), burials, combustion and storage features, paving and gravel lenses, various negative features (post holes, depressions, trenches, and pits). If some interpretation intervenes in the creation of the principal features, we underline our intention to remain the most neutral possible at the time of their definition. The preceding table presents the number of principal features per sector, sorted according to the quoted categories.

455 principal features were created for the whole excavation. A principal feature unites on average 6.24 features. This average is significant because it provides an immediate check on the validity of the principal features created. If this average was equivalent to the average of each sector (with + or – 2 features), we could consider that each sector has been processed in the same way, which is essential for the validity of the final interpretation. However, according to a simple observation of the data, it appears essential to balance this result, which seems too low. In order for it to be representative of reality, we exclude from this average the sectors near the edge of the excavation, those with little stratigraphy (sectors C, D, H, L, O, P, T, R and S), and sector F, disturbed by the 1981 trial trench. After weighting, (using only sectors A, B, E, G, I, K, M and N), the average is 9.38 features per principal feature. So, if this average indicates an effective homogenisation for 7 sectors (A, B, E, G, I, K and N), it still remains quite distant for sector M with an

Figure 10. Sheet resulting from the File Maker Pro file "principal structures"

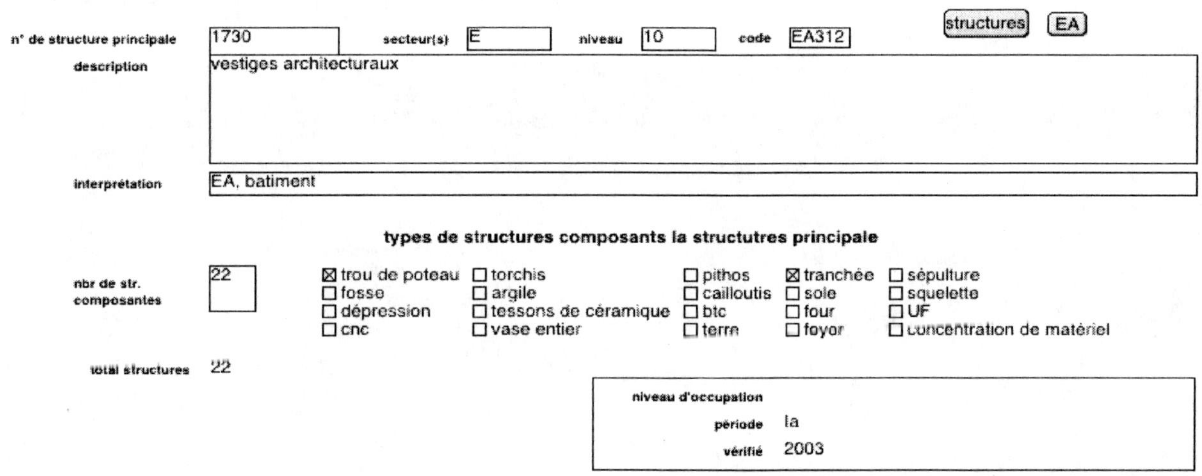
n° de structure principale 1730 secteur(s) E niveau 10 code EA312 structures EA
description vestiges architecturaux
interprétation EA, batiment
types de structures composants la structutres principale
nbr de str. composantes 22
☒ trou de poteau ☐ torchis ☐ pithos ☒ tranchée ☐ sépulture
☐ fosse ☐ argile ☐ cailloutis ☐ sole ☐ squelette
☐ dépression ☐ tessons de céramique ☐ btc ☐ four ☐ UF
☐ cnc ☐ vase entier ☐ terre ☐ foyer ☐ concentration de matériel
total structures 22
niveau d'occupation
période Ia
vérifié 2003

Figure 11. "Principal structures" coding

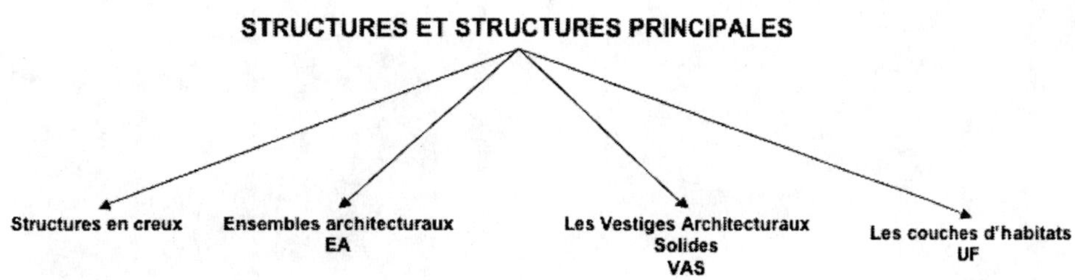

average of 14.6 features. This average number of features is possibly explained by the presence of a "central" baulk which split the sector in two parts (installed to help understand this sector with a strongly disturbed stratigraphy). Even if an attempt was made to unite a maximum of features without taking account of this baulk, this number reflects the difficulty of the task.

The principal features are recorded in the "principal features" file which belongs to the "spatial analysis" data base. This file is linked to the "architectural units" file, which belongs to the same base, and to the "features" file of the "excavation" data base. It enables recording of the data necessary for the description of the principal features. The classification is carried out starting from the feature numbers ("features" file): the number of a principal feature corresponds, in the large majority of the cases, to the number of the first feature included (e.g., the principal feature made up of features 568, 580, 589, 594 and 598 has the principal feature number 568). This file is composed of 13 headings. Three of them make it possible to locate the principal feature (n°, sector(s), and level(s)). The other headings enable the description of the principal feature (number of features that compose it, their type, the dating and the code assigned to the principal feature).

A code is accorded to each principal feature. This coding was applied to make it possible to homogenize the data from the file "principal features." It was established while trying to remain as far as possible on a descriptive rather than interpretative level. The basic level is the principal feature divided later into four main categories: negative features, settlement layers, architectural units and architectural remains. Figure 12 presents the coding of the "architectural units" and the "architectural remains" and Figure 14 the coding of the "negative features" and the settlement layers.

Figure 12. Coding of the "architectural units" and the "solid architectural vestiges"

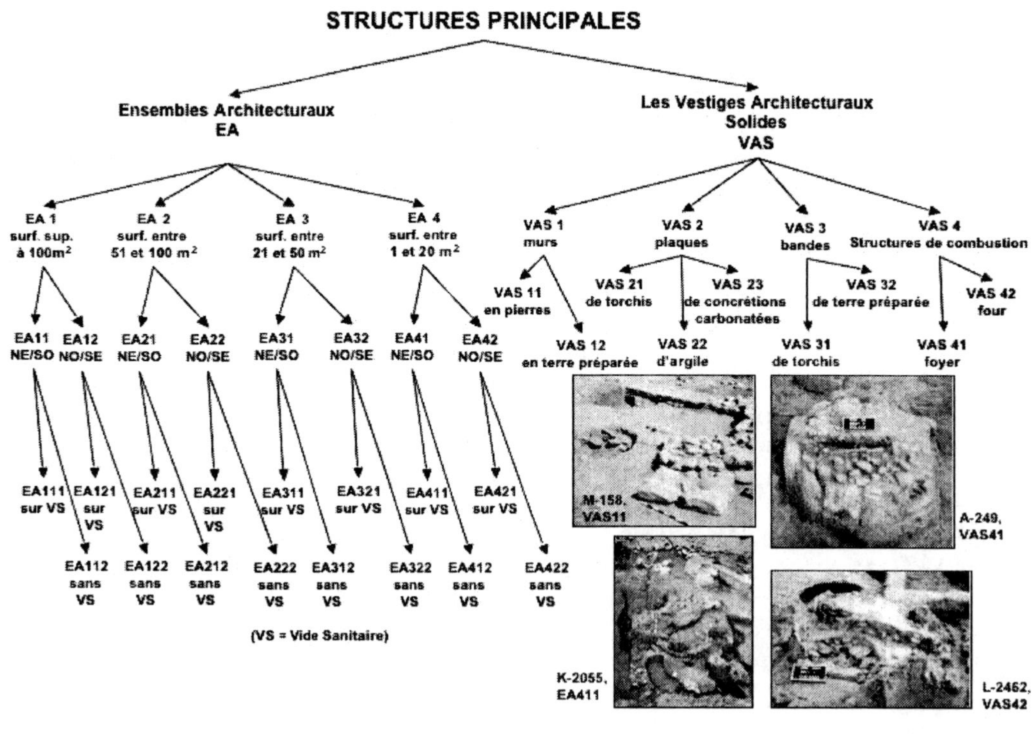

The "architectural units," which correspond to potentials buildings, are divided in four large subcategories created according to the surface of the units: EA1 (surface superior to 100 m^2), EA2 (surface ranging between 51 and 100 m^2), EA3 (surface ranging between 21 and 50 m^2) and EA4 (surface inferior to 21 m^2). These four subcategories are still subdivided according to the orientation of the unit (north-east/south-west or north-west/south-east) then according to the presence or not of a subjacent sanitary space. The architectural units are the subject of a description more thorough than the other types of principal structures. The descriptive criteria necessary for the full exploitation of these units are recorded in a file pertaining to the "space analysis" data base. These descriptive criteria relating exclusively to the architectural units allow an analysis on the scale of the unit of habitat. They are on the one hand very general (dimensions and types of structures which compose them) and on the other hand specific (floor installation, hard work and construction techniques, external installations and quantities of furniture).

The "solid architectural remains" are divided into four subcategories: VAS1 (walls) subdivided according to building materials (stones and prepared soil), VAS2 ("slabs") subdivided into daub, clay and carbonated concretions, VAS3 ("bands") into daub and prepared soil, and VAS4 (combustion features) into hearth and oven.

Figure 13. Sheet resulting from the File Maker Pro file architectural units

Ensembles architecturaux — SP

n° SP 2199 — secteur K — niveau 4,5 — datation Ia — code typo. EA322

GENERALITES

longueur estimée 8,75m. — largeur estimée 5m. — surface au sol estimée 43,75m².

orientation NW-SE

nombre de structures composantes 32

types de structures composantes
☒ planchers de CNC
☒ planchers de terre battue seule
☐ vide sanitaire
☒ fosse
☐ trou de poteau
☐ UF
☐ plaque d'argile cuite
☐ tranchée de fondation

recollage céramique intra SP

recollage céramique inter SP

AMENAGEMENT DU SOL

présence d'un vide sanitaire ◉ oui ○ non — vide sanitaire rempli ○ oui ○ non — taux de remplissage ☐ très dense ☐ dense ☐ peu dense

place du VS dans le bâtiment

nbr de fosse composant le vide sanitaire — fosse polylobée ○ oui ○ non

nombre de planchers conservés 6

GROS OEUVRE

technique d'édification ☐ pisé ☐ torchis ☐ briques ☐ indéterminée

aménagement préalable à l'édification du mur ☐ soubassement en pierres ☐ tranchée de fondation ☐ soubassement en BTC

présence de trous de poteau ◉ oui ○ non — trous de poteau internes 2 — trous de poteau mur 1

AMENAGEMENTS EXTERNES

proximité d'une structure de combustion ○ oui ◉ non — présence d'une structure de combustion interne ○ oui ◉ non

proximité d'une structure liée à la gestion de l'eau ○ oui ○ non

MOBILIER

P-L S	30	G-L	8	O-O	30
type P-L sur représenté		P-L RO	3	type O-O sur représenté	poinçon
nbr P-L sur représenté		autel	1	nbr O-O sur représenté	22
pds céramique		pintaderas		parure	19
nbr d'individus		fus/jetons	2	type parure	☒ céramique ☐ RO
		figurines	6		

Figure 14. Coding of the "structures in crevices" and the "layers of habitat"

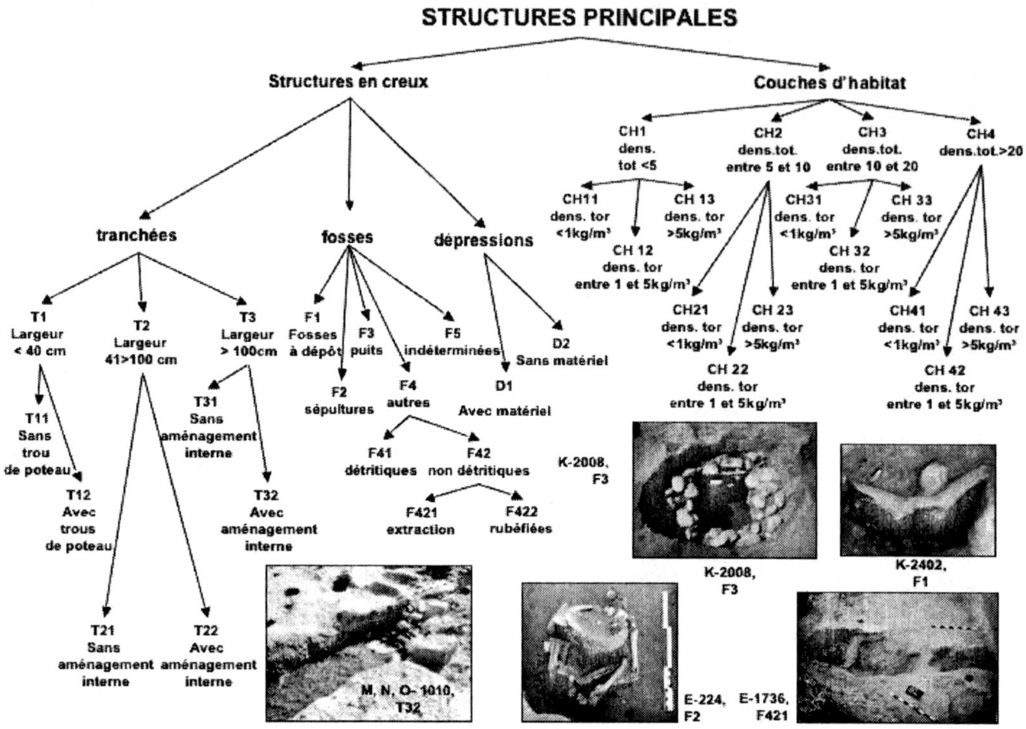

The third coding concerns the "negative features." They are divided into three subcategories: trenches, pits, depressions. The trenches are subdivided according to their width: T1 (less than 40 cm), T2 (41-100 cm) and T3 (over 100 cm). Then, this coding is specified according to their "installation" (presence or absence of post holes, presence or absence of a built internal installation).

The next coding is that of the pits. It begins with their functional aspect. However, it is very difficult to define the exact function of this type of feauture. In the large majority of cases, the attribution of a function to a pit is based on the observation of two descriptive criteria: dimensions and type of filling. Unfortunately, these criteria do not always present sufficiently discriminating characters to allow the attribution of a function to a pit. Moreover, one pit seldom presents a single (primary) function. Secondary functions, even tertiary, are very often identified. For example, the pits known as "extraction," whose primary function is the extraction of sediment for building purposes, can be also used secondarily for refuse disposal. The establishment of this coding of pits was only possible through our experience of the site. Pits are subdivided in five subcategories: pits with deposits (F1), burials (F2), wells (F3), "others" (F4) and "unspecified pits." The subcategory "others" is divided into two: refuse pits (F41) and nonrefuse pits (F42). The coding of the F42 pits is refined by additional information: sediment extraction (F421) and particular use involving burning of the pit walls (supposed storage pits) (F422).

Finally, the last subcategory of negative features, the depressions, is subdivided simply by the presence of finds corresponding to a particular use of this depression (with finds [D1] or without finds [D2]).

The coding of the settlement layers was carried out according to their density of finds. After importing all the excavation units from the "features" file into a "layers volume" file, we calculated as precisely as possible the volume (in m^3) of each excavation unit. Once the import (from the "finds" file) of quantities of daub, ceramics and bone has been carried out, an automatic calculation provides the densities in kg/m^3 of each category of find. The settlement layers are subdivided first of all according to the total density of finds and then according to the density of daub (architectural remains). Four subcategories are initially created: settlement layers of which the total density is less than 5 kg/m^3 (CH1), settlement layers for which the total density is between 5 and 10 kg/m^3, settlement layers of which the total density is between 10 and 20 kg/m^3 and settlement layers of which the total density is higher than 20 kg/m^3. Each subcategory is then ordered according to the density of daub: less than 1 kg/m^3, between 1 and 5 kg/m^3 and higher than 5 kg/m^3.

Stratigraphic and Planimetric Diagrams

Having characterized the settlement units by defining the principal features and attributing

Figure 15. Chart codes and legend of the stratigraphic schemes

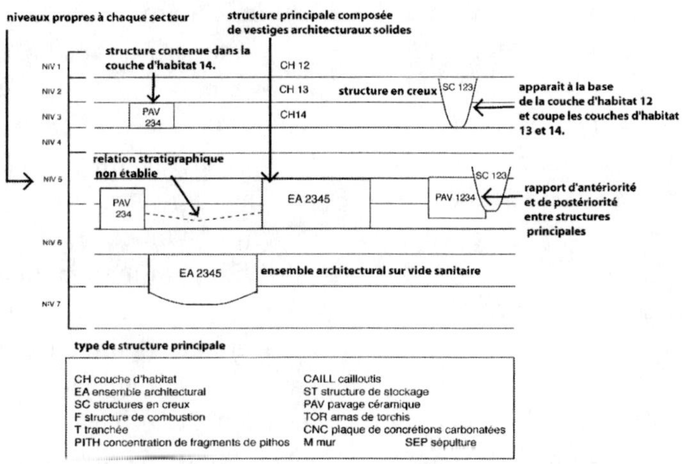

Figure 16. Chart codes and legend of the planimetric schemes

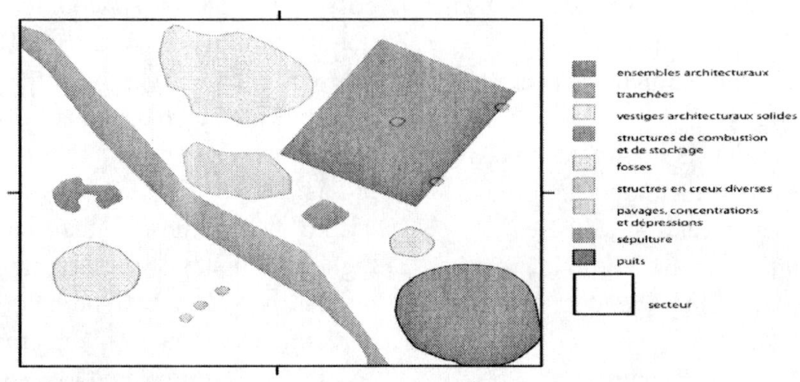

a code for each one, it is important to organize these data in space. The nature of the data led us to implement "diagrams." These are made according to two planes: vertical and horizontal. Three dimensions are thus taken into account.

The representation of the horizontal plane corresponds to the planimetric organization of the principal structures. These schemes make it possible to apprehend the horizontal stratigraphy of the vestiges thanks to the observation of their in between organization (superpositions, partial overlappings, interruptions, etc.). All the principal structures and the various structures in crevices which are associated to them are also represented. Each principal structure is drawn (contour of its maximum extension) and is coded by a color according to its type. Initially, the planimetric schemes present all the principal structures without taking into account any codings and ratios of anteriority or posteriority. It is only after the extraction of the data necessary to the various processes of analysis, essential to answer the general issues that the thematic schemes are carried out.

Data Extraction and Analysis of the Sectors

Although the objective of this article is mainly methodological, it can be illustrated through a "typical example" of analysis. The internal chronology of the site is not yet definitively established and the various finds studies are not finished, so we are not able to present an analysis using the real data from the site.

This "standard" analysis is directed toward chronological issues: to understand the organization of settlement units dating to the earliest Neolithic period on the site and try to approach the settlement phases using the data from a "standard sector."

This first phase of analysis consists of a brief description of the sector in question, using the stratigraphic and planimetric diagrams. Figure 17 presents the stratigraphy and planimetry of principal features in the standard sector dating to the earliest Neolithic. The quantities of certain categories of finds are illustrated graphically (flint industry, grinding equipment, bone industry, ornaments, hard stone industry, spindle whorls and figurines). A vertical bar chart (heights of the bars proportional to the values) and a circular graphic (pie-chart of percentage values of the data) are made for each architectural unit. The second type of graphic presents only three categories of finds (flint industry, grinding equipment and bone industry). The aim of these graphics is to represent the proportion within each architectural unit of finds categories relating to particular functions. These data make it possible to direct the analysis toward a functional interpretation of the architectural units.

The description of the "standard sector" which follows is invented and does not correspond to reality. It is just an example, which enables us to illustrate the method of analysis as clearly as possible.

This "standard sector" presents a stratigraphy of 2,50 m maximum and 1,70 m minimum. Twenty-one principal features were defined from 90 features identified during excavation. The stratigraphic diagram shows 10 settlement layers, distributed over 7 levels. There are 3 architectural units, occurring in levels 5 to 7. The low density of principal features in the higher levels (1 to 4) possibly reflects two phenomena: poor preservation of remains or a hiatus in the occupation of this sector. The earliest Neolithic period of the site is represented by 6 principal features: 2 architectural units, one gravel and three pits. One of the pits is a well and is coded F3. The distribution of finds within the architectural units reveals the higher frequency of certain categories. One of the units (EA XXXX) is characterized by a higher percentage of flint tools than the average for the architectural units dated to the earliest Neolithic period of the site.

Figure 17. Standard analysis of a sector

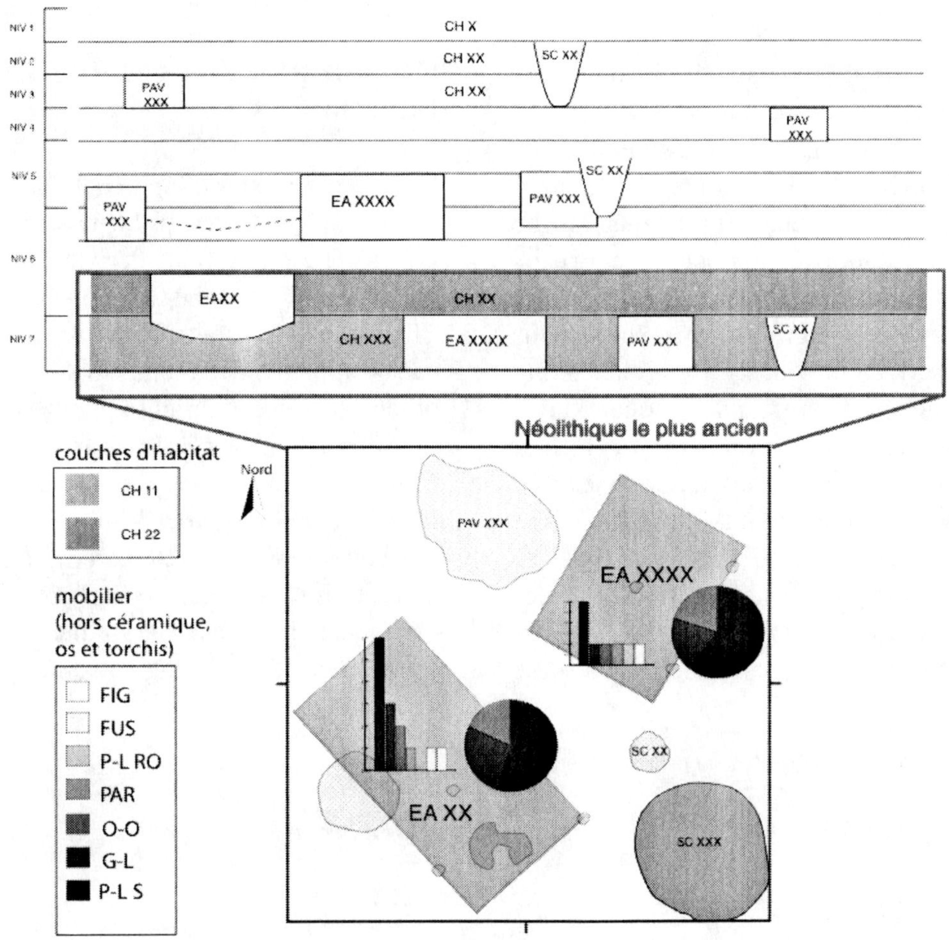

THE ORGANIZATION OF THE HABITAT: INTERPRETATION

Once the data are sorted, extracted and analyzed, it is then possible to propose an interpretation of the organization of the principal features dated from the earliest Neolithic period on the site. The general organization of these features is described in terms of three axes.

A "spatial" axis which consists in establishing links between the architectural units and looking for patterns in the distribution of features within the site. The scale involved here is the excavated area.

A "functional" axis, justified by the need to understand the units, makes it possible to examine the interrelationships of features. This axis concerns the architectural units. This aspect is treated with the data resulting from coding the features and the quantities of finds. The scale here is the principal feature.

Lastly, a chronological axis defines the settlement phases and provides thus a detailed image of the village at a given moment. This is where interpretation comes in.

Organization According to a Space Axis

Here, the aim is to address certain questions relating to the initial research problems. These questions revolve around a fundamental issue: what is the function of the buildings? The functional aspect of the architectural units can be apprehended thanks to the characteristics of each unit. The identification of these characteristics is based on synthesis of results from the various analyses described previously. Here, the coding of the architectural units and the quantitative information relating to the finds from each unit are used. The studied characteristics were selected according to questions about the function of the architectural units: do the dimensions of the buildings and the presence of underfloor spaces have a chronological or functional explanation? Do the quantities and types of find from these units present characteristics which can provide a functional definition for the units?

Organization According to a Functional Axis

Here, it is a matter of approaching certain questions which make it possible to answer the initial issues. These questions derive from a principal question: Which is the function of the buildings? The functional aspect of the architectural units can be apprehended thanks to the characteristics of each unit. The highlighting of these characteristics is based on the synthesis of the data resulting from the various types of exploitation described in the preceding part. Within this framework, the coding of the architectural units and the quantitative information relating to the furniture of each unit are used. The studied characteristics were selected according to some questions the

Figure 18. Methodologic synthesis: from the processes of extraction and analysis till the interpretation

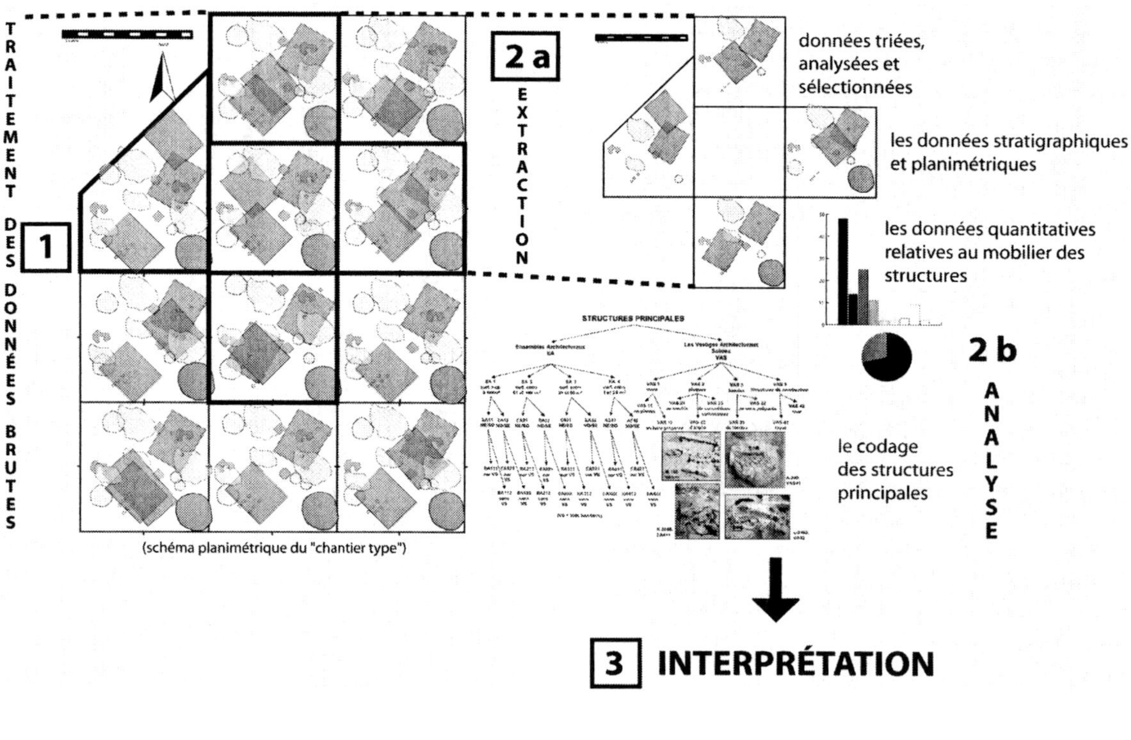

function of the architectural units raises: do the dimension of the buildings and the presence of subjacent sanitary spaces have a chronological or functional explanation? Do the quantities and the types of furniture collected in these units present characteristics capable of bringing a functional definition to the units?

General Space Organization of the Principal Structures of the Oldest Neolithic Period of the Site: Interpretation

The proposed general interpretation is the response to the questions posed at the beginning of this article. The patterns on a spatial axis and on a functional axis lead to suggestions about how the architectural units were organized.

Above all, is it still necessary to use neutral terms for what are certainly "buildings?" While the use of terms like "principal feature," "unit" or "architectural unit" was necessary to avoid an erroneous interpretation, some of these remains were better understood after analysis on the spatial axis. This study was necessary to be sure that each "architectural unit" corresponded to a building. It is their position within the stratigraphy, the distribution of the remains in plan and the identification of numerous refits and links which make it possible to specify whether or not there is a building for each architectural unit. Yet it is obviously very difficult to call them "houses," especially as some show characteristics relating to functions other than housing the inhabitants of the village.

The architectural characteristics of the buildings do not all point toward the same interpretation. While some contain functional information, others contain chronological information. The function of the buildings can be perceived thanks to the specific architectural characteristics of the finds. Chronological interpretation combines architectural characteristics, the stratigraphic organization of the buildings and the refitting of ceramics.

The quantity and the representativity of certain categories of finds within the buildings can also indicate function. For example, the buildings which reveal a significant proportion of a particular finds categories may be intended for a particular activity, or at least more so than the other buildings.

The chronological interpretation of the buildings of the earliest Neolithic period on the site, that is, the establishment of the occupation phases, is quite difficult. Nevertheless, there are clues as to the existence of occupation phases. This involves a combination of several observations: the distribution of the buildings, their orientation, their organization within the stratigraphy (relationships of posteriority/anteriority), and refitting finds.

The possible phases can be highlighted by the study of the spatial distribution of the remains. Their validity must be checked through detailed chronological study of the ceramics.

FURTHER RESEARCH DIRECTIONS

The archaeological research problem defined in the beginning of this chapter has been approached through application of a method of spatial analysis adapted to the data from the site of Kovačevo. The data are examined from the **observation** phase, on site, up to the **interpretation** phase. Although use of a geographical information system had been planned to treat the data, this spatial study was carried out without this type of software. However, the computer is omnipresent and the work could not have been accomplished without it: the method of analysis could not have been applied because the data management would have been too difficult. Data base software, computer graphics, and spreadsheets were used. Obviously, a geographical information system could have been applied, but the technical investment (expensive software, long apprenticeship) proved too important for a task, which ultimately, is feasible without this tool. However, for the general interpretation of the site, that is, the synthesis of all the studies in progress, a geographical information system will be applied because its use will be very beneficial for the huge quantity of data.

Consequently, a geographical information system should be used when there are clearly defined research issues. It must be applied when the data are rich and varied, and when their interpretation requires multiple cross analyses.

ACKNOWLEDGMENT

The author expresses her gratitude to the French and Bulgarian leaders involved in the research project of Kovačevo for permitting the use of the databases and the documentation of the excavation results. She is particularly grateful to Professor Marion Lichardus-Itten who introduced her to the methodological procedures and watched constantly over the development of ideas and interpretations. Finally, she thanks Dr. Michael Ilett for the translation of these lines into English language.

REFERENCES

Beeching, A., & Brochier, J.L. (2003). Espace et temps de la Préhistoire: biaisage et problèmes de representation. In Gasco J., Gutherz X. et de Labriffe P.A. (dir.), *Temps et espaces culturels du 6° au 2° millénaire en France du Sud, Actes des quatrièmes rencontres méridionales de Préhistoire récente* (pp. 21-32), 28 et 29 octobre 2000, Nîmes.

Brochier, J.L. (1988). Les sédiments, documents archéologiques. *Nouvelles de l'Archéologie*, pp. 15-17.

Brochier, J.L. (1994). *Étude de la sédimentation anthropique. La stratégie des ethnofaciès sédimentaires en milieu de constructions en terre. Le site de Kovačevo* (pp 619-645) Bulletin de Correspondance Hellénique, n°118.

Brochier, J.L. (1999). Taphonomie de sites : fossilisation et conservation de l'espace habité, In Beeching A. et Vital J. (dir.), *Préhistoire de l'espace habité en France du Sud, Travaux du centre d'Archéologie préhistorique de Valence*, pp. 19-28.

Demoule, J.P., & Lichardus-Itten, M. (1994). Fouilles franco-bulgares du site néolithique ancien de Kovačevo, Bulgarie du Sud-Ouest. In *rapport préliminaire (campagnes 1986-1993)*, Bulletin de Correspondance Hellénique, n°118, pp. 561-618.

Demoule, J.P., & Lichardus-Itten, M. (2001). Kovačevo (Bulgarie), un établissement du néolithique le plus ancien des Balkans. In Guilaine J. (dir.),*Communautés villageoises du Proche-Orient à l'Atlantique* (pp. 85-99) (8000-2000 avant notre ère), Séminaire du Collège de France.

Leroi-Gourhan, A., & Brézillon, M. (1972). *Fouilles de Pincevent: essai d'analyse d'un habitat magdalénien: la section 36*, Gallia-Préhistoire, suppl. 7.

Djindjian, F. (1997). L'analyse spatiale de l'habitat pré- et protohistorique, perspectives et limites des méthodes actuelles. In Auxiette G., Hachem L et Robert B.(dir.), *Espaces physiques espaces sociaux dans l'analyse interne des sites du Néolithique à l'âge du fer, actes du 119ème Congrès national des sociétés historiques et scientifiques*, Amiens, 26-30 octobre 1994, pp. 13-21.

Lichardus-Itten, M., Demoule, J.P., Perničeva, L., Grebska-Kulova, M., & Kulov, I. (2002). The Site of Kovačevo and the Beginnings of the Neolithic Period in South-Eastern Bulgaria, the French-Bulgarian excavation 1986-2000. In Licharchus-Itten M., Lichardus J. & Nikolov V. (dir.), *Beiträge zu Jungsteinzeitlichen Forschungen in Bulgarien, Saarbrücker Beiträge zur Altertumskunde*, Bonn, pp. 99-158.

KEY TERMS

Geographical Information System (GIS): A set of procedures used to store and process information with geographical reference. More specific, it is a combination of computer hardware, software, data, and user interfaces designed to analyze, manipulate, and display geographic information in many ways.

Stratigraphy: A superposition of layers (natural layers in geology), which are deposited one over the other following the chronology of the events that took place.

Feature: It can be conceived as a *significant grouping* of evidence, the relevance of which is based on the *repetition of similar situation*.

Planimetric Schemes: Visualizations that present all the principal structures without taking into account any codings and ratios of anteriority or posteriority.

Interpretation Organization: Described in terms of three axes, it comprises a spatial axis which consists of establishing links between the architectural units, a functional axis concerning the architectural units and lastly, a chronological axis defining the settlement phases and providing thus a detailed image of the village at a given moment.

Chapter VII
Databases for Multiple Archaeological Excavations and Internet Applications

Athanasios Karamalis
Computer Scientist and Researcher, Germany

INTRODUCTION

The science of Archaeology has been in existence for a long time and the way an archaeological excavation is conducted hasn't changed much. However, the way archaeological data is recorded has changed dramatically by the progress of technology and the widespread use of computers. Nowadays, almost any archaeological excavation uses databases to record not only the objects which have been found, but also the various data which come up during the excavation process (Lock, 2003).

Many remarkable researches have been conducted by archaeologists who developed standards and methods for recording the data which was produced during an archaeological excavation. Although many excavators use particular standards and methods for data recording, these usually cannot be completely implemented and have to be adapted to the particular requirements of the excavation. The reasons why this is happening are the various differences excavations have; in how archaeologists excavate a site, which data is recorded and how the data is characterized (we will discuss further this topic in the following chapters).

Therefore, databases that have been used have been developed by archaeologists and database developers, in order to satisfy the particular data recording requirements of each excavation. To achieve this, databases are commonly developed completely from scratch and separately for each excavation, in order to come up with the different needs archaeologists have. It is obvious that different databases have different structures, which basically means that they consist of different tables with different columns.

In order to create a database which can handle multiple excavations, the above differences make it necessary to provide archaeologists the capability of recording data according to their needs. Therefore, a database should be indirectly modified by archaeologists in order to meet their needs, without changing the database structure. This means that archaeologists do not intervene within the database structure in order to modify it, which results in the structural integrity of the database (we will discuss further this topic in the following chapters).

The main purpose of such a database is to improve the capability of sharing archaeological data and knowledge of different excavations with other archaeologists, scientists and generally with other people. Also, a multiple excavation database can improve the collaboration between archaeologists, by letting them work on a specific database structure which can be indirectly modified (Burenhult, 2001). Another issue is the compatibility between databases and other information systems. By using different databases, existing systems like GIS systems, Internet applications or simple database queries have to be modified in order to work or may even not work due to the different database structures. Having a database with distinct structure, information systems can be developed once and reused for any other excavation with its corresponding data (Richards, 1998).

In the following sections, we make a brief introduction in archaeological excavations. We describe first the analysis that has been done to create a database which can record multiple archaeological excavations, second how the database was realized and finally how the archaeologists can be assisted in their work by using the capabilities Internet provides.

INTRODUCTION TO ARCHAEOLOGICAL EXCAVATIONS

As mentioned before, archaeological excavations may vary in different ways, but the principles of archaeological working methods remain generally the same. In this chapter, we have an introduction of how a site is excavated and which data come up during this process.

Let's begin with the most important spatial entity of an archaeological excavation, which is the section. At this point, notice that not all archaeologists use the term section, but they may use other terms to describe this entity (the same applies for the following entities). Sections are the parts of an excavation site which have been removed and studied. We can think of them as the soil that has been removed from the excavation during a digging process. Those part's dimensions can vary and they usually have the shape of a square, but they can also have any other shape. A section is defined by the points which define its shape and the depth of each point. Obviously, archaeologists record the coordinates of these points and the depth.

A section gives specific information about a particular part of the excavation that has been removed, for example, what type of soil and objects have been found. Additionally, a section can belong to a phase, to a layer and to a construct. These are entities that define chronologically and spatial an excavation (we will discuss this entities later on). Any objects that have been found in a section do "belong" to this section and inherit many of its chronological and spatial information. So when an archaeologist knows a section or an object, he can gain additional information on a specific part of the excavation. This gives the section a key role, which enables the archaeologists to create spatial and chronological analysis on the entire excavation or on objects which have been found. Also, sections enable archaeologists to keep track of the excavation progress. Notice at this point that the way sections are created may vary, depending on the excavation (Figure 1).

We mentioned before the term layer. The layers are 2-dimentional or 3-dimentional representations of the excavation, which have been defined by the archaeologists. Layers are used by archaeologists to define characteristics and consequently information for particular parts of the excavation. For example, layers are used to separate a part of the excavation which is believed

Figure 1. Image of a section from the excavation of the Toumpa site in Thessaloniki

Figure 2. In this example layers are defined considering the chronological period in which they belong

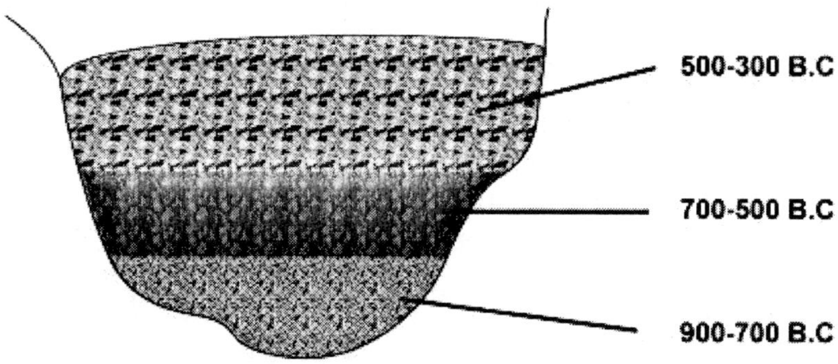

to belong to an earlier time period than the rest of the excavation (Figure 2). Furthermore, a layer can contain multiple sections and a section can belong to multiple layers. Therefore, knowing in which section an object was found also allows us to know in which layer it belongs to. This clearly shows us the important role sections have.

Constructs refer to spatial entities which existed in the past at the location of the excavation (archaeologists may also refer to constructs as architectures). For example, constructs can be streets, wells, and buildings like temples and houses which existed in the past and have been found during the excavation, or clues may indicate their former existence (Figure 3). During the excavation of a site, a part of a construct might be revealed in a section. In order to reveal the whole construct, more than one section is needed. Therefore, a construct belongs usually to multiple sections. Furthermore, a section might contain more than one construct, which usually is not the fact.

Phases are chronological periods which have been defined by archaeologists for the excavation

Figure 3. Construct representation of a part of the excavation

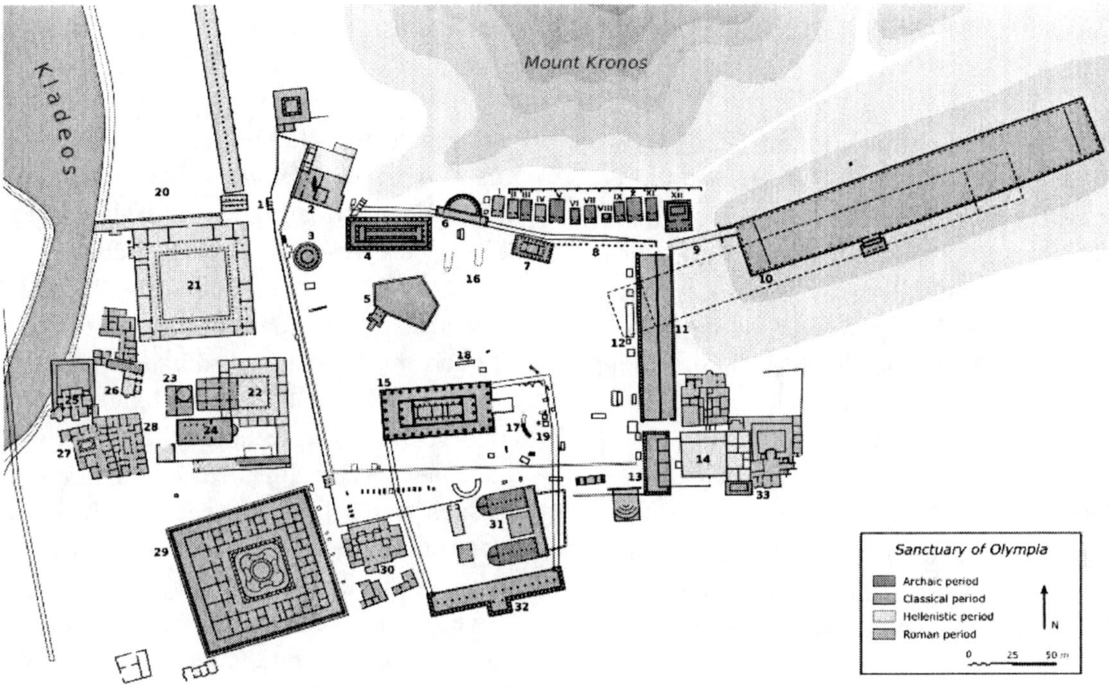

and they are important to chronological analysis. For example, a phase, named A11, stands for the time period 500-400 B.C. A phase contains multiple sections that belong to the same chronological period.

To sum all the latter up:

- **Section:** Part of an excavation site which has been removed and studied. A section is defined by the points which define its shape and the depth of each point.
- **Layer:** N-dimensional (usually N =1, 2, 3) representations of the excavation, which have been defined by the archaeologists. Layers are used by archaeologists to group parts of an excavation based on a set of characteristics. A layer can contain multiple sections and a section can belong to multiple layers.
- **Construct:** Spatial entity which existed in the past at the location of the excavation. A construct belongs usually to multiple sections, while a section might contain more than one construct.
- **Phases:** Chronological period defined by archaeologists for the excavation. A phase contains multiple sections that belong to the same chronological period.

This was a very brief and general introduction of archaeological excavations, which is necessary for those who are not skilled in the science of Archaeology, in order to understand the following chapters. The generality of this introduction has been practically used for the development of the database, in order to handle multiple excavations. Later on we will see how this generality was actually implemented.

PROBLEMS WHEN HANDLING MULTIPLE ARCHAEOLOGICAL EXCAVATIONS USING ONE DATABASE

As mentioned before, the differences in various archaeological databases, which are mainly the result of the different data recording methods and the different working procedures, make it difficult to have multiple excavations recorded by a single database. In this chapter, we will take a closer look at the problems which show up and give some examples.

The main problem is the structural difference in the various archaeological databases. Different databases likely have different table names, column names, relations and a different number of tables and columns. This also means that a database may not contain data on an entity that another database has, by simply not having the appropriate column (Date, 2004). Furthermore, these differences make it difficult to combine various archaeological databases into one. Also, archaeologists won't use a fixed database structure because they can't record the desired data according to their needs, so these differences are necessary for them. This makes it difficult to apply a fixed database structure for multiple excavations. The following example gives us an idea of possible differences that may occur between two databases.

Consider the following two databases, namely "*database 1*" and "*database 2*." While it is obvious that both contain data referring to almost identical objects, they present structural differences. For example, the X,Y,Z coordinates of the stored objects in database 1 are stored in the fields coordinate X, coordinate Y and coordinate Z of the object table, while in database 2, the latter information is stored in a separate table called "coordinates," in the fields X,Y,Z. Furthermore, database 1 uses one table for all objects and specifies their category in one column; whereas database 2 uses separate tables for each object category.

The differences in the database structures make the collaboration among archaeologists more difficult, because they deal with different databases to which they are not used. Additionally, different column and table names may confuse them, which means that they have to spend more time to understand a different structure (Figure 4 and Table 1).

Figure 4. Example of two different databases that use different tables for the same information

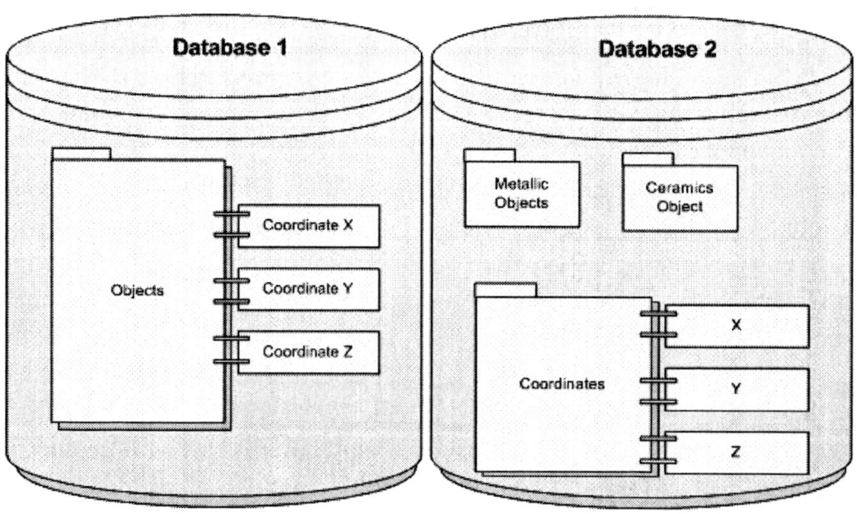

Table 1. Example of two different databases that use different tables for the same information

Database 1	Database 2
Tables	**Tables**
Objects	Category Objects
-Category	Metallic Objects
-Coordinates X	....
-Coordinates Y	Coordinates
-Coordinates Z	-X
	-Y
	-Z

Furthermore, these differences have a large impact on other information systems that use archaeological databases like GIS systems, Internet applications or mobile devices (Politis et al, 2005). This is because information systems have been designed to work with a particular database structure that has specific tables, table names and field names. Already existing information systems have to be changed in order to cooperate with other databases, which is a very time consuming task. What's more, information systems designed to manipulate data from a specific database cannot be used at the same time for multiple databases, because of their different structures. This makes it necessary to use multiple applications that are slightly different, actually performing the same tasks on different databases. This leads to significant cost increase as more licences and software packages are required to be purchased.

In order to deal with these problems and to gain the benefits of handling multiple excavations with one database, a unified relational database was designed and developed. This database gives the archaeologists the necessary capability of indirectly modifying the database in order to record their excavation data based on their needs.

DESIGNING AND REALIZING A MULTIPLE ARCHAEOLOGICAL EXCAVATION DATABASE

Before creating the actual database, a careful and time-consuming analysis has taken place to identify the requirements that are set by recording data from different archaeological excavations. Having these requirements in mind, the database has been developed to meet the archaeologist's needs in data recording and analysis.

To better comprehend the design and implementation of the database, we'll describe what relational databases are about. Relational databases are based on the relational model which was introduced by Codd in 1970 (Codd, 1970). The model is based on the mathematical sense of relations. In the relational model, information is represented as data in relations and can be retrieved by performing queries on those. We won't focus on the model itself, but rather on its implementation for databases.

When designing a relational database, we divide our set of data into domains which share the same characteristics or set of criteria. The definition of a domain depends on our set of data and how we want to use it; from here on we will refer to domains as entities for a database-oriented context. Furthermore, each entity has attributes which define the entity. The database implementation of relations and entities are tables and for attributes columns. To store information/data for each entity, we add rows with the corresponding data for each column. Furthermore, the relational concept implies that tables should always have a primary key which make each instance (row) of the table unique. Usually, the primary keys are auto increasing numbers (the first entry entered in the table will get id# 1, the second id# 2, etc.), but they can also consist of more than one column. To get a better insight, let's continue with an example. Consider that we want to model the sales of a car salesman (Figure 5).

After we create our first data representation we normalize our tables; meaning we apply normal forms (NF). Normal forms describe rules for relational databases and help developers avoid logical inconsistencies and data operation anomalies to a certain degree. The degree depends on the degree of the normal form that is reached (1NF to 8 NF). Further reading can be found in Date (2004) and Codd (1970).

When normalizing the table of our previous example, we soon come up with separating the sales with the cars and therefore having two separate entities (Figure 6).

As we can see the *Sales* table contains a column with a reference to the primary key of the *Cars* table, namely *car_ID*. This is a so called foreign key; used to establish relations between tables. Now, what are the benefits of this implementation? In our previous implementation let's consider that the salesman wanted to add a new car to his collection and therefore in his database. He couldn't do so because there was only one table, *Sales*, in which a new row was only added when a car was sold. This example demonstrates the importance of the relational database design in order to avoid problematic implementations of a database.

Say that the following records where retrieved from our previous implementation of the *Sales* and *Cars* Tables 2 and 3. We notice that we have repeating values in the *Manufacture* column of the *Cars* table. Again, we can make a separation, and hence separate the *Cars* entity into the *Cars* and the *Manufacture* tables (Figure 7).

By doing so we save storage space, which may not be obvious in this example, but in a table with thousands of rows the difference becomes obvious. Apart from saving disk space, this implementation allows us to add new manufactures to our database, without having to wait for a new car to arrive. Most of the possible data operation anomalies and logical inconsistencies are not addressed; however, the interested reader can find additional information on this topic in Date (2004) and Codd (1970). Closing this brief presentation of the functionality of the relational databases, we will delve into our approach for storing archaeological data.

Figure 5. Initial design for the database

Figure 6. References between two entities

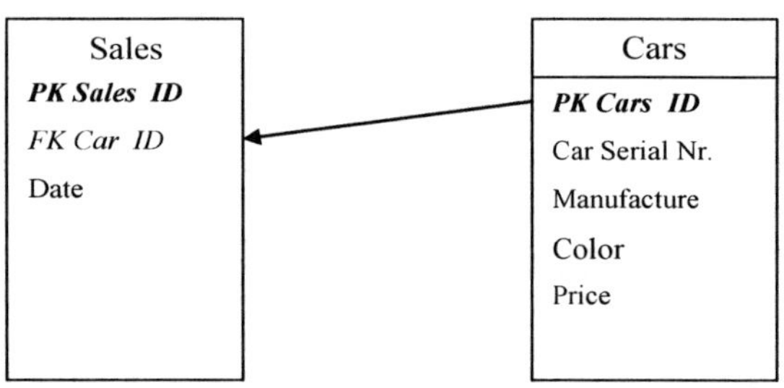

Table 2. Sales' records

Sales_ID	Car_ID	Date
1	1	07/02/2006
2	3	08/02/2006
3	2	10/02/2006

Table 3. Cars' records

Cars_ID	Car Serial Nr.	Manufacture	Colour	Price [$]
1	DE80771211	BMW	Metallic Silver	69995.00
2	JAP9175246	Honda	Metallic Black	49998.00
3	DE84464917	BMW	Red	59995.00

Figure 7. Separating one entity into two

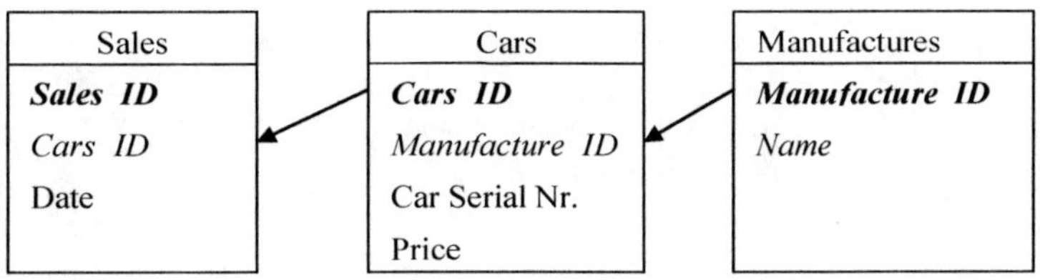

Figure 8. Stored data for an Object

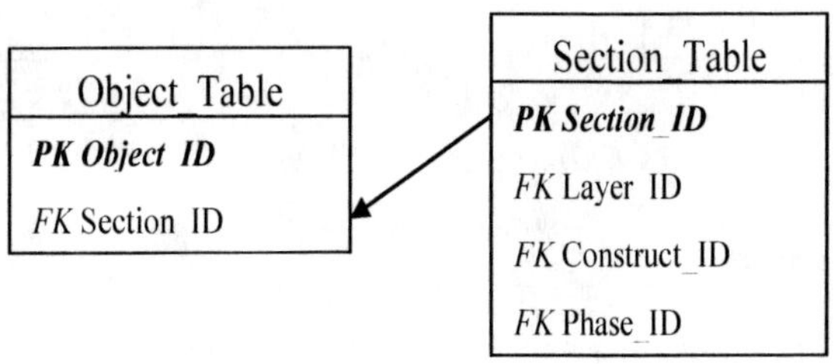

As mentioned before, the sections, which describe chronologically and spatially the excavations, play a very important role in archaeology. To implement this key role of the section entity a *section_table* is created. Its primary key is set to the Section_ID field, while the other fields are foreign keys to other tables. This way, in order to store data for an object we specify its corresponding section by using the FK (foreign key) to the *Section_Table*; as shown in the Figure 8.

The following example is more enlightening using some data and columns of the actual Tables 4 and 5 to show how these relations are actually implemented (Figure 9).

At this point we notice that the section Table 6 contains the foreign keys to the layer, construct and phase tables to realize the relations above. This can be visualised as in Figure 10.

As we can see, sections that belong to more than one layer, have in the layer column a combination of the layers they belong to. Other excavation databases may implement a different approach, by creating layer keys that correspond to multiple layers (Table 7).

Table 4. Actual data of object table

Object_Table	
Object_ID	Section_ID
1981	426
1982	291

Table 5. Actual data of section table

Section_Table			
Section_ID	Layer_ID	Construct_ID	Phase_ID
426	512	21	87
427	12	341	231

Figure 9. Visualization of tables relations

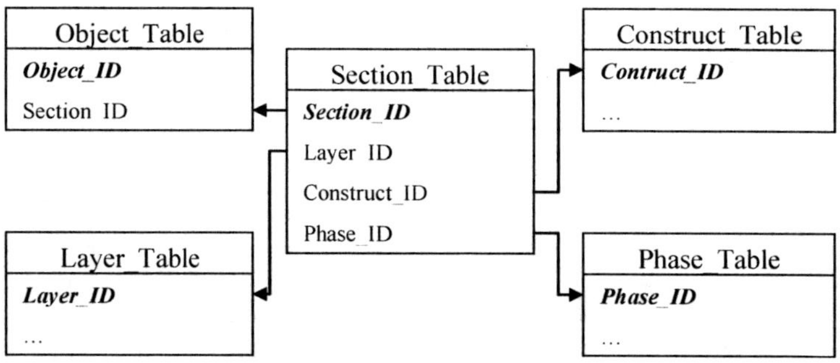

Table 6. Combination of different layers that sections belong to

Section			**Layer**	
ID	**Layer**		**ID**	**Data**
145	A21		A11	……..
146	A11,A13,A14		A12	……..
147	B2,B3		A13	……..

Figure 10. ER-Diagram of the relations between Section, Object, Layer, Construct and Phase

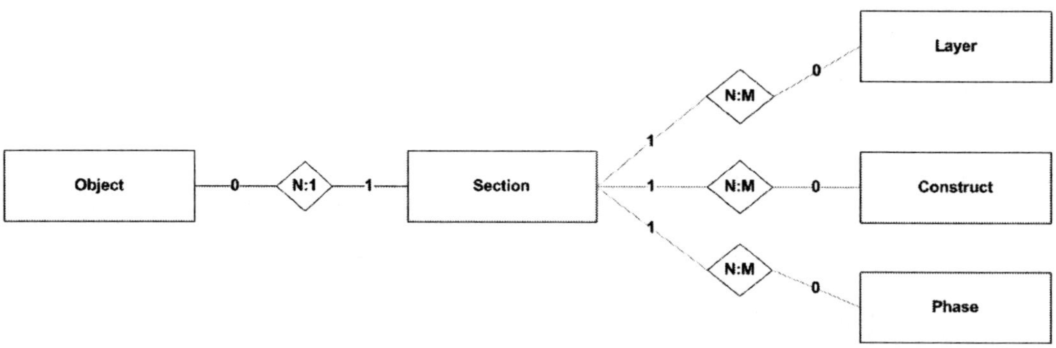

Table 7. Layer keys to multiple layers

Multi_Layer	
ID	Multilayer
AM1	A1,A2,A3
BM1	B6,B7,B9

Figure 11. ER-Diagram of Section, Excavation and Location relations

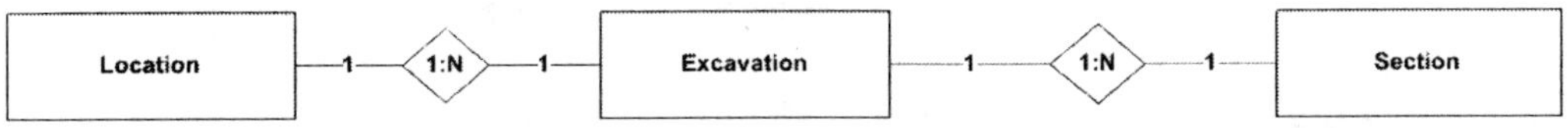

Later on we will see how the database can also handle this approach.

The section entity is related to the excavation entity, which contains all the excavations. Furthermore, the excavation entity is related to the location entity, which represents all the locations at which excavations are conducted. These relations are similarly created as the described section relations in Figure 11.

As mentioned before there are many differences in the way archaeologists record and characterize their data and therefore there are many differences between archaeological databases. The question now lies on how archaeologists can modify the existing multiple excavation databases according to their needs, without actually changing anything in the database structure. The answer lays the realization of a relational database where modifications can be performed by altering (i.e., adding, deleting and editing) rows in already existing tables. The main tables for each entity contain only the necessary columns for data recording, while the remaining data are being characterized and stored in separate tables. In order to better comprehend this method, we will further describe it using examples from the database.

For the first example, we use the *Object* table, which is one of the most important tables, considering that it stores the entire collection of objects which have been found. These objects can belong to any category of findings like metallic, crockery, ceramic and stone. The main table *object* consists of the columns described in Table 8. It is obvious that the columns *object_id, section_id* and *category_id* are defined by the database and the columns *custom_id, discovery_data* and *description* can be altered by archaeologist. The column *custom_id* allows archaeologists to import existing primary keys from other databases consequently to import existing objects into the database.

As we can see in Table 8 the object table consists of a small number of columns to record data for objects. It is possible that archaeologists might want to add additional columns, which in any other case would corrupt the structural integrity of the designed database.

Therefore, if we want to add a new attribute to the objects, with its corresponding data, we shall use the tables *object_attribute* and *object_data.* We can think of these attributes as the columns which are used in regular databases. The first table *object_attribute* characterizes the additional data and can be considered as the table that contains all the existing attributes for all the objects (Table 9). The second table *object_data* is used to store the data for each object (Table 10).

The following example has tables that come from the database and show how this approach is implemented. The main idea behind the example is this: Relational database views allow the user to combine data from different tables and data types

Table 8. Table's object columns

Object_ID	Custom_ID	Section_ID	Category_ID	Discovery_Data	Description

Object_ID	Primary keys which are set by the database
Custom_ID	Possible former primary keys used by an existing database of an excavation
Section_ID	Foreign keys of the *section_table* in order to assign objects to specific sections
Category_ID	Foreign keys of the *object_category* table to assign categories to objects
Discovery_Data	Date of the object
Description	Can be used to store a description for an object

and present them as if they were originated from a single table. In fact, you can image the database views as a table which is populated by data stored in other tables. In this example, the originating tables are *object_data* and *object attribute*, with the *attribute_ID* field in the *object_data* table being a foreign key from the *object_attribute* table (Figure 12). We are interested in presenting a view which contains the *object id*, the *object attributes* and the *object attributes_values.*

So, we extract the following fields: *Object_data_.object_ID*, *object_data_.attribute_ID* and *object_data.mydata* combined with *object_data.unit.* (Note that the *object_data_.attribute_ID* will eventually lead us to the data stored in the *object_attribute* table, as it is a foreign key to this table). After the latter data have been extracted they are combined into a data view, the so called *object_data_attribute_view,* which will present the results in a unified way.

As we can see in the example in Figure 12, in order to add additional data for an object we combine the desired object's *object_id* with the

Table 9. Table of object attributes

Object_Attribute		
ID	**Attribute**	**Description**
1	Weight	Total Weight of Object
2	Color	Object Color
3	NumP	Number of pieces of a ceramic object

Table 10. Table of objects data

Object_Data_			
ID	**Attribute_ID**	**My_Data**	**Unit**
1	1	3.450	kg
1	2	5 YR 4/4	
1	3	4	
...	......	......	....

Figure 12. Extracted fields and data view of object table

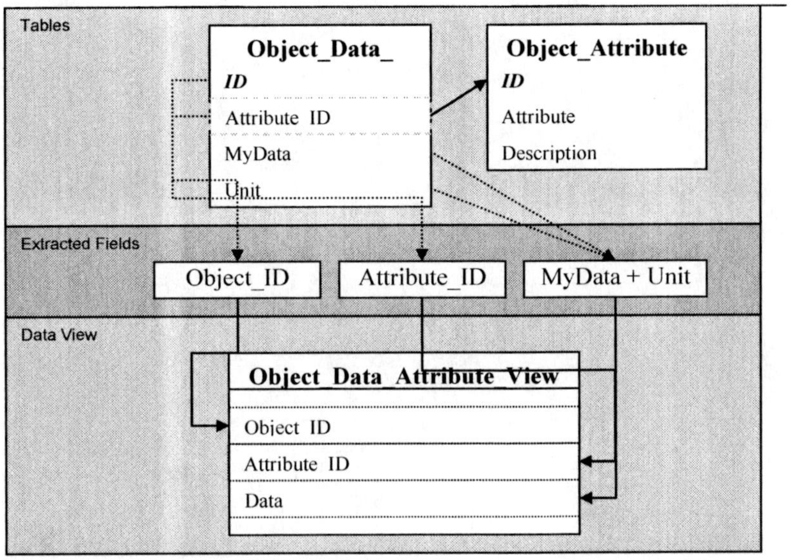

desired attribute's *attribute_id* and store the data in the *my_data* column with a possible unit in the unit column. The *attribute_id* refers actually to the attribute of the *object_attribute* table. Therefore, if we want for example to store the weight for an object which has the *object_id* 1, we combine the *object_id* 1 with the *attribute_id* 1, which stands for the weight, and enter the objects weight and unit. Afterward, recombining the tables with SQL views, we get the additional data for the objects displayed with the attribute names and not with the attribute_id, which would be confusing. The concept of entities and attributes is furthermore visualized by the diagram in Figure 13.

The above described implementation for the object entity is applied to the other main entities of the database, named archaeologist, construct, excavation, layer, location, object, phase and section.

Using this implementation, archaeologists can freely modify any attribute for any entity and record whatever data they want, by adding, deleting and editing rows of the already existing tables. As there is no need to create new tables or to alter the existing ones in any way, the archaeologists can adopt the database to meet the different requirements of various excavations in an easy way. Furthermore, the database does not change when additional excavations are being recorded, because the new data are stored in already existing tables. Therefore, information systems that have been developed as database front-ends can handle many excavations at once as the database structure remains firm and unchanged. What's more, as the database does not have to be altered in any way, there is no need for the archaeologist to delve into technicalities as the database schema, or its scripting language.

As mentioned before, the proposed database schema is able to handle various and multiple excavations. It is now obvious that the archaeologists may store all the objects that have been found into one table and use a column to determine their category (e.g., metallic, ceramic) or use separate tables for each category of objects. To enable them with the ability to add or freely edit categories and to assign a specific desired category to each object, the tables' *object_category* and *object_category_attribute* have been created. In Figure 14

Figure 13. Diagram of entities with attribute and data tables. This is the example for the section entity. This method is similarly applied to the other entities too

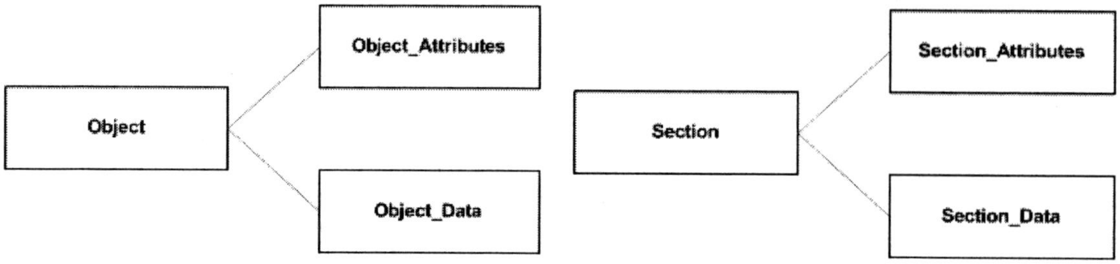

Figure 14. Object categories separated of the object table

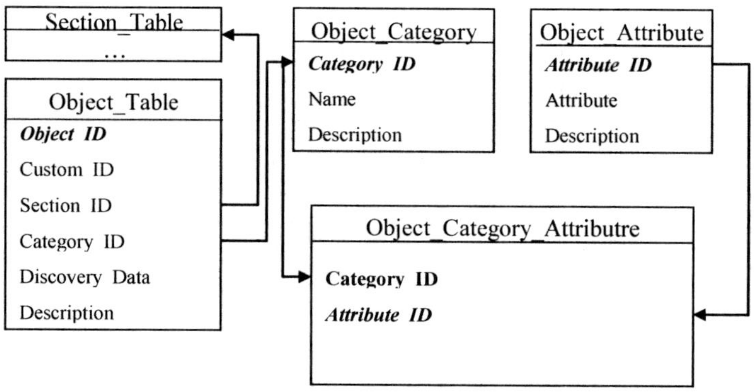

Table 11.

Object_Table					
Object_ID	**Custom_ID**	**Section_ID**	**Category_ID**	**Discovery_Data**	**Description**
149	1881	12	1	7/21/1997	
150	421	314	3	11/3/1988	

Tables 12, 13.

Object_Category		
Category_ID	**Name**	**Description**
1	METALLIC	
2	CERAMIC	
3	CERAMIC	

Object_Category_Attribute	
Category_ID	**Attribute_ID**
1	12
1	13
1	26

the schema of the object table is depicted, helping the reader clarify any dark spots.

In the above example we can see the main object table and the *object_category* and *object_category_attribute* table. When an object is being recorded the id of the category it belongs to, is assigned to it and therefore the combination of those two tables returns the category name of each object. Having the object categories separated of the object table, the archaeologists gain again the freedom of changing the categories, however they desire to meet their needs. The table *object_categoty_attibute* combines *category_id* and the *attribute_id* of the *object_attribute* table. Thus, attributes can be freely assigned by archaeologists to the desired categories. This does not only determine which attributes describe each category, but it also helps with the creation of numerous database queries that can be used by archaeologists. Also using this table, attributes can quickly be assigned to a selected category of objects.

Another important issue is how coordinates are recorded by the various excavations; what system and what units are used. Different approaches are used by archaeologists to determine the coordinates of an object, therefore again an implementation that gives the archaeologists the freedom to define and use their own coordinate system is needed. Thus, the tables' *object_coordinates* and *coordinate_definition* have been created (Figure 15, and Tables 14 & 15).

Figure 15. Object Coordinates and their definition

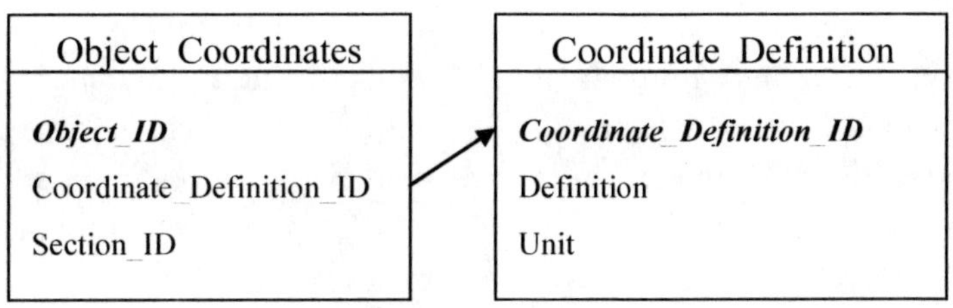

Table 14.

Object_Coordinates		
Object_ID	**Coordinate_Definition_ID**	**Coordinate_Data**
11	1	17.88
11	2	20.95
11	3	4.7

Table 15.

Coordinate_Definition		
Coordinate_Definition_ID	**Definition**	**Unit**
1	South	m
2	West	m
3	Depth	m
4	LAT	float

In the above example, we can see again that the object coordinates are separately stored for the objects using the *object_id*, the *coordinate_definition_id* and the corresponding data. The *coordinate_definition* table is used to define which coordinate system corresponds to the given *coordinate_definition_id* and which unit is used. As before archaeologists can freely create and modify existing coordinate systems and assigned the desired system to the objects they record. The combination of those two tables gives the actual coordinate definition for each object. Therefore, excavations that use different coordinate systems can be stored in the same database. The *coordinate_definition* table is also used to define the coordinate system that is used to store section coordinates. The difference in this implementation is that sections are defined by more than one point, so the following table named *section_coordinates* is created. For each point that defines the section, the coordinate system is defined and the appropriate data are stored (Table 16).

In almost any excavation, a large number of photos are taken by archaeologists, which mostly are photos of objects and sections. Moreover, there might be images of the excavation, the location and images that refer to layers, constructs and phases (e.g., hand-drawn layer representations) (Brown and Perrin, 2000).

Nowadays, most of them are digital or being digitized by archaeologists and stored. To give archaeologists the capability to store digital images in the database, image tables have been created for the above entities in order to store these images. Also, the above described implementation of attribute and data tables is used for the image tables, in order to allow archaeologists to store whatever additional data they want for their images.

The table *object_image* stores the image and its most important data, the table *object_image_data* and *object_image_attribute* work in the same way as previously described for the attribute and data tables. The above tables have been created in the same way for the remaining entities, which are the section, phase, layer, construct, excavation and location entities. The only difference these tables have is found in the second column of each image table. For the *section_image* table the second column is *section_id*, for the *layer_image* table the *layer_id,* and so forth.

Lastly, there are two more entities, the archaeologist and *web_user* entities. The first one handles data that is relevant to the archaeologists, like name and occupation. Also, this entity determines at which excavation an archaeologist works. As before, this entity uses the attribute and data table implementation. The second entity handles the necessary security data, in order to give archaeologists and other personal access to the database, through the Internet or through other information systems.

Table 16.

Section_Coordinates			
Section_ID	**Coordinate_Definition_ID**	**Point_ID**	**Coordinate_Data**
1	1	1	12.44
1	1	2	13.50
1	2	1	17.44

Figure 16. System overview

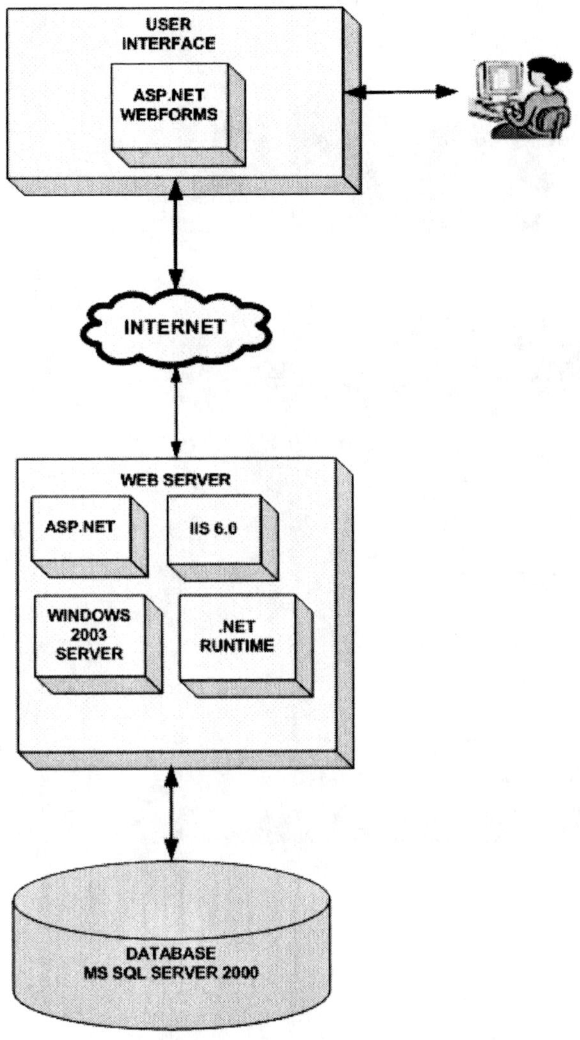

THE MULTIPLE ARCHAEOLOGICAL EXCAVATION DATABASE AND INTERNET APPLICATIONS

As mentioned in the introduction, the main purpose of a database that can handle multiple excavations is to allow archaeologists to easily share their data and knowledge with colleagues and other people. To realize this capability Internet applications have been developed using Microsoft Asp.Net to be connected with the Microsoft SQL Database and therefore to allow archaeologists and authorized users to gain remote access to the data of many excavations (Kauffman & Farr, 2002). Furthermore, these Internet applications allow archaeologists to record their excavation data on the remote database and (to) use advanced database queries, in order to search the database and all the excavations it contains. Later on we will see how these Internet applications have been implemented, how they can be used by archaeologists and what benefits the database structure offers to those Internet applications.

In Figure 16, we can see which kind of software packages have been used to develop the multiple excavation database and the Internet applications that use the database. All software packages have been provided by Microsoft. Of course, the final user does not need to have any of these software packages. The user only interacts with Web forms that are accessible through the Internet, using a simple Web browser like Internet Explorer. Furthermore, archaeologists and database developers can gain proper authorization and connection to the database system remotely, to create additional queries and functions for the system.

Users can register and log into the Web system through the main page, which is currently hosted at http://www.seearchweb.net → modules → multimediadb (Figure 17). To prevent unauthorized access, the Web system compares the username and password which are provided by a given user, with those which are stored in the database. If the username and password are correct, the user gains access to the Web system by using Asp.Net Form-Authentication. Once a user has logged into the system, he can choose among a variety of existing forms to access the database.

Almost every archaeological database contains huge amounts of data; so for a database that stores multiple excavations, the capability of searching the database must be provided, in order to help the archaeologists find objects based on a variety of criteria. Despite the quick search Web form (Figure 18) that allows archaeologists

Figure 17. Index page of the web system

Figure 18. Quick Search page

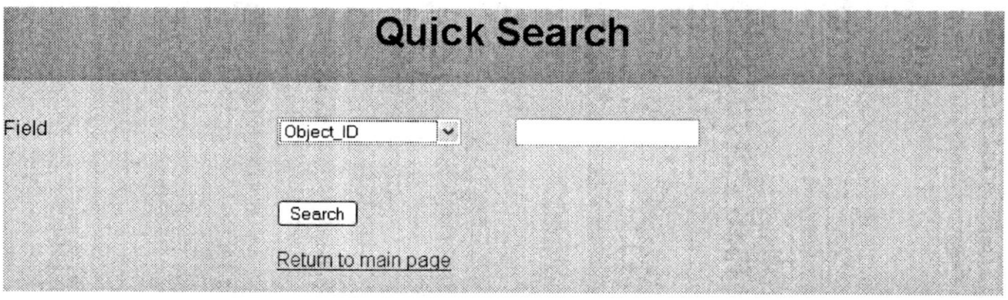

Figure 19. Advanced search web form with results after a search

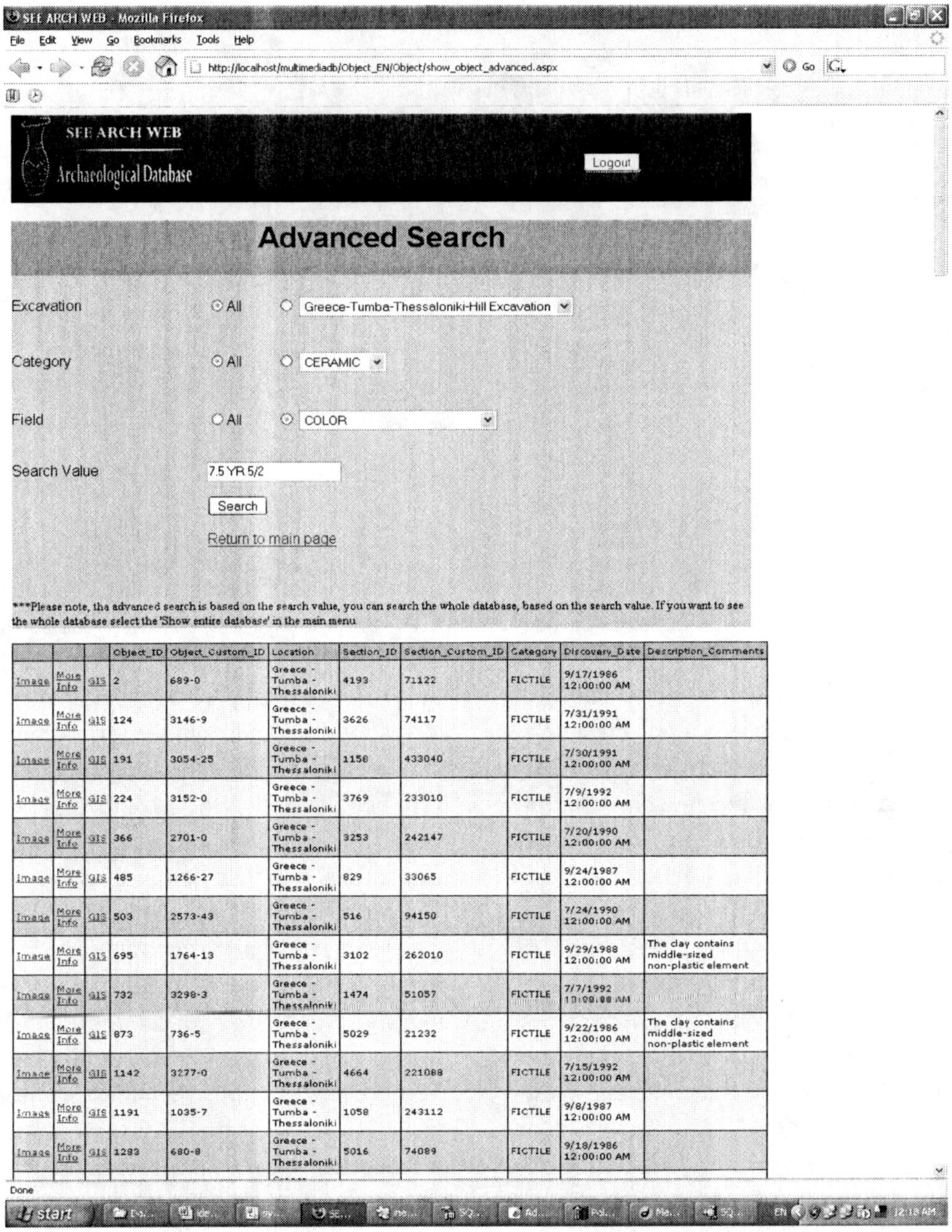

Figure 20. "More info" view of an object

Attribute	My_Data	Unit
BISCUIT		
CLOUDS		
COLOR	7.5 YR 5/2	
FABRIC	MEDIUM	
FIRING	UNEVEN	
INTEGRITY	1	
MANUFACTUR	HANDMADE	
ORIGIN		
SURFACE CONDITION	SCALED	
TYPE	WHORL	
WORKTRACES		

Return

Figure 21. Advanced Search web form

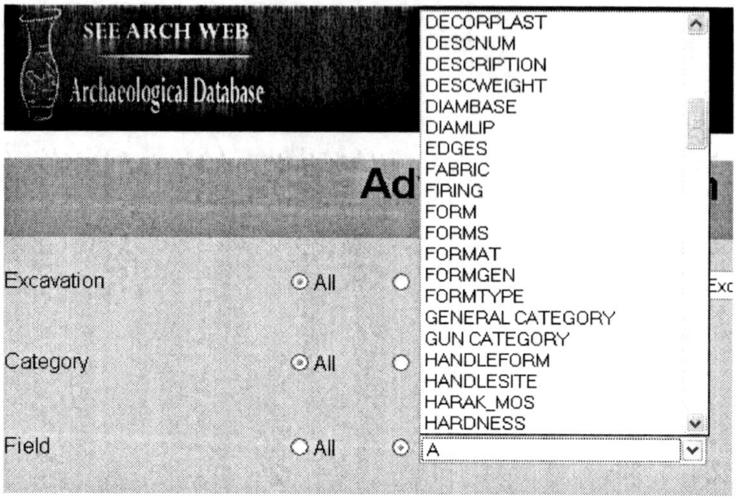

to find objects based on very simple criteria, the Web system offers an advanced search feature (Schloen, 2004).

The advanced search gives users the capability of searching the entire database for objects with a specific value (Figure 19). The search value can be anything like the discovery data, the object color or the length of the handle of a vase. In addition to this users can set additional criteria for the search, by selecting the desired excavation, by selecting the object category or by selecting the exact attribute of the objects they are interested in. The user can access through these hyperlinks additional information on any object, view the image of an object, if there exists one, and view its coordinates.

This implementation is not just handy to quickly view additional information of an object, but it is also necessary. The reason for this is that not all objects have the same attributes. Therefore, by having all attributes displayed in the results table, it would lead to a table that consists at this point of over 160 columns, which is confusing and not user friendly.

In Figure 20 a snapshot of the additional data of an object is shown; it appears when the "more info" hyperlink is used. As we can see attributes have been assigned to this particular object category, and therefore there are displayed as the additional data of the particular object. The corresponding additional information's view for an object is created according to what attributes have been assigned to the object.

In this snapshot of Figure 21 we can see the drop-down list that contains all the attributes which are currently available in the database for all the objects. The excavation and the category drop-down list have all the available excavations and object categories. The significance of these drop-down lists lies in the fact that the source of their content are not lists which are stored in the Asp.Net source script. In other words, the content of those drop-down lists is not a preprogrammed set of available data. These drop-down lists are populated through SQL queries that access the database. Considering the attribute (field) drop-down list, the Asp.Net script runs a simple SQL query which returns all the attribute names of the *object_attribute* table and populates the list with them. As mentioned before, archaeologists can freely modify the *object_attribute* table. Any modifications in the object_attribute table are automatically applied to the attribute drop-down list, because its source is the attribute names of the attribute table. The same method is also used for the other drop-down lists, by using the appropriate excavation and *object_category* tables. Using this method enables archaeologist to freely modify the object categories and attributes and to add or remove excavations, without the need of continuously changing the Web page script, in order to handle changes that occur. We realize that this advantage is a result of the database structure, which enables modifications to be applied only to rows of existing tables. It is obvious that the same information system, at this point the Internet applications, can be used for more than one excavation, without the need of reprogramming the Web forms.

It might be noticed that the complex database structure, which was described in previous sections, does not appear in the Web forms. Specifically, if we take a look at the category drop-down list we do not see the primary keys of the object_category table, but actually we see the attribute names (Figure 19). Also, if we take a look at the "more info" view we do not have the complex data representations of example object_id =1, attribute_id = 15 and My_Data = 'UNEVEN' (Figure 20). Instead, we have a simple

Figure 22. Chronological and spatial search web form

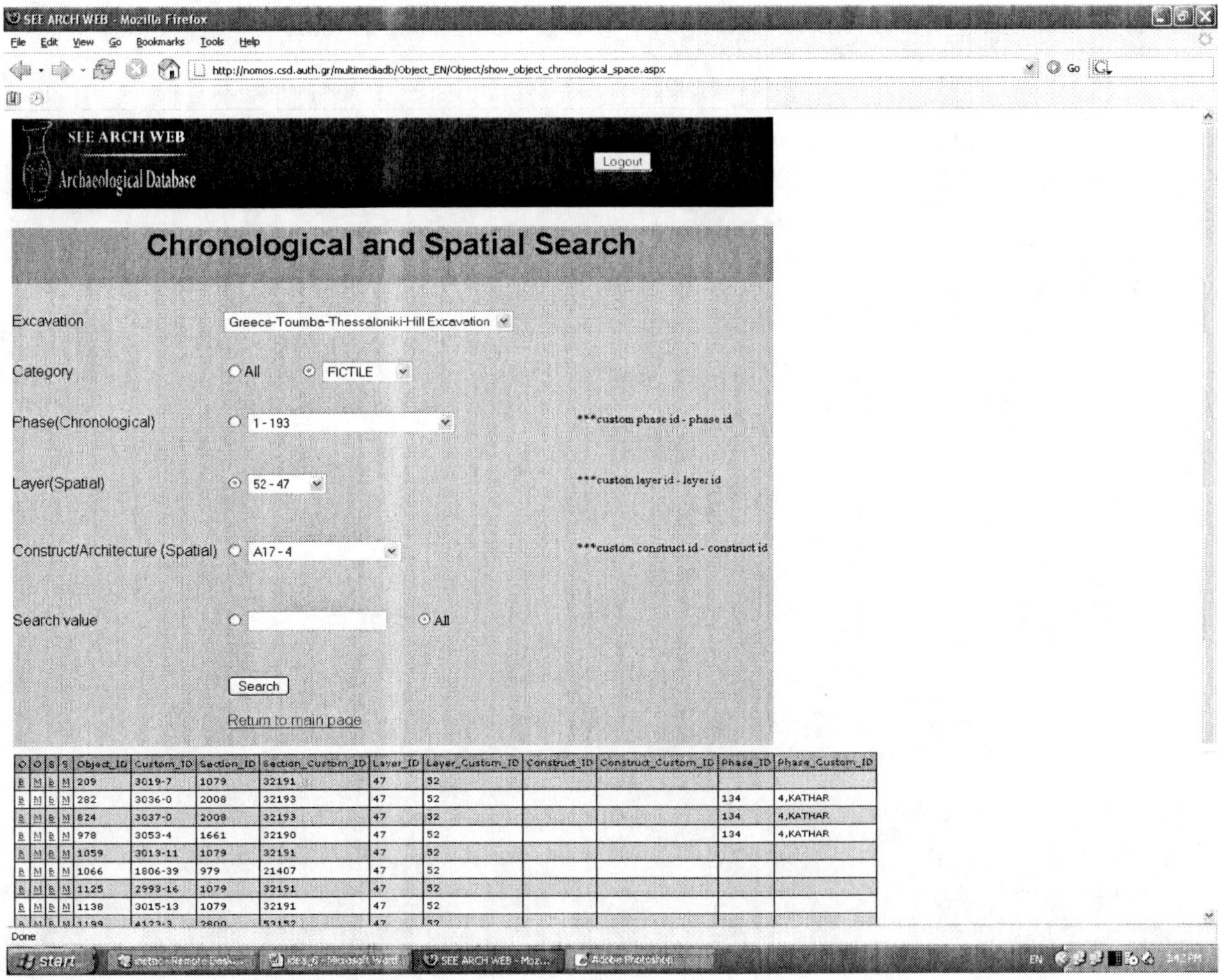

view of the attributes with their corresponding data. This capability was implemented by using views in the database that join and select specific tables and columns; and by using a small number of simple SQL queries in the Web forms. This implementation also works for multiple excavations, because its data sources are the database tables, which are only modified by altering rows and not the tables.

The chronological and spatial analyses of excavations are of great importance to archaeologists. In order to assist archaeologists in this task, the Web system offers an advanced search Web form in which chronological and spatial criteria can be set. Archaeologists can set the excavation and the category the objects belong to, in order to specify their search. Furthermore, they can use the layer, construct and phase drop-down lists in order to select the desired chronological or spatial entity, in which objects belong. By doing so, they can select objects, which belong to the chronological or spatial entity of their interest, and fulfill the criteria which have been set. Also, archaeologists can use a search value for the desired data of the attribute of an object, in order to specify even more their search results. In the above example (Figure 22) we can see a part of the results that have been returned, by selecting as search criteria the object category fictile and as layer 52-47. The layer 52-47 stands for the layer which has the custom_id 52 and the layer_id 47. The reason for this is to help archaeologists to find quickly desired layers, by using their own custom key or the primary key that has been assigned to a layer by the database. This also applies to the construct and phase drop-down lists. As we can see the result table contains basic chronological and spatial data. In order to gain quick access

Figure 23. Snapshot of the web form used to store images for objects

Figure 24. Snapshot of the remote edit web form, which allows archaeologists to edit remotely the data of the database

	Object_id	section_id	category_id	discovery_date	description_comments
OK Cancel	5974	425	8	7/5/1993 12:00:00 AM	

to additional data, hyperlinks are used to obtain and display additional data on the objects and the sections they belong to. Archaeologists can view quickly the corresponding basic and additional data for an object in the result table. Also they can view quickly the basic and additional data of the section an object belongs to, by using the appropriate hyperlinks. The method of populating the drop-down lists by using queries on the database, as mentioned before for the advanced search Web form; is also applied to these drop-down lists. Therefore changes which occur in the database tables are automatically applied to the Web form.

Using the advantages of the relational structure of the multiple excavations database, developers and archaeologists can create additional features for the database, without the need of changing the database. These additional features can be additional Web forms (Figures 23, 24), GIS systems or mobile device support by using mobile ASP .NET Web applications.

FUTURE RESEARCH DIRECTIONS

In conclusion, this chapter presented a general insight in archaeological excavations, in order to provide the unfamiliar reader with the basic concepts in this field. Furthermore, through this introduction we pointed out the most important data sets which are recorded at excavations. Taking into consideration the different archaeological approaches and the different data recording concepts, we introduced a relational database design to deal with these differences. The implementation of the database showed that archaeologists can make adjustments in form of table operations on a fixed database in order to record their data, without compromising the structural integrity of the database. The design and implementation resulted in a database that can record multiple archaeological excavations. The realized Web application demonstrated that except from recording archaeological data, the database provides many benefits for processing data through Internet applications. Furthermore, multiple excavations can be processed by using the same system, without the need for readjustments.

The new challenge lies in recording and processing advanced external archaeological data models that are created by archaeologists for the chronological and spatial analysis of excavations. Although the database can record most of these data models, the question lies in how their functionality can be used for all excavations at the same time, without compromising the database structure. Currently the focus lies on building these external models into external applications and Internet applications that access the mutliple excavation database and provide their functionality to all excavations. Furthermore, research is being conducted on using the database for complex GIS visualizations, for auto generated virtual museums and for archaeological social modelers.

REFERENCES

Brown, A., & Perrin, N, K. (2000). A model for the description of archaeological archives. *English Heritage Centre for Archaeology.* Retrieved October 25, 2007, from http://www.english-heritage.org.uk

Burenhult, G. (2001). *Archaeological informatics: Pushing the envelope.* CAA 2001. Computer Applications and Quantitative Methods in Archaeology. BAR International Series. Oxford: Archaeopress.

Codd, E.F. (1970). A relational model of data for large shared data banks. *Communications of the ACM, 13*(6), 377-387.

Date, C. J. (2004). *Introduction to database systems* (8th ed.). Addison Wesley.

Kauffman, J., Ferrachiati, F. C., Matsik, B., Mintz, E. N., Narkiewicz, J. D., Tegels, K., et al. (2002). *Beginning ASP.NET Databases Using VB.NET.* Wrox.

Lock, G. (2003). *Using computers in archaeology: Towards virtual pasts.* New York: Routledge.

Politis, D., Gkatzogias, M., Karamalis, A., & Pyrinis, K. (2005). GIS driven Internet multimedia databases for multiple archaeological excavations in Greece and the region of South-Eastern Europe: The SEEArchWeb project. *WSEAS Transactions on Advances in Engineering Education, 2*(2), 54-61.

Richards, J.D. (1998). Recent trends in computer applications in Archaeology. *Journal of Archaeological Research, 6*(4), 331-382. Springer-Verlag.

Schloen, J. D. (2004). Archaeological data models and Web publication using XML. *Computers and the Humanities, 35*(5), 123-152. Springer Netherlands.

ADDITIONAL READING

Andrefsky, B. (2003). Archaeological field methods. Retrieved October 25, 2007, from Department of Anthropology Washington State University, http://www.indiana.edu/~arch/saa/matrix/afm.html

Atarashi, R.S., Imai, M., Sunahara, H., Chihara, K., & Katana, T. (2004). Building archaeological photograph library. In *Proceedings of the Research and Advanced Technology for Digital Libraries: 4th European Conference*, Lisbon, Portugal, (Vol. 1923/2000). Berlin/Heidelberg: Springer-Verlag.

Dobson, R. (2002). *Programming Microsoft SQL Server 2000 with Microsoft Visual Basic .NET.* Microsoft Press.

Heckerman, D. *(1996). Advances in knowledge discovery and data mining* (pp. 273-305). Cambridge, MA: MIT Press.

Hynst, S., Gervautz, M., Grabner, M., & Schindler, K. (2001). A work-flow and data model for reconstruction, management, and visualization of archaeological sites. In *Proceedings of the 2001 Conference on Virtual Reality, Archeology, and Cultural Heritage*, Glyfada, Greece, (pp. 43-52). ACM Press.

Shaper, R., & Ashmore, W. (1993). *Archaeology: Discovering our past.* California: Mayfield Publishing Company.

KEY TERMS

Relational Database: A database which has been designed and implemented according to the relational model and makes use of normal forms. Relations and entities are implemented as database tables and attributes as table columns. Also primary and foreign keys are used in the tables.

Multiple Excavations Database: A database that can store and handle data from multiple archaeological excavations. The database uses a fixed set of tables for all archaeological excavations, whereas additional attributes can be added by archaeologists on the existing tables in form of rows. The excavations can be completely independent, at different locations and can be conducted based on different archaeological approaches.

Internet Applications: In the present context we refer to Internet applications as a general term to describe dynamic Web pages and Web applications, which are used to request process of data on a server and to respond the results back to the client by using a Web browser (e.g., Internet Explorer).

Section: Part of an excavation site which has been removed and studied. A section is defined by the points which define its shape and the depth of each point. They play an important role in excavations by spatially binding the other entities to them. Furthermore, through sections the excavation progress can be monitored and reconstructed later on.

Layer: Are used to group parts of the excavation which share characteristics defined by the archaeologists. They result in N-dimensional representation of the excavation; mostly N =1, 2, 3.

Construct: Spatial entity which existed in the past at the location of the excavation. For example, constructs can be streets, wells, buildings like temples and houses which existed in the past and have been found during the excavation, or clues may indicate their former existence.

Phase: Chronological periods defined by archaeologists, which contain section that belong to them. Chronological periods can be, for example, 500-400 B.C., Roman Period or even short term periods like May 15, 1998- January 15, 1990.

SQL (Structured Query Language): SQL is a data manipulation language (DML) and a data definition language (DDL) for relational database management systems.

GIS (Geographical Information System): A computer system which handles spatial (geographical) data and corresponding information. Main purpose of the system is to associate information with its spatial attributes and execute queries on those. The results are geographical depend information representations, which can be visualized in several ways like on maps and on 2D/3D graphs. In the visualization, layers are used to filter information.

Multilayer: In the present context a multilayer is a collection/group of other layers.

Chapter VIII
Geographical Information Systems (GIS) and Learning Applications in Archaeology

Dimitrios Margounakis
Computer Scientist and Researcher, Greece

INTRODUCTION

Progress made in the fields of designing and geometrically analyzing earth maps, has lead to the development of automatic techniques which are applied in collecting analyzing and representing any information relevant to geographical interest. Such a collection of techniques sets the frame of what we call geographical information system (GIS).

GIS is a well organized collection of computer hardware and software along with the appropriate human resources that stores, updates, process, analyzes, and displays spatial data from a variety of sources. Two very popular definitions of GIS are:

...a powerful set of tools for collecting, storing, retrieving at will, transforming, and displaying spatial data from the real world for a particular set of purposes. (Burrough, 1986)

...an information system that is designed to work with data referenced by spatial or geographic co-ordinates. In other words a GIS is both a database system with specific capabilities for spatially-referenced data as well as a set of operations for working (analysis) with the data. (Star & Estes, 1990)

With a GIS, we can link information to location data, such as time to archaeological places, different earth surface levels to excavation periods, or different border lines within eras. We can then layer that information to give a better understanding of how it all works together. This is done by choosing what layers to combine based on what questions we need to answer. ArcGIS (which is the approach of the leading ESRI corporation to the field of GIS) is presented later in the chapter. A GIS module of SeeArchWEB can be found and used in the Web site www.seearchweb.net.

There are 2 basic types of geographic information:

- **Spatial information** (topologies and networks)**:** By the term spatial information we mean the determination of the position of different geographical data on a map, according to a reference system. Spatial relationships, such as topologies and networks, are also crucial parts of a GIS database. Topology is employed to manage common boundaries between features, define and enforce data integrity rules, and support topological queries and navigation. Topology also is used to support sophisticated editing and construct features from unstructured geometry. Much, if not all, of the data that archaeologists recover is spatial in nature, or has an important spatial component (Wheatley & Gillings, 2002).
- **Descriptive information:** On the other hand, descriptive information is the term used to handle the quantitative and qualitative attributes of a specific geographical space. In addition to geographic representations, GIS data sets include traditional tabular attributes that describe the geographic objects. Many tables can be linked to the geographic objects by common fields (keys). These tabular information sets and relationships play a key role in GIS data models, just as they do in traditional database applications.

A major change which derived from GIS implementation is that for the first time spatial information is linked with non-graphical one and in addition to that, logical and arithmetical operations are made possible between them.

Apart from the above change, a GIS is most often associated with maps. However, a map is only one type of product produced by a GIS. This product provides one way to work with geographic data in a GIS. As it can be easily understood, a GIS can provide more problem-solving capabilities than using a simple mapping program or adding data to an online mapping tool.

According to Marble (1990) GIS comprise four major subsystems:

- The Data Entry subsystem
- The Spatial Database
- The Manipulation and Analysis subsystem
- The Visualisation and Reporting subsystem.

A GIS can be viewed in three ways:

- **The database view:** A GIS is a new kind of database—a geographic database (geodatabase). A GIS is based on a relational database that includes information for the world in geographic terms. This can be considered as the IS (information system) of geography.
- **The map view:** A GIS can produce and manipulate maps enriched with artificial intelligence, so that by changing views they can show different perspectives of the earth's objects and the relationships between them. These different perspectives support what is called geovisualization, which is the term to describe the ability to form queries, and analyze and edit information in a user friendly way.
- **The model view:** Finally, a GIS can be used as a tool to transform existing geographic information into new one by implementing a model on pre-existing datasets. This is done by using geoprocessing functions made to correspond with the needs of the desired model.

By implementing the above three ways, we are able to pass from the simplicity of a single map to the interactivity of GIS information. So, every time we are ready to answer the following question about the objects in which we are interested:

- What is it?
- Where is it?
- How it relates with other objects?

But which are the fundamental ingredients of a GIS (Figure 1)?

- **Users:** They develop any indispensable process need for the system to work efficiently.
- **Data:** There are many kinds of data to be served by a GIS. Their accuracy is essential for the reliability of the results.
- **Equipment:** It includes all the computers, network and peripheral devices need to integrate a GIS. They determine the speed of the calculations, the usability level and the accuracy of the results.
- **Software:** It refers to all the specific GI programs and to all the supplementary programs needed for image processing, database management and statistic analysis.
- **Processes:** They are standardised series of actions engaged for accurate conclusion drawing.

Finally, the answers to the question "what are the archaeologists doing with GIS?" could be summarized in the following list of options (Wheatley & Gillings, 2002):

Figure 1. GIS fundamental ingredients

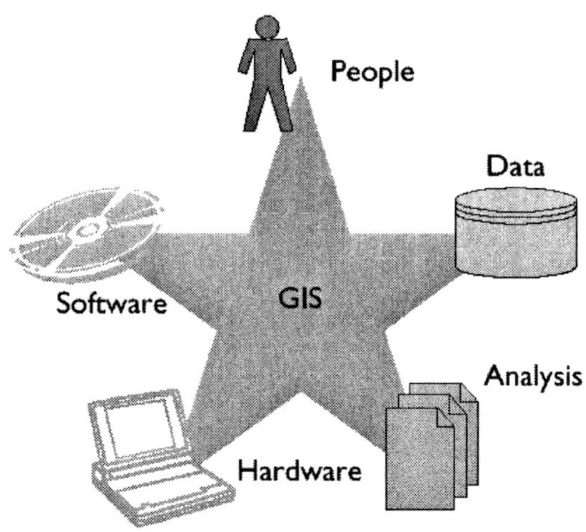

- Rediscovering the quantitative spatial statistical approaches characteristic of the "new" and "spatial" archaeologies of the 1960s and 1970s
- Predictive modeling – privileging environmental information
- "Humanistic analysis" – privileging cultural information.

LINKING BETWEEN SPATIAL AND DESCRIPTIVE DATA

The major difference between GIS and CAD (computer aided design) systems is that GIS managed to link spatial information with specific descriptive material. This is done by using databases with two separate views: the spatial one and the tabular. There are more fundamental differences between CAD and GIS clearly explained in Lock (2003).

Any spatial object on a map is connected with any descriptive information by one unique arithmetic value known as key. With these keys, records in the database are linked to map objects. The whole process is automatic and needs no effort.

WHAT IS ARCGIS?

ArcGIS is a corporate approach to the field of GIS. It covers the needs of GIS users by providing a scalable and unified platform for inserting, analysing, process, maintain, store and publish geographic information. Figure 2 represents this scalable working environment, which is integrated with a series of tools for one or more users and with no dependence to the machine used.

In our SeaArchWeb project we take advantage of more than one of these programs. First of all, by using ArcInfo we obtain advanced capabilities of geographical processing and spatial analysis. It is the basic tool for creating the appropriate

Figure 2. Linking by key

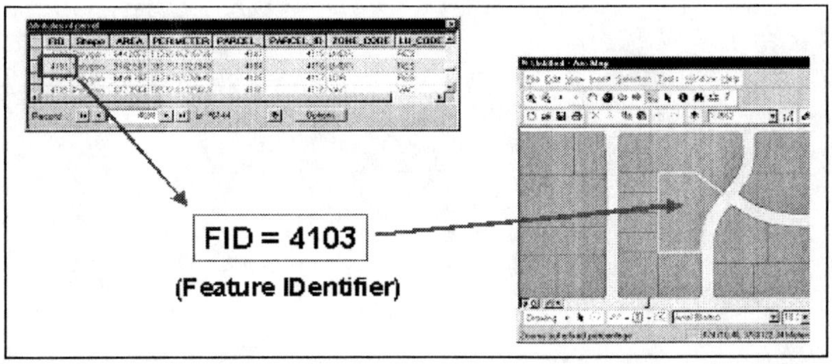

maps and linking them with the provided (by the archaeologists) descriptive data.

Spatial analyst provides a wide variety of tools for spatial modeling and analysis which are used for analysing raster data representing the excavations related with the project.

After all the processing described earlier, ArcIMS is the ultimate solution, so that the core of a GIS can publish its integrated information to the Internet. It is a powerful tool for creating Web sites and managing the Web application server and its spatial data, with the eventual aim to provide geographic information to the end user. Simultaneously it is a common platform for exchanging and interacting with the geo-information by a wide variety of interested people.

Because of its importance, an analysis of this program takes place; its behaviour and its tools are extensively presented in the next paragraphs.

INTERNET MAPPING SERVICES

Introduction to Internet Mapping Services

Internet is becoming an important channel of communication and offers greater possibilities for transmitting and receiving all kinds of information. Thus, geographical information systems are being complemented with this development, and consequently, replacing interactive means of communication through the network.

In a very few years, the World Wide Web has evolved from a hypermedia system to a complete information platform. For users of geographical information this means that a lot of the work that is done on a local computer can be obtained through the Internet. This third step in the development of the client-server technology has made it possible to implement applications that have allowed us to move forward from prepared and static documents to an interactive and dynamic platform. In virtual form, any computer connected to the Internet can offer a service and, using a navigator such as Netscape or Internet Explorer, we can access it.

The key factor that has permitted this achievement has been the use of the technology internet map server (IMS). Starting from this technology, various systems have been developed that are described in the section on IMS Technology. They allow us to create GIS applications on Internet to visualize, consult, and analyze geographical information through the Net.

Internet Map Server (IMS) Technology

With IMS technology, the spatial information published on the Net is dynamic. The distribution of geographical information via Internet allows

Figure 3. Scalable working environment

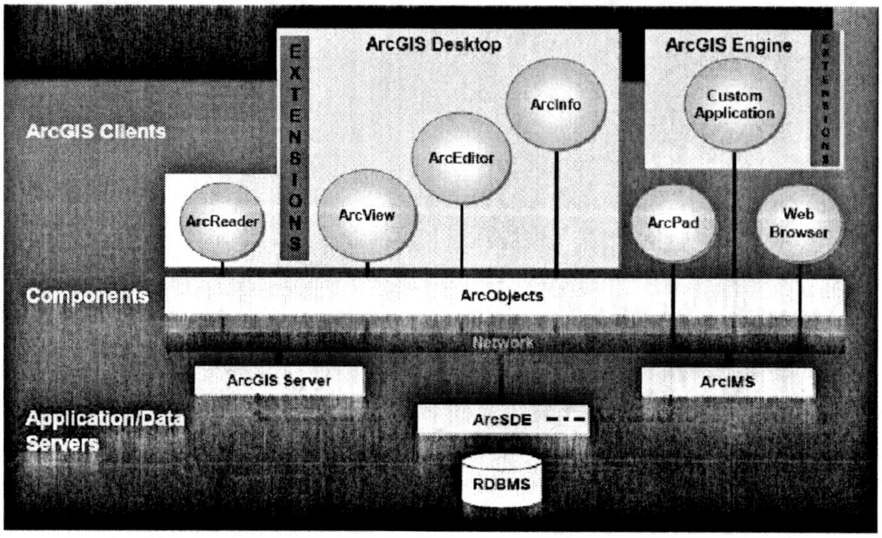

the integration in real time of data originating in any part of the world. The user has access to WWW resources, moves freely through all the information with functional tools, changes graphic representation online, links graphic elements with information from databases, and works in real time with analysis functions.

The options of exchanging, integrating, or analyzing data in a new form through the network facilitate, expedite, and favour the process of decision taking. Users can combine data and information accessible via Internet with local data, see them, and make consultations and the pertinent analysis.

This distributive system of information, compared with tools that are installed in a personal computer, offers the following advantages, among others:

- Sharing and exchange of data
- Access to applications and tools for analysis and decision taking for a much more extensive public
- Facilitates continued updating of information, helping to reduce redundancies (duplications) and improving access to databases
- Facilitates updating of applications and disclosed information

The IMS architecture comprises three levels:

- **Client Applications**: Work environment of the user. Any navigator that supports standard HTML can act as client. It will also need to support Applet of Java or ActiveX technology if the services being accessed contain these components. Through the Internet, and with the navigator as interface, the client sends requests to the server application to obtain the information that the client wants to see, consult, or analyze.
- **Server Applications**: These are responsible for channelling and attending the operations that the user requests on the data.
- **Databases**: The server applications access the data that can be stored in files or in spatial databases (spatial data engine, SDE).

Arc Internet Map Server: ArcIMS (ESRI)

A key characteristic of a system for publishing maps on Internet is its capacity to establish a common platform for the exchange of GIS data and services on the Web. The ArcIMS technology is based on the multitier (multilevel) architecture, widely distributed and scalable, and its system is composed of clients, services, and database, in a structure of three tiers.

These tiers are:

- **Presentation tier:** Includes the ArcIMS client viewers for accessing, viewing, and analyzing geographic data.
  ArcIMS is delivered with two clients:
  - *HTML Viewer*: The HTML Viewer consists of almost 10,000 lines of JavaScript code that are able to construct and parse ArcXML requests and responses. It provides many of the familiar map tools that allow users to interact with geospatial data within a Web browser. The HTML Viewer can handle responses from the image and the extract servers. Only a single image server can be displayed at any time, and any additional functionality required must be written in JavaScript within the context of the existing code base.
    The biggest drawbacks to the HTML Viewer are:
    - It is slow when parsing large responses during which time it does not provide any feedback to the user that it is even doing anything; frequently, the browser simply appears to be locked.
    - The level of interactivity for certain operations such as measuring or selecting by shape is kludgy at best. (Each mouse click on the map requires a complete request and response cycle to the application server.)
    - If the request/response cycle is broken for any reason, usually due to user impatience while using the interactive tools or the user presses the back or refresh buttons on the browser, then the page must be completely reloaded. (Frequently, this requires closing and restarting the Web browser.)
    - JavaScript is not the best language for developing large complex systems, because it is interpreted (slow), loosely typed, variable declaration is not required, undeclared variables automatically become global, and is not uniformly supported across all Web browsers.
  - *ArcExplorer*: ArcExplorer is a Java application that is able to act as a client to both the image and feature servers. When ArcExplorer is deployed in the context of a Web page it is referred to as the Java Viewer. It can be downloaded from sites deploying it and requires the Java run-time environment from Sun.
    The advantage of ArcExplorer is its ability to connect to a feature server. When a connection is established, all the vector data in the defined extent is downloaded to the client. Therefore, further requests to the server are no longer required, dramatically increasing client performance.
    ArcExplorer can connect to multiple image and feature servers simultaneously, although its behaviour with image servers is the same as the HTML Viewer. Clients using ArcExplorer can also display shapefiles on their local hard drives and connect to SDE

enabled relational databases. When ArcExplorer is deployed in a Web page, it is only available for Web browsers that are able to script Java applets. A number of methods are exposed on the applets that comprise the Web page. This provides capability for developing custom functionality. JavaScript is used to interact with the applets, but the desired functionality must fall within the scope of what is provided by ESRI. Both of these are designed to work with the Java servlet connector.

- **Business logic tier:** The components in this tier are used for handling requests and administering the ArcIMS site. The **ArcIMS site management applications** provide access to components in the business logic tier for authoring maps, administering ArcIMS services and spatial servers, and designing Web sites.
  The components of the ArcIMS server include:
  - *Web Server*: This is the component that communicates directly with the Viewer, and is required in order for ArcIMS to work. It is not included with ArcIMS, and can be any number of Web servers, including Microsoft Internet Information Server, Netscape Enterprise Server, iPlanet and Apache.
  - *Spatial Server*: It creates digital images of vector and raster data. It gives access to geographical elements and processes consultations in the database.
  - *Applications Server*: Handles the balance of the processes and incoming demands, and maintains a registration of the map services executed in the spatial servers.
  - *ArcIMS Monitor*: This is a background process that tracks the state of the spatial servers and starts or restores map services.
  - *ArcIMS Tasker*: This is a background process that is used to periodically delete the output image files.
  - *Connectors to the Applications Server*: It connects the Web server to the applications server. ArcIMS provides various types of connectors:
    - *Java Servlet (default connector):* The default connector for ArcIMS is the Java servlet connector. The servlet passes ArcXML requests from a calling application, usually a Web browser, onto the application server and returns the ArcXML response. The servlet connector is not able to process or modify the request/responses at all. It simply acts as a conduit. All clients to the servlet connector must be able to compose and parse valid ArcXML requests and responses. The servlet connector must be used in order to deploy spatial data with the feature server.
    - *ColdFusion*: The ColdFusion connector is similar to the ActiveX connector, in that it allows for some of the processing to be moved off the client Web browser, and onto the server, but the author has no experience with this product. ColdFusion is available for both the UNIX and Windows platforms.
    - *ActiveX*: The ActiveX connector is a set of COM objects that expose interfaces to the application server. Some of the interfaces can be used to construct, pass, and process ArcXML requests/responses to the application server; others can simply act as a middleman like the servlet connector. The ActiveX connector offers a lot of capabilities for people who are committed

to the Microsoft platform. The one drawback is that it is unable to take advantage of the HTML Viewer client delivered with ArcIMS. The connectors ActiveX and ColdFusion work with their own clients and translate their internal language to ArcXML.

- *WMS Connector*: The WMS connector is a collection of additional Java classes that work with the default servlet connector to allow ArcIMS to be compliant with the OpenGIS Web mapping specification. This also has an *Administrator* function, a group of assistants of easy use for the management of all the functions and tasks related to the server. Assistants exist to create and manage map services, to design the maps to publish, to create the Web sites that provide user access, and to administer the spatial servers.

- **Data storage tier:** Consists of the file servers that hold the shape files and image files, as well as the server running Oracle (or other RDBMS) and spatial data engine (SDE). Depending on how you want to think about it, the spatial server can also be considered part of the data storage tier.

These tiers describe logical groupings of the functionality of the various application components and do not necessarily correspond to their physical location.

Generally, ArcIMS has a complex architecture and the author might gloss over some the details in the interest of clarity (Figure 4). It should be noted that any reference to a server means a software application that responds to client software requests. For example, a Web server (apache) responds to client Web browser (Internet Explorer) request for a specific Web page.

Figure 4. ArcIMS architecture

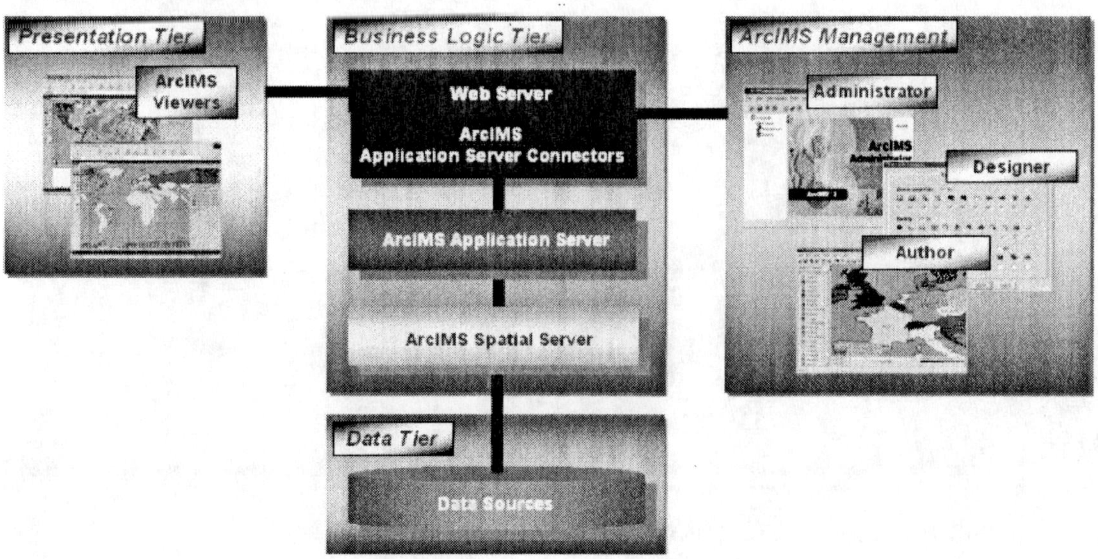

ARCXML

The ArcXML is the language of ArcIMS. It is used for communication between the different components of ArcIMS, and it is used to define map services. ArcXML uses a hierarchical system of tags and subtags which is in some ways similar in appearance to HTML.

There are five root tags in ArcXML:

- *ARCXML*: Used in every ArcXML statement to declare what it is.
- *CONFIG*: Used to configure a Map Service by defining the data to be included and how it will appear.
- *REQUEST*: Used to make a request from the client to the server.
- *RESPONSE*: Used to make a response from the spatial server to the client.
- *MARKUP*: Used to describe changes made on the client through EditNotes. This is only used when a feature server and Java client viewer are employed.

USING THE ARCIMS HTML VIEWER

Figure 5 depicts the navigation elements of a GIS systems, as seen by an ordinary HTML browser. They are:

- **Map Title** = Displays the name of the map project.
- **Overview Map** = Displays the position of the view map.
- **Map Display** = The map display view window.
- **Layer List & Legend** = Lists all data layers available to use and view.
- **Scale Bar** = Displays the mapping scale of the Map Display.
- **Data Display** = Displays any data information of a layer when you use the identify tool or make a query. Some features may be asociated with multiple records.
- **Selected Tool Display** = Displays which tool you have selected in the tool bar area.

Figure 5. ArgIMS html viewer

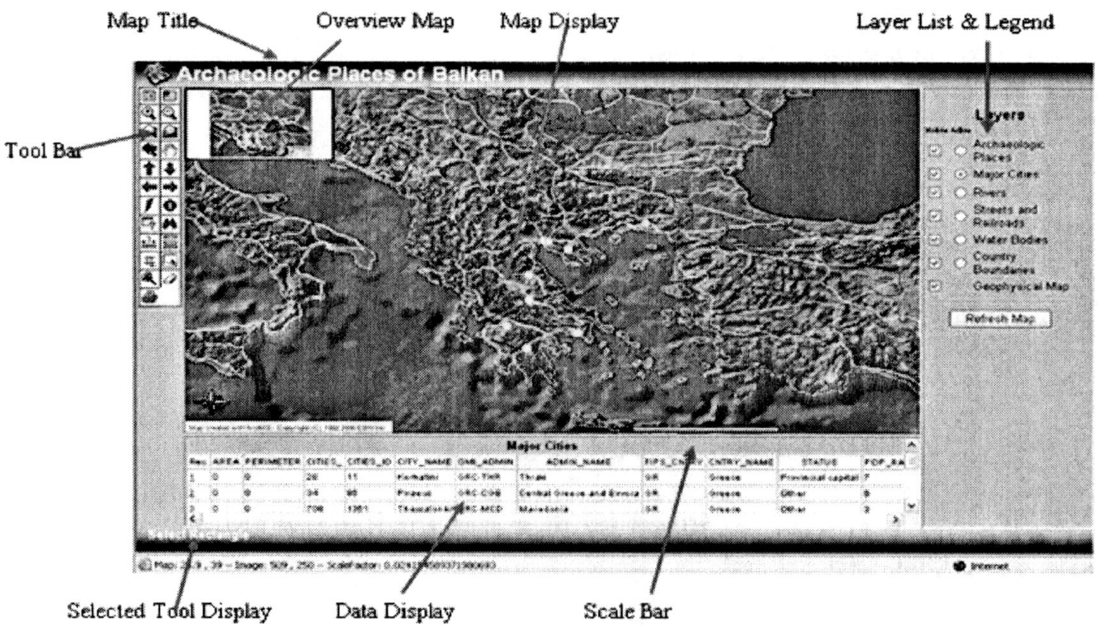

- **Tool Bar** = Displays various buttons that allow you to interact with the map, such as zooming in and out or pan around the map.

Interested readers can use the system from the SeeArchWEB site (www.seearchweb.net) and perform a navigation of its capabilities, especially in performing *spatial queries*.

Tool Bar Frame

If you hold your cursor over a tool for a few seconds a name will pop up for that tool. The information, find, and query buttons can be used to find information in the database for the active layer. The other tools present are for navigating and measuring the maps. To use these tools it is necessary to make the layer you are interested in active. To activate a layer, simply click on the radio button in the layer list on the right side of the screen. A message should appear in the text box on the bottom left hand side of the page.

Important notes:

- Many tools are dependent on whether or not a layer is visible or active. To make layers visible, check the box next to the layer name, and then click the Refresh Map button at the bottom of the TOC. To make a layer active, click the radio button next to the layer name. Only one layer can be active at a time.
- Tool icons with a red outline are persistent, which means these tools remain enabled until another tool is selected. The name for the currently enabled tool, or tool mode, is displayed to the left of the toolbar. When the map page first loads, the Zoom In tool is automatically selected.

Next is a description of how each toolbar button operates. They are ordered, starting at the top of Figure 6, from left to right.

- Clicking on the first icon will result in the right side of the ARCIMS window toggling between the "Layer" and "Legend" views.
- **Toggle Overview Map:** This button toggles the overview map in the upper left hand corner of the map. By default, the Overview map is turned on. Click once on this button with the mouse and the overview map with disappear. Click again and the overview map will reappear.
- **Zoom In:** There are two ways to use this tool to zoom in on the map:
  - **Zoom to Point:** Click anywhere on the map image to recenter the view on that point, and zoom in by a factor of two.
  - **Zoom to Box:** Use this mode to define a rectangular region to zoom in on. Hold the mouse cursor over the map image at the top left corner of the new viewing rectangle. Click and hold down the left mouse button, then drag the cursor across the map to create a zoom box. Release the mouse button to complete

Figure 6. Tool Bar frame

the rectangle and produce a new map image.

- **Zoom Out:** This button works similarly to the Zoom In tool, allowing you instead to zoom out.
- **Zoom to Full Extent:** This button allows you to see the full extent of the map.
- **Zoom to Active Layer:** Each spatial data set occupies some region, or extent, on the map. Clicking the Zoom to Active Layer button will produce the map with the smallest scale at which the selected layer is entirely visible.
- **Back to Last Extent:** This tool returns the map to the previous spatial extent and scale.
- **Pan:** Select the pan tool, and then hold the mouse cursor over any part of the map. The mouse cursor will appear as a pair of arrows. By clicking and holding down the left mouse button, you can drag the map image around the map frame. Release the mouse button to recenter the map in a new position.
- **Pan to North:** Pans the map in north direction.
- **Pan to South:** Pans the map in south direction.
- **Pan to East:** Pans the map in east direction.
- **Pan to West:** Pans the map in west direction.
- **Identify:** More than just graphics, features on the map are related to a database record of attribute information. This information can be displayed by using the Identify tool. Any visible map features that are part of the currently active layer can be identified by selecting the Identify tool and clicking on a map feature that belongs to the active layer. The database record for that feature will be retrieved and displayed below the map.
- **Query:** Use this tool to formulate a Boolean query for searching the attributes of map features. In this query form, you can build the conditions for a query on attributes in the currently active layer. Use these steps to build a query:
    - Choose a field name, comparison operator, and enter a value in the top part of the query dialog.
    - Click the Add to Query String button to add the selected conditions to the query. Use the And, Or, Not, and parentheses buttons to link multiple query conditions together. The syntax for these queries conforms to the rules of Boolean logic.
    - Click the Undo button to remove unwanted conditions from the query, or the Clear button to start over.
    - Choose a query region from the options entire state, visible area, or selected area. Only query results that are within the query region will be returned. The selected area refers to selections made with the Select by Rectangle tool.
    - Choose a color and click Execute to generate a new map with the matching features drawn in the selected color.
    - Matching database records will be displayed in the area below the map, and the query will be added to the end of the layer list in the table of contents. Multiple queries will be grouped together in a queries folder.
    - The check box next to the query name allows you to toggle the query results on or off of the map. The radio button allows you to display the results of the query in the area below the map.
- **Search:** Searches for features based on the information you enter.
- **Find:** This tool allows you to search the active layer by entering a case-sensitive key word to match against database records. Matching records, if any, are displayed in the area below the map, and the corresponding map features are highlighted in yellow

on the map. Clicking the record number in the table of retrieved records will highlight in red the feature matching that particular record, and also recenter the map on that feature.

- **Measure:** The measure tool is used to determine the distance along a line segment or series of connected line segments, or path. Select the Measure tool and click once on the map to create a starting point. A new map image will be retrieved showing this starting point. On the new map, click again to mark the ending point of the line segment. A new map will again be retrieved showing the line segment. Continue this process of adding points to create a path. Near the top of the map are two boxes showing the length of the current path, as well as the distance from the last point added to the position of the mouse cursor. The current path may be cleared at any time using the Clear Selection tool, described below.
- **Set Units:** The map units can be changed to feet, miles, meters, or kilometres by selecting this tool and completing the set units dialog that appears. A drop-down menu provides the various options for units, and a submit button is provided to apply the changes to the map display units.
- **Buffer:** The buffer tool allows you to locate map features from any layer within a chosen distance from features selected from some other layer. To buffer a feature, first select one or more features using the select tool (mode 1 only), as described below. Next, click on the buffer tool icon. In the buffer dialog that appears below the map, choose a layer from the drop-down list, enter the distance to buffer in the text box, and click the Create Buffer button. Features in from this layer that are in the selected proximity to the selected feature will be highlighted. If you wish to see the database records for those features located within the buffer zone, make sure the Display Attributes check box is checked before creating the buffer.
- **Select by Rectangle:** Features in the currently active layer can be selected with this tool for additional manipulation with the query and buffer tools. There are three modes for selecting by rectangle:
  - **Mode 1:** Select features within a small rectangle. Click on any map feature from the active layer to select it. The rectangle in this case will be very small, appearing almost like a single point.
  - **Mode 2:** Select features within a single rectangle. Starting with the cursor over the map, click and hold down the left mouse button. Drag the cursor across the map to create a rectangle. Release the mouse button and all features within that rectangle from the active layer will be selected. A new map is generated with the selected features highlighted in yellow, and the records associated with those features are shown in the area below the map image.
  - **Mode 3:** Select features from multiple rectangles. Hold down the shift key and move the mouse cursor over the map. Click and hold down the left mouse button, and drag the cursor across the map to create a rectangle. Release the mouse button to complete the rectangle, and then release the shift key. This will highlight the features within the rectangle on the map, and display the attributes of those features in a table below the map. Allow the map to refresh, and then hold down the shift key and draw another rectangle. Continue this process as many times as necessary to build a compound selection set. Each rectangle added to the selection is displayed in red on the map image. This compound selection set can be reset by using the Clear Selection tool,

or by selecting more features without holding down the shift key.

- **Select by Line/Polygon:** This tool allows you to draw a line or polygon to select features in the active layer that intersect the shape drawn. Select this tool, and use the following method to select features:
    - Click on the map to create a starting point for a line or polygon. A new map image will be retrieved showing the starting point in red.
    - Repeat the first step to continue adding points to the line segment, path, or polygon. At least two points will be required.
    - Unwanted points can be removed one-at-a-time by clicking the Delete Last Point button. You can start over by clicking the Restart button.
    - Once the desired number of points has been added to the map, choose from the buttons Complete Line & Select or Complete Polygon & Select in the dialog.
    - Features from the active layer that are located on the path or inside the polygon will be shown highlighted in yellow on a new map image.
    - The attributes of the selected features are displayed in a table below the map.
- **Clear Selection:** This button clears the current selected features and compound select areas from the map image, resets the measure tool, and clears any buffers from the map.
- **Locate Address:** Locates a street address on the map.
- **Print:** Opens the print dialog for printing the current map image. A title can be added before creating the print page. The print page opens in a new browser window, and the File menu of the new window may be used to print the map image.
- **Hyperlink:** The hyperlink tool allows you to view documents related to features in some designated layers on the map.

Legend/Layer Frame

Map layers are listed on the right side of the screen (Figure 7).

The Legend/Layer List button allows you to toggle between the layer list (left) or a legend (right), which shows the symbology for each layer.

Each layer has two interactive modes: Visible and active. (Image types like satellite images do not have attributes, and therefore do not have an active mode.) Most layers are initially turned off to keep the download time reasonable. To view layers, simply click on the Visible check box and then refresh the map with the button found on the bottom of the list.

The active circle column allows you to make a specific layer active to work with certain tools in the tool bar area. For example, if you wanted to find out when Web pages are hotlinked to the "Vibracore" layer, you would need to click on the circle to the left of "Vibracore," click on the lightening bolt tool in the tool bar, and then click on the Vibracore feature in the map to view the hotlinked Web page associated with the feature.

Some layers are scale dependent. They are not viewable until you zoom in or out to a mapping scale threshold.

- **Refresh Map button:** For the map display, to reflect your command when you change the visibility of a layer, you must use the Refresh Map button.

Results Frame

The Results frame is the area below the map image that is used to display several kinds of textual information (Figure 8), such as:

Figure 7. Legend Layer Frame

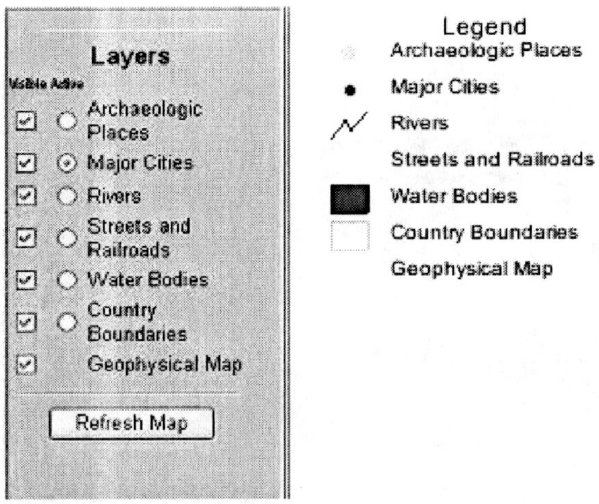

- Diagnostic messages
- Tabular results from identifying, selecting, and querying features
- Forms for user input
- Hyperlinks to related documents

Below is a screen capture of the results from a selection by rectangle on the All Sand Samples layer. The Select By Rectangle tool is described in detail in the toolbar frame section.

GIS LEARNING PROCESSES

The number of e-learning applications is rapidly increasing as the main advantage is the time and place independency of education and individual learning speed. In awareness of the deficiencies of e-learning, the project SeeArchWeb has a strong focus on interactivity and media didactic. The main targets of the project are the development of an Internet platform for e-learning, support of self-study, sustainable integration in the curricula, development of specific learning modules, creating a virtual landscape which demonstrates the phases of excavations and finally the useful inset of multimedia and interactivity through a media didactic concept.

Methods and technologies in the fields of GIS and modeling are playing the leading roles in this interdisciplinary learning platform. To unify all the different aspects of the involved disciplines, the above mentioned virtual landscape serves as a common base to explain and to visualize the processes, the interactions and their effects that are taking place in complex excavations. The participating institutes have the chance for a more attractive, up-to-date and transparent tuition. The final target is the development of a learning module on remote sensing. This special module is aims at creating an Internet platform to improve teaching in archaeology issues.

Conception of the Learning Platform

The students can easily access project through the Internet by a registered username and password. Dependant on their respective study course they can choose the learning modules they would like to work on. The students can easily navigate through the module's specific structure. The ArcIMS toolbar and layer bar make it easy for

Figure 8. Results frame

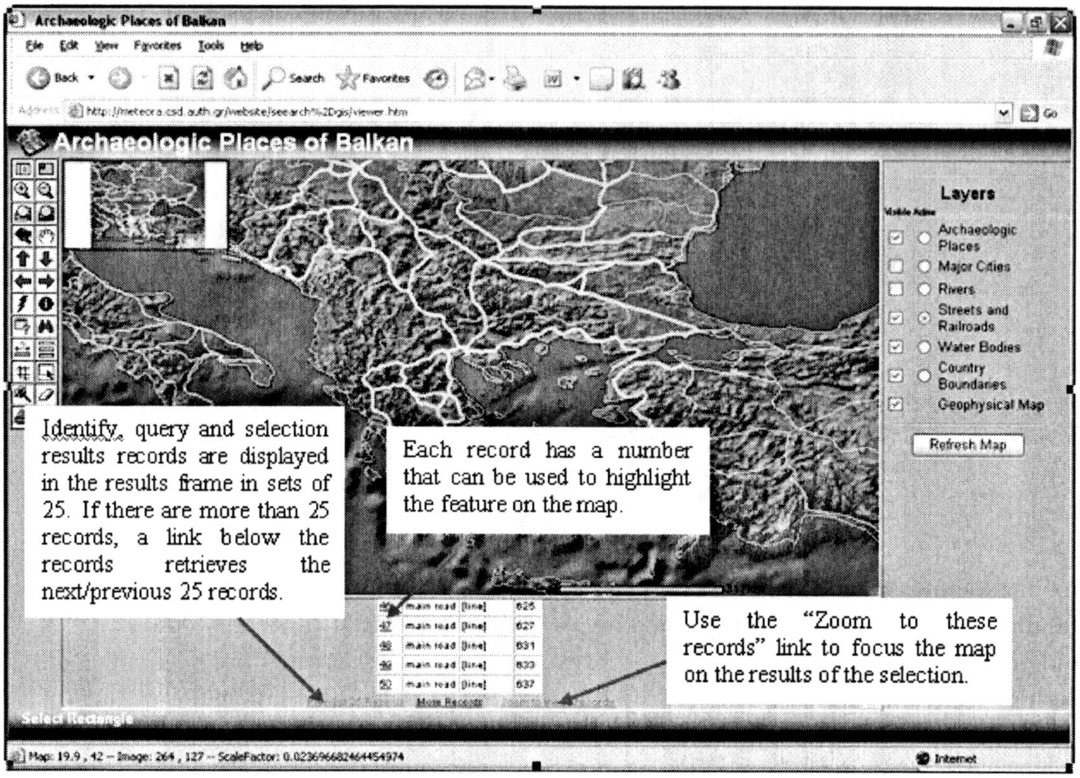

the user to follow his path during his work on an archaeological place of interest. All letters, buttons and icons are developed with regard to usability and functionality.

To explain spatial and time processes in different environmental sciences, a virtual landscape represents an ideal base. The virtual landscape is presented by realistic landscape located in Southeastern Balkans. For this region a geo-database exists, which contains all kinds of data like countries, borders, roads, cities, rivers and archaeological places. It is planned to visualize this landscape also in 3D. Another important component is the communication with other students or tutors to get a feedback while working on a specific module. Communication techniques either asynchronous ones like e-mail, mailing list or newsgroup or synchronous ones like chat and videoconferencing will be implemented into the platform insofar as it is useful for practical use in education of each of the institutes involved.

Architecture of the Platform

The integration of GIS is mainly based on the use of components from ArcGIS. The latest available clients for Arc Internet Map Server (ArcIMS) allow extensive configurable reading access on geo-data with Java or HTML-based "viewers." As mentioned above, even a client for 3D-visualization of the virtual landscape is provided. The data management is realized through a combination of a database (MSSQL) and file server systems. Complex elements like flash animations, server side scripts such as PHP, JSP or Java applets will be anchored in the XML module file.

Learning Methods

A map is a two dimensional graphic representation of the three dimensional configuration of the earth's surface. As an abstract representation, maps reduce the number of variables and simplify reality into an understandable bit of information. Even a simple map, however, contains a great deal of information. Students need help and guidance as they try to interpret and understand this complex visualization, whether the map is on paper or generated from a database in a geographic information system. It is possible to design GIS that supports for all levels of existing classroom instruction. But how can we design a project so that students could use it efficiently? The answer to this question comes from a series of actions that should be made in order to achieve the learning goals. These actions are (Figure 9):

- **Presentation:** The display of a static map
- **Exploration:** A simple examination of data presented in the GIS
- **Analysis:** Selection of features based upon criteria
- **Synthesis:** Recombination of existing data or creating one's own data into a new map
- **Visualization:** A dynamic process of searching for new spatial patterns by altering the way the data is represented

The actions mentioned above match in some way with Bloom's (1956) classification of intellectual behaviour:

- Knowledge
- Comprehension
- Application
- Analysis
- Synthesis
- Evaluation

This sequence represents a general structure of intellectual behaviour of great value that should be applied as we develop a GIS process framework.

Presentation of GIS maps is relatively stable, with relatively few chances of technical problems or errors. This can be delivered easily through a user friendly Web interface of map. But in such an environment maps are not static. This gives the opportunity to students to start to play with GIS software and data. They can turn layers on and off, make layers active, or even add/delete existing data layers in a GIS. Exploration is a stage where students can check out immediately available data layers and simply see the result of their actions. For example, a student may wish to turn on a layer representing state boundaries, as an overlay for other geographic features, later adding cities, fault lines, and points of archaeological interest.

After exploring though the map, they can move to the phase where data layers are compared and contrasted against one another. In some cases, data are identified based upon relationships with

Figure 9. Learning methods

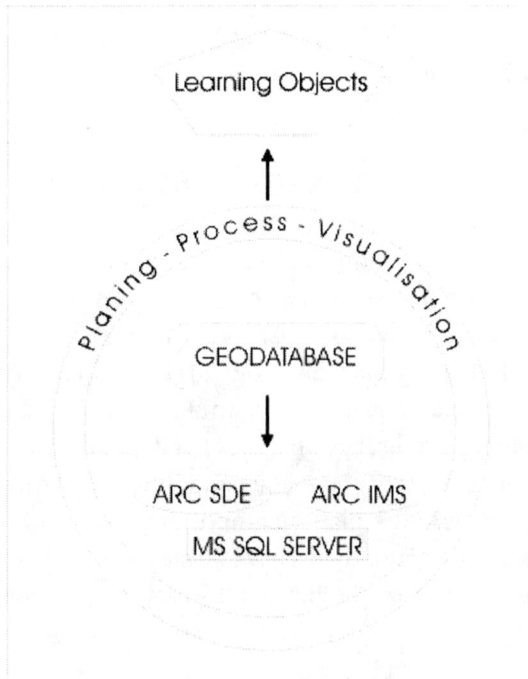

other data. For example, a common analysis task is the selection of a suitable location, based upon some criteria. Tasks could include identifying what's inside, outside, or nearby another object. For example, someone may want to identify archaeological places within 100 km of primary today's cities. After such queries, synthesis is the idea of creating new data layers and recombining existing data layers into new. In the processes of synthesis, students take the knowledge they have previously learned about science and GIS use and apply the knowledge to a new, unknown situation. A simple synthesis activity may include adapting a previous study to conform to the question of the current research. For example, some could see which would have been the major cities of today if the population density was distributed according to past eras, as they presented by excavation findings. Finally, by using visualization methods, a virtual reality environment can be created so that the user can become a member of the described situation. For example, a virtual flight over the ancient city of Troy can give someone the feeling of how the things were then. Visualization requires substantial computing power and memory, high bandwidth and advanced skills in the use of a GIS, and detailed knowledge of cartographic and design principles.

FUTURE RESEARCH DIRECTIONS

It is generally admitted that although the educational purposes have not changed over time, the educational needs are continuously growing, following the technological revolution. This has led the educational community to focus on students' preferences in order to adapt new ways to use technology so that it supports the learning objectives. GIS play an important role in this scenario, especially in case of time issues arising in certain scientific fields. GIS provide a simple interface to manipulate data collected through time in reference to geographic information. A GIS Web site requires less training for teachers to learn to use, as well as less expertise for them to teach in their classrooms. In addition, less time is required to present lessons to students in the classroom, and as a result more teachers may be likely to adopt the technology into their teaching, provided they have the computer resources to do so. The same good will seems to have students involved in such courses.

A Web GIS also addresses some of the issues regarding resources. Less software is required on the computers that students use because a Web GIS simply requires a Web browser and the Internet to access the functionality. Computers still need to be powerful enough to effectively handle processing time, but do not require the necessary space to store GIS software and data sets. GIS functionality can even be accessed from homes.

Unfortunately, ArcIMS offers limited capability compared to ArcView, but it offers a simple interface, which is ideal for the beginners. Combining GIS and the Internet provides an easy first touch to GIS technology and enriches study with Internet links for further exploration from different resources. The whole environment has the potential of communication with others in order to discuss, analyse the results or findings and generally collaborate with others.

A great advantage of Web GIS is the ability to update data in real time. For example, photos of an archaeological place of interest can be instantly published by using advanced mobile technologies such as handheld devices and wireless communication networks. This is a very important issue as time is the enemy in archaeology. It could take ages for an excavation's findings to be known to the general public. But by implementing projects like SeeArchWeb, a first view of some findings can be laid out in matter of minutes.

REFERENCES

Bloom, B. (1956). Taxonomy of educational objectives. *Handbook I: The cognitive domain*. New York: David McKay.

Burrough, P. A. (1986). *Principles of GIS for land resources assessment*. Oxford: Clarendon Press.

Lock, G. (2003). *Using computers in archaeology: Towards virtual pasts*. New York: Routledge.

Marble, D. F. (1990). The potential methodological impact of geographic information systems on the social science. In K.M.S. Allen, S.W. Green, & E.B.W. Zubrow (Eds.), *Interpreting space: GIS and archaeology, applications of geographic information systems*. London: Taylor & Francis.

Star, J., & Estes, J. (1990). *Geographic information systems*. New Jersey: Prentice Hall.

Wheatley, D., & Gillings, M. (2002). *Spatial technology and archaeology: The archaeological applications of GIS*. London: Taylor & Francis.

ADDITIONAL READING

Conolly, J, & Lake, M. (2006). *Geographical information systems in archaeology*. Cambridge University Press.

Maschner, D. G. (Ed.). (1996). *New methods, old problems: Geographic information systems in modern archaeological research*. Southern Illinois University.

Mehrer, M. W., & Wescott, K.L. (Eds.). (2006). *GIS and archaeological site location modeling*. Boca Raton: CRC Press.

KEY TERMS

Geographical Information System (GIS): A system for capturing, storing, analyzing and managing data and associated attributes which are spatially referenced to the earth.

Spatial Information: The determination of the position of different geographical data on a map.

Descriptive Information: Information about the quantitative and qualitative attributes of a specific geographical space.

Computer Aided Design (CAD): The use of a wide range of computer-based tools that assist engineers, architects and other professionals in their design activities.

Internet Mapping Service (IMS): A GIS that is designed to serve maps across the Internet.

Results Frame: The area below the map image that is used to display several kinds of textual information.

Chapter IX
Virtual Reconstructions in Archaeology

Dimitrios Margounakis
Computer Scientist and Researcher, Greece

INTRODUCTION

The rapid evolution of virtual reality (VR) in computer systems is one of the major technologies of our century. New ways of learning, living and working are on their way to be put on the map. virtual reality comprises an extension of static modeling, where the user can interact with a simulated environment. This type of computer modeling constitutes a major area of simulation in Archaeology. The new methods and computer practices allow the visualization and virtual reconstruction of artefacts, buildings, sites, landscapes and objects.

This chapter analyzes the computational methods used for recreating virtual worlds from the past. Terms, like *photogrammetry, rendering* and *digital elevation models,* are introduced and explained. The collaboration between archaeologists and computer graphics designers has to offer a lot to the wide spreading of cultural heritage by using innovative and appealing 3D technologies. In Section 1, several possible applications of virtual reconstructions in archaeology are discussed. Section 2 presents the methods and techniques for recreating a virtual world, while Section 3 mentions some examples and related work on the field from literature.

DIGITIZING THE ANTIQUITY

Technology advances have to show many admirable achievements. The continuously increasing computing power together with the multimedia applications of boundless capabilities is already offering a lot to archaeology, as well as other sciences. It is interesting to examine the ways of reviving the antiquity through technology and computers. Technology provides us today with the means to see pictures from the past, listen to sounds and music of another historical time, get known with our cultural heritage and interact with it.

The term "reconstruction" means here the recreation of some landscape, object, or situation by digital means. The physical reconstructions (e.g., the reconstruction of a tool from a previous era by physical means, like wood) are absolutely different from the digital virtual reconstructions that are mentioned in this chapter.

Next, some cases of digitization of the antiquity are presented. All these cases are supported by multimedia applications (computer applications that contain text, images, sounds, animations and videos) and may be either 2-dimensional or 3-dimensional[1]. These applications could have a range from educational to entertaining character. Virtual reality (VR) models may lead to educational applications, didactic aids for heritage diffusion, or even helpful applications for scholars in order to address research issues.

Landscapes and Archaeological Monuments

Pictures and representations from antiquity can be seen on a visual display unit. These particular reconstructions are based on today's salvaged monuments, the excavations and the archaeological research. The creation of exact representations (especially in cases of 3D images) on a computer is a laborious process, because something that does not exist today should be visualized in many details, while most of the time the opinions of the specialists about them diverge. Techniques, which are used for such visualisations, are: 3D scanning, photogrammetry, and so forth.

Situations – Events

Nowadays, the art of digital animation, as well as virtual reality, allows the live representation of occasions with the participation of virtual characters in the nature of animation, video, or even 3D virtual worlds where the user can actively take part. Fetes, ceremonies, rites, games and everyday life's moments from the ancient years come to life in front of user's eyes with photorealistic visualizations, movements and sounds. The resources of such applications lie on historical records and archaeological research. The latest trends of these applications are Virtual Cinemas, where the user interacts with the environment and resurrects moments of previous eras (Figure 1).

Figure 1. Visualization of an event: Live scenario of Ostracism in ancient Athens within a virtual environment (Sideris, 2006)

Video Games

A combination of the two previously mentioned cases concerning the entertainment field results to video games that are based on ancient times. 3-Dimensional worlds, imposing graphics, objects and characters from the past and strong doses of imagination compose a unique gaming experience for the user (usually it is about adventure, or role playing games).

There are many video games of that kind, because the ancient civilizations and landscapes have always been an attractive theme for designers and gamers. "Wrath of the Gods" (Figure 2) was first presented about 20 years ago (1994)! The game treats the Greek mythology through a virtual world with temples and landscapes of the ancient Greece and may fairly be considered an electronic encyclopaedia. Other titles concerning the antiquity are: "Titan Quest," "Spartan," and so forth.

Virtual Museums

The digitization of treasures from antiquity comprises a recent trend. Objects like vessels, weapons, coins, tools, musical instruments, and so forth, are converted into their digital version and create thereby electronic museums, which are available worldwide. One of the advantages of virtual museums is that objects, which are not solidly saved nowadays, may also be reconstructed (e.g., broken vessels can be digitally restored under the guidance of archaeologists). Virtual museums are created either by using a 3D scanner on real objects, or by electronically designing the objects from scratch (using descriptions and feature variables).

Music from Antiquity

Melodies and songs from antiquity may be digitally revived in our personal computer with sound applications, which are reposed on archaeological research and musicological writings that have survived until now. Virtual representations of ancient musical instruments, as well as physical voice modeling, create sounds from eras that have no sound recordings now available.

Two applications for modeling, composition and reproduction of ancient Greek music are ORPHEUS and ARION (Margounakis 2006). Both of them are part of a project of Aristotle University of Thessaloniki for Ancient Greek Music.

Figure 2. A snapshot from the PC game "Wrath of the Gods"

METHODS AND TECHNIQUES FOR ARCHAEOLOGICAL RECONSTRUCTIONS

This section describes the methods to reconstruct an archaeological site or object. Examples of each case are next presented.

Reconstruction modeling of buildings, landscapes and so forth, is an increasingly used method of visualising 3D archaeological data (Lock, 2003). The newly created integrated software applications can include together CAD, reconstruction modeling and virtual reality elements. There are two types of modeling software (Ryan, 1996):

- **Surface modeling.** Wire-frame or line modeling is an extension of a 2D drawing in three dimensions. A surface model consists of polygons, which are made of lines, points and surfaces, and can later be given texture or colour, and be rendered to achieve realistic lighting conditions. More about rendering and wire-frame models are explained later in this section.
- **Solid modeling**. Solid models use shapes (instead of surfaces) because they are real 3D representations and properties like mass, volume and centre gravity can be calculated. Solid models have limited use in archaeology reconstructions.

Virtual reality (VR) projects aim at the design of a 3D environment, in which the visitor is able to interact with it. Sideris (2006) describes the production process in VR representations of archaeological sites in five steps (Figure 3).

- **Step 1: Definition of time and space of the site.** The area to be designed is analyzed along with the buildings and the natural environment at the selected historical period. Also, at this step, the target groups and their needs are analyzed, defining that way the (educational or scientific) scope of the project (Sidiropoulos & Sideris, 2002; Sideris & Roussou, 2002).
- **Step 2: Documentation.** All the necessary documents are collected and analyzed. These include: pictures, excavational data, historical writings and previously made models.
- **Step 3: Building of 3D models.** It is about the actual design phase, where the architectural patterns are built. The forms are simplified as much as possible, falling into simple geometry shapes, and then textures and details are added.
- **Step 4: Integration.** Adjustments are made at this step on the 3D model. A 2D horizon

Figure 3. The five steps of a Virtual Reconstruction process

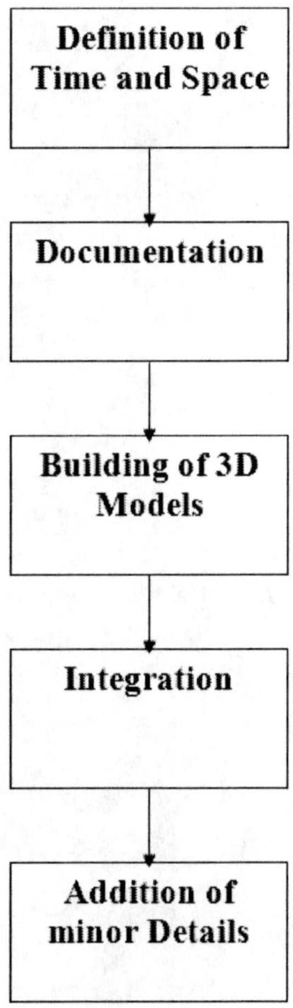

(distant structures and surroundings) is added.

- **Step 5: Addition of minor details.** The last step includes the final additions in order for the model to liven up. Walls, steps, light structures, as well as organic forms (trees, people, animals) are added according to a given scenario of varying flexibility and interactivity (Sideris, Roussou, & Gaitatzes, 2004).

Snapshots from the process of reconstructing an ancient site for Steps 3-5 can be seen in Figures 4 and 5.

When it comes to space, it is crucial to design in detail the landscape and the terrain model. Although the use of geographic information systems (GIS) are suggested for modeling and analysis of landscapes, the boundaries between software categories is blurring so that GIS, modeling and VR are becoming integrated tools for the appreciation of sites and landscapes (Lock, 2003). Especially in virtual worlds, real time rendering should give the user the feeling of really moving into the world, while accuracy should not be ignored. Because the computational power has increased, interactive visualizations of terrain models are now available. Examples of tools for

Figure 4. A wire-frame model of the Stoa of Attalos (Sideris 2006)

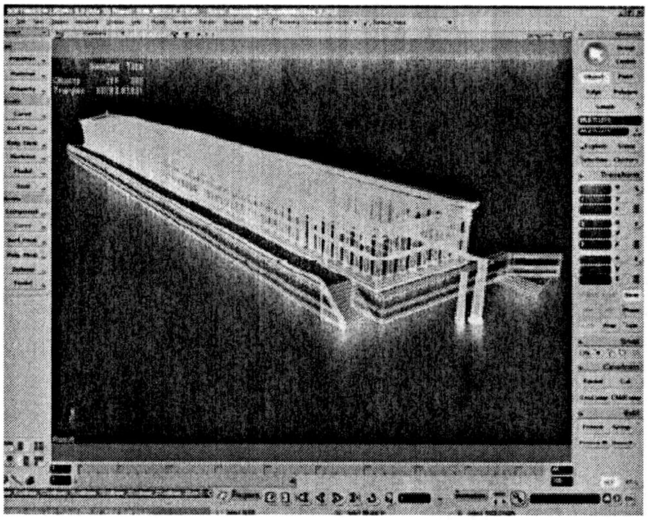

Figure 5. Real-time VR rendering of Stoa of Attalos (Sideris 2006)

interactive 3D terrain representations are "SG3D," "NVIZ," and so forth.

Wheatly and Gillings (2002) discuss the digital elevation models as methods to store and manipulate terrain data. The term digital elevation model (DEM) is the most widely used term for models of the earth's surface, although it need not necessarily refer solely to surface topography or landform. It should be mentioned that any empirically measurable variable that varies continuously over space can be regarded as an elevation model (pottery density, distance from water, etc.). DEMs can be applied in GIS and, as an extension, in VR archaeological recreations.

Elevation models can generate some secondary products of great value to archaeological reconstructions (Wheatley & Gillings, 2002):

- **Slope and aspect:** Slope consists of two components: *gradient*, which is the maximum rate of change of altitude, and *aspect*, which is the direction in which the maximum rate of change occurs. Both slope and aspect are estimated from the geometry of a local neighbourhood.
- **Analytical hill shading:** It uses slope and aspect in order to estimate the intensity of reflected light, given the light source. Hill shading is a very useful feature for the visual interpretation of landform. That way, the digital landscape is presented in a way familiar to the eye.
- **Hydrological and flood modeling:** Such simple or complex models have an impact on virtual archaeological reconstructions because they could estimate the course of ancient rivers, or identify the parts of certain sites that are at risk of erosion.

A project of reconstruction of an archaeological site could also use the method of photogrammetry. The term photogrammetry actually refers to a large field of study concerned with obtaining accurate measurements from photographs (Wheatley & Gillings 2002). Technological evolution allows yet the automatic scanning of photographs and output of accurate data. This method of digital photogrammetry needs little intervention from the designer. Output of this method could be contours and triangulated irregular networks (TINs).

Two very important processes during the third step of 3D modeling are the pre-image design and the final image rendering. Creating the pre-image usually results in a *wireframe sketch*, while the addition of bitmap and procedural textures, lights, bump mapping and relative position to other objects results in a complete image for the viewer (Figures 6 and 7). The addition of the detailed futures on the preliminary sketch is called *rendering*. Rendering is defined as the creative process of generating an image from a model (a description of 3D objects in a strictly defined language or data structure) by means of software projects. The main steps of image rendering are: *projection* and *realism*. Rendering is applied in most of the 3D visualizations and produces the realism associated with good computer reconstructions. A common use in archaeology is virtual museums. A very useful survey about rendering is presented by Karagkiozidis et al. (2006).

Rendering is not a simple process, especially when it is about recreating virtual worlds where the user should acquire the feeling of actually moving in the 3D space and interact with several objects. Several features are directly related to rendering process (Karagkiozidis et. al., 2006):

- Shading
- Texture – mapping
- Bump – mapping
- Fogging/participating medium
- Shadows
- Soft shadows
- Reflection
- Transparency
- Translucency
- Refraction
- Indirect illumination

- Caustics
- Depth of field
- Motion blur
- Photorealistic morphing
- Nonphotorealistic rendering

Research on 3D visualization has revealed several rendering techniques, each of them serving different applications and uses. Known rendering techniques are next presented (Karagkiozidis et. al., 2006):

- **Polygon rendering:** It is the oldest method, where objects are reduced in polygons that are then smoothed and rendered. Lock (2003) states that "realistic lighting, shadows and

Figure 6. A wire-frame model of pottery, enriched with a primitive kind of texture (Rowe and Razdan 2003)

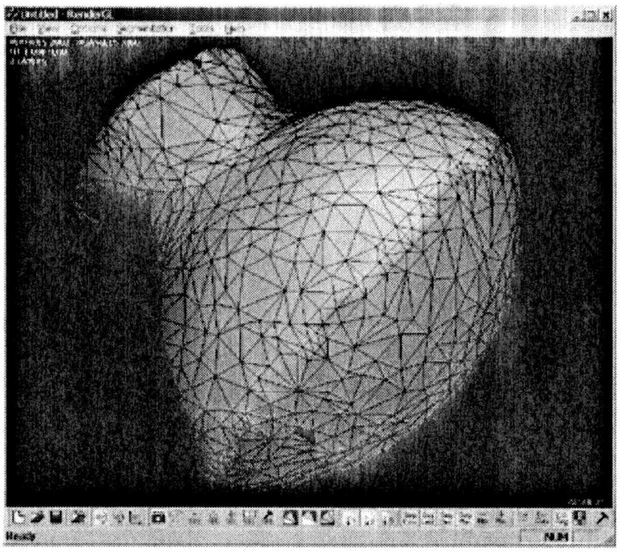

Figure 7. A wire frame reconstruction model of Symon's Castle (Guo-Yuan 1998)

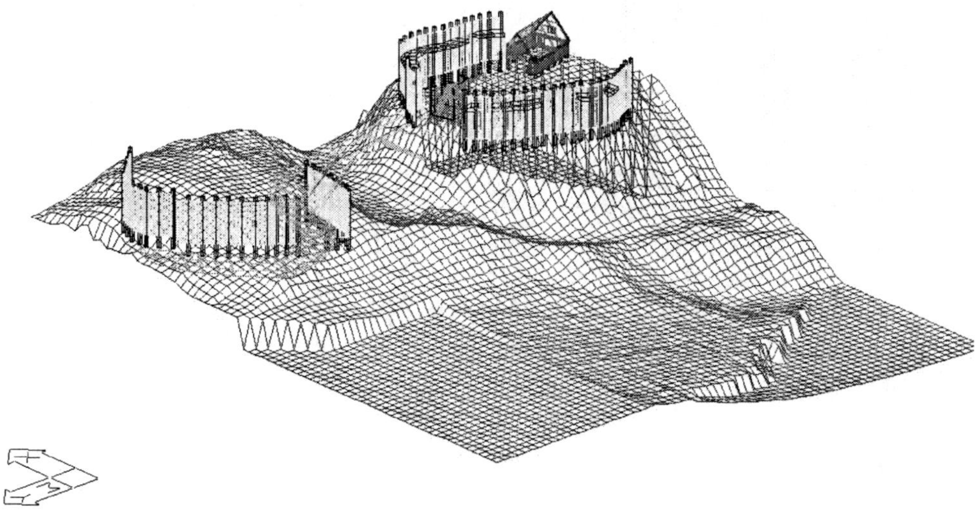

reflections are difficult to achieve with polygon rendering as is tends to produce a 'blocky' appearance."

- **Rasterization:** Rasterization is a primitive-by-primitive approach to rendering where looping through the primitives of an image determines the pixels to be affected and modifies them accordingly. It is faster than pixel-by-pixel approach, but may result in images of lower quality.
- **Ray casting:** This technique calculates the prementioned features from a particular point-of-view, using geometry elements and basic optical laws of reflection intensity. It applies to real time simulations (3D video-games, VR environments, etc.).
- **Radiosity:** Radiosity is the rate at which energy leaves a surface, and more specifically, the rate at which the surface emits, reflects and transmits energy from itself or other surfaces. This technique produces more realistic scenes and is therefore considered as the leader in real-time rendering methods. Archaeological reconstructions may use *particle tracing*, which is a development of radiosity that introduces smoke and fog in the atmosphere based on absorbed and re-radiated light (Chalmers & Stoddart, 1996).
- **Ray tracing:** An extension of ray casting that handles complicated mathematically described objects. It is based on calculating the average of the variables of many randomly generated samples of a model and this is why it is too slow for real-time applications. Another disadvantage is that it produces crisp images with harsh boundaries. A solution to this is multiple light sources, but then even more processing time is needed. Nevertheless, it suits well to the modeling of photorealistic objects of a virtual museum collection.

Other rendering techniques (not so well-known yet), such as *spherical harmonics,* still lack of practical use (Moller & Haines, 2002).

EXAMPLES AND RELATIVE WORK

Lock (2003) presents in detail the steps for reconstructing ancient Greek pottery. Stages are presented again here in order to be understood by the reader[2]:

1. A 2D profile is generated by a computer
2. A 3D wire-frame model is spun from the profile
3. The model is rendered using ray-tracing to produce the solid effect with light and shade which can be manipulated in space. Parameters such as transparency, reflectance and index of refraction determine the final look.
4. Surface decoration is created either freehand within a paint program or as a digital image from a photograph
5. The decoration is applied to the model as a surface texture

Several projects are under construction or already in use. The methods mentioned above comprise the most common techniques used in order to produce 3D virtual environments. Some examples are next presented. The ARCHAVE system, developed at the SHAPE lab at Brown University, presents archaeological excavation data from Temple excavations in Petra and site information via a virtual reality interface (Acevedo et. al., 2000). The virtual world allows the user (researcher or visitor) to experiment with various tasks: explore objects (such as pottery finds), transfer to several historical moments of the archaeological site (variables of time and space-step 1 of previous section), and so forth.

Several VR models of buildings and monuments in ancient Rome have been developed by the UCLA Virtual Reality Lab. The so called "Rome Reborn" project aims to develop open standards for cultural VR so that a chronologically and geographically full model of ancient Rome can be created by many scholars publishing their work in a digital, scientific format (Frischer et. al., 2000).

Apart from the techniques presented above, many researchers work on new innovative ways of reconstructing the antiquity. Several projects are in progress aiming at different tasks and different users.

VITA (visual interaction tool for archaeology), for example, is a collaborative system, which combines virtual and augmented reality. VITA provides a hybrid interface that uses both 2D and 3D visualization and interaction metaphors (Benko, Ishak, & Feiner, 2003). Special accessories (like instrumented gloves, etc.) allow users to interact with the virtual environment using both gestures and speech. The visualised excavation data of this project was collected at Monte Polizzo in Italy.

A fine collection of high profile archaeological sites from all over the world that have been virtually reconstructed is presented by Forte and Siliotti (1997). Of course, because then much more has been achieved on that field and the results nowadays are impressive. Technological achievements in Archaeology have created a new way of experiencing the past. VR worlds are now too successful, too convincing, and too believable (Lock, 2003)!

FUTURE RESEARCH DIRECTIONS

The interest for virtual reconstructions in archaeology becomes greater day-by-day. Because technology allows for more innovations to appear, we will see more amazing achievements on that field. Computer database systems, high-level graphics systems and artificial intelligence techniques are already beginning to allow archaeologists and scholars to ask new types of questions and to look at their data from positions which were previously impossible (Reilly, 1989).

More intelligent systems will create answers and different situations in a virtual reconstructed world to "IF" queries. What would have happened if...? Different scenarios would give answers to the archaeologists taking into account many complicated parametrical values. The interaction with these hypothetical new worlds could predict similar situations in future, or compare different situations where the views of the experts are conflicted. We will experience systems able to visualise uncertainty and fuzzy data. Living characters of another era (avatars) will interact with the user in many ways.

Most archaeologists would want to emphasise the uncertainty of knowing the past, that there can be different, and equally valid, views of the past. The final concern and aim of archaeologists and computer experts in the field of virtual reconstructions is one: to finally *deal with the unknowable*.

REFERENCES

Acevedo, D., Vote, E., Laidlaw, D.H., & Joukowsky, M.S. (2000). ARCHAVE: A virtual environment for archaeological research. *Work in Progress report presented at IEEE Visualization*, Salt Lake City, Utah.

Benko, H., Ishak, E., & Feiner, S. (2003). Collaborative visualisation of an archaeological excavation. In *Proceedings of the Workshop on Collaborative Virtual Reality and Visualisation (CVRV 2003),* Lake Tahoe, CA.

Chalmers A. and Stoddart S.K.F. (1996). Photo-realistic graphics for visualising archaeological site reconstructions. In A. Higgins, P. Main, and J. Lang (eds.), *Imaging the Past. Electronic imaging and computer graphics in museums and archaeology,* British Museum occasional paper 114, pp. 85-93. London: British Museum

Forte, M., & Siliotti, A. (1997). *Virtual archaeology: Great discoveries brought to life through virtual reality.* London: Thames and Hudson.

Frischer, B., Abernathy, D., Favro, D., Liverani, P., & De Blaauw, S. (2000). *Virtual reality and Ancient Rome: The UCLA cultural VR lab's Santa Maria Maggiore project* (pp. 155-162). Barcelo: Forte and Sanders.

Guo-Yuan, C. (1998). *3D reconstruction modelling from varied data sources.* Doctoral dissertation, University of Glasgow.

Karagkiozidis, A., Mpampouklis, K., Triantafyllou, V., Loli, M., Grivas, I., & Printziou, E. (2006). Virtual museums: A flash presentation about rendering. In D. Politis (Ed.), *The e-learning dimension of computer applications in archaeology* (pp. 111-122). The SEEArchWeb project. Athens: Kleidarithmos.

Lock, G. (2003). *Using computers in archaeology: Towards virtual pasts.* New York: Routledge.

Margounakis, D. (2006, September 29-30). ARION – the Ancient Greek singer. In *Proceedings of the 1st SEEArchWeb Conference E-Learning and Computer Applications in Archaeology,* Thessaloniki, Greece.

Moller T., & Haines, E. (2002). *Real–time rendering.* London: AK Peters.

Reilly, P. (1989). Data visualization in archaeology. *IBM Systems Journal, 28*(4), 569-579.

Rowe, J., & Razdan, A. (2003). A prototype digital library for 3D collections: Tools to capture, model, analyze, and query complex 3D data. *In Museums and the Web 2003: Selected Papers from 7th International Conference*, Charlotte, NC.

Ryan, N. (1996). Computer based visualisation of the past: Technical "realism" and historical credibility. In P. Main, T. Higgins, & J. Lang (Eds.), *Imaging the past: Electronic imaging and computer graphics in museums and archaeology* (pp. 95-108). London: The British Museum.

Sideris, A. (2006). A virtual cradle for democracy: Reconstructing the ancient agora of Athens. In *E-learning and computer applications in archaeology, Proceedings of 1st SEEArchWeb Conference*, Thessaloniki, Greece.

Sideris, A., & Roussou, M. (2002). Making a new world out of an old one: In search of a common language for archaeological immersive VR representation. In *CREATIVE Digital Culture, Proceedings of 8th International Conference on Virtual Systems and Multimedia*, Gyeongju, Korea.

Sideris, A., Roussou, M., & Gaitatzis, A. (2004). The virtual reconstruction of the Hellenistic Asklepieion of Messene. *Imeros, 4*, 208-216.

Sidiropoulos, G., & Sideris, A. (2002). Requirements and assumptions in visualization process of urban and surrounding areas (The case of Greek city in time). In *Proceedings of the CAA 2002 The Digital Heritage of Archaeology, Computer Applications and Quantitative Methods in Archaeology Conference*, Heraclion, Crete, Greece.

Wheatley, D., & Gillings, M. (2002). *Spatial technology and archaeology: The archaeological applications of GIS.* London: Taylor & Francis.

OTHER RESOURCES

- http://www.mythweb.com/teachers/learning/wrath/index.html
- http://www.titanquest.net/
- http://www.gamespot.com/pc/strategy/spartan/index.html
- http://ligwww.epfl.ch/teaching/teaching_index.html

KEY TERMS

Virtual Reconstruction: The act or process of reproducing by new technologies the exact form and detail of a vanished building, structure, or object, or a part thereof, as it appeared at a specific period of time.

Surface Model: A mesh of polygons, which are made of lines, points and surfaces, and can later be given texture or colour, and be rendered to achieve realistic lighting conditions.

Solid Model: An unambiguous representation of the solid parts of an object. It uses shapes (instead of surfaces) since they are real 3D representations and have properties like mass, volume and centre of gravity. Accordingly, overall such properties can be calculated for the whole model.

Photogrammetry: The output of photogrammetry is typically a map, drawing or a 3D model of a real-world object or scene. The term actually refers to a large field of study concerned with obtaining accurate measurements from photographs.

Rendering: It is the creative process of generating an image from a model (a description of 3D objects in a strictly defined language or data structure) by means of software projects.

ENDNOTES

1 3D applications are usually referred to as a *virtual* and support interactivity with the user.

2 Reader should not be confused here as these are not the 5 steps previously mentioned. They describe in detail steps 3-5 from the production process (Sideris, 2006).

Chapter X
The Use of Virtual Museums, Simulations, and Recreations as Educational Tools

Dionysios Politis
Aristotle University of Thessaloniki, Greece

Ionnis Marras
Aristotle University of Thessaloniki, Greece

INTRODUCTION

The idea of creating a virtual museum is far from new. However, creating a museum that an archaeologist could customize to match his needs is quite innovative. Here we present a system which can be used for online visualization of museums. Although there are plenty of online virtual museums, none of them is customizable. These museums are designed statically and represent certain museums, which makes it rather difficult to change.

On the contrary, our Dynamic Virtual Museum is easily managed through database entries, which provide all necessary variables (rooms, models, exhibits) and interact with the renderer through scripts. Therefore, the virtual museum can be easily transformed to match any given exhibition or a visitor's specific choices.

The system consists of two main elements, a database where all information about the exhibits, models, and so forth, is kept and a renderer which is responsible for graphically representing all this information on the computer screen.

The database part is handled by MySQL(Rose, Buchanan, & Sarrett, 1999), whereas VRML(Moschos, Nikolaidis, & Pitas, 2004) is responsible for all the graphics. In order to easily connect MySQL and VRML through an easy to use Web interface, php (Wang, Zhang, Wang, Lee, Pejun, & Wang, 2005) is used. Our goal is to create a fully customizable museum, which will be easy to navigate and control by any archaeologist or visitor. It could be used in a wide range of occasions, such as an exhibition centre where exhibits are changed quite often, and it could be an important help to a museum executive who needs to rearrange some or all of the exhibits, or it could be used by any visitor who wants an exhibit to match his certain needs.

THE RENDERER

The graphics subsystem of the application is responsible for rendering the museum rooms and the exhibits displayed therein. It also handles the interaction of the user with the virtual world. This would allow, for example, a verbal description to be played back, whenever the user clicks on an exhibit. The render is implemented using VRML (virtual reality modeling language), a Web-based network protocol for working with three dimensional (3D) scenes or data sets. It allows the creation of platform-independent 3D objects, described in text files, which can then be displayed on any computer platform for which an appropriate browser exists. VRML browsers come in two types: stand-alone and plugins for HTML browsers. They allow a user to walk into a VRML scene using a mouse or keyboard and navigate, as he or she does in the real world. A VRML document, like an html document, is a formalized text description of a Web page's contents. Unlike html however, VRML is not "marked up" text. It contains descriptions of three-dimensional objects and their interrelationships.

THE DATABASE SUBSYSTEM

The database subsystem of the application is responsible for the storage of all elements important to the museum model. It is organized in a way which makes it possible for the system to easily extract information about the exhibits and how they should be displayed in the virtual museum.

The database used is MySQL, the most commonly used database in conjunction with php. It's architecture makes it extremely fast and easy to customize.

Using a database, it is quite a simple task to record a large number of data and information about an object, without necessarily having to use them all in the construction of the model or the display of the object in the museum. Therefore, we can create a well organized library of all of our artifacts and exhibits.

The most important records that describe an object should be the object's type (whether it's a painting, a sculpture, a mask, etc.), its measurements (height, width, weight, etc.), a title (if there is one e.g., "Mona Lisa") and a short description of the artifact.

The description could be simple text or even a path (relative or not) to an audio file, which could be used in the museum model. The visitor then could hear a narrated description of the artifact by interacting with it. Other characteristic features that could be recorded as well are the artifacts' distinguishing features, creation date or period (if known), its origin, maker's name and the materials which were used. These descriptive items could be easily added even after the creation of the database through the Web interface or any other administration tool for MySQL databases. Such a tool is eskuel[1], a MySQL database administration interface written in PHP. It allows users to simply and fully manage one or more databases without any advanced knowledge of SQL language.

SCRIPTING

VRML was created for describing interactive, but static, 3D objects and worlds. Therefore, there was no need for variables when the specification was written. When creating a dynamic virtual museum you need to be able to process data and change many of the models' attributes (size, translations, geometry, materials, etc.). You must also have the capability of extracting specific fields from a database record and provide the field values to the VRML model. Hence, the need for a scripting language to solve these problems was born. For all the scripting tasks, php is used. PHP is an HTML-embedded scripting language. Much of its syntax is borrowed from C, Java and Perl with a couple of unique PHP-specific features thrown in.

It has built-in functions that allow you to perform various functions on a MySQL database and can be used to solve complex mathematical equations using libbcmath, which is bundled with PHP (since version 4.0.4). Both of these characteristics made the use of php for the virtual museum an easy choice.

MATHEMATICS

```
Coordinate { exposedField MFVec3f point [
] (-INF,INF)}
```

This node defines a set of 3D coordinates to be used in the coordinate field of vertex-based geometry nodes, including IndexedFaceSet, IndexedLineSet, and PointSet.

The VRML 2.0 naming philosophy is to give each node the most obvious name and not try to predict how the specification will change in the future. If carried out to its logical extreme, then a philosophy of planning for future extensions might give coordinate the name CartesianCoordinate3Float, because support for polar or spherical coordinates might possibly be added in the future, as might double-precision or integer coordinates.

```
ElevationGrid
ElevationGrid {
eventIn MFFloat set _ height
exposedField SFNode color NULL
exposedField SFNode normal NULL
exposedField SFNode texCoord NULL
field MFFloat height []
field SFBool ccw TRUE
field SFBool colorPerVertex TRUE
field SFFloat creaseAngle 0
field SFBool normalPerVertex TRUE
field SFBool solid TRUE
field SFInt32 xDimension 0
field SFFloat xSpacing 1.0
field SFInt32 zDimension 0
field SFFloat zSpacing 1.0
```

The ElevationGrid node specifies a uniform rectangular grid of varying height in the Y=0 plane of the local coordinate system.

The geometry is described by a scalar array of height values that specify the height of a surface above each point of the grid.
The `xDimension` and `zDimension` fields indicate the number of elements of the grid height array in the X and Z directions. Both `xDimension` and `zDimension` must be greater than or equal to zero. The vertex locations for the rectangles are defined by the height field and the `xSpacing` and `zSpacing` fields:
Thus, the vertex corresponding to the point `P[i, j]` on the grid is placed at:

```
P[i,j].x = xSpacing / i
P[i,j].y = height[ i + j / xDimension]
P[i,j].z = zSpacing / j
```

where `0 <= i < xDimension` and `0 <=j < zDimension`, and `P[0, 0]` is `height[0]` units above/below the origin of the local coordinate system.

The `colorPerVertex` field determines whether colours specified in the colour field are applied to each vertex or each quadrilateral of the ElevationGrid node. If `colorPerVertex` is FALSE and the color field is not NULL, the color field shall specify a Color node containing at least (xDimension − 1)/(zDimension − 1) colors; one for each quadrilateral, ordered as follows:

```
QuadColor[i, j] = Color[i+j/(xDimension-1)]
```

where `0 <= i < xDimension - 1` and `0 <= j < zDimension - 1`, and `QuadColor[i, j]` is the colour for the quadrilateral defined by `height[i + j/xDimension]`, `height[(i + 1) + j/xDimension]`, `height[(i + 1) + (j + 1)/xDimension]` and `height[i + (j + 1)/xDimension]`. If `colorPerVertex` is TRUE and the color field is not NULL, the color field shall specify a Color node containing at least `xDimension` / `zDimension` colours, one for each vertex, ordered as follows:

```
V ertexColor[i, j] = Color[i+j/xDimension]
```

where `0 <= i < xDimension` and `0 <= j < zDimension`, and `V ertexColor[i, j]` is the colour for the vertex defined by `height[i+ j/xDimension]`.

The `normalPerVertex` field determines whether normals are applied to each vertex or each quadrilateral of the ElevationGrid node depending on the value of `normalPerVertex`. If `normalPerVertex` is FALSE and the normal node is not NULL, the normal field shall specify a Normal node containing at least `(xDimension-1)/(zDimension-1)` normals; one for each quadrilateral, ordered as follows:

```
QuadNormal[i, j] = Normal[i + j/(xDimension
- 1)]
```

where `0 <= i < xDimension - 1` and `0 <= j < zDimension -1`, and `QuadNormal[i, j]` is the normal for the quadrilateral defined by `height[i + j/xDimension]`, `height[(i +1) + j/xDimension]`, `height[(i + 1) + (j + 1)/xDimension]` and `height[i + (j + 1)/xDimension]`.

If `normalPerVertex` is TRUE and the normal field is not NULL, the normal field shall specify a Normal node containing at least `xDimension / zDimension` normals; one for each vertex, ordered as follows:

```
V ertexNormal[i, j] = Normal[i +j/xDimen-
sion]
```

where `0 <= i < xDimension` and `0 <= j < zDimension`, and `V ertexNormal[i, j]` is the normal for the vertex defined by:

```
height[i + j/xDimension].
```

The `texCoord` field specifies per-vertex texture coordinates for the ElevationGrid node. If `texCoord` is NULL, default texture coordinates are applied to the geometry. The default texture coordinates range from (0,0) at the first vertex to (1,1) at the last vertex. The S texture coordinate is aligned with the positive X-axis, and the T texture coordinate with positive Z-axis. If `texCoord` is not NULL, it shall specify a TextureCoordinate node containing at least (`xDimension`)/(`zDimension`) texture coordinates; one for each vertex, ordered as follows:

```
VertexTexCoord[i, j] = TextureCoordinate[i
+ j/xDimension]
```

where `0 <= i < xDimension` and `0 <=j < zDimension`, and `V ertexTexCoord[i, j]` is the texture coordinate for the vertex defined by `height[i + j/xDimension]`.

Group

```
Group {
eventIn MFNode addChildren
eventIn MFNode removeChildren
exposedField MFNode children []
field SFVec3f bboxCenter 0 0 0
field SFVec3f bboxSize -1 -1 -1}
```

A Group node contains children nodes without introducing a new transformation. It is equivalent to a Transform node without the transformation fields.

The `bboxCenter` and `bboxSize` fields specify a bounding box that encloses the Group node's children. This is a hint that may be used for optimization purposes. If the specified bounding box is smaller than the actual bounding box of the children at any time, the results are undefined. A default `bboxSize` value, (-1, -1, -1), implies that the bound-in box is not specified and, if needed, is calculated by the browser.

IndexedFaceSet

```
IndexedFaceSet {
eventIn MFInt32 set _ colorIndex
eventIn MFInt32 set _ coordIndex
```

```
eventIn MFInt32 set _ normalIndex
eventIn MFInt32 set _ texCoordIndex
exposedField SFNode color NULL
exposedField SFNode coord NULL
exposedField SFNode normal NULL
exposedField SFNode texCoord NULL
field SFBool ccw TRUE
field MFInt32 colorIndex []
field SFBool colorPerVertex TRUE
field SFBool convex TRUE
field MFInt32 coordIndex []
field SFFloat creaseAngle 0
field MFInt32 normalIndex []
field SFBool normalPerVertex TRUE
field SFBool solid TRUE
field MFInt32 texCoordIndex []
}
```

The IndexedFaceSet node represents a 3D shape formed by constructing faces (polygons) from vertices listed in the coordinate field. The coordinate field contains a Coordinate node that defines the 3D vertices referenced by the coordIndex field. IndexedFaceSet uses the indices in its coordIndex field to specify the polygonal faces by indexing into the coordinates in the Coordinate node. An index of "-1" indicates that the current face has ended and the next one begins. The last face may be (but does not have to be) followed by a "-1" index. If the greatest index in the `coordIndex` field is N, the Coordinate node shall contain N+1 coordinates (indexed as 0 to N). Each face of the IndexedFaceSet shall have:

1. At least three noncoincident vertices
2. Vertices that define a planar polygon
3. Vertices that define a nonself-intersecting polygon

Otherwise, results are undefined.

IndexedLineSet

```
IndexedLineSet {
eventIn MFInt32 set _ colorIndex
eventIn MFInt32 set _ coordIndex
exposedField SFNode color NULL
exposedField SFNode coord NULL
field MFInt32 colorIndex []
field SFBool colorPerVertex TRUE
field MFInt32 coordIndex []
}
```

The IndexedLineSet node represents a 3D geometry formed by constructing polylines from 3D vertices specified in the coordinate field. IndexedLineSet uses the indices in its `coordIndex` field to specify the polylines by connecting vertices from the coordinate field. An index of "-1" indicates that the current polyline has ended and the next one begins. The last polyline may be (but does not have to be) followed by a "-1". IndexedLineSet is specified in the local coordinate system and is affected by ancestors' transformations.

OrientationInterpolator

```
OrientationInterpolator {
eventIn SFFloat set _ fraction
exposedField MFFloat key []
exposedField MFRotation keyValue []
eventOut SFRotation value _ changed
}
```

The OrientationInterpolator node interpolates among a set of rotation values specified in the `keyValue` field. These rotations are absolute in object space and therefore are not cumulative. The `keyValue` field shall contain exactly as many rotations as there are key frames in the key field.

An orientation represents the final position of an object after a rotation has been applied. An OrientationInterpolator interpolates between two orientations by computing the shortest path on the unit sphere between the two orientations. The interpolation is linear in arc length along this path. If the two orientations are diagonally opposite results are undefined. If two consecutive key value values exist such that the arc length between them is greater than PI, the interpolation will take place on the arc complement. For example, the interpolation between the orientations (0, 1, 0, 0) and (0, 1, 0, 5.0) is equivalent to the rotation between the orientations (0, 1, 0, 2_) and (0, 1, 0, 5.0).

Shape

```
exposedField SFNode appearance NULL
exposedField SFNode geometry NULL
```

The Shape node has two fields, `appearance` and `geometry`, which are used to create rendered objects in the world. The `appearance` field contains an Appearance node that specifies the visual attributes (e.g., material and texture) to be applied to the geometry. The `geometry` field contains a Geometry node. The specified Geometry node is rendered with the specified Appearance nodes applied. If the `geometry` field is NULL, the object is not drawn.

TextureCoordinate

```
TextureCoordinate
exposedField MFVec2f point []
```

The TextureCoordinate node specifies a set of 2D texture coordinates used by vertex based geometry nodes (e.g., IndexedFaceSet and ElevationGrid) to map textures to vertices. Textures are two dimensional color functions that, given an `(s, t) coordinate`, return a color value `color(s, t)`. Texture map values (ImageTexture, MovieTexture, and PixelTexture) range from [0.0, 1.0] along the S-axis and T-axis. However, TextureCoordinate values, specified by the point field, may be in the range (–1,1). Texture coordinates identify a location (and thus a color value) in the texture map. The horizontal coordinate s is specified first, followed by the vertical coordinate t. If the texture map is repeated in a given direction (S-axis or T-axis), a texture coordinate `C (s or t)` is mapped into a texture map that has `N` pixels in the given direction as follows:

```
Texturemaplocation = (C - floor(C))/N
```

If the texture map is not repeated, the texture coordinates are clamped to the 0.0 to 1.0 range as follows:

```
Texturemaplocation =
= N, ifC > 1.0,
= 0.0, ifC < 0.0,
= C/N, if0.0 <= C <= 1.0.
TextureTransform
TextureTransform {
exposedField SFVec2f center 0 0
exposedField SFFloat rotation 0
exposedField SFVec2f scale 1 1
exposedField SFVec2f translation 0 0
}
```

The TextureTransform node defines a 2D transformation that is applied to texture coordinates. This node affects the way textures coordinates are applied to the geometric surface. The transformation consists of (in order):

1. A translation
2. A rotation about the centre point
3. A nonuniform scale about the centre point

In matrix transformation notation, where Tc is the untransformed texture coordinate, Tc′ is the transformed texture coordinate, C (center), T (translation), R (rotation), and S (scale) are the intermediate transformation matrices,

```
Tc' = -C/S/R/C/T/Tc
```

Transform

```
Transform {
eventIn MFNode addChildren
eventIn MFNode removeChildren
```

```
exposedField SFVec3f center 0 0 0
exposedField MFNode children []
exposedField SFRotation rotation 0 0 1 0
exposedField SFVec3f scale 1 1 1
exposedField SFRotation scaleOrientation
0 0 1 0
exposedField SFVec3f translation 0 0 0
field SFVec3f bboxCenter 0 0 0
field SFVec3f bboxSize -1 -1 -1
}
```

The Transform node is a grouping node that defines a coordinate system for its children that is relative to the coordinate systems of its ancestors.

The `bboxCenter` and `bboxSize` fields specify a bounding box that encloses the children of the Transform node. This is a hint that may be used for optimization purposes. If the specified bounding box is smaller than the actual bounding box of the children at any time, the results are undefined. A default `bboxSize` value, (-1, -1, -1), implies that the bounding box is not specified and, if needed, must be calculated by the browser.

The `translation`, `rotation`, `scale`, `scaleOrientation` and `center` fields define a geometric 3D transformation consisting of (in order):

1. A (possibly) nonuniform scale about an arbitrary point
2. A rotation about an arbitrary point and axis
3. A translation

The `center` field specifies a translation offset from the origin of the local coordinate system (0, 0, 0). The `rotation` field specifies a rotation of the coordinate system. The `scale` field specifies a nonuniform scale of the coordinate system. Scale values shall be > 0.0. The `scaleOrientation` specifies a rotation of the coordinate system before the scale (to specify scales in arbitrary orientations).

The `scaleOrientation` applies only to the scale operation. The translation field specifies a translation to the coordinate system.

The translation/rotation/scale operations performed by the Transform node occur in the "natural" order each operation is independent of the other.

Given a 3-dimensional point P and Transform node, P is transformed into point P' in its parent's coordinate system by a series of intermediate transformations. In matrix transformation notation, where C (`center`), SR (`scaleOrientation`), T (`translation`), R (`rotation`), and S (`scale`) are the equivalent transformation matrices,

```
P' = T/C/R/SR/S/ - SR/ - C/P
```

The second operation, in order, is the `scaleOrientation`. The `scaleOrientation` temporarily rotates the object's coordinate system (i.e., local origin) in preparation for the third operation, `scale`, and rotates back after the scale is performed.

The fourth operation is `rotation`. It specifies an axis about which to rotate the object and the angle (in radians) to rotate.

The last operation is `translation`. It specifies a translation to be applied to the object. "Spaces" is kind of like a coordinate system. Well, it actually *could* be a coordinate system, but not always, though in your case it most likely will be. Also, the system I am describing follows the "camera moves in space" concept, sure the math is all the same no matter what you do, but *how* the math is implemented can lead to interesting problems if you accidentally switch between "camera moves" and "camera stays still."

Definitions

- **Object Space:** The vertex data of an object usually set up so that 0, 0, 0 is the center of rotation you desire.

- **World Space:** A space where all object's vertex data (for all objects) are represented with respect to ONE coordinate system centered at 0, 0, 0.
- **View Space:** Almost like a world space, but what happens is you translate the camera to the World Space 0,0,0 position and align it to the cardinal axes. All of the objects in the world are moved such that they are in their relative locations and orientations with respect to the camera (which is now at 0, 0, 0).
- **Screen Space:** This is the result you get when you project the view space coordinates of the vertex data for each object via projection equations.

  Rotation about the X axis by an angle a:

$$\begin{bmatrix} 1 & 0 & 0 & 0 \\ 0 & \cos(a) & -\sin(a) & 0 \\ 0 & \sin(a) & \cos(a) & 0 \\ 0 & 0 & 0 & 1 \end{bmatrix}$$

  Rotation about the Y axis by an angle a:

$$\begin{bmatrix} \cos(a) & 0 & \sin(a) & 0 \\ 0 & 1 & 0 & 0 \\ -\sin(a) & 0 & \cos(a) & 0 \\ 0 & 0 & 0 & 1 \end{bmatrix}$$

  Rotation about the Z axis by an angle a:

$$\begin{bmatrix} \cos(a) & -\sin(a) & 0 & 0 \\ \sin(a) & \cos(a) & 0 & 0 \\ 0 & 0 & 1 & 0 \\ 0 & 0 & 0 & 1 \end{bmatrix}$$

- Projection Matrix: $$\begin{bmatrix} 1 & 0 & 0 & 0 \\ 0 & -1 & 0 & 0 \\ 0 & 0 & \frac{1}{d} & 0 \\ 0 & 0 & 0 & 1 \end{bmatrix} * \begin{bmatrix} Transformation \\ Matrix \end{bmatrix} * \begin{bmatrix} x \\ y \\ z \\ 1 \end{bmatrix} = \begin{bmatrix} x' \\ -y' \\ \frac{z'}{d} \\ 1 \end{bmatrix}$$

where , $d = \frac{W}{2*\tan(a/2)}$,

W is the screen width in pixels, a is a desired field of view (normally $\frac{\pi}{3}$ to π rad)

A WEB APPLICATION FOR THE DYNAMIC VIRTUAL MUSEUM

At this part of the chapter we present the Web application through which the user can dynamically administrate or use the virtual museum we described earlier. All the tasks concerning the administrating or use of the virtual museum are completed through an easy to use Web interface. There are three types of users in the application, the administrator, the constructor and the simple user. The role of each type of user is discussed exclusively below in this chapter. As mentioned in the introduction, this application restricts not to the presentation of a static, online virtual museum, but it expands to its customization. The basic idea here is that the users have the capability to construct the museum according to his preferences by choosing the virtual objects they like from a database, where they are stored. More specifically, after search, based on different criteria, they can select the objects they want to view at the virtual museum. After this selection, the virtual objects are extracted to an XML file, which in turn is used for the visualization of the museum.

In order to build the above Web application a lot of new technologies have been used. The DBMS that we used for the creation of our database is MySQL, which has full server support for Windows XP and other operating systems. MySQL was combined with Apache Server and PHP. PHP is an HTML-embedded scripting language and has built-in functions that allow the performance of various functions on a MySQL database. After the creation of the database we used the XML language. XML stands for extensive markup language and is designed to describe data and to focus on what data is. XML is a cross-platform, software and hardware independent tool for transmitting information. As far as our application is concerned, the XML file contains the selected by the user objects that finally leads to the creation of the desired in each case virtual museum. Another state of the art technology that was used in our application is Ajax, shorthand for Asynchronous JavaScript and XML. It is a Web development technique for creating interactive Web applications. The intent is to make Web pages feel more responsive by exchanging small amounts of data with the server behind the scenes, so that the entire Web page does not have to be reloaded each time the user makes a change. This is meant to increase the Web page's interactivity, speed, and usability.

The Basic Functions of the Application

After describing the Web application in brief, in this part of the chapter are described the basic functions of the application. Firstly, one should login either as an administrator or a constructor or a simple user to identify oneself to the system.

The rights of each user vary proportionately. Secondly, it is given the capability to add VRML objects-artefacts from a local drive to the database. Thirdly, one can search for the virtual objects that are already stored in the database, select these ones one wants for his or her museum and then preview them in a VRML browser. The searching depends on different criteria such as the period during which these artifacts were constructed. Another option that is provided in this Web application is the extraction of the VRML objects to XML files. These files are used later for the visualization of the museum.

Apart from the plain insertion of objects into the database new fields can be added in the database, new categories of objects can be defined and general one can intervene to the structure of the database.

Figure 1. The login page

Categories of Users and Their Functions

After describing the Web application in brief, in this part of the chapter is described the basic functions of the application. Firstly, one should login as an administrator, a constructor or a simple user to identify oneself to the system. The rights of each user vary proportionately.

After an administrator is identified several options are presented. To begin with, the administrator is the one who is responsible for the creation or deletion of constructors and users. That means, he or she decides whether somebody can be a user or constructor and how many users or constructors the system can support.

An administrator can also add or remove new VRML artifacts from a local drive in the database. Apart from the plain insertion of objects into the database they can define a new category of objects and general intervene to the structure of the database. That means, the database is dynamically constructed so that it can be possible for the administrator to add new fields, which are characteristic for each object. To be more specific, if administrators wish to add a painting to their collection, first they have to define a field for the name of the painter, whereas if they wants to add a sculpture, they have to define a field for the name of the sculptor. They can also view in a VRML browser the selected records with the necessary details in each case and if desired they can modify them. Viewing all the records should be considered an obvious option, given the built-in MySQL functions that PHP has, thus making it possible for the users to sort and view all records by their id number, type, title or any other field An administrator can also, after viewing the first, automatically constructed model, rearrange manually the position of certain artifacts. Finally, they are in charge of the extraction of the files to XML. This is also the last stage of the application, because after that follows the visualization of the museum.

Figure 2. Preview of items for creating a virtual museum

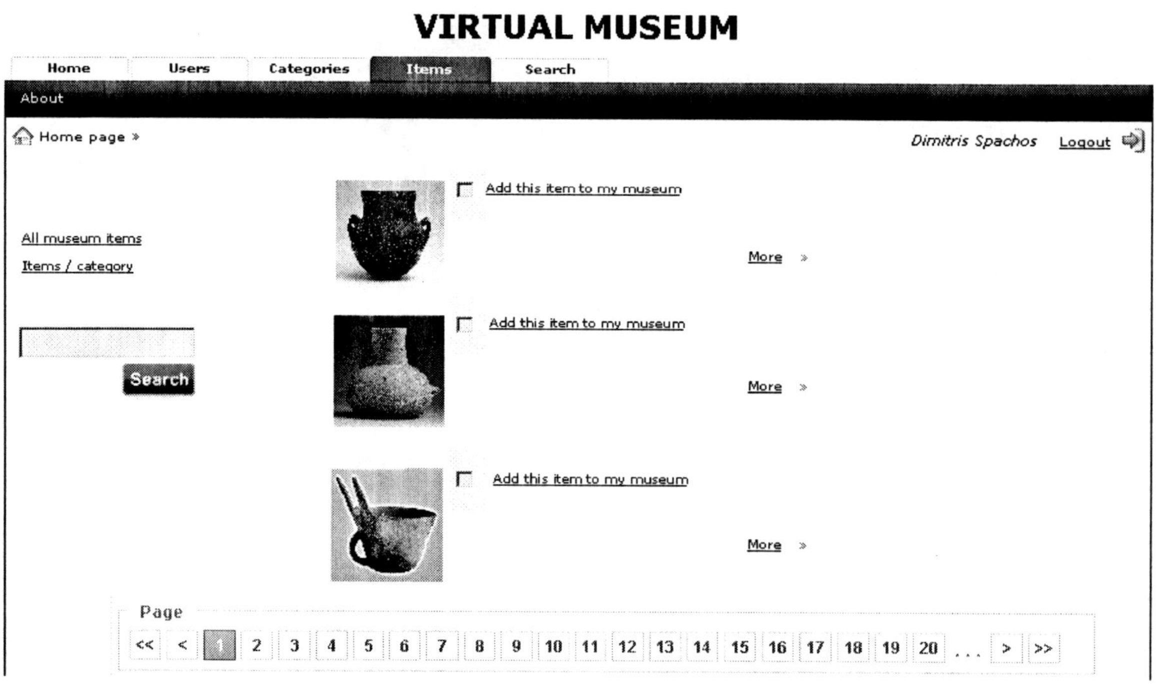

The constructors in turn, have less rights than the administrator. They can do the same things with the administrator, except from creating new users or deleting them. That means they can add new VRML artifacts from a local drive in the database, change some attributes of the selected objects, completely remove them from the database and general interfere in the structure of the database like the administrator. Furthermore, they can view in a VRML browser the existing records with their details. They do their selections for the creation of their own exhibition and finally the virtual objects are extracted to an XML file.

Finally, the simple users have the most restricted rights. All they can do is dynamically construct the database, define a new category of objects, add or change the objects of the database and view the selected objects in a VRML browser. They have neither the right to manage the other users of the system, nor the right to extract their selection to an XML file.

Search and Preview

In this application all kind of users have the ability to search the desired objects under specific criteria. For example, if users were interested in viewing an exhibition of the Roman period, they would then customize their selection to this criterion, namely to the period of time the specific artifacts are included. Another criterion could be the type or the title of the object. For this purpose, the database is constructed in such a way that data is organized into tables with the appropriate fields.

After search, based on specific criteria each time, the user can preview the desired objects in a VRML browser. The VRML viewer that has been chosen for this purpose is the Cortona client from Parallel Graphics. Cortona(r) VRML client is a fast and highly interactive Web3D viewer that is ideal for viewing both simple 3D models and complex interactive solutions on the Web. Cortona VRML client works as a VRML plug-in

Figure 3. Dynamic creation of users

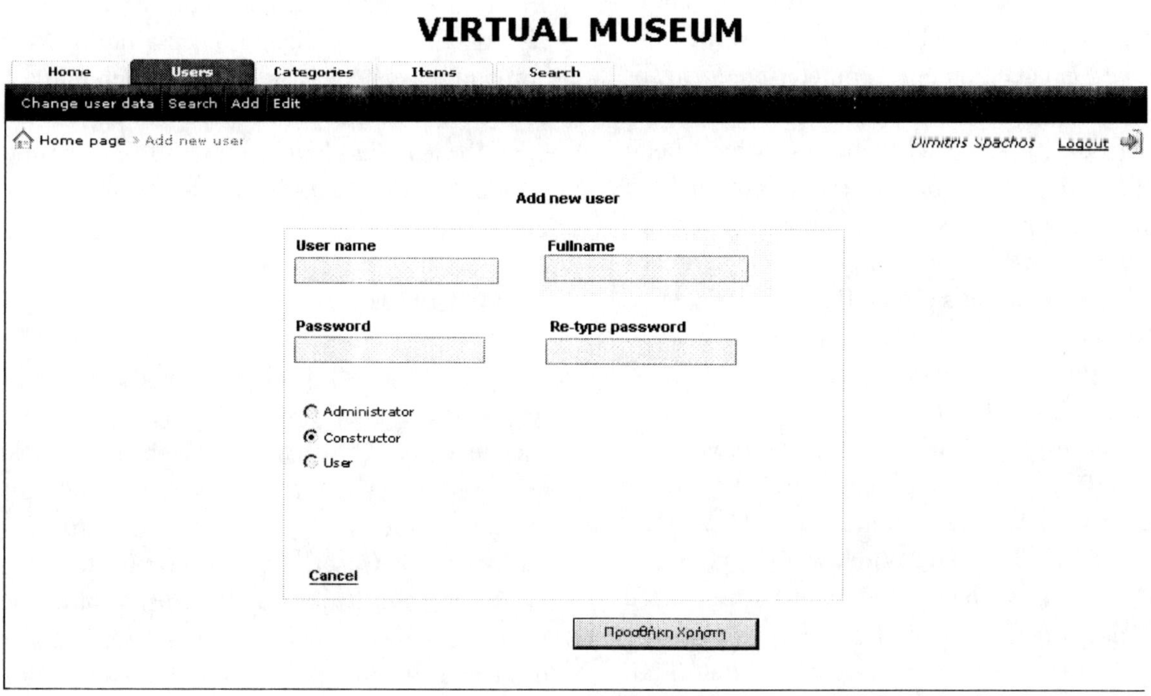

for popular Internet browsers (Internet Explorer, Netscape Navigator, Mozilla and Opera) and office applications (Microsoft PowerPoint, Microsoft Word, etc.). Cortona VRML client will start automatically when you open a file containing VRML world.

Extraction to XML

This function is the administrator's and constructor's responsibility. It is the last step of the construction of the dynamic museum. After previewing the desired objects in a VRML viewer and having concluded to the ones for our exhibition, the extraction to XML follows. More specifically, the xml files contain the basic attributes that are necessary for the description of each VRML object. These attributes, the number of which ranges from 7 to 12, are important for the visualization of the museum, because they depict the details of each object.

INTEROPERABILITY

VRML allows the creation of platform independent 3D objects, described in text files, which can then be displayed on any computer platform for which an appropriate browser exists or plugin. Since today, many VRML browsers have been created and for different platforms.2 Some of these browsers are ported to a great number of popular platforms, like Windows, Linux, MacOSX, Java or Unix and its variants (BSD, IRIX, Solaris, etc.).

Similar is the case with MySQL which has full server support forWindows XP/2003, MacOSX, Solaris, Linux, BSD, HP-UX, AIX, Netware, OpenServer, IRIX and others3. The most common PHP installation is probably the PHP module running with Apache on Linux or a UNIX-variant. But PHP also works on Windows NT and 9x, as well as with a number of other Web servers. You'll find more documentation floating around on the Web that's specific to the Apache/Linux/PHP combo, but it isn't by any means the only platform on which PHP is supported.

A CULTURAL JOURNEY IN THESSALONIKI: USING THE DYNAMIC VIRTUAL MUSEUM BASED ON A COGNITIVE WALKTHROUGH METHOD

A cultural journey is a dynamic hypermedia environment, which proposes the electronic roads as a metaform for exploring cultural information that can form cultural journeys. The electronic roads metaform facilitates travellers to explore the information space in a natural and continuous way very similar to the exploration of physical roads. This metaform is advantageous over existing cultural exploration approaches, which usually apply only to discrete information spaces, failing to provide users with continuous explorations and as a result users may lose their intended destinations.

In the present section we propose an environment based on the Dynamic Virtual Museum which provides extendable cultural and historical content for the city of Thessaloniki, Macedonia. The system is based on a method called cognitive walkthrough. Such a system could be ideal for teaching history and culture; therefore several learning activities can be developed in this context

Introduction

The cognitive walkthrough method is a usability inspection method used to identify usability issues in a piece of software or Web site, focusing on how easy it is for new users to accomplish tasks with the system. The method is rooted in the notion that users typically prefer to learn a system by using it to accomplish tasks, rather than, for example, studying a manual. The method is prized for its ability to generate results quickly with low cost, especially when compared to usability testing, as well as the ability to apply the method early in the design phases, before coding has even begun.

A cognitive walkthrough starts with a task analysis that specifies the sequence of steps or actions required by a user to accomplish a task, and the system responses to those actions. The designers and developers of the software then walk through the steps as a group, asking themselves a set of questions at each step. Data is gathered during the walkthrough, and afterward a report of potential issues is compiled. Finally, the software is redesigned to address the issues identified.

The method was developed in the early nineties by Wharton et al., and reached a large usability audience when it was published as a chapter in Jakob Nielsen's seminal book on usability, "Usability Inspection Methods." The Wharton et al. method required asking four questions at each step, along with extensive documentation of the analysis. In 2000, there was a resurgence in interest in the method in response to a CHI paper by Spencer who described modifications to the method to make it effective in a real software development setting. Spencer's streamlined method required asking only two questions at each step, and involved creating less documentation. Spencer's paper followed the example set by Rowley et al. who described the modifications to the method that they made based on their experience applying the methods in their 1992 CHI paper "The Cognitive Jogthrough."

The effectiveness of methods such as cognitive walkthroughs is hard to measure in applied settings, as there is very limited opportunity for controlled experiments while developing software. Typically measurements involve comparing the number of usability problems found by applying different methods. However, Gray and Salzman called into question the validity of those studies their dramatic 1998 paper "Damaged Merchandise," demonstrating how very difficult it is to measure the effectiveness of usability inspection method. However, the consensus in the usability community is that the congnitive walkthrough method works well in a variety of settings and applications.

In the case of the Dynamic Virtual Museum a number of users are asked to select which virtual museum of the city of Thessaloniki they want to walk through. Each one of the above is referred to different historic period and its exhibition contains different kinds of artefacts varying from paintings, illustrations, monuments and sculptures. The process of walk-through in this case can be divided into three steps:

1. Firstly, the user of the Web environment can see in a form of a film strip the museums/sightseeing of Thessaloniki. (Figure 4). The photos of the museums and the sightseeing are real and the user can click on the one he or she is interested in.
2. Right below the "advertisement" of the most important museums/sightseeing of Thessaloniki there is a map of the city of Thessaloniki, where the user can see where each one is located, how far is one from another and which roads connect them. Every time the user clicks on the photo of a museum/sightseeing, presented in the first step, an arrow emerges that points to the appropriate location in the map. Hence, the user is given a total overview of the museum-map and can see the comparative to the whole map location of the desired museum/sightseeing.
3. Lastly, the user can enter into the virtual museum, out to which the arrow has pointed in the previous step. Clicking on the pointed location, described at step 2, starts the Web application for the Dynamic Virtual Museum. That means the user can walk through the rooms of the museum, add new items and locate them in the museum or add a new room if it is demanded.

Figure 4.

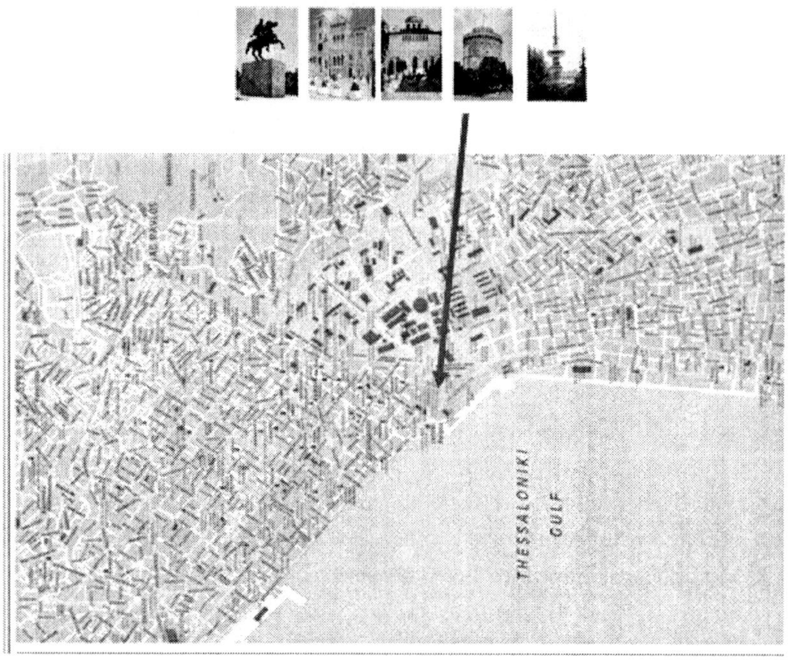

Structure of the Cultural Journey Environment

A cultural journey is an amalgam of the series of ERs that the user selected to explore (i.e., the series of information units the user explored). At every ER stop, a new set of dynamic ERs and an information unit are presented to the traveler. The user explores the information unit content and proceeds by selecting a new ER.

The system presents ERs in groups: Route roads continue the exploration of the information space in the same thematic direction by giving more specific information. The system produces the following different types of exploration roads:

- **Historic period lateral roads** present information of the same thematic context but of different historic periods.
- **Geographical lateral roads** present information of the same thematic context from different geographical areas.
- **Cross-lateral roads** present the cross-linked roads of the selected road.
- **Previous stops** is a list of stops where the traveler changes route by selecting an exploration road.

Information Unit

Information units are the building blocks of the information of the system and consist of the actual content and an attached metadata index. The system contains thousands of information units, which are collected and entered to the system by the cultural experts (Miller, 1998; Weibel & Cathro, 1997).

Part of the information unit of our system could be some historical evidence about Thessaloniki. So, according to the history of Thessaloniki its emergence dates into five eras. Each era could be stored in a different information unit. Five virtual museums were created based on different historic periods, during which Thessaloniki.

When we want, we can add later information units to our system through the Semantic Dictionary Entry tool, which is described later. Below follows the presentation of each historic era.

Hellenistic Era

The city was founded circa 315 BC by Cassander, the King of Macedon (Μακεδών), on or near the site of the ancient town of Therma and 26 other local villages. He named it after his wife Thessalonica, the sister of Alexander the Great. She gained her name from her father, Philip II of Macedon, to commemorate her birth on the day of his gaining a victory (Gr. Nike) over the Phocians, who were defeated with the help of Thessalian horsemen, the best in Greece at that time. Thessalonki means the "victory of Thessalians" (where Thessalians derives from Thessaly which means thesi alos, i.e., "a land that was sea").

Thessaloniki developed rapidly and as early as the 2nd century BC the first walls were built, forming a large square. It was, as all the other contemporary Greek cities, an autonomous part of the Kingdom of Macedon, with its own parliament where the King was represented and could interfere in the city's domestic affairs.

Roman Era

After the fall of the kingdom of Macedon in 168 BC, Thessalonica became a city of the Roman Republic. It grew to be an important trade-hub located on the Via Egnatia, a Roman road that connected Byzantium (later Constantinople), with Dyrrhachium (now Durres in Albania), facilitating trade between Europe and Asia. The city became the capital of one of the four Roman districts of Macedonia. It kept its privileges but was ruled by a praetor and had a Roman garrison. For a short time in the 1st century BC, all the Greek provinces came under Thessalonica. Due to the city's key commercial importance, a spacious harbour was built by the Romans, the famous Burrow Harbour (Σκαπτός Λιμήν) that accommodated the city's trade up to the eighteenth century; later, with the help of silt deposits from the river Axios, it was reclaimed as land and the port built beyond it. Remnants of the old harbour's docks can be found nowadays under Odos Frangon Street, near the catholic church.

Thessaloniki's acropolis, located in the northern hills, was built in 55 BC after Thracian raids in the city's outskirts, for security reasons.

Thessaloniki acquired a patron saint, St. Demetrius, in 306. He is credited with a number of miracles that saved the city. He was the Roman Proconsul of Greece under the anti Christian emperor Maximian and was martyred at a Roman prison, where today lays the Church of St. Demetrius, first built by the Roman subprefect of Illyricum Leontios in 463.

Other important remains from this period include the Arch and Tomb of Galerius, located near the center of the modern city.

Byzantine Era

When the Roman Empire was divided into eastern and western segments ruled from Byzantium/Constantinople and Rome, respectively, Thessaloniki came under the control of the Eastern Roman Empire (Byzantine Empire). Its importance was second only to Constantinople itself. In 390 it was the location of a revolt against the emperor Theodosius I and his Gothic mercenaries. Botheric, their general, together with several of his high officials, were killed in an uprising triggered by the imprisoning of a favorite local charioteer for pederasty with one of Botheric's slave boys.[3] 7,000-15,000 of the citizens were massacred in the city's hippodrome in revenge, an act which earned Theodosius a temporary excommunication.

At that time, despite the various invasions, Thessaloniki had a large population and flourishing commerce. That resulted in an intellectual and artistic florescence that can be traced in the numerous churches and their frescoes of that era and also by the names of scholars that taught there (Thomas Magististos, Dimitrios Triklinios, Nikiforos Choumnos, Kostantinos Armenopoulos, Neilos Kavassilas, etc.). Many fine examples of Byzantine art survive in the city, particularly the mosaics in some of its historic churches, including the basilica of Hagia Sophia and the church of St. George.

Ottoman Era

The Byzantine Empire, unable to hold it against the Ottoman Empire advance, sold it to Venice, which held it until it was captured by the Ottoman Sultan Murad II on March 29, 1430, after a 3-day-long siege. The Ottomans had captured Thessaloniki in 1387, but lost it after the Battle of Ankara against Tamerlane in 1402.

During Ottoman times, the city received an influx of Muslims and Jews. Architectural remains from the Ottoman period can be found mainly in the "Ano Poli" (upper town) which has the only traditional wooden houses and fountains that survived the great fire. In the city centre, a number of the stone mosques survived, notably the "Hamza-Bey Camii" on Egnatia (under restoration), the "Alatza Imaret Camii" on Kassandrou Street, "Bezesteni" on Venizelou Street, and "Yahoudi Hamam" on Frangon Street. Almost all of the more than 40 minarets collapsed in the fire, or were demolished after 1912; the only surviving one is at the Rotonda (Arch and Tomb of Galerius). There are also a few remaining Ottoman hammams (bathhouses), particularly the "Hamam Bey" on Egnatia Avenue.

Modern Era

Thessaloniki was the main "prize" of the First Balkan War, as a result of which it was united with Greece on October 26, 1912. This date has an immense importance for the city as, in addition to the aforementioned historic event of the unification, it also marks the nameday of Saint Demetrius, its patron saint.

Semantic Dictionary

The semantic dictionary structures the cultural information of the system (i.e., information units) in a hierarchical manner from general to specific and also captures the multicontextual dimensions (i.e., crosslinks) that each information unit may have. The system provides a user friendly Semantic Dictionary Entry Tool that assists the culture experts to easily construct it. A universal cultural Semantic Dictionary has been developed that could be applied to any country's culture. It is classified by country, historic period and a repetitive standard part that describes science, architecture, arts, folk arts/food and history (Fakas et al., 2004).

After the creation of the museums, the group of users asked to categorized each one of the following landmarks and monuments in the correct historic period time or in the correct virtual museum. The landmarks and the monuments were the following:

Landmarks

- **The White Tower of Thessaloniki** (Lefkos Pyrgos), widely regarded as the symbol of the city. It has been known by many names and is now home to the Museum of Byzantine Cultures. The top of the tower has excellent views of the city.
- **The Arch and Tomb of Galerius** is more commonly known as the "Kamara," is ornately decorated and made with a reddish coloured stone.
- The upper town or "**Ano Poli**" is what remains of Ottoman Thessaloniki, beautiful wooden houses overhang the winding streets all the way up to the Eptapyrgio at the top of the city. The Ano Poli also contains some of the city's oldest and most important church-

es, particularly Osios David, St. Nicolaos Orphanos and Vlatades Monastery.

- **The Church of Aghios Demetrios** is the most important church in the entire city. Lying above the remains of the agora and the Roman Forum, the church has three side-chapels, a museum, and underground catacombs that also include Saint Demetrios' imprisonment chamber. He is the patron saint of the city.
- **OTE Tower**, a TV tower is the centre of the Thessaloniki Expo Centre. A revolving restaurant offers great views of the city.
- The **waterfront** is Thessaloniki's major drawcard. The promenade of Nikis Avenue runs from the White Tower of Thessaloniki to the giant palace that is now a ferry terminal. Numerous shops and cafes line the waterfront.
- **The Rotonda** or the **Church of Aghios Georgios**, which is a circular church lacking the classic Orthodox iconostasis. The church is built upon former Roman and Greek pagan ruins.
- **Aristotelous Square**, extending all the way from Nikis Avenue on the waterfront to the Church of Panayia Halkeion. The square, shaped like a bottle, is lined with tall archondika, or mansions of the rich, that have now been converted to shops and hotels. A large park lies at the north end of the square, and Thessaloniki's thriving old market is just one block away to the east and west.
- The area surrounding the **Church of Aghia Sofia**, also located in the city centre, includes the large church and paved alleyways that make the few blocks around it famous.
- The extensive **Byzantine walls** of the upper town (Ano Poli) and kastro.
- **The Kyvernion** (little palace); former residence of the King and Queen of Greece; in the Karabournaki area, in Eastern Thessaloniki
- **The Modern Concert Hall of Thessaloniki** in the East side of the city, near the Posidonion sports center.
- **Thessaloniki Intemational Trade Fair** held every September, organised by Helexpo.

Monuments

- The Arch and Tomb of Galerius
- The extensive city walls
- Trigonian Tower and the Castra area
- The ancient Agora
- The Rotunda
- The Roman Palace and Hippodrome
- The Church of Hagia Sofia

Discussion and Conclusion

Through the process of constructing the virtual museums, users were able to learn the most important historic information for the city of Thessaloniki. They learn that in the history of Thessaloniki there were five important eras, for each one of them the developed a virtual museum using the Dynamic Virtual Museum Web application described in the previous section. Then, the next task was to collect the most important landmarks and monuments, information and at least one picture for each one of them.

The last task was to categorize the list of the landmarks and the monuments and insert each one of the list items in the correct virtual museum or in the correct historic era.

The result was five virtual museums, one for each of the five historic eras. A visitor who wants to take a virtual tour on the Byzantine era, for example, is able to choose the Byzantine virtual museum and learn about the most important remains that this period includes.

The above was just an example on how the Dynamic Virtual Museum can be used for learning purposes based on usability inspection methods, like the cognitive walkthrough method.

ARION & ORPHEUS: VIRTUAL ENVIRONMENTS FOR THE RECREATION OF ANCIENT GREEK MUSIC

In recent years several efforts have been recorded in Greece and elsewhere in reconstructing AGM instruments, both physically and with physical modeling techniques (Tsahalinas et al., 1997). The most notable was the reconstruction of the ancient hydraulis by the European Cultural Centre of Delphi in 1999[2]. A wide range of other instruments has been also presented in exhibitions and live performances (Halaris). As prototypes for this restoration have been used fragments of AGM instruments found in excavations or descriptions of them in papyri. Some other indicative efforts of AGM instruments physical reconstruction are mentioned next:

- The Greek band "Lyraulos" has reconstructed and demonstrated 40 ancient Greek musical instruments, for example, lyra, barbitos, phorminx, and so forth.
- Michalis Georgiou and the AGM orchestra "Terpandros" work on an effort to revive the sounds of the antiquity.
- Nikolaos Bras constructs copies of the AGM instruments and cooperates with the band "Demonia Nymphi" for live performances.
- The instruments Aulos and Kithara were reconstructed in projects of the Austrian Academy of Sciences.
- The ensemble Musica Romana reconstructed and played instruments (e.g., water organ).
- Ensemble Kerylos and Annie Belis, who has reconstructed ancient instruments for her archaeological works.

The Museum of Ancient, Byzantine and Meta-Byzantine Musical Instruments, which was established in 1977, exhibits more than 200 copies of musical instruments that are dated from 2800 BC until the beginning of the 20th century. Their construction is based on evidence and sources that were collected and studied by the Aristotle University of Thessaloniki, Greece. The museum hosts a collection of instruments, like lyra, kithara, phorminx, the 6-stringed pandouris, and so forth.

The aim of the ORPHEUS project is to digitize the musical instruments presented in physical exhibitions and demonstrate their use and sounds to the public. ORPHEUS is an interactive presentation of Ancient Greek Musical Instruments and comprises a multimedia application, which revives antiquity, just like virtual museums. The virtual environment of ORPHEUS allows the experimentation with the use and the sounds of the becauseed ancient instruments. The ancient Greek guitar ("Kithara"), which was the first becauseed instrument, can be virtually strummed using the mouse or the keyboard. The auditory result is ancient Greek melodies. The application, which is accompanied by information about the history of ancient Greek Music and a picture gallery relative to the ancient Greek instruments, has mainly educational character. Its main scope is to demonstrate the ancient Greek musical instruments to the audience.

Complementary to the ORPHEUS project, another application (ARION) has been produced. ARION provides a unique interface for ancient Greek music composition and reproduction. ARION can accurately reproduce ancient Greek melodies, using the sound of avlos, as well as vocal elements. The function of the application is based on the mapping and conversion of each ancient Greek music symbol to the modern western notation system. ARION can also be used for music synthesis, as the reverse process (from western music to ancient Greek symbolism) is feasible. The user can experiment with the various scales, symbols and frequencies having the total freedom to "imagine" and hear how ancient Greek music really was. ORPHEUS and ARION together revive ancient Greek music.

Introduction

It is true that we know very little about ancient Greek music (from this point and forth: AGM) primarily because we have no actual recordings or hearings and secondly because sources about eastern music, the successor of AGM, are scattered and not thoroughly indexed, as is the case with its counterpart, western music. Furthermore, it is difficult for researchers with a profound musical education in western music and culture, well advanced in diatonicism and tempered scales to understand the chromatic (Politis, Margounakis, & Mokos, 2004; Politis & Margounakis, 2003) and enharmonic background of AGM (West, 1992). On the other hand, researchers and pioneers like West (1992) and Pöhlmann and West (2001) have managed to collect and organize a very large amount of documents and actual music scores and have given a scientific insight for a music system over 2,000 years old. This project takes their work and tries to make a connection between that music and prevailing modern western music. Two software instruments are produced: ORPHEUS and ARION.

According to Greek mythology, Orpheus (son of Apollo and the muse Calliope) was a poet and musician. After his wife Eurydice's death, he went to the underworld to ask for her return. The guard dog Cerberus fell asleep listening to his music, while Hades was moved by it and let her go under a condition: Orpheus should not look at her eyes until they were back to the sunshine. Orpheus couldn't resist and as he turned around to look at her, she died again forever.

Arion was a famous musician at the court of Periander, king of Corinth. A dolphin saved his life, after he tried to commit suicide by springing into the sea from a boat. Before his drowning attempt, he played lyre and sang on the boat. His music was so wonderful that it fascinated the dolphins in the sea. So, they just followed the boat and one of them saved him.

Music in Ancient Greece

An Overview

A first elementary clue, which is extracted from the research on AGM, is that the singer possessed the main role on a musical performance. The soloist's voice was the basic "instrument" in a performance. The melody came indispensably from singing. A musical instrument accompanied the sung Greek poetry. Ancient Greek poetry and tragedy was inseparable from music (Borzacchini & Minnuni, 2001). The term "lyric" stems from the word "lyre."

In ancient Greece, the roles of composers and performers intertwined with each other. The reason why not so many handwritten scores from this era exist today, is that performers used to improvise on the musical instrument, while the soloist was singing the melody, and not read notes from papers. In general, the performer followed the singer's tempo and sound, but he also tried to achieve heterophony (by improvising). So, the performer was also the composer at the same time.

As it can be easily conceived from the above, the nature of ancient Greek music was purely melodic and rhythmic. Aristides Quintilianus states: "Music is the science of melody and all elements having to do with melody" (Winnington-Ingram, 1932). This definition of music goes all the way with the monophonic and melodic structure of ancient Greek music.

Although not so many handwritten scores of AGM have been saved, there are (luckily) abundant about AGM theory. Numerous treatises in Greek, Latin and Arabic have survived which, mingled with the study of other material, became integrated into the cultures of all Western peoples, the heirs of Hellenic learning (Harmonia, 1979).

Musical Instruments

There are several references about the musical instruments, which were used in AGM. Some of them namely are: the lyra, the avlos, the kithara, the hydravlis, the monochordon, the trichordon, and so forth.

The monochordon, the lyra, the kithara and the trichordon constitute some examples of ancient stringed instruments. The monochordon (or monochord) was a rectangular sound box of arbitrary length with a single string, which could be derived by a movable bridge (Rieger, 1996). The kithara was a plucked string instrument and consisted of a square wooden box that extended at one end into heavy arms. Originally it had five strings, but additional strings were later added to include seven and finally eleven strings. These were stretched from the sound box across a bridge and up to a crossbar fastened to the arms (San Francisco Performances).

The avlos and its variations were a kind of wind instruments. In this first version of ARION, the sound of the musical instrument, which accompanies the ancient Greek singer, is an approach of the sound of avlos, while the ancient kithara is the first instrument that was modeled in ORPHEUS.

Ancient Greek Musical Notation

The Greeks had two systems of musical notation, which correspond note for note with each other: one for the vocal and one for the instrumental melody. The instrumental system of notation is comprised of numerous distinct signs probably derived from an archaic alphabet, while the vocal system is based on the 24 letters of the Ionic alphabet.

The whole system covers a little over three octaves. In particular, it contains notes between Eb-3 (155, 6 Hz) and G-6 (1568, 1 Hz). This range of notes has been implemented and appears on the default form of ARION. The symbols form groups of three. The first symbol (from the left) in each triad represents a "natural" note on a diatonic scale. The symbol in the middle represents the sharpening of the "natural" note, while the third symbol represents the flattening of the "natural" note.

Problem Formulation

The Challenge of ARION

The challenge of the project is to be consistent to the source material and create an AGM composer with scientific accuracy and the same time to produce a synthesizing instrument with an easy to use interface targeting noncomputer science experts.

How can you faithfully reproduce ancient music when you had never heard something like it[3]? The only safe way is to follow the work of experts in the field and the actual musical scores. But even these are usually incomplete. Also, the instruments used at the time were very different than modern or even medieval ones. Moreover, the true ancient Greek accent is different from the modern Greek one and from the one used by foreigners today (the so called Erasmian) (Devine & Stephens, 1994), so extended research had to be carried out on the vocal reproduction of the lyrics.

The synthesis of the singing voice is a research area that has evolved over the last 30 years. Different aspects of this implicative field involve the interdisciplinary area of musical acoustics, signal processing, linguistics, artificial intelligence, music perception and cognition, music information retrieval and performance systems (Georgaki, 2004).

Development Issues

ARION was built using Microsoft's .NET framework and more particularly the object-oriented language Microsoft Visual Basic .NET 2005. The framework is a set of libraries engineered specifically to enhance the development of Microsoft Windows oriented applications. It provides smooth interconnectivity to the underlying application programming interface of the operating system and the means to manipulate each aspect of it. This application implements extensive use of the GDI+ calls that affect the graphical user interface and provide us the ability to create our own controls or to extend pre-existing ones. The application also uses XML tables for storing the data of the ancient Greek notes and their association to modern ones. The development has been done in Windows XP Professional environment, but its function is not limited to this operating system. The application works properly under all versions of Windows XP (since .NET Framework 2.0. is installed), Windows 2003 and Windows Vista.

Moreover, the following programs have been used during the construction phase of the application for the creation and processing of graphics, setup files and help files:

- Corel PhotoPaint 12
- Microsoft FrontPage 2003
- High-Logic Font Creator 5.5
- Microsoft HTML Help Workshop 1.3
- Macrovision InstallShield 12
- Macrovision DemoShield 8

As far as the programming structure is concerned, the application code is object-oriented in order to provide a better structure and flexibility in case of future changes.

ARION's interface comprises of: 13 forms that are used for the appearance of all necessary information for the user, 6 user controls that represent the notes on staff and the Symbol Repertory, as well as the "*Insert Note*" and "*Insert Lyrics*" fields, and four files that contain the auxiliary classes, which are necessary for the storing of several kinds of data and the implementation of peripheral functions.

The 13 forms are namely: *Main (frmMain.vb), Edit Note 1 (frmEditNote.vb), About, Export Settings, Properties, Delete Note, Ancient Duration, Modern Duration, Manage, Panel Description, frmAddInstrument, Synchronize, Edit Note 2 (frmEditNote2.vb)*. Their use would become more tangible in the Tutorial section.

The creation of six new user controls was qualified as necessary, because the predefined Windows controls were not able to fulfil all the requirements of the application in terms of functionality and usability. In particular, the drag & drop functions and (mainly) the controls that correspond to the instruments and their containing notes could not be implemented via the predefined user controls, because the required functions are too complicated. If the predefined user controls were to be used, the result would be a hard to use and dysfunctional code. Therefore, the new complicated user controls were created aiming at the simplicity of the required functions by grouping the functions in two categories: those that concern notes and those that concern musical instruments. Several techniques, which have been implemented in order for the final application to be produced, are mentioned later on the chapter.

Lots of decisions have been taken concerning the *usability engineering* in order to achieve an easy-to-use and easy-to-learn interface. Also, testing led the development team to the implementation of designing prediction solutions for the avoidance of possible misuses of the user, which may lead to unexpected results during the running of the application. The components, which are used in all forms of ARION, have been chosen in order for the "creation" of mistakes by the user not to be feasible. For instance, the application contains locked combo boxes that do not allow the choice of an invalid value and UpDown boxes with strictly defined bounds that discard far-out values, which may corrupt the normal execution of the application. Also, most of the possible usability rules have been applied, for example, the mapping of the *enter* and *escape* keys to the buttons *OK* and *cancel*, or the existence of shortcut keys for the menu commands.

The graphics device interface (GDI) is the Microsoft Windows subsystem, which undertakes the graphics designing. By the term *graphics*, we mean the beelines, the curves and the fonts that may comprise a window. To all intents, it is about an application programming interface (API), which intervenes between the applications and the hardware of a computer and accomplishes all the necessary functions for the appearance of graphics on the user visual display unit. Therefore, there is no need for the programmer to handle the diversification of the hardware (and primarily the graphics card) of each computer system.

GDI+ (the successor of GDI) for Windows XP comprehends advanced capabilities of 2-dimensional vector graphics processing, such as line smoothing methods, object transparency, and so forth. GDI was originally designed to allow the use of only C/C++ applications. Nevertheless, .NET Framework (on which ARION is based) disposes the System.Drawing library, which allows the access to the GDI+ functions. It should be mentioned that GDI+ API comprises of 40 classes, which are used to execute all the offered functions.

ARION makes extensive use of GDI+, because this system is used in order to draw:

- The **Symbol Repertory notes**, which also change colour when the cursor "touches" them, or when the user drags them for inserting them in an instrument melody.
- The modern western music **staff**, including the clefs.
- The **ancient Greek notes** and their duration.
- The **modern western notes**, which may also contain extra auxiliary staff lines.
- The **frames** and the **icons** of Music panels and Lyrics panels, which represent the instruments and the lyrics.
- The **about** window, which is dynamically created during the application execution.

The GDI+ capabilities are separated in 3 categories:

- Those concerning the 2-D vector graphics
- Those concerning the (nonvector) images
- Those concerning the fonts' appearance (typography)

ARION uses functions from all three categories, although the main capabilities used fall on the first and the third category.

The GDI+ functions of **2-dimensional vector graphics** are used in the application for the drawing of the staff and its possible necessary extensions in certain notes, as well as the design of several Symbol Repertory elements, without however the symbol of the note. Moreover, the background and the Music panels and Lyrics panels frames make use of the same functions.

GDI+ defines a system of rectangular coordinates, using *pixel* as measure and the upper left corner of the surface as a start, in order to draw the graphics on the surface of the prementioned components (Box 1).

This is feasible by using a Visual Basic command (just like the following one) that creates a graphics object *g*, on which all the GDI+ functions can be applied.

```
Dim g As Graphics = e.Graphics
```

Next, functions like *DrawLine* (Box 2) could be called for the object *g*, in order to draw a line. The next figure shows the result of the DrawLine call for drawing a black line with width of

Box 1.

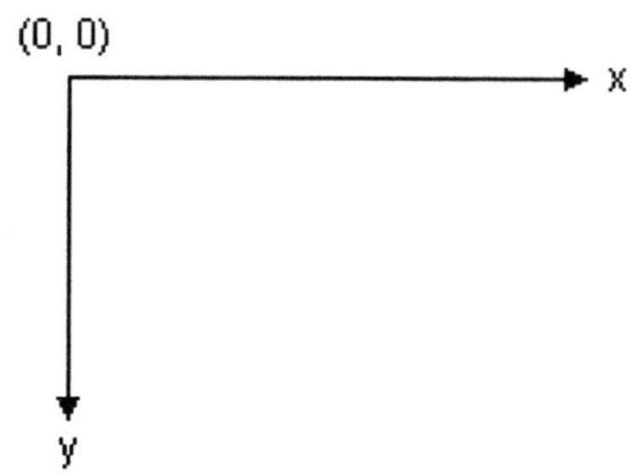

1 pixel, which would start from the pixel with coordinates (4,2) and end at the pixel (12,8). It should be mentioned here that the creation of an object that belongs to the *Pen* class and has the desirable properties is necessary for configuring the color and the line width.

In ARION, all the object frames of Symbol Repertory (that is the user components of Note Repertory type), MusicPanel and LyricsPanel, and the staff (on the frame dedicated to modern western music) are designed using *DrawLine*. Moreover, using the *DrawRectangle* function that draws rectangles of a certain colour value, the colours of the objects on Symbol Repertory, MusicPanel and LyricsPanel are defined.

The **imaging** (nonvector) functions are used for difficult to present in a vector manner graphics, when the use of bitmap images is much easier. The use of such function in the application is limited. In particular, they are used for the appearance of two images at the left side of MusicPanel. Those images make clear whether the particular object (MusicPanel) is related to an instrument or voice. In addition, indirect use of the Imaging functions is made for the occurrence of the toolbars icons and the application menus, from Visual Basic's Form Designer.

The **typography** functions (third category) are used in several different occasions in ARION. Specifically, the DrawString function (whose aim is to draw characters on GDI+'s objects surface) is used for:

Box 2.

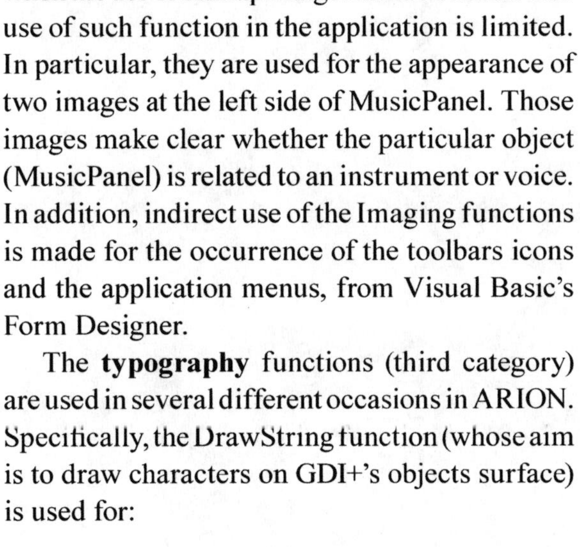

- **Symbol Repertory**, in the order the notes symbols to appear
- **Ancient Greek musical instruments**
- **Staff**, in the order the modern notes to appear
- **About** window, where the information appears dynamically during the execution of the application.

This solution, that is, the embedment of different necessary symbols in the *MusicSymbols* and *ModernMusic* fonts, has been chosen because it offers a flexible way of usage, as it is about vector graphics that may appear "clearly" in any necessary size, but is also relatively easy to add new musical symbols in the future, without interfering at the inner structure of ARION's executable file. *Pen* objects are used in order to form the fonts in GDI. In some occasions though, *Rectangles* (in which the character to appear is centered) are used. Depending on each occasion's needs, any of the different versions of *DrawString* may be used.

ARION's interface has been designed in such a way that future changes are as easy as possible (if this is necessary). The modular architecture of the interface minimizes the possibility of future extensive programming code interferences that may result in a problematic normal execution. Besides, the most important fact about this programming style is that the application does not undertake any function of music or voice production itself, but assigns them to independent parsers, which use the data of the user's music composition as input. Moreover, the music symbols that correspond to notes are registered in font files, so as any modification to be easy and platform-independent. That way, recompilation of the application code proves to be unnecessary for any changes embedment.

The CSound Music Language

The sound of the instruments that this project performs was made with the use of CSound. CSound is a programming language designed and optimized for sound rendering and signal processing. The language consists of over 450 opcodes, the operational codes that the sound designer uses to build "instruments" or patches. Usually, two text files are created, an .orc (orchestra) file containing the "instruments," and a .sco (score) file containing the "notes." The CSound interpreter works by first translating the set of text-based instruments, found in the orchestra file, into a computer data-structure that is machine-resident. Then, it performs these user-defined instruments by interpreting the list of note events and parameter data that the program "reads" from: a text-based score file, a sequencer-generated MIDI file, a real-time MIDI controller, real-time audio, or nonMIDI devices such as the ASCII keyboard and mouse.

Depending on the speed of the used computer (and the complexity of the instruments in your orchestra file) the performance of this "score" can either be auditioned in real-time, or written directly into a file on your hard disk. This entire process is referred to as "sound rendering" as analogous to the process of "image rendering" in the world of computer graphics.

The original sound fonts used in ARION were taken from reconstructed AGM instruments.

The Phoneme Modeler

ARION uses 32 synthesized phonemes for the voice production of the ancient Greek singer. The default phoneme configuration of ARION were designed in a special interface for this purpose; the Phoneme Modeler.

The Phoneme Modeler is a TCL/TK interface for the modeling and processing of phonemes. It makes use of the syntmono server, which manipulates SKINI messages and is part of the synthesis toolkit (STK) in C++ (Scavone &

Figure 5. The graphical user interface of Phoneme Modeler

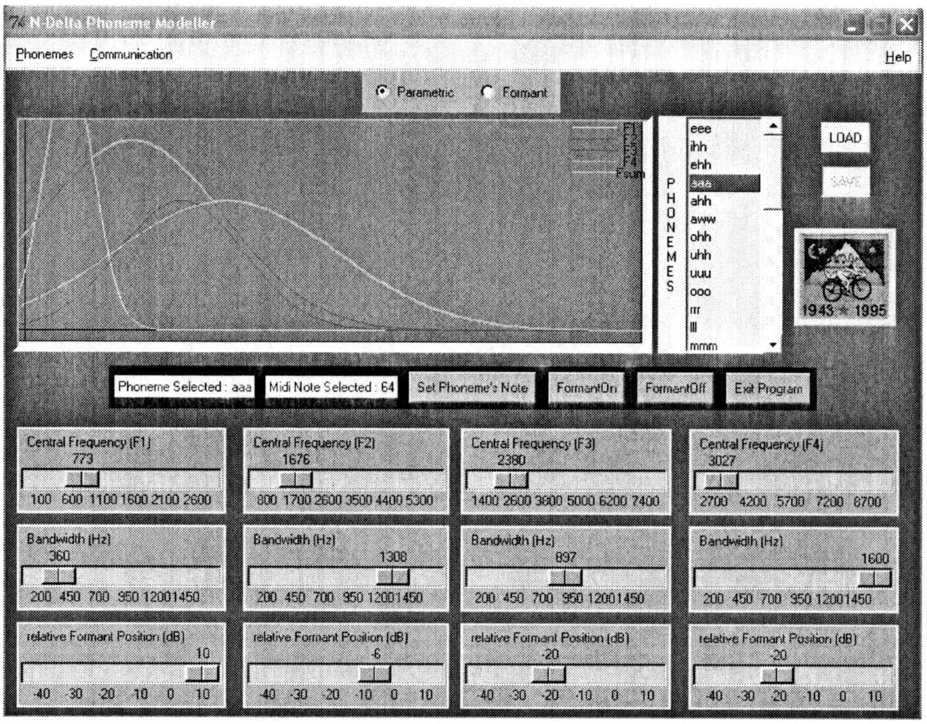

Cook, 2004). These messages are created in the Phoneme Modeler application and are sent to the server, where their processing results to the auditory reproduction of the phoneme. The Phoneme Modeler interface can be seen in Figure 5.

As it can be seen, the interface represents the attributes of each phoneme with sliders. The user may define the central frequency, the bandwidth and the relative position of the 1st, 2nd, 3rd and 4th formant of each of the 32 phonemes.

The default configuration of ARION phonemes has been achieved by analyzing (by means of sound processing) recordings of several historians and archeologists' reciting on Homer and Plato's works, and resynthesizing their accent on the Phoneme Modeler.

Ancient Greek Music Sources

After the latest important additions of the last years, the total amount of original AGM texts comes up to 61. The melodies, most of them fragmented, have survived as stone inscriptions or musical papyri (scraps of papyrus, the ancient equivalent of paper) containing musical notation. The most recent and full edition of the AGM extant texts bears the thoroughness of the two universally recognized AGM experts Egert Pöhlmann and Martin West (2001). The "Song of Seikilos" is the only fully extant musical text of antiquity. Substantially, it is about a small column dated in the AD 2nd century. The preserved poem—engraved on the small pillar—is a small verse that comments on the meaning of life, praising mostly at the welfare. It is about a very small, but indicative of the ancient Greek music, composition. The column is exhibited in the Museum of Copenhagen.

While it is certainly true that the hearings are lost, recent research has satisfactorily deciphered AGM notation and rhythm. In fact, we know quite a lot: we know a great deal about the rhythms and the tempo of the music, because these are reflected in the metrical patterns of Greek verse (Pöhlmann & West, 2001). Adequate knowledge has been gathered about the musical system, that is, how the scales were conceived and the like, since the works of several Greek musical theorists survive, like those of Aristoxenus and Archytas, which are dated in 4th century BC (Winnington-Ingram, 1932; Burkert, 1972; Barker, 1989). Instead of using ratios, Aristoxenus divided the tetrachord into 30 parts, of which, in his diatonic syntonon, each tone has 12 parts, each semitone 6 (Barbour, 1972). Some of the musical intervals that were used are even smaller than the space between two keys on our piano, a common feature of oriental scales. There are several writers, like Otto Gombosi (1939) that managed to interpret and recognize the microtonal nature of ancient Greek music theory and practice. Ancient Greek music theorists, like Archytas, Eratosthenes, Didymus and Ptolemy propose exact ratios for the intervals of nondiatonic ancient greek music systems, and even versions of the diatonic with microtonal modifications (Franklin, 2005).

We can infer much about the instruments, using as evidence surviving fragments of ancient instruments (Halaris; Tsahalinas et al., 1997), depictions on vases and wall paintings, literary descriptions, and cross-cultural comparison.

In AGM scripts, above each line of Greek is notation that looks mostly like Greek letters, but is in fact vocal musical notation. Interestingly, as it has been mentioned before, ancient musicians had two completely separate systems of musical notation, the one meant for voice, and the other for instruments (West, 1992). Some of these symbols can be seen in Figure 6.

Related Work

Lots of research has been done in recent years on the field of text-to-speech synthesis. The digitized speaking voice and vocoders are a major aspect of this area.

One step ahead, the research has performed an amazing evolution over the last decades on

Figure 6. Notes for vocal performance, chosen from a pool of symbols comprising the Instrumental and Vocal Repertory

the synthesis of the singing voice. The efforts of the scientists were focused on the separation of the speaking and the singing voice, taking into account the special characteristics the singing voice has (e.g., frequency, vibrato, tempo, etc.). There are plenty of works worldwide on singing synthesis (Carlson, Ternstrom, & Sundberg, 1991; Chowning, 1981; Cook, 1993).

There is also some relative work on Greek music. Two text-to-speech/singing projects on Greek music are IGDIS (Cook, Kamarotos, Diamantopoulos & Philippis, 1993) and AOIDOS (Xydas & Kouroupetoglou, 2001). The latter is a virtual Greek singer (vocal synthesizer) for analysis and synthesis of Greek singing.

ORPHEUS

The first of the two AGM applications is about the modeling and presentation of the AGM instruments to the audience. ORPHEUS is a multimedia application, designed with Macromedia Flash MX, which also incorporates Microsoft Agents Technology. ORPHEUS has mainly an educational character.

The central user interface of ORPHEUS is presented in Figure 7. The music track that can be listened to during the introduction of the presentation has been exclusively written for the application and is about a musical composition with contemporary hearings, which is influenced from AGM in many ways (melody, instruments, modes, rhythm).

The six circles / buttons correspond to the six different functions of the application. After selecting a submenu by clicking one of the six pictures, the user can confirm the selection in the next screen or return to the main menu by pressing the "Back" button.

The first circle contains a rich photo gallery with pictures that are relative to the Ancient Greek Music. The user can get acquainted with the way AGM instruments looked, as well as the way they were used by musicians, through snapshots from angiographies and wall paintings. The photographic material comes from real archaeological treasures of ancient Greece. Information about the AGM instruments can be found in the second circle.

The third circle leads to the interactive surface, where the ancient Greek instruments are presented. The virtual library of "ORPHEUS" contains 11 ancient Greek musical instruments right now:

- Lyra
- Barbitos
- Kithara
- Phorminx
- Pandouris (madoline)
- Diaulos (Double Aulos)
- Triangle
- Syntono
- Halkeofono
- Tympanon
- Hydravlis

The instruments are also supported in the "ARION" application for AGM composition, as it

Figure 7. The graphical user interface of ORPHEUS

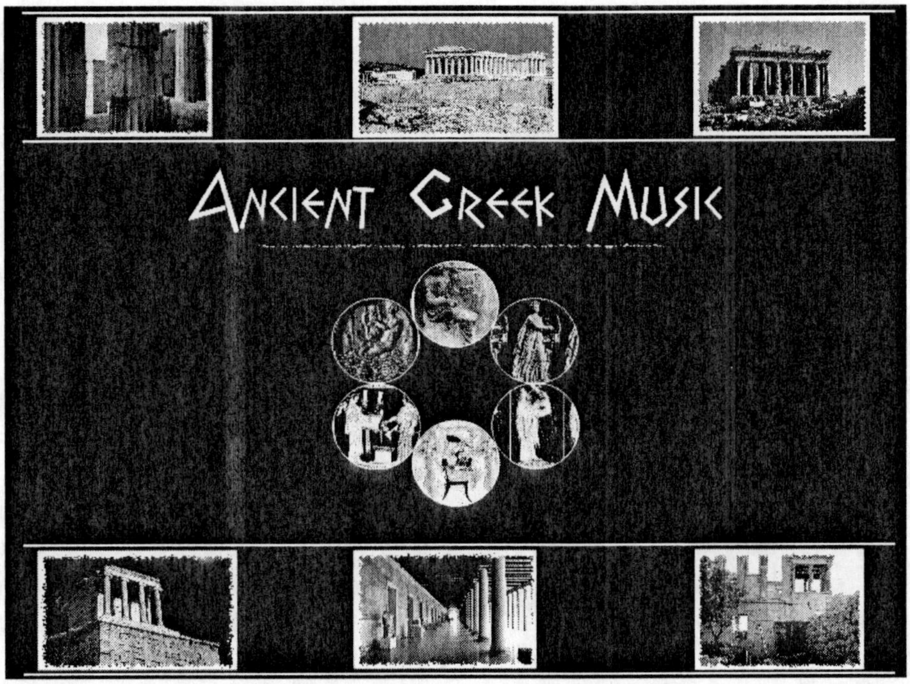

Figure 8. The ancient Greek guitar (Kithara)

is shown next. The first modeled instrument, which is the ancient Greek kithara, is demonstrated here (for more information about kithara, see section Musical Instruments).

The electronic visualization of the ancient guitar is based on information that was extracted from writings and angiographies, which have survived from that era. The user is able to "touch" the strings of the guitar (either using the mouse or the keyboard shortcuts) and create that way ancient Greek melodies and sounds.

As the figure shows, the modeled guitar represents the latest version of the instrument: the one with 11 strings. The microtonal nature of the ancient guitar's strings (the sound has been materialized with physical modeling) has been implemented according to the correspondence of the ancient Greek symbols to the modern notes (West, 1992), which can be seen in Table 1.

The last three circles – menus of the application concern the common functions "Help," "About" and "Credits."

ARION – A Tutorial

The graphical user interface of ARION can be seen in Figure 9.

The application consists of three major surfaces: The Symbol Repertory surface, the Ancient Greek Music surface and the Modern Greek Music surface.

The Symbol Repertory is the container of all AGM symbols used by the application. It holds the instrumental and the vocal symbols. While browsing through the symbols the user can see as a tool tip the symbols frequency and the corresponding modern note.

By right-clicking the Edit Ancient Note Dialog Box is invoked (Figure 10). In that dialog box, the user can modify the type of the note and the note's frequency. The AGM drawing surface consists of three fields, vocal symbols, instrumental symbols and lyrics. The user can either drag'n'drop a symbol from the Symbol Repertory to the corresponding field or use the Text tool (which is located in the Toolbar) to change each field (Figure 11).

Concerning the instrumental part, ARION supports 11 already defined musical instruments, which have been mentioned. Their sound comes from CSound files. The default selection of the application consists of just one instrument (aulos) and the vocal part, because ancient Greek music was monophonic. Nevertheless, the use of many instruments for orchestral composition is supported. As a fully parametrical application, the user is able to add as many instruments as he wishes to his project, as well as to define new instruments by mapping new CSound files to the newly created musical instruments. Also, the sound parameters of the already defined AGM instruments can be reconfigured.

The modern music surface has two modes, the vocal mode and the instrumental mode. The user can interact with only one mode at a time.

By right-clicking on a note the Edit Modern Note Dialog Box is invoked where the user can modify the note's duration and frequency shifting it from double flat to double sharp and in between (Figure 12).

Table 1. Mapping of AGM symbols to modern notes for the ancient Greek guitar.

AGM symbol	E	⊢	Γ	μ	F	C	K	⊳	<	⊏	N
Modern Note	C	D	E	F	G	A	B	C	D	E	F

Many notes of AGM have difficulty in their correspondence with their western music counterparts. Especially in modes like Phrygian and Lydian, a creeping substrate for the development of oriental music systems can be detected. Because no accurate correspondence can be made, the instrument gives its users the flexibility to experiment by assigning different pitch levels, and therefore the fuzziness of scales can be resolved in a trial and error manner by hearing the note.

The toolbar of the application has six functions (Figure 13). The first three (New, Open, Save) manipulate the music document. The other two (Select, Text) are used to drag'n'drop symbols

Figure 9. The graphical user interface of ARION.

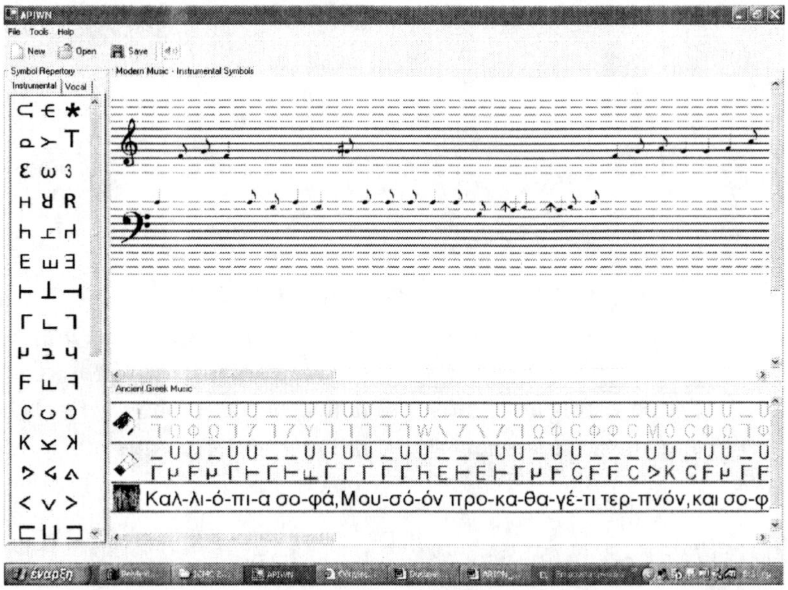

Figure 10. Editing an AGM note – the dialog box.

Figure 11. AGM surfaces: Notes for vocal and instrumental melodic scripting along with the lyrics.

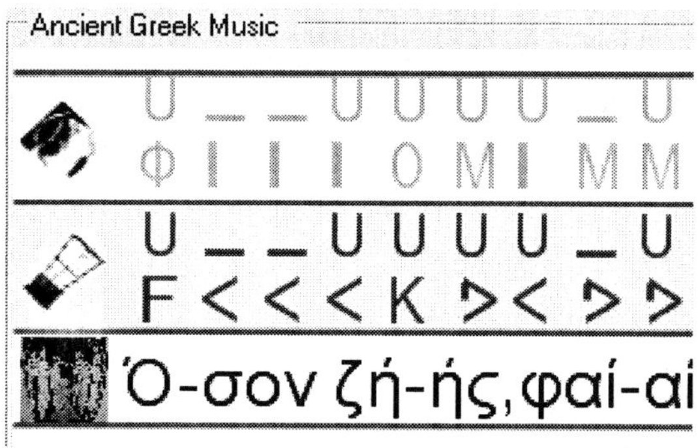

Figure 12. Altering AGM note's pitch and duration

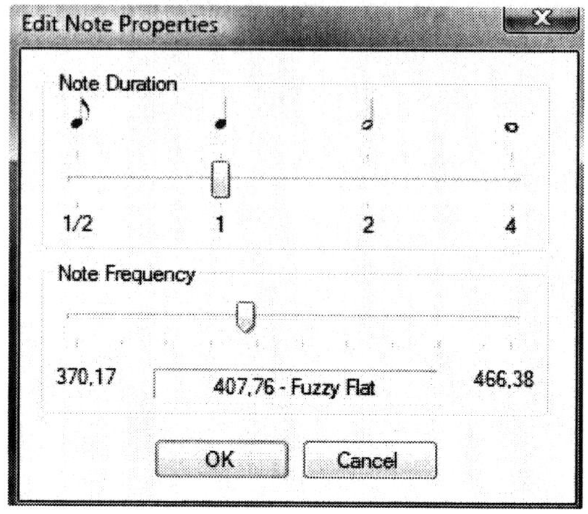

Figure 13. Application toolbar

from the Symbol Repertory to the AGM surface (Select) or to change the text in the AGM surface (Text).

The last function is used for creating an audio representation of the current music document. By clicking it, a dialog box about the status of the output file appears (Figure 14). The user can configure the final audio output by choosing which musical elements it should contain: instrumental, vocal and lyrics. Users can also define the tempo of the song (the default value is 60). By clicking on "Export," a Microsoft Wave file is created in the current working directory and a message about successful creation appears on the screen (see Figure 15). The user can then listen to the file from any audio player on his or her system. The audio file is produced by using CSound's rendering processes.

Last but not least there is the menu bar, which has three menus. The File menu deals with file handling as well as the document's identity, which contains information such as the date of creation of the document and the composer. The Tools menu has the Edit Association Table command and the Export to Wave command. The association table is the table from which the mapping function reads the data and maps AGM notes to western music notes. The last menu is the Help menu, which at the moment contains a very useful manual and the credits for this application.

ARION allows the user to alternate any attribute of a note and adjust it according to his or her needs, so as to produce the desirable melody. This way, even if (for example) different attributes for a music symbol are discovered (e.g., frequency, etc.) there will not be any problem for the user. The default form of the note (as it is consistent to current research and literature) may be corrected by the user using the association table. Moreover, the user is allowed to add new notes or delete existing ones at will.

All the (available to the user) notes are registered in the association table. Each note bears the following attribute values:

- **ID** (the unique code for each note – primary key)

Figure 14. Defining the attributes of the file to be produced – The dialog box

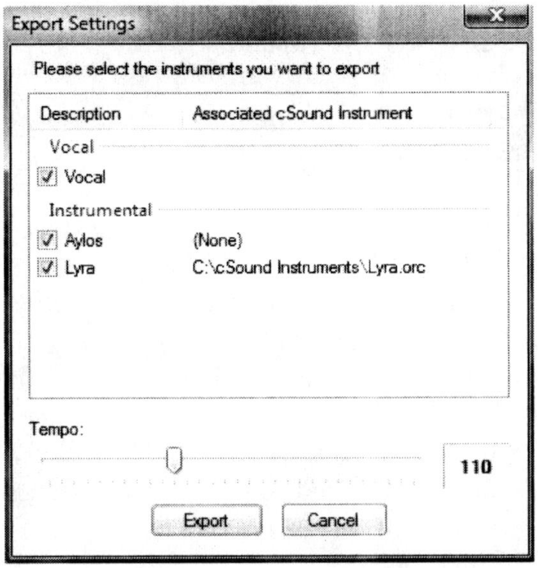

- **Character ID** (the code that defines the symbol of the note)
- **Frequency**
- **Vocal**/Instrumental (the note's category)
- **Double Flat Frequency**
- **Double Sharp Frequency**
- **Type** (the default type, e.g., sharp)
- **Note** (the corresponding note according to western music system)
- **Octave** (the octave of the note)
- **Corresponding ID** (the code of the corresponding vocal or instrumental note, which is used for synchronization)

It should be mentioned here that the attributes **note** and **octave** are those that define the position of the note on staff and do not affect the sound of the note at the final sound file, which is produced.

The next sections present a short tutorial on how to use ARION.

Figure 15. Successful event handling of real–time CSound audio rendering

Working with Compositions

Creating a New Composition

To create a new composition on the File menu, click New, or click the button on the toolbar. If you have a modified open composition, you will be prompted to save any changes done.

Saving a Composition

To save a composition, just click Save on the File menu or the button on the toolbar.

The very first time that you save a new composition, you will need to give your composition a file name. Follow these steps:

1. On the File menu, click Save or click the button on the tool bar.
2. In the File name box, type a name.
3. Click Save.

If you want to save a composition using a new filename, click Save as on the File menu.

Opening a Composition

To open a saved composition:

1. On the File menu, click Open, or click the button on the toolbar. If you have a modified open composition, you will be prompted to save any changes done.
3. Select the file you want to open.
4. Click Open.

Setting the Composition's Properties

To set the properties of a composition:

1. On the File menu, click Properties.
2. Set the desired Title, Author and Comments. You cannot modify the creation date.
3. Click OK and then save your composition.

Working with Instruments

Each new ARION composition consists of only one instrument. However, you can add up to nine instruments, which can be associated with CSound synthesis instruments to create a more complex song.

Adding a New Instrument

To add new instruments in your composition follow these steps:

1. On the Instruments menu, click Add Instrument.
2. Type a description for the new instrument.

At this step, you will be prompted to associate the new instrument with a CSound synthesis instrument. If you want to proceed:

3. Select a CSound synthesis instrument file (a file with .orc extension).
4. Click Open.

Otherwise, you can do this at a later time as described in the following section.

Associating with CSound Synthesis Instruments

At anytime, you can associate an instrument with a CSound synthesis instrument, which will be

Figure 16. Meta-data of an ARION composition

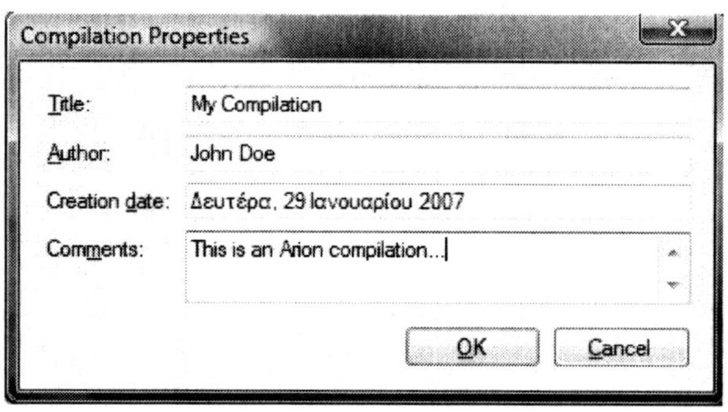

Figure 17. Managing musical instruments

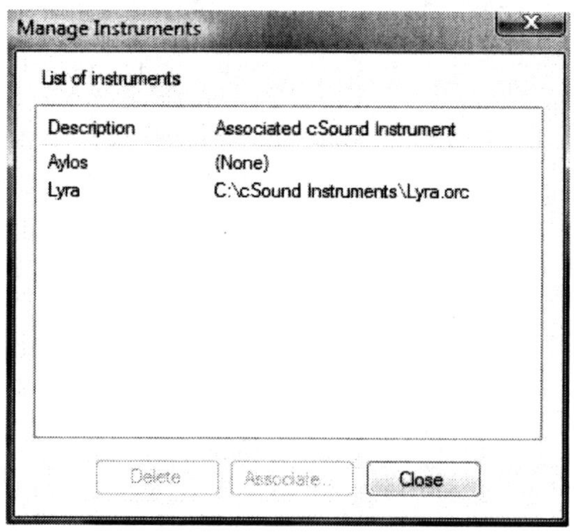

used to export the composition to a wave file. To do so, follow these steps:

1. On the Instruments menu, click Manage Instruments (Figure 18).
2. Select the instrument you want to associate with the CSound file.
3. Click Associate.
4. Select a CSound synthesis instrument file (a file with .orc extension) Click Open.

Deleting an Instrument

To delete an instrument:

1. On the Instruments menu, click Manage Instruments.
2. Select the instrument you want to delete.
3. Click Delete and OK to confirm.

Alternatively, you can delete an instrument by right-clicking on its icon in the Ancient Music Panel, and selecting Delete.

Synchronizing Two Instruments

You can synchronize two instruments, so that the notes of the first instruments are "copied" to the second. Additionally, you can synchronize vocal notes with an instrument, so that the music of the instrument "follows" the voice.

To synchronize two instruments:

1. On the Instruments menu, click Synchronize Instruments (Figure 19).
2. Select the source and destination instruments.
3. Click OK.

Changing the Description of an Instrument

To change the description of any instrument:

1. Right-click the instrument's icon in the Ancient Music Panel and select Change Instrument Description.
2. Type the new description.
3. Click OK.

Remarks

- You cannot delete or change the description of the Vocal Panel.
- You cannot have two instruments with the same description.

Figure 18. Deleting a defined musical instrument

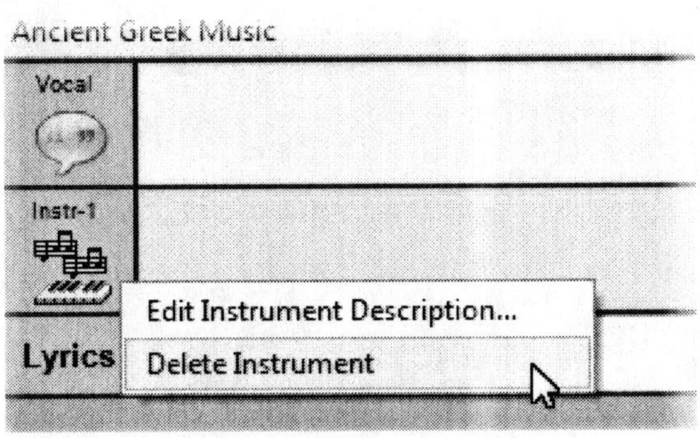

Figure 19. Synchronization of two instruments

Working with Notes

Adding a New Note in the Composition

To add a new note in your composition:

- Drag and Drop the note from the Symbol Repertory to the destination instrument

- or -

- Double-click the note in the Symbol Repertory and it will be added in the last position of the active instrument

The default duration of a new note is full.

Changing the Frequency of a Note

Arion enables you to set any intermediate frequency to the note between its double flat and its double sharp.

To set the frequency:

1. Right-click the note on the modern (upper) panel and select Change Note Duration/Frequency.
2. Using the lower slider, set the desired frequency.
3. Click OK.

Figure 20. The user can place a new note anywhere in the composition using the drag-n-drop technique

Changing the Duration of a Note

For each note you can select one of the four available durations.

To set the duration:

- Right-click the note on the modern (upper) panel and select Change Note Duration/Frequency

- or -

1. Right-click the note on the ancient (lower) panel and select Change Note Duration.
2. Using the slider, set the desired duration.
3. Click OK.

Deleting a Note from the Composition

To delete a note from your composition:

- Right-click the note (on either the ancient or modern panel) and click Delete

- or -

- Select the note by clicking it and press delete on your keyboard.

Figure 21. Editing the duration of an AGM note

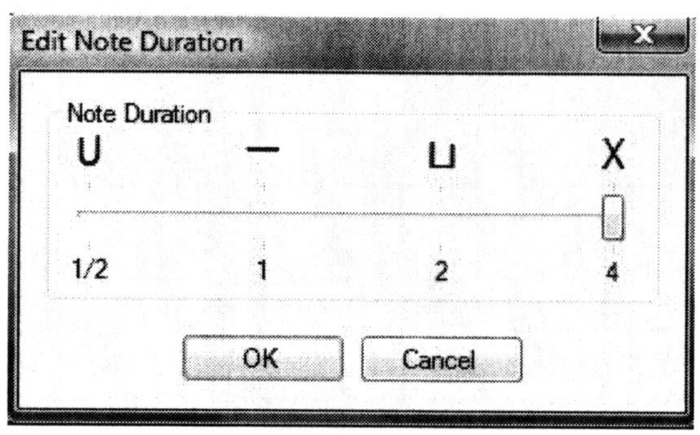

Bars

In the modern music, you can add bars to group the notes. The bars are independent for each instrument.

To add or remove a bar:

- Right-click the note on the modern (upper) panel and select Insert/Remove Bar

  - or -

- Double-click in the white space between two notes.

Export a Composition

To create an audible wave file, you must first export the composition.

How to Export a Composition to WAV File

To export compositions follow these steps:

1. On the Tools menu, click Export to WAV or click the button on the toolbar (Figure 14).
2. Select the instruments you want to export by clicking the corresponding checkboxes. Note that if an instrument is not associated with a valid CSound synthesis instrument, it will not be exported.
3. Set the desired tempo by dragging the slider.
4. Click Export.
5. In the File Name box, type a name.
6. Click Save.

Remarks

- You cannot export an empty composition.
- You must export at least one instrument or the lyrics.

Edit Note Attributes

ARION enables you to customize the properties of every note to adjust them to your needs.

How to Edit a Note's Attributes

To edit a note's properties follow these steps:

1. Right-click on the note which you want to edit in the symbol repertory (Figure 6).
2. Set the values you want. If you want to automatically calculate the double flat and double sharp frequencies, after you set the original frequency click the appropriate button.
3. Click OK.
4. You will be prompted to update any notes already added in the composition.

Figure 22. Options for handling bars on staff

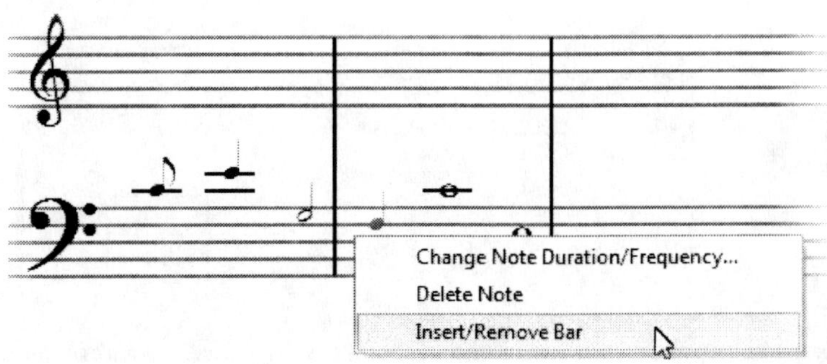

Remarks

- When unchanged, the first column of the symbol repertory contains the original notes, the second the sharp of the note and the third the flat of the note.
- When you want to change the basic attributes of a note, for example, the symbol or the type, you must use the Edit Association Table option,
- A note's double flat frequency must be lower than its original frequency, which must be lower than the double sharp frequency.

Edit the Association Table

All the notes you can use in a composition, are stored in the association table. You can add or remove notes at the association table or edit the attributes of an existing note.

Viewing the Association Table

To view the association table, on the Tools menu, click Edit Association Table. The following window appears:

Adding a New Note

To add a new note, follow these steps:

1. Click the Add New Note button (Figure 23).
2. Set the attributes you want. If you want to automatically calculate the double flat and double sharp frequencies, after you set the original frequency click the appropriate button.
3. Click OK.

Deleting a Note

To delete a note, follow these steps:

1. Select the note you want to delete
2. Click the Delete button and confirm your choice

Editing a Note's Attributes

To edit a note's attributes, follow these steps:

Figure 23. The dialog box for adding a new note to the application. User-defined notes and symbols can be stored for later use.

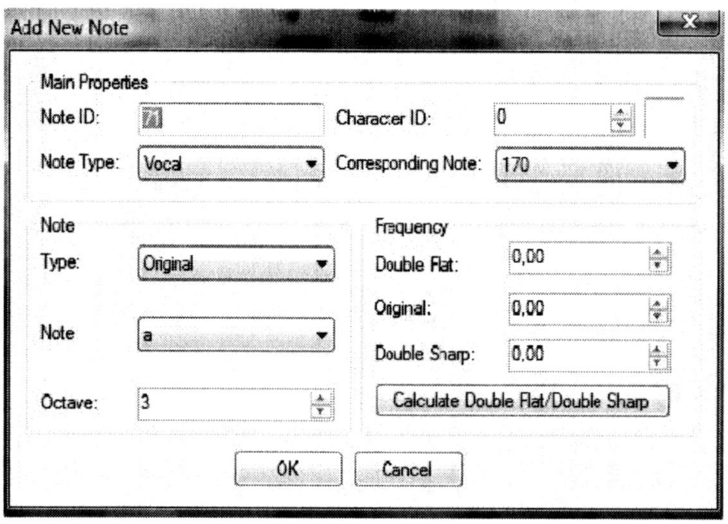

1. Select the note you want to edit
2. Click the Edit button
3. On the window that appears, set the attributes you want
4. Click OK

Remarks

- The Corresponding Note attribute corresponds a vocal note to an instrumental one or an instrumental note to a vocal one. This is necessary to enable synchronizing vocal notes with instruments or vice versa.
- In order to avoid any inconsistencies, it is recommended to edit the association table only when no composition is open.
- A note's double flat frequency must be lower than its original frequency, which must be lower than the double sharp frequency.

Lyrics and the Polytonic System

One unique characteristic of ARION is that the user can add the lyrics of his or her AGM composition on their original format, that is, on the polytonic system of writing at the ancient Greek language. Of course, the tool gives the option to write immediately on modern Greek language.

The polytonic system (with accents and breathings) was invented by Aristophanes- the Byzantine- in about 200 B.C., in order to help the foreign students of the ancient Greek language read and spell it correctly, because the ancient Greek accent was musical and tonal, which means that the vowels were spelled in a very different way from nowadays.

The Help section of ARION contains explicit instructions on how to install a polytonic ancient Greek font. Once installed, the user can write on the ancient Greek format of writing, using the key combinations for the polytonic symbols on Table 2.

While writing the lyrics of the composition, the user has to specify each syllable, so as the virtual singer can sing it together with the corresponding instrumental note. That means that one note of the instrument can be indexed either on a vocal syllable or a pause. The separation of syllables in ARION can be done in four ways: by dash (-), by dot (.), by comma (,) or by nothing ( ). An instrumental note that is not to be sung must be denoted by (p) (=pause) in the Lyrics section.

Figure 24. The Association Table stores the notes and their properties.

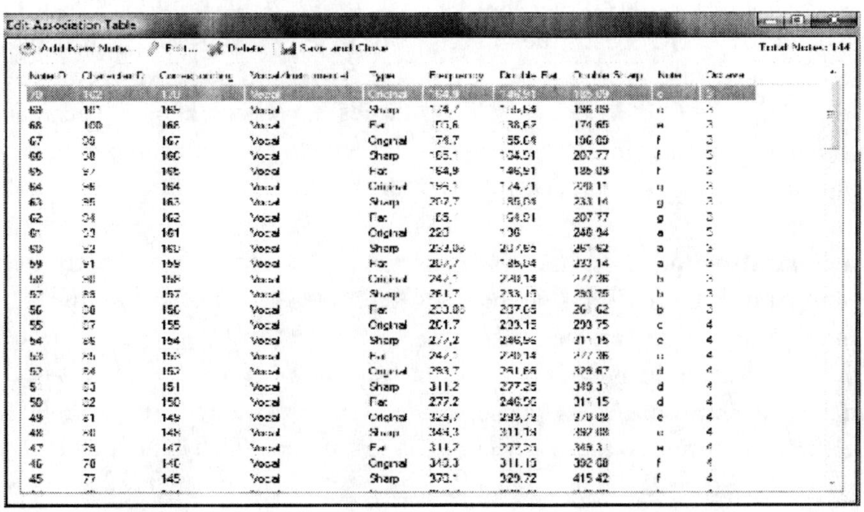

Table 2. Correspondence of keys and symbols in the Ancient Greek Polytonic system

Key	Produced Breathing
“	Rough breathing
‘	Smooth breathing
+	Rough breathing +circumflex
-	Long
/	Smooth breathing + the acute accent
:	Dieresis
;	The acute accent
=	Smooth breathing + circumflex
?	Rough breathing + the acute accent
[	Circumflex
\	Smooth breathing +grave
]	Grave
_	Breve
`	Dieresis + grave
{	Subfix
|	Rough breathing + grave
~	Dieresis + the acute accent

File Structure and Attributes

In this section, the attributes of the files that the application creates and uses are presented shortly. More particularly, ARION uses files in three cases:

1. To **store a musical composition**, so as the user to be able to continue with processing at a later time.
2. To **export a musical composition** (as an intermediate temporary means of transferring the necessary data to the parsers that take charge of the synthesis of the melody)
3. To **store an association table**, so as its use is available at a later time, either by the users themselves, or other users, who wish to use an association table that is different from the application's default one.

In all of these three cases, the created files are of XML type and fulfill the version 1.0 of the XML language requirements. The discussed types have been chosen because this particular type of files offers some advantages, which are critical for the application:

- First of all, the strictly defined structure of XML files allows their "facile" reading by a third-party application with the use of an XML reader. This is necessary because the extracted files from ARION are later processed by independent parsers, before the final music file is created.

- The application has been designed in a way that its architecture is as "open" as possible and allows changes at its functionalities because such a decision is essential in the future. The choice of the XML language was a one-way choice because of that fact. XML files are the only type of files that may keep compatibility (with minor changes) to modified versions of ARION.
- Finally, it is also more practical for the application itself to use this particular type of file, because no additional methods of reading and writing files (that could lead to problematic unexpected situations) were necessary. The built-in XML reader and writer, whose reliability has been tested repeatedly in other applications, have been chosen.

A short discussion on the three previously mentioned types of files follows.

Save Files

These files are created when the user saves his composition, so as to continue its processing at a later time. The extension of those files is *.anc* (ARION Compilation). It is self-evident that they should include data that define:

- The **musical instruments** that comprise the composition of the user, as well as their attributes: the name and the corresponding CSound file.
- The **notes** that are assigned to each instrument, together with the attributes that the user may have altered, like the frequency and the duration.
- The **lyrics** of the composition.
- The **properties** of the composition: The name, the composer, the creation date and any comments of the user.

Intermediate Export Files

The particular files are temporary, which means they are only used during the process of converting a composition into a melody, and they are aiming at data transferring from the application to the parsers that undertake the music synthesis and the lyrics synthesis. This solution has been chosen so as the process of music synthesis to remain independent of the application, which comprises the main tool for writing music and lyrics.

Export files have much in common to the previous type (save files), because the data used here are also related to the instruments and the notes. Though, there are some differences that intend to facilitate the parsing process.

Association Table Files

Files of this type are created when a user exports an association table (i.e., a sum of notes with certain attributes), so as to be available for future use. The extension of these files is *.aat* (ARION Association Table).

Requirements and Features of ARION

Requirements

In order to run correctly, ARION's minimum requirements are:

- Windows XP, 2003 or Vista
- .NET framework 2.0 or a latest release (which can be found in the application CD)
- A Windows compatible sound card
- Installed audio player software, for example, Windows Media Player (optionally)

Features

Next, a list with the unique characteristics of ARION follows:

- Capability of music or voice isolation in the final .wav file
- The option Synchronize copies the notes from the Instrumental field and pastes them into the vocal field, or the opposite
- Freedom of choice of any intermediate frequency for each note
- Freedom to edit the parameters on the association table
- Capability of using all the idioms of the ancient Greek language
- Three already prepared compositions-demos with the program
    - "The Song of Seikilos"
    - "Innovation of the Muse"
    - "Innovation of Calliope and Apollo"

Usage

The usage of the application is quite trivial. It works into two modes, the Vocal and the Instrumental mode. The user chooses the current mode by clicking on the desired Symbol Repertory page. When the application starts the default mode is Vocal mode. The user can add a note to the ancient Greek music drawing surface.

Because ancient Greek notes do not provide any information on their duration the user can simply change the duration by right-clicking on the modern note and choosing the desired duration in ♪. When the composition is complete he or she can convert the composition to a Wave file and listen to it via his or her audio player of choice.

FUTURE RESEARCH DIRECTIONS

We have presented a dynamically created virtual museum. Building a custom museum is now easy for every visitor of the museum or any museum executive, through an easy to use interface.

VRML was chosen primarily because it's an open, Web-based protocol. Although there is a newer protocol available, called "x3d," designed by the same team (w3c) as a replacement for VRML, we believe that VRML is more mature, with more tools and viewers available.

Although, the whole project was build using nonproprietary tools, a step forward to improving would be to support more databases and probably export both VRML and X3D models.

REFERENCES

Ahlberg, J. (2001). Candide-3 – an updated parameterized face, T*echnical report no. lith-isy-r-2326.*

Banvard, R. (2002, September 29-October 3). The visible human project image data set: From interception to completion and beyond. In *18th International Conference CODATA 2002: Frontiers of Scientific and Technical Data,* Montréal, Canada.

Barbour, J. M. (1972). *Tuning and temperament: A historical survey.* New York: Da Capo Press.

Barker, A. (1989). *Greek musical writings II.* Cambridge.

Bathe, K. J. (1982). *Finite element procedures in engineering analysis.* Upper Saddle River, NJ: Prentice Hall.

Borzacchini, L., & Minnuni, D. (2001). *A mathematica notebook about ancient Greek music and mathematics.* University of Bari.

Burkert, W. (1972). *Lore and science in Ancient Pythagoreanism.* Cambridge, MA: Harvard University Press.

Carlson, C., Ternstrom, S., & Sundberg, J. (1991). A new digital system for singing synthesis allowing expressive control. In *Proceedings of ICMC 91, International Computer Music Conference,* Montreal.

Chowning, J. (1981). Computer synthesis of singing voice, ICMC 81. In *Proceedings of the*

International Computer Music Conference, La Trobe University, Melbourne.

Conti, F., Barbagli, F., Morris, D., & Sewell, C. (2005). CHAI: An open-source library for the rapid development of haptic scenes demo. In *paper presented at IEEE World Haptics,* Pisa, Italy.

Cook, P. (1993). Spasm, a real-time vocal tract physical model controller, and singer the companion software synthesis system. *Computer Music Journal, 17*(1). Boston: MIT Press.

Cook, P. R., Kamarotos, D., Diamantopoulos, T., & Philippis, J. (1993). IGDIS: A modern Greek text to speech/singing program for the SPASM/Singer instrument, ICMC 93. In *Proceedings of the International Computer Music Conference*, Tokyo.

Devine, A.M., & Stephens, L.D. (1994). *The prosody of Greek speech.* New York: Oxford.

Fakas, G.J., Lamprianou, I., Andreou, A., Pampaka, M., & Schizas, C. (2005). The evaluation of the cultural journeys in the information society environment as an educational aid. *Computers & Education*, (45), 123-139.

Franklin, J. C. (2005). Hearing Greek microtones. In S. Hagel & Ch. arrauer (Eds.), *Ancient Greek music in performance*. Vienna: Wiener Studien Beiheft 29.

Georgaki, A. (2004). Virtual voices on hands: Prominent applications on the synthesis and control of the singing voice. In *Proceedings of SMC 2004, Sound and Music Computing 2004*, Paris, France.

Gombosi, O. (1944). *Johannes. New light on Ancient Greek music*. International Congress of Musicology, New York 1939, New York, p. 168.

Halaris, C. *Music of Ancient Greece, booklet and CD.* Halaris has reconstructed Ancient Greek Music instruments. He has exhibited them and his ensemble performs with them.

Harmonia, M. (1979). *Musique de la Grece Antique*, booklet and CD, HMA 1951015, France.

Montani, R., Scateni, & Scopigno, R. (1994). Discretized marching cubes. In *Proceedings of Visualization 94,* (pp. 281-287). Washington: IEEE Computer Society Press.

Moschos, G., Nikolaidis, N., & Pitas, I. (2004). Anatomically-based 3D face and oral cavity model for creating virtual medical patients. In *Proceedings of IEEE ICME 2004*, Taipei, Taiwan, (pp. 867-870).

Nikopoulos, N., & Pitas, I. (1997). An efficient algorithm for 3D binary morphological transformations with 3D structuring elements of arbitrary size and shape. In *Proceedings of the 1997 IEEE Workshop on Nonlinear Signal and Image Processing* (NSIP'97).

Pöhlmann, E., & West, M. L. (2001). *Documents of ancient Greek music.* USA: Oxford University Press.

Politis, D., & Margounakis, D. (2003). Determining the chromatic index of music. In *Proceedings of WEDELMUSIC 2003, 3rd International Conference on the Web Delivering of Music*, Leeds, UK.

Politis, D., Margounakis, D., & Mokos, K. (2004). Vizualizing the chromatic index of music. In *Proceedings of WEDELMUSIC 2004, 4th International Conference on the Web Delivering of Music*, Barcelona, Spain.

Ranta, J. F., & Aviles, W. A. (1999). The virtual reality dental training system—simulating dental procedures for the purpose of training dental students using haptics. In *Proceedings of the 4th PHANTOM Users Group Workshop.*

Rieger, M. (1996). *Music before and after Solesmes*. Penn State University: STS Working-Papers.

Rose, J. T., Buchanan, J., & Sarrett, D. C. (1999). Software reviews – the DentSim system. *Journal of Dental Education, 63*, 421-423.

San Francisco Performances. Guitar trek: Ancient origins. Retrieved October 27, 2007, from www.performances.org

Scavone, G., & Cook, P. (2004). Synthesis toolkit in C++ (STK). In K. Greenebaum & R. Barzel (Eds.), *Audio anecdotes* (Vol. 2). Natick, MA: A.K. Peters Press.

Tsahalinas, K. et al. (1997). Physical modeling simulation of the Ancient Grek Auloi. In *ICMC 97: International Computer Music Conference,* Thessaloniki.

Vlachos, A., Peters, J., Boyd, C., & Mitchell, J. L. (2001). Curved PN triangles. In *Proceedings of the ACM Symposium on Interactive 3D Graphics.*

Wang, D., Zhang, Y., Wang, Y., Lee, Y.-S., Peijun, L., & Yong, W. (2005). Cutting on triangle mesh: Local model-based haptic display for dental preparation surgery simulation, *IEEE Transactions on Visualization and Computer* Graphics, *11*(6), 671-683.

West, M. L. (1992). *Ancient Greek music.* Oxford: Clarendon Press.

Winnington-Ingram, R.P. (1932). Aristoxenos and the intervals of Greek music. *The Classical Quarterly, 26*(3-4), 195-208.

Xydas, G., & Kouroupetroglou, G. (2001). The DEMOSTHENES speech composer. In *Proceedings of the 4th ISCA Tutorial and Research Workshop on Speech Synthesis*, Perthshire, Scotland, (pp. 167-172).

KEY TERMS

Virtual Reality: A technology which allows a user to interact with a computer-simulated environment.

Virtual Reconstruction (in Archaeology): The recreation of buildings, artifacts and landscapes through their digital visualization with complex three-dimensional archaeological data.

Photogrammetry: A large field of study concerned with obtaining accurate measurements from photographs.

Digital Elevation Model: A model of the earth's surface.

Wire-Frame Model: A visual presentation of an electronic representation of a three dimensional or physical object used in 3D computer graphics.

Rendering: The creative process of generating an image from a model by means of software projects.

Rasterization: A rendering technique.

Ray Casting: A rendering technique.

Radiosity: A rendering technique.

Ray Tracing: A rendering technique.

ENDNOTES

1 http://www.phptools4u.com/scripts/eskuel/?lang=english

2 It is about the first model of reconstructed hydravlis. The team that reconstructed hydravlis consisted of M. Mavroeidis, G. Paraschos, P. Vlagkopoulos and C. Stroux and was based on the excavation of Dion (carried out by Professor Dimitrios Pandermalis) in 1992. Since then, three more models have been reconstructed.

3 Having heard several CDs from bands all over the world claiming that they sing more or less AGM, we have concluded that they are strongly biased by their musical tradition rather than by the AGM acquis.

Chapter XI
Social Modeller:
The Use of Expert Systems in Archaeology

Panagiotis Linardis
Aristotle University of Thessaloniki, Greece

INTRODUCTION

Computer applications and especially artificial intelligence (AI) in archaeology is a scientific field that emerged in the late 1970s. This fact came in response to several simultaneous needs, opportunities and interests that result from the systematic development of methodologies relative to excavating, recording and restoration of findings, and also the increasing amount of information gathered in excavation areas. One of the first uses of artificial intelligence on a practical level was the coupling of expert archaeological knowledge with computer-based applications such as expert systems (ES), in order to simulate archaeologist's reasoning for a specific problem. Nowadays, the evolvement of the Internet provides a novel platform convenient for the development of new intelligent software and for offering valuable services in archaeology (Gardin, 1988; Huggett & Ross, 2004; Huggett & Ryan, 1994; & Wilcock, 1985, 1990).

Archaeology is a problem-oriented discipline, which tries to solve questions such as "What social action has caused the material effect that we are observing?" The goal of archaeology is to discover what cannot be seen in terms of what is actually seen (Barcelo, 2004). Answers are unobservable social causes, such as actions and processes, related to observable elements, such as items found in excavation areas. Problem solving can be conceptualized as a form of learning, because it can be defined as the acquisition of knowledge (decision rules) that derives from existing data (facts) and is inserted in an intelligent information system. The prerequisite of building an information system is the existence of a formal and systematic knowledge relative to a very narrow subject that will be encapsulated in an expert system (Huggett, 1985). In this chapter, we present a rule-based system implemented as a service that offers to experts and nonexperts the ability to formulate, organize, initialize and test hypothetical social scenarios, based on items that were gathered and facts that were concluded from excavation areas. The presented tool is called ArchES and is part of the Social Modeller module of the SeeArchWeb project (URL: http://www.seearchweb.net).

Expert systems are "software systems (or subsystems) that simulate as closely as possible the output of a highly knowledgeable and experienced human functioning in a problem-solving mode within a specific problem domain" (Lane, 1986). Expert systems were found to be ideal for integrating different programs in a domain, resulting in the development of decision support systems. Decision support systems integrate heuristic knowledge-based inference, description of scenarios and situations using a network of frames, objects or scripts, conventional programs and databases (Jackson, 1999; Liebowitz, 1997; Smith & Kandel, 1993; Waterman, 1986). The process of building an expert system typically involves a special form of interaction between the expert-system builder (knowledge engineer) and the expert in the specific area (domain expert). The knowledge engineer extracts from the domain expert strategies and rules for solving the problem. Extracting information (knowledge) is usually in the form of facts and rules.

For example (Barcelo, 2001):

Facts:

- Site x has pottery.
- Pottery is of type A.

Rules:

- IF site x has pottery
- AND pottery is of type A
- THEN site x chronology is 5th century.

Facts and rules may not always be true/false with absolute certainty. A degree of certainty/uncertainty is commonly used, to express the validity of a fact or the accuracy of the rule. The collection of the domain knowledge is called knowledge base, while the problem-solving tool that is based on knowledge emulates human capabilities to arrive at a conclusion by reasoning is called inference engine.

THE SOCIAL MODELLER TOOL

SeeArchWeb is a MINERVA project that aims to develop and present a new instructional approach for the subject domain of Archaeology based on networked technologies. The project emphasizes on a pilot study for the prehistoric archaeology of southeastern Europe. In order to accomplish this aim, the SeeArchWeb infrastructure has four parts:

- The Web Course module which is the basic learning resource for use by students, teachers and lecturers.
- The Social Modeller module that provides the users (learners, social scientists and archaeologists) with a new instrument for analysis, comparison and testing of hypothetical social scenarios.
- The Excavation Cataloguer module which is a standardized digital database used as a storage of archaeological excavation data.
- The Educational and Community Resources module which presents to the general public resources about the archaeology of southeastern Europe through the development of a current fund of archaeological community related information.

ArchES, the social modeller tool, is a novel instrument that formulates and tests hypothetical social scenarios provided by the expert archaeologist. ArchES analyses different variables as social factors in southeastern Europe in the past, as well as the present. The social modeller use knowledge management techniques to analyse large amounts of information available through the Excavation Cataloguer Module database. The detailed defining of the social values provides a better understanding of past processes and offers benefits such as more inclusive understanding of the region today.

In terms of computer science, the Social Modeller module includes an intelligent interface capable of accepting questions for social scenarios of the form: what would have happened if …? Based on an expert system that takes into account the knowledge database deposited at the project's central server, ArchES deploys a rule-based decision taking mechanism for social scenarios to supply the answers to questions.

Modeling scenarios could be related to the:

- Representation of accumulation of wealth
- Representation of social inequality and equality
- Representation of exchange and trade mechanisms
- Representation of settlement patterns (regional and local)
- Role of technology in society

The Social Modeller module was designed for European graduate students in European archaeology and related disciplines, professional researchers and other social scientists.

AN EXEMPLAR SCENARIO

In this section, we present a general purpose example scenario to use in the ArchES system. Our scenario is motivated by the story of the lost continent, Atlantis. The story of Atlantis begins quite literally with two of Plato's dialogues, Timaeus and Critias (Atlantis, 1999). These accounts are the only known written records which refer specifically to a lost civilization called Atlantis.

According to Plato, over 11,000 years ago there existed an island nation, larger than Libya and Asia combined and located in the middle of the Atlantic Ocean, outside the "Pillars of Heracles," populated by a noble and powerful race. The people of this land possessed great wealth thanks to the natural resources found throughout their island. The island was a center for trade and commerce. The rulers of this land held sway over the people and land of their own island and well into Europe and Africa. This was the island of Atlantis.

To facilitate travel and trade, a water canal was cut through of the rings of land and water running south for 5.5 miles to the sea.

The city of Atlantis sat just outside the outer ring of water and spread across the plain covering a circle of 11 miles. This was a densely populated area where the majority of the population lived.

Beyond the city laid a fertile plain 330 miles long and 110 miles wide surrounded by another canal used to collect water from the rivers and streams of the mountains. The climate was such that two harvests were possible each year. One in the winter fed by the rains and one in the summer fed by irrigation from the canal.

Surrounding the plain to the north were mountains which soared to the skies. Villages, lakes, rivers, and meadows dotted the mountains.

Besides the harvests, the island provided all kinds of herbs, fruits, and nuts. An abundance of animals, including elephants, roamed the island.

For generations the Atlanteans lived simple, virtuous lives. But slowly they began to change. Greed and power began to corrupt them. When Zeus saw the immorality of the Atlanteans, he gathered the other gods to determine a suitable punishment.

Soon, in one violent surge it was gone. The island of Atlantis, its people, and its memory were swallowed by the sea.

Derived Rules

Based on this section of Plato's scripts, decision rules can be derived. In Table 1, we report a nonexhausted list of possible rules.

Furthermore, certainty factors should be invoked for the listed rules in order to express the weight of each one of the left hand side (premises) and right hand side (consequent) facts in the process of concluding the rules' contribution to the extracted conclusion.

ARCH ES

In this section, we present the ArchES system architecture and its relation with the overall SeeArchWeb project. We explain knowledge representation model and rules execution mechanism that ArchES supports. Finally, we present in detail the execution workflow for the Atlantis scenario.

System Architecture

ArchES Web tool is part of the Social Modeller module of the SeeArchWeb project. ArchES works in cooperation with the Excavation Cataloguer's module digital database, which ensures that our data are in a form that is suitable for our use and are organized in a way that facilitates data analysis, data categorization and relationships mining in available datasets.

The tool consists of (i) two independent user-friendly intefaces (see Figure 1), one for the domain expert—ArchaeologistUI—and one for the learner visitor—VisitorUI, and (ii) the intelligent component (expert system shell).

A domain expert that logs in the system has the ability to:

- Create new social scenarios in combination with available excavations data
- Manage formerly stored scenarios that he/she owns.

Scenarios are organised by defining rules and the way they activate and act. As a result, a deduction system is formulated. Rules are stored in the rule base, that is, the system's relational database. On the other hand, system behavior is defined in the control module that can be expressed either as a tree-like structure or by providing a salience factor related to each rule.

ArchES visitor that enters the system, after a welcoming message, has the ability to:

- Execute a social scenario that he or she chooses
- View all initial facts that are relative to the chosen scenario
- View all rules that where initial entered in the system's inference engine
- View just the fired rules that drive the system to a conclusion jointed with their computed certainty factor
- View rules' activation order that offers services of an reasoning tool

Table 1. Rules for Atlantic scenario

ID	Rule
Rule 1	If site's name is Atlantis then site is Atlantis.
Rule 2	If site's age is 11,000 years then site is Atlantis.
Rule 3	If site is on island and island is in Atlantic Ocean then site is Atlantis.
Rule 4	If site is on plain and plain is enormous and plain is fertile then site is Atlantis.
Rule 5	If site was destroyed and site was swallowed by the sea then site is Atlantis.
Rule 6	If site was surrounded by water channels then site is Atlantis.
Rule 7	If site had army or site was powerful then site is Atlantis.
Rule 8	If site was trade centre or site was rich then site is Atlantis.

- View the final conclusion and its certainty factor
- Modify scenario's social factors (certainty factors) and reactivate the inference engine, in order to come to an new conclusion.

The intelligent component of the ArchES is implemented in Jess (Java Expert System Shell) [16]. Jess is a rule engine and scripting environment written entirely in Sun's Java language by Ernest Friedman-Hill at Sandia National Laboratories. It supports the development of rule-based systems

Figure 1. ArchES users web tools.

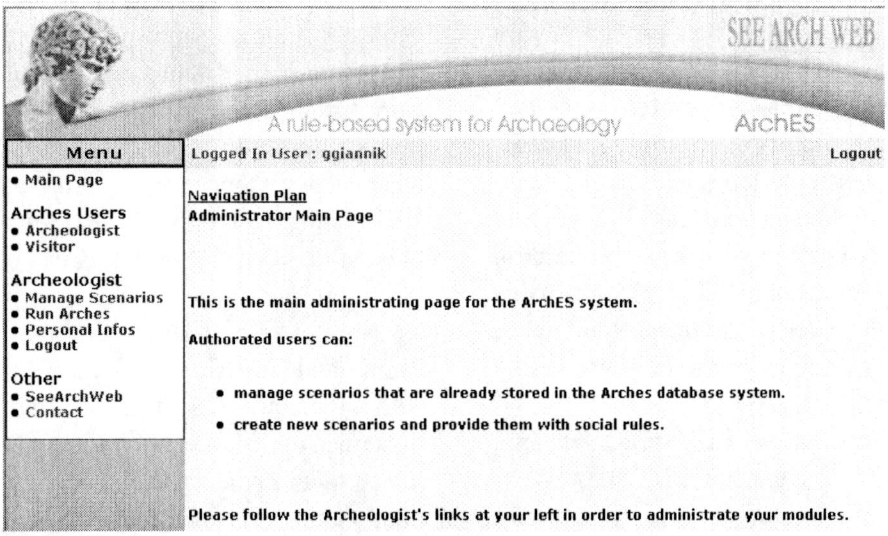

(a) ArchaeologistUI

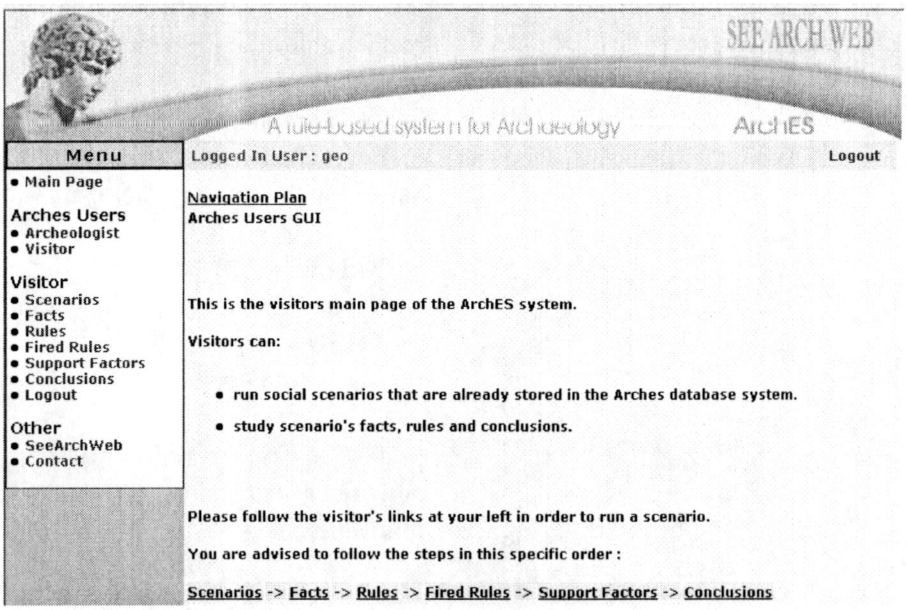

(b) VisitorUI

which can be tightly coupled to code written in the powerful and portable Java language. Jess is a fast and powerful rule engine so it is an ideal tool for adding rules technologies to Web-based software systems.

Jess was originally inspired by the CLIPS expert system shell, which has a successful history as a tool for expert system development (Clips). Later, Jess grows into a complete, distinct, dynamic environment of its own. By using Jess, we build a Java Web tool that has the capacity to "reason," using knowledge that was supplied in the form of declarative rules by experts. Jess supports both forward and backward reasoning and has the full features of a programming language. The syntax of Jess rule language is similar to Lisp, that is a simple language, easy to learn and well-suited to both defining rules and procedural programming. Jess uses a special algorithm called Rete to match the rules to the facts. Rete makes Jess much faster than a simple set of cascading if... then statements in a loop.

There are different ways to embed Jess in a Web application (Friedman-Hill, 2003). Web-based systems architecture is divided into two main categories: client-side and server-side. By choosing the first, Jess can be deployed as an applet. By choosing the second, Jess can be embedded using technologies as servlets, Java server pages (JSP) and Web services (WS). Usually, a combination of them is preferable. In our application, a combination of Java servlets and JSPs were used in the way described in Figure 2. Particularly, Java servlets were used to deploy Jess Engine and to query the engine's state and JSPs are an intermediate factor in order to present the engine's state.

Figure 2. Embedding Jess in ArchES

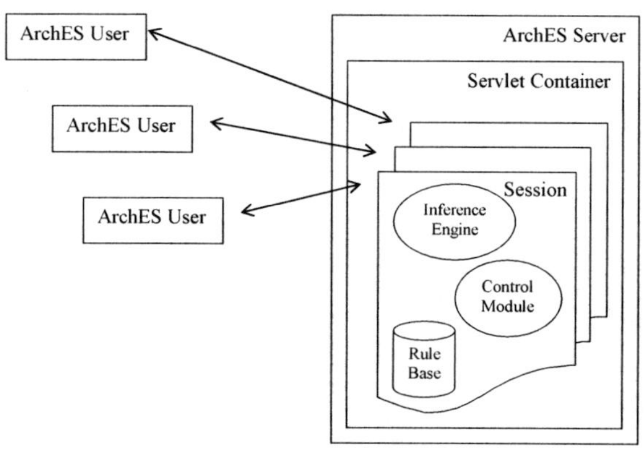

Rule Model and Activation Mechanism

Rules provide a formal way of representing recommendations, directives, or strategies. They are appropriate when the domain knowledge results from empirical associations developed through years of experience solving problems in a specific area (Waterman, 1986). Rules are expressed as if... then statements as shown. Rules of this manner are supported by ArchES.

Moreover, both rule's left hand side (lhs) and right hand side (rhs) portions are enhanced with certainty factors (CF). Certainty factor is a number that measures the certainty or confidence one has that a fact or rule is valid. For our tool, certainty factors can take a value in the range of [-1,1].

Certainty factor value equal to -1 considers the premise fact as false. In the same manner certainty factor value equal to +1 means that premise fact is true. On the other hand, a 0 value certainty factor expresses complete ignorance.

For instance, rule 1 from Table 1 could be enhanced with certainty factors as shown below.

Rule 1:
IF site's name is Atlantis with CF=1
THEN
site is Atlantis with CF=0.95

In this case, the certainty factor for the hypothetical conclusion of rule 1 is computed as follows:

$$CFrule = CFif * CFthen \quad (1)$$

If more than one facts exists in the rule's lhs portion and are combined with an AND/OR boolean operand, then the rule's CFif value is considered as the minimum value of CF1 and CF2.

$CFif = min(CF1, CF2)$ (2)

For instance, rule 3 could be enhanced with support factors and represented, as shown in Figure 3.

Rule 3:
IF site is on island with CF1=0.7
AND
island is in Atlantic Ocean with CF2=0.8
THEN
site is Atlantis with CFthen=0.7

The certainty factor for the hypothetical conclusion of rule 3 is:

$CFrule = min(CF1, CF2) * CFthen$ (3)

Besides rule's premises facts, initial facts are also enhanced with a certainty factor. For example, consider that among other initial facts are the below two:

Initial Fact 1:
Excavation site is on island with CF= 0.8.
Initial Fact 2:
Island is in Atlantic Ocean with CF= 0.9.

Figure 3. ArchES rule model

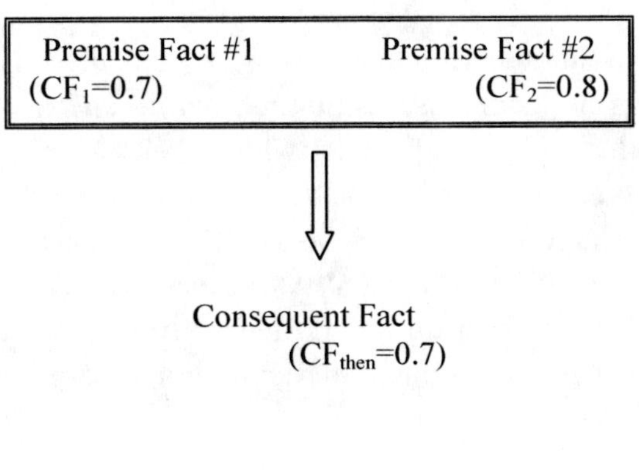

According to the presented model, a rule should only fire (activate) if:

- The if portion of the rule is satisfied by initial or intermediate (facts that were inserted in the inference during execution) facts
- The facts' certainty factors are equal or greater than the certainty factor of the rule's premises facts.

When a rule fires, the action specified by the lhs portion performs and the rule's certainty factor is computed as explained. We should note that in equation (3) certainty factors of rule's premises facts are being replaced with the real certainty factor values of initial facts (see Figure 4).

$CFrule = min(CFfact1, CFfact2) * CFthen$ (4)

Moreover, if the activation of a rule with CF_{r_j} conclude to the same hypothetical consequent as another, already, activated rule with CF_{r_i}, then the overall certainty factor of this specific consequent is defined as follows:

- if $CF_{r_i}, CF_{r_j} > 0$ then

  $$CF_{r_{ij}} = CF_{r_i} + CF_{r_j} - CF_{r_i}CF_{r_j}$$

- if $CF_{r_i}, CF_{r_j} < 0$ then

  $$CF_{r_{ij}} = CF_{r_i} + CF_{r_j} + CF_{r_i}CF_{r_j}$$

- if CF_{r_i}, CF_{r_j} have opposite signs then

$$CF_{r_{ij}} = \frac{CF_{ri} + CF_{r_j}}{1 - min(|CF_{r_i}|, |CF_{r_j}|)}$$

In addition to this, each rule associates with a salience value that defines rule's priority in the control module. Variations in priority help us to construct a tree-like structure scenario, where rules with greater salience value have priority in activation (see Figure 5).

Figure 4. ArchES rule execution model

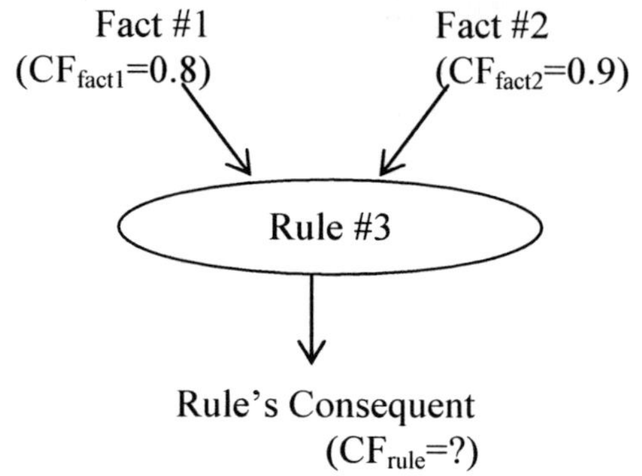

Figure 5. Tree-like structure scenario

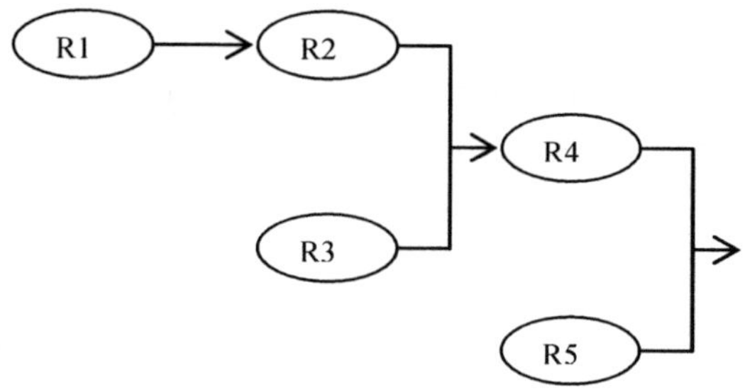

Knowledge Representation

A special way inspired by RDF (resource description framework) documents, is used to represent facts, both for initial facts, premises facts (lhs) and consequent facts (rhs) in rules. A fact is represented by a triplet that contains a subject, a predicate and a value. Facts are formatted in a line-based plain text format.

(*<subject>,<predicate>,<object>*).

According to the formerly presented rule model, all facts are enriched with a certainty factor. By embedding this parameter in the triplet, a quadruplet comes up having the form shown below:

(*<subject>,<predicate>,<object>,<CF>*).

Rules are stored in a relational database; they are gathered by the expert who formulates the applicable scenarios. During initialization of the Jess Engine, rules are extracted from the database, transformed into an intermediate form (XML) and imported into the engine using the XML-based rule representation that Jess supports [16, 18]. A typical XML representation of a simple rule, that is, Rule 1, according to Jess XML DTD (data type definition) [16] is shown in Table 2.

Besides rules, facts should also be imported in Jess Engine. Initial facts come from Excavation Cataloguer module relational database, follow the same quadruplet format and are represented in XML too.

Scenario Execution

As soon as the insertion of social rules from the domain expert completes, the ArchES rule system is ready for execution.

Let us concern that Atlantis scenario rules, shown in Table 3 are stored in the ArchES rule base. Rules are enhanced with certainty factors and a salience value. For example, rule 1, means that:

Rule 1:
IF a fact supports, with absolute confidence, that site's name is Atlantis
THEN the site should be Atlantis
with certainty 95%.

When the system executes, stored rules and facts are loaded in Jess Engine, an inference rule chain is produced, rules, which their premises facts are satisfied, fires and a final consequent fact with its certainty factor conclude. Apart from this, ArchES user has the ability to check initial facts and rules, fired rules and their activation order, conclusion facts and their computed factors.

Table 2. XML rule representation

```
<?xml version="1.0"?>
<!DOCTYPE rulebase SYSTEM "jess.dtd">
<template>
  <name>MAIN::subject</name>
  <multislot>
    <name>__data</name>
  </multislot>
</template>
<rulebase>
<rule>
  <name>MAIN::Rule1</name>
  <lhs>
    <group>
      <name>and</name>
      <pattern>
        <name>MAIN::subject</name>
        <slot>
          <name>__data</name>
          <test><type>eq</type>
             <value><type>STRING</type>
               site's name</value></test>
          <test><type>eq</type>
             <value><type>SYMBOL</type>
                predicate</value></test>
          <test><type>eq</type>
             <value><type>STRING</type>
                is</value></test>
          <test><type>eq</type>
              <value><type>SYMBOL</type>
                object</value></test>
          <test><type>eq</type>
              <value><type>STRING</type>
                atlantis</value></test>
          <test><type>eq</type>
```

continued in next column

Table 2. (cont.)

```
              <value><type>SYMBOL</type>
                cf</value></test>
          <test><type>eq</type>
              <value><type>VARIABLE</type>
                cf1</value></test>
        </slot>
      </pattern>
    </group>
  </lhs>
  <rhs>
    <funcall>
      <name>assert</name>
      <fact>
        <name>MAIN::subject</name>
        <slot>
          <name>__data</name>
              <value><type>STRING</type>
                site</value>
              <value><type>SYMBOL</type>
                predicate</value>
              <value><type>STRING</type>
                is</value>
              <value><type>SYMBOL</type>
                object</value>
              <value><type>STRING</type>
                atlantis</value>
              <value><type>SYMBOL</type>
                cf</value>
              <value><type>VARIABLE</type>
                cf</value>
        </slot>
      </fact>
    </funcall>
  </rhs>
```

Scenarios can be executed iteratively, while modifying their values will drive them to an alternative definition of hypothetical scenarios and different conclusions

RELATED WORK

During the last 15 years, a rapid growth of research activity related to rule-based systems in archaeology has occurred. Selected former research and implementation efforts that exceed classification and typology purposes and inquire functionality and social criteria are briefly presented in this section. Patel and Stutt (1988) developed the KIVA system, which by given a description of the spatial context of an area interprets the function of the areas and the activities that took place in an archaeological deposit. Frankfurt (1992) with the PALAMEDE system was able to analyse some effects of social processes on the archaeological record, notably, the concepts of wealth and hierarchy. Roger Grace (1996) produced a tool for classifying the shape and the technology of prehistoric tools, and to explain their functionality

Table 3. Enriched rules for Atlantis scenario

ID	Sal	Rule
Rule1	100	If site's name is Atlantis (CF=1) then site is Atlantis (CF=0.95).
Rule2	60	If site's age is 11,000 years (CF=0.8) then site is Atlantis (CF=c).
Rule3	60	If site is on island (CF=0.7) and island is in Atlantic Ocean (CF=0.8) then site is Atlantis (CF=0.8).
Rule4	70	If site is on plain (CF=0.6) and plain is enormous (CF=0.8) then site is Atlantis (CF=0.8).
Rule5	70	If site is on plain (CF= 0.6) and plain is fertile (CF=0.8) then site is Atlantis (CF=0.8).
Rule6	90	If site was destroyed (CF=0.9) and site was swallowed by the sea (CF=0.9) then site is Atlantis (CF=0.9).
Rule7	90	If site was surrounded by water channels (CF=0.95) then site is Atlantis (CF=0.9).
Rule8	50	If site had army (CF=0.7) or site was powerful (CF=0.8) then site is Atlantis (CF=0.8).
Rule9	50	If site was trade centre (CF=0.7) or site was rich (CF=0.8) then site is Atlantis (CF=0.8).

FUTURE RESEARCH DIRECTIONS

Expert systems and artificial intelligence applications are very common in the archaeological domain. Some of the most popular applications are related with the implementation of classification systems (typologies), virtual archaeology (virtual reality) and knowledge discovery in archaelogical databases (KDD). Computers can execute iterative procedures that an archaeologist considers excellent. In other words, machine intelligence reproduces operations designed by a human. The combination of various technologies such as intelligent software (expert systems and agents), machine vision (MV) and geographic information systems (GIS) on a common Web-based platform (enviroment) can lead us to the implemention of powerful, operative and reliable software solutions.

In this chapter, an extension of the ArchES intelligent system was presented. ArchES, is a novel rule-based system implemented as a Web tool for formulating and testing hypothetical archaeological social scenarios. Scenarios are formatted and organized by archaeologists and are based on rules and facts that experts derive from findings in excavation areas.

The advantages that ArchES offers are its:

- Multipurpose: The system was designed to provide to different users, learners, social scientists and archaeologists, with the ability to analyse, compare and test hypothetical social scenarios.
- Ability of reasoning: Rules' activation order offer explanation of reasoning to the final conclusion.

Figure 6. ArchES storage architecture

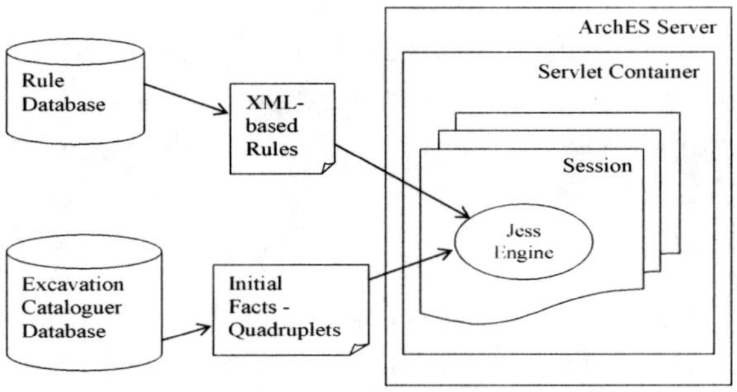

- Ability of manipulating uncertain or fuzzy knowledge with the use of certainty factors
- Scalability: As the number of findings grows up, archaeologists can add more social scenarios or alter and extend already stored rules.
- Ability for extension and revision of knowledge, because control module is separated from knowledge module
- Availability as a Web tool

Our aim for future work is the extension of the presented software to have the capability to learn, accumulate knowledge and combine observations with information derived from the project's database and by using adaptive pattern matching techniques to apply this knowledge to new situations and scenarios. Moreover, a software agent module capable of accepting questions, in the form of human speaking, for social scenarios will be of utmost importance.

REFERENCES

Atlantis - Fact, fiction or exaggeration? (1999). Retrieved October 27, 2007, from http://www.activemind.com

Barcelo, J. A. (2001). *Expert systems as cognitive emulation.* An archaeological viewpoint. Retrieved October 27, 2007, from http://seneca.uab.es/prehistoria/Barcelo/

Barcelo J. A. (2004). *The nature of archaeological problems.* Retrieved October 27, 2007, from http://seneca.uab.es/prehisto ria/Barcelo/

Barcelo, J. A. (2004). *Notes about the use of neural networks for archaeological modelling.* Retrieved October 27, 2007, from http://seneca.uab.es/prehistoria/Barcelo/

CLIPS: A tool for building expert systems. Retrieved October 27, 2007, from http://www.ghg.net/clips/CLIPS.html

Frankfurt, H.P. (1992). Palamede: Application of expert systems to the archaeology of prehistoric urban civilizations. In K. Lockyear & S. P. Q. Rahtz, (Eds.), *Computer applications and quantitative methods in archaeology 1990,* (pp. 211-214), BAR International Series, No. 565. Oxford.

Friedman-Hill, E. (2003). *Jess in action, rule-based systems in Java.* Manning Publishing Company.

Gardin, J. C. (1988). *Artificial intelligence and expert systems: Case studies in the knowledge domain of archaeology.* Prentice Hall.

Grace, R. (1996). Expert systems for Lithic analysis. Retrieved October 27, 2007, from http://www.hf.uio.no/iakk/roger/lithic/expsys.html

Huggett, J. (1985). Expert systems in archaeology. In J. Richards & M. Cooper (Eds.), *Current issues in archaeological computing* (pp. 123-142). Oxford: British Archaeological Reports.

Huggett, J., & Ross, S. (Eds.). (2004). Archaeological informatics: Beyond technology. *Special Issue, Internet Archaeology, 15.*

Huggett, J., & Ryan, N. (Eds.). (1994). *Computer applications and quantitative methods in Archaeology.* British Archaeological Reports Int. Ser. 600.

Jackson, P. (1999). *Introduction to expert systems* (3rd ed.). Addison-Wesley.

Lane, N.E. (1986). Global issues in evaluation of expert systems. In *Proceedings of the IEEE International Conference on Systems, Man, and Cybernetics IEEE,* (pp. 121-125). Piscataway, NJ: Computer Society Press.

Liebowitz, J. (1997). *Handbook of applied expert systems*. Boca Raton, FL: CRC Press.

Patel, J., & Stutt, A. (1998). *KIVA: An archaeological interpreter Human Cognition* (Research Laboratory Tech. Rep. No. 35). Milton Keynes: The Open University.

Smith, S., & Kandel, A. (1993). *Verification and validation of rule-based expert systems*. Boca Raton, FL: CRC Press.

Waterman, D. A. (1986). *A guide to expert systems*. Reading, MA: Addison-Wesley.

Wilcock, J. D. (1985). A review of expert systems, their shortcomings, and their possible applications in Archaeology. *Computer applications in Archaeology* (pp. 139-144). University of London.

Wilcock, J. D. (1990). A critique of expert systems, and their past and present use in archaeology. In R. Ennals, & J. C. Gardin (Eds.), *Interpretation in the humanities: Perspectives from artificial intelligence* (pp. 130-142). LIR Rep. 71. London: British Library Board.

KEY TERMS

Artificial Intelligence: The science of engineering aiming to understand the nature of intelligence, to engineer systems that exhibit such intelligence by utilising vision, language, and so forth.

Computer Architecture: It is the conceptual design and fundamental operational structure of a computer system.

Expert Systems: These software modules represent the expertise knowledge as data or rules within the computer. In the expert system approach, all of the problem related expertise is encoded in data structures only; none lay in programs.

Knowledge Representation: It is fundamentally a surrogate, a substitute for the thing itself, used to enable an entity to determine consequences by thinking rather than acting, that is, by reasoning about the world rather than taking action in it.

Rules: The most common form of expert systems is a program made up of a set of rules that analyze information (usually supplied by the user of the system) about a specific class of problems.

Chapter XII
Machine Translation Systems

Athanasios Tryferidis
Electrical and Computer Engineer, MLS SA, Greece

Theofanis Korlos
Aristotle University of Thessaloniki, Greece

INTRODUCTION

Machine translation, sometimes referred to by the acronym MT, is a subfield of computational linguistics that investigates the use of computer software to translate text or speech from one natural language to another. At its basic level, MT is performed as a simple substitution of atomic words in one natural language for words in another. Using corpus techniques, more complex translations may be attempted, allowing for better handling of differences in linguistic typology, phrase recognition, and translation of idioms, as well as the isolation of anomalies (Mitkov, 2003).

The European Association for Machine Translation (EAMT) defines machine translation (MT) as "the application of computers to the task of translating texts from one natural language to another."

It is obvious that MT is not a simple process. It has to overcome several problems such as to:

- Analyze the complexity of human/natural languages
- Clarify syntactical/referential ambiguities
- Decide on different word meanings
- Decide on polysemy, homonymy
- Detect and deal with metaphors, anomalies

At this point, it should be noted that MT is not a mere substitution for each word, such as a dictionary lookup.

The rest of the chapter is organized as follows: in Section 2 we give some information about the history of MT. In Section 3 we present the way in which the MT works. In Section 4 we mention the two major applications of MTS. In Section 5 we present the techniques that can make MT work better. In Section 6 we present Systran the worldwide leader and one of the first independent MT developers. In Section 7 we focus on expectations users may have and we present feature MTS applications. Finally, in Section 8 we give some details about the way the dictionaries are used in the process of machine translation, and we focus on the operation of the SEEArchWeb forum.

HISTORY

The history of machine translation generally starts in the 1950s after the Second World War. The Georgetown experiment in 1954 involved fully automatic translation of more than 60 Russian sentences into English. The experiment was a great success and ushered in an era of significant funding for machine translation research. The authors claimed that within 3 or 5 years, machine translation would be a solved problem (Asher, 1994).

However, the real progress was much slower, and after the ALPAC report in 1966 (ALPAC, 1966), which found that the 10 years long research had failed to fulfill the expectations, the funding was dramatically reduced. Starting in the late 1980s, as computational power increased and became less expensive, more interest began to be shown in statistical models for machine translation.

Currently, machine translation continues to progress. Large companies are now using it more, which also increases software sales to the general public. This situation has led to the creation of online machine translation services such as Altavista, which offer rapid e-mail services, Web pages, and so forth, in the desired language, as well as to the availability of multilingual dictionaries, encyclopaedias, and free, direct-access terminology databases.

HOW MACHINE TRANSLATION WORKS

The translation process can be stated simply as:

- Decoding the meaning of the source text
- Re-encoding this meaning in the target language

The diagram that follows in Figure 1 explains the procedure of MT in 5 steps.

It is understandable that MT is not a simple process. It takes advantage of computer power to perform complex procedures based on genetic algorithms and artificial intelligence in order to analyze some basic concepts such as:

- Morphology of words used
- Grammatical structure
- Source text syntax
- Semantics of words
- Word ambiguities, idioms, anomalies

Morphology is concerned with the ways in which words are built up from small meaning-

Figure 1. The procedure of MT

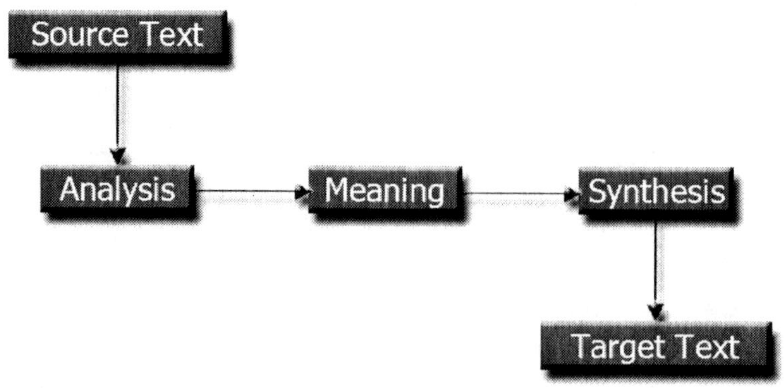

bearing units. Two types are distinguished: the inflectional morphology and the derivational morphology (Bennett, 1993).

Semantics is the study of the ways in which individual words (lexical items) have meaning, either in isolation or in the context of other words, and the ways in which phrases and sentences express meanings. A common assumption is that word meanings involve semantic features. For example, words such as man, woman, boy, girl share a common feature "human" in contrast to animals (Chierchia & McConnell-Ginet, 1990).

Syntax comprises the rules or principles by which words (lexical items) may combine to form sentences. Rules apply to the grammatical categories. It is common to distinguish between the grammatical categories of individual lexical items such as noun, determiner (article), adjective, verb, adverb, preposition, and so forth, and the constituents indicating groupings of items, for example, noun phrase, subordinate clause, and sentence (Bennett, 1993).

The grammatical structure is the set of rules and principles with which we can decide whether a sentence structure is correct or not. Finally, it is necessary to use rules and assumptions in order to solve possible problems with idioms, anomalies and ambiguities (Chierchia & McConnell-Ginet, 1990).

But how can we decide what is the best translation of an ambiguous word? And how we solve possible semantic or syntactic problems? The answers to these questions are quite simple. In the first occasion the selection of the words is based on the context (corpus) of each word. We have to consider the surroundings of each word to decide on the most appropriate translation of an ambiguous word. In the second occasion the translation semantic output is based on lexicons (dictionaries) with morphological, semantic and syntactic information.

HOW MACHINE TRANSLATION IS USED

There are two major situations in which machine translation is used today, regardless of the type of the domain or document concerned. In the first place MS is used as a means of "information dissemination." Translations of this type are generally used for publication or mass distribution. The quality requirement is generally high in every respect: accuracy, readability, smoothness, and style. On the other hand, MT's use is focused on "information assimilation." Translations of this type are mostly used for information scanning purposes. For example, automatically translated scientific and technical papers allow researchers and engineers to follow trends in their respective fields in foreign countries. For this type of translation, the quality requirement for the finished product may be less demanding. The translations output, however, should still remain at a high level, presenting text that is at least easily understandable.

To take things further, we present some basic features for the two different applications of MTs.

For publishing:

- Used as a powerful assistive tool for human translators
- Better MT output can be achieved by the use of specialized / customized dictionaries
- Documents require high quality translation (e-learning, technical support documents)

For understanding / content scanning:

- Obtain a rough draft, to get the general gist of a text
- Fast understanding of foreign content (Web pages, e-mails)

- Fast and immediate way to access multilingual information/news
- Draft translation: Aid when writing in a foreign language
- Solution when publication quality is not necessary

There are some objections stated by professionals on the field on how machine translated text can be used for publishing. The answer is simple: "Even where the quality is lower, it is easier, faster and cheaper to revise 'draft quality' MT output than to translate entirely by hand."

HOW TO MAKE MT WORK BETTER

There are several techniques that can be used in order to make MT work better for us, such as:

- *Pre-editing.* Typically pre-editing involves checking source texts for foreseeable problems for the system and trying to eradicate them. For instance, this may imply the identification of names, the marking of grammatical categories of homographs and the indication of embedded clauses.
- *Post-editing.* The task of the post-editor is to parse and correct MT output so that it meets an agreed quality standard.
- *Domain restriction.* With the use of specialized dictionaries we reduce ambiguities by specifying the field or topic of the text. In these dictionaries every source language word is given a complete morphological, syntactic and semantic description.
- *Customized dictionaries.* The user can build up and maintain personal specialized dictionaries, so as to adapt and fit to special needs, thus gradually increasing output accuracy.

Summing things up, we should quote a saying from Systran's Web site so as to state that: "No automated translation is perfect nor is it intended to replace human translators. The quality of the source text significantly affects the translation output."

WHO OFFERS MACHINE TRANSLATION

Systran was founded in 1968 in La Jolla. SYSTRAN SA, which is located in Paris, is one of the first independent MT developers, with more than 30 years of experience. It is undoubtedly the worldwide leader in the field of MT.

Some statistical information about Systran:

- In SYSTRAN SA work approximately 60 employees worldwide
- Systran supports at least 40 language combinations (new combinations are added)
- 25M pages are translated daily from the different Systran applications (systransoft.com, Altavista Babelfish, Google).

But what are the characteristics that make the different Systran applications so competitive? Some of Systran's competitive features are:

- Many language pairs (including Chinese, Korean, Arabic, Russian, Greek, etc.).

- Specialized domain dictionaries. In addition, Systran offers tools for creating customized user dictionaries by utilizing Systran's Intuitive Coding Technology.

- Customizable professional versions. For example, the European Commission uses Systran to handle the automatic translation of a large volume of preliminary drafts of documents for internal use.

The Systran MT engine is also offered online as a service. Some examples are the WorldLingo, AltaVista's Babelfish, Google, and Yahoo.

There are three separate stages in Systran's MT engine process: analysis, transfer and synthesis. In the analysis stage, source text is preprocessed and a variety of other functions take place, such as character set conversion, spelling correction, sentence segmentation, tokenization, and POS tagging. After the analysis, the process of transfer aims to match with the target language through dictionary lookup. Rules are then applied to re-order the words according to the target language syntax, such as restructure propositions and expressions. The final synthesis stage tidies up the target text and determines grammatical choice to make the result coherent. This stage relies heavily on large tables of rules to make its decisions.

WHAT TO EXPECT IN THE FUTURE FROM MTS

Although MT systems have already come to a mature state, there are still a lot to expect in the near future. Focusing on the quality of MT output, the more important expectations of users are:

- Steady quality improvement
- More language pairs
- More specific domain dictionaries
- Better covering and more complex ambiguity

On the other hand, there are also more innovative and challenging expectations from MT systems that focus on the integration of linguistic and advanced computer technologies, in the attempt of producing new applications. For example, the first challenge is the spoken language translation, where speech recognition and text-to-speech linguistic technologies cope together to produce an integrated all-in-one end-user application, that will help users in real time spoken conversations in cross-languages. A similar application is a scanner translator, where MT and OCR (optical character recognition) technologies can work together so that text can be automatically scanned-translated-printed in an all-in-one machine. Another future application of MT can be automatic real-time television subtitling.

The future of MT system applications is based on the fact that machine translation technology is growing very fast, offering better and better output day by day. So, MT technology is expected to be integrated soon in many advanced systems, offering a lot new MT applications (Nirenburg, 1993).

THE SEEARCHWEB FORUM

In the previous sections of this chapter, we focused on machine translation systems. We concentrated on the history, the applications, the different technologies, the future expectations of machine translation systems, and presenting an analysis of the way these systems work. We specially described the SYSTRAN machine translation technology, which is considered today's worldwide leader in the field. In the following sections, we will try to focus on some basic machine translation systems' features that we met before, such as the dictionary in use, the specialized fields and the pre-editing and post-editing techniques. All of these things will be described in the scope of SEEArchWeb forum, which is a tool mainly for archaeologists.

Defining the Domain of Archaeology

As mentioned before, SEEArchWeb forum is a tool specially designed to cover the needs of the science of archaeology. For the same reason, the machine translation system used should take into account two different aspects, when coming to the automatic translation of archaeological text: "*region*" and "*time*." More specific, based on the "time" factor, we can define different archaeology subfields, such as: Prehistoric, Paleolithic, Classic, and so forth. In the same way, based on the

Table 1. Adding a new term

Greek	English
Αμφορέας	Vase
Αμφορείς	Vases

"region" factor, we can define different subfields such as Greek, Roman and Judaic archaeology. This discrimination has to do with the fact that a word may have different meanings in every period. For example, the English word "vase," that can be translated as "βάζο" in the Greek language, can also be translated as "αμφορέας", "δοχείο", or "αγγείο" in a different, more specialized, archaeological subfield. This depends on the certain category or period in which the source text is referred to. In order to outcome this problem, which is indeed very vital for the quality of the translation output, we come to use specialized dictionaries, corresponding to different archaeology subfields.

Creating a Database for Archaeologists

Making a simple survey in the different automatic translation systems, one can easily notice the absence of a specialized dictionary in the domain of archaeology. This has an obvious impact on the output quality of an automatically translated text. The purpose of the SEEArchWeb forum is to provide a solution to problem. To be more specific, we follow the model of the Systran dictionaries in different domains. The goal is to create a corresponding specialized dictionary, which will be created from scratch and filled word by word by expert translators on the archeology field. This dictionary will feed the process of automatic translation, in order to obtain better translating results. In the following sections, we will describe the way this is done and also focus on some of the rules that have to be taken into account in order to build a well-organized dictionary. The dictionary mechanism adopted is similar to the one used by the Systran translation system.

Creating a Dictionary

The use of dictionaries in automatic translation systems provide the users with the means of increasing the vocabulary recognized and also adjusting the translation output to a specific or specialized field. Creating and maintaining specialized dictionaries in the long run lead to better and more accurate translation output for all associated target languages. Dictionaries allow the user to:

- Complete the main dictionary, by providing custom translation for words not currently available NFWs (not found words) in the main dictionary.
- Override the target-language meaning of a word or expression as found in the main dictionary, a capability that allows the customizing of translation output to fit specific needs.

We should note here that, when adding a new term (a single word or an expression, that is, group of words with no verb) to a dictionary, only the simplest verbal form of the word is added. The dictionary manager engine is capable of providing all the different verbal forms a single word or expression may appear in a text, thus incorporating the added terms in the main dictionary.

For example, by adding the following word (Table 1), the translation engine can automatically produce the plural form of the word "Αμφορείς" as "Vases" when met in a text, providing the appropriate translation output text.

A dictionary entry consists of the following parts:

- The word or expression in both the source and target language

- The grammatical correctness and the confidence factor of the meaning of a word or phrase
- The domains that are essentially dynamic contextual terminology specifications

Apart from the lexical terms, a user can add to a dictionary a number of useful information for each entry, as presented in Table 2.

The user can also add entries in a do-not-translate dictionary, when using a term that should remain untouched and therefore not translated throughout an automatic translation. For example, if the phrase "Princess of Mykonos" refers to a unique Greek statue found on the island and given that name, then it should remain unchanged in the target translation into Greek, instead of using the term «Βασίλισσα της Μυκόνου».

There are other, more advanced grammatical and syntactical rules that can be applied to a dictionary. For example, one can specify the part of speech of a certain dictionary entry (e.g., [n] for nouns, [v] for verbs, [a] for adjectives), applying different meaning in each case. In this case, we can explicitly define the category of each entry, as shown in Table 3.

A second rule can be used with fixed words or phrases which have certain meanings and should not be analyzed during the translation, such as the example in Table 4.

Table 3. Specifying grammatical information

English	Greek
Empty(v)	Αδειάζω
Empty(a)	Άδειος

Table 4. Fixed phrases

English	Greek
"US"	"ΗΠΑ"

USER GROUPS OF THE SEEARCHWEB FORUM

The user groups of the SEEArchWeb forum are the following:

- Visitor
- Registered Member
- Author
- Translator
- Administrator

Visitors can wonder in the forum and are restricted to only viewing the published posts in any language of the supported languages. After a short registration process (the user fills in some information about himself/herself and activates

Table 2. Useful information in the dictionary

Category	Description
Source-language entry	Contains the word or phrase of the source language, in the simplest verbal form
Target-language entry	Contains the desired translation of the word or phrase of the target language, in the simplest verbal form
Category	Indicates the part of speech for the word or phrase (i.e., noun is displayed for an English entry of cat, expression is displayed for a French entry of c'est pas grave), as understood by the dictionary manager engine.
Confidence	Displays a graded measurement of the syntactical quality of the entry. The scale used is Green LED-style, with the greater illumination representing the greater levels of confidence. The measurement is the result of a matching made against SYSTRAN's Linguistic Resources database.

the newly created account following an e-mail link) visitors can become registered members.

Registered members besides other personal information also set a default language, in order to view mainly the content originally posted or translated in this language. The personal information given when the user registered into the system can be changed anytime just as his primary language. What's more, registered members can post replies or comments to each of the published posts and exchange personal messages with any other registered member. Finally, registered members can become authors or translators or both by applying for this through a specialized link.

Once an author, a registered member is able to post new and unique content in each content category. The created content must be of the language which the registered member specified when registered. Authors also have the ability to request translation for any content published in the SEEArchWeb forum.

When applying to become a translator, each registered member specifies the languages that he can translate content from and to. Based on this information, when a translation request is issued, an e-mail is sent to each of the translators which are eligible for translating from the primary content language to the requested language. When the translator is logged into the system he or she can view all the pending translation requests through a specialized interface. Through this interface, translators can request machine translation of the untranslated content.

Machine translation occurs periodically, in intervals set by the system administrator, for example, every 24 hours. When a translation request is marked as machine translated, the issuing translator can finalize it and publish it to the SeeArchWeb forum. The machine translated version of the text is presented in a rich text editor. There, the translator can fix any translation errors created by the machine translator.

When this procedure is finished, the translator can use the created text to populate the SEEArchWeb dictionary. More specifically, the dictionary editor presents the translated text highlighting all the recognized words. Here, the translator can add new dictionary entries by right clicking on a word. This dictionary entry consists of:

- The word in the original language
- The word in the translated language
- The type of each word (i.e., noun, verb, gerund)

Finally, the translator can also edit or delete all the dictionary entries.

In closing, the administrator is able to perform all the latter tasks while controlling the forum. He can ban/delete users, delete categories, promote or denote users into user groups, change their contact information (note none can view the user's password as it is not stored in clear text by in a heavily encrypted form). The administrator can also create forum categories, move posts, edit them and delete them. Generally, the administrator has full control over the SEEArchWeb forum.

REFERENCES

ALPAC. (1966). *Language and machines: Computers in translation and linguistics* (ALPAC report). A report by the Automatic Language Processing Advisory Committee. Division of Behavioral Sciences, National Academy of Science. National Research Council. Washington D.C.

Asher, R. E. (1994). Machine translation: History and general principles. *The encyclopedia of languages and linguistics.* Oxford: Pergamon Press.

Bennett, P. (1993). The *interaction of syntax and morphology in machine translation.* London: Pinter.

Chierchia, G., & McConnell-Ginet, S. (1990). *Meaning and grammar: An introduction to semantics.* Cambridge, MA: MIT Press.

Mitkov, R. (2003). Machine translation: General overview. *The Oxford handbook of computational linguistics*. Oxford: University Press.

Nirenburg, S. (1993). *Progress in machine translation*. Amsterdam: IOS Press.

ADDITIONAL READING

Arnold,D.J., Balkan, L., Meijer, S., Humphreys, R.L., & Sadler, L. (1994). *Machine translation: An introductory guide* (PDF version of the book). London: Blackwells-NCC.ISBN: 1855542-17x. Retrieved October 27, 2007, from http://www.essex.ac.uk/linguistics/clmt/MTbook/PostScript/

EAMT - European Association for Machine Translation. Retrieved October 27, 2007, from http://www.eamt.org/

Hutchins, J. (2006). Computer-based translation in Europe and North America, and its future prospects. *JAPIO 2006 Yearbook* (Tokyo: Japan Patent Information Organization, 2006) (pp. 170-174). Retrieved October 27, 2007, from http://www.hutchinsweb.me.uk/JAPIO-2006.pdf

Microsoft Research on MT. Retrieved October 27, 2007, from http://research.microsoft.com/nlp/Projects/MTproj.aspx

SYSTRAN SA. Corporate site and free Web translation services. Retrieved October 27, 2007, from http://www.systransoft.com

KEY TERMS

Machine Translation: A subfield of computational linguistics that investigates the use of computer software to translate text or speech from one natural language to another.

Information Assimilation: The term refers to a process of combining the sensory and non-sensory information obtained from asynchronous multifarious sources using the context and past experience.

Morphology: It is the study concerned with the ways in which words are built up from small meaning-bearing units. Two types are distinguished: the inflectional morphology and the derivational morphology.

Semantics: It is the study of the ways in which individual words (lexical items) have meaning, either in isolation or in the context of other words, and the ways in which phrases and sentences express meanings.

Syntax: It comprises the rules or principles by which words (lexical items) may combine to form sentences.

Section III
Electronic Publishing and Copyright Protection over Archaeological Computer Networks

Chapter XIII
Legal Issues of Electronic Publishing in Virtual Environments

Ioannis Iglezakis
Aristotle University of Thessaloniki, Greece

INTRODUCTION

Electronic publishing is a new concept, aiming at replacing traditional publishing media and making available the electronic delivery of digital content. Initially, e-publishing did not yield expected economic outcomes (Zahrt, 2003). The increase in the use of information and communication technologies, however, and the development of fast network connections, has provided electronic publishing new opportunities. Furthermore, e-publishing changed from text-based applications into multimedia presentations, which can be disseminated in various forms over network environments such as the Internet (Ramaiah, Foo, & Choo, 2003).

In more particular, e-publishing is the application of computing software by a publisher to information content and packaged for a specific audience, and the distribution of the final product through electronic means (Ramaiah et al., 2003). While the earliest applications of e-publishing were stand alone off-line applications, distributed through CD-ROMs and other storage media, today e-publications are far more than that. They include multiple information resources and their distribution takes place over networks, so that the information is able to reach a wider circle of users. It is also notable that file-sharing (peer-to-peer) technologies can be used for the distribution of information, independent from centralized Web servers. Individual authors can benefit from such technologies; however, due to copyright infringement committed by users of P2P systems, the future of such systems remains unclear.

With these appealing characteristics, it is not a coincidence that applications of e-publishing are increasing. It should also be mentioned that major advantages of e-publishing compared to paper publishing are the reduction of cost and the great amount of information that can be put together into such products. On the other hand, commercial publishers have to invent appropriate business models for e-publishing, which may be proven to be complicated.

The applications of e-publishing include the publishing of digital text, electronic versions of books, online newspapers, electronic magazines, electronic journals, electronic newsletters via e-mail, database publishing and courseware publishing (Vitiello, 2001). The distribution of electronic content may take different forms, including Internet bookshops, digital publishing on print-on-demand basis, direct publishing on the Web and wireless Internet publishing on wireless and mobile handheld devices.

E-publishing raises also legal issues referring to the reinforcement of copyright provisions. In particular, publishing of copyright protected material should be authorized by right holders or permitted under a legal exception such as those exceptions concerning teaching or research, and so forth. Other issues concern the protection of content electronically published and licensing agreements between the copyright owner and the organization that is about to exploit the material. The aforementioned issues will be dealt with in this section.

COPYRIGHT PROTECTION OF CONTENTS IN E-PUBLICATIONS

General Requirements

Like print publications, electronic publications also consist primarily of text, photographs and illustrations, but also of animations or musical compositions, which are being digitized and consequently undergo electronic processing. The question which arises is whether such content can be protected by copyright law.

According to the Berne Convention for the Protection of Literary and Artistic Works (the "Berne Convention"), protection of authors refers to literary and artistic works (article 1), and this protection extends to every production in the literary, scientific and artistic domain, whatever may be the mode or form of its expression, such as books, pamphlets and other writings, lectures, dramatic works, musical compositions with or without words, cinematographic works, works of drawing, painting, architecture, sculpture, engraving and lithography, photographic works, illustrations, maps, plans, sketches and three-dimensional works relative to geography, topography, architecture or science.

It is beyond any doubt that works included in e-publications fall within the realm of literary and artistic works, which deserve protection from copyright legislation (Zahrt, 2003). It should be noted that copyright protection does not exclude works of a more practical character, which are protected similarly to fiction (Loewenheim, 1999).

The criterion for eligibility of copyright protection is that the said works are original. The legal term of originality is difficult to define; nevertheless, it can be said that a work is original if it is not commonplace, or in other words, if the bringing together and the arrangement of the material in question is original. According to the theory of statistical uniqueness of *Kummer*, a work is original if it is highly unlikely that another person could create the same or similar work. In common law countries like the UK there is a lower level of originality, since it is required that the author has afforded "skill and labour."

In particular, texts from books, segments of texts and articles underlie copyright protection as literary works. There are no stringent requirements of protection, while also works with lower originality deserve protection ("small coins"). On the contrary, simple information or news do not deserve any protection; also, scientific and technical texts are only protected if they present a high level of originality (Zahrt, 2003).

Collections of texts are protected as collections of literary works in the sense of article 2 para. 5 of the Berne Convention, that is, if, by reason of the selection and arrangement of their contents, they constitute intellectual creations. This is without prejudice to the copyright in each of the works forming part of such collections.

Also, photographs which constitute photographic works in the sense of article 2 para. 1 section 7 of the Berne Convention. Graphic elements are protected under article 2 para. 1 section 9 (illustrations, maps, plans, sketches and three-dimensional works relative to geography, topography, architecture or science). Animations and musical pieces underlie also the protection of copyright law (article 2 para. 1 sections 5, 6 of the Berne Convention).

The Reproduction Right and the Right of Making Available to the Public

The dissemination of copyright protected works in open networks such as the Internet should comply with rules of copyright law as any other type of publication. In more particular, the reproduction right was redefined by Directive 2001/29[1] in order to be adapted to reproduction which is typical in the Internet environment. Under article 2 of the directive, authors and rightholders have the exclusive right to authorize or prohibit direct or indirect, temporary or permanent reproduction by any means and in any form, in whole or in part of their works or other subject-matter.

Accordingly, a publisher may only publish content with permission of the author or rightholder. In most occasions, a nonexclusive license, granting the right to publish a work, will be sufficient. Publishers may not exploit their right to publish in the electronic environment works already published by traditional means, because this constitutes a new type of exploitation of works that should be explicitly permitted by the author.

More particular, scanning of print publications or other copyright protected material and their digitization in order to be used in virtual environments represents a reproduction, regardless of whether it leads to a permanent fixation or not, because the right of reproduction includes also temporary reproduction (Lehmann, 2000).

It should be mentioned, however, that Directive 2001/29 provides for optional exceptions or limitations to the reproduction right, which are also relevant in our case study; nevertheless, they have not been implemented by all EU member states, as there are not mandatory. An exception applies, firstly, to specific acts of reproduction made by publicly accessible libraries, educational establishments or museums, or by archives, which are not for direct or indirect economic or commercial advantage (article 5 para. 2 lit. c). Furthermore, exceptions or limitations to the right of reproduction may be provided in the case regarding use for the sole purpose of illustration for teaching or scientific research, as long as the source, including the author's name, is indicated, unless this is impossible and to the extent justified by the noncommercial purpose to be achieved (article 5 para. 3 lit a.).

These exceptions are indeed important, because they allow reproduction of copyright protected material by educational establishments, such as universities, and also by research institutions or by academics. Projects which are organized under the umbrella of educational or research institutions may benefit from the exceptions and limitations in order to include protected works in their presentations.

Moreover, a new right established by the directive is the right of making available to the public of works in such a way that members of the public may access them from a place and at a time individually chosen by them (article 3). This right applies in particular to publication of works in the online environment and it grants authors the right to decide whether to grant their permission to make available their works over the Internet or not. Regarding this right, the sole exception that may be provided by national legislation concerns the use for the purpose of illustration for teaching or scientific research (article 5 para. 3 lit a).

DATABASE PROTECTION

The development of e-publishing is intertwined with the existence of full-text databases (Zahrt, 2003). Furthermore, Web sites containing collections of information or other resources, which have search possibilities, are able to be characterized as databases.[2] The legal protection of databases is therefore a crucial issue. In the EU, databases are protected under Directive 96/9[3], which provides for twofold protection; namely, databases are protected by virtue of copyright law and by virtue of a sui generis right.

The term "database" is defined as a collection of independent works, data or other materials arranged in a systematic or methodical way and individually accessible by electronic or other means (article 1 para. 2 of the directive). In this sense, it covers both protected works, as well as the collection of simple data.[4]

Copyright protection of databases differs from sui generis protection in that the former requires that a database is original, in the sense that by reason of the selection or arrangement of their contents, constitutes the author's own intellectual creation. The sui generis protection does not require originality, but rather that a database shows that there has been qualitatively or quantitatively a substantial investment in either the obtaining, verification or presentation of the contents (article 7 para. 1). The database right protects the "sweat of the brow" of the database producer, that is, the skill, energy and money invested in the database (Hugenholtz, 2006).

Beneficiary of protection according to copyright law is the author of the database, who shall be the natural person or group of natural persons who created the base or, where the legislation of the member states so permits, the legal person designated as the rightholder by that legislation (article 4 para. 1). Under the sui generis right, the maker of the database is the beneficiary of protection. Beneficiaries are granted rights, which are different in any particular case.

Under copyright law, the author of a database is granted the exclusive right to carry out or to authorize:

- Temporary or permanent reproduction by any means and in any form, in whole or in part; (b) translation, adaptation, arrangement and any other alteration
- Any form of distribution to the public of the database or of copies thereof
- Any communication, display or performance to the public
- Any reproduction, distribution, communication, display or performance to the public of the results of the acts referred to in (b) (article 5)

In contrast, the maker of the database has the right to prevent extraction or re-utilization of the whole or of a substantial part, evaluated qualitatively or quantitatively, of the contents of that database (article 7 para. 1).

LOOPHOLES OF PROTECTION?

In case the e-publishing product fulfils the requirements for protection, the author has specific exclusive rights on his/her product. The core right of copyright is the right to reproduction, but also the right of making available to the public deserves our attention. A specific right is, of course, the right of the maker of a database to prevent extraction or reutilization of the whole or of a substantial part.

Consequently, any reproduction of an e-publising product or of the contents of the database and the presentation to the public of works is not permitted without permission of the author, which has to decide how to exploit his/her work, in general. There are no formal requirements for the recognition of copyright protection or whether it is compulsory to add a copyright note.

However, loopholes of protection may appear in the case of e-publishing products, which are classified as multimedia. In particular, multimedia products are works which combine on a single medium more than one kind of expressions in an integrated digital format, and which allow their users to manipulate the contents of the work with a substantial degree of interactivity (Stamatoudi, 2000). E-publishing products in virtual environments may take the form of multimedia, in case they consist of different expressions, for example, sound, image, texts, and provide extended possibilities to users allowing them to interact with the content of the publication.

As a new category of works, multimedia products have to be classified into one of the existing categories of works, because there are no specific provisions in copyright law for multimedia products. The legal framework for databases would serve for the protection of multimedia products to some extent, but in cases where multimedia products are more sophisticated, they would not fall into the category of databases. The difference between the two categories is that where a database requires elements that are individually accessible, this may not exist in a multimedia product, whose contents are merged inseparably, and which is characterised by a high degree of interactivity (Stamatoudi, 2000).

Other categories of works, such as audiovisual works or computer programs, are also not providing appropriate solutions. In particular, audiovisual works are consisting of a linear predefined sequence of images, and this element does not exist in multimedia products (Latreille, 2000). And furthermore, computer programs differ extensively from multimedia products, which do not consist of source code alone and which include an artistic input (Latreille, 2000).

So where the classification process has failed to provide an adequate solution, it would be suitable to consider multimedia products as derivative or composite works, that is, as works composed of segments separately created by several creators (Kallinikou, 2005; Latreille, 2000; Marinos, 2004). It may also possible to classify multimedia products as collective works, particularly in cases where the final product is created by many persons (Latreille, 2000).

LIMITATIONS OF EXCLUSIVE RIGHTS

Exploitation rights of e-publishers are conceived as exclusive rights, but these rights also underlie certain exceptions, which aim at the protection of the press, of broadcasting organisations and of the freedom of information right. Such exceptions are established in legislations that implement the international copyright conventions. Such limitations of exploitation rights apply, firstly, to reproduction by the press or making available to the public of published articles or of broadcast works in cases in which the reproduction, broadcasting or such communication thereof is not expressly reserved (article 5 para. 3 lit. c of Directive 2001/29, article 10bis of the Berne Convention). Other exceptions and limitations refer to research and teaching, and so forth, which have been already mentioned.

An important limitation of the reproduction right is the one concerning copying for private use. This right has been reformulated by Directive 2001/29 in order to cover acts of reproduction not specifically leading to a fixation of the copy. Article 5 para. 2 lit. b states that exceptions or limitations to the reproduction right may be provided in respect of reproductions on any medium made by a natural person for personal use and for ends that are neither directly nor indirectly commercial, on condition that the rightholders receive fair compensation.

The regulation of the private copy takes into account the legitimate users' rights and it introduces a right that concerns use of copyright protected works that takes place in the private sphere of users with the aim to cover personal needs (Zahrt, 2003). This should be respected also in regard with e-publishing products, which may not restrict the right of users to make copies for own use, for example, through technological measures.

CONTRACTS

Finally, an important issue concerns the contracts for the exploitation of e-publishing products. At first hand, the copyright owner of e-publishing products is entering into contracts with end-users, in order to exploit the material. There are different types of agreements, for example, agreements in which the user buys a subscription, or in which he pays for every use or for use of a work at a particular site, and so forth (Ramaiah et al., 2006). It is notable that there are no legal rules establishing the rights of legitimate users, in contrast to other technology products like software.

Regarding contracts for the exploitation of e-publishing products, it is also possible that problems may occur (Zahrt, 2003). The author or authors of such products have to agree with the party exploiting the product. As a general rule, the author is not able to give a license for not yet known forms of exploitation or obligations in this respect. In this sense, the creation of e-publishing products represents a new from of exploitation of works. This general principle obliges contracts for the exploitation of works to be precisely defined and foresee the specific uses of works.

FUTURE RESEARCH DIRECTIONS

It has been pointed out that the contracts for the exploitation of e-publishing products are not regulated by specific law provisions, as other products of Information Technology do, for example, databases, computer software. It would be, therefore, advisable to analyse the main issues at stake in regulating the relationships between authors and users and try to find a balance between the rights of both.

Such contracts, in particular, will be governed by the general rules of copyright and contract law. The terms of e-publishing licences have to be scrutinized, in order to develop a methodology for the treatment of such licences, including the type of use, specific contract types which are applied to, and standard terms regulating pricing, payment, warranty, possible limitations of liability, and so forth. Cross border licensing also creates problems, which have to be addressed.

Establishing limitations of exclusive rights, in our case of the rights of e-publishers, is another field of research. Particularly, the private copy exemption should be applied in e-publishing products and DRMs should not restrict this right. This should be taken into account in the development of e-publishing products and a theory has to be developed concerning its application in this field.

And finally, the gaps which have been identified have to be further analysed. This regards e-publishing products classified as multimedia, especially those functioning in virtual environments, for which there is currently no legal instrument that will apply. This issue is linked to the more general issue of lack of protection for multimedia products and has to be surveyed in this perspective. Also, the application of database protection to e-publishing products has to be further investigated, because the requirements to afford such protection need to be determined.

REFERENCES

Hugenholtz, P. B. (2006). The new database right: Early case law from Europe. Retrieved October 26, 2007, from http://www.ivir.nl

Kallinikou, D. (2005). *Copyright and related rights* (in Greek) (p. 84).

Latreille, A. (2000). The legal classification of multimedia creations in French law. In I. Stamatoudi & P. Torremans, *Copyright in the new digital environment* (p. 58). London: Sweet & Maxwell.

Lehmann, M. (2000). Digitisation and copyright agreements. In I. Stamatoudi, & P. Torremans. *Copyright in the new digital environment* (p. 195; Zahrt, op. cit, pp. 1674-1675).

Loewenheim. (1999). In Schricker (Ed.), *Urheber Gesetz*, § 2, 1999, nr. 1.

Marinos, M. T. (2004). *Copyright law* (in Greek) (p. 105).

Oberlandesgericht. (1999). (Court of Appeal) Düsseldorf 29 June 1999 (baumarkt.de).

Ramaiah, C., Foo, S., & Choo, H.P. (2006). Trends in electronic publishing. In H. S. Ching, P. Poon, & C. McNaught (Eds.), *E-learning and digital publishing* (p. 111). Dordrecht: Springer.

Stamatoudi, I. (2000). *To what extend are multimedia products databases.* In I. Stamatoudi, & P. Torremans (Eds.), *Copyright in the new digital environment* (pp. Op. cit, pp. 21-22).

Vitiello, G. (2001). A European policy for electronic publishing. *Journal of Electronic Publishing, 6*(3). Retrieved October 26, 2007, from http://www.press.umich.edu/jep/06-03/vitiello.html

Zahrt, M. (2003). Elektronisches Publizieren. In G. Gounalakis (Ed.), *Rechtshandbuch Elektronic Business* (pp. 1663 et seq.). München: Beck Juristischer Verlag.

ADDITIONAL READING

Benett, S. (1993, May 19). Copyright and innovation in electronic publishing: A commentary. *The Journal of Academic Librarianship*, 87-91.

Bider, M. (2003). Copyright and the network. *Learned Publishing, 16*(2), 103-109.

Böhle, K., Riehm, U., & Wingert, B. (1997). Vom allmählichen Verfertigen elektronischer Bücher. Ein Erfahrungsbericht, Frankfurt am Main u. a.

Deloughry, T. J. (1995, September 15). Copyright in cyberspace. *The Chronicle of Higher Education*, A22, A24.

Desmarais, N. (2001). Copyright and fair use of multimedia resources. *The Acquisitions Librarian, 26*, 27-59.

Fiedler, H. (1991). Zukunftsperspektiven des Fachkommunikation. In H. Fiedler (Ed.), *Rechtsprobleme des elektronischen Publizierens.* Köln.

Frazier, K. (1995, June 30). Protecting copyright and preserving fair use in the electronic future. *The Chronicle of Higher Education*, A40.

Früschütz, J. (1997). *Dynamik des elektronischen Publizierens, Daten, Märkte, Strategien.* Frankfurt a.M. 1997.

Haupt, S. (2002). *Electronic Publishing*, München.

Jensen, M. B. (1992). Making copyright work in electronic publishing models. *Serials Review,* 18, 1-2, 62-65.

Kaestner, J. (Ed.). (1999). *Legal aspects of intellectual property rights in electronic commerce.* München.

Kahin, B., & Varian, H. (Eds.). (2000). *Internet publishing and beyond: The economics of digital information and intellectual property.* Cambridge, MA: MIT Press.

Katzenberger, P. (1996). *Elektronische Printmedien Und Urheberrecht: Urheberrechtliche Und Urhebervertragsrechtliche Fragen Der Elektronischen Nutzung Von Zeitungen Und Zeitschriften.* Verlag: Schäffer-Poeschel.

Kindler, P. (2000). „Leistungsschutz für Datenbanken ohne Werkcharakter – Eine Zwischenbilanz.“ *Kommunikation & Recht 2000*, 265-272.

Litman, J. (2001). *Digital copyright*. Amherst, NY: Prometheus Books.

Lutzker, A. (2002). *Content rights for creative professionals: Copyrights & trademarks in a digital age*. Burlington, MA: Elsevier Science.

Riehm, U., Böhle, K., Gabel-Becker, I., & Wingert, B. (1992). *Elektronisches Publizieren. Eine kritische Bestandsaufnahme*. Berlin u. a.

Riehm, U., Böhle, K., & Wingert, B. (2004). Elektronisches Publizieren. In R. Kuhlen, T. Seeger, & D. Strauch (Hg.), *Grundlagen der praktischen Information und Dokumentation*. München: Band 1.

Smith, M. (2005). Fair use and distance learning in the digital age. *The Journal of Electronic Publishing*. Retrieved October 26, 2007, from http://www.press.umich.edu/jep/05-04/smith.html

Strauch, A.B. (2001). (Ed.). *Publishing and the law: Current legal issues*. New York: Hawork Information Press.

KEY TERMS

E-Publishing: The process of creating messages, distributing them, and reproducing them entirely online, often with a capability for feedback.

Copyright: It is a set of exclusive rights granted for a limited time to protect the particular form, way or manner in which an idea or information is expressed. Copyright is an attribute or type of intellectual property.

Loophole: An ambiguity (especially one in the text of a law or contract) that makes it possible to evade a difficulty or obligation

Contract: A legally-enforceable promise or set of promises made by one party to another and, as such, reflects the policies represented by freedom of contract. In the civil law, contracts are considered to be part of the general law of obligations.

ENDNOTES

1. OJ L 167/10.
2. Oberlandesgericht (Court of Appeal) Düsseldorf 29 June 1999 (baumarkt.de).
3. OJ. L 077/20.
4. However, protection of databases does not to computer programs used in the making or operation of databases accessible by electronic means (article 1 para. 3 of Directive 96/9).

Chapter XIV
Drama-Merdžumekja: A Southeast Bulgarian Monument of the European Culture Heritage and Its Publication

Rudolf Echt
University of Saarland, Germany

20 YEARS OF EXCAVATION AT DRAMA-MERDŽUMEKJA: THE MAIN RESULTS

The archaeologists, when excavating, find themselves in a dilemma: they have to dig up from above, but should understand from below. They discover the life cycle of a site always "downside up," first the latest, and in the end the first. But understanding history means to recognize in the first the origins of the latest, in other words, to comprehend the causal relationships in order to be able to explain the reason why the one arose from the other. Understanding the life cycle of a site means, first of all, to chronologically divide the finds and features as accurately as possible. It is only on the basis of a reliable chronological sequence, progressively from one period to the other, that the causal, coherent developments can be described or, in a case they are lacking, the gaps in the cultural sequence. Many years or even decades may pass from the first spade cut, until the archaeologists find themselves in this position.

Let us take as an illustration of this the excavations at Tell Merdžumekja and its surroundings near Drama, southeast Bulgaria[1]. Covering an area of less than 20,000 m², Drama-Merdžumekja is one of the smaller tells in southeast Europe, and its five occupation periods don't demonstrate an especially long sequence[2]. Nevertheless, it took 20 years to the German-Bulgarian excavation team directed by the late Jan Lichardus and the late Alexander Fol, to completely dig up the sites whose life cycles are still only outlined here.

Thanks to the enterprising perseverance of the German excavation director Jan Lichardus as well as to the participation of many archaeologists and more than 110 German and Bulgarian students, and to the diligence of the excavation labourers, we now know that, after a hesitant beginnings in the middle Neolithic, a densely built up permanent settlement was created in the late Neolithic, on a small natural hill on the outskirts of a river valley. This period is referred as Karanovo V in

Thrace and according to the 14C dates, belongs to the fifth millennium cal BC. Certain sporadic finds and features indicate that people had settled down for the first time on the hill in the Karanovo IV period. Pottery sherds of the Karanovo IVb period were recovered from a palisade ditch in the northwestern part of the tell as well as from a pit in its southwestern part, and were scattered in other areas. Pottery sherds of the following Karanovo IVc phase were rare as well. Remains of house structures from that time, however, have not been found at Merdžumekja.

The Middle Neolithic Settlement (Karanovo III-IV)

Before that, however, there existed a settlement barely 300 m south of Merdžumekja, in the Gerena locality (now a meadow), on the bank of the Kalnitsa River. Only a part of this site could be excavated, and only to the point where the water-table hindered excavation to greater depths[3]. We also know for sure that this flat site was occupied for a longer period of time and that it already existed in the Karanovo III period, but we cannot define exactly when it had been created. It is certain, indeed, that the lowest layer excavated is virgin soil. Several pits, however, had been dug up in the virgin sand by the first occupants of the site; these pits contained animal bones and pottery sherds from the classical Karanovo III period as well as several other pottery shapes representing an earlier stage of the Karanovo III or Karanovo II period. We refer to the earliest occupation evidence at this site as Gerena A. Just like the later settlements of Gerena B and Gerena C, Gerena A dates back to the 6th millennium BC.

The Gerena B phase consists of two construction layers. The lowest construction layer Gerena B1 yielded the remains of four houses built at the ground level. When these had already been ruined, three new houses were constructed; two of them were also built at the ground level whereas the third one had a sunken floor. Diagnostic pottery vessels and sherds date both building layers to the Karanovo IIIb phase. After the end of the Gerena B2 construction level, the settlement was deserted and ca. 20 cm earth layer covered the collapsed wattle-and-daub walls of the houses.

Only after this layer had been formed, the site was resettled. The remains of two houses were excavated close to each other, also having sunken floors. Their walls had been burned and destroyed by fire, and they could thus be so easily distinguished from the surrounding deposit that it was possible to measure their height, which amounted to 2.40 m. The ceramic assemblages of both these Gerena C houses clearly differ in shapes and decoration from the ones of the Gerena B phase. They already belong to the Karanovo IV period and represent the Karanovo IVa phase.

After the end of Gerena C, these settlements were abandoned forever. We can only guess why people were forced to leave this area. It is possible that a climate change led to frequent inundations or to a rise of the water table. To answer this question, archaeologists cooperate with physical geographers who evaluate the evidence of climate history acquired from the analyses of soil samples, as well as with palaeozoologists who draw conclusions about the biotope and thus indirectly about the climate from the wild fauna.

The Late Neolithic Settlement (Karanovo V)

Between the end of Gerena site and the beginning of human activities at Merdžumekja, there must have passed a certain period of time, because, as stated above, the earliest finds at Merdžumekja only date back to the Karanovo IVb phase. However, a constant use of this area or even the creation of an organized settlement on the hill could be proven neither for this phase nor for the next Karanovo IVc phase. An organized, densely built-up village[4] existed at Merdžumekja only in the Karanovo V period; a ring ditch separated it from the outside world (Figure 1).

Figure 1. Map of the Karanovo V settlement with the main features.

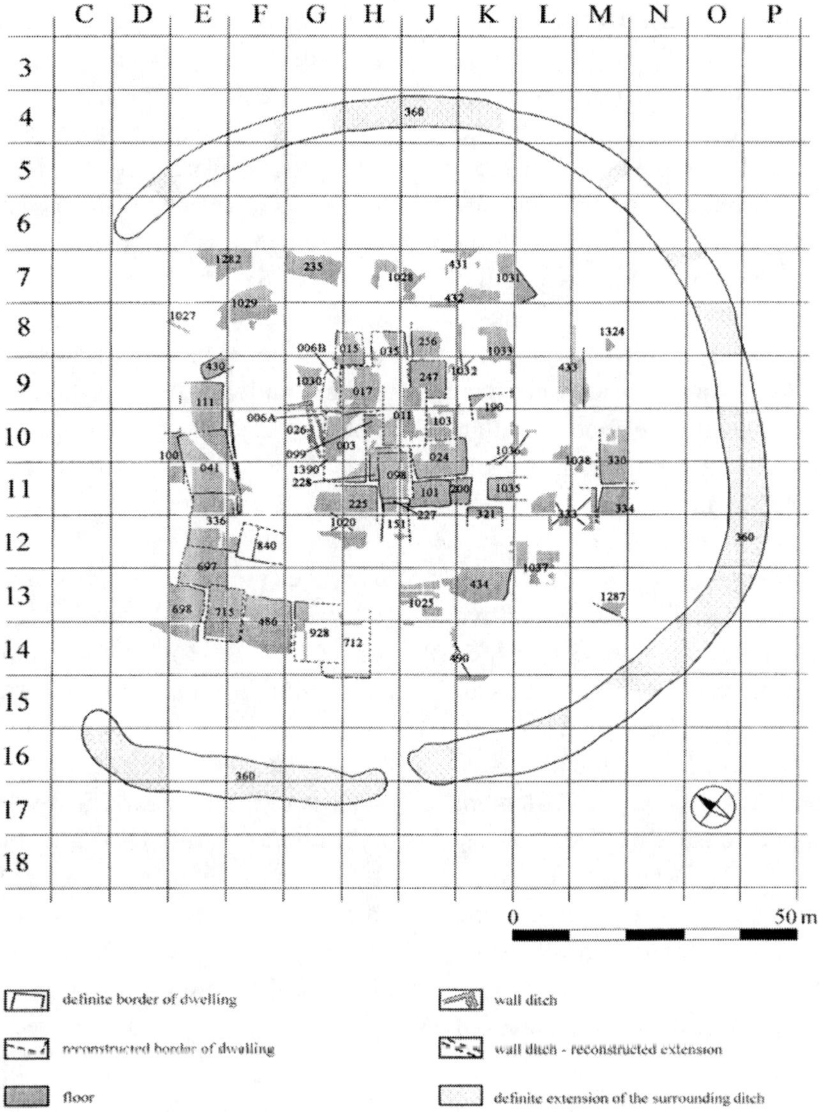

Before the construction of the first houses, measures were taken to make the ground—until then uneven and in places steep—inhabitable inside but difficult to penetrate from the outside world. Natural ground depressions were filled up and slopes were terraced, whereas the northwest slope of the hill was artificially made steeper. On the more slanting slopes of the hill, a ditch was dug up around the settlement, at least two meters deep, and the earth dug up was raised as ramparts. It was not possible to determine the original width of the ditch because during its existence it had been silt up several times, and had to be dug up again. However, taking into consideration its total length of more than 250 meters, we can estimate that the total earth excavated in the area amounts to 20,000 or 30,000 cubic meters.

The remains of 48 houses were discovered and excavated in the settlement. A dozen other areas yielded traces of houses, of which hardly anything was left. Altogether, we estimate that there were originally ca. 60 dwelling houses in the settlement of Merdžumekja during the Karanovo V period.

Settlement's centre was so densely built up that it was difficult to define at first sight the ground plans of neighbouring houses as their ruins covered an undifferentiated area. Sometimes the ground plans could not be defined until the building pits—from 0.20 to 0.60 m deep—that had been dug up before the building of the house, were outlined on the already cleared, flat surface. The construction pits of some houses were partially overlapping; it was therefore impossible that these two buildings existed simultaneously. The first house must have already been ruined when the other one was built on its remains.

This kind of successions was seen in other parts of the settlement as well. Sequences of five successive houses were revealed twice, and once a sequence of three houses. From that one can deduce that the number of houses existing simultaneously was considerably lower than the above number. Moreover, it is sure that the settlement existed for at least five house life cycles.

Besides, the partial overlapping between an older and a newer house means—due to the practice of digging up a construction pit before building a house—that the older feature was disturbed. But also many of the newer houses of the Karanovo V settlement were touched by later disturbances. This makes it twice as difficult for the excavator to define the settlement pattern of the oldest village at Tell Merdžumekja.

All the dwelling houses, the preservation of which allows such an assessment, had one room. The ground plan is rectangular or slightly trapezium-shaped, and only rarely approximately square. Most of the houses had a surface area of 35 to 65 square meters. However, this area has obviously been exceeded three times. The biggest house had a surface area of 94 square meters and was built in the settlement's centre; both the second and the third biggest habitations were located in the western periphery. All of the houses featured ovens. Usually, only the thermal installation's base was preserved, representing a very well smoothed and fired clay layer covering a thermal insulation consisting of pottery sherds or pebbles. Seven houses contained the remains of more than one oven, and one yielded a total of four ovens. But this doesn't mean that these were all used simultaneously because most of the houses of the Karanovo V settlement have been renovated several times, a fact that is evidenced by the number of successive floors. We could recover up to seven successive floors in the same house, each of them consisting of a packed clay layer and a lime plastering. When the old oven

Figure 2. Diagnostic Karanovo V ceramics from house no. 003 (left) and house no. 486 (right).

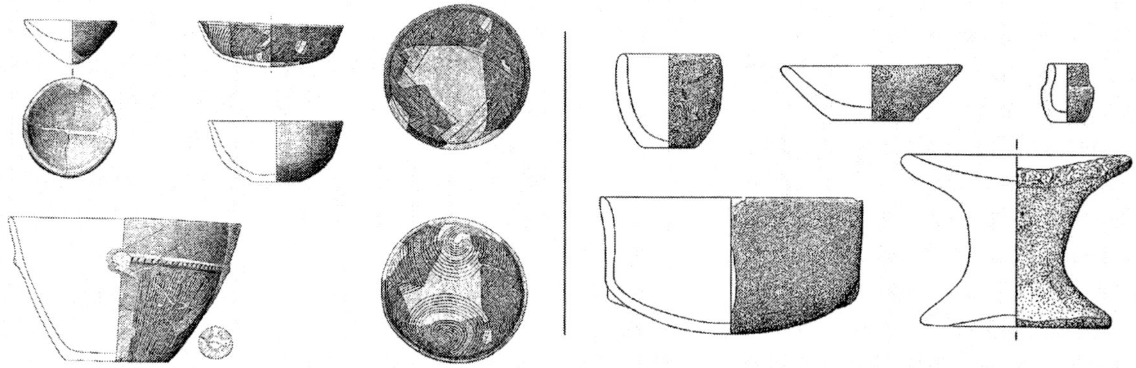

sank in the floor as it was, the house's occupants had to construct another one.

A Karanovo V house usually yielded hundreds to thousands of potsherds. Even entire ceramic vessels or at least complete shapes were found there. Once, two unbroken pottery vessels were found that had intentionally been deposited in a pit under the house floor. Houses number 003, 486, and 715 yielded more than 10 complete pottery vessels (Figure 2). However, these are only a part of the original house inventories. Because in many houses, under the ruins of the collapsed walls, no bigger vessels were found in situ, it seems that these ones were abandoned on purpose; except for the further useless things, only small objects were left behind that could be easily ignored.

Some houses yielded pendants, beads, bone clothing accessories, and fragments of bracelets made of Spondylus, a shell that is not to be found in the Black Sea but in the Mediterranean Sea. The presence of adornments made of Spondylus at Drama suggests that contacts between southeast Bulgaria and the Aegean had taken place during the Karanovo V period.

Besides their houses, the settlers at Drama also erected a special building ca. 8.50 meters long and 7.25 meters wide on the area surrounded by the enclosure. It was located in the western part of the settlement, on an artificially made terrace. We were able to excavate the base of the walls of this building that had still been preserved in a vertical position. They were made of clay mixed with such a big amount of lime that they had a whitish colour. They were on the average 0.45 m thick; the western short wall, however, was only 0.25 to 0.30 m thick. The building was open to the east. It was the only building in the settlement divided by a partition into a bigger anteroom and a narrow back room. In contrast to the dwelling houses it had no oven. It is not possible to make an educated guess regarding the function of this particular building until the conclusion of the general analysis of the Karanovo V site at Drama-Merdžumekja.

The Early Chalcolithic Settlement (Karanovo VI)

The Karanovo V settlement was abandoned, without traces of violence as a possible cause. The tell must have stayed afterward deserted for some time because material of the latest Karanovo

Figure 3. This profile at the eastern border of the settlement shows the cross-section through five different ditches. The older ones (Karanovo V?) have a rounded form, while the younger ones (Karanovo VI) are V-shaped.

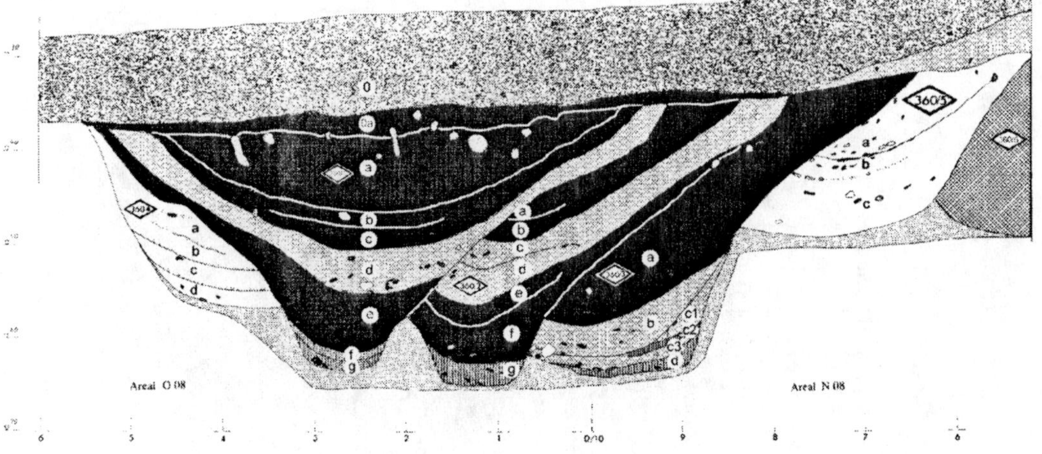

V phase, as it was recovered from Tell Marcheva in Yambol, which is about 40 km away, does not appear at Merdžumekja. This gap, however, could not have lasted very long. When Merdžumekja was resettled, the ring ditch of the Karanovo V settlement must have still been seen on the surface. The new settlers dug up their village ditch where their predecessors had already made theirs (Figure 3).

The newcomers brought some innovations: a new construction technique for their houses, new technologies and new ceramic shapes, which define the Karanovo VI period in Thrace.

The Karanovo VI settlement, which was completely excavated after 20 years hard work, had consisted of at least 25 houses, whose remains were more or less well preserved (Figure 4). There are some more features, which are so badly destroyed that they cannot safely be interpreted as house remains. Besides, some house remains in the northwest part of the settlement could later have been totally removed. That is why the number of 25 houses is less than the real one; the actual number could easily have amounted to more than 30[5].

A belt 20 meters wide remained empty between the ditch, which enclosed the village from the east, south, and west, and the first houses. The area was covered by a clay layer which differed from the usual settlement deposits because it didn't contain pottery sherds and animal bones. The clay layer ended with a stone setting near the edge of

Figure 4. Karanovo VI settlement, with houses and clay pits (outside the enclosing ditch)

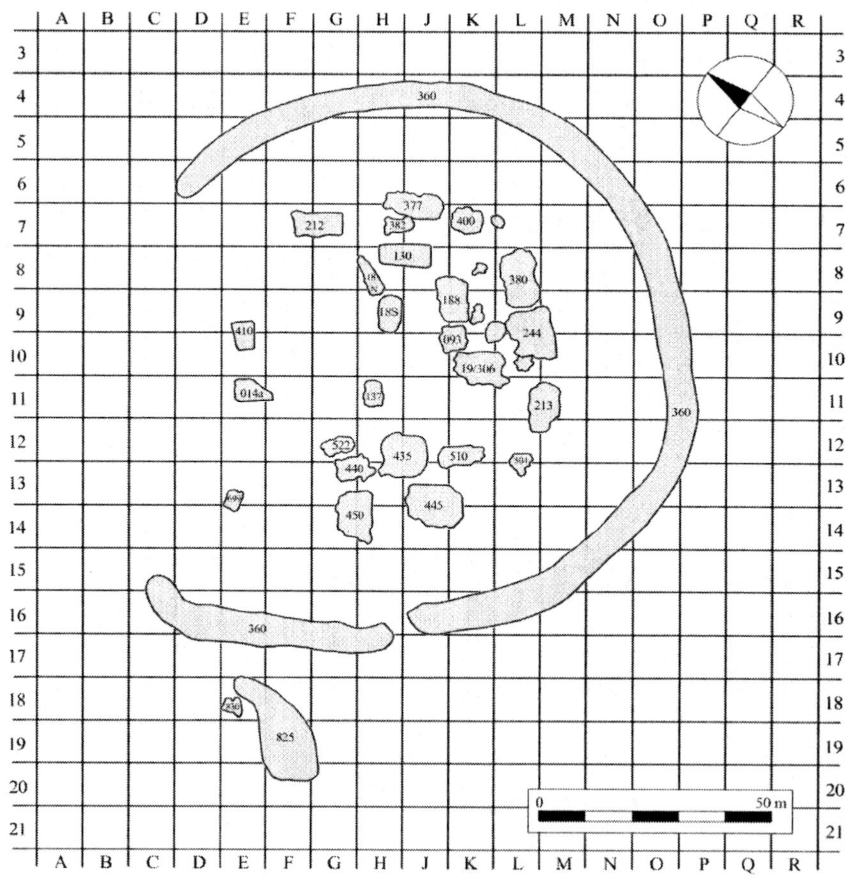

the ditch. As far as this finds lacking clay layer is concerned, these are the remains of ramparts, which rose behind the ditch and whose base was fortified with stones. To the southwest, we were able to find both ends of the ring ditch; the space between them, ca. 4 m wide, represented the entrance to the settlement. Remains of the gate behind it were recovered in the form of small wall ditches as well as postholes. A 1-meter wide strip of plastered pebbles and pottery sherds, which stretches out to the northeast of the gate, indicates the way to the centre of the settlement.

The settlement was designed in such a way that the outer ring of houses has run almost parallel to the village ditch. In the middle, clusters of three to five houses each surrounded an open area. An L-shaped open area of about 500 square meters formed the centre of the settlement. The fact that only a few houses were found to the north of the centre could have been due, as suggested, by later disturbances. Except for the dwelling houses, more than 100 pits were excavated at the settlement, 17 of which can unambiguously be interpreted as storage pits. Some of them have been dug up close to the houses, whereas others were far away from them. We interpret two big pits, which were found beyond the village ditch and outside of the settlement, as clay extraction pits supplying raw material for building and pottery making. If a pit was no longer used, it was filled with rubbish and earth. This also happened with both of the clay extraction pits outside the village.

We found out that a building pit up to one meter deep had been dug up before the construction of each house. This caused serious disturbances to some Karanovo V features. The house floor was constructed above the pit and usually consisted of three layers; a flooring of wooden planks was plastered with a 7 or 8 centimetres thick layer of packed clay; its smoothed surface has been subsequently "whitewashed" with a thin lime layer. Both sides of the wattle-and-daub walls of the houses were plastered with ochre coloured clay. Under good conditions, we were able to observe in several cases that the plastering had been renewed several times by applying a fresh layer. In one of the most centrally located houses, the white plastered inner walls were decorated with red paint. The few preserved plaster fragments allow no reconstruction of the pattern; it was possible to establish, however, that the paintings had been renewed nine times. None of the houses yielded clear evidence about the roof constructions. However, such clay house models as those found at Drama-Merdžumekja feature variously sloping gabled roofs (Figure 5). It is thus plausible to assume that roofs were gabled. The bigger stones that were found in large numbers in the settlement debris suggest a light roof covering of straw, brushwood or reed which has been pressed down with stones against the sometimes rather violent wind.

All houses but one were one-storey, the only exception being the big house in the southeastern

Figure 5. A clay house model from the Karanovo VI settlement at Drama-Merdžumekja with a gabled roof, which can be taken as evidence of contemporaneous roof building.

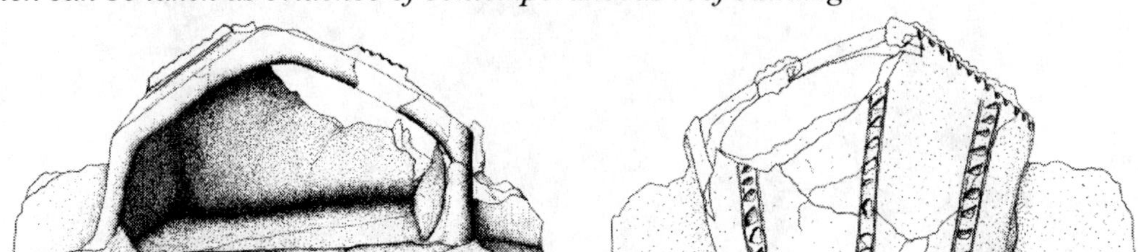

edge of the village, which we refer to as feature No. 244; it had also a second floor. After first excavating the badly damaged remains of the upper storey mixed together with household goods, and then after the removing of a layer consisting of fired clay, we were very much surprised to find a better preserved lower storey ca. 0.30 m under the remains of the upper floor. Whole sets of fine pottery were recovered there, partially still stacked to each other and partially red burned as a result of the secondary firing (Figure 6). Both storeys of house No. 244 yielded more than 200 pottery vessels. A well preserved oven with its dome intact was found on the ground floor of this house. The smashed remains of a second oven revealed that the upper floor featured a thermal installation as well.

The interior furnishing of a Karanovo VI house normally consisted of such an oven, from which often the base has survived only, but in some cases the dome was preserved as well. An oven was built on a low clay pad and could be surrounded by a clay podium. A cooking place has been added to the podium in one of the houses. Millstones were found near the oven. In several houses we could perfectly observe that the oven stood on an earth bank, which had been intentionally left when the construction pit had been dug up. This was also the case with house no. 244; this is why the oven on the ground floor was so well preserved. The above situation reveals a farsighted planning during the digging of the building pit.

This brief description of the architecture features is the result of numerous detailed observations in 25 houses. Of course there are also many other details, which would be interesting only for archaeologists. What has to be emphasized at this point, however, is that there are almost no house remains in situ which is why we had to reconstruct most of the features from the fallen settlement debris. As described above, there was a deep hollow under each house. It was not filled in during the construction process but formed a hollow cavity under the house. This may have served as isolation against rising ground dampness in winter and for cooling in summer. It is also possible that supplies were stored there. The evidence rules out an access from outside. When the houses of the Karanovo VI settlement collapsed, everything came down in these hollows, the floor together with the oven on it (provided that it was not built on an earth bank), and with the furniture that was still in the house, the roof and, in the end, the walls. A profile section of a house demonstrates

Figure 6. Set of fine ceramics, put into one another, found in the burnt debris of house no. 244 (left); the central pot after cleaning (right). The bright red colour is due to its secondary firing.

the following: the wooden construction of the house floor, charred and pressed down, lies on the ground and on the flanks of the hollow. It is covered by the burst chunks of the packed clay layer and the immovable house facilities. They are followed by the crashed household goods overlaid by the often charred remains of the roof and the orange clay of the collapsed walls. From all this becomes clear that the Karanovo VI settlement of Drama-Merdžumekja must have been destroyed in a fire.

A new period at Merdžumekja has been heralded not only by a different settlement structure and building technique, but also by two finds from houses in the western and southern periphery of the site: two small copper chisels! A new period in history began with the discovery of metals, the production of metal tools, and the high value of metals. A farming society, which changed to such an extent that it developed an extensive metallurgy production, could not avoid a certain measure of social division of labour. Craft and trade originated from metallurgy as well as perhaps a class of professional warriors that protected the raw material deposits and secured the commercial routes[6]. All this is evidenced by the finds, and it is the task of the excavator to recognize and interpret the traces. Thus, we found not only copper tools at the Karanovo VI site of Drama-Merdžumekja, but also small thick-walled ceramic vessels, which might be pouring crucibles, as well as some small pottery sherds with sticking slag splashes. Physical-chemical analyses proved that this is copper slag[7]. We can assume that inhabitants of the settlement not only used copper but poured and forged it as well. However, we found no signs of primary metallurgy. The site was completely excavated and therefore this can only mean that the smelting of the ore must have taken place somewhere else, probably near the deposits. The nearest copper deposits, where prehistoric mining has been proved by the Russian archaeologist E.N. Černych, are located at Aibunar in the hills northwest of Stara Zagora, about 80 km away from Drama[8].

The Karanovo VI settlement of Merdžumekja does not seem to have existed very long. All pottery from the houses follow clearly the Karanovo V tradition and date in the earliest phase of the Karanovo VI period, as it is known from Kodžadermen, Ovčarovo, Poljanica, and Sadievo. Later Karanovo VI pottery like that at Ruse, Smyadovo, and Vinitsa does not appear at Drama-Merdžumekja. However, the Karanovo VI settlement must have lasted many decades because, as the trenches in the eastern slope of the tell demonstrated, the village ditch had been dug up several times after it was filled in with material washed down of the accompanying ramparts as well as with windblown and washed down earth (Figure 3).

The amount of the pottery in the houses is noteworthy. As it was already mentioned, more than 200 pottery vessels were found in house No. 244. Other houses also yielded dozens of vessels each. The number of pottery sherds per house can easily exceed 10,000. In house No. 244, there were 43,393 sherds! All the sherds were carefully examined by house or pit assemblages, checked for the right fittings, and the appropriate sherds were fixed to form whole vessels or at least bigger vessel parts. This work has just finished. Almost 1,000 vessels are now at our disposal, their shape being complete or could be reconstructed using close parallels. All pottery vessels are photographed and drawn on a scale of 1:1 in front view and cross section. The visually distinguishable signs of production technology, shape, and decoration of each complete vessel and more than 400,000 pottery sherds have been recorded using an elaborated model. The evaluation of the extensive data is the subject matter of a PhD dissertation at the University of Saarland[9]. The respective physical-chemical analyses will provide information about the composition of the clay and the firing procedures. We can confidently elaborate a ceramic typology based on the detailed analysis of shapes, decorations and technologies, with the help of which it will be possible to objectively compare the ceramic assemblages of the houses, on the one hand, with view of houses' chronology within the settlement, and on the other hand, with view of the social status of houses' occupants, because the ceramics of the Karanovo VI settlement is not homogeneous at all. Besides the relatively simple and quickly made vessels, which were produced to fulfil their purpose, there were others, for the production and decoration of which a lot of efforts, manual skills and knowledge have been invested; this is why they were considered as more valuable. It becomes clear that not only the number of vessels has considerably varied, but also the number of such prestige items in the ceramic assemblages of houses. It will therefore be examined if the cause for this was the different economic power and the related social status of a household.

Besides pottery vessels, the ruins of the houses also yielded implements and tools of stone, animal bones, antler, and clay. Simple polished axes and wedges of local rocks like amphibolites, gabbros and diabas were used in wood processing. Blades and points with bilateral retouch were made of flint. Needles, awls, and chisels were made of animal bone, hammers and toggles of antler[10]. An oven model of clay and a house model on stilts belong also to the assemblage of the Karanovo VI settlement, as well as clay stamp seals and clay plaques interpreted as amulets. In many houses, we found clay figurines and other artefacts whose meaning is to be found in the spiritual and religious beliefs of prehistoric people.

More than 30,000 animal bones come from the house debris; they were examined by the archaeozoologist N. Benecke[11]. 93% of the bones belong to domestic animals: bovines, sheep/goat, pig, and dog. Only 7% belong to wild animals: wild boar, aurochs, fallow- and red deer, brown hare, fox, brown bear, wolf and wildcat. On the one hand, these data indicate what kind of animal husbandry has been practiced and what significance had different animal species for the subsistence; on the other hand, they reveal the natural environment of the settlement.

We were able to collect such a huge amount of data due to the fact that the Karanovo VI settlement had been burned down. It was not rebuilt, but on the place of the burned village, a cult place was established on the top of the hill. The sanctuary consisted of a platform and a building southwest of it. On a large area further eastward, pottery sherds as well as animal bones have been deposited together with tools, figurines, clay horns, and fragments of the so-called cult tables; all this was covered with stones. Following the stone concentrations, we could distinguish 26 single places of deposition. To the southwest, a narrow access ramp, which was flanked on both sides by two basins made of clay and lime, led to a clay podium measuring 3.00 x 4.40 meters. To the northeast, the podium was enclosed by a clay wall ca. 2 m high that was collapsed en bloc beside it. A few steps before the access ramp leading to the podium, we excavated the remains of a big two-room building; in contrast to the dwelling houses of the Karanovo VI settlement, it contained no oven but a round, open fireplace of 1.20 m diameter. Both this building and the podium have been burned up. The chronological distance to the burned settlement must be very short because the pottery assemblages both of the cult place and the settlement are generally similar.

When the former village ditch, which had probably still encircled the sanctuary, was filled up again, new houses were built at the foot of the tell; however, only fragmentary preserved features remained that can hardly be interpreted. When this latest Karanovo VI settlement was created, the tell itself had been deserted. From this last early Chalcolithic settlement at Drama-Merdžumekja comes a golden pendant, which has close parallels, for instance, to the famous Varna cemetery on the Black Sea coast[12].

Remains of the Early Bronze Age Settlement (Cernavoda III)

Many years had to go by before people returned to Merdžumekja. Again, we did not find the traces of their presence on the top of the tell, but on its southeast slope, which faces the Kalnitsa River. The evidence was unclear at first because of the appearance of a black layer up to 1.35 m deep, and was clarified only after its removing. We were able to localize a house and a pit at some distance from it, the latter yielding, besides the usual pottery sherds and stones, fragments of clay nozzles, ladles and copper droplets that prove the existence of a local metallurgy production. The pottery from the house dates to the Early Bronze Age (according to the Near Eastern/Aegean chronology) and belongs to a culture formation common from the lower Danube to the Carpathian basin. In Romania and northwest Bulgaria, it is referred to as Cernavoda III, and in Hungary and Slovakia, as Baden-Boleráz. According to the 14C dates, we can date this formation to the mid fourth millennium cal BC.

The Middle Bronze Age Ritual Enclosure (Nova Zagora culture)

The Early Bronze Age Cernavoda III settlement remained only a short episode. After a long gap, new building activity on the tell could be proven again at the beginning of the second millennium BC. As toward the end of the Karanovo VI settlement, a cult place has been installed at Merdžumekja, almost 2,000 years having passed in between. This evidence was the subject matter of F. Bertemes' habilitation submitted to the University of a Saarbrücken; it was considered in its Aegean context[13]. The study will be published shortly.

The ritual enclosure has an oval shape with a diameter, 41.50 m west to east and 38.50 m north to south (Figure 7). It consists of a V-shaped ditch 3 m deep that is open to the south. The enclosed area could be entered by a passage 3.60 m wide between the two ends of the ditch. Apart from some pits, there are no contemporary building remains in this area. A circle of 13 postholes was recorded opposite the entrance, but there were

Figure 7. The Middle Bronze Age ritual enclosure and the remains of the contemporaneous building outside the ditch.

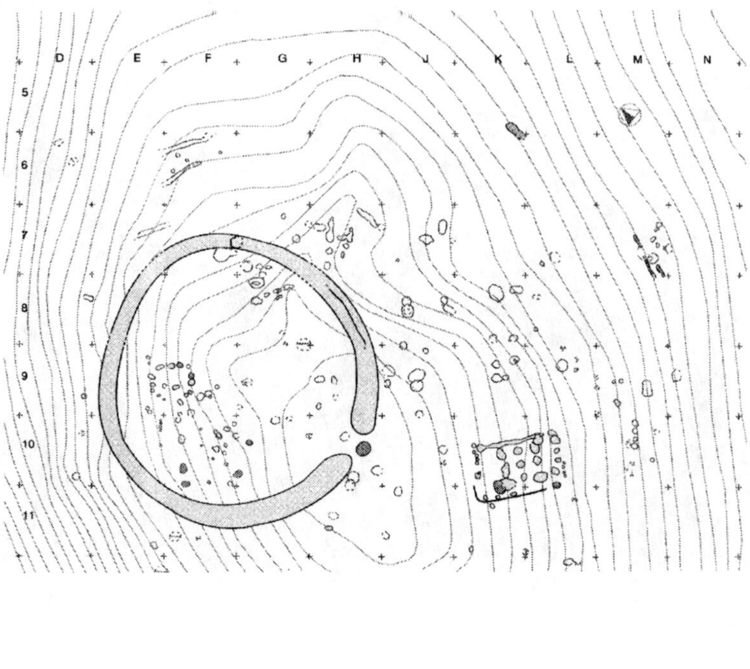

neither remains of walls nor pieces of wattle-and-daub constructions. F. Bertemes thus interprets this feature as a circle of free standing poles[14]. It was not possible to establish whether the site of the ritual enclosure was levelled in advance, for modern-times cultivation has repeatedly disturbed the soil up to that depth. In any case, it is noteworthy that only at the outmost edge of this area, the remains of two Karanovo VI houses were found, while on the enclosed area itself no remains of Karanovo VI buildings were recorded but a number of houses belonging to the Karanovo V settlement.

About 15 m in front of the entrance to the encircled area, the remains of a building with an area of almost 100 square meters and with a NW-SE orientation were visible in the form of wall ditches and postholes. The entrance was located in the northwest; the opposite side had slightly apsidal form. Three rows of posts, which divided the inside of the building into four bays, supported the timbering. Except for subterranean traces of the roof-supporting posts and the walls, nothing else was preserved; the floor with its associated installations was destroyed by ploughing. Accordingly, there were no in situ finds contemporary with the building.

The number of finds from the ditch, however, is much larger. A complex analysis of the 56 graphically recorded profiles of the ditch made by F. Bertemes yielded the conclusion that this whole feature had contained the same sequence of four layers, while in some places there could be four more layers, locally restricted. Many completely preserved pottery vessels were recovered from the upper two of the overall layers, above all askoi and jars, more rarely bowls, bottles, high jugs, cups with spouts, large carinated vessels, sieves, funnels, beakers and pots (Figure 8). All vessel types can be found in the ceramic assemblage of the Middle Bronze Age (according to Bulgarian terminology) Nova Zagora culture, to which this enclosure can be attributed. This period is simultaneous with the Early Helladic II–III in the Aegean dating to the second half of the 3rd millennium BC.

Some vessels contained grain. While it is already unusual to find entirely preserved pottery vessels in a ditch, these contents indicate without any doubt that they were not rubbish disposed of in the ditch but intentionally deposited goods. Loom weights, spindle whorls and perforated pottery sherds also belong to the depositions in the ditch. They were concentrated to the right and

Figure 8. Various types of Nova Zagora pottery from the ditch of the Middle Bronze Age sanctuary.

to the left of the entrance as well as in the eastern and western parts of the ditch.

Especially informative are fragments of life-size clay figures of humans and animals as well as of clay basins from the ditch, which may have been used as ritual images and cult equipment. Packed layers of stones and chunks of daub covered the depositions. The observation that the earth around the chunks of daub was exposed to fire leads to the conclusion that when the daub had been dumped on the deposited vessels, it was still hot. Whether it came from the walls of the described building, which would afterward have been burned, is only a speculation.

Settlement Remains of the Early Iron Age (Pshenichevo)

The Early Iron Age Pshenichevo culture has left the latest settlement traces at Merdžumekja. It is represented not only with characteristic pottery vessels decorated with cord and stamp impressions, zoomorphic figurines and a mould for sleeve hatchets, but also with several dozen pits. Some of them can be interpreted as storage pits; others outlined a rectangular area and might therefore had marked the location of the posts of rectangular houses although their average diameter is up to 1 m. Two pits definitely contained burials. Burial no. 1 contained the skeletons of a woman and child interred together, both lying in a contracted position on the right side, the woman oriented north-south and the child oriented south-north, that is, facing each other. Burial no. 2 yielded a child between 5 and 9 years old, lying in a contracted position on the left side, on the bottom of a storage pit. It is possible to date these burials on the basis of Pshenichevo pottery sherds that were recovered from the backfill of the pits. This channelled and stamp impressed pottery is diagnostic for the centuries before and after 1000 BC.

Thus ends the settlement activity at Merdžumekja. The latest remains of human presence at the tell are some Roman Age pits. However, they cannot be connected with any building remains and therefore must be considered as evidence of temporary presence of people at Merdžumekja. A contemporaneous settlement must have existed in the vicinity, as can be proven by stray finds in the Drama-Jurenja locality and elsewhere in this micro region.

A Roman cemetery dating from the late 1st to the 5th century AD was discovered and partially excavated on the Kajrjaka hill, at the southern edge of the micro region. At the same place an earlier cult centre was located where offerings had been deposited from the times of the Pshenichevo culture to the end of the pre-Roman Iron Age. This site can serve as evidence that people have steadily been occupying this micro region in the 1st millennium BC when Merdžumekja had been deserted.

FROM EXCAVATION TO PUBLICATION

This short summary of a southeast European site's life cycles dating from the 6th to the 1st millennium BC is the result of 20 years of excavation and research. It relies on the extensive records of the excavated features and finds. How this was achieved and what is it based on will be generally explained below.

Excavations and Finds Processing

According to the modern standards, a square grid of areas measuring 10 x 10 meters was laid out on Tell Merdžumekja before the beginning of the excavations. Every 20 m, the vertices of the grid were marked with short iron posts fixed in concrete. The southwest vertex of area J11 on the top of the tell was selected as the datum. Its height, which is 120.32 m above sea level, was the point of reference for all height measurements at Merdžumekja.

The 10 x 10 m areas constituted the excavation units. Each area was labeled with a distinct alphanumeric combination; the letter sequence proceeds from west to east and the numbers from north to south. Correspondingly, the above mentioned area J11 is located in the centre of the tell, B3 to the northwest, and R20 to the southeast.

After the beginning of excavation in an area, strips 0.25 m remained unexcavated on each side. In this way, earth banks of 0.50 m were left between the neighbouring areas. On the vertical walls of these earth banks, the sequence of excavated layers could be controlled and recorded.

Measuring distances from the southwest vertex of each area, the north and east coordinates of all features and finds in this area were recorded with measuring tape, and the depths below datum (BD) were determined with a leveling device. In this way, all features and finds were recorded three-dimensionally, both in their relative and absolute position.

As soon as the surface humus layer was removed, locally restricted, differentiated discolorations in the cleaned surface were outlined as indications of anomaly. They could be sign for a filled-up pit, ditch or building spot, or they could have emerged naturally through alluvial material. The established anomalies were recorded with photographs and drawings, and after that were excavated. First, only half of the smaller features were excavated, and only a quarter of the larger ones, so that from each feature could be obtained at least a cross section; larger features should have had both cross section and longitudinal section. After the features were completely excavated, a new situation plan was drawn. Each artificial feature received a consecutive number ("object no."), for its clear identification and fixed referring. Finds within such features were recorded with the same object numbers, permitting a quick assessment in further considerations.

Considering the small finds, they were distinguished into two categories. Each complete or almost complete artefact, as well as potsherds found together, fragments of special finds such as figurines, plaques or amulets, and such made of rare materials like Spondylus shell, copper or gold, were regarded as small finds of category one. They were measured three-dimensionally.

Small finds of category two are single pottery sherds and animal bones from defined contexts, that is, from settlement features. In the case of larger features, they were collected from units of a square meter and delivered as a collection. Likewise, we proceeded with potsherds and animal bones found in the deposit outside of features. They were generally collected from units of one square meter. For that purpose, each area was divided with cords into 100 squares, which were consecutively numbered from 00 to 99. This procedure enabled us, during later pottery analyses, to lay out the sherds in a manner corresponding to the original situation of their finding, and facilitated the search for fitting pieces.

While processing the ceramic finds, potsherds from undefined contexts were downgraded to small finds of category three. This means that they were considered in a simplified procedure where only size, body part (rim, wall, or bottom) and technology of decoration were recorded and where the collection was considered as a whole. All potsherds of category two were determined in more detail according to criteria like size, weight, firing, thickness, shape, technologies of decoration, decoration patterns, and combinations of decoration patterns based on permanently updated catalogues. In the course of this, a data sheet was filled in for each potsherd. The data sheets form the database for a more detailed statistical analysis of all pottery sherds from defined contexts.

Recording and Consideration

A couple of figures should give the nonprofessionals an impression of the large extent of the recording, which has to be conducted for the scientific consideration of excavations of this size.

Areas represent the units not only of the excavations themselves but of the recording as well. This means that the excavations conducted, the observed results and the small finds are recorded separately for each area. For each area excavated field logs are kept, in which the everyday work progress and the observed results are recorded. After the day records, the label duplicates were fixed in the field log that were made for small finds of category one and closed collections. The original labels accompanied the finds through all stages of their processing, until they were stored in depositories.

The excavated features were recorded with 2124 scale drawings; all of them were drawn manually on millimetre paper, on a scale of 1:20 (burials and very important features, on a scale of 1:10) with pencil, and were coloured with crayons. Situation plans record the features in the area, whereas profile drawings illustrate the cross sections through the layers' sequence at the area's borders or the sequence of soil layers in pits and ditches. Each drawing corresponds to a respective description in the field log. The completed drawings were consecutively numbered and these numbers were recorded in a drawing log.

The graphic records of the features were complemented with 1,348 excavation photos (colour slides) and 2,448 field photos (black and white negatives). Photo numbers were recorded together with the date of photographing and a short description of the respective situation in a general excavation photo log and in a field photo log, as well as in the day records of the respective field log.

The small finds records also include drawings, photographs and descriptions. All artefacts of stone and bone, metal and clay (stamp seals, plaques, spoons, loom weights, etc.), all anthropomorphic and zoomorphic clay figurines, complete pottery vessels, and all pottery sherds having a distinguishable profile from rim to bottom, were drawn in front view and cross section on a scale of 1:1 (Figure 9). Only for those vessels higher than 0.40 m, a scale of 1:2 was used. In addition, many other single sherds were drawn because of their interesting decoration or special shape or because they characterize certain contexts. 16,500 small finds have hitherto been drawn. Because some find assemblages have not been finally processed—among them large parts of the material from the Karanovo V settlement as well as from the flat site at the foot of Merdžumekja and the Cernavoda III settlement—this number is going to increase.

Because drawings do not record the surfaces of small finds in detail, each drawn artefact was also photographed. In addition, some sherds that

Figure 9. Example of a line drawing. Cross-section, orthoptic front and side view, and complete ornamentation of the vessel in Figure 6.

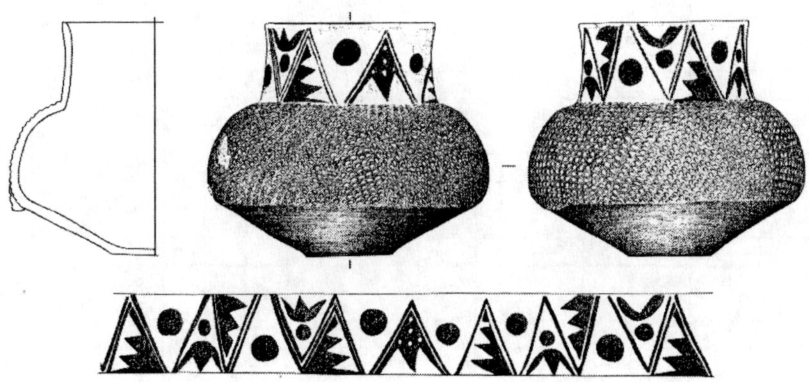

were not suitable for drawing were photographed to work with. A total of 15,050 small finds have been photographed so far. All these photos are part of the archives and are stored together with drawings and descriptions for the further consideration of the excavation finds.

The description of finds has a standard form. For this purpose a numerical code was developed, as can be illustrated, for example, with the description of the pottery. The information from Drama, which has been recorded on the data sheets (Figure 10), is fed into dBase files in Saarbrücken, which enables an automated analysis process. Pottery from the Karanovo VI settlement of the early Chalcolithic alone comprises 442,918 records! 26,915 of them refer to bottom sherds, 270,046 to decorated wall sherds and 79,677 to undecorated wall sherds, 46,589 to undecorated and 16,539 to decorated rim sherds. Further 3,152 records refer to complete vessels and sherds of vessels whose profile could be completely distinguished from the bottom to the rim.

It is clear that the collection and processing of such an amount of data require time, a lot of time and personnel. A trained person can determine 2,000 or 3,000 sherds in 4 weeks, depending on the degree of difficulty. Taking the average into account, it is concluded that a person determines 625 sherds per week. A single person would need approximately 709 weeks or almost 14 years uninterruptedly in order to describe only the Karanovo VI pottery from Drama-Merdžumekja. The same holds true for the drawings of the finds. A talented and trained person needs 90 minutes for a drawing in average; small artefacts can be drawn in 10 minutes, whereas the drawing of a big artefact with a more complex geometry and variant surface may need some days. When averaging 90 minutes for a drawing, 24,840 hours are needed for 16,560 drawings or, for a 48-hour week, approximately 10 years, without a single day of holiday or sick leave.

Because so much time is needed already for the consideration and processing of data, it becomes clear that the analysis requires plenty of time as well, even if an automated process is employed. To analyze the data means first to deduce established standard combinations of characteristics

Figure 10. Example of a data sheet of decorated potsherds numerically coded.

DRAMA MERZUMEKJA — VERZIERTE WANDUNG Seite: 13

DATUM: 04.09.98 Bearb.: D. Meyer Obj.Nr.: 699 Bemerkungen:

B.Nr	Ar.	Str.	Qua.	KL-NR	Z.NR	Erh	Disp	VT	ME	Komb	Grö	Gew	Mag	Bra	OBi	OBa	Fai	Faa	Wa	
177	E13	/	/	96.0171		8-13	5	PL 29	5	6	3	55	4	2	4	2	9	9	39	
							5	Kn 26												
							6-8	Ge 5		35										
178						7	/	Kn 2 fay			4	6	3	3	3	3	12	15	12	
179						7	/	Kn 26		34	3	28	5	2	3	3	9	9	39	
							/	Gx 5		35										
180						9	/	Kn 10			3	14	4	2	4	3	8	8	39	
181						9	/	Kn 7			4	14	4	2	4	3	12	10	6	
182						9	/	Kn 58			4	9	5	2	4	4	12	12	4	
183						9	/	Ri 3.1	5	9	3	12	2	1	4	4	6	15	1	
							/	Ka 11 inkr.	4											
184						15	3	Ka 5			4	14	12	3	3	2	2	2	24	
185						9	/	Ka 16			3	24	2	2	4	3	12	12	5	
186						15	3	Ka 3			4	11	4	2	4	3	15	9	3	
187						9	/	Ei 32	5		4	9	3	3	3	3	12	12	13	
188						7	/	Ka 19			5	4	4	3	3	3	14	14	14	
189						7	/	Ka 3			4	8	2	2	3	3	10	10	10	
190						13-15	13	Ka 21			3	15	4	2	3	3	12	12	5	
							3	Ge 12		35										

from the visual information stored in drawings and photos and from the codified conceptual information stored in databases. The result of this process is what the archaeologists characterize as "types," namely standard combinations of certain shapes, technologies and decorations, established by custom and followed for a while.

Because all standards change with time, it is expected that types correspond to a chronological sequence. In order to solve this problem, the finds classified in types must be related according to their context; it should be examined what types existed together in the same house–and therefore were contemporaneous during only a few decades–and what types could never be found together in the same house. As a solution to this problem we use statistical procedures like a presence/absence matrix and correspondence analysis. The mapping of distribution patterns of types and combinations of types within the settlement should finally show where were the houses of each period, which resulted from time specific type combinations. On the basis of a chronology as precise as possible, the archaeologists, who are also historians, can tackle questions like number of inhabitants of the settlement excavated, their social structure, subsistence economy and religion.

Publication

From what has been mentioned above it becomes clear that two things cannot be achieved when excavating a site like Drama-Merdžumekja. There will be no complete catalogue containing all features and finds; such a catalogue would not only be almost unaffordable but also hardly useful. It would be of no use to anyone, for example, to publish 270,000 undecorated wall sherds from the Karanovo VI period. And second, it is not possible to publish a single book in which the interested reader could find everything about Drama-Merdžumekja. Therefore, a publication of 16 volumes is planned which will gradually appear. Each volume will contain certain parts of the results; all settlement features and finds will be considered there, together with plans and drawings, partially complemented with photos, as far as they are necessary for the understanding of the excavation results and for the reasoning of their interpretation. Everything else will only appear as a number in statistics. Two volumes are being prepared for printing and their publication can be expected within the next year. The first volume, which will appear in English, summarizes the main results of the excavation and analysis until now, according to the current knowledge. This volume differs from all the others to the extent that it serves professionals and students from all over the world as an introduction to the research and the variety of the problems encountered. In the second volume, the ritual enclosure of the middle Bronze Age will be published. A third volume, which contains the results of the Karanovo V settlement, is making good progress. Four more volumes are currently being worked on. They concern the settlement and pottery vessels of the Karanovo VI period, the pottery of the Pshenichevo culture group at Drama and in the lower Tundzha area[15], as well as the results of geological and palaeozoological investigations[16]. The remaining volumes can be premeditated only after work on the above volumes is finished. We must calculate realistically that as much time will be needed for the complete publication of the Drama excavation results as for the excavations themselves.

As not to leave the professionals for so long in a state of uncertainty, three detailed preliminary excavation reports have been published in an internationally widespread German journal, the *Bericht der Römisch-Germanischen Kommission* (Ber. RGK): in Ber. RGK 70, 1989, a preliminary report about the excavations 1983-1988; in Ber. RGK 77, 1996, a preliminary report about the excavations 1989-1995; and in Ber. RGK 84, 2003, the last preliminary report about the excavations 1996-2002. All these reports have inevitably preliminary nature, reflecting the prevailing interpretations before the end of the excavations and long before the end of the final analyses of the finds. Similarly, this is also true for the small comprehensive monograph published under the title *Forschungen in der Mikroregion Drama 1983-1999* in 2000, with the Dr. Rudolf Habelt Publishing House, and in Bulgarian in 2001, with the St. Kliment Ochridski University Publishing House, Sofia. Besides, since 1988, Jan Lichardus and various researchers involved in the excavation project have published articles in scientific journals or congress proceedings that consider single aspects or subproblems. A permanently updated list of all publications about Drama is available at the Internet address http://www.phil.unisb.de/fr/vfgeschichte/dramlit.html.

These preliminary reports, like the planned publication, address to professionals, as well as students, and not to the general public. This is why the text prevails over the figures. Black and white images are exclusively used, mainly in the form of line drawings like Figures 3 and 9. Certainly the two-dimensional reproduction of three-dimensional objects means a reduction, connected with a schematic reproduction of the surface marks. Professionals, however, have no problem with that; they are used to this kind of representation of features and finds. The planimetral representation of finds drawn on a scale offers the advantage to the professional to objectively compare large series of finds with the help of drawings on the same scale. The various features of the surfaces, often brought about by lying in the earth, are of smaller importance for the typological consideration and can therefore often be ignored. For the scientific publication of larger amounts of finds, one will therefore still prefer the drawing of correctly oriented and measured objects to every other type of illustration.

The general public has other requirements, and the archaeologists who are financed by its taxes should take them seriously into account. In an ideal case, they present their finds to the public in the museum. Since 1988, important finds assemblages from Drama were shown in three international exhibitions: "Power, Domination, and Gold. The Varna cemetery (Bulgaria) and the beginning of a new European civilization" at the Saarland Museum in Saarbrücken in 1988; "Drama—7000 years between the Pontic and the Aegean" at the Yambol Museum of History in 2000 and at the National Museum of History, Sofia, in 2001; and finally "The Thracians—Orpheus' Golden Empire" at the Art and Exhibition Hall of the Federal Republic of Germany, Bonn, in 2004. Since 2005, the finds from Drama are the heart of the Prehistoric Department of the Kabyle Museum near Yambol. This type of publication creates the closest contact between the archaeological find and its viewer. The disadvantage is, however, that this contact can take place only at a single location and only for a short time. In order to balance this disadvantage, museum and exhibition catalogues are being printed, with colour, nicely arranged photos and descriptive text[17]. Meanwhile, the photographs represent the viewpoint that the photographer has selected to photograph, and they also reduce the artefacts to the two dimensions of a book page. The same is true for electronic publication on the Internet.

New Media

Modern technology enables an imaging method nowadays that does not know this restriction any more: three-dimensional scanning, shortly named 3D-scanning. 3D-scanning is an efficient technology that depicts in a very short time photo-realistically the surface of an object in the form of clusters of pixels. A three-dimensional computer model of the object is created through the large amount of received data in real colour and with all the available features of the surface. It can be animated and therefore observed by the user from every desired view angle. In this regard, the presentation of an animated 3D-model even exceeds the direct presentation of the object in the museum. That is why this technology should undoubtedly be used. The question is, for what kind of finds its use is appropriate and meaningful?

This question can be answered by a comparison between the advantages of an orthographic projection, a conventional photograph, and a 3D scan. When it is a matter of comparing large series of similar objects irrespective of their colour and surface texture, an undistorted scale drawing will be preferred. Because conventional photos can never overcome distortion, they are less suitable in this case. They are suitable when an exact colour illustration of a surface in a very high resolution is needed, for example, for the recording of painted figurines or vessels. 3D-scanning combines an exact colour illustration of the surfaces in a middle resolution and the possibility to determine and represent an object in all of its dimensions. The advantages of the 3D-technique are interesting when dealing with objects of complicated geometry that cannot be grasped with just one view. Moreover, objects with strongly differentiated, or multicoloured surfaces can be better represented through 3D-scanning than through the conventional technologies of the visual recording. This kind of publication on the Internet is especially suitable for anthropomorphic and zoomorphic figurines, as well as for coloured small finds, for example, the graphite painted and white incrusted pottery of the late Neolithic and the early Chalcolithic at Drama-Merdžumekja and other sites where such pottery has been recovered. The possibility to exemplarily observe such finds as computer models from all angles is interesting not only for the general public but also gives students and professionals in Europe and all over the world a completely new impression of finds they often don't know in original and which they can see only on long and expensive trips to several museums.

Hence, the completely clear demand of the SEEArchWeb project to 3D-scan exemplary finds from southeast Europe which are typical of certain period of time, certain area or certain culture. For Drama, we suitably selected a series of artefacts to illustrate a 7,000-year history of civilization in southeast Europe using prominent examples. If not unfeasible, it is very difficult to transport the finds to the location of the 3D-scanner at the AUB in Blagoevgrad. As far as the three-dimensional presentation of the above mentioned artefacts on the Internet is concerned, these unique, thousands-of-years-old remains of the European culture heritage are often very fragile due to their age and for that reason can only be transported by experts with great care. Their material value is not insignificant and this should additionally be taken into consideration; in any case, it means high insurance costs. For these reasons, it is better to go the opposite way, visiting the relevant museums of southeast Europe with a 3D-scanner and scan the finds there. That also requires a lot of money because the 3D-scanner must be operated by a trained person. However, the costs are manageable and there is no danger that the project would fail because of a museum director's veto.

FURTHER DIRECTIONS

The methods of electronic data processing will doubtlessly play an ever more important role in the documentation of excavation features, the analysis of the small finds and the communication of excavation results. Archaeologists will have to take this into account in the planning of larger, long lasting excavations.

This begins with the use of electronic total stations, the data of which is saved and processed by graphic producing software allowing for the production of contextual plans, feature plans and even three dimensional topographic models with as yet impossible speed. Analogue photographic documentation is already augmented by the use of digital cameras in the graphic documentation of the features and the finds in the creation of internal reference material. With the development of high resolution digital cameras is to be expected that one may rely solely on digital photographic information in the not too distant future.

These developments extend their utility to the use of databanks and their implementation in geographic information systems (GIS). These systems serve not only the feature-linked registration of all small finds, but are also an important instrument in the spatial analysis thereof.

If all of these prerequisites have been completed, it would not be so difficult in the future to represent the main excavation results on the Internet, besides the usual publication of book[18].

REFERENCES

Benecke N., & Lichardus, J. (1999). Der „arme" Hund von Drama. Bemerkungen zu einem früheisenzeitlichen Hundeskelett aus Südost-Bulgarien. In C. Becker u. a. (Hrsg.), *Historia animalium ex ossibus. Festschrift für Angela von den Driesch.* Internat. Arch. Stud. Honoraria, 8, 67-77.

Bertemes, F. (1998). Der mittelbronzezeitliche Kultgraben von Drama und seine kulturhistorische Stellung in Südosteuropa. *Arch. Nachrbl.* 3, 322-330.

Bertemes, F. (2002). Heiligtum und Kultplatz in der thrakischen Ebene im 3. Jahrtausend v. Chr. *Ber. RGK* 83, 23-144.

Bertemes, F., & Krastev, I. (1998). Die bulgarisch-deutschen Ausgrabungen in Drama, Bez. Burgas - Katalog. In A. Fol & J. Lichardus (Hrsg.), Macht, *Herrschaft und Gold. Das Gräberfeld von Varna (Bulgarien) und die Anfänge einer neuen europäischen Zivilisation*, 241-266.

Echt, R. (2001). Die eisenzeitliche Kultanlage von Drama-Kajrjaka - ein thrakisches Heiligtum im Wandel der Zeit. In *Thrace and the Aegean: Proceedings of the Eighth International Congress of Thracology*, Sofia - Yambol, 25-29 September 2000. Sofia, 187-205.

Fecht, F. (2002). Die Karanovo V-zeitlichen Öfen in Drama-"Merdžumekja". In Lichardus-Itten, M., Lichardus, J., & Nikolov V. (Hrsg.) *Beiträge zu jungsteinzeitlichen Forschungen in Bulgarien.* Saarbrücker Beitr. Altkde. 74. Bonn, 511-528.

Fecht, F. (2004). F. Fecht, Karanovo V-zeitliche Häuser von Drama-Merdžumekja. In V. Nikolov, K. Băčvarov, & P. Kalchev (Eds.), *Prehistoric Thrace. Proceedings of the International Symposium in Stara Zagora*, 30.09 - 04.10.2003. Sofia-Stara Zagora, 283-291.

Fol, A., Katinčarov, R., Lichardus, J., Bertemes, & Iliev, I. (1989). Bericht über die bulgarisch-deutschen Ausgrabungen in Drama (1983-1988). Neolithikum - Kupferzeit - Bronzezeit. *Ber. RGK* 70, 1989, 5-127.

Lichardus, J., Echt, R., Iliev, I.K., Christov, Ch. J., Becker, J.S., & Thiele, W.- R. (2002). Die Spätbronzezeit an der unteren Tundža und die ostägäischen Verbindungen in Südostbulgarien. *Eurasia Antiqua*, 8, 133-182

Lichardus, J., Fol, A., Getov, L., Bertemes, F., Echt, R., Katinčarov, R., & Iliev, I.K. (1997). Bericht über die bulgarisch-deutschen Ausgrabungen in Drama (1989-1995). *Ber. RGK* 77, 1996 (1997), 5-106 Taf. 1-30 Beil. 1-8.

Lichardus, J., Fol, A., Getov, L., Bertemes, F., Echt, R., Katinčarov, R., & Iliev, I.K. (2000). 18 Jahre bulgarisch-deutsche Forschungen in Drama, obština Tundža (Kurzer Bericht). 18 godini bălgarsko-germanski archeologičeski izsledovanija kraj s. Drama, obština Tundža. *Vesti na Jambolskija muzej* 3, 3-14.

Lichardus, J., Fol, A., Getov, L., Bertemes, F., Echt, R., Katinčarov, R., & Iliev, I.K. (2000). *Forschungen in der Mikroregin von Drama (Südostbulgarien). Zusammenfassung der Hauptergebnisse der bulgarisch-deutschen Grabungen in den Jahren 1983-1999.* Bonn.

Lichardus, J., Fol, A., Getov, L., Bertemes, F., Echt, R., Katinčarov, R., & Iliev, I.K. (2001). *Izsledvanija v mikroregiona na s. Drama (Jugoiztočna Bălgarija). Obobštenie na osnovnite rezultati na Bălgaro-germanskite razkopki ot 1983 do 1999 g.* Sofia.

Lichardus, J., Fol, A., Getov, L., Bertemes, F., Echt, R., Kubiniok, J., & Iliev, I.K. (2004). Die bulgarisch-deutschen Forschungen in der Mikroregion von Drama (1983-2003). In *Die Thraker. Das goldene Reich des Orpheus [Katalog der Ausstellung vom 23. Juli bis 28. November 2004 in der Kunst- und Ausstellungshalle der Bundesrepublik Deutschland in Bonn].* Mainz, 37-60.

Lichardus, J., Fol, A., Getov, L., Echt, R., Gleser, R., Katinčarov, R., et al. (2003). Bericht über die bulgarisch-deutschen Ausgrabungen in Drama (1996-2002). Neolithikum - Kupferzeit - Bronzezeit - Eisenzeit - Römerzeit. *Ber. RGK.* 84, 155-221.

Lichardus, J., Gatsov, I., Gurova, M., & Iliev, I. K. (2000). Geometric Microliths from the Middle Neolithic Site Drama-Gerena (South Bulgaria) and the Problem of Mesolithic Tradition in South Eastern Europe. *Eurasia Antiqua.* 6, 1-12.

Lichardus, J., & Iliev, I.K. (1993). Tonamulette aus Drama und das Problem der nordöstlichen Einflüsse in der Kupferzeit an der unteren Tundža. In Nikolov, V. (Hrsg.) *Praistoričeski nachodki i izsledvanija. Sbornik v pamet na prof. Georgi I. Georgiev.* Sofia, 141-149.

Lichardus, J., & Iliev, I. K. (1994). Frühe Vorgeschichte auf dem Gebiet der heutigen Stadt Jambol in Zusammenhang mit der Entwicklung an der unteren Tundža. In Draganov, D. (Ed.) *Studies on Settlement Life in Ancient Thrace.* Jambol, 13-20.

Lichardus, J., & Iliev, I. K. (2000). Das frühe und mittlere Neolithikum an der unteren Tundža (Südostbulgarien); ein Beitrag zu den chronologischen und kulturellen Beziehungen. In Hiller, S., & Nikolov, V. (Hrsg.) *Österreichisch-bulgarische Ausgrabungen und Forschungen in Karanovo 3: Beiträge zum Neolithikum in Südosteuropa.* Wien, 75-108.

Lichardus, J., & Iliev, I. K. (2001). Die Cernavoda-III-Siedlung von Drama-Merdžumekja in Südostbulgarien und ihre Bedeutung für Südosteuropa. In *Symposium Cernavodă III - Boleráz - ein vorgeschichtliches Phänomen zwischen dem Oberrhein und der Unteren Donau Mangalia, Neptun 18. - 24. Oktober 1999.* Stud. Danubiana Pars romaniae Ser. symposia 2.Bucureşti, 166-198.

Lichardus, J., & Iliev, I. (2004). Die relative Chronologie des Neolithikums und der Kupferzeit in der Mikroregion von Drama und die Verbindungen zu Zentralthrakien. In Nikolov, V., Băčvarov, K., Kalchev, P. (Eds.) *Prehistoric Thrace. Proceedings of the International Symposium in Stara Zagora.* 30.09 - 04.10.2003. Sofia-Stara Zagora, 34-45.

Lichardus, J., Iliev, I.K., & Christov, Ch. J. (2002). Die Karanovo I-IV-Perioden an der unteren Tundža und ihre chronologische Stellung zu den benachbarten Gebieten. In Lichardus-Itten, M., Lichardus, J., & Nikolov, V. (Hrsg.) *Beiträge zu jungsteinzeitlichen Forschungen in Bulgarien.* Saarbrücker Beitr. Altkde. 74. Bonn: Habelt, 325-410.

Vollmann, D. (2004). Die neolithischen Häuser von Drama-"Gerena". In: Nikolov, V., Băčvarov, K., Kalchev, P. (Eds.) *Prehistoric Thrace. Proceedings of the International Symposium in Stara Zagora, 30.09 - 04.10.2003.* Sofia-Stara Zagora, 269-277.

ADDITIONAL READING

Bailey, D.W., & Panayotov, I. (Eds.). (1995). *Prehistoric Bulgaria.* Monogr. World Arch. 22. Madison, Wisconsin.

Bonev, A. (1998). *Trakija i egejskijat vjat prez vtorata polovina na II chiljadoletie pr. n.e.* Razkopki i proučvanija 20. Sofija.

Boyadziev, Y. (1995). Chronology of prehistoric cultures in Bulgaria. In D.W. Bailey & I. Panayotov (Eds.), *Prehistoric Bulgaria.* Monogr. World Arch. 22. Madison, Wisconsin, 149-191.

Čičikova, M. (1972). Nouvelles données sur la culture Thrace de l'époque du Hallstatt en Bulgarie du Sud. *Thracia* 1, 79-100.

Fol, A. (Ed.). (2001, September 25-29). Thrace and the Aegean. In *Proceedings of the Eighth International Congress of Thracology. Sofia - Yambol, 25-29 September 2000.* Sofia

Fol, A., &. Lichardus, J. (Eds.). (1998). *Macht, Herrschaft und Gold. Das Gräberfeld von Varna (Bulgarien) und die Anfänge einer neuen europäischen Zivilisation.* Saarbrücken.

Georgiev, G.I. (1961). Kulturgruppen der Jungstein- und der Kupferzeit in der Ebene von Thrazien (Südostbulgarien). In *L'Europe à la fin de l'âge de la pierre; actes du Symposium Consacré aux Problèmes du Néolithique Européen, Prague, Libice, Brno 5. - 12. oct. 1959.* Praha, 45-100.

Georgiev, G.I. (1967). Beiträge zur Erforschung des Neolithikums und der Bronzezeit. *Arch. Austriaca* 42, 90-144.

Görsdorf, J., & Bojadžiev, J. (1996). Zur absoluten Chronologie der bulgarischen Urgeschichte. Berliner 14C-Datierungen von bulgarischen archäologischen Fundplätzen. *Eurasia Antiqua*, 2, 105-173.

Hachmann, R. (Ed.). (1969). *Vademecum der Grabung Kāmid el-Lōz.* Saarbrücker Beitr. Altkde. Bonn.

Hänsel, B. (1976). *Beiträge zur regionalen und chronologischen Gliederung der älteren Hallstattzeit an der unteren Donau. Teil 1 Text; Teil 2 Tafeln, Karten und Beilagen mit Erläuterungen.* Beitr. ur- u. frühgesch. Arch. Mittelmeer-Kulturraum. Bonn, 16-17.

Hänsel, B. (Ed.). (1982). *Südosteuropa zwischen 1600 und 1000 v. Chr.* Prähist. Arch. Südosteuropa, 1. Berlin.

Hiller, S., & Nikolov, V. (Eds.). (1970). *Karanovo 1: Die Ausgrabungen im Südsektor 1984-1992.* Salzburg: Sofia.

Hiller, S., & Nikolov, V. (Ed.). (2000). *Karanovo 3: Beiträge zum Neolithikum in Südosteuropa.* Wien.

Krauss, R. (2006). *Die prähistorische Besiedlung am Unterlauf der Jantra vor dem Hintergrund der Kulturgeschichte Nordbulgariens.* Prähist. Arch. Südosteuropa 20. Rahden/Westfalen.

Lichardus, J. (Ed.). (1991). *Die Kupferzeit als historische Epoche. Symposium Saarbrücken und Otzenhausen 6-13.11.1988.* Saarbrücker Beitr. Altkde. 55. Bonn.

Lichardus-Itten, M., Lichardus, J., & Nikolov, V. (Eds.). (2002). *Beiträge zu jungsteinzeit-lichen Forschungen in Bulgarien.* Saarbrücker Beitr. Altkde. 74. Bonn.

Merkyte, I. (2005). Lîga. Copper Age Strategies in Bulgaria. *Acta Arch. København* 76, 1, 1-194 = Centre World Arch. Publ. 2. København.

Nikolov, V. (1998). *Proučvanija vărchu neolitnata keramika v Trakija. Keramičnite kompleksi Karanovo II-III, III i III-IV v konteksta na Severozapadna Anatolija i Jugoistočna Evropa.* Sofia.

Nikolov, V. (Ed.). (2000). *Trakija i săsednite rajoni prez neolita i chalkolita.* Sofia.

Nikolov, V., Băčvarov, K., & Kalchev, P. (Eds.). (2004). Prehistoric Thrace. *Proceedings of the International Symposium in Stara Zagora, 30.09 - 04.10.2003.* Sofia - Stara Zagora.

Nikolova, L. (Ed.). (1995-1997). *Early Bronze Age settlement patterns in the Balkans (ca. 3500-2000 BC, Calibrated Dates)* vol 1-3. Sofia.

Nikolova, L. (1999). *The Balkans in later prehistory. Periodization, chronology and cultural development in the Final Copper and Early Bronze Age (Fourth and third millenia BC).* BAR Internat. Ser. 791. Oxford.

Panajotov, I. (1989). Zur Chronologie und Periodisierung der Bronzezeit in den heutigen bulgarischen Gebieten. *Thracia* 9, 74-103.

Parzinger, H. (1993). *Studien zur Chronologie und Kulturgeschichte der Jungstein-, Kupfer- und Frühbronzezeit zwischen Karpaten und mittlerem Taurus.* Röm.-Germ. Forsch. 52. Mainz.

Roman, P. (Ed.). (1997). The Thracian World at the Crossroads of Civilizations. *Proceedings of the Seventh International Congress of Thracology Constanța, Mangalia, Tulcea, 20 - 26 May 1996.* Bucureşti.

Roman, P. (Ed.). (2001). *Symposium Cernavodă III-Boleráz - ein Vorgeschichtliches Phänomen zwischen dem Oberrhein und der Unteren Donau: Mangalia, Neptun (18.-24. Oktober 1999).* Stud. Danubiana / Pars romaniae / Ser. symposia 2. Bucureşti.

Stefanovich, M., Todorova, H., & Hauptmann, H. (Eds.). (1998). *In the steps of James Harvey Gaul* (Vol. 1). Sofia.

Todorova, H. (1981). Das Chronologiesystem von Karanovo im Lichte der neuen Forschungsergebnisse in Bulgarien. *Slovenská Arch.* 29, 203-216.

Todorova, H. (1982). *Kupferzeitliche Siedlungen in Nordostbulgarien.* Mat. Allg. Vergl. Arch. 13. München.

Todorova, H. (1986). *Kamenno-mednata epocha v Bălgarija.* Sofia.

Todorova, H. (1989). *Durankulak 1.* Sofia.

Todorova, H. (2002). *Durankulak 2. Die prähistorischen Gräberfelder.* Sofia.

KEY TERMS

Cultural Heritage: The legacy of physical artifacts and intangible attributes of a group or society that are inherited from past generations, maintained in the present and bestowed for the benefit of future generations.

Karanovo (Bulgaria): Settlement mound (arab.: "tell") in Thrace, partly excavated by V. Mikov (1936), G. I. Georgiev (1947-1957), G. I. Georgiev and S. Hiller (1984-1988), V. Nikolov and S. Hiller (since 1992). The stratigraphy of the tell, first published in 1961 by G.I. Georgiev, has since become referential for the neolithic and chalcolithic periods in Thrace and beyond. Settlement periods Karanovo I and II are Early Neolithic, Karanovo III and IV are Middle Neolithic, Karanovo V is Late Neolithic and Karanovo VI is Chalcolithic, while Karanovo VII represents the southeast European Early Bronze Age.

Cernavodă (Romania): Settlements at the mound "Dealul Sofia," uncovered during rescue excavations (1954-1962). Cernavodă I (Late Neolithic) in area A, Cernavodă II (Bronze Age) in area B and Cernavodă III (Early Bronze Age) in area C and D. Cernavodă III is connected with the Boleráz stage of the Baden culture in the Carpathian basin.

Nova Zagora (Bulgaria): Settlement mound "Ciganska mogila," excavated by R. Katinčarov and M. Kănčev (1969-1987) with building layers from the Early (Michalič-Phase) and Middle Bronze Age. The Middle Bronze Age finds of the site have become eponymous for the Nova Zagora Period in Thrace.

Pshenichevo (Bulgaria): Settlement mound in the Chaskovo region, partly excavated by D.P. Dimitrov, eponymous findplace of the Pshenichevo group, distinguished by channelled and stamp-decorated pottery. The Pshenichevo group represents the Early Iron Age in large parts of Bulgaria.

ENDNOTES

1 This contribution is completely based on the published and unpublished preliminary results of the Bulgarian-German joint excavation project at Drama, near Yambol, directed by Jan Lichardus (Saarbrücken) and Alexander Fol (Sofia), in which the author has taken part as assistant director since 1993. This summarized information can be found in detail in Lichardus, Fol, Getov, Bertemes, Echt, Katinčarov, and Iliev (2000). I have to emphasize that the evaluation of the extensive material is still in process and therefore these results cannot be considered as definite.

2 For comparison, in the Neolithic and Copper Age of Thrace, seven occupation periods have been distinguished at the eponymous tell at Karanovo by its first excavator, G. I. Georgiev.

3 For the above data as well as for the periodization of the IVa, IVb and IVc phases, see Lichardus, Iliev, and Christov (2002, pp. 331-334) and Taf. (pp. 11-16). Dr. Dieter Vollmann has typologically classified and stratigraphically evaluated the pottery from Drama-Gerena (forthcoming).

4 The settlement features of the Karanovo V period are considered in a PhD dissertation to be submitted to the University of Saarland by Frank Fecht. The settlement plan, which features here, has been reproduced from his work. It represents an improved version of earlier publications that have now been critically revaluated in Fecht's dissertation. I am grateful to F. Fecht for his permission to refer to important results of his work.

5 The work on the Karanovo VI settlement evidence has been done since 2005 at the University of Saarland by Dr. Dominik Meyer, in the framework of a project sponsored by the German Research Council.

6 Cf. J. Lichardus, Der Westpontische Raum und die Anfänge der kupferzeitlichen Zivilisation. In: A. Fol / J. Lichardus (Hrsg.), Macht, Herrschaft und Gold. Das Gräberfeld von Varna und die Anfänge einer neuen europäischen Zivilisation (Saarbrücken 1988) 79-129.

7 I am grateful to Dr. Wolf-Rüdiger Thiele from the Institute of Material Science at the University of Saarland, for the results of the analyses.

8 Cf. E.N. Černych, Frühester Kupferbergbau in Europa. In: A. Fol / J. Lichardus (Hrsg.), Macht, Herrschaft und Gold. Das Gräberfeld von Varna und die Anfänge einer neuen europäischen Zivilisation (Saarbrücken 1988) 145-150.

9 I am grateful to Manuela Kraus M.A., for the information about the current state of her work.

10 Special research on each of these categories of finds is in progress or already finished. Dr. I. Sidéra (Paris) has examined the tools of animal bone, Prof. Dr. I. Gatsov and Dr. M. Gurova (Sofia) have carried out the typological and use-wear analyses of the flint tools, and Ch. Jung is in charge for the research on the ground stone tools.

11 See the preliminary report in N. Benecke, Archäozoologische Untersuchungen in der Siedlungskammer von Drama. Ber. RGK 84, 2003, 212-217.

12 Cf. R. Echt / W.R. Thiele / I. Ivanov, Varna: Untersuchungen zur kupferzeitlichen Goldverarbeitung. In: J. Lichardus (Hrsg.), Die Kupferzeit als historische Epoche. Symposium Saarbrücken und Otzenhausen 6-13.11.1988. Saarbrücker Beitr. Altkde. 55 (Bonn 1991) 633-691.

13 Bertemes (1998; 2002).

14 Bertemes (2002, p.130).

15 This analysis is conducted as a PhD thesis by Dagmar Wilhelm at the University of Saarland and has progressed far.

16 Prof. Dr. Jochen Kubiniok from the Department of Physical Geography at the University of Saarland analyzes the results of his pedologic investigations. The archaeozoologist Prof. Dr. Norbert Benecke, head of the Department of Natural Sciences of the German Archaeological Institute, Berlin, has determined and analyzed the animal bones.

17 J. Lichardus, in collaboration with the Bulgarian project partners and colleagues, published two lavishly illustrated catalogues: A. Fol. / J. Lichardus (ed.), Macht, Herrschaft und Gold. Das Gräberfeld von Varna (Bulgarien) und die Anfänge einer neuen europäischen Zivilisation (Saarbrücken 1988); A. Fol / J. Lichardus / V. Nikolov, Die Thraker. Das goldene Reich des Orpheus. Katalog der Ausstellung vom 23. Juli bis 28. November 2004 in der Kunst- und Ausstellungshalle der Bundesrepublik Deutschland in Bonn (Mainz 2004).

18 I like to express my very best thanks to Dr. Krum Bachvarov for "brushing up" the English version of this paper.

Chapter XV
Posting Articles about Excavations in Electronic Forums

Charilaos Thomos
Computer Scientist and Researcher, Greece

Alexandros Gouniotis
Computer Scientist and Researcher, Greece

Konstantinos Kechagias
School of Second Chance, Greece

INTRODUCTION

This chapter presents how forums can expand authors' or speakers' ability to reach new audiences with their lecture series, conferences and workshops. Focused on archaeological purposes, this chapter aims to show how learning communities could support knowledge by mixing different electronic media of communication.

Defining as an electronic journal (e-journal) one which is distributed to some or all of its primary subscribers in electronic form and as a paper journal (p-journal) one that is distributed exclusively in paper form (Kling & Covi, 1995), we can quickly understand that the number of e-journals is growing rapidly, including fields purely theoretical, such as archaeology. Although debate swirls around questions of copyright (see chapter 13), peer review, and publishing costs, individual authors are taking action in this arena by posting their articles to personal or institutional Web pages and to disciplinary repositories.

Electronically enhanced forums provide more sources of information and communication, but also alter the ways that people speak and interact. As a result of the audience's scale-up in size, space and time, the informal give and take between speakers and listeners becomes more difficult. On the other hand, people reading an article may privately revise sections to enhance their comprehension, while in a face-to-face meeting they may have to ask questions.

To this direction, this chapter firstly describes the problem of designing a system to support archaeological knowledge, shows the way that this problem could be solved and proposes SEE-ArchWeb as a system for posting hypermedia articles.

"BALKANIZATION" AS A CONTEMPORARY SOCIAL REALITY

Having taken its name from the fragmentary and divisive nature of the 20th century Balkans, the geopolitical term "balkanization" has come to refer to any region or society with internal turmoil or divisions. At the same time, it is being used to express the divergence over time of languages.

In both cases, "balkanization" is an indisputable reality nowadays and reflects current relationships among nations. In this sense, although the unification process of the EU is believed to be a given today, problems such as the downgrading of less widespread languages such as Balkan languages and dialects still remain unsolved, mostly due to the predominance of English, French or German in the scientific, political, economical and commercial world. Indicatively, there are nine officially acknowledged languages today in the Balkans, whose even existence is ignored by the majority of EU citizens. Some have no apparent relation to the other. Whatever the case is, the Balkans have to and will survive this "Babel," together with all European Union states. Maintaining a country's language is a multilateral case and duty of nations nowadays; it also concerns a place's culture and its specific characteristics and lifestyle, which differentiate it from other nations. It has to do with ethnic identity and understanding of one's existence over time.

It is exactly at this point where one could wonder how this notion of "balkanization" links to the scientific world and more specifically to the field of archaeology; the answer lies on a variety of levels. Despite the turmoil that shattered political stability in the Balkans, there is an indisputable linking factor which binds Balkan countries, a common point of reference: their past. The rich historical background and traditions in the Balkans are of great value and this is confirmed by the discovery of significant archaeological findings. However, political and economical circumstances have hindered and undermined the spreading of their heritage.

Therefore, it is an urgent need to design a system that focuses exactly on supporting this aim and helping publish these countries' history and culture. The implementation of such a scientific forum, fostering multilingual projects and equally promoting them comprises an effort toward this direction; to equate "balkanization" with the need for sustenance of different ethnic groups and societies. This system has to regard "balkanization" as a positive challenge: to show the potential of this term for the establishment of democratic processes, starting from the scientific world.

DESIGNING A SYSTEM TO SUPPORT ARCHAEOLOGICAL KNOWLEDGE

The idea of creating an exhibition with visual content of archaeological findings from all around the globe, displaying full size pictures and copies of important Balkan artefacts, currently, located in foreign museums, seems that should take less time and money than actually gathering the artefacts and exhibiting them. In fact, a global exhibition with artefacts from different sites is considered impossible, as today's museums are very reluctant in transporting and exhibiting artefacts into others' exhibitions. Moreover, this transportation process would raise some threats to the artefacts (imagine the case where a truck transporting some of those valuables had an accident). Finally, some artefacts require special environmental circumstances in order to be kept and exhibited to the public.

An exhibition of photographs overcomes the bureaucracy issue and the dangers of transportation, as a simple gather and display of some photos of artefacts should not be so difficult. However, there are some other obstacles that should be taken into consideration; for example, photos' high quality and set-up depend on museums willing to provide such original and high quality photos. Instead, they usually choose the low quality photos presented into their brochures.

Supposing that the photos are gathered, another problem quickly arises. Not many visitors would be attracted to visit an archaeological exhibition presenting just photographs of items. So, some interior decorators should be hired in order to produce a very pleasing environment for the presentation of the photographs, which will enhance their contents and make the visitors overcome the fact that they see just photographs and not the items themselves.

Finally, the advertising campaign faces the same difficulties. It is difficult to advertise a photo exhibition of archaeological artefacts and persuade the potential visitors to come over and visit. As a matter of fact, the actual visitors are only a fragment of the potential visitors. The rest choose to see some artefact photos in easily reachable media (such as books, specialized magazines, and of course, the Internet). So it becomes clear that the procedure of organizing such an event is as tedious, difficult and time consuming as organizing an exhibition of the actual items. As a matter of fact, all around processes may take about 5 to 6 years and involve all the latter mentioned difficulties.

So the question finally posed is: *Is there a quick, easy and cheap way to exhibit various archaeological artefacts in a sole exhibition?* It is quite possible to overcome all these drawbacks just by changing the medium of the photo exhibition: from paper photographs to digital photographs and from a physical museum to a virtual museum, residing on the Internet. This transition would definitely bring lots of advantages:

- Each archaeologist could upload the images of retrieved artefacts directly after the dig site. This approach not only separates the museum factor, but also enables the virtual museum to have a really larger photo exhibition than the real museum. As each archaeologist would like to promote his work, appealing and high quality photographs are almost guaranteed.
- The virtual exhibition requires only a Web hosting service. These services are quite cheap and accessible to anyone.
- There is no need for special decoration in order to compensate the lack of physical items presence. Moreover, as is the virtual museum case, the Web site content is much more important than the Web site visual design; some decoration expenses could also be kept down.
- A virtual exhibition is totally accessible from all around the globe. Every interconnected person, no matter where he is physically connected, is just a few clicks away from the exhibition.
- Finally, one of the main Internet's advantages is the ability to interact both with the content and other Web surfers. Each image exhibit can be commented on by any visitor. These comments could also be questions, leading to conversations either with other visitors or the archaeologists themselves. An Internet community could be built around the visual exhibition, discussing and sharing information and ideas. And all this through a personalized experience.
- As the images in the exhibition are digitized, each user can download them, share them, use them in personal essays and, generally, promote them (whenever copyright problems do not occur). So, the virtual exhibition could allow the spreading of archaeological findings quickly to an even greater audience.

So, the solution is to move toward the new digital era of the Internet. This is not an easy procedure which can be accomplished by the exhibition managers. Some IT specialists (Web application developers and Web masters) are required in order to provide solid ground for the transition.

Building such an application framework (or choosing from the ones already created) is not an easy task for Web developers. In fact, the development process might seem quite easy for an outsider, but it may prove to be a serious headache for the programmers that will undertake this task.

Apart from the regular quality requirements (software security and stability), the Web developers should also implement the following:

- Ability to present and manipulate multimedia content (images, streaming sounds/videos, Flash/Apollo/WPF presentations). This will ensure a rich user experience.
- Ability for some users (archaeologists) to upload such rich and copyrighted content to the server (which may lead to security problems).
- Multilingual support. A must for the "balkanization" reality which involves various countries with different languages.
- Translation support. The content uploaded in one language should be translated, and thus accessible, to other languages too.
- Author rights. Each author should have explicit rights to his work.
- Visitor community feedback. The content should be commentable by the users, who are encouraged to form a community.
- Easily spread. The content should be easily "broadcast" and become known to a large number of people.

So, what kind of Internet technology should be used? To the best of our knowledge there is no specific Web software which provides an adequate solution to all the latter problems and requirements. Some of them are solved by forum software, others by blog software, and others by content management systems.

Web Software for Virtual Exhibition

As it has already been mentioned, what is actually needed in order to build a virtual exhibition is Web software, a mixture of forum, blog and content management systems. There is a brief look at each of the systems below, describing their functionality and pointing out their advantages and disadvantages when they are used solely.

Internet Forum

The Internet forum software takes it name from the forum, the public space set in the centre of Roman cities. This place was thriving with people sharing views, discussing, exchanging ideas and communicating.

The **Internet forum** just like its real life predecessor, the Roman forum, is a facility on the Internet for holding discussions on specific topics. Web-based forums, which date from around 1995, perform a similar function as the dial-up bulletin boards and Internet newsgroups that were numerous in the 1980s and 1990s.

An Internet forum is maintained on a server that is accessible through an ordinary Web browser from any location with an Internet connection. The interaction language between server and user is HTML, enhanced usually with a Web scripting

Figure 1. A thread is made by a topic and replies either to the topic itself or to other replies.

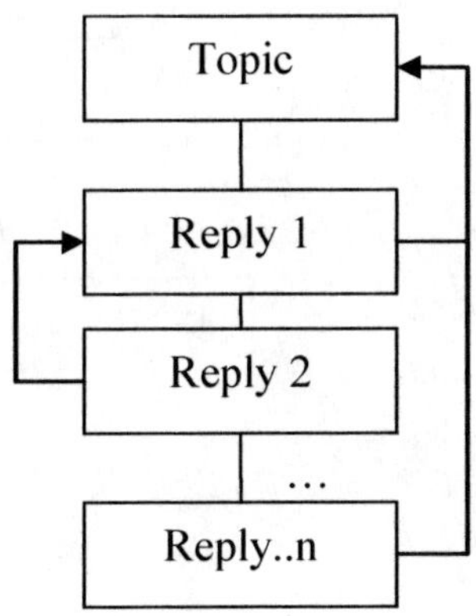

language that allows the server to generate Web pages dynamically in order to display results, graphs and other information. Cookies, small blocks of data that are transmitted to and stored on the user's machine by the server software, are used to link Web page requests to users thus making sure that players receive the correct pages during and between sessions (Hare et al., 2001).

Content Management in Internet Forums

The main information entity in the Internet forum software is the *topic*. Each topic is, actually, the beginning of a conversation created by a user. The user logs in into the system and commences the beginning of the conversation, often by posing some questions or by asking other users to comment on facts. Other users log in into the forum, locate the topic and *reply* either to it or to other topic replies. This way each user can participate into the conversation by creating a *reply*. A topic together with all its replies is called a *thread* (Figure 1).

While the title of each thread is often able to guide a user to the desired conversation, some forums may reach up to thousands of threads. Therefore, it is important that the user can browse these threads by subject field. This is done by grouping the threads into *categories* which contain threads referring to the same or near subjects (Figure 2).

Yet, this grouping may still prove inadequate for large forums containing lots of threads and categories. So another level of organization was introduced: *subforums* (subfora). Subforums are group of categories which contain threads referring to the same of near general subjects (Figure 3).

To sum all the latter up, the information in forums is grouped into threads → categories → subforums → forums as shown in Figure 4, the information pyramid in Internet forums.

User Roles in Internet Forums

As Internet forums don't host articles but threaded conversations, they lead to the creation of virtual communities. Regular users get to meet each other, and by exchanging personal messages through the Internet Forum engine they reach a more personal communication.

Figure 2. Each topic is grouped into a category.

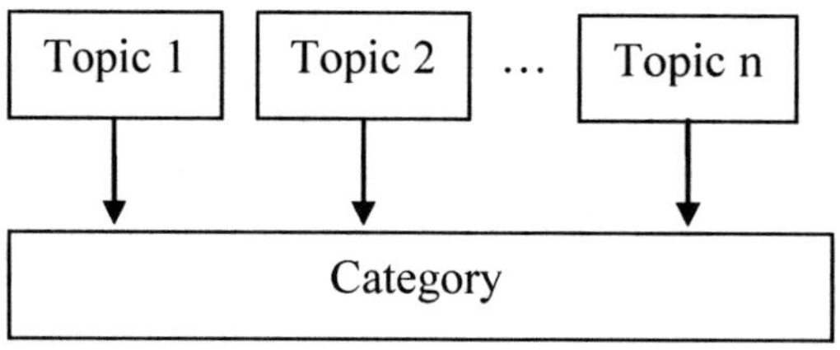

Figure 3. Each category is grouped into a subforum.

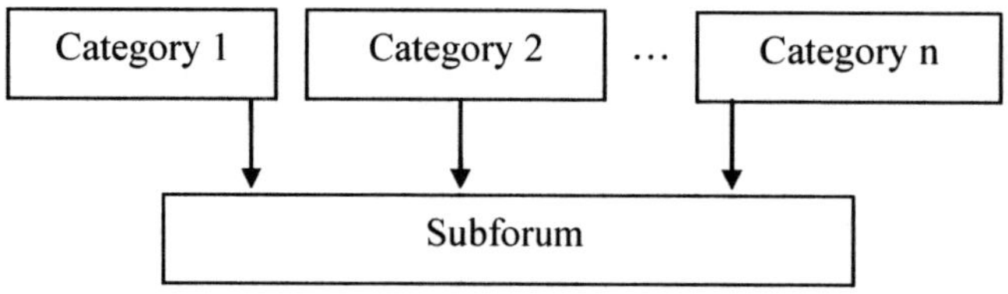

Figure 4. Internet forum content management pyramid

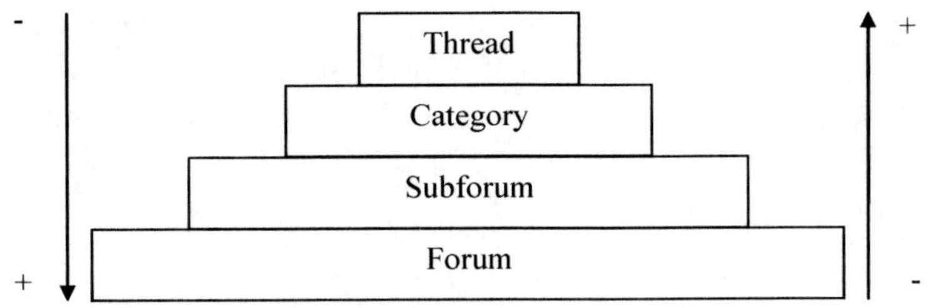

Table 1. User groups and roles in Internet forums

User group	User role
User	The heart of the Internet Forums: • Creates threads • Replies to thread posts
(Super) Moderator	Makes sure forum rules are applied: • Edits user posts • Moves user posts • Deletes user posts • Bans users
Administrator	Highest forum authority: • Creates/edits/deletes/moves subforums/categories • Makes sure the forum is technically well being • Promotes and denotes (super) moderators • Takes care of technical user issues

The latter fact makes the Internet forums an ideal network place to spend time on, get together with other same-interested users, exchange ideas, gather information and perform research.

Yet, as the number of users grows in an Internet forum and as they get more personal by being members of the community, they tend to leave the subjected conversation and start other, more personal conversations. So, the greater the number of users discussing in a forum, the greater the chance is that their interest field grows beyond the forum subject.

In order for this phenomenon to be avoided, the moderator user role has been introduced. Moderators are special users, authorized by the forum owner, to keep an eye on the content of the forum. *Moderators* can either moderate content on a category, a subforum, or even on the whole forum (the so-called *super moderators*). According to a (usually public) set of rules, they can move threads from category to category, edit other users' posts and, finally, ban users from forum access when their behavior is unacceptable.

As mentioned before, moderators and (super moderators) are, usually, promoted users which show exceptional interest in the well being of the community. These users are promoted by the forum administrator(s). Forum administrator(s) not only have the ability to promote and denote users, but also are in charge of the primary content management, as they can create, edit, move and delete content categories. Moreover, they are technically in charge of the forum and are obliged to solve technical user problems and monitor its well-being. One could say that administrators are the highest authority in an Internet forum. So the roles in Internet forums can be summarized in Table 1.

Table 2. Advantages and disadvantages of Internet forums

Pros	Cons
Personalized user experience	Administrative and moderative overhead
Promotes discussion and sharing among members	Lack of strict control on the authoring process
Easy to use	Not suitable for article publishing
Supports multimedia content	Limited translation services

Some famous, open source forum engines are: PHPBB (PHP Bulleting Board), SMF (Simple Machines Forum), myForum, YAF.NET (Yet Another Forum.NET)

Yet, the roles are not restrictive in the hierarchy of the user groups in the Internet forums, and thus a moderator can always take part in discussions and an administrator can always moderate forums. This is simplified in the following diagram.

So, we conclude that a forum engine can provide the best place to discuss, share ideas and views. But as these summarize the main purpose of the Internet forums we can also conclude that Internet Forums cannot efficiently satisfy the requirements posed in our problem. Moreover, the fact that there is no strict authoring process does not provide us with a strict content control which is required for the system we have described. What's more, they require a large moderation and administration overhead. Finally, forums, to the best of our knowledge, have very limited translation services

The pros and of the Internet forums are summarized in Table 2.

Blog

The word *blog* is a portmanteau of the term "Web log" and refers to a Web site where the author shares his or her personal (usually) views with the public presenting them in chronological order.

Blogs, today, have become synonyms to the "personal Web site" term. Each netizen can sign up in a free blog hosting provider and start posting his personal thoughts, opinions and views in his blog. Blog software was designed for users which don't have special training in computer and Internet systems, and therefore it is really simple to set up, use and maintain. Yet, this does not limit its potential, as blog software is really powerful

Figure 5. User roles are a subset of the moderator, super moderator and administrator roles

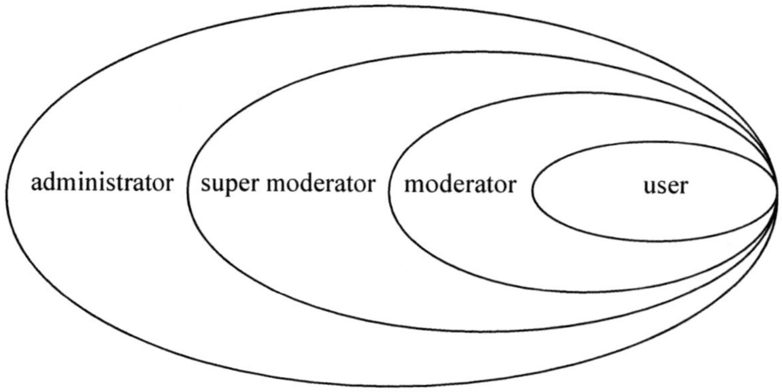

Figure 6. Users can reach a blog article either by browsing through categories, publish dates or by looking for a specific tag

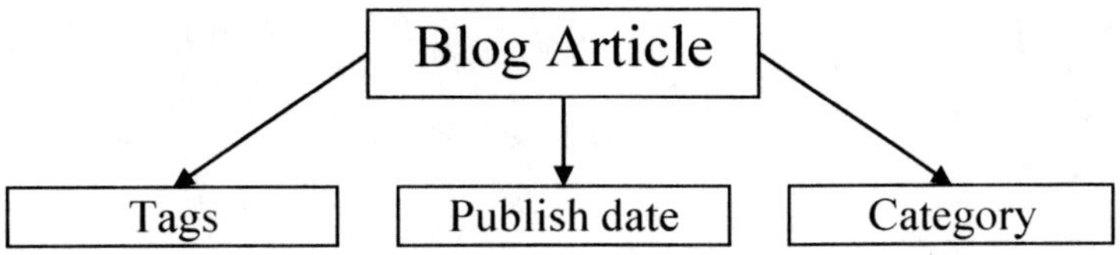

in presenting articles of personal thoughts in chronological order.

Content Management in Blogs

As it is designed for personal use, a blog does not impose very strict rules in content management, but being a relatively new software (the first self-aware blogs popped up in the Web around 2001) has 3 powerful management mechanisms:

The first mechanism is the conventional "*subject category:*" Blog articles are (or at least supposed to be) grouped by subject into specific content categories. Yet, the case is that most blog owners utilize a very small number of categories, each one covering an enormous subject field (e.g., "miscellaneous" or "personal"). This raises a great difficulty to the blog visitors, as they cannot easily navigate in the content by browsing a subject category, as this involves them shuffling on general categories, each one containing a large volume of articles.

The second mechanism is the "*publish date*" of each blog article. The main purpose for the blog software was to provide the means for a Web journal, containing content organized in chronological order. This is done automatically when the author publishes articles, as the publish date is recorded and according to this a navigation calendar is built. While this functionality is quite adequate for the purpose, the way blogs were designed does not provide any means of subject control to the blog visitor. Therefore, the date archiving of the articles may seem useful to regular blog visitors only.

The third and most powerful mechanism for content management in blog software is the "*tagging*" mechanism: When a new article is published, the author is called to write some key words that summarize or describe its subject field. These tags can prove to be very efficient to the visitor who can browse blog articles by tag. Another, less conventional, but equally powerful article browsing method is the so-called tag cloud.

The *tag cloud* is a specific area in a Web page which contains the tags of the most popular articles. Most popular article tags are presented with larger fonts (this way gaining immediate attention from the viewer) while the less popular articles are presented with smaller fonts (Figure 7).

Yet, the tagging mechanism is not only a content management mechanism, but it also enables the content to be easily indexed by specialized search engines or directories, and thus to automatically spread and become accessible to vast numbers of potential visitors.

When an article is published, the blog software can automatically forward the article tags along with the article URL to a directory service, where they are stored. Later, when users visit the directory service and perform a search related to one of these tags, they will be presented with the article title and URL. This way they can navigate to the article. Moreover, if the users visit another page having similar content tags, they can ask the directory service to forward them to a similar page, which could be the authored article. The latter procedure is clarified in Figure 8.

Besides the main content that is written by the blog owner, another content type, equally

Figure 7. Tag clouds provide an efficient visual way of content navigation

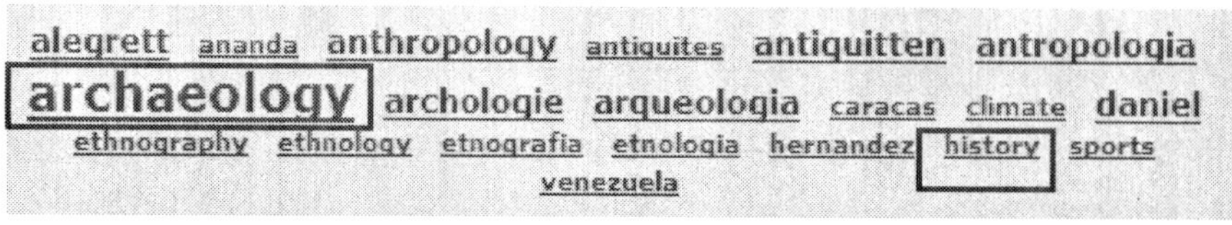

Figure 8. Content tagging and directory publishing may lead to an increased number of visitors

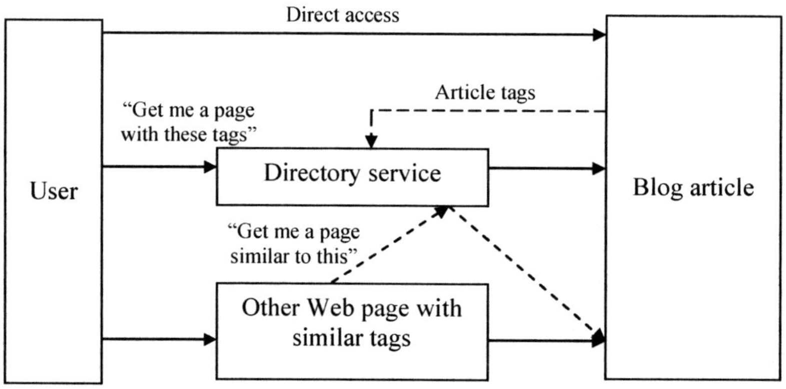

important, is also hosted in blogs. This is the user feedback, expressed by article comments. After an article is presented, visitors can choose to express their thoughts/opinions about the content they just read and to add a note for other visitors to see. This can be done through a commenting system in which every visitor can add something to the content of the blog.

The latter feature makes the blog somewhat similar to the Internet forum, in the way that users can gather up and discuss on certain subjects as they derive from the blog owner articles. Taking under consideration the fact that the blog is much easier to set up, that makes content more widely available and enables user interaction triggered by content articles we could say that blogs can easily replace the Internet forums.

But this is not the case. Blogs do not give the community feel to the user, as they are just personal points of presence in the World Wide Web. When users comment into a blog, they cannot create a new thread, and they are confined to comment on the owner's articles. As private messaging is also not supported, no personal feel and communication could raise between the blog article commenters. Moreover, users cannot easily express themselves and communicate with other users as they do not consider themselves to be in their "Web home" (i.e., forum) but they are invited into a foreign place. Moreover, translation and multilanguage utilities are not present in the blog application space as there is no need to publish someone's thoughts in more than one language.

In closing, blogs do a great job as personal Web sites, some of them thriving with information. But they are not community Web sites, but they are more personal Web sites where visitors come to talk with the blog owner, something that does not encourage communication and sharing of knowledge and ideas.

Content Management Systems

Introduction to Content Management

Content management, in general, is a set of processes and technologies that realize and support

Table 3. Advantages and disadvantages of blogs

Pros	Cons
Really easy to set up and maintain	No user community feel
Support rich multimedia content	No Multilanguage/translation services
Powerful content management techniques	No personalized user experience
Support user feedback	Not suitable for article publishing

Famous blog engines: Wordpress, Lifetype, Blogger
Famous tag directories: Technorati, Blogcatalog

the evolutionary life cycle of information (content) when presented onto a medium (magazine, TV channel, etc.). In our case, the information is related to archaeological issues and the medium is the Internet. As the Internet consists of a digital medium, the managed content is also digital. Due to this, the content management procedure becomes far more complex compared to traditional "print" content, as digital content is consisted not only by text and static photos, but also by videos, sounds, music, interactive presentations and, of course, any combination among them.

No matter the presentation medium, according to content management, content life cycle consists of six primary phases (Figure 9):

- **Creation:** The general idea is conceived by the content author who imprints it into the desired medium, usually through the procedure that is called *art* (Musician → Music, Writer → Text, Painter → Image, Photographer → Photo, etc.).
- **Update:** As the time span required to create content varies (from very small to very large amounts of time) it is quite possible that the initial circumstances which triggered the content creation have changed. Some specific types of content are required to reflect the publishing epoch, so some updates are required.
- **Publish:** This is when the content is introduced to the public, the most important step of content management.
- **Translate/Reform:** Once the content is published, it may be reformed in order to fill some other needs, not reflected in the initial creation procedure. For example, written text should be translated in order to be accessible by people not speaking the initial text language, or, an original music score could be remixed in order to be used in advertising campaigns.
- **Archive:** All the published content can be archived for future reference, both by content creators or by content consumers. The archive is usually publicly accessible.
- **Retire:** This is where the content has finished its purpose and is being removed from public access, in order for other newer content to be promoted.

As it is evident, content management is a fairly complex process which involves many coordinated steps performed by an equal number of specialists, all of them collaborating seamlessly together. These specialists are:

- **Content Author:** Person or group of persons responsible for the *creation* of original (or revised) content.
- **Editor:** Person who spots any problems (semantic, morphologic, etc.) in the created content and sends created content back to the content author for *update*.
- **Publisher:** Decides when the content should be *published* and pushes edited content to the

Figure 9. The lifespan of managed digital content is a circular path

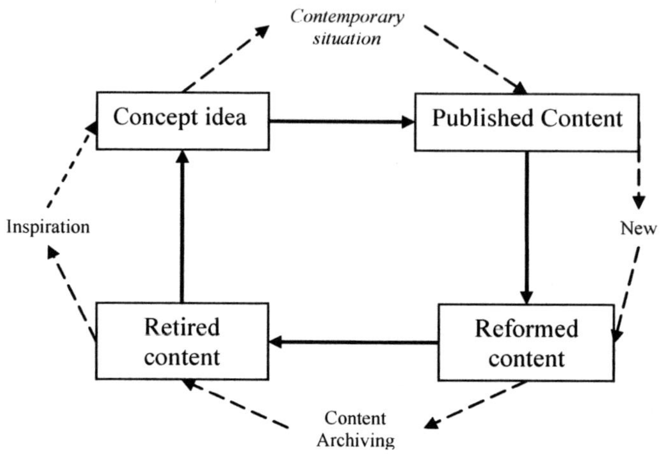

Figure 10. Specialist relationships and content-oriented roles

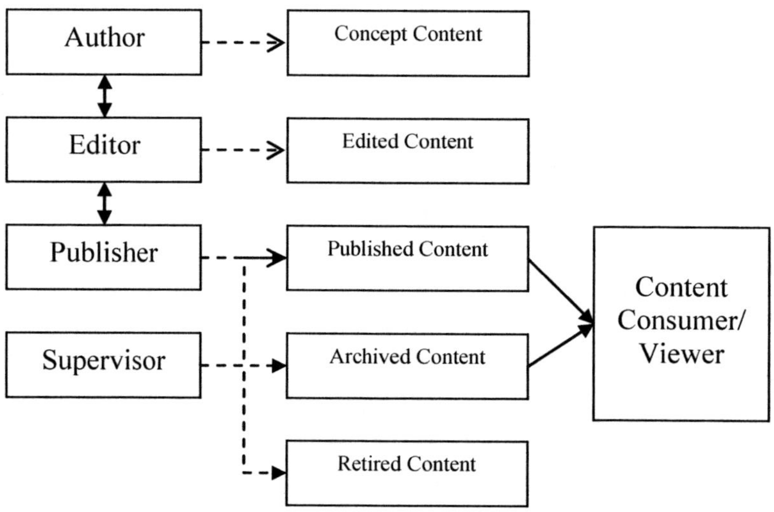

presentation medium. He is also responsible for predicting any required content *reformation/translations*, which are forwarded to the *editor* and after that published.

- **Supervisor:** He decides for how much content is published and when it should be *archived* and *retired.*

The specialist roles are reflected in Figure 10.

Content Management Systems (CMS) and CMS Structure

Content management systems (CMS) is a computer software system which realizes the above procedure, offering facilities and utilities for the organization of created content and providing an adequate collaboration environment for the creation, editing, updating, publishing and archiving of digital content (Figure 11).

Figure 11. The overall structure and functionality of a CMS system

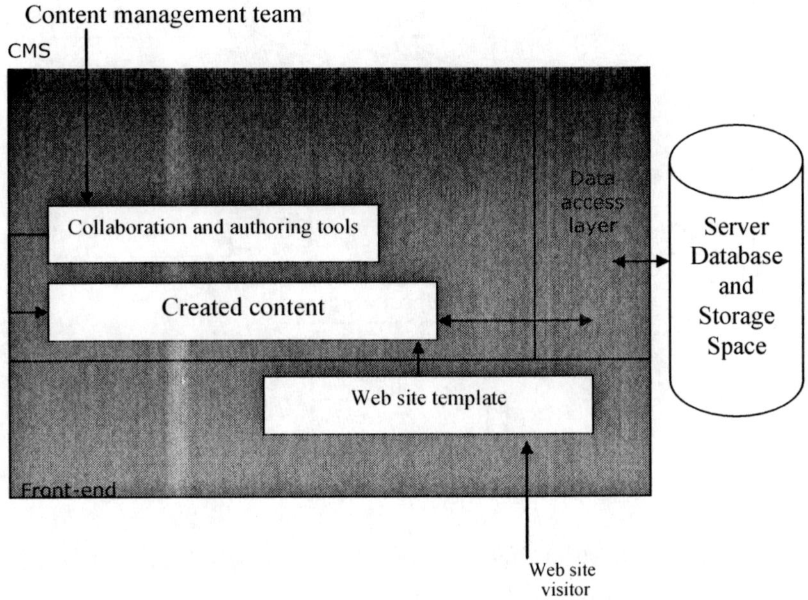

As mentioned before, the Internet is a very competitive content management medium, and therefore many Web sites and portals are realized through the technology of the CMS. The role in a CMS is double:

- As a *Front-End* or *Presentation Layer*: CMS present the content in an appealing and aesthetically pleasing way in order to attract visitors and provide a rich user experience. The CMS presentation layer is often designed by specialized Web designers who have nothing to do with the CMS itself.
- As a *Back-End* or *Business Logic Layer*: CMS provide the content management team with the appropriate tools to create, update, publish and archive digital content. Each of these tools is provided through content management panels tailored to each role of the CM team.

The CM team utilizes the collaboration and authoring tools to create, edit and publish content. This content is stored either in a database or in a raw storage space located in the server (usually a transparent procedure implemented through the "*data access layer*"). When a user visits the CMS powered Web site and requests some content, the CMS retrieves it from the database (through the data access layer), blends it with the Web site graphical template and then serves it to the user.

CMS Collaboration and Authoring Tools

The success of a CMS depends on the ability to serve rich multimedia content to the end user, together with its ability to coordinate and simplify the content creation and management process.

First of all, in order for the CM team to collaborate efficiently, a *messaging system* is required in each CMS. These messaging systems can also be used by the CMS engine itself in order to provide automatic notification on CM team according to specified events. These automatic notification messages are either hard coded, or created by the CMS administrator using specialized scripting languages.

Figure 12. Tools provided by the CMS, and used by special members of the CM team

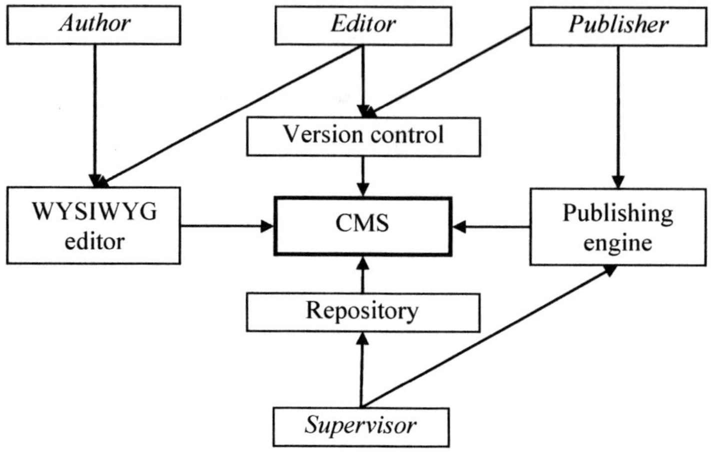

The content creation is usually supported by *What-You-See-Is-What-You-Get* (WYSIWYG) editors. These are powerful visual editors embedded in the back-end panels which allow the content creators and editors to view something very similar to the end result while the content is being created. For example, Web page content can be created without the WYSIWYG user having to be familiar HTML, CSS or XML markup languages (Figure 12).

Content editors usually use the same WYSIWYG editors in order to make comments on the created content. Yet, saving comments on the same document may prove inadequate, especially when the need to track the evolution of a document has risen. In order to satisfy this need, commercial large scale CMS systems also maintain a *version control* engine which enables editors to see a document in all its development stages. Yet, as this feature is very specialized, it is not supported by many generic CMS engines.

Publishers and supervisors require total control on when a document (content) will be published, for how much time it will stay published, when it will be moved to the archive section, and finally when it will retire and become unpublished. All the latter functionality is usually implemented through a scripting language powered by embedded *calendar* controls.

Finally, as the retired content is never deleted but kept for internal archiving reasons, a repository component is also required. Besides the actual content, some version control information (number of revisions, etc.) together with some statistics (publishing date, number of user read it, etc.) must also be kept for bookkeeping reasons.

Many CMS have been introduced to the IT technology, other commercial and other open source. Most of them lack the full functionality of CMS system, as it was described before in their core packages. Yet, this functionality can easily and seamlessly be provided to the CM team and visitors using various plug-ins.

CM systems are, usually, complex and sophisticated Web applications, which can fully support the organized rich multimedia content distribution from its early stages of creation to its full maturity. Moreover, thanks to their modular application they enable collaboration among different groups of specialists over the delivered content. In this context, CMS can also provide with sophisticated translation services in order to ensure that the final content is delivered in various languages.

Table 4. Advantages and disadvantages of CMS

Pros	Cons
Powerful and modular	No user community feel
Support of translation facilities	Very complicated (usually)
Ability to publish rich multimedia content	No author rights preserved (usually)
Support collaboration between experts	

Yet, the complicated structure of the CM systems makes them inappropriate for use with non IT familiar groups, like archaeologists. Moreover, CMS do not present a warm feel to the user (because of the fact that they are used mainly by corporations, and by the fact that the user can merely interact and provide feedback to the content, usually by some poor commenting or rating system). What's more, author rights are not well preserved in CMS as, usually, the content belongs to the CM team and not to the content author (Table 4).

Combining Web Software

The answer to the question posed before would actually be a mix of a content management system, an Internet forum and a blog. Internet forum offers simplicity, preserves author rights and welcomes users into the community. Moreover, CMS can provide the collaboration of experts required for the translation of rich multimedia content, while the powerful blog management and spread mechanisms would allow for content to become known through Internet directories.

As our system should be used by a group of non IT experts, the Internet forum architecture is used as a framework for our proposed answer (Figure 13).

This system was designed to be a user group managed with simple user (visitor), author, translator, moderator and administrator being the available user groups. Each one is provided with a specialized view of the system, together with a set of function panels and utilities.

- For the first two roles, we adapt the Internet forum model: threaded conversations between users which can be started only by archaeologists-authors (in order to ensure author rights).
- These threaded conversations are moderated by the moderators user group who can move threads from category to category, while editing/deleting abusing comments and banning users with unacceptable behavior.
- The translators have a somewhat more CMS-oriented approach as they can collaborate on the translation of authored content, in order to present it to a language different from the original.
- Finally, administrators face a CMS view of the system, which enables them to create/edit/move forums and subforums and to

Figure 13. Architecture and access to the proposed system

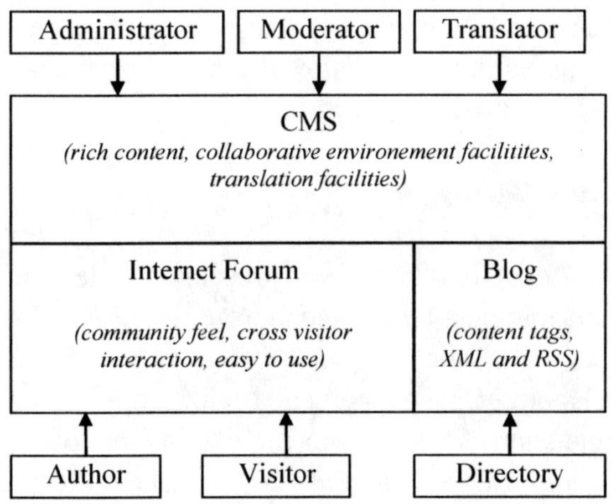

promote and denote users to the translator and administrator user roles.

The designed system sketched out above is the **SEEArchWeb forum**, a hybrid Web application that embraces the evolving new Web technologies and uses them for the sake of archaeological science.

POSTING HYPERMEDIA ARTICLES VIA THE SEEARCHWEB FORUM

So Another Forum: What is it all about?

Readers could rightfully pose questions such as the one above and reserve reasonable doubts on the concept and implementation of another specialized forum among the innumerable ones one can access on Internet.

Yet, specialized forums were designed with a specific target use group in mind, taking under consideration its technical expertise and affiliation to theinformation technology.

From this point of view, the use of a specialized Internet forum, especially for an author of a theoretical background, may prove extremely valuable, as it brings him in controlled and carefully crafted contact with the field of IT and Internet publishing. As a matter of fact, it clarifies the established in people's consciences as perplex and complicated world of computer technologies and humanizes it, to make use of a term related to Humanities.

The Framework

The aim of this chapter is to present this scientific archaeological forum and thoroughly explain its mode of use on the part of its designers and a collaborator, who intervened with remarks and suggestions for improvement, playing the role of an "inquisitive" potential user. Thus, not only the results of this effort are being publicly presented, but at the same time this effort has already been at least once tested and scrutinized, and open to a constructive and beneficial criticism. Apart from the practicalities involved within this task, meaning the navigation around the multimedia options and tools offered by ArchForum, one should not ignore the discourse emerging from the multilingual nature of the forum and the translation database it introduces; it is about the "balkanisation" of modern world and societies and subsequently the "balkanisation" of scientific world and the extent to which it is receptive and inclusive.

The authors will attempt to shed light on all these issues in the following paragraphs in an effort to introduce ArchForum and present the context and basis of its implementation.

What Actually is the SEEArchWeb Forum?

A quick search on the Internet is indicative of the current situation regarding the field of archaeology. To the best of our knowledge, there has been no organized attempt to create a coherent, well-conceived multimedia powered and at the same time multilingual archaeological forum. Without being disrespectful toward efforts of the sort and already existing organized and information thriving Web sites, one should not, however, ignore a considerable number of "adventurous" archaeology Web sites with hints of "antiquarianism" and a desire to discover the "wonders" and "mysteries" of archaeology. Thus, the significance of ArchWeb forum goes far beyond the integration of modern technologies in the domain of archaeology; it re-establishes and confirms its scientific entity.

But, before getting drawn into theoretical discourses, one should clarify the exact meaning and design purpose of the SEEArchWeb forum: what does a multilingual and multimedia archaeological Web forum mean?

- **Forum:** A virtual space where people state their opinions on specialized issues.
- **Web:** This forum resides on the World Wide Web.
- **Archaeological:** Containing articles about archaeological sites and findings, publications and current issues concerning archaeologists, researchers and the whole of academic community.
- **Multimedia:** The published articles can also contain pictures and animations, complementing the traditional "text" layout.
- **Multilingual:** Provides for multilingual translation of articles and of the interface itself.

In brief, this forum is a Web environment where archaeologists and researchers can post articles about their scientific work, and support and enhance it with pictures, photographs, animations and audio-tools. Translators then rewrite the articles in another language which helps build the first dictionary in the domain of archaeology, which is continually updated and enriched thanks to the flow of new articles and terms.

What Does this Forum Offer?

- **Quality archaeology-oriented content:** Researchers, archaeologists, academics and authorized authors can post their announcements, research work, publications, articles and findings in a "hypermedia" way, even as simple as a word document. Thus, one benefits from modern computer technologies without the prerequisite of expertise on handling complicated tools.
- **An archaeology-oriented publishing directory:** ArchWeb forum comprises a gratis and effortless way for anyone to officially post an article and state an opinion within the context of archaeological scientific community. In other words, it gives the answer to the question: "Where should I address to, to present my work to the public?"
- **Quick and easy content publication:** Publication takes a matter of seconds; it requires no time-consuming procedures, and the same applies for the translation process.
- **Knowledge spreading:** It "democratises" knowledge, providing open access to everyone interested in archaeology, no matter where he or she lives and regardless of his or her academic, social, ethnic and age background.
- **Archaeology online community builder:** Subsequently, this inclusiveness provides the opportunity for a fertile problematic and discourse among users.
- **Content reference authority:** SEEArchWeb forum is actually to become a database containing a vast amount of information regarding archaeological issues.
- **Machine aided translation facilities:** The auto-translate function greatly enhances the translation process, and by the moment new terms are continually being added to the dictionary.

In general, SEEArchWeb forum is an invaluable resource for students, academics, archaeologists and researchers. Altogether, with all elements mentioned above, it radically changes the so far solidified perceptions of approaching Archaeology, meaning the exclusively old-fashioned study in libraries and the lack of a coherent and consistent database.

Presenting the SEEArchWeb Forum

At this point, we follow the presentation of SEEArchWeb forum's functions and mode of use.

The user interface composes of four groups / user types: simple user, author, translator and administrator. The presentation starts from the simple user level up to the author and translator

Figure 14. Home page of the forum

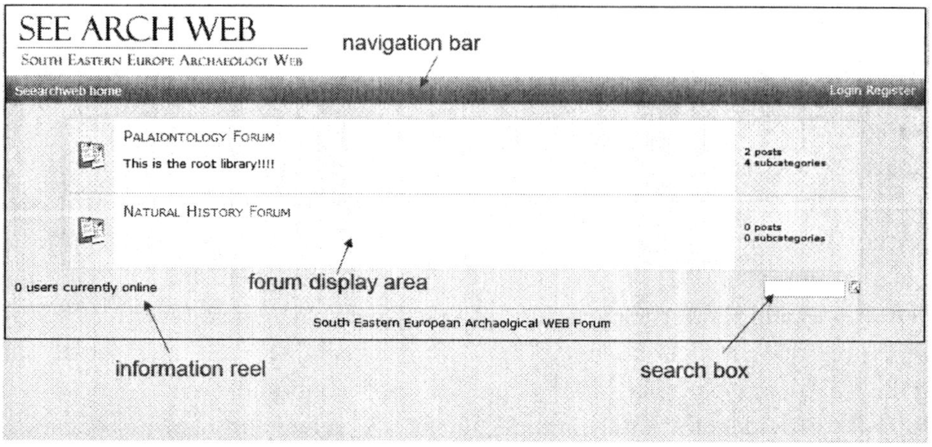

Figure 15. The login screen

level. Each presentation contains a tutorial of the basic functions each one of the users can perform. The administrator level functions are not being presented, because it does not apply to external users, except for the design team.

The simple users group consists of all people interested in Archaeology and can access the Web page through Internet. No registration is required; access and navigation is gratis. Yet, in order for someone to be able to post comments/replies to threads and to experience a translated view of each article, registration is required.

Basic parts of this page are the following:

- Navigation bar
  - This bar contains the path to the current category/thread viewed, together with links to the home page.
  - The login and register links, enabling registered users to login and non registered users to sign up.
- Search box
  - Ability to search for a word or phrase in the title or content of an article.
- Information reel
  - Various information about the logged in user and the forum state
- Forum display area
  - The main content area of the forum. Here one can find:
    - Links to subforums/subcategories
    - Information about each subforum/subcategory (number of threads, posts, replies, etc.)
    - A list of the titles in the various languages and their corresponding flags

The next page is the "About Us" page. This page contains information about the creators of this site and helpful information. This page is of no significant function; there is therefore no need for further description.

The last page is the "contact form." This form is used to contact the administrator, in order to make a request or a remark, even to subscribe to this site as a more advanced user.

The **author** group consists of archaeology scientists and individuals wishing to publish their work to the public. The functionality of this user type is the most crucial one, because the author writes the original articles and subsequently "builds up" the forum. "Author" users therefore need to register in order to keep track of their announcements and articles and assist them with the writing process.

Authors need to log into the system to be authorized. By pressing the Login link on the home page one can see the login screen.

As long as the administrator supplies authors with credentials, by clicking the Login button the author can enter this Web environment and view the authors' home-page:

The next page is the "About Us" page. This page contains information about the creators of this site and helpful information. Because this page is of no essential use to users, there is no need for further description.

The next page is the "contact form." This form is used to contact the administrator in order to make a request or a remark as well as to subscribe to this site as a more advanced user. One only has to follow the steps below: (1) Fill in the textbox voids; (2) Write his or her comment; (3) Press the Send button. The info icon emerges again for quick help assistance.

The next page is the "manage account" form, which is invoked by clicking on the username of the registered user. This form is used to update personal data like username, password, e-mail, and so forth. To process is simple. Just fill in the textbox and then press the Save button to update the data. If you don't change a value, leave it blank.

The last page is the "add new content form." This is the most essential page of the whole forum, because this actually provides the space available for the composition of new articles. The author needs to fill in the content title, tags, description and main body.

Archaeology scientists and researchers, or even polyglots, compose the **translator** group. These are responsible for valid translations from one language to another, and this is what makes this user type of crucial importance. This is the reason these users have to register, that is, to keep track of their repostings and assist them with the translation process. Translators need to log into the system to be authorized. By pressing the Login link on the home page, one can see the login screen.

The navigation menu with the navigation options:

- The dropdown with the interface languages
- **The View Untranslated Articles link:** Presents all the articles the user can translate
- **The View Pending Translations link:** Presents all the articles the user can check for their translation
- **The Manage Dictionary link:** Navigates to the "manage dictionary" page
- **The Home link:** Goes back to the default page
- **The About Us link:** Shows information and help
- **The Contact link:** Brings up a form to contact the administrator
- **The Manage Account link:** Navigates to the manage account page
- **The Logout link:** Logs out the current user
- **The search box:** Searches for a word or phrase in the article title or its content

In the forum, each article has the following sections:

- A list of the article titles in the various languages offered and their corresponding flags
- Information about the article
- The number of replays, a button to navigate the replays, another one to navigate the translation form and a last one to navigate the check translation form

The next page is the "check translation form." This page enables the user to check the accuracy of a translation implemented by another translator. The last page is the "translation form" is where

Table 5. List of all the icons in the editor and their function

Source	Display the html, behind the document.	**B**	Bold text.		Remove link from text.
	Initialize a new page.	*I*	Italic text		Display the anchor dialog.
	Preview this page.	U	Underline text		Display the image edit/add dialog.
	Open the templates dialog.	abc	Strike through text.		Display the flash edit/add dialog.
	Cut the selected text.	x_2	Subscript text.		Display the table edit/add dialog.
	Copy the selected text.	x^2	Superscript text.		Insert horizontal rule.
	Paste the text.		Numbering list.	Ω	Display the special character dialog.
	Paste as plain text.		Bullet list.		Insert page break.
	Paste from word.		Decrease indent of text.		Display the universal keyboard dialog.
	Undo last action.		Increase indent of text.		Change text color.
	Redo last action.		Left justify text.		Change background color.
	Display the find dialog		Center justify text.	Style	Change text style.
	Display the replace dialog		Right justify text.	Format	Change text format.
	Select all content.		Block justify.	Font	Change text font.

the original or approved article is translated to a new language (see more detailed information in the SEEARCHweb forum Web site tutorial).

The **editor** (Table 5) used by the SEEArchWeb forum is not very difficult to handle because it is very similar to the Office Word functionality.

FUTURE RESEARCH DIRECTIONS

This chapter indicates that, across a variety of disciplines, posting articles in forums have a greater research impact than articles that are not Web available. Although this is just a part of ongoing changes in scholarly communication, it can help to inform academicians in working on networked information environment. Particularly, archaeologists self posting is nowadays a response to the benefits in sharing research output.

New ways that would promote the idea of virtual exhibitions are needed. A system that would mix better Web software, and would be more appealing to a greater audience, is the goal. Probably a system with an easy user's interface to support archaeological knowledge is a system with well structured forums, blogs and content management structures where users could be informed about archaeological discoveries from the whole world separated in time, place and kind. SEEArchWeb forum is a system which with some improvements (e.g., concerning more items, combine other Web software) it could have a serious impact on scholarly communication.

REFERENCES

Antelman, K. (2004). Do open-access articles have a greater research impact? *College & Research Libraries News*, *65*(5), 372-382.

Avern, G. (2001). *Progress report on a new technique for recording archaeological sites and excavations*. Belgium: Université Libre de Bruxelles.

Bampton, M., & Mosher, R. (2001). A GIS driven regional database of archeological resources for research and CRM in Casco Bay, Maine. In Z. Stancic & T. Veljanovski (Eds.), *Computing archaeology for understanding the past, CAA 2000, BAR International Series 931, 28th Conference*, Ljubljana, Slovenia, (pp. 139-142).

Baxter, M.J., & Freestone, I.C. (2006). Log-ratio compositional data analysis in archaeometry. *Archaeometry*, *48*(3), 511-531.

Börner, W. (2000). Vienna archaeological GIS. In *Proceedings of the 28th CAA Conference*, op.cit., (pp. 149-152).

Clarke, J. (2001). Questions raised by electronic publication in archaeology. *Journal Bar International Series*, *931*, 351-356.

Hare, M., Gilbert, N., Medugno, D., Asakawa, T., Heeb, J., & Pahl-Wostl, C. (2001). The development of an Internet forum for long-term participatory group learning about problems and solutions to sustainable urban water supply management. In L.M. Hilty & P.W. Gilgen (Eds.), *Sustainability in the Information Society, 15th International Symposium Informatics for Environmental Protection, Part 2: Methods/Workshop Papers*, (pp. 743-750). Marburg: Metropolis Verlag.

Kling, R., & Covi, L. (1995). Electronic journals and legitimate media in the systems of scholarly communication. *The Information Society, Special Issue on Electronic Journals and Scholarly Publishing, 11*(4), 261-271.

KEY TERMS

Balkanization: Balkanization is a geopolitical term originally used to describe the process of fragmentation or division of a region into smaller regions that are often hostile or noncooperative with each other [Webster online dictionary]. The term has arisen from the conflicts in the 20th century Balkans, when in 1912–13, two short wars, fought for the possession of the European territories of the Ottoman Empire, elapsed mainly between the national entities and the counties of the Balkan Peninsula, in the southeastern part of Europe. The wars heightened tensions in the Balkans and helped spark World War I. The term was reaffirmed in the recent Yugoslav wars (1989-2000).

Blog: It refers to a Web site where the author shares his personal views with the public, presenting them in chronological order

E-Journal: It is a journal which is distributed to some or all of its primary subscribers in electronic form. Issues like copyright protection, royalties, and subscription and distribution policies are still a concern to the academic community.

Internet Forum: It is a facility on the Internet for holding discussions on specific topics. It simulates the way a *forum* functioned in antiquity. Although the plural of forum is fora, in computer jargon the morpheme *forums* is used.

Tag Cloud: A specific area in a Web page which contains the tags of the most popular articles.

Thread: a *thread* with all its replies. In a more computer science oriented approach, a *thread* can be defined as a separate stream of execution that takes place simultaneously with and independently of everything else that might be happening.

Topic: Entity in the Internet forum software. Each topic is actually the beginning of a conversation created by a user.

Section IV
Selected Readings

Chapter XVI
Communication Barriers and Conflicts in Cross-Cultural E-Learning

Rita Zaltsman
International Center of Modern Education - Prague, Czech Republic

ABSTRACT

The present chapter assesses the key questions of communication barriers in distance learning virtual communities. To examine their cultural aspects, a Web-survey for distance learners has been conducted. The principal areas of interest were a cultural dichotomy of West/East; discrepancies in educational cultures (teacher-centered vs. learner-centered); mismatches in communication and educational traditions in different cultures; conflict paradigm and methods of conflict resolution. The findings of the survey are summarized and interpreted and some implications for further research are discussed.

COMMUNICATION BARRIERS AND CONFLICTS IN CROSS-CULTURAL E-LEARNING

Ignoring cultural factors inevitably leads to frustrating and ultimately ineffective learning experiences (Dunn & Marinetti, 2002).

Along with the stunning success, the most striking thing about cross-cultural e-learning is how many initiatives have failed. Dropout rates are as high as 80% ("sources estimate anywhere from a 60 to 80 percent dropout rate for online courses"—Braley-Smith, 2004) resulting not only from terrible content (Dunn, 2003), inefficient instruction (Clay, 1999; Cook, 2001), technological barriers (Mayes, 2001), but also lack of students' motivation (Harasim, 1990; Mehrotra, Hollister, & McGahey, 2001), language barriers (Meierkord, 2000; Young, 2002), cognitive discrepancies (Coomey, Stephenson, 2001) and psychological difficulties (Suler, 2002).

A fundamental reason for this is a poor understanding of how e-learning actually works. The solutions offered to avoid communication pitfalls (Berge, 1998; Mason, 2003) place the main responsibility on online tutors who do not encourage and facilitate collaborative work. The latter seem to be little effective as it is culturally absolutely insensitive (Dunn, et al 2002).

The last two years have produced a growing body of research that studies cultural and cross-cultural dimensions of e-learning (Cook, 2001; Dunn, 2003; Edmundson, 2003; Thorne, 2002) and provides case study analyses with instances of miscommunication between culturally-diverse e-students (Chase, Macfadyen, Reeder, & Röche, 2002; Macfadyen, Chase, Reeder, & Roche, 2003). The Internet is not "a culture-free zone" (Reeder, Macfadyen, Roche, & Chase, 2004), and it influences the whole spectrum of communication on both interpersonal and group level. Accordingly, a conflict in the cyber environment differs greatly from its offline counterpart due to additional barriers such as text-based communication in the absence of visual and auditory cues, the new technology as well as anonymity and invisibility, and others. Still, the cause of most misunderstandings in cross-cultural education stems from differing cultural dimensions.

GOAL AND OBJECTIVE OF CHAPTER

In the present chapter, the analysis of cross-cultural communication pitfalls has been extrapolated into the area of distance learning virtual communities. To examine their cultural aspects, a WWW-survey for distance learners has been conducted. The principal areas of interest were the dichotomy of Western vs. Eastern cultures; discrepancies in learning cultures (teacher- vs. learner-centered); mismatches in communicational and educational traditions in different cultures; conflict paradigms and peculiarities of conflict resolution.

It should be noted that for the purpose of this research, the notions of *e-learning, online learning, distance learning, and distance education* denoting the process of learning at a distance on the Internet without face-to-face communication between online students are used interchangeably.

BACKGROUND

"Culture is always a collective phenomenon ... it is the collective programming of the mind which distinguishes the members of one group or category of people from another...it is learned, not inherited" (Hofstede, 1991, p. 5). G. Hofstede's classical definitions and his comparative cultural analyses remain the benchmark for discussion of national cultures. According to Hofstede, culturally-diverse groups have less similarity than monocultural groups due to different orientations to nature, environment, time, relationships, activities, and so forth. The adaptation of the cross-cultural teams to virtual learning is often accompanied by psychological discomfort, stress, frustration, the feeling of being isolated (Munro, 2002; Suler, 2002). Due to discrepancies in conflict management traditions in different cultures, their inter- and intra-communication sometimes result in intercultural conflicts.

In this chapter, intercultural conflict is defined as the perceived or actual incompatibility of values, norms, processes, or goals between a minimum of two cultural parties over content, identity, relational, and procedural issues. (Ting-Toomey, 1999).

To better understand the nature of communication pitfalls in learning communities, several dimensions for cultural comparison have been offered:

1. Power-distance; collectivism vs. individualism; femininity vs. masculinity; uncertainty avoidance (high vs. low); long-term vs. short-term orientation (Hofstede, 1997).
2. Universalism vs. particularism; achievement vs. ascription; individualism vs. commu-

nitarianism; affective vs. neutral cultures; specific vs. diffuse cultures; sequential vs. synchronic cultures (Trompenaars, 1998).
3. High/low context theory (Hall, 1981).
4. Time factor: monochronic/polychronic cultures (Hall & Hall, 1989).

According to Hofstede (1986), Eastern cultures (China, Taiwan, Thailand, etc.) are collectivistic, intuitive, and indirect, traditionally focused on relationships, roles, and status; whereas Western cultures (e.g., U.S., Germany, UK) have a definite orientation towards individualism, are logical, rational, direct, and success-oriented. The opposing cultural distinctions complicate effective communication and learning collaboration within online teams. In addition, Western cultures base their ethics on competitiveness; whereas the ethics of Eastern cultures are based on calmness and humility: Easterners value cooperation and harmony more than competition between individuals. Consequently, the following tactic in offline conflict situations is practiced in Eastern cultures: conflict avoidance as an appropriate behavior which aims at maintaining relational harmony ("lose face" phenomenon); Western cultures favor conflict openness: the Westerners are opened for communicating points of disagreement, and view conflict as an efficient way to solve problems.

There is also a contrast between educational preferences based on the Eastern/Western paradigm: "*listen and reflect,*" "*learn by heart*" (Eastern) vs. "*express a personal opinion,*" "*criticize and discuss*" (Western) (Hofstede, 1986). These preferences generate a conflict potential for online learners as well. To minimize this, some scholars advocate an idea of a constructivist approach to online learning. The term refers to the idea that learners construct knowledge for themselves—each learner individually (and socially) constructs meaning—as he or she learns (Hein, 1991). This is manifested in active dialogues in groups, between learners, tutors, and other actors. A constructivist learning environment presupposes the learners' personal initiative and their responsibility for their own learning. Such learning is not limited to data or facts transfer, when the students are expected only to "digest" knowledge, is directed at solving problems and active collaboration in online communities.

Jin, Mason, and Yim (1998) argue that the Internet can bridge cultural differences and illustrate this with the following example:

Most Chinese, even if they speak English, are much weaker conversationally than in reading and writing. They also are clumsy when put into positions to respond or react publicly, without prior preparation. In contrast, the Americans are generally very good at this. Consequently, if something is written down and a Chinese is given the time to read and to produce a written response, he/she will be able to come up with reasoned, well-thought-out responses. (Jin & Mason, 1998, Language and Interactions with Non-Chinese Section, para. 1)

The time zones difference (12 hours between the U.S. and China) which normally hinders communication plays a positive role here: The Chinese are given additional time to think their answers over. Thus, the Internet turns into an ideal communication setting for these two contextually opposite cultures.

This means that the Internet can play not only *a destructive role* but also *a constructive role*, making online communication across cultures less problematic.

METHODOLOGY

The present survey was a part of a doctoral research conducted in 2001-2004 (Zaltsman, 2004) in which the main objective was to investigate and comprehend communication barriers and conflicts in online cross-cultural distance learning communities. The study was based on three research methods: participation-observation, Web-based survey, and case study research (discourse analysis). This combination of methods has provided a more holistic view on the research subject, and contributed to a better understanding of the issues. Consequently, the data validity has been ensured. Some of the research results have already been reported in several print and online publications (Zaltsman, 2005; Zaltsman & Belous, 2004).

The survey was available via the Internet from March to June 2004. Participation in the study was confidential and voluntary. It should be emphasized that global online research is very complex in regard to methodological aspect: The majority of Web surveys attract mostly international students attending one particular university or college. Some researchers, however, through the results obtained from samples of students, make conclusions concerning all representatives of a certain culture, or even generalize them to all cultures. Hence, the findings they obtain may be inaccurate. Second, the present survey, undertaken at the global level, differs from the ones conducted for a certain academic institution: Filling it out was not compulsory, and participants did not benefit from their participation, compared with the University of Windsor survey pretext: "A raffle for a $100 Campus Bookstore gift certificate or University (...) sweatshirt would be offered as an incentive for filling out the survey"—Sloniowski, 1993, Methodology Section, para. 1). This accounted for a relatively limited number of survey participants.

Invitations to complete the survey have been sent to potential respondents over:

1. Listservs (e.g., ITFORUM@LISTSERV.UGA.EDU)
2. FIDO newsletters (e.g., psychology, education, instructional psychology)
3. Online Communication Yahoo Groups: Intercultural Communication, Intercultural Insights, Distance Learning
4. Learning communities for intercultural communication: www.dialogin.com, www.sietar-germany.de, www.learningcircuits.org, www.learningtimes.com, etc.

The participants, students, online tutors and PhD learners, psychologists, sociologists, distance learning researchers and administrators, were contacted by email and directed to the www.surveymonkey.com Web site where the survey had been placed.

To gain first-hand information and more understanding of the subject matter, the author has taken part in several distance learning courses designed for cross-cultural virtual learners in the U.S. (Carrollton) and Germany (Saarbrücken). Participants of both programs constituted later the majority of the survey respondents.

1. **"Distance Learning Certificate Program 10"** (January - June, 2003) conducted by the University of West Georgia, USA (http://distance.westga.edu/) for distance learning tutors and administrators. Conflict paradigm: learning cultures discrepancies (learner vs. teacher-centered) between American and Italian online students.
2. **"Ikarus: Teaching and Learning in Virtual Learning Environments"** (March - June, 2004)—intercultural online seminar funded by the European Community and conducted by Saarland University, Germany (http://www.online-seminar.net/index.html) together with its partners from European universities and educational research centers in Sweden, Greece and Spain. The entire seminar was concentrated on learning environments based on the Internet. The students were discussing the subject of teaching and debating the issues of learning in the virtual learning settings. Conflict paradigm: differences in time orientation between Austrian and Chinese students.

Both programs were offered completely online with no residency requirement. The project development was tracked from the inside: The researcher was working alongside with the students. Such field research is known as participant-observation. "The empirical approach to participant observation emphasizes participation as an opportunity for in-depth systematic study of a particular group or activity" (Garson, 2005, Key Concepts and Terms Section, para. 3). This research strategy has contributed to active virtual collaboration with course participants and tutors, direct observation of communication proceeding, and its barriers.

Thus, the data of a relatively neutral online survey were backed up with the researcher's own experiences and impressions. Such an approach, among other things, has led to alterations in objectives and contributed to obtaining valid data.

SURVEY RESULTS AND DISCUSSION

The findings are a result of responses from 91 survey participants (270 invitations to participate have been sent) from 23 countries (response rate: 30.3%). It took each participant an average of 15 minutes to respond to the entire survey. (The obtained results are provided in Appendix A.)

Demographic data. Fifty point seven percent of the respondents were young people between 20 and 40 years old, which coincides with the results obtained by other studies (Hamdorf, 2003). The rest were aged over 40. This indicated that learning in virtual settings is gradually attracting a greater amount of the elderly. The reason for it is that at this age most employees are threatened with unemployment and are forced to continuously update their skills profiles and general abilities. The desire to study on the Internet and the interest in online learning for people over 40 was a predictable parameter (Hamdorf, 2003). However, a high percentage of respondents of this age group was not anticipated.

There was a balance of male and female respondents. Women comprised 51.4% of the total number who took part in the survey. This reflected the standard concept about an equal interest from both genders in e-learning, for example, the gender parameter gave anticipated results. Seventeen persons ignored the question and did not identify their gender.

Cultural profile of the respondents. The results clearly showed that the majority of respondents (66.3%) were Westerners: Out of 68 responses to this question, 35.4% came from European countries with Germany being well represented, more than one third (31%) came from the U.S. and Canada, and the remaining 33.3% came from the rest of the world. Fifty-two point two percent of the participants identified that their cultural values focused on individual's views, decisions, and tasks and, consequently, belonged to individualistic cultures. It is notable, that some respondents did not know what category they should be referred to—individualistic or collectivistic: In their comments, some Easterners indicated that they had been living for years mostly abroad, in the West, under the conditions of a non-native culture. Subsequently, 19.4% of respondents experienced difficulties with this question and either skipped it or have marked a "*don't know*" option.

Online communication issues. The overwhelming majority of respondents were satisfied with communication online indicating that "*it is substantially the same as talking face-to-face to people*" or "*online has its own qualities as has "is-à-vis"*.... Significantly, communication in forum (asynchronous) is more preferable than that in chat (synchronous). The following reasons for that were indicated:

Time Factor

- *[...] I have a chance to carefully consider my responses, as opposed to relying on 'knee-jerk' reactions characteristic of face-to-face interactions.*

- *There is [plenty] of time to work on a response, unlike face-to-face. And my accent does not get in the way.*
- *As a non-native speaker, online communications give me more time to think and write more clearly than communication in a face-to-face environment.*

Decisive Role of Successful Collaboration

- *I find the collaboration and feeling of learning from the whole group to be much more effective than "sage on the stage" teacher-centered learning.*
- *Some students watch rather than participate; class is too lethargic.*
- *It is a matter of context and others' personality more than a stable situation. With some people I feel comfortable, with others not.*

Interestingly, the feeling of being protected (35.4%) or anonymous (25.4%) has been emphasized as criteria for communication comfort and learning success.

Communication barriers. The data suggested that the participants view new technology on the whole as a positive force. Nonetheless, the limitations of e-learning were mentioned; some considered a lack of non-verbal dimension of online communication as the most important barrier:

- *I'm feeling quite comfortable, but I feel it is a very difficult task to avoid misunderstandings—more than in face-to-face (where you can transfer more than words through gestures, mimic etc. and you also receive immediate response via mimic, etc.).*
- *Often the online forms of communication do not offer sufficient richness to communicate as well as in a class. Needs to be even more open.*

In their comments, several respondents advocated the idea that online communication was of inferior quality, and mentioned a perception that online education is too impersonal. Also, the results indicating the attitude to online conflict and conflict resolution revealed dissimilarities: The majority of participants (66.2%) preferred an open dialogue and would rather "*communicate the point of disagreement*," "*share the point of difference*," "*voice out openly*" or "*confront the individual*" as it is practiced in the Western cultures rather than "*keep silent though disagreeing* or *carry out a public confrontation*." Thus, the Westerners did not feel uneasy sharing their points of difference, whereas the Easterners preferred to avoid conflict "*to save face*."

Other responses included:

- *Tell the person who doesn't agree with me via @-mail.*
- *My response would depend on the nature of the disagreement and the culture within the class and the school. I am not opposed to being forthright, provided I can do it tactfully. Also, my behavior would differ quite a bit depending on whether I were a student or a teacher. As a teacher, I would be less inclined to say, "I disagree." I would need to be much more focused on equanimity and tact.*

The most striking data were a set of figures indicating that every second student (46 out of 91 persons) would need the assistance of the class tutor in case of communication pitfalls. Probably, the idea of asking a tutor to help with conflict resolution was caused by discomfort, frustration, and stress which the participants reported as the predominant feelings experienced by them in e-learning. So, they needed support of a senior person who had much more life experience; many participants were accustomed to this practice in traditional class and felt a lack of it in online settings. The presence of a tutor or a mentor seemed to be an integral part of the educational process for these students, whereas his/her absence turns into a communication barrier.

Learning styles as communication barriers. The question: *Which activity characterizes best the educational tradition in your culture?* has given results which were not anticipated. A high percent (54.3%) of the variant "*listen and reflect*" has shown that in most classrooms (even in Western cultures), a reproductive way of knowledge acquisition through memorizing, listening to instructor, rote learning, and drill testing was being traditionally practiced. It should be noted that there were no more relevant options, for example: "*learning by doing*" which was a limitation of this survey.

- The overwhelming majority (70.6%) of respondents have stated that the educational tradition in their cultures was teacher-centered. Thus, taking into account that most of the responses came from the Westerners, it can be concluded that in the Western classrooms teachers remain the main "source of knowledge," whereas the learners are still unable to confront new challenges and take the responsibility for their learning achievements. Learning process is supposedly only shifting from teacher to learner ("*probably somewhere in the middle at present but moving towards learner-centered*"; "*there seems to be a development towards student-centered*").

Example Excerpts from the Survey Responses

- *Never considered it a Western or Eastern phenomenon. I encounter both in the States. I think in the U.S., many teachers* pretend *to be learner-centered but are very teacher-centered anyway.*
- Elementary education is learner-centered, secondary and beyond is teacher-centered
- *Given the diffusion of constructivist ideals into the educational system, especially in colleges/universities, I don't think that selecting either teacher-centered or learner-centered would be accurate. It is difficult to know if one style predominates, given by subjective experience at a school of education that emphasizes a learner-centered approach.*
- Combination of both: Structured learning through authority as well as critical discussions
- *Well, it's worked effectively in many regions (University of London courses in Africa, Indian Open University, United Kingdom Open University, etc.). It's more a matter of appropriate design—and then there's the access problem.*

The question of suitability to a greater degree Western or Eastern culture to online learning has resulted in a number (n = 15) of comments. Some respondents did not see any necessity for such a dichotomy, since the choice, in their view, depended on: (a) the age and background of the students; (b) the learning objectives; (c) the purpose of teaching; (d) the individualities of concrete persons. Nevertheless, 43.3% of all participants reported a Western style, 7.8% reported an Eastern style, which clearly indicated that the question was legitimate.

Culture and new technology. The question whether the Internet will dissolve all national differences and create a monolithic modern Internet culture resulted in 54.9% of negative responses; slightly more than 36.3% of participants expressed some level of agreement, with another 8.8% remaining neutral. A clear majority (75.8%) felt that the Internet would stimulate cultural contacts, provide communication, and a cross-cultural dialogue. The students have demonstrated a very thoughtful approach to this issue and showed that they did not view the Internet as a panacea or a machine for learning, but as an environment where various cultures could successfully cooperate to achieve their educational objectives.

CONCLUSION

The research presented a starting point for exploring the factors inherent in mismatches in intercultural online learning that can affect the success of it. The findings suggested that:

1. Online learners tend to be older, there is no statistically-significant difference between male and female students
2. The Western/Eastern division of cultures based on contrasts of communication and educational cultures is quite legitimate
3. Communication barriers and conflicts in online settings are based on the West vs. East paradigm: Eastern communication is based on conflict avoidance, whereas Western is characterized by the ability to criticize or communicate the point of disagreement
4. Online communities have an intermediate ("cosmopolitan") group of students who have cross-cultural experiences of living and learning. As such, they can act as conflict mediators along the cultures and help Westerners and Easterners accommodate to cultural diversity of online settings
5. The majority of respondents feel positive about online communication and perceive it (in spite of the lack of visual and sensitive contact) as an equivalent to face-to-face or not less qualitative
6. The survey has confirmed that, at present, the teacher occupies a leading position in the virtual class: Most online learning is still teacher-centered
7. The findings also has suggested that teachers play a more important role in conflict resolution as anticipated

The findings and implications of this study need to be considered in light of their limitations. Unfortunately, no data were collected about the professional background of the respondents. Also, the question about the time of distance learning experience had to be included in the survey; it would have helped us to examine how it could influence the perception of the distance learning.

Furthermore, in order to obtain more exact data, a five-point Likert scale would have been necessary to indicate the extent to which the respondents agreed or disagreed, from strongly disagree to strongly agree.

Additional research is necessary in tracking the dynamics of conflict processes and studying the characteristics of conflict discourse and communication pitfalls between English native and non-native speakers. We are currently conducting a case study research exploring a stress retrieval function of humor in intercultural e-learning conflicts. Some implications that the major findings raise will be discussed and related to a widely-disputed theme of global Internet culture.

REFERENCES

Allen, I., & Seaman, J. (2004). *Entering the mainstream—The quality and extent of education in the United States, 2003 and 2004.* Needham, MA: Sloan-C. Retrieved September 10, 2005, from http://www.sloan-c.org/resources/entering_mainstream.pdf

Baumeister, H. -P., Williams, J., & Wilson, K. (Eds). (2000). *Teaching across the frontiers. A handbook for international online seminars.* Tübingen: Deusches Institut für Fernstudienforschung an der Universität Tübingen.

Birkenbihl, M. (1990). *Train the trainer: Arbeitsbuch für Ausbilder und Dozenten.* Darmstadt: Moderne Industrie Verlag.

Chase, M., Macfadyen, L., Reeder, K., & Röche, J. (2002). Intercultural challenges in networked learning: Hard technologies meet soft skills. *First Monday, 7*(8). Retrieved September 10, 2005, from http://firstmonday.org/issues/issue7_8/chase/index.html

Correia, A. (2003). *"When differences collide"—Lessons learned from a cross-cultural team.* Retrieved September 10, 2005, from http://www.indiana.edu/~gist/conference2003/Documents/Correia.pdf

Edmundson, A. (2003). *Decreasing cultural disparity in educational ICTs: Tools and recommendations.* Retrieved November 10, 2005, from http://tojde.anadolu.edu.tr/tojde11/articles/edmundson.htm

Garson, G. (2005). *Participant observation (PA 765 research methodology).* Retrieved November 10, 2005, from http://www2.chass.ncsu.edu/garson/pa765/index.htm

Guertler, L. (2003). Conference note: Third workshop "Qualitative psychology: Research questions and matching methods of analysis" (34 paragraphs). *Forum qualitative sozialforschung / forum: Qualitative Social Research (online journal), 4*(1). Retrieved September 10, 2005, from http://www.qualitative-research.net/fqs-texte/1-03/1-03tagung-guertler-e.htm

Hall, E. (2000). *Monochronic and polychronic time.* In L. A. Samovar & R. E. Porter (Eds.), *Intercultural communication: A reader* (9th ed.). Belmont.

Hall, E., & Hall, M. (1989). *Understanding cultural differences.* Yarmouth, ME: Intercultural Press.

Hamdorf, D. (2003). Towards managing diversity: Cultural aspects of conflict management in organizations. *Conflict & Communication Online, 2*(2).

Hein, E. (1991, October 15-22). Constructivist learning theory (The museum and the needs of people). *CECA (International Committee of Museum Educators) Conference*, Jerusalem. Retrieved September 10, 2005, from http://www.exploratorium.edu/IFI/resources/constructivistlearning.html

Hofstede, G. (1986). Cultural differences in teaching and learning. *International Journal of Intercultural Relations, 10*(3), 301-320.

Hofstede, G. (2001). *Culture's consequences: Comparing values, behaviors, institutions, and organizations across nations* (2nd ed.). Thousand Oaks, CA: Sage Publications.

Jin, Z., Mason, R., & Yim, P. (1998). *Bridging USA-China cross-cultural differences using Internet and groupware technologies.* Retrieved September 10, 2005, from http://www.cim-oem.com/bridge_8c18c.html

Macfadyen, L., Chase, M., Reeder, K., & Roche, J. (2003). Matches and mismatches in intercultural learning: Designing and moderating an online intercultural course. In *Proceedings of the UNESCO Conference on International and Intercultural Education,* Jyvaskyla, Finland.

Marinetti, A., & Dunn, P. (2002). *Cultural adaptation—A necessity for e-learning.* Retrieved September 10, 2005, from http://www.linezine.com/7.2/articles/pdamca.htm

Mehrotra, C., Hollister, D., & McGahey, L. (2001). *Distance learning: Principle for effective design, delivery, and evaluation.* London; New Delhi: Sage Publications.

Munro, K. (2002). *Conflict in cyberspace: How to resolve conflict online.* Retrieved September 10, 2005, from http://www.kalimunro.com/article_conflict_online.html

Porter, L. (1997). *Creating the virtual classroom (distance learning with the Internet).* Wiley: Computer Publishing.

Reeder, K., Macfadyen, L., Roche, J., & Chase, M. (2004, May). Negotiating cultures in cyberspace: Participation patterns and problematic. *Language Learning and Technology, 8*(2) 88-105. Retrieved September 10, 2005, from http://llt.msu.edu/vol-8num2/reeder/default.html

Reeves, T. (1997). *Evaluating what really matters in computer-based education.* Retrieved September 10, 2005, from http://www.educationau.edu.au/archives/cp/reeves.htm

Rösch, O., Loew, R., & Pfeifer, A. (2003). Interkulturelle Kompetenz—heute eine unerlässliche Schlüsselqualifikation. Zwischenbericht zu einem Forschungsprojekt an der TFH Wildau. In: *Wissenschaftliche Beiträge der Technischen Fachhochschule Wildau.*

Schmidt, D., Gruhler, G., & Fearns, A. (Hrsg.) (2003). *E-Learning Experimente und Laborübungen zur Automatisierungstechnik über das Internet: Nutzungsmöglichkeiten, Beispiele und die Simulation am Bildungsmarkt*: Europa-Lernmittel Verlag.

Sloniowski, L. (1993). *Report of findings: Distance education working group student survey project.* Retrieved September 10, 2005, from http://artemis.uwindsor.ca/kits/gailj/99009a/vck13materials.nsf/0/875ef62fa9e00a5185256e01005aa78a/$FILE/dereport_of_findings.doc

Suler, J. (2002). The online disinhibition effect. In *The psychology of cyberspace.* Retrieved September 10, 2005, from http://www.rider.edu/~suler/psycyber/dis inhibit.html

Ting-Toomey, S., & Oetzel, J. (2001). *Managing intercultural conflict effectively.* Thousand Oaks, CA: Sage.

Trompenaars, F. (1998). *Riding the waves of culture: Understanding the waves of cultural diversity in global business.* New York: McGraw-Hill.

Zaltsman, R. (2004). *Conflict paradigm in distance learning cross-cultural online settings.* Doctoral dissertation, Academy of Personnel Management, Kiev: IAPM.

Zaltsman, R. (2005, August). The challenge of intercultural electronic learning: English as lingua franca. *Cybercultures: Exploring Critical Issues, 3rd Global Conference,* Prague, (under review). Retrieved September 10, 2005, from http://www.inter-disciplinary.net/ci/cybercultures/c3/prog.htm

Zaltsman, R., & Belous, A. (2004, June). Considerations to the applications possibilities of E-learning in TRIZ. *QFD-/TRIZ-Kongress,* Kassel, Germany.

APPENDIX A.

Summary of Survey Results

You're a male/female	**Total**	**Percent**
Male	36	48.6%
Female	**38**	**51.4%**
You are		
20-30	18	24.7%
30-40	19	26%
40-55	**27**	**37%**
55+	9	12.3%
What country are you from?		
USA	**27**	**30.9%**
Germany	8	11.8%
Austria, Malaysia, Thailand	à 3	13.5%
Australia, Great Britain, Italy, The Netherlands, Poland, Sweden, Switzerland	à 2	20.4%
Canada, China, Colombia, Egypt, Greece, Venezuela, Mexico, Russia, Spain, Taiwan, Turkey	à 1	23.4%
Do you think your home country is individualistic (focused on individual's views, decisions, tasks, etc.) or rather collectivistic (focused on relationships, roles, status)?		
Individualistic	**24**	**52.2%**
Collectivistic	16	34.8%
Not applicable	1	2.1%
Other (please specify)	5	10.9%
Do you think you belong to the Western cultural tradition?		
Yes	**51**	**70.8%**
No	7	9.7%
Don't know	14	19.4%
Are you comfortable with the communication in your online class? (multiple responses are allowed)		
Yes, absolutely, as I feel anonymous	22	25.4%
Yes, it's just for me absolutely, as I feel protected as compared to face-to-face contacts	**30**	**34.5%**
No, I feel more comfortable when communicating face-to-face	16	18.4%
No, I'm often frustrated: it's stressful to learn in a "global village"	5	5.1%
Don't know	4	4.6%
Other (please specify)	14	12%
What do you think is an ideal medium for communication in an online class? (multiple responses are allowed)		
E-mail	44	62.9%
Voice mail	13	18.6%
Chat	33	47.1%
Video	26	37.1%
Forum	**51**	**72.9%**
Blogs	16	22.9%
Other (please specify)	10	14.3%

Suppose that you feel misunderstood in your online class. Which of the following would you do? (multiple responses are allowed)		
Write an e-mail	**60**	**83.3%**
Use a voice mail	10	13.9%
Chat	18	25%
Meet in video-conference	13	18.1%
Ask for a telephone number	15	20.8%
Meet face-to-face if it's possible	25	34.7%
Other (please specify)	5	6.9%
In case you disagree with somebody in your online class you will:		
Tell the class openly that you don't feel at ease about it	**47**	**66.2%**
Keep silent as confrontation is seen negatively in your culture	14	19.7%
Other (please specify)	10	14.1%
In case you feel misunderstood in your online class, you will apply for help to:		
Your tutor	**46**	**50.5%**
Some student from your class	13	14.3%
The whole group	24	26.4%
Other (please specify)	8	8.8%
Which activity characterizes best the educational tradition in your culture? (multiple responses are allowed)		
Listen and reflect	**38**	**54.3%**
Learn by heart	23	32.9%
Tell your opinion	16	22.9%
Criticize, discuss	24	34.3%
Other (please specify)	10	14.3%
Educational tradition in your culture is:		
Teacher-centered	**49**	**70.6%**
Learner-centered	10	14.3%
Other (please specify)	11	15.1%
Which educational tradition is more appropriate for distance learning?		
Western	**39**	**43.3%**
Eastern	7	7.8%
Don't know	29	32.2%
Other (please specify)	15	16.7%
Do you agree that the Internet is a melting pot - it dissolves all national differences and creates a monolithic modern Internet culture?		
Yes	33	36.3%
No	**50**	**54.9%**
Don't know	8	8.8%
Do you agree that the Internet is an environment where hundreds of national cultures can blossom and enrich each other?		
Yes	**69**	**75.8%**
No	10	11%
Don't know	12	13.2%

Sample Qualitative Comments by Survey Respondents

- I believe that there is an element of trust that is often missing from online instruction. I think building trust is important although difficult.
- I think education, due mainly to technology, must become student centered to be competitive.
- I have both been a student in an online degree program, and am currently involved in creating online higher education. My background is in cultural anthropology and I am interested in your idea that there may be a 'western' vs. 'eastern' methodology for online education—the idea may be too generalized. I don't necessarily see a dichotomy. For US respondents, you should also ask if they're based on the West coast or the East coast of the country—because US Westerners are more influenced by Asian and Native/Hispanic culture, and US Easterners are more influenced by European culture.
- I am fine with online communication but sometimes the lack of proximity is felt.
- Great survey—however, there are still areas that have ambiguous answers and do not fit into choices allowed. Interesting subject. Hope that you get what you need.
- I think that online is a different mode of communication, and as oral or body communication one has to learn the code. I am in the process of learning this code, and as in everything the start is more difficult than the end of the process. I don't think that the distinction Eastern-Western as the role of the teacher concerns is appropriate as there are differentiations in every country (and I find that it indicates a racism).
- These last questions are too narrow, of course Internet and communication technologies have great advantages—but... there are a number of buts.
- Cultural aspects do survive, however, some cultures are reticent to get involved fully.
- U (you) didn't clarify what u meant by western/eastern tradition; I am Egyptian (eastern, but not like Japan) and educated in UK and U.S. institutions, so I'm eastern relative to U.S. but Western relative to my own country...
- Language barriers can hinder multicultural communications. I only speak and read English. When communicating via the Internet, I am not judged by my ethnicity.

This work was previously published in Globalizing E-Learning Cultural Challenges, edited by A. Edmundson, pp. 291-306, copyright 2007 by Information Science Publishing (an imprint of IGI Global).

Chapter XVII
Multimedia, Cognitive Load, and Pedagogy

Peter E. Doolittle
Virginia Polytechnic Institute & State University, USA

Andrea L. McNeill
Virginia Polytechnic Institute & State University, USA

Krista P. Terry
Radford University, USA

Stephanie B. Scheer
University of Virginia, USA

ABSTRACT

The current emphasis, in education and training, on the use of instructional technology has fostered a shift in focus and renewed interest in integrating human learning and pedagogical research. This shift has involved the technological and pedagogical integration between learner cognition, instructional design, and instructional technology, with much of this integration focusing on the role of working memory and cognitive load in the development of comprehension and performance. Specifically, working memory, dual coding theory, and cognitive load are examined in order to provide the underpinnings of Mayer's (2001) Cognitive Theory of Multimedia Learning. The bulk of the chapter then addresses various principles based on Mayer's work and provides well documented web-based examples.

INTRODUCTION

Improving the efficiency and effectiveness of instruction has consistently been a primary goal of education and training. In pursuit of this goal, cognitive psychology has provided considerable insight regarding the processes that underlie efficient and effective instruction. The past 50 years are replete with empirical studies addressing the characteristics inherent in human learning and the influence of these characteristics on instruction. Unfortunately (Anderson, Reder, & Simon, 1998), this "science of human learning has never had a large influence upon the *practice* of education [or training]" (p. 227; italics added). This gap between research and practice is lamentable and serves to deny learners and teachers access to powerful forms of teaching, training, and learning.

Fortunately, the current emphasis on the use of instructional technology has fostered renewed interest in integrating human learning and pedagogical research (see Abbey, 2000; Rouet, Levonen, & Biardeau 2001). As Doolittle (2001) has stated, "it is time to stop professing technological and pedagogical integration and to start integrating with purpose and forethought" (p. 502). One area within instructional technology that has begun this integration is multimedia. The domain of multimedia has matured beyond technology-driven applications into the realm of cognition and instruction. As stated in Rouet, Levonen, and Biardeau (2001), "There is a subtle shift of attention from what *can* be done with the technology to what *should* be done in order to design meaningful instructional applications" (p. 1). This shift has involved the technological and pedagogical integration between learner cognition, instructional design, and instructional technology, with much of this integration focusing on the role of working memory in the development of comprehension and performance.

Specifically, a focus has developed addressing the limited resource nature of working memory and cognitive load. Cognitive load simply refers to the working memory demands implicitly and explicitly created by instruction and how these demands affect the learning process. Those learning tasks that are poorly designed or involve the complex integration of multiple ideas, skills, or attributes result in increased cognitive load and decreased learning. This relationship between cognitive load, working memory, and instruction/training has proved to be especially significant when the instruction is in the form of multimedia. According to Mayer (2001), "the central work of multimedia learning takes place in working memory" (p. 44).

This chapter focuses on multimedia and the mitigating effects of cognitive load on teaching, training, and learning. A central organizing theme throughout the chapter is the development of theoretically sound pedagogy (see Figure 1). Theoretically sound pedagogy involves instruction that is based on empirical research and sound theory designed to illuminate the nature of human learning and behavior. Such theoretically sound pedagogy may then be molded to fit specific learning environments, learning goals and objectives, and learners.

WORKING MEMORY, DUAL CODING AND COGNITIVE LOAD

When pursuing theoretically sound pedagogy, it is essential to ground one's conclusions in the human memory literature. Unfortunately, while there is a plethora of research findings exemplifying the structure and function of human memory, a singular model of memory to which one can refer has yet to emerge. Currently, the three most prevalent models are Atkinson and Shiffrin's (1968) dual-store model, Baddeley's (Baddeley, 1986; Baddeley & Hitch, 1974) working memory model, and Anderson's (1983, 1990, 1993) functional ACT-R model. Each of these models has roots in the early information-processing work of Broadbent (1958) and Peterson and Peterson (1959).

Figure 1: The development of theoretically sound pedagogy

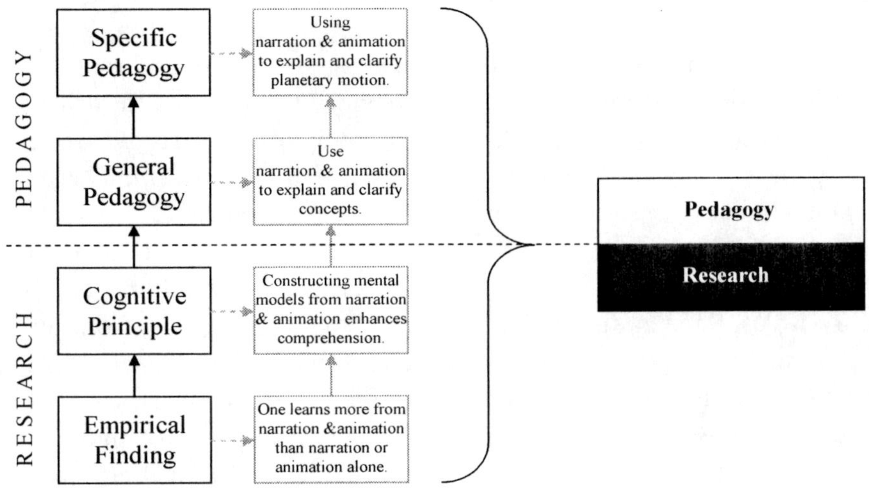

Memory Models and Working Memory

Atkinson and Shiffrin (1968) emphasized the structural nature of memory, delineating three essential structures, *sensory memory*, *short-term memory*, and *long-term memory*. Atkinson and Shiffrin asserted that individuals experience the world through their senses, momentarily storing these senses in raw sensory formats at their sensory sites. These sensations, if attended, may then be encoded into a mind-friendly format and consciously held in short-term memory, where if the individual rehearses this encoded experience, the experience may be transferred to long-term memory. The *dual-store* of Atkinson and Shiffrin's model refers to the short-term memory store, where a small amount of information or experience may be held temporarily, and the long-term memory store, where an unlimited amount of information or experience may held indefinitely. This idea that there were two storage components, each with different processing capabilities, was developed from Broadbent in the 1950s through Atkinson and Shiffrin in the 1960s and was well accepted in the early 1970s. Unfortunately, in the 1970s, testing of the dual-store model revealed inconsistencies in the need for two storage components. By the 1980s, the dual-store model, with its two storage components, was being replaced by a unified working and long-term memory model.

Two separate memory stores were eliminated, and what remained was a single memory store, long-term memory, and a constellation of related processes, termed working memory, responsible for the regulation of reasoning, problem solving, decision making, and language processing (Miyake & Shah, 1999). Working memory is often confused with, or made synonymous with, short-term memory, as working memory has retained certain short-term memory characteristics. For example, a central characteristic of short-term memory was a limited capacity due to a hypothesized small storage space. This limited capacity is also a characteristic of working memory, but the rationale has changed from a limitation based on structure (i.e., space) to a limitation based on function (i.e., processing). Working memory limitations are currently seen as a function of ongoing processing and the nature of the information being processed (see Miyake & Shah, 1999). While working memory and short-term memory share certain similar characteristics, although for differing reasons, they are also significantly different.

Perhaps the most obvious difference between short-term memory and working memory is that short-term memory was construed as a storage location or "box," while working memory is defined as a set of cognitive processes responsible for the support of complex cognition. A second, and related, difference involves purpose. Typically, short-term memory is described as subservient to long-term memory, where long-term memory is responsible for the cognitive processing and short-term memory is merely a workspace for memorization (Baddeley, 1999). Working memory, however, is interpreted as working synergistically with long-term memory, playing a primary role in control and regulation functions (Cowan, 1999). This emphasis on synergy underlies the third difference, which is related to the influence of long-term memory on short-term and working memory. The traditional relationship between short-term memory and long-term memory is one of *independence*, where short-term and long-term memory communicate, as two individuals talking on the telephone, sharing ideas but each operating in only distantly related realms. The relationship between working memory and long-term memory, however, is one of *interdependence* (Baddeley & Logie, 1999; Ericsson & Kintsch, 1995). The interplay between working memory and long-term memory is integrated to such an extent that any discussion of human cognitive performance in the absence of either working or long-term memory would be incomplete.

Thus, an exploration of human cognitive performance in a multimedia environment would need to address this working and long-term memory interdependence. This interdependence is evident in two theories that are currently guiding the development of multimedia instructional technology—dual-coding theory and cognitive load theory.

Dual-Coding Theory

Building on working and long-term memory interdependence, Paivio (1971, 1990) created a theory of cognition that emphasizes the mind's processing of two types or codes of information, verbal and nonverbal. Specifically, Paivio (1990) stated that memory and cognition are represented within two functionally independent, but interconnected, processing systems (see Figure

Figure 2. A schematic representation of Paivio's (1990) dual-coding model, including both verbal/nonverbal channels and representational, associative, and referential processing

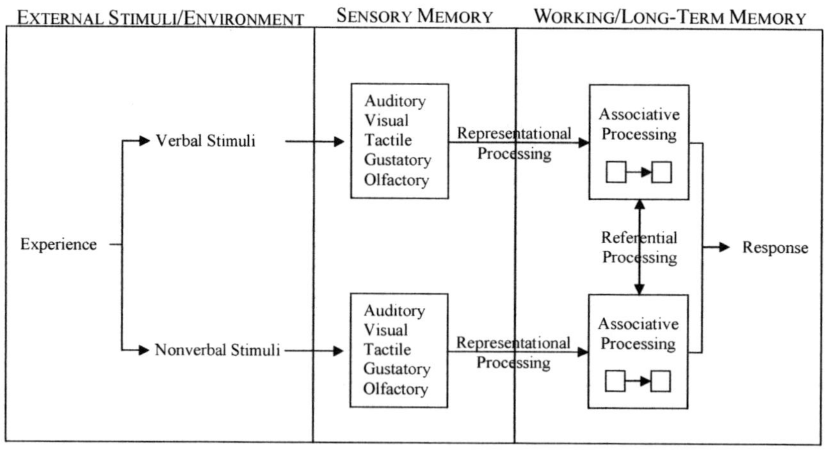

2). One system, the *verbal system*, is specialized for the representation and processing of verbal information (e.g., words, sentences, stories), while the other system, the *nonverbal system*, is specialized for the representation and processing of nonverbal information (e.g., pictures, sounds, smells, tastes). Each system holds and processes representations that are modality-specific (i.e., visual, auditory, tactile, gustatory, olfactory), that is, the representations retain certain properties of the concrete sensorimotor events on which they are based (Clark & Paivio, 1991). It is important to note that these representations are not exact copies of one's experiences, but rather they represent imprecise facsimiles (Paivio, 1990).

The interaction between the verbal/nonverbal processing and modality-specific perceptions can be somewhat confusing. A central point is that regardless of modality, verbal experiences are processed by the verbal system, and nonverbal experiences are processed by the nonverbal system (see Table 1). An everyday example of dual coding would include an individual looking at a weather map on the computer while listening to a weather report (e.g., http://www.weather.com/activities/verticalvideo/vdaily/weeklyplanner.html). The words encountered listening to the weather report would be processed by the verbal system, while the visual images encountered looking at the weather map would be processed by the nonverbal system.

Paivio (1990), upon delineating this relationship between verbal/nonverbal processing and modality-specific perceptions, focused primarily on the verbal/nonverbal processing aspects of the dual-coding theory. According to Paivio (1990), three levels of processing enable verbal and nonverbal representations to be accessed and activated during cognitive tasks (see Figure 2). *Representational processing* is characterized by direct activation; that is, a verbal or linguistic sense experience directly activates a verbal representation and a nonverbal or nonlinguistic sense experience directly activates a nonverbal representation. For instance, reading on-screen text (verbal) directly activates the verbal system, while seeing an on-screen image (nonverbal) directly activates the nonverbal system. *Referential processing* refers to the indirect activation of the verbal system through experience with nonverbal information and the indirect activation of the nonverbal system through experience with verbal information. For example, reading on-screen text (verbal) may indirectly activate a mental image (nonverbal) based on the on-screen text; similarly, viewing an on-screen image (nonverbal) may indirectly activate a concept label (verbal) for that image. Consequently, referential process-

Table 1. Examples of verbal/nonverbal cognitive processing based on specific modality experiences

	Cognitive Processing	
Modality	Nonverbal	Verbal
Visual	Looking at pictures, animations, or clouds	Reading a book, a billboard, or the label on clothing
Auditory	Listening to music, airplanes taking off, or nature sounds	Listening to a speech, a song, or a conversation
Haptic	Touching silk, another's hair, or the texture of wood	Reading Braille, finger spelling, or sign language
Gustatory	Tasting food, licking an envelope, or eating snow	NA
Olfactory	Smelling food, a rainstorm, or noxious gases	NA

ing is indirect in nature, because it requires crossover activity from one symbolic system to another. Finally, *associative processing* refers to the activation of representations within either system by other representations within that same system. For example, for a student with an aversion to technology, the word "computer" (verbal) might elicit verbal associations such as "hate" or "stupid" (verbal); conversely, the sight of a computer (nonverbal) might elicit images or visceral responses (nonverbal) reminiscent of unpleasant experiences using the computer.

Studies examining verbal/nonverbal processing have revealed two central findings (Mayer, Heiser, & Lonn, 2001; Sadoski & Paivio, 2001). First, processing experiences verbally and visually lead to greater learning, retention, and transfer than do processing experiences only verbally (Clark & Paivio, 1991; Paivio, 1975). For instance, in studying the process of osmosis, viewing an animation with a text description of the process (see http://edpsychserver.ed.vt.edu/5114web/modules/slideshows/slideshows.cfm?module=4) results in better learning, retention, and transfer than simply reading a text description. Second, both verbal and visual channels of information processing are subject to memory limitations such that each channel may be overloaded, reducing processing capacity and speed, and learning, retention, and transfer. For example, a multimedia slide show that includes auditory narration (verbal), subtitles of the auditory narration (verbal), and text within the slides themselves (verbal) is certain to overload an individual's verbal channel (http://edpsychserver.ed.vt.edu/5114web/modules/memory5_apps1/slideshow1.cfm). These two findings play a central role in multimedia pedagogy (see Mayer & Anderson, 1991; Schnotz, 2001) and are further explored in the next section, which addresses cognitive load theory. The construct of cognitive load is a means for assessing the memory limitations mentioned previously and for understanding the beneficial effects of adding visual information to verbal information.

Cognitive Load Theory

Cognitive load is a multidimensional construct that refers to the memory load that performing a task imposes on the learner (Paas & van Merrienboer, 1994; Sweller, van Merrienboer, & Paas, 1998). Inextricably linked with cognitive load theory is the notion that working memory is a limited resource; therefore, a careful distribution of the cognitive load within working memory is needed to successfully perform a given task (Chandler & Sweller, 1991, 1992). Further, cognitive load theory is based on several assumptions concerning human cognitive architecture (Mousavi, Low, & Sweller, 1995), including the following:

1. People have limited working memory and processing capabilities
2. Long-term memory is virtually unlimited in size
3. Automation of cognitive processes decreases working memory load

Ultimately, the central premise of cognitive load theory is that working memory is limited and, if overloaded, learning, retention, and transfer will be negatively affected.

Cognitive load theory posits that instructional materials impose upon the learner three independent sources of cognitive load—intrinsic cognitive load, extraneous cognitive load, and germane cognitive load (Gerjets & Scheiter, 2003; Paas, Renkl, & Sweller, 2003). Together, intrinsic, extraneous, and germane cognitive load comprise the total working memory load imposed on the learner during instruction (Tindall-Ford, Chandler, & Sweller, 1997) (see Figure 3).

Intrinsic cognitive load represents the inherent working memory load required to complete a task. As an inherent component of a given task, intrinsic cognitive load is beyond the direct control of the instructional designer. Sweller (1994) suggested that the amount of interaction between learning elements, element interactivity, is a critical fac-

Figure 3. Scenarios of the relationship between working memory capacity and the three components of cognitive load (i.e., intrinsic, extraneous, and germane cognitive load)

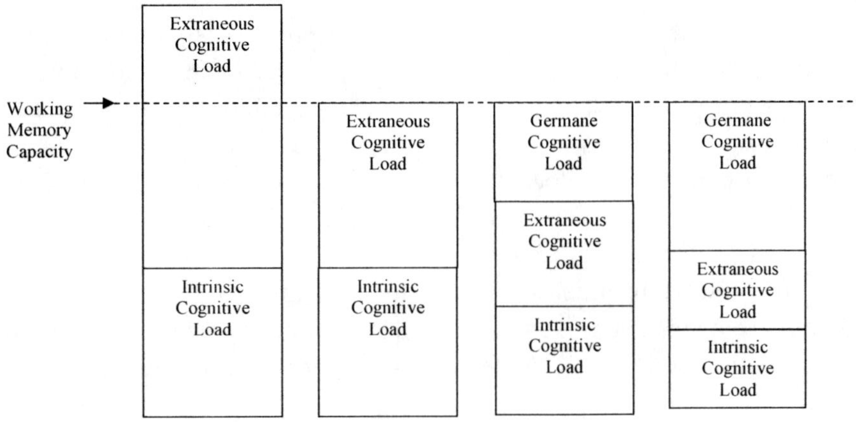

tor influencing intrinsic cognitive load. Element interactivity (Tindall-Ford et al., 1997) occurs when the "elements of a task interact in a manner that prevents each element from being understood and from being learned in isolation and, instead, requires all elements to be assimilated simultaneously" (p. 260). For example, learning the syntax of a computer language imposes a heavy intrinsic cognitive load, because to learn word and rule orders, all the words and rules must be held in working memory simultaneously.

What constitutes an element does not depend solely on the nature of the material, but it also depends on the expertise of the learner (Gerjets & Scheiter, 2003; Tindall-Ford et al., 1997). High element interactivity may not result in high cognitive load if expertise has been attained, thus allowing the learner to incorporate multiple elements into a single element, or "chunk," through schema acquisition or automaticity. This may be evidenced in the use of online simulations. For example, the Neurodegenerative Disease Simulation Model, a Java applet, can be daunting and create significant cognitive load for the novice due to the multiple options available, the complexity of the graphs, and the lack of automated skills related to the operation of the simulation (http://www.math.ubc.ca/~ais/website/guest00.html). For the experienced Neurodegenerative Disease Simulation Model user, however, the cognitive load is significantly reduced as the options are incorporated into schemas that act as an independent element, and the actual operation of the simulation is automated. Thus, using the simulation may result in extremely high intrinsic cognitive load for novices while imposing very little cognitive load on experts.

In addition to intrinsic cognitive load, the manner in which information is presented to learners and the activities required of learners can impose additional cognitive load (Paas, Renkl, & Sweller, 2003). While intrinsic cognitive load is determined by the nature of the material, *extraneous cognitive load* reflects the effort required to process instructional materials that do not contribute to learning the material or completing the task. In this sense, extraneous cognitive load can be seen as "error" in the overall instructional process. Fortunately, extraneous cognitive load is, to a large extent, under the control of instructional designers (Sweller et al., 1998). For example, when animation and text are combined, extraneous cognitive load is increased if the animation and text are not presented simultaneously (Moreno & Mayer,

1999). Specifically, imagine a simulation in which the directions are presented first, followed by the simulation (see http://webphysics.ph.msstate.edu/jc/library/2-6/index.html). In this case, the learner must read the directions, maintain the relevant directions in working memory, and then attempt to use the simulation. The simulation has an innate level of cognitive load, intrinsic cognitive load, to which is being added an additional cognitive load, extraneous cognitive load, as the result of having to maintain the directions in working memory. A simple solution to this extraneous cognitive load would be to provide the directions on the same page as the simulation.

The third type of cognitive load is *germane cognitive load*. Germane cognitive load is the cognitive load appropriated when an individual engages in processing that is not designed to complete a given task, but rather, is designed to improve the overall learning process (e.g., elaborating, inferencing, or automating). Engaging in processes that generate germane cognitive load is only possible when the sum of intrinsic and extraneous cognitive load is less than the limits of an individual's working memory. In addition, like extraneous cognitive load, germane cognitive load is influenced by the instructional designer. The manner in which information is presented to learners and the learning activities are factors relevant to the level of germane cognitive load. However, while extraneous cognitive load interferes with learning, germane cognitive load

Figure 4. The Advanced Search page of the Social Justice Resources Center that when used by novices to search for social justice resources results in high intrinsic and extraneous cognitive load

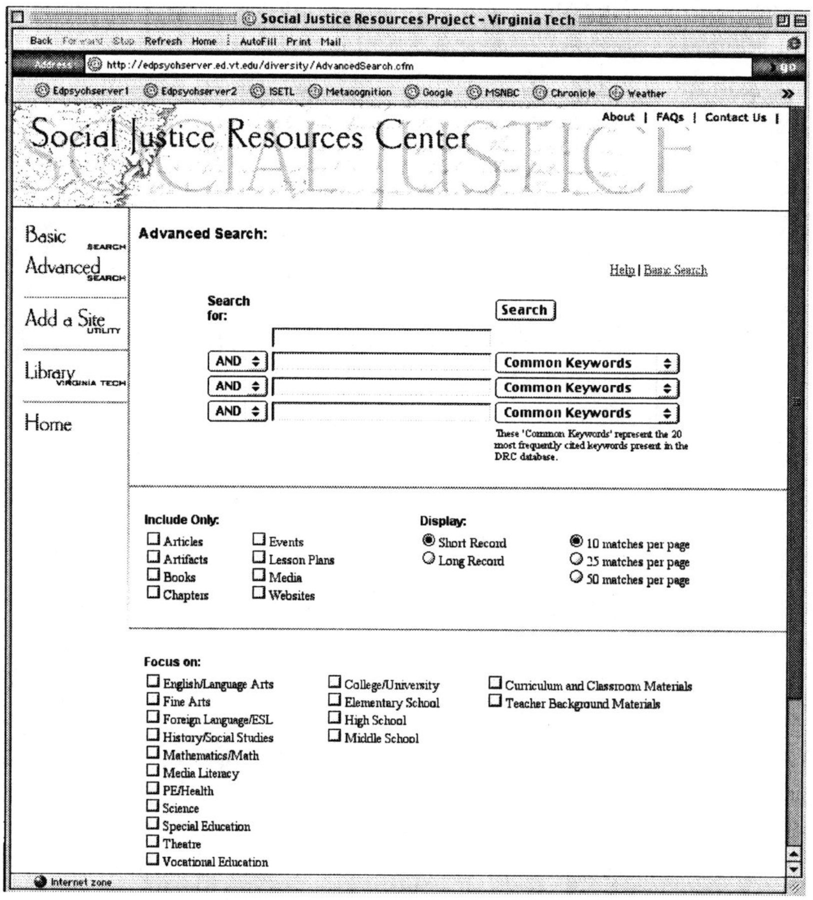

enhances learning by devoting resources to such tasks as schema acquisition and automation (Paas et al., 2003). For example, a student may engage in solving an historical murder mystery (http://web.uvic.ca/history-robinson/), resulting in both intrinsic and extraneous cognitive load. If sufficient working memory capacity remains, the student may also engage in practicing a metacognitive strategy for assessing the primary sources that serve as data for solving the murder mystery. Using a metacognitive strategy is not essential to engaging the murder mystery, however, this use will lead to greater automaticity of the strategy, elaboration on the primary sources, and ultimately, enhanced learning.

Overall, total cognitive load is comprised of the sum of intrinsic, extraneous, and germane cognitive load. This summative nature leads to several interesting scenarios (see Figure 3), all limited or constrained by an individual's working memory capacity (see Figure 3a). These differing scenarios will all be examined using a common example, a Social Justice Resource Center database site (see http://edpsychserver.ed.vt.edu/diversity/).

In the first scenario, if the sum of the intrinsic and extraneous cognitive loads exceeds one's working memory capacity, then learning and performance of the given task will be adversely affected (see Figure 3b). In the case of the Social Justice site, the Advanced Search page could easily overwhelm the working memory capacity of a database/search novice (Figure 4). The Advanced Search page contains complex functions for Boolean searches, data restriction, and layout control, all possibly contributing to excessive extraneous cognitive load.

If, however, the sum of intrinsic and extrinsic cognitive load is equal to one's working memory capacity, then one should be able to complete the given task successfully (see Figure 3c). Continuing the Social Justice example, the extraneous cognitive load may be reduced by instructing a student to focus only on understanding and using the Boolean operator search fields and ignoring the data restriction and layout options. Providing or focusing on fewer options is likely to reduce extraneous cognitive load.

Figure 5. The Basic Search page of the Social Justice Resources Center that when used to search for social justice resources results in low intrinsic and extraneous cognitive load

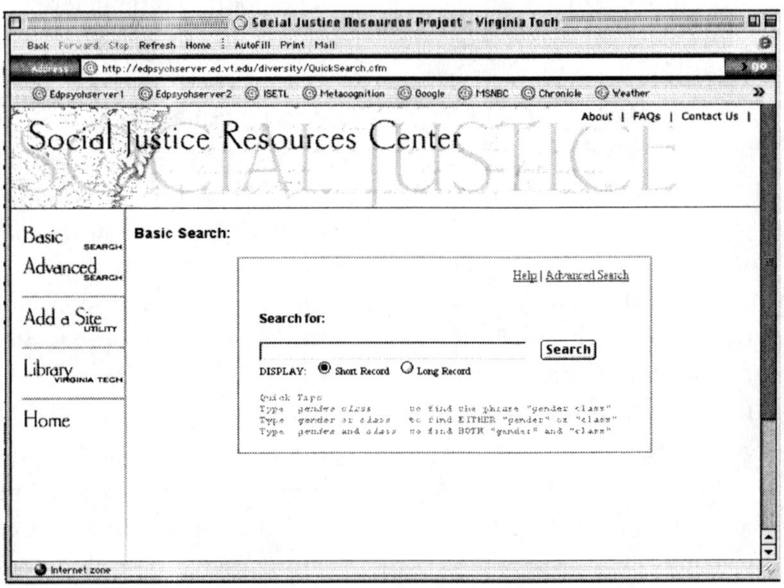

While this situation is acceptable, it does not provide any cognitive resources for engaging in additional and beneficial processing beyond the mere completion of the task. If cognitive load is reduced further, such that the sum of intrinsic and extraneous cognitive load is less than one's working memory capacity, then one may engage in additional synergistic processing, yielding germane cognitive load, resulting in increased overall performance (see Figure 3d). For a database/search novice, no use of the Social Justice Advanced Search page is likely to result in germane cognitive load. To facilitate germane cognitive load, a new Web page may need to be developed that simplifies the task at hand, such as a Basic Search page (Figure 5). The Basic Search page has only one field to complete with very simple directions. The use of the Basic Search page would allow the user to engage in secondary processes, generating germane cognitive load, such as generating a schema of database use, elaborating on potential keywords, and combining keywords into more precise search phrases.

Thus, the ultimate goals of instruction are to (a) create tasks that have inherently low to moderate intrinsic cognitive load, (b) develop instructional designs that reduce extraneous cognitive load, and (c) foster engagement in active processing that facilitates germane cognitive load (see Figure 3e). An example that satisfies all three of these criteria would include searching the Social Justice Resources Database using the Basic Search page that combines a manageable task with an efficient environment to produce effective learning and performing.

This effective and efficient learning and performing is shaped by careful attention to the constraints and guidelines provided by dual-coding theory and cognitive load theory. And, just as dual-coding theory informs cognitive load theory, cognitive load theory informs the cognitive theory of multimedia (see Mayer, 2001). By considering factors that may place an undue burden on the learner while engaged in multimedia cognition, designers can develop multimedia environments that promote effective and efficient learning.

A COGNITIVE THEORY OF MULTIMEDIA

Creating multimedia that balances the constraints of human memory (e.g., dual coding and cognitive load) with the goals of education and training (e.g., meaningful learning, retention, and transfer) requires a theory of multimedia instruction grounded in the science of human learning. Until recently, multimedia meant multiple media *devices* used in a coordinated fashion (e.g., cassette tape player and a slide show) (Moore, Burton, & Myers, 1996). However, advances in technology have combined these media so that information previously delivered by several devices is now integrated into one device (e.g., computer, kiosk) (Kozma, 1994). Thus, multimedia is now typically defined as the integration of more than one medium into a common computer-based communication framework; specifically (von Wodtke, 1993), "multimedia refers to the integration of media such as text, sound, graphics, animation, video, imaging, and spatial modeling into a computer system" (p. 3).

This common computer-based communication framework for multimedia instruction resulted in early research on multimedia focusing on capturing the capabilities of this new framework to deliver instruction (Moore, Burton, & Myers, 1996). However, the current focus of multimedia instruction has shifted away from this technology-centered approach to a more learner-centered approach, where the emphasis is on how to design multimedia frameworks to aid human cognition (see Abbey, 2001).

This learner-centered approach to multimedia instruction focuses on the cognitive processing of multimedia messages and the influence of this processing on learning, retention, and transfer. This processing of multimedia messages within a computer-based instructional environment is typically reduced to two channels of presentation/sensation—auditory and visual. Within this limited two-channel environment, *words* and *pictures* comprise the two main formats available for engaging in multimedia instruction. Words, or verbal information, include primarily auditory speech or printed text, whereas pictures, or visual information, include primarily static graphics (e.g., illustrations and photos) and dynamic graphics (e.g., animation and video). Fortunately, advances in computer technology have resulted in the emergence of numerous ways of presenting these words and pictures. These advances allow designers to combine words and pictures in ways that were not previously possible. As a result, new research has emerged concerning the effectiveness of presenting instruction using both words and pictures.

Research focusing on exploiting the benefits and limitations of the mind's verbal and visual-processing channels in multimedia instructional environments has been championed by Richard Mayer and his colleagues (see Mayer, 2001). Mayer (2001), in pursuing this dual-channel multimedia research, specifically defines multimedia as "the presentation of material using both words and pictures….I have opted to limit the definition to just two forms—verbal and pictorial—because the research base in cognitive psychology is most relevant to this distinction" (pp. 2–3). This research base to which Mayer refers is centered on Baddeley's *working memory model* (Baddeley, 1986, 1999), Paivio's *dual-coding theory* (Clark & Paivio, 1991; Paivio, 1990), and Sweller's *cognitive load theory* (Chandler & Sweller, 1991; Sweller, 1994). As mentioned previously, these three theories are not independent but rather overlap, creating theoretical interdependencies. This interdependency is evident in Mayer's construction of the *cognitive theory of multimedia learning* (Mayer, 2001).

Mayer's (2001) *cognitive theory of multimedia learning* is premised on the following three assumptions: (a) learners process visual and auditory information in different cognitive channels—the dual-channel assumption; (b) each cognitive channel has a limited processing capability—the limited-capacity assumption; and (c) learners actively process this visual and auditory information—the active-learning assumption.

The *dual-channel assumption* holds that individuals have separate cognitive channels for processing auditory and visual information. For example, if a learner is watching a video clip with auditory narration, then the visual channel will process the video images, while the auditory channel will process the narration. This dual-channel assumption is consistent with Baddeley's (1986) working memory model and Paivio's dual-coding theory (Paivio, 1990).

The *limited-capacity assumption* builds on the premise that humans are limited in the amount of information that can be processed in either channel at one time. For instance, if a learner is watching a video clip with subtitled text, the visual channel could easily become overloaded attempting to process both the video images and the subtitled text, because the images and the text are processed visually. This limited-capacity assumption is consistent with Baddeley's (1986) working memory model and Sweller's (1994) cognitive load theory.

The *active-processing assumption* posits that learners actively engage in processing multimedia environments by (a) *selecting* relevant information from the environment, (b) *organizing* the information into coherent representations, and (c) *connecting* both visual and verbal representations (Mayer, 1997). For example, if a learner is watching a video clip with auditory narration, the learner will select relevant pictures from the video and relevant words from the narration, organize the pictures and words into coherent representations, and then combine these coherent representations into an overall conceptual model of the video clip. The active-learning assumption is consistent with Paivio's (1986) dual-coding theory and Baddeley's (1986) working memory model.

These three assumptions combine to create a model of multimedia processing based on a dual-channel, limited-capacity, active-processing learner. It is important to think of these three assumptions as an integrated whole, not as isolated factors, as each affects the other and in turn affects learning within multimedia instructional environments. For example, if too much visual information is presented (e.g., animation and on-screen text; http://basepair.library.umc.edu/movies/mitosis1.mov), then the visual channel's capacity will be exceeded, leading to insufficient processing of that visual information (i.e., either the animation or on-screen text will not be attended to in their entirety). This situation could be corrected, however, by either eliminating some of the visual information (e.g., removing the on-screen text) or switching some of the visual information to an auditory channel (e.g., using audio narration instead of on-screen text (http://basepair.library.umc.edu/movies/mitosis.mov).

Within these three assumptions, Mayer (2001) posited five cognitive processes necessary for the generation of meaningful learning, retention, and transfer. These five processes are evident in the cognitive theory of multimedia and include the following: (a) selecting relevant words from the multimedia environment, (b) selecting relevant images from the multimedia environment, (c) organizing the selected words into a coherent representation, (d) organizing the selected images into a coherent representation, and (e) integrating the word and image representations with prior knowledge into a coherent mental model (Mayer, 2001). A learner watching a narrated slide show demonstrates these five processes (see http://edpsychserver.ed.vt.edu/5114web/modules/classical/slideshow1.cfm). The learner selects relevant words from the narration and relevant images from the slide show. The learner then generates meaningful representations of the words and images. Finally, the learner integrates the words, pictures, and relevant prior knowledge into a coherent mental model of the narrated slide show.

These three assumptions and five processes, based on working memory, dual-coding theory, and cognitive load theories, serve as the framework for much of Mayer's work in multimedia learning. Mayer's work addressing multimedia learning has resulted in several principles of multimedia learning. It is important to note that Mayer's research focuses on the derivation of cognitive principles from empirical research, where the principles may then be used to create general pedagogy (see Figure 1). This clarification is important, as Mayer uses short tutorials within his research. However, the principles that are derived are not limited to tutorial-based instructional environments. The benefit of focusing on the derivation of cognitive principles is that these principles have generalizability beyond the contexts in which they are originally demonstrated. In the following section, several cognitive principles of multimedia are delineated and examples are provided that extend these principles into nontutorial instructional environments.

MULTIMEDIA, PRINCIPLES AND PEDAGOGY

The development of cognitive principles of multimedia is essential in the quest for theoretically sound pedagogy for multimedia instructional environments (see Figure 1). These cognitive principles serve as the bridge between empirical findings and general pedagogical principles. Over the past 15 years, Richard Mayer, Roxana Moreno, and their colleagues have continued in their efforts to generate empirical findings relative to multimedia learning. These empirical findings have coalesced into a series of cognitive and pedagogical principles relevant to learning and instruction within multimedia environments. The following section will introduce seven cognitive principles of multimedia that have emerged from their work. These seven principles include the multimedia principle, the modality principle, the redundancy principle, the coherence principle, the contiguity principle, the segmentation principle, and the signaling principle (see Table 2).

Multimedia Principle

The multimedia principle simply states that individuals learn, retain, and transfer information better when the instructional environment involves words and pictures, rather than words or pictures alone. Specifically, individuals who experienced a short tutorial explaining how bicycle tire pumps worked, where the instruction was in the form of words and pictures or narration and animation, learned, retained, and transferred the knowledge within the tutorial significantly better than individuals who experienced a tutorial where the instruction was in the form of narration or animation only (Mayer & Anderson, 1991, 1992). Thus, when constructing multimedia instructional environments, learning, retention, and transfer are facilitated by the use of both words and pictures, or narration and animation.

Theoretically, these results and the multimedia principle may be explained based on Paivio's (1990) dual-coding theory. When an individual experiences instruction both verbally and visually, the individual constructs verbal and visual representations of the explanations and subsequently integrates the two representations into a coherent model. This dual-channel integration has been demonstrated to provide for increased learning when compared to learning based on a single-channel representation (Clark & Paivio, 1991; Paivio, 1991). Further, these results and the multimedia principle are consistent with Mayer's (2001) cognitive theory of multimedia. Mayer posits that verbal and visual representations are informationally distinct, such that the informational sum of the integration of verbal and visual representations always exceeds the information present in the verbal or visual representations alone. This integration of distinct verbal and visual representations, in turn, leads to greater learning, retention, and transfer. As Mayer (2001) stated, "In short, our results support the thesis that a deeper kind of learning occurs when learners are able to integrate pictorial and verbal representations of the same message" (p. 79).

Table 2. Brief definitions of the cognitive principles of multimedia

Principle	Definition
Multimedia principle	Individuals learn, retain, and transfer information better when the instructional environment involves words and pictures, rather than word or pictures alone.
Modality principle	Individuals learn, retain, and transfer information better when the instructional environment involves auditory narration and animation, rather than on-screen text and animation.
Redundancy principle	Individuals learn, retain, and transfer information better when the instructional environment involves narration and animation, rather than on-screen text, narration, and animation.
Coherence principle	Individuals learn, retain, and transfer information better when the instructional environment is free of extraneous words, pictures, or sounds.
Signaling principle	Individuals learn and transfer information better when the instructional environment involves cues that guide an individual's attention and processing during a multimedia presentation.
Contiguity principle	Individuals learn, retain, and transfer information better in an instructional environment where words or narration and pictures or animation are presented simultaneously in time and space.
Segmentation principle	Individuals learn and transfer information better in an instructional environment where individuals experience concurrent narration and animation in short, user-controlled segments, rather than as a longer continuous presentation.

This integration has ramifications for pedagogy, specifically, that multimedia instructional environments should utilize words or narration and pictures or animation. Combining words or narration and pictures or animation can be as simple as using static images to clarify on-screen text. For example, ACKY.NET provides a wealth of information regarding Web design, including several effective tutorials that consist primarily of static images and text (http://www.acky.net/tutorials/flash/bouncing_ball/). Another basic method of combining words or narration and pictures or animation is the use of streaming video for disseminating lectures (http://sinapse.arc2.ucla.edu/streaming/cnsi/seminars/spring2003/mceuen-rm8-mbr.ram). The video lecture scenario may be made more complete through the use of streaming video, with a concurrent slide show and hyperlinks (http://ra.okstate.edu:8080/ramgen/zayed/leadership_skills_a/trainer.smi). The key in these instances is that words or narration and pictures or animation are being combined for the purpose of enhancing instruction.

Modality Principle

The modality principle, which further clarifies the multimedia principle, states that individuals learn, retain, and transfer information better when the instructional environment involves auditory narration and animation, rather than on-screen text and animation. Specifically, individuals who experienced a short tutorial explaining the creation of lightning, where the instruction was in the form of auditory narration and animation, learned, retained, and transferred the knowledge within the tutorial significantly better than individuals who experienced a tutorial where the instruction was in the form of on-screen text and animation (Mayer & Moreno, 1998; Moreno & Mayer, 1999). Thus, when constructing multimedia instructional environments, learning, retention, and transfer are facilitated by the use of auditory narration and animation.

Theoretically, these results and the modality principle may be explained based on Baddeley's (1986) working memory model and Sweller's (1991) cognitive load theory. When on-screen text and animation are presented simultaneously, an individual is confronted with the task of attending to and creating two visual representations, which can easily overload the visual channel. When the visual on-screen text is transformed into auditory narration, the cognitive load of the visual channel is reduced, and the overall cognitive load of the instructional environment is better balanced between the auditory and visual channels. Further, these results and the modality principle are consistent with Mayer's (2001) cognitive theory of multimedia. Mayer supports the limited-capacity, dual-channel structure of memory responsible for the cognitive overload created by the presentation of two visual stimuli: on-screen text and animation. According to Moreno and Mayer (1999), "When learners can concurrently hold words in auditory working memory and pictures in visual working memory, they are better able to devote attentional resources to building connections between them" (p. 366).

Pedagogically, using both channels to foster connections implies that multimedia instructional environments should utilize narration and animation, as opposed to on-screen text and animation, whenever possible. Integrating audio and video in multimedia environments is reasonably common these days. Stanford University's Center for Professional Development provides a series of *Online Seminars* that consist of simple streamed lectures, which combine narration and video, on a variety of topics (http://stanford-online.stanford.edu/murl/cs547/). Another example that demonstrates the blending of narration and animation is the International Association of Intercultural Education's *The Big Myth* that provides lessons on creation myths and cultural pantheons from around the world (http://www.mythicjourneys.org/bigmyth/1_webmap.swf). In each of these instances, the multimedia instructional environment is enhanced through the use of concurrent auditory narration and animation.

Redundancy Principle

The redundancy principle, which provides an extension of the multimedia and modality principles, states that individuals learn, retain, and transfer information better when the instructional environment involves narration and animation, rather than on-screen text, narration, and animation. Specifically, individuals who experience a short tutorial explaining the creation of lightning, where the instruction was in the form of auditory narration and animation, learned, retained, and transferred the knowledge within the tutorial significantly better than individuals who experienced a tutorial where the instruction was in the form of on-screen text, auditory narration, and animation (Mayer, Heiser, & Lonn, 2001; Moreno & Mayer, 2002). Thus, when constructing multimedia instructional environments, learning, retention, and transfer are facilitated by the use of auditory narration and animation, without on-screen text.

Theoretically, these results and the modality principle may be explained based on Baddeley's (1986) working memory model and Sweller's (Chandler & Sweller, 1991) cognitive load theory. When on-screen text, auditory narration, and animation are presented simultaneously, an individual is confronted with the task of attending to and creating two visual representations based on the on-screen text and the animation, and attending to and creating an auditory representation based on the auditory narration. The task of attending to and creating two visual representations can easily overload the visual channel and impair the individual's ability to attend adequately to the auditory channel. When the visual on-screen text is eliminated, the cognitive load of the visual channel is reduced, and the overall cognitive load of the instructional environment is better balanced between the auditory and visual channels. Further, these results and the modality principle are consistent with Mayer's (2001) cognitive theory of multimedia. Mayer supports the limited-capacity, dual-channel structure of memory responsible for the cognitive overload created by the presentation of two visual stimuli: on-screen text and animation. According to Mayer et al. (2001), "in this case, learners are less likely to be able to carry out the active cognitive processes needed for meaningful learning" (p. 195) (e.g., elaboration, organization, reflection).

While the redundancy principle has significant ramifications for pedagogy, these ramifications will be combined with the recommendations from following principle, the coherence principle, and will be discussed at the end of the next section.

Coherence Principle

The coherence principle, which refines the redundancy principle, states that individuals learn, retain, and transfer information better when the instructional environment is free of extraneous words, pictures, or sounds. Specifically, individuals who experienced a short tutorial explaining either the creation of lightning or the workings of a hydraulic break, where the instruction was in the form of narration and animation, learned, retained, and transferred the knowledge within the tutorial significantly better than individuals who experienced a tutorial where the instruction was in the form of narration, animation, and interesting, but irrelevant, words, pictures, or sounds (Mayer, Heiser, & Lonn, 2001; Moreno & Mayer, 2000). Thus, when constructing multimedia instructional environments, learning, retention, and transfer are impeded by the inclusion of extraneous, irrelevant materials; therefore, multimedia should be kept simple and include only those attributes necessary for the instruction.

Theoretically, these results and the coherence principle may be explained based on Baddeley's (1986) working memory model and Sweller's (Chandler & Sweller, 1991) cognitive load theory. When extraneous materials are introduced into the multimedia instructional environment, these extraneous materials compete with the instructional materials for the limited resources of the individual's working memory. If these extraneous materials are significant, then cognitive overload can occur, and learning and performance will be negatively affected. According to Moreno and Mayer (2000), "these findings suggest that auditory overload can be created by adding auditory material that does not contribute to making the lesson intelligible" (p. 121).

The redundancy and coherence principles each have a common message for the building of pedagogy, specifically, that multimedia instructional environments should be clear and concise, avoiding the duplication of information and the inclusion of extraneous, noninformative elements. While the tendency in creating multimedia instructional environments is often to add "bells and whistles" (multiple representations of the same content, interesting sounds, or moving text), simple designs that are focused on the learner's attention and process are more effective. A simple, yet effective multimedia instructional environment is the *Who Killed William Robinson?* Web site at the University of Vancouver, British Columbia Web address (http://web.uvic.ca/history-robinson/). This site is composed of primarily static text and pictures, yet the design and implementation of the project is simple and straightforward. There is no redundant or extraneous material. Another that is simple, yet effective is the Advanced Education Psychology site at the Virginia Tech Web address (http://edpsychserver.ed.vt.edu/5114web/modules/classical/). These particular sites are prime examples of effective multimedia instructional environments that are not "tech heavy," that is, sites that do not rely on advanced technology but rather on effective multimedia design.

Signaling Principle

The signaling principle, which is related to the coherence principle, states that individuals learn and transfer information better when the instructional environment involves cues, or signals, that guide an individual's attention and processing during a multimedia presentation. Signaling (Meyer, 1975) "serves as guides…by giving emphasis to certain aspects of the semantic content or pointing out aspects of the structure of content so that the [individual] can see the relationships stated in the passage more clearly" (p. 1). Specifically, individuals who experienced a short tutorial explaining the creation of lift in aeronautics, where the instruction was in the form of narration and animation, and included auditory signals (e.g., intonation changes, pausing) and visual signals (e.g., arrows, color emphasis, summary icons), learned and transferred the knowledge within the tutorial significantly better than individuals who experienced a tutorial where the instruction was in the form of narration and animation but did not include signals (Mautone & Mayer, 2001). Thus, when constructing multimedia instructional environments, learning and transfer are facilitated by the use of auditory and visual cues and signals.

Theoretically, these results and the signaling principle may be explained based on Baddeley's (1986) working memory model and Sweller's (1991) cognitive load theory. When signals or cues are provided that focus an individual's attention on relevant, rather than irrelevant, information, the individual's expenditure of cognitive resources is more efficient, thus reducing cognitive load. In addition, this reduction in cognitive load, when coupled with cues and signals designed to make explicit relational links within the presentation information, results in the increased generation of connections between auditory and visual representations. According to Mautone and Mayer (2001), "signals encourage learners to engage in productive cognitive processing during learning, including selecting relevant steps in the explanation, organizing them into a coherent mental structure, and integrating them with existing knowledge" (p. 387).

Pedagogically, the signaling principle posits that multimedia instructional environments should include cues to assist in focusing learner's attention and fostering appropriate learner processing of the relevant information. Students often find Web pages and online instruction overwhelming, with too much to see and do. Using cues to guide a learner's attention and processing provides the learner with instructional scaffolding and learner support. As part of the online experience in the Department of Entomology, students have the option of participating in an online "course" called *The Whole Student*. This course combines streaming audio with static slides and provides cues for students through the use of effective navigation and by placing on the static slides the main points discussed in the audio (http://www.ento.vt.edu/ihs/distance/lectures/whole_student/). Another site that provides effective cues is Biology in Motion's *Evolution Lab*. This site provides cues through section headers, color, and graphics (http://biologyinmotion.com/evol/). The Whole Student and Evolution Lab sites both provide effective cues through strategic use of text and text attributes (e.g., boldface, color).

Contiguity Principle

The contiguity principle states that individuals learn, retain, and transfer information better in an instructional environment where words or narration and pictures or animation are presented simultaneously in time and space. Specifically, individuals who experienced a short tutorial explaining the creation of lightning, where the instruction was in the form of integrated on-screen text and animation (i.e., the text was presented spatially within the animation), learned, retained, and transferred the knowledge within the tutorial significantly better than individuals who experienced a tutorial where the instruction was in the form of separated on-screen text and animation (i.e., the text was presented spatially separated from the animation) (spatial contiguity effect; Moreno & Mayer, 1999). In addition, individuals who experienced a short tutorial explaining the creation of lightning, where the instruction was in the form of simultaneous narration and animation, learned, retained, and transferred the knowledge within the tutorial significantly better than individuals who experienced a tutorial where the instruction was in the form of narration *followed by* animation (temporal contiguity effect; Moreno & Mayer, 1999). The contiguity principle, as stated here, combines what Mayer and Moreno referred to as the spatial contiguity principle and the temporal contiguity principle (Mayer & Anderson, 1991; Moreno & Mayer, 1999). Thus, when constructing multimedia instructional environments, learning, retention, and transfer are facilitated when text or narration and pictures or animation are concurrent and are not separated in either time or space.

Theoretically, these results and the contiguity principle may be explained based on Baddeley's (1986) working memory model and Sweller's (Chandler & Sweller, 1991) cognitive load theory. When on-screen text is presented spatially separate from animation, the individual is forced to split attention between the two sources of information (Mayer & Moreno, 1998). This attention split requires extra working memory and processing resources and is more likely to result in cognitive overload than when the on-screen text and animation are integrated. Similarly, when narration is provided *prior to* viewing an animation, the individual must maintain the narration in working memory while viewing the animation if any connections between the narration and animation are to be created. This narration maintenance is cognitive resource intensive and is likely to result in cognitive overload at the onset of the animation. Mayer's (2001) cognitive theory of multimedia is consistent with these findings and rationales: "If we want students to build cognitive connections between corresponding words and pictures it is helpful to present them contiguously in time and space—that is, to present them at the same time or next to each other on the page or screen" (p. 112).

Applying the contiguity principle implies that multimedia instructional environments should be constructed such that words and pictures or narration and animation are displayed simultaneously and close together. Prime examples of this synchronization of time and place include the fusion of audio and video. For example, Brainware.tv's *Boardband Business Videos* (http://www.brainware.tv/previews/p1harn2.asx) and the Electronic Scholar's *Study of Teaching Videos* (http://www.electronicscholar.com/videos.html). Another example of synchronization includes the synthesizing of text and animation, where the text is integrated into the animation. An example of this type of synchronicity includes the *Projectile Motion* Java applet (http://galileoandeinstein.physics.virginia.edu/more_stuff/Applets/ProjectileMotion/jarapplet.html). This applet plots the path of a simulated projectile, given specific parameters (i.e., velocity, angle, mass), and provides integrated feedback on the projectile's maximum distance, maximum height, end velocity, and time aloft. The previous video examples represent temporal contiguity, where multimedia are experienced simultaneously, while the applet example represents spatial contiguity, where multimedia are experienced close together in space. It is important that multimedia instructional environments be both temporally and spatially contiguous.

Segmentation Principle

The segmentation principle states that individuals learn and transfer information better in an instructional environment, where individuals experience concurrent narration and animation in short, user-controlled segments, rather than as a longer continuous presentation. Specifically, individuals who experienced a short tutorial explaining the creation of lightning, where the instruction was in the form of 16 short, user-controlled segments of concurrent narration and animation, learned and transferred the knowledge within the tutorial significantly better than individuals who experienced the tutorial as a single, continuous narration and animation presentation (Mayer & Chandler, 2001; see also Mayer & Moreno, 2003). Thus, when constructing multimedia instructional environments, learning and transfer are facilitated by the user being able to control the rate of information presentation.

Theoretically, these results and the segmentation principle may be explained based on Baddeley's (1986) working memory model and Sweller's (Chandler & Sweller, 1991) cognitive load theory. When an individual has control over the rate of information presentation, the individual may pace the presentation such that time and cognitive resources are allotted for making connections between verbal and visual representations. Alternatively, during an automatically paced presentation, the individual may lack sufficient time and cognitive resources to make representational connections, resulting in cognitive overload. Mayer and Moreno (2003), in discussing the segmentation principle in light of the cognitive theory of multimedia, stated that "the learner is able to select words and select images from the segment; the learner also has time and capacity to organize and integrate the selected words and images" (p. 47).

The segmentation principle, pedagogically, supports the position that multimedia instructional environments should be created to allow the user control over the pacing of the environment, if the environment is likely to foster cognitive overload. A well-constructed example of allowing user control includes Virginia Tech's *Critical Media Literacy in Times of War* site (http://www.tandl.vt.edu/Foundations/mediaproject/). This site integrates text, graphics, animation, and audio, while providing the learner with step-by-step navigational control. Similarly, the Joliet Junior College tutorial *Using a Secant Line to Approximate a Tangent Line* provides the learner with the ability to experience the tutorial in small steps (http://home.attbi.com/~waterhand/tangent.html). In each of these cases, the user is provided with the ability to slow his or her interaction with the multimedia instructional environment and thus provide added time and resources for active cognitive processing.

Summary

The explanations and examples of pedagogy based on the cognitive principles of multimedia provide an initial framework for creating multimedia instructional environments that are empirically and theoretically well grounded. This grounding is essential, as it has been demonstrated repeatedly that media itself, even multimedia, has little effect on learning unless the pedagogy that drives the media is focused on student learning (see Clark, 1983, 1994).

Collectively, these seven cognitive principles of multimedia provide a grounded framework within which to begin to build this learner-centered pedagogy. The multimedia and modality principles clearly delineate the benefits of using concurrent narration and animation in multimedia instructional environments. Furthermore, the redundancy principle extends the multimedia and modality principles by demonstrating that providing redundant information in both auditory and visual-processing channels is detrimental when the visual channel also needs to process images. Further, the coherence principle refines the redundancy principle by demonstrating that irrelevant stimuli, as well as redundant stimuli, are detrimental to learning, retention, and transfer. However, the signaling principle may provide a potential solution to the overload caused by irrelevant or redundant stimuli by providing cues that may focus the learner's attention and processing and thus ameliorate the cognitive overload. While signaling may ameliorate the presence of extraneous stimuli, the coherence principle demonstrates, more generally, that proximity in time and space of narration and animation is beneficial to learning, retention, and transfer. Finally, the segmentation principle demonstrates that when a narration and animation sequence is likely to proceed too quickly for the learner to process information adequately, then allowing the user to control the progress of the narration and animation sequence pace is beneficial.

CONCLUSION

Improving instruction has been a primary goal of education and training. To foster this goal, educators have employed cognitive principles to highlight effective instructional practices. Unfortunately, a disconnect continues to exist between this science of human learning and daily educational practice. This gap denies learners and teachers access to powerful forms of teaching, training, and learning.

Fortunately, the field of instructional technology, generally, and the domain of multimedia learning, specifically, is providing an avenue for bridging this educational gap. Current research into pedagogical and technological integration within multimedia instructional environments is yielding significant and meaningful findings related to the improvement of learning, retention, and transfer. As discussed previously, the cognitive principles of multimedia, derived from Mayer's (2001) cognitive theory of multimedia, provide a solid foundation upon which to build a theoretically sound pedagogy. This process, however, of creating pedagogy from theory is fraught with difficulty and thus must be undertaken with care and forethought. According to William James (1899-1958):

I say moreover that you make a great, a very great mistake, if you think that psychology, being the science of the mind's laws, is something from which you can deduce definite programmes and schemes and methods of instruction for immediate schoolroom use. Psychology is a science, and teaching is an art; and sciences never generate arts directly out of themselves. An intermediary inventive mind must make the application, by using its originality. (p. 23)

Thus, pedagogy of any type is at least once removed from its theoretical underpinnings. With this caution in mind, it is necessary that we not only apply the pedagogy arising from the cognitive principles of multimedia with due diligence, but that we also continue to further investigate and refine the pedagogy of multimedia.

REFERENCES

Abbey, B. (Ed.). (2000). *Instructional and cognitive impacts of web-based education*. Hershey, PA: Idea Group.

Anderson, J. R. (1983). *The architecture of cognition*. Cambridge, MA: Harvard University.

Anderson, J. R. (1990). *The adaptive character of thought*. Hillsdale, NJ: Erlbaum.

Anderson, J. R. (1993). *Rules of the mind*. Hillsdale, NJ: Erlbaum.

Anderson, J. R., Reder, L. M., & Simon, H. A. (1998). Radical constructivism and cognitive psychology. In D. Ravitch (Ed.), *Brookings papers on educational policy: 1998* (pp. 227–255). Washington, DC: Brookings Institute.

Atkinson, R. C., & Shiffrin, R. M. (1968). Human memory: A proposal system and its control processes. In K. W. Spence, & J. T. Spence (Eds.), *The psychology of learning and motivation: Advances in research and theory* (pp. 89–195). New York: Academic Press.

Baddeley, A. D. (1986). *Working memory*. Oxford: Oxford University Press.

Baddeley, A. D. (1999). *Essentials of human memory*. East Sussex, UK: Taylor and Francis.

Baddeley, A. D., & Hitch, G. J. (1974). Working memory. In G. H. Bower (Ed.), *Recent advances in learning and motivation*. New York: Academic Press.

Baddeley, A. D., & Logie, R. H. (1999). Working memory: The multiple-component model. In A. Miyake, & P. Shah (Eds.), *Models of working memory: Mechanisms of active maintenance and executive control* (pp. 28–61). Cambridge, UK: Cambridge University Press.

Broadbent, D. E. (1958). *Perception and communication*. London: Pergamon.

Chandler, P., & Sweller, J. (1991). Cognitive load theory and the format of instruction. *Cognition and Instruction, 8*(4), 293–332.

Chandler, P., & Sweller, J. (1992). The split-attention effect as a factor in the design of instruction. *British Journal of Educational Psychology, 62*(2), 233–246.

Clark, R. E. (1983). Reconsidering research on learning from media. *Review of Educational Research, 53*(4), 445–459.

Clark, J. M., & Paivio, A. (1991). Dual coding theory and education. *Educational Psychology Review, 3*(3), 149–210.

Clark, R. E. (1994). Media will never influence learning. *Educational Technology Research and Development, 42*(2), 21–29.

Cowan, A. (1999). An embedded-process model of working memory. In A. Miyake, & P. Shah (Eds.), *Models of working memory: Mechanisms of active maintenance and executive control* (pp. 62–101). Cambridge, UK: Cambridge University Press.

Doolittle, P. E. (2001). The need to leverage theory in the development of guidelines for using technology in social studies teacher education. *Contemporary Issues in Technology and Teacher Education, 4*(1), 501–516.

Ericsson, K. A., & Kintsch, W. (1995). Long-term working memory. *Psychological Review, 102*, 211–245.

Gerjets, P., & Scheiter, K. (2003). Goal configurations and processing strategies as moderators between instructional design and cognitive load: Evidences from hypertext-based instruction. *Education Psychologist, 38*(1), 33–42.

James, W. (1958). *Talks with teachers.* New York: Norton. (Originally published in 1899.)

Kozma, R. (1994). Will media influence learning: Reframing the debate. *Educational Technology Research and Development, 42*(2), 7–19.

Mautone, P. D., & Mayer, R. E. (2001). Signaling as a cognitive guide in multimedia learning. *Journal of Educational Psychology, 93*(2), 377–389.

Mayer, R. E. (1997). Multimedia learning: Are we asking the right questions? *Educational Psychologist, 32*(1), 1–19.

Mayer, R. E. (2001). *Multimedia learning.* Cambridge, UK: Cambridge University Press.

Mayer, R. E., & Anderson, R. B. (1991). Animations need narrations: An experimental test of a dual-coding hypothesis. *Journal of Educational Psychology, 83*(4), 484–490.

Mayer, R. E., & Anderson, R. B. (1992). The instructive animation: Helping students build connections between words and pictures in multimedia learning. *Journal of Educational Psychology, 84*(4), 444–452.

Mayer, R. E., & Chandler, P. (2001). When learning is just a click away: Does simple user interaction foster deeper understanding of multimedia messages? *Journal of Educational Psychology, 93*(2), 390–397.

Mayer, R. E., & Moreno, R. (1998). A split-attention effect in multimedia learning: Evidence for dual processing systems in working memory. *Journal of Educational Psychology, 90*(2), 312–320.

Mayer, R. E., & Moreno, R. (1998). Nine ways to reduce cognitive load in multimedia learning. *Educational Psychologist, 38*(1), 43–52.

Mayer, R. E., Heiser, J., & Lonn, S. (2001). Cognitive constraints on multimedia learning: When presenting more material results in less understanding. *Journal of Educational Psychology, 93*(1), 187–198.

Meyer, G. J. F. (1975). *The organization of prose and its effects on memory.* New York: Elsevier.

Miyake, A., & Shah, P. (Eds.). (1999). *Models of working memory: Mechanisms of active maintenance and executive control.* Cambridge, UK: Cambridge University Press.

Moore, D. M., Burton, J. K., & Myers, R. J. (1996). Multiple-channel communication: The theoretical and research foundations of multimedia. In D. H. Jonassen (Ed.), *Handbook of research for educational communications and technology* (pp. 851–875). Mahwah, NJ: Lawrence Erlbaum Associates.

Moreno, R., & Mayer, R. E. (1999). Cognitive principles of multimedia learning: The role of modality and contiguity. *Journal of Educational Psychology, 91*(2), 358–368.

Moreno, R., & Mayer, R. E. (2000). A coherence effect in multimedia learning: The case for minimizing irrelevant sounds in the design of multimedia instructional messages. *Journal of Educational Psychology, 92*(1), 117–125.

Moreno, R., & Mayer, R. E. (2002). Verbal redundancy in multimedia learning: When reading helps listening. *Journal of Educational Psychology, 94*(1), 156–163.

Mousavi, S. Y., Low, R., & Sweller, J. (1995). Reducing cognitive load by mixing auditory and visual presentation modes. *Journal of Educational Psychology, 87*(2), 319–334.

Paas, F., & van Merrienboer, J. J. G. (1994). Instructional control of cognitive load in the training of complex cognitive tasks. *Educational Psychology Review, 6*(4), 351–371.

Paas, F., Renkl, A., & Sweller, J. (2003). Cognitive load theory and instructional design: Recent developments. *Educational Psychology, 38*(1), 1–4.

Paivio, A. (1971). *Imagery and verbal processes.* New York: Holt, Rinehart, and Winston.

Paivio, A. (1975). Coding distinctions and repetition effects in memory. In G. H. Bower (Ed.), *The psychology of learning and motivation* (Vol. 9, pp. 179–214). New York: Academic Press.

Paivio, A. (1990). *Mental representations: A dual coding approach.* New York, NY: Oxford University Press.

Peterson, L. R., & Peterson, M. J. (1959). Short-term retention of individual verbal items. *Journal of Experimental Psychology, 58*, 193–198.

Rouet, J., Levonen, J., & Biardeau, A. (Eds.). (2001). *Multimedia learning: Cognitive and instructional issues.* London: Pergamon.

Sadoski, M., & Paivio, A. (2001). Imagery and text: A dual coding theory of reading and writing. Mahwah, NJ: Erlbaum.

Schnotz, W. (2001). Sign systems, technologies, and the acquisition of knowledge. In J. Rouet, J. JU. Levonen, and A. Biardeau (Eds.), *Multimedia learning: Cognitive and instructional issues* (pp. 9–30). New York: Pergamon.

Sweller, J. (1994). Cognitive load theory, learning difficulty, and instructional design. *Learning and Instruction, 4*, 295–312.

Sweller, J., van Merrienboer, J. J. G., & Paas, F. G. W. C. (1998). Cognitive architecture and instructional design. *Educational Psychology Review, 10*(3), 251–296.

Tindall-Ford, S., Chandler, P., & Sweller, J. (1997). When two sensory modes are better than one. *Journal of Experimental Psychology: Applied, 3*(4), 257–287.

von Wodtke, M. (1993). *Mind over media: Creative thinking skills for electronic media.* New York: McGraw-Hill.

This work was previously published in Interactive Multimedia in Education and Training, edited by S. Mishra & R.C. Sharma, pp. 184-212, copyright 2005 by IGI Publishing, formerly known as Idea Group Publishing (an imprint of IGI Global).

Chapter XVIII
Knowledge Through Evolution

Russell Beale
University of Birmingham, UK

Andy Pryke
University of Birmingham, UK

ABSTRACT

This chapter argues that a knowledge discovery system should be interactive, should utilise the best in artificial intelligence (AI), evolutionary, and statistical techniques in deriving results, but should be able to trade accuracy for understanding. Further, it needs to provide a means for users to indicate what exactly constitutes "interesting", as well as understanding suggestions output by the computer. One such system is `Haiku`*, which combines interactive 3D dynamic visualization and genetic algorithm techniques, and enables users to visually explore features and evaluate explanations generated by the system. Three case studies are described which illustrate the effectiveness of the* `Haiku` *system, these being Australian credit card data, Boston area housing data, and company telecommunications network call patterns. We conclude that a combination of intuitive and knowledge-driven exploration, together with conventional machine learning algorithms, offers a much richer environment, which in turn can lead to a deeper understanding of the domain under study.*

INTRODUCTION

In this modern world, information is collected all the time: from our shopping habits to web browsing behaviours, from the calls between businesses to the medical records of individuals, data is acquired, stored, and gradually linked together. In this morass of data, there are many relationships that are not down to chance, but transforming data into information is not a trivial task. Data is obtained from observation and measurement, and has no intrinsic value. But from it we can create information: theories and relationships that describe the relationships between observations. And from information we can create knowledge: high-level descriptions of what and why, explaining and understanding the fundamental data observations. The mass of data available allows us to potentially discover important relationships between things, but the sheer volume dictates that we need to use the number-crunching power of computers to assist us with this process.

Data mining, or knowledge discovery as it is sometimes called, is the application of artificial intelligence and statistical analysis techniques to data in order to uncover information. Given a number of large datasets, we are fundamentally interested in finding and identifying interesting relationships between different items of data. This may be to identify purchasing patterns, which are then used for commercial gain through guiding effective promotions, or to identify links between environmental influences and medical problems, allowing better public health information and action. We may be trying to identify the effects of poverty, or to understand why radio-frequency observations of certain stars fluctuate regularly. Whatever the domain of the data, we are engaged in a search for knowledge, and are looking for interesting patterns in the data.

But what is "interesting"? One day, it may be that the data falls into a general trend; the next it may be the few outliers that are the fascinating ones. Interest, like beauty, is in the eye of the beholder. For this reason, we cannot leave the search for knowledge to computers alone. We have to be able to guide them as to what it is we are looking for, which areas to focus their phenomenal computing power on. In order for data mining to be generically useful to us, it must therefore have some way in which we can indicate what is interesting and what is not, and for that to be dynamic and changeable. Many data mining systems do not offer this flexibility in approach: they are one-shot systems, using their inbuilt techniques to theorise and analyse data, but they address it blindly, as they are unable to incorporate domain knowledge or insights into what is being looked for; they have only one perspective on what is interesting, and report only on data that fit such a view. Many such systems have been utilised effectively, but we believe that there is more to data mining than grabbing just the choicest, most obvious nuggets.

There are further issues with current approaches to data mining, in that the answers are often almost as incomprehensible as the raw data. It may be that rules can be found to classify data correctly into different categories, but if the rules to do so are pages long, then only the machine can do the classification: we may know how to do the classification, but have no insight into why it may be like that. We have gained information, but not knowledge. We believe that we should be able to understand the answers that the system gives us. In order to achieve this, it may be that we need broader, less accurate generalisations that are comprehensible to the human mind, but then feel confident in the main principles to allow the machine to do classification based on much more complex rules that are refinements of these basic principles. For example, "if it's red and squishy, it's a strawberry" is easy to understand. Even if that's true only 80% of the time, it's a useful rule, and easier to grasp than:

```
red, deforms 4mm under 2N pressure,
>3cm diameter = strawberry &
red, deforms 1mm under 2N pressure,
<6cm diameter = cherry &
red, deforms 3 mm under 4N pressure,
>5cm diameter = plum
else raspberry
```

which may be 96% correct but is hardly memorable. For many data mining systems, the rules developed are far more complex than this, each having numerous terms, with no overall picture able to emerge. For statistical-based systems, the parameter sets are even harder to interpret.

Since "interesting" is essentially a human construct, we argue that we need a human in the data mining loop; if we are to develop an effective system, we need to allow them to understand and interact with the system effectively. We should also take advantage of the capabilities of the user, many of which we have tried to emulate with AI systems for many years, and are still a long way from reproducing effectively. A key example is the human visual system, which is very effective at picking out trends within a mist of data points, capable of dealing with occlusion, missing values, and noise without conscious effort. On the other hand, processing vast numbers of points and deriving complex statistics is something much better suited to computers.

This leads us to conclude that a knowledge discovery system should be interactive, should utilise the best in artificial intelligence, evolutionary, and statistical techniques in deriving results, but should be able to trade accuracy for understanding; it also needs to provide a way of allowing the user to indicate what is interesting and to understand the suggestions that the computer makes. An ideal system should be symbiotic, each benefiting from the intrinsic abilities of the other, and holistic, producing results that are much more powerful than each could achieve on their own (Pryke & Beale, 2005).

KNOWLEDGE DISCOVERY WITH HAIKU

The `Haiku` system was developed with these principles in mind, and offers a symbiotic system that couples interactive 3D dynamic visualization technology with a novel genetic algorithm. The system creates a visualisation of the data which the user can then interact with, defining which areas are of interest and which can be ignored. The system then takes this input and processes the data using a variety of techniques, presenting the results as explanations to the user. These are in both textual and visual form, allowing the user to gain a broader perspective on what has been achieved. Using this information, they can refine what the system should look at, and slowly focus in on developing knowledge about whatever it is they are interested in. As well as using conventional rule generation techniques, Haiku also has a specifically designed genetic algorithmic approach to producing explanations of data. Each of these components is described in more detail as follows.

VISUALISATION

The visualisation engine used in the Haiku system provides an abstract 3D perspective of multi-dimensional data. The visualisation consists of nodes and links, whose properties are given by the parameters of the data. Data elements affect parameters such as node size, mass, link strength, elasticity, and so on. Multiple elements can affect one parameter, or a sub-set of parameters can be chosen.

Many forms of data can be visualisated in `Haiku`. Typical data for data mining consists of a number of individual "items" (representing, for example, customers) each with the same number of numerical and/or nominal attributes. What is required for `Haiku` visualisation is that a distance can be calculated between any two items. The distance calculation should match an intuitive view of the differences between two items. In most cases, a simple and standard distance measure performs well: with data elements $= [x_1, x_2, ... x_n]$, the distance d between elements $\overline{x_a}$ and $\overline{x_b}$ is:

$$d = \left|\overline{x_a} - \overline{x_b}\right| = \sum_{i=1}^{n} x_{ai} - x_{bi} \qquad (1)$$

An example of this is shown in Table 1.

The total distance d = -26.53. Clearly, many variations of this exist — a weighted sum can be used, and so on. One of the characteristics of the system is that the user can choose which parameters are used to create the distance metric, and which ones affect the other characteristics of the visualisation.

Table 1. Calculating distance between two data items

Data Item	Phone bill	Shopping	Petrol	Children	Age	Sum distance
Customer1	124.23	235.12	46.23	2	34	
Customer2	34.56	281.46	123.09	0	29	
Distance	89.67	46.34	76.86	2	5	219.87

In the visualisation, a node is created that represents an item. These nodes may be all equivalent, or may have characteristics inherited from the data (for example, number of children may be used, not in the standard distance measure, but in the mass of the node). Links are created between all the nodes, which act as springs and try to move the nodes about in the space.

To create the visualisation, nodes are initially scattered randomly into the 3D space, with their associated links. This 3D space obeys a set of physical-type laws, which then affect this initial arrangement. Links tend to want to assume a particular length (directly related to the distance measure between the nodes), and tend to pull inwards until they reach that length, or push outwards if they are compressed, just as a spring does in the real world. Nodes tend to repel each other, based on their mass. This whole approach can be seen as a force-directed graph visualisation. This initial state is allowed to evolve, and the links and nodes shuffle themselves around until they reach a local minimum, low-energy steady state. The reasoning behind these choices of effects is that we want related things to be near to each other, and unrelated things to be far away. Therefore, by creating links that are attractive between data points with similar characteristics, we achieve this clumping effect. The data points themselves, the nodes in the visualisation, are made repulsive so that the system does not collapse to a point, but instead are individually distinguishable entities, slightly separated from their similar neighbours.

This approach achieves a number of things. It allows us to visualise high-dimensional data in a comprehensible and compact way. It produces results that are similar to those achieved using approaches such as multi-dimensional scaling, but is somewhat more comprehensible because it tries to cluster "similar" things with other "similar" ones. It is certainly true that the choice of distance metric, and particularly which items to include and which to map to node characteristics, can affect the resulting visualisation, but we are searching for insight and meaning, not trying to come up with a *single* right solution. At different times, different features can be examined, and different results achieved; this is an inherent characteristic of searching for information, rather than an intrinsic problem with the approach. In any move from a high-dimensional space to a lower one, information will have to be lost; this approach at least preserves some of the main similarity characteristics of the original datasets.

The physics of the space are adjustable, but are chosen so that a steady state solution can be reached that is static; this is unlike the real world, in which a steady state exists that involves motion, with one body orbiting another. This is achieved by working in a non-Newtonian space. In the real physical world (a Newtonian space), we have the following condition:

$$F = ma \qquad (2)$$

where F is the force applied to a body, m the mass of that body, and a is the acceleration produced. This can be re-written as:

$$F = m\frac{dv}{dt} \quad (3)$$

where v is the velocity of the object.

When the visualisation is in a local minimum, there is no net force on any of the bodies (in other words, all the spring-like forces from the links and repulsive nodal forces balance each other out), and so for each node, $F = 0$. Thus:

$$0 = m\frac{dv}{dt} \Rightarrow \frac{dv}{dt} = 0 \Rightarrow v = \text{constant} \quad (4)$$

Therefore, in a steady-state Newtonian space, each node may potentially have zero or a constant velocity. In other words, the steady state solution has dynamic properties, with bodies moving in orbit, for example.

In our space, we redefine (2) to be:

$$F = mv \quad (5)$$

When we reach the steady state, we have (for non-zero masses):

$$0 = mv \Rightarrow v = 0 \quad (6)$$

Thus, in our representations the steady state that the arrangement evolves to is static.

This representation can then be explored at will by rotating it, zooming in, and flying through and around it. It is a completely abstract representation of the data, and so has no built-in preconceptions. Different data-to-attribute mappings will clearly give different structures, but the system can at least produce a view of more than three dimensions of the raw data at once. A typical structure is shown in Figure 1.

To evolve the structure, each node is checked for links to other nodes, and the forces of those links is added vectorially to give a net force, and the node is then moved according to that force using equation (5) above. Computationally, the process scales exponentially with the number of links, which is usually proportional to the number of data points, so the evolution to the stable structure moves from being a real-time process that you can watch towards one that has to be allowed to run for a long period of time as the dataset increases in size.

In general, this is not a problem, since the initial arrangement of data is random and the evolutionary process is not in itself informative (although it is interesting to observe). However, when the visualisation is used as a component in the data mining tool, this is designed to be an interactive process, so we have taken a number of approaches to speeding up the relaxation to steady state. The first involves re-coding the system into `OpenGL/DirectX`, to take advantage of the power of modern graphics processors, especially for 3D work. The second places the nodes into the space in a non-random position initially; each node is placed "near" a node it has a link to. This is marginally more computationally expensive initially, but reduces the numbers of nodes that have to move a large amount through the visualisation, and hence cause large scale changes in other nodal positions. The most effective approach is to use predominantly local relaxation; however, instead of considering all the forces to act over infinite

Figure 1. Nodes and links self-organised into a stable structure

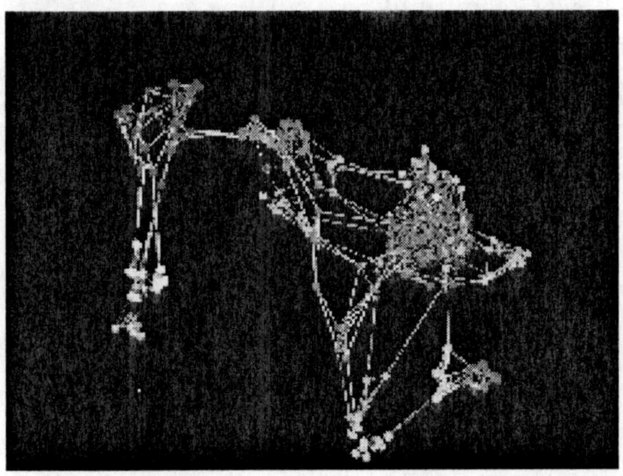

distance, we can limit nodal interactions to be very local, so that nodes which are a long way away do not exert any forces on the ones in question (much like assuming that the gravitational effects of all the stars except the sun are negligible).

Once the system has undergone some initial relaxation, which provides some level of organisation, we can also focus on the local neighbourhood much more, and occasionally recompute the longer-range interactions. This is akin to organising a tight cluster properly, but then treating that as one structure for longer-range effects. A combination of these approaches allows us to produce an effective steady state representation, even with large datasets, in interactive time.

PERCEPTION-ORIENTED VISUALISATION

The interface provides full 3D control of the structure, from zooming in and out, moving smoothly through the system (flyby), rotating it in 3D, and jumping to specific points, all controlled with the mouse. Some typical structures emerge, recognisable from dataset to dataset. For example, a common one is the "dandelion head": a single central node connected to a number of other nodes with the same strength links. The links pull the attached nodes towards the central one, but each node repels the others, and so they spread out on the surface of a sphere centred on the main node. This looks much like a dandelion head. Another typical structure occurs when a number of dandelion heads are loosely linked together. The effect of the other heads in the chain forces the outer nodes away from being equidistantly spaced on the sphere and makes them cluster together somewhat on the side away from the link, and a series of "florets" are created, all linked together. It is because of this that some users have termed the visualisation "cauliflower space".

The visualisation in itself provides a lot of information about the dataset. We have used the visualisation in isolation for a number of tasks (Hendley, Drew, Beale, & Wood, 1999). One of the more effective ones has been the visualisation of users' internet browsing behaviour. Each page visited is represented by a node, and their page transitions are represented by the links. Typically, users start on a home or an index page, and move out and back a number of times before moving off down a promising thread: this behaviour, when visualised in real time, produces a dandelion head with increasing numbers of "seeds" (the outer nodes) and then switches towards a floret as the thread is followed. A new index-type page is reached (sometimes after one hop, sometimes after many, and another floret is created. Often, there are links back to the originally explored pages, and when the user follows these, the visualisation pulls itself into a ring, representing a notion of closure and returning that has an exact analogy in the real world (Wood, Drew, Beale, & Hendley, 1995). A different representation is formed if we visualise the structure of web pages: pages themselves are nodes again, but hyperlinks map to visualisation links. A Web site has a fairly typical cauliflower image, caused by closely interrelated and interlinked sections, tied back to a common home or index page, with links off to other cauliflowers where the site links externally to other sites.

The system has also been used to assist users to comprehend their progress in information retrieval tasks. Using a digital library as our domain, for each query a representation of the results was returned. A large node represented the query, and was fixed in the 3D space. Each document that matched the query was a mobile node, with a link attaching it to the query, with the link strength being how relevant the document was to that query. An initial query would return a number of documents, so a distorted dandelion head would appear. However, a second query that returned some of the same documents would show links from those documents to both fixed nodes, and hence the degree of overlap could be easily seen. Such an approach allowed the user, in real time, to see how effectively they were exploring the space of documents, and how those were interrelated to the queries made (Beale, McNab, & Witten, 1997; Cunningham, Holmes, Littin, Beale, & Witten, 1998). This is important as subsequent searches are often dependent on the results of the previous ones, so having a representation of the history and its relationships to the present search matches more closely what the user is doing internally. A walkthrough of the process is shown in Figures 2 through 5.

Interaction with the Data Visualisation

When features of interest are seen in the visual respresentation of the data, they can be selected using the mouse. This opens up a number of possibilities:

- Data identification
- Revisualisation
- Explanation

The simplest of these (data identification) is to view the identifiers or details or items in the

Figure 2. Visualising the result of a single query: "visualisation colour graphics"

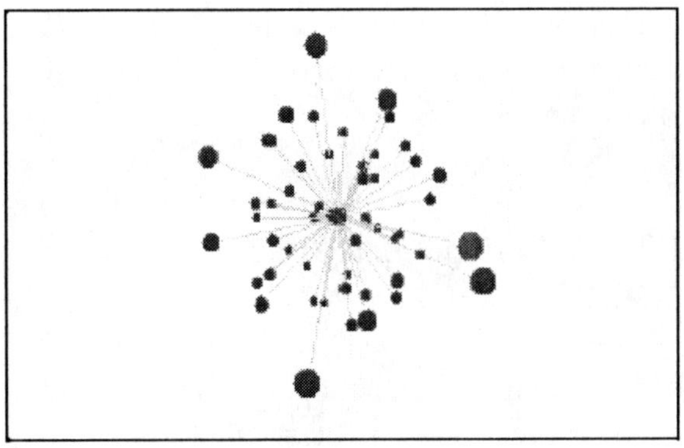

Figure 3. Adding a second query: "3D surface graphics"

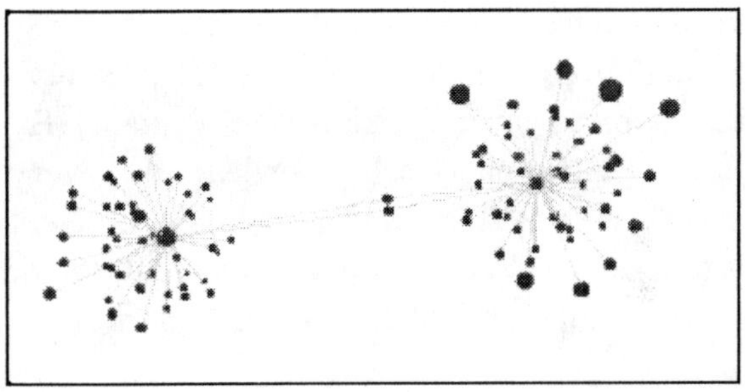

Figure 4. Adding a third, unrelated query: "agents"

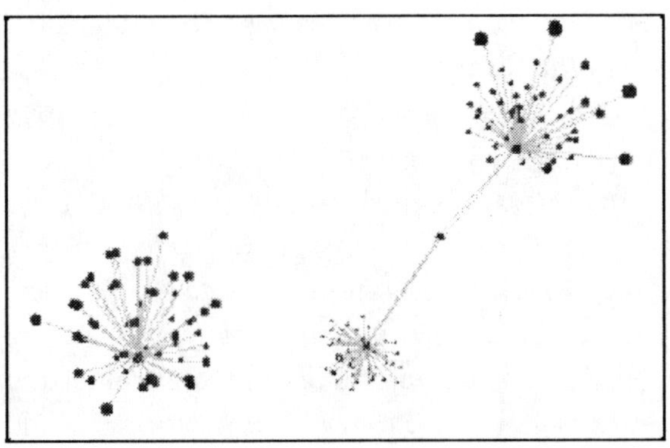

Figure 5. A sequence of four queries

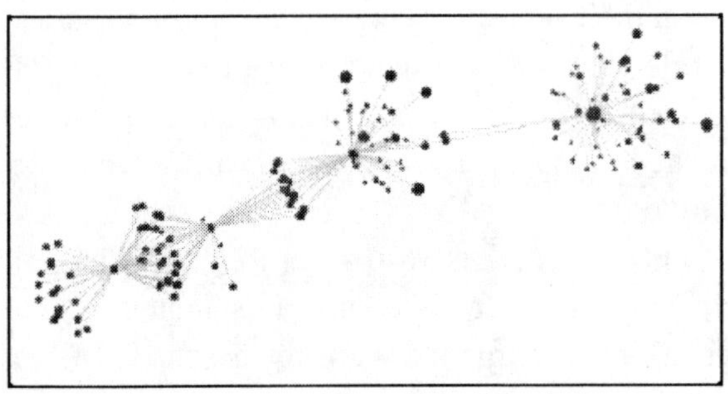

feature, or export this information to a file for later use.

Another option is re-visualise the dataset without the selected data or to focus in and only visualise the selected data. This can be used to exclude distorting outliers, or to concentrate on the interactions within an area of interest. Of course, we can data mine the whole dataset without doing this, the approach taken by many other systems. One of the features of the `Haiku` system is this interactive indication of the things that we are currently interested in, and the subsequent focussing of the knowledge discovery process on best describing that data only.

A key feature of the system is that this user selection process takes full advantage of the abilities of our visual system: humans are exceptionally good at picking up gross features of visual representations. Our abilities have evolved to work well in the presence of noise, of missing or obscured data, and we are able to pick out simple lines and curves, as well as more complex features such as spirals and undulating waves or planes. By allowing user input into the knowledge discovery process, we can effectively use a highly efficient system very quickly as well as reducing the work that the computational system has to perform.

Explanation

The most striking feature of the system is its ability to "explain" why features of interest exist. Typical questions when looking at a visual representation of data are: "Why are these items out on their own?", "What are the characteristics of this cluster?", "How do these two groups of items differ?". Answers to these types of question are generated by applying a machine learning component.

The interaction works as follows: First, a group or number of groups is selected. Then the option to explain the groups is selected. The user answers a small number of questions about their preferences for the explanation (short/long) (highly accurate/characteristic), and so on. The system returns a set of rules describing the features selected.

As an alternative, the classic machine learning system `C4.5` (Quinlan, 1992) may be used to generate classification rules. Other data mining systems may be applied by saving the selected feature information to a comma-separated value file.

Rule Visualisation

Rules generated using `C4.5` or the GA-based method can be visualised within the system to give extra insight into their relationships with the data. Rules are usually represented by massive nodes that do not move far in space, and are regularly spaced. Links show which rules apply to which data, and hence unclassified data and multiply-classified data are shown well.

From this, the processing moves towards the computer, as the genetic algorithm-based process takes over.

GENETIC ALGORITHMS FOR DATA MINING

We use a genetic algorithm (GA) approach for a number of reasons. The first is that a GA is able to effectively explore a large search space, and modern computing power means we can take advantage of this within a reasonable timeframe. We use a special type of GA that evolves rules; these produce terms to describe the underlying data of the form:

```
IF term OP value|range (AND …) THEN term
OP value|range (AND …)                    (7)
```

where `term` is a class from the dataset, OP is one of the standard comparison operators ($<$, $>$, $=$, $\leq$, $\geq$), `value` is a numeric or symbolic value, and `range` is a numeric range. A typical rule would therefore be:

```
IF colour = red AND consistency = soft THEN
fruit = strawberry                        (8)
```

A set of these rules can, in principle, describe any arbitrary situation. There are two situations that are of interest to us; classification, when the left hand side of the equation tries to predict a single class (usually known) on the right hand side, and association, or clustering, when the system tries to find rules that characterise portions of the dataset. The algorithm follows fairly typical genetic algorithmic approaches in its implementation, but with specialised mutation and crossover operators, in order to explore the space effectively. We start with a number of random rules, and evolve the population through subsequent generations based on how well they perform.

The genetic algorithm aims to optimise an objective function, and manipulation of this function allows us to explore different areas of the search space. For example, we can strongly penalise rules that give false positive results and achieve a different type of description, than rules that may be more general and have greater coverage but make a few more mistakes. Each rule is analysed in terms of the objective function and given a score, which is its *fitness*. The fittest rules are then taken as the basis for the next population, and new rules are created. Crossover points are chosen to be in syntactically-similar positions, in order to ensure that we are working with semantically-meaningful chunks. Mutation is specialised: for ranges of values, it can expand or contract that range; for numbers, it can increase or decrease them; for operators, it can substitute them with others.

Statistically principled comparisons showed that this technique is at least as good as conventional machine learning at classification (Pryke, 1999), but has advantages over the more conventional approaches in that it can perform clustering operations as well. One of the key design features is to produce a system that has humanly-comprehensible results. Rules of the form in equation (7) are inherently much more understandable than decision trees or probabilistic or statistical descriptions. It is also true that short rules are going to be easier to comprehend than longer ones. Since the GA is trying to minimise an objective function, we can manipulate this function to achieve different results. If we insist that the rules produced must be short (and hence easier to understand), then the system will trade off accuracy and/or coverage but will give us short rules, because they are "fitter", which provide a general overview that is appropriate for much of the data. Because the `Haiku` system is interactive and iterative, when we have this higher level of comprehension, we can go back into the system and allow the rules to become longer and hence more specific, and accuracy will then increase.

FEEDBACK

The results from the GA are fed back into the visualisation: identified clusters can be coloured, for example, or rules added and linked to the data that they classify, as in Figure 6.

In this figure, rules are the large purple (left and centre), fuschia (rightmost) and green (top) spheres, with the data being the smaller spheres. Links are formed between the rules and the data that is covered by the rule, and the visualisation has reorganised itself to show this clearly. We have additionally coloured the data according to its correct classification (clear in colour, harder to see in greyscale).

A number of things are immediately apparent from this visualisation, much more easily than would be the case from a textual description. On the very left of Figure 6, one rule covers exactly the same data as the second sphere from the left, except it also misclassifies one green data point. But this second sphere, while correctly classifying all its own data correctly, also misclassifies

Figure 6. Rules and classified data

much of the other data as well, shown by the many links to the different coloured data items. The visualisation shows us that we can remove this rule, simplifying the description, without reducing coverage and improving accuracy. On the right hand side of the picture, the rule clearly does very well; it covers all its data and does not misclassify anything. The rule at the top has mixed results.

The system is fully interactive, in that the user can now identify different characteristics and instruct the GA to describe them, and so the process continues.

This synergy of abilities between the rapid, parallel exploration of the structure space by the computer and the user's innate pattern recognition abilities and interest in different aspects of the data produces a very powerful and flexible system.

CLASSIC CASE STUDY 1: WELL KNOWN DATASETS

Several machine learning datasets from the UCI Machine Learning Repository (Blake & Merz, 1998) were used to benchmark the performance of data mining and classification. It should be noted that it focuses on quantitative performance, whereas the qualitative experience and use of perception-based mining techniques is not assessed. However, good results on these datasets in quantitative terms will give us confidence when analysing new datasets.

The GA-based approach gave perfectly acceptable results, with statistical analysis showing it performed better than `C4.5` (Quinlan, 1992) on the "Australian Credit Data" ($p=0.0018$). No significant difference in performance was found for the other two datasets. These results are summarised in Table 2.

CASE STUDY 2: INTERACTIVE DATA MINING OF HOUSING DATA

Figure 7 shows a 2D view of the system's visual clustering of the Boston housing data. Two user selected groups have been indicated.

GA-based data mining was then applied to these user identified groups. The fitness function was chosen so as to bias the system towards the discovery of rules which are short and accurate (Table 3).

This case study illustrates the following qualitative aspects of the system. The interactive visual discovery approach has revealed new structure in the data by visual clustering. Subsequent application of the data mining algorithm has generated concrete information about these "soft" discoveries. These rules look at a variety of aspects of the system, from their location to their tax rates to their social status, and provide rules that are accurate, short, and cover much of the data, and they are comprehensible. Together, interactive data mining has delivered increased knowledge about a well-known dataset.

Having proven its worth on known datasets, we have used the system to try to discover *new* phenomena.

Table 2. Quantitative benchmarking performance

Dataset	Genetic algorithm % correct	C4.5 % correct
Australian Credit (Quinlan, 1987)	86%	82%
Boston Housing (Quinlan, 1993)	64%	65%
Pima Indians Diabetes (Smith et al., 1988)	73%	73%

CASE STUDY 3: APPLYING HAIKU TO TELECOMS DATA

Justification

Massive amounts of data are generated from monitoring telecommunications switching. Even a small company may make many thousands of phone calls during a year. Telecommunications companies have a mountain of data originally collected for billing purposes. Telecoms data reflects business behaviour, so is likely to contain complex patterns. For this reason, `Haiku` was applied to mine this data mountain.

Data

The data considered detailed the calling number, recipient number, and duration of phone calls to and from businesses in a medium sized town. Other information available included business sector and sales chanels. All identity data was anonymized.

Call Patterns of High Usage Companies

Visualisation

A number of companies with particularly high numbers of calls were identified. These were

Figure 7. Clusters selected in the Boston housing data

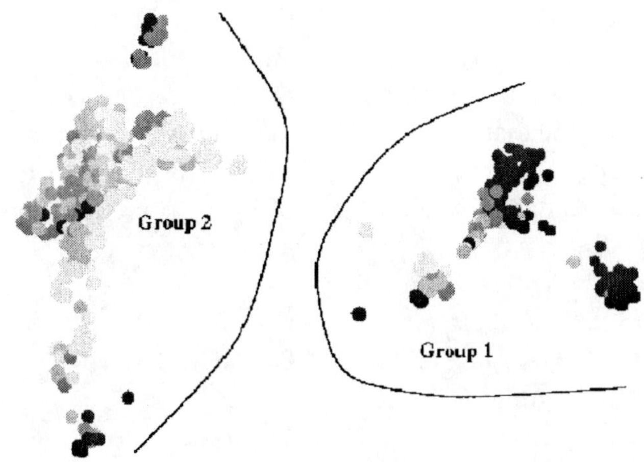

Table 3. Rules generated from Boston housing data

Rule A	ccuracy (%)	Coverage (%)
Bounds_river=true ⇒ GROUP_1	100	43
PropLargeDevelop = 0.0 AND 9.9 <= older_properties_percent <= 100.0 AND Pupil_teacher_ratio = 20.2 ⇒ GROUP_1	94	83
Bounds_river=false AND 4 <= Highway_access <= 8 ⇒ GROUP_2	100	77
Bounds_river=false AND 264 <= Tax_rate <= 403 ⇒ GROUP_2	100	69
2.02 < Industry_proportion <= 3.41 ⇒ GROUP_2	98	13
5.68 <= Lower_status_percent <= 6.56 ⇒ GROUP_2	96	75
Bounds_river=false ⇒ GROUP_2	73	100

visualised separately to identify patterns within the calls of individual companies.

Figure 8 shows a clustering of calls from a single company. The most immediately obvious feature is the "blue wave" to the right of the image; this has been labelled "A".

Also visible are various other structures, including the two clusters labelled "B" and "C".

Discoveries

After identifying these features, we then asked the system to "explain" their characteristics. The following rules were discovered by the system, and translated into sentence form for clarity:

- All calls in group A are to directory enquiries.
  - Further investigation, selecting parts of the "blue wave" showed that the wave structure was arranged by hour of day in one dimension and day of week in the other.
- Within group B, about 70% of calls are to two numbers. 90% of calls to these numbers fall into the group B. Almost all of the remaining 30% of calls in group B are to another two numbers.
- Most long-distance ISDN calls are in group B. All but one call in the group has these properties. Most calls in the group are also charged at the same rate.
- About 80% of Group C calls are ISDN calls, and about 10% are from payphones. About one third occur between 21:00 and 22:59, and about one half start at 15 minutes past the hour. Most are long-distance calls. About 50% of the calls are very long, lasting between 8 and 15.5 hours.

For this dataset, `Haiku` discovers some very interesting facts about the calling patterns of a company. Notice that we can produce short, comprehensible rules that cover a significant portion of the dataset, which are intrinsically much more usable than detailed descriptions of 100% of the data. These insights can then be used by the company to optimise their phone usage, or, as for this study, to feed back to the telecoms company some concepts for marketing and billing strategies.

CONCLUSION

The `Haiku` system for information visualisation and explanation provides a useful interface for

Figure 8. Calls from one company, automatically clustered by Haiku (three areas are apparent — labelled A, B and C)

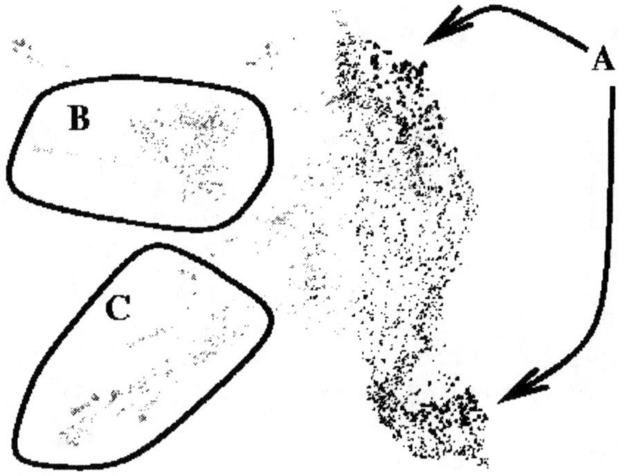

interactive data mining. By interacting with a virtual data space created dynamically from the data properties, greater insight can be gained than by using standard machine learning- based data mining. It allows users to explore features visually, to direct the computer to generate explanations and to evaluate the results of their exploration, again in the visual domain. By using a novel genetic algorithmic approach, we can bias rules generated to give us first a general overview and then progressively refine their accuracy and coverage as our understanding increases. This combination of intuitive and knowledge-driven exploration with the mechanical power of the learning algorithms provides a much richer environment and can lead to a deeper understanding of the domain.

ACKNOWLEDGMENT

This work was partially supported by grants from British Telecom, Integral Solutions, Ltd., and British Maritime Technology. Thanks to Nick Drew and Bob Hendley for their work on the visualisation parts of the system, and to colleagues for their comments and help.

REFERENCES

Beale, R., McNab, R. J., & Witten, I. H. (1997). Visualising sequences of queries: A new tool for information retrieval. *Proceedings of the IEEE Conference on Information Visualisation,* London, August (pp. 57-62).

Blake, C. L., & Merz, C. J. (1998). UCI repository of machine learning databases. *University of California, Irvine, Department of Computer Science*. Retrieved from http://www.ics.uci.edu/~mlearn/MLRepository.html

Cunningham, S. J., Holmes, G., Littin, J., Beale, R., & Witten, I. H. (1998). Applying connectionist models to information retrieval. In S. –I. Amari

& N. K. Kasabov (Eds.), *Brain-like computing and intelligent systems* (pp. 435-457). Berlin: Springer-Verlag.

Hendley, R. J., Drew, N., Beale, R., & Wood, A. M. (1999). Narcissus: Visualising information. In S. Card, J. Mackinlay, & B. Shneiderman (Eds.), *Readings in information visualization* (pp. 503-511). San Mateo, CA: Morgan Kaufmann.

Pryke, A. N. (1999). *Data mining using genetic algorithms and interactive visualisation.* PhD thesis, Department of Computer Science, University of Birmingham, UK.

Pryke, A. N., & Beale, R. (2005). Interactive comprehensible data mining. In C. Yang (Ed.), *Ambient intelligence for scientific discovery: Foundations, theories, and systems* (pp. 48-65). Berlin: Springer-Verlag.

Quinlan, J. R. (1987). Simplifying decision trees. *International Journal of Man-Machine Studies, 27*, 221-234.

Quinlan, J. R. (1992). *C4.5: Programs for machine learning.* San Mateo, CA: Morgan Kaufmann.

Quinlan, J. R. (1993). Combining instance-based and model-based learning. *Proceedings of the 10th International Conference of Machine Learning, University of Massachusetts, Amherst* (pp. 236-243). San Mateo, CA: Morgan Kaufmann.

Smith, J. W., Everhart, J. E., Dickson, W. C., Knowler, W. C., & Johannes, R. S. (1988). Using the ADAP learning algorithm to forecast the onset of diabetes mellitus. *Proceedings of the Symposium on Computer Applications and Medical Care* (pp. 261-265). Piscataway, NJ: IEEE Computer Society Press.

Wood, A. M., Drew, N. S., Beale, R., & Hendley, R. J. (1995). HyperSpace: Web browsing with visualisation. *Proceedings of the 3rd International World-Wide Web Conference*, Darmstadt, Germany, April (pp. 21-25).

This work was previously published in Advances in Applied Artificial Intelligence, edited by J. Fulcher, pp. 234-250, copyright 2006 by IGI Publishing, formerly known as Idea Group Publishing (an imprint of IGI Global).

Chapter XIX
Collaborative Geographic Information Systems:
Origins, Boundaries, and Structures

Shivanand Balram
Simon Fraser University, Canada

Suzana Dragicevic
Simon Fraser University, Canada

It is the theory that decides what can be observed.

Albert Einstein (1879-1955)

The scientists of today think deeply instead of clearly.

Nikola Tesla (1857-1943)

ABSTRACT

This study describes the origins, boundaries, and structures of collaborative geographic information systems (CGIS). A working definition is proposed, together with a discussion about the subtle collaborative vs. cooperative distinction, and culminating in a philosophical description of the research area. The literatures on planning and policy analysis, decision support systems, and geographic information systems (GIS) and science (GIScience) are used to construct a historical footprint. The conceptual linkages between GIScience, public participation GIS (PPGIS), participatory GIS (PGIS), and CGIS are also outlined. The conclusion is that collaborative GIS is centrally positioned on a participation spectrum that ranges from the individual to the general public, and that an important goal is to use argumentation, deliberation, and maps to clearly structure and reconcile differences between representative interest groups. Hence, collaborative GIS must give consideration to integrating experts with the general public in synchronous and asynchronous space-time interactions. Collaborative GIS provides a theoretical and application foundation to conceptualize a distributive turn to planning, problem solving, and decision making.

INTRODUCTION

Definitions within a community of practice have multiple benefits. Definitions reduce differences in semantics, and focus a community of practice towards goals that reinforce individual and collective efforts, make knowledge accessible to those at the edges of the community, and expand a study area by integrating related external concepts (Sager, 2000). Moreover, clearly defined concepts in a knowledge domain can better facilitate theory building. There are five types of definitions, and we have chosen to specify a *theoretical definition* for collaborative GIS since this type of definition aims to capture a commonality in the research area, and to relate that commonality to a broader intellectual framework (Sager, 2000). This chapter is organized as follows: firstly, a theoretical definition of collaborative GIS is presented; secondly, a historical footprint is established to reinforce the theoretical definition; and thirdly, the linkages between collaborative GIS and its broader conceptual framework are outlined.

What is Collaborative GIS?

There is a mutual influence between geographic information science and collaborative geographic information systems. GIScience is the rationale or science (axioms, theories, methods) that justifies the design and application of geographic information systems (Goodchild, 1992). Geographic information systems on the other hand are the physical designs and processes that integrate people and computer technology to manage, transform, and analyze spatially referenced data to solve ill-defined problems (Wright, Goodchild, & Proctor, 1997). Collaborative GIS are influenced by both GIS and GIScience. Hence, the name collaborative GIS will be used as systems, science, or both, depending on the context.

Collaborative GIS can be defined as *an eclectic integration of theories, tools, and technologies focusing on, but not limited to structuring human participation in group spatial decision processes*. In particular, the aim is to probe at the participant-technology-data nexus, and to describe, model, and simulate effects on the consensual process outcomes. The participants are typically a mixture of technical experts and the public, the technological tools being computers that are networked or distributed, and the data being spatially referenced maps and attributes. The outcomes do not result from implementing a task-oriented approach, but rather they emerge from a joint and structured exploration of ill-defined problems to benefit planning, problem solving, and decision making. In planning, the intention is to develop steps to achieve a desired outcome, while problem solving deals with the formulation of plans in new contexts. Decision making is the process of choosing among a set of alternatives.

Structuring is defined in the Webster Online Dictionary (http://www.m-w.com) as "the act of building, arrangement of parts, or relationship between parts of a construction." In this regard, structuring in collaborative GIS deals with the creation of process designs, how those designs enable the participant-technology-data interactions, and the relationships between the component parts of the designs. Hence, collaborative GIS is situated within the enhanced adaptive structuration theory 2 (EAST2) framework (Jankowski & Nyerges, 2001a). The framework outlines a detailed set of concepts and relationships linking the content, process, and outcome of collaborative spatial decision making. The content constructs of EAST2 examine the socioinstitutional, group participant, and GIS technology influences. The process constructs examine the social interactions between humans and computers. The outcome constructs address societal impacts of the decisions. Constructs five (group processes) and six (emergent influence) are important for collaborative GIS because they deal with "idea exchange as social interaction" and "emergence of sociotechnical information influence" respectively. The interactions that occur in these constructs are more collaboration rather than cooperation.

Questions that engage collaborative GIS research activities include "What collaborative spatial decision making structures can generate meaningful outcomes? How can the attitudes and needs of participants be integrated into the group process? What are the effects of spatial data and cognitive overload on participation quality? How can prior solutions be integrated into the designs of collaborative spatial decision making systems? How can the outcomes of the process be evaluated and assessed for quality?"

The Collaboration vs. Cooperation Distinction

Some of the earliest works of educational psychologists attempted to distinguish collaboration from cooperation within teaching and learning contexts. The notion of "associated life" by John Dewey made the important recognition that human relationships are a key to welfare, achievement, and mastery (Dewey, 1916). This associative educational enterprise was the predecessor of the modern day interpretation and application of collaboration and cooperation in interactions that deal with groups of individuals (Bruffee, 1995).

The difference between collaboration and cooperation is subtle, but important. John Smith (1994) suggests that collaboration is an expectation of a common purpose, and this occurs at the implementation level with a close integration of component parts. On the other hand, cooperation does not come with an expectation of close integration as individual tasks are combined at the hierarchically higher goal level. This means that for cooperative process, individuals can complete subtasks without being in close interaction with other supporting individuals. Bruffee (1995) points out that both collaboration and cooperation encourage group participation, but while cooperation guarantees accountability and risks maintaining authoritative structures, collaboration encourages self-governance and places guarantees of accountability at risk. Moreover, both collaboration and cooperation assume knowledge is socially constructed.

In the participatory GIS literature, collaboration and cooperation have been conceptualized in a hierarchical and cumulative arrangement consisting of four levels (Jankowski & Nyerges, 2001b). These participatory levels are communication, cooperation, coordination, and collaboration. Communication is meant to exchange ideas in social interactions, while cooperation uses the ideas generated from communication to develop an overall agreement, despite individuals may not interact with each other. Coordination occurs when there is a planned implementation of cooperative activity to reinforce collective group gains. Collaboration deals with a shared sense of meaning and achievement in the group process. The goal of collaborative GIS is to leverage collaboration towards a *collective* process. In collective participation, the participatory group, technology, and data operate as a single fused system.

Philosophical Orientation of Collaborative GIS

Understanding the philosophical orientation of a study area is important because it dictates what can be measured, and how measurements can be integrated and synthesized. A philosophical description can be characterized along four dimensions: ontology, epistemology, methodology, and praxeology. Based on a historical examination of collaborative GIS, a description of its philosophical dimensions is proposed in Table 1.

Ontology is about the essence of existence and its explicit specification when conceptualized concretely (Gruber, 1992). The ontology is usually organized into a hierarchy of top (general concepts), domain (specific knowledge domain), task (vocabulary), and application (context dependent) levels (Gómez-Pérez, Fernández-López, & Corcho, 2004; Torres-Fonseca & Egenhofer, 2000).

Table 1. The philosophical orientation of collaborative GIS

Philosophical Dimension	Summary Description
Ontology	RELATIVIST In this interpretation, the real world exists in the form of multiple mental constructions that are based on social and experimental processes. These constructions are local and context specific because of the individual perspectives from which they are formed.
Epistemology	SUBJECTIVIST In this interpretation, the investigator and the investigated are combined into a single entity. Knowledge is created from the interaction processes between the investigator and the investigated.
Methodology	HERMENEUTIC and DIALECTIC The individual reality constructions are processed hermeneutically (interpreted based on experience and experiments) and assessed dialectically (synthesis of opposing assertions) for the purposes of achieving one or more consensus constructions.
Praxeology	PLANNING, PROBLEM SOLVING, DECISIONS The consensus constructions guide individual and collective action. The actions (with associated individual reflections) take the form of problem solving, planning and management, and decision making with the aim to improve human, societal and environmental conditions.

For collaborative GIS, the ontology is relativist where the real word is socially and experimentally formed from multiple mental constructions.

Epistemology is the study of knowledge and its associations to truth and belief (Rescher, 2003). The interaction of the investigator and the investigated is a crucial consideration in the knowledge formation process. For collaborative GIS, the epistemology is subjectivist where the investigator and investigated are integrated as one entity.

Methodology is the study of methods, and seeks to examine how knowledge is obtained and verified (Fuller, 2002). The processing and assessment of mental constructions of reality are of importance. For collaborative GIS, the methodology is such that the processing is hermeneutic and the assessment is dialectic, with the outcome being a reduced set of consensus constructions.

Praxeology is the science of human action, and considers how that action can impact societal, human, and environmental situations (Oakeshott, 1975). Collaborative GIS has been applied extensively in the knowledge domains of geography and environmental studies. The three predominant action-oriented aims that can be synthesized for GIS applications are planning, problem solving, and decision making (Duckham, Goodchild, & Worboys, 2003).

COLLABORATIVE GIS: ORIGINS AND BOUNDARIES

The origins of collaborative GIS are diverse and some level of aggregation is therefore necessary to clearly understand its origins and boundaries. A first strand of relevant knowledge is from the planning and policy analysis arena where environmental decisions are made. A second strand of knowledge is the aggregation of decision support systems, geographic information systems, and geographic information science. The key concepts from these strands of knowledge are chronologically presented in Figure 1 and summarized in Table 2.

The history shown in Figure 1 can be categorized into four cumulative and overlapping periods: argumentation, reasoning, representation, and synthesis, which can be mapped to data, information, knowledge, and intelligence (Klosterman, 2001). The argumentation period covered the 1950s and 1960s and focused on logical structures to construct lexical arguments, and to use those arguments in planning and decisions. The reasoning and representation period covered the 1960s and 1970s, with much effort directed to showing relationships between arguments and processing those arguments with mathematical formalisms. During the 1970s and 1980s, the practical integration of planning concepts and computer-based decision making began to take hold. This was partly due to earlier progress made in decision support systems and geographic information systems. With the planning and computer integration solidifying, the 1980s and early 1990s were the synthesis years when the spotlight was turned towards groups and computer technology in decision interactions. The synthesis was further accelerated by the increasing importance of environmental matters during the time; integrated management using computer based data integration was seen as a promising way to manage the environment. With the emergence of Web GIS and supporting communication technologies during late 1990 and early 2000, the collaborative GIS focus is now converging towards a distributive paradigm, where systems and processes are aligned to incorporate a wider cross section of participants in the planning and decision making process.

Table 2 provides a summary of key concepts that have influenced the evolution of collaborative GIS. The integration of these concepts provided the foundation for contemporary spatial group decision systems (Balram, 2005). An early form of collaborative spatial decision making was the Strabo technique, designed to elicit and forecast planning strategies based on a consensus of expert opinions (Luscombe & Peucker, 1975). The Strabo technique produced map and error summaries to aid decision makers in assessing a group's perspective about geographic planning problems. Technological limitation presented an immediate hurdle for the Strabo technique, with a critical challenge being how best to quickly obtain

Figure 1. A historical footprint of concepts related to collaborative GIS

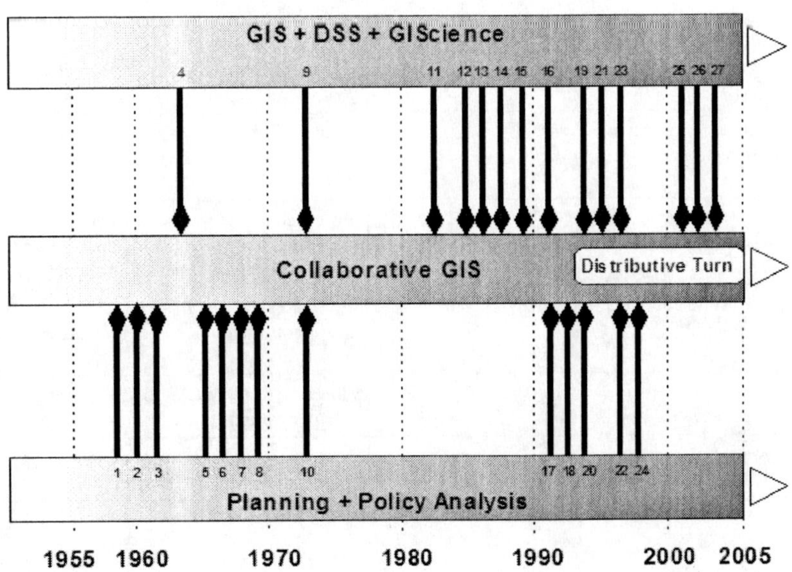

Table 2. Summary description of key concepts that influenced collaborative GIS (Note: The timelines represent the best estimate. There are time lags between when the concepts were formed and when they appeared in some published format.)

ID	Year	Concepts of influence	Summary Description
1	1958	Argumentation (Toulmin, 1958)	Sets out to establish a conclusion based on facts. The facts are connected to the conclusion by another argument called a warrant. The warrant is further supported by a backing. Together these form an argumentation structure.
2	1960	Sketch planning and modeling (B. Harris, 1960)	Deals with the rapid and partial description of scenarios using computer modeling methods. This was the precursor to present day Planning Support Systems (PSS).
3	1960 - 1970	The Delphi process (Linstone & Turoff, 1975)	The Delphi process is used to explore consensus among decision making groups. It consists of multiple iterations and feedbacks.
4	1963	Geographic Information Systems (Tomlinson, 1967)	A collection of computer tools and approaches to capture, manage, and transform spatially referenced data for planning and decisions.
5	1966	Mental maps (Gould, 1966)	Maps in the form of mental images are stored in our consciousness and they seem to document spatial environmental relationships. Research was focused on clarifying the characteristics and uses of mental maps.
6	1968	Communicative rationality (Habermas, 1971)	A theory that assumes human rationality is a necessary consequence of successful communication. In the theory, implicit knowledge can become explicit through communication and discourse.
7	1969	Design with nature (McHarg, 1969)	Proposed a method for land use and human settlements planning that involved manual inclusion and exclusion of map based features. The layered analysis approach suggested here has been adopted by geographic information systems (GIS) design.
8	1969	Ladder of citizen participation (Arnstein, 1969)	Clarified the levels of participation and non-participation using a ladder metaphor. The bottom rung corresponds to manipulation and the top rung corresponds to citizen control.
9	1971	Decision matrix framework (Gorry & Scott Morton, 1971)	Used a matrix to show the interaction between levels of management and decision-making structure at multiple levels. This was the precursor to Decision Support Systems (DSS)
10	1971	Wicked problems (Rittel & Webber, 1973)	A class of problems for which no analytical solutions exist. These problems possess 10 characteristics. One characteristic is that a wicked problem has no definitive formulation.
11	1982	Human computer interaction (Badre & Shneiderman, 1982)	Deals with the design, evaluation and implementation of interactive computer systems for use by humans.
12	1985	Group decision support systems (DeSanctis & Gallupe, 1985)	Proposed a system design where the purpose and configuration depended on the length and duration of the decision process, and on the physical proximity of the group members.
13	1985	Computer supported cooperative work (Bannon & Schmidt, 1989)	Addresses the design and deployment of computer technologies to support interactions between groups, teams, and organizations.
14	1985	Hypermaps (Laurini & Milleret-Raffort, 1990)	The spatial referencing of documents and cartographic products in a networked (Internet) environment.
15	1989	Multicriteria spatial analysis (Jankowski, 1989; Malczewski, 1996)	An approach integrating qualitative and quantitative information with MCE in a group decision making structure.

continued on following page

Table 2. continued

16	1992	Geographic Information Science (Goodchild, 1992)	The science that deals with geographic information technologies, designs, and their impacts on individuals and society.
17	1992	The argumentation turn in planning (Fischer & Forester, 1993)	An approach using argumentation to define problems and structure viable solutions. Argumentation deals with rational persuasion towards changing the perspectives of others.
18	1992	The communicative turn in planning (Healey, 1992)	An approach that used communication to resolve disagreements and conflicts towards consensual solutions. A key goal is to improve local participation in policy processes.
19	1993	Virtual reality GIS (Faust, 1995)	A traditional GIS with a virtual reality interface and interaction method. The intention is to improve communication and collaboration in decision making and simulation contexts.
20	1993	Bioregional mapping (Aberley, 1993)	An approach using biophysical and cultural knowledge as a basis to construct maps of environmental places and spaces. The maps combine scientific and traditional information.
21	1993	Web geographic information system (Palo Alto Research Center, 1994)	Uses a distributed network (LAN, internet, wireless) to share, process and transform spatially referenced data.
22	1996	The deliberative turn in planning (Forester, 1999)	An approach where participants deliberate under conditions that support reasoned reflection. Deliberation is the process where individual reflection on issues can lead to a change in perspective.
23	1996	Collaborative spatial decision making (T. L. Nyerges & Jankowski, 1997)	A framework integrating aspects and concepts relevant to group spatial decision making.
24	1997	Ladder of empowerment (Rocha, 1997)	Clarifies various levels of empowerment by using a ladder metaphor. The bottom rung of the ladder is individual empowerment and the top rung is community empowerment.
25	2001	Geovisualization (A. M. MacEachren & Kraak, 2001)	Methods and techniques focusing on the novel display and integrated understanding of large volumes of spatial data.
26	2002	Geocollaboration (A. MacEachren, Brewer, Cai, & Chen, 2003)	A visual approach to collaboration using geospatial technologies in group processes.
27	2002	Agent interactions (Gimblett, 2002)	A paradigm where human entities are represented as agents in computer environments and possible collaboration scenarios are explored through simulations.

geographical summaries of expert feedback for input into the next iteration of the workshop group discussion. Nevertheless, the Strabo demonstrated the valuable contributions of expert groups in the spatial planning process.

The rapid advances in GIS software, hardware, and networking technologies have resulted in many new opportunities to integrate spatial mapping and analysis tools into group decision-making processes. In this respect, Armstrong (1994) argued for a greater integration of group mapping and visualization technologies into spatial decision making. Godschalk, McMahon, Kaplan, and Qin (1992) reported on a group design that allowed participants to manipulate criteria during the decision-making process. The key role of data in the decision-making process was also recognized, and collaborative multimedia technologies were used to make data more accessible (Shiffer, 1992). A loose-coupled electronic meeting and map overlay system was also designed for land-use planning applications (Faber, Watts, Hautaluoma, Knutson, Wallace, & Wallace, 1996). The issues of qualitative and quantitative data integration using multicriteria analysis was also at the forefront of research efforts in collaborative spatial decision making (Carver, 1991; Jankowski, 1989; Malczewski, 1996). These developments highlight stages in the evolution of a research area that would later come to benefit from a coordinated research direction.

The collaborative spatial decision making (CSDM) research initiative of the National Center of Geographic Information and Analysis (NCGIA), USA, and the first specialist meeting in September 1995 added focus to the research direction of CSDM by emphasizing the design of "highly interactive group-based decision making environments." The research thereafter reflected this new focus, and there now exists a well-established and growing body of literature on the theory and application of collaborative, spatial, decision making (Densham & Rushton, 1996; Feick & Hall, 1999; Horita, 2000; Jankowski, 1995; Jankowski & Nyerges, 2001b; Jankowski, Nyerges, Smith, Moore, & Horvath, 1997; Jiang & Chen, 2002; Klosterman, 1999; Kyem, 2000, 2004; Malczewski, 1996). However, the multitude of variables that are usually involved in the CSDM process makes it a challenge to conduct experimental studies and compare results across implementations. This was a driving factor in the development of the Enhanced Adaptive Structuration Theory 2 by Jankowski and Nyerges (2001a). The EAST2 framework outlined a detailed configuration of "concepts and relationships linking the content, process and outcome of collaborative spatial decision making." The content constructs examined the socioinstitutional, group participant, and GIS technology influences. The process constructs examined the social interactions between humans and computers, and focused on structuring the group decision-making process. The outcome constructs addressed societal impacts of the outcome decision.

Geographic data and the structure of the collaborative group process are two important micro-level factors that influence the group constructs of the EAST2 framework. Effective participation and decision making is dependent on access to scientific data and information (Craig, Harris, & Weiner, 2002; Jankowski & Nyerges, 2001b; Nyerges, Jankowski, & Drew, 2002; Sieber, 2000). During group deliberations, many alternative scenarios are generated as a result of the diversity in participant beliefs and interests, and as these scenarios become less distinct, more data and knowledge is required to develop informed solutions. But obtaining this knowledge is difficult, and when available, it is usually partial, transitory, and contested. New and synergistic opportunities for generating relevant knowledge are obtained by aggregating participant knowledge and spatial map data (Jankowski & Nyerges, 2001a). The merging of context-dependent participant knowledge and context-independent spatial data with digital maps and user-friendly exploration tools enhances critical thinking and creativity, producing a comprehensive understanding of values and change structures. The result is broader participant satisfaction, better management plans, and improved decision making (Geertman, 2002).

In recent times, a number of studies have reported on integrating digital map data into the group modeling and decision-making process (Fall, Daust, & Morgan, 2001; Horita, 2000). The general trend has been to use this data either to support existing arguments, or to choose among a predefined set of alternatives. When the data is not integrated into the decision-making process, two negative consequences occur. First, arguments and counterarguments among participants using independent data can lead to more confrontation, due to inherent differences in knowledge sources. Second, participants do not have the flexibility to define or explore common spatial scenarios and therefore, opportunities to develop new perspectives and understanding about an environmental situation are restricted. Despite these disadvantages, the use of prepackaged data in the process has persisted because of the perceived cognitive difficulties that digital map data and supporting technologies impose on participants. However, practical experience has shown that embedded digital-map technology can be modified to suit the needs of a targeted end-user, and that the technologically uninitiated is capable of adapting to new levels of sophistication in short time intervals (Mitcham, 1997; Talen, 1999).

The explicit integration of spatial map data and visual exploration tools into the group decision-making process can be achieved by embedding a collaborative geographic information system into the participatory structures of the process. A collaborative GIS is a tool and a system consisting of a networked collection of computer hardware, software, and user groups with the objective to capture, store, manipulate, visualize, and analyze geographically referenced data and knowledge, so as to provide new information in an institutional setting for solving unstructured planning problems (Armstrong, 1994). As a sociotechnical system, the collaborative GIS facilitates synchronous interactions, as stakeholder and scientific knowledge are combined using exploratory tools to share, annotate, analyze, and visualize numeric, text, and map data in search for solutions within shared geographic place and space (Faber et al., 1996). The collaborative GIS allows for elicitation of knowledge, simulation of data, scenario development, and encouraging spatial critical thinking about all issues. In order to best implement the collaborative GIS to articulate participant ideas, a careful structuring of the group decision-making process is needed for equitable and sufficient issues representation.

Structuring the group decision-making process can help focus the discussions so that constructive ideas are generated during argumentation. Usually, the structuring is conducted in stages involving shared understanding of the environmental situation, criteria identification and ranking, data and knowledge availability, and the generation of alternative scenarios (Godschalk et al., 1992). This is an effective way to integrate individual perspectives, resources, institutions, and organizations towards common solutions. A consequence of integration has been process structuring using top-down, bottom-up, and facilitator-based workshop settings, with advisory committees (Vasseur, LaFrance, Ansseau, Renaud, Morin, & Audet, 1997), participatory democracy (Moote, McClaran, & Chickering, 1997), and cooperative strategies (Lejano & Davos, 1999) being a few of the implementation strategies. Not surprisingly, critics have suggested that some of these implementations are inherently confrontational, and can stall the decision process. But many researchers have pointed out the many long-term partnerships and planning benefits that can accrue by carefully embedding discursive strategies into the participatory decision making process (Healey, 1993; Webler, Tuler, & Krueger, 2001; Wilson & Howarth, 2002).

The Delphi method is a focus-group approach that has been applied in a number of recent studies to structure and incorporate discursive strategies into decision making processes (Gokhale, 2001; Hess & King, 2002). The focus group assembles a small number of individuals in a face-to-face collaborative setting to elaborate the details about a particular issue that is initially chosen for discussion by an investigator who structures or moderates the discussions. The Delphi uses a collaborative approach to create a process of building relationships, awareness, learning, and negotiation. During the Delphi, a neutral facilitator elicits individual, anonymous judgment about an issue from a group by using iterative feedback involving a series of rounds of questioning, in order to explore ideas or achieve a convergence of group opinion (Linstone & Turoff, 1975). There are four phases to the Delphi, with the first phase emphasizing the exploration of ideas through individual comments in a structured, brainstorming session. The second phase captures the collective opinions of the group, focusing on agreements and disagreements. The reasons for the disagreements are explored in the third phase. In the fourth phase, an analysis of the opinion convergence on the issues is presented back to the group for final evaluation. The Delphi allows for improved understanding of the decision problems, goals, and objectives, and is useful when there is limited knowledge and data, strong conflict, and when interpersonal interaction is difficult to organize (Linstone & Turoff, 1975). The Delphi has been integrated within a collaborative GIS design to structure environmental planning and decision-making processes (Balram, Dragicevic, & Meredith, 2003, 2004).

Participation in the collaborative, spatial, decision-making process has been an ongoing issue of concern in environmental and community planning (Brandt, 1998; Ghose, 2001; Harris & Weiner, 1998; Sieber, 2000; Talen, 2000). At the basic level, participation can be interpreted to mean the inclusion of a wide range of stakeholder inputs to all stages of the planning and decision-making process. In order to structure and operationalize the concept of participation, Arnstein's "Ladder of Citizen Participation" (Arnstein, 1969) and Rocha's "Ladder of Empowerment" (Rocha, 1997) are two frameworks of analysis widely used in the planning and decision-making literature. The central arguments of both "ladders" and their adaptations to specific contexts is that through a process of collaboration, participation becomes a knowledge sharing and knowledge producing activity capable of initiating social and political change (Baum, 1999; Healey, 1997). Also, a useful adaptation to Arnstein's ladder is presented in Whitman (1994). Whitman attributes varying levels of expert (those possessing "specialist knowledge" of relevance) involvement in each stage of the Arnstein ladder. At the lower end (individual involvement) of the Arnstein ladder, Whitman attributes a detached expert who is removed from the end user in the decision-making process. At the upper end (community involvement) of the Arnstein ladder, Whitman attributes an absent expert, and action is initiated from collective community initiatives. Collaborative GIS targets a middle ground and works at the "partnership" level of the Arnstein ladder, which has been mapped to the "expert as a team member" in the Whitman ladder. Adopting this position in the "ladder" hierarchy makes the focus one of balancing issues of concern gathered at the individual, expert, and public levels.

COLLABORATIVE GIS: A STRUCTURE OF THE RESEARCH AREA

The intellectual landscape of collaborative GIS can be structured by considering two scales. The first scale can be termed a local interdisciplinary view, where the research agenda of geographic information science situated in the upper hierarchy guides the research directions of collaborative GIS located at a lower level in the hierarchy (Figure 2). The second scale can be termed a global transdisciplinary view, where the adoption of new ideas into group spatial decision support systems (GSDSS) from diverse disciplines, coupled with improvements in Internet and wireless technologies are evolving towards a *distributive turn* to planning, problem solving, and decision making.

GIScience is now fairly well established as a discipline, with a diverse set of themes and subareas complete with research challenges and agendas (McMaster & Usery, 2005). Figure 2 shows the themes of GIScience and the subareas, such as spatial data acquisition and integration, cognition, scale, and so on. Of the subareas, GIS and Society is the most relevant for collaborative GIS (Elmes, Epstein, McMaster, Niemann, Poore, Sheppard et al., 2005). GIS and Society addresses institutional, legal and ethical, intellectual history, critical social theory, and participatory GIS issues. There may be some disagreement on whether participatory GIS or public participation GIS should be higher in the GIScience hierarchy. We suggest that PGIS is a more general concept, and should appear higher in the hierarchy. Both GSDSS (small groups) and PPGIS (large groups)

Figure 2. The intellectual structure containing collaborative GIS

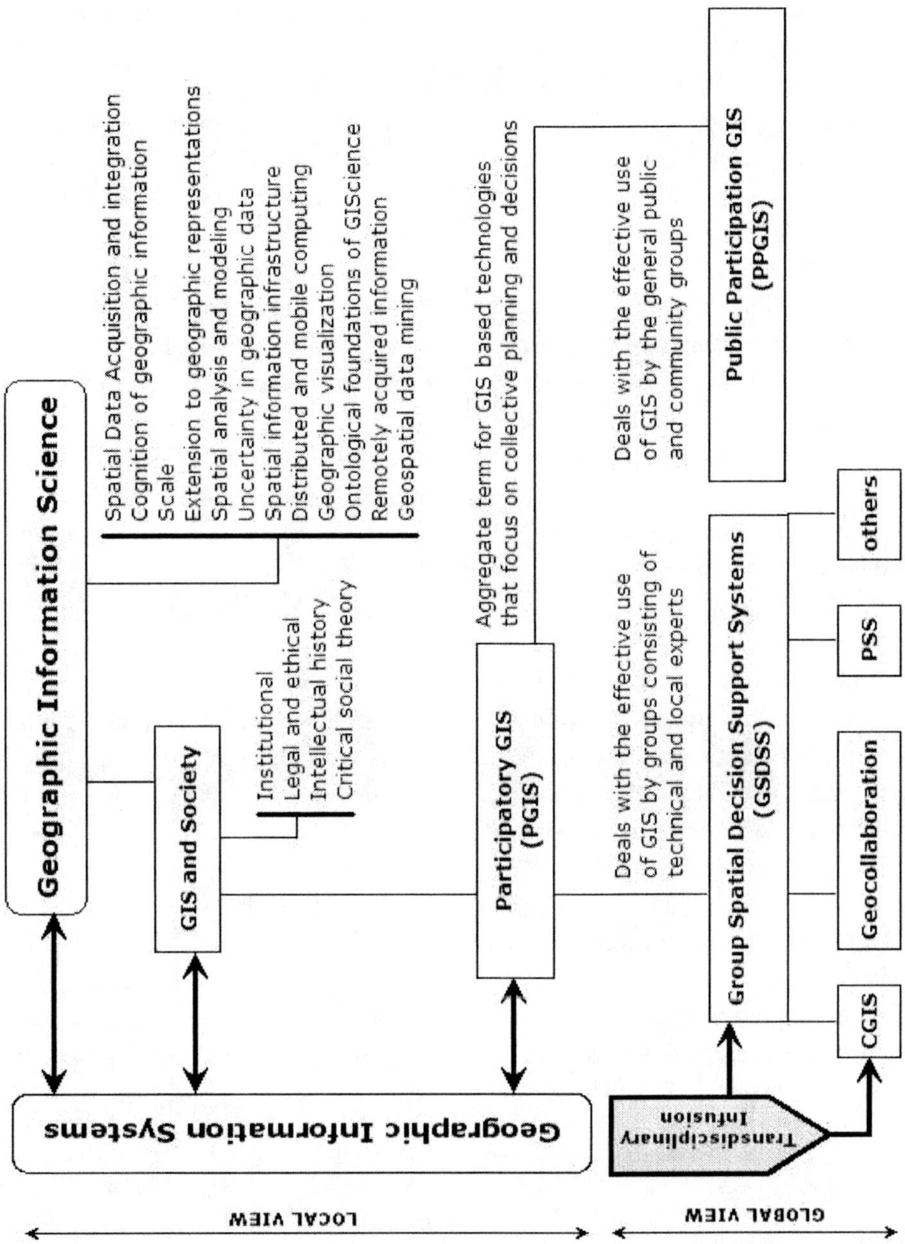

are directly related to group decision making, and are members of the participatory GIS category. Collaborative GIS, geocollaboration, and planning support systems are all GSDSS implementations. However, the presence of fuzzy linguistic terms such as "small," "groups," and "public" will make the structure presented here open to further refinement.

The local interdisciplinary view of collaborative GIS is guided by the geographic information science research agenda. The concepts are interdisciplinary, meaning that the goal is to synthesize two or more disciplines with the intention of creating a coordinated whole. In this view, the research and application focus of collaborative GIS is towards establishing stronger linkages with GIScience. Geographic information systems intervene at all levels of the hierarchy.

The global transdisciplinary view of collaborative GIS is guided mostly by the concepts of theory, experimentation, and simulation as means to explore reality. The concepts are transdisciplinary, meaning that multiple perspectives are integrated and transformed to create new knowledge to solve complex societal problems. It is in this transdisciplinary direction that current collaborative GIS initiatives seem to be focused. The most likely scenario is a *distributive turn* to planning, problem solving and decision making. There are already signals in the research literature (for example: Dymond, Regmi, Lohani, & Dietz, 2004; Schafer, Ganoe, Xiao, Coch, & Carroll, 2005) to suggest that a distributive turn is underway.

CONCLUSION

Progress in collaborative GIS is hinged on an understanding of the historical background of concepts, and the dynamics that are shaping its future. This study has proposed a working definition of collaborative GIS, and presented a philosophical description of the research area. A discussion about the historical background adds justification to the proposed definition. Conceptual linkages between GIScience, public participation GIS, participatory GIS, and CGIS are also presented. An important conclusion is that collaborative GIS is centrally positioned on a participation spectrum that ranges from the individual to the general public, and that argumentation, deliberation, and maps are the common means used to structure and reconcile differences between representative interest groups. Collaborative GIS must give consideration to integrating experts and the general public in synchronous and asynchronous space-time interactions. It is suggested that collaborative GIS theory provides a foundation to conceptualize a *distributive turn* to planning, problem solving, and decision making.

ACKNOWLEDGMENT

This work was supported by the Natural Sciences and Engineering Research Council (NSERC) of Canada Discovery Grant awarded to Suzana Dragievi.

REFERENCES

Aberley, D. (1993). *Boundaries of home: Mapping for local empowerment*. Gabriola Island, British Columbia, Canada: New Society Publishers.

Armstrong, M. P. (1994). Requirements for the development of GIS-based group decision support systems. *Journal of the American Society for Information Science, 45*(9), 669-677.

Arnstein, S. R. (1969). A ladder of citizen participation. *Journal of the American Institute of Planners, 35*(4), 216-224.

Badre, A., & Shneiderman, B. (Eds.). (1982). *Directions in human-computer interaction*. Norwood, NJ: Ablex Pub. Corp.

Balram, S. (2005). *Collaborative GIS process modelling using the Delphi method, systems theory and the unified modelling language (UML).* PhD Thesis, McGill University, Montreal, Canada.

Balram, S., Dragicevic, S., & Meredith, T. (2003). Achieving effectiveness in stakeholder participation using the GIS-based collaborative spatial Delphi methodology. *Journal of Environmental Assessment Policy and Management, 5*(3), 365-394.

Balram, S., Dragicevic, S., & Meredith, T. (2004). A collaborative GIS method for integrating local and technical knowledge in establishing biodiversity conservation priorities. *Biodiversity and Conservation, 13*(6), 1195-1208.

Bannon, L. J., & Schmidt, K. (1989). CSCW: Four characteristics in search of a context. In J. Bowers & S. Benford (Eds.), *Studies in computer supported cooperative work: Theory, practice and design* (pp. 3-16). Amsterdam: North-Holland.

Baum, H. S. (1999). Community organizations recruiting community participation: Predicaments in planning. *Journal of Planning and Education Research, 18*, 187-199.

Brandt, M. (1998). Public participation GIS - Barriers to implementation. *Cartography and Geographic Information Systems, 25*(2), 105-112.

Bruffee, K. A. (1995). Sharing our toys: Cooperative learning vs. collaborative learning. *Change,* (January/February), 12-18.

Carver, S. (1991). Integrating multicriteria evaluations with geographical information systems. *International Journal of Geographical Information Systems, 5*(3), 321-339.

Craig, W. J., Harris, T. M., & Weiner, D. (Eds.). (2002). *Community participation and geographic information science.* London: Taylor and Francis.

Densham, P. J., & Rushton, G. (1996). Providing spatial decision support for rural public service facilities that require a minimum workload. *Environment and Planning B-Planning & Design, 23*(5), 553-574.

DeSanctis, G., & Gallupe, R. B. (1985). Group decision support systems: A new frontier. *Database, 16*(1), 377-387.

Dewey, J. (1916). *Democracy and education.* New York: The Macmillan Company.

Duckham, M., Goodchild, M. F., & Worboys, M. F. (Eds.). (2003). *Foundations of geographic information science.* New York: Taylor & Francis.

Dymond, R. L., Regmi, B., Lohani, V. K., & Dietz, R. (2004). Interdisciplinary Web-enabled spatial decision support system for watershed management. *Journal of Water Resources Planning and Management, 130*(4), 290-300.

Elmes, G. A., Epstein, E. F., McMaster, R. E., Niemann, B. J., Poore, B., Sheppard, E., et al. (2005). GIS and Society: Interrelation, integration, and transformation. In R. B. McMaster & E. L. Usery (Eds.), *A research agenda for geographic information science* (pp. 287-312). Boca Raton, FL: CRC Press.

Faber, B. G., Watts, R., Hautaluoma, J. E., Knutson, J., Wallace, W. W., & Wallace, L. (1996). A groupware-enabled GIS. In M. Heit, H. D. Parker, & A. Shortreid (Eds.), *GIS applications in natural resources 2* (pp. 3-13). Fort Collins, CO: GIS World Inc.

Fall, A., Daust, D., & Morgan, D. G. (2001). A framework and software tool to support collaborative landscape analysis: Fitting square pegs into square holes. *Transactions in GIS, 5*(1), 67-86.

Faust, N. L. (1995). The virtual reality of GIS. *Environment and Planning B: Planning and Design, 22*, 257-268.

Feick, R. D., & Hall, B. G. (1999). Consensus-building in a multiparticipant spatial decision support system. *URISA Journal, 11*(2), 17-23.

Fischer, F., & Forester, J. (Eds.). (1993). *The argumentative turn in policy analysis and planning.* Durham, NC: Duke University Press.

Forester, J. (1999). *The deliberative practitioner: Encouraging participatory planning processes.* Cambridge, MA: MIT Press.

Fuller, S. (2002). *Social epistemology* (2nd ed.). Bloomington, IN: University Press.

Geertman, S. (2002). Participatory planning and GIS: A PSS to bridge the gap. *Environment and Planning B: Planning and Design, 29*(1), 21-35.

Ghose, R. (2001). Use of information technology for community empowerment: Transforming geographic information systems into community information systems. *Transactions in GIS, 5*(2), 141-163.

Gimblett, H. R. (Ed.). (2002). *Integrating geographic information systems and agent-based modeling techniques for simulating social and ecological processes.* New York: Oxford University Press.

Godschalk, D. R., McMahon, G., Kaplan, A., & Qin, W. (1992). Using GIS for computer-assisted dispute resolution. *Photogrammetric Engineering & Remote Sensing, 58*(8), 1209-1212.

Gokhale, A. A. (2001). Environmental initiative prioritization with a Delphi approach: A case study. *Environmental Management, 28*(2), 187-193.

Gómez-Pérez, A., Fernández-López, M., & Corcho, O. (2004). *Ontological engineering.* London; New York: Springer-Verlag.

Goodchild, M. F. (1992). Geographical information science. *International Journal of Geographical Information Systems, 6*(1), 31-45.

Gorry, G. A., & Scott Morton, M. S. (1971). A framework for management information systems. *Sloan Management Review, 13*(1), 55-70.

Gould, P. R. (1966). *On mental maps.* Ann Arbor: University of Michigan.

Gruber, T. R. (1992). A translation approach to portable ontology specifications. *Knowledge Acquisition, 5*, 199-220.

Habermas, J. (1971). *Knowledge and human interests* (J. J. Shapiro, Trans.). Boston: Beacon Press.

Harris, B. (1960). Plan or projection: An examination of the use of models in planning. *Journal of the American Institute of Planners, 26*, 265-272.

Harris, T., & Weiner, D. (1998). Empowerment, marginalization and community-integrated GIS. *Cartography and Geographic Information Systems, 25*(2), 67-76.

Healey, P. (1992). Planning through debate: The communicative turn in planning theory. *Town Planning Review, 63*(2), 143-162.

Healey, P. (1993). Planning through debate: The communicative turn in planning theory. In F. Fischer & J. Forester (Eds.), *The argumentative turn in policy analysis and planning* (pp. 233-253). Durham, NC: Duke University Press.

Healey, P. (1997). *Collaborative planning: Shaping places in fragmented societies.* Vancouver, BC: UBC Press.

Hess, G. R., & King, T. J. (2002). Planning open spaces for wildlife I: Selecting focal species using a Delphi survey approach. *Landscape and Urban Planning, 58*, 25-40.

Horita, M. (2000). Mapping policy discourse with CRANES: Spatial understanding support systems as a medium for community conflict resolution. *Environment and Planning B: Planning and Design, 27*, 801-814.

Jankowski, P. (1989). Mixed-data multicriteria evaluation for regional planning: A systematic approach to the decision-making process. *Environment and Planning A, 21*, 349-362.

Jankowski, P. (1995). Integrating geographical information systems and multiple criteria decision-making methods. *International Journal of Geographical Information Systems, 9*(3), 251-273.

Jankowski, P., & Nyerges, T. (2001a). *Geographic information systems for group decision making: Towards a participatory geographic information science*. New York: Taylor and Francis.

Jankowski, P., & Nyerges, T. (2001b). GIS-supported collaborative decision making: Results of an experiment. *Annals of the Association of American Geographers, 91*(1), 48-70.

Jankowski, P., Nyerges, T., Smith, A., Moore, T. J., & Horvath, E. (1997). Spatial group choice: An SDSS tool for collaborative spatial decision-making. *International Journal of Geographical Information Science, 11*(6), 577-602.

Jiang, J., & Chen, J. (2002). A GIS-based computer-supported collaborative work (CSCW) system for urban planning and land management. *Photogrammetric Engineering & Remote Sensing, 68*(4), 353-359.

Klosterman, R. E. (1999). The What if? Collaborative planning support system. *Environment and Planning B: Planning and Design, 26*(3), 393-408.

Klosterman, R. E. (2001). Planning support systems: A new perspective on computer-aided planning. In R. K. Brail & R. E. Klosterman (Eds.), *Planning support systems: Integrating geographic systems, models, and visualization tools* (pp. 1-23). Redlands, CA: ESRI Press.

Kyem, P. K. (2000). Embedding GIS applications into resource management and planning activities of local and indigenous communities: A desirable innovation or a destabilizing enterprise? *Journal of Planning Education and Research, 20*, 176-186.

Kyem, P. K. (2004). On intractable conflicts and participatory GIS applications: The search for consensus amidst competing claims and institutional demands. *Annals of the Association of American Geographers, 94*(1), 37-57.

Laurini, R., & Milleret-Raffort, F. (1990, July 23-27). Principles of geomatic hypermaps. In K. Brassel (Ed.), *Proceedings of the 4th International Symposium on Spatial Data Handling* (pp. 642-651). Zurich.

Lejano, R. P., & Davos, C. A. (1999). Cooperative solutions for sustainable resource management. *Environmental Management, 24*(2), 167-175.

Linstone, H. A., & Turoff, M. (1975). *The Delphi method: Techniques and applications*. Reading, MA: Addision-Wesley.

Luscombe, B. W., & Peucker, T. K. (1975). *The Strabo technique*. Burnaby, Canada: Simon Fraser University, Department of Geography Discussion Paper Series.

MacEachren, A., Brewer, I., Cai, G., & Chen, C. (2003, August 10-16). Visually enabled geocollaboration to support data exploration and decision-making. Paper presented at the *Proceedings of the 21st International Cartographic Conference*, Durban, South Africa.

MacEachren, A. M., & Kraak, M. (2001). Research challenges in geovisualization. *Cartography and Geographic Information Science, 28*(1), 3-12.

Malczewski, J. (1996). A GIS-based approach to multiple criteria group decision-making. *International Journal of Geographical Information Systems, 10*(8), 955-971.

McHarg, I. L. (1969). *Design with nature*. Garden City, NY: Natural History Press.

McMaster, R. B., & Usery, E. L. (Eds.). (2005). *A research agenda for geographic information science*. Boca Raton, FL: CRC Press.

Mitcham, C. (1997). Justifying public participation in technical decision making. *IEEE Technology and Society, 16*(1), 40-46.

Moote, M. A., McClaran, M. P., & Chickering, D. K. (1997). Theory in practice: Applying participatory democracy theory to public land planning. *Environmental Management, 21*(6), 877-889.

Nyerges, T. L., & Jankowski, P. (1997). Enhanced adaptive structuration theory: A theory of GIS-supported collaborative decision making. *Geographical Systems, 4*(3), 225-257.

Nyerges, T., Jankowski, P., & Drew, C. (2002). Data-gathering strategies for social-behavioural research about participatory geographical information system use. *International Journal of Geographical Information Science, 16*(1), 1-22.

Oakeshott, M. (1975). *On human conduct*. Oxford, UK: Oxford University Press.

Palo Alto Research Center. (1994). *Xerox PARC map viewer*. Retrieved November 11, 2005, from http://www2.parc.com/istl/projects/mapdocs/

Rescher, N. (2003). *Epistemology: An introduction to the theory of knowledge*. Albany: State University of New York Press.

Rittel, H., & Webber, M. (1973). Dilemmas in a general theory of planning. *Policy Sciences, 4*, 155-169.

Rocha, E. M. (1997). A ladder of empowerment. *Journal of Planning and Education Research, 17*(1), 31-44.

Sager, J. C. (Ed.). (2000). *Essays on definition*. Amsterdam; Philadelphia: J. Benjamins Publishers.

Schafer, W. A., Ganoe, C. H., Xiao, L., Coch, G., & Carroll, J. M. (2005). Designing the next generation of distributed, geocollaborative tools. *Cartography and Geographic Information Science, 32*(2), 81-100.

Shiffer, M. J. (1992). Towards a collaborative planning system. *Environment and Planning B: Planning and Design, 19*(6), 709-722.

Sieber, R. E. (2000). GIS implementation in the grassroots. *URISA Journal, 12*(1), 15-29.

Smith, J. B. (1994). *Collective intelligence in computer-based collaboration*. Hillsdale, NJ: Lawrence Erlbaum and Associates.

Talen, E. (1999). Constructing neighborhoods from the bottom up: The case for resident-generated GIS. *Environment and Planning B: Planning and Design, 26*(4), 533-554.

Talen, E. (2000). Bottom-up GIS: A new tool for individual and group expression in participatory planning. *Journal of the American Planning Association, 66*(3), 279-294.

Tomlinson, R. F. (1967). *An introduction to the geographic information system of the Canada Land Inventory*. Ottawa, Canada: Department of Forestry and Rural Development.

Torres-Fonseca, F., & Egenhofer, M. (2000). Ontology-driven geographic information systems. *Computers, Environment and Urban Systems, 24*(3), 251-271.

Toulmin, S. E. (1958). *The uses of argument*. Cambridge, UK; New York: Cambridge Press.

Vasseur, L., LaFrance, L., Ansseau, C., Renaud, D., Morin, D., & Audet, T. (1997). Advisory committee: A powerful tool for helping decision makers in environmental issues. *Environmental Management, 21*(3), 359-365.

Webler, T., Tuler, S., & Krueger, R. (2001). What is a good public participation process? Five perspectives from the public. *Environmental Management, 27*(3), 435-450.

Whitman, P. (1994). Experts and their interventions: A model of the field of urban improvement. *Environment and Planning B: Planning and Design, 21*(6), 759-768.

Wilson, M. A., & Howarth, R. B. (2002). Discourse-based valuation of ecosystem services: Establishing fair outcomes through group deliberations. *Ecological Economics, 41*, 431-443.

Wright, D. J., Goodchild, M. F., & Proctor, J. D. (1997). Demystifying the persistent ambiguity of GIS as "tool" vs. "science." *Annals of the Association of American Geographers, 87*(2), 346-362.

This work was previously published in Collaborative Geographic Information Systems, edited by S. Balram and S. Dragicevic, pp. 1-23, copyright 2006 by IGI Publishing, formerly known as Idea Group Publishing (an imprint of IGI Global).

Chapter XX
Towards an Ontology for Information Systems Development:
A Contextual Approach

Mauri Leppänen
University of Jyväskylä, Finland

ABSTRACT

This chapter presents an ISD ontology, which aims to provide an integrated conceptualization of ISD through anchoring it upon a contextual approach. The ISD ontology is composed of concepts, relationships, and constraints referring to purposes, actors, actions, and objects of ISD. It is presented as a vocabulary with explicit definitions and in meta models in a UML-based ontology representation language. We believe that although not complete the ISD ontology can promote the achievement of a shared understanding of contextual aspects in ISD. It can be used to analyze and compare existing frameworks and meta models and as a groundwork for engineering new ISD methods, and parts thereof.

INTRODUCTION

To advance the understanding, management, and improvement of an information system development (ISD) process, a large number of frameworks, meta models, and reference models, in short ISD artifacts, have been suggested for ISD and ISD methods. Most of these artifacts view ISD from perspectives that are based on some specific approaches, such as a transformation approach (e.g., Moynihan, 1993; Saeki, Iguchi, Wen-yin, & Shinokara, 1993; Song, & Osterweil, 1992), a decision-making approach (e.g., Grozs et al., 1997; Jarke, Jeusfeld, & Rose, 1990; NATURE Team, 1996; Rolland, Souveyet, & Moreno, 1995), a problem-solving approach (e.g., Bodard et al., 1983; Jayaratna, 1994; Sol, 1992), or a learning approach (e.g., Iivari, 1990). In consequence of this, ranges of concepts and constructs in these artifacts are rather narrow. To enable a more comprehensive view on ISD, ISD should be conceived as a context with all its meaningful facets, distinguishing purposes, actors, actions, objects, facilities, locations, and time aspects.

The purpose of this study is to present an ISD ontology that is based on a contextual approach. An ontology is a kind of framework unifying different viewpoints, thus functioning in a way like a lingua-franga (Chandrasekaran, Josephson, & Benjamins, 1999). More specifically, an ontology is an explicit specification of a conceptualization of some part of reality that is of interest (Gruber, 1993). The *ISD ontology* provides a conceptualization of contextual aspects of ISD through a vocabulary with explicit definitions. To enhance the clarity and preciseness of the ontology, we deploy a UML-based ontology representation language to describe the ISD ontology in meta models.

The ISD ontology is intended for descriptive, analytical, and constructive use. For the descriptive purposes, the ontology offers concepts and a vocabulary for conceiving, understanding, structuring, and presenting contextual aspects of ISD. In the analytical sense, the ontology can be used to analyze and compare existing ISD artifacts. In the constructive sense, the ontology is to support the engineering of new ISD artifacts, such as ISD models, techniques and methods, by providing a coherent and consistent groundwork for them. The ISD ontology is not yet a complete ontology. It should be enhanced with more specialized concepts and constructs and assessed for validity and applicability by empirical tests.

The rest of the chapter is structured as follows. In the next section, we define the notions of context and contextual approach and apply them to define the ISD ontology. Moreover, we discuss the process of engineering the ISD ontology. In the next five sections, we specify four main ISD domains (i.e., ISD purpose domain, ISD actor domain, ISD action domain, and ISD object domain) and inter-relationships between them. After that, we make a comparative analysis of current ISD artifacts to find out how comprehensive they are in terms of contextual features and demonstrate the usability of the ISD ontology as an analytical means. The chapter concludes with discussions and implications to research and practice.

CONTEXTUAL APPROACH AND ENGINEERING OF THE ISD ONTOLOGY

Based on a large literature review on the notion of context in several disciplines, such as knowledge representation and reasoning (e.g., Brezillon, Pomerol, & Saker, 1998; Sowa, 2000), pragmatics (e.g., Levinson, 1983), computational linguistics (e.g., Clark & Carlson, 1981), sociolinguistics (e.g., Halliday, 1978), organizational theory (e.g., Weick, 1995), and information systems (e.g., Kyng & Mathiassen, 1997), we came to the following generic conclusion: *context* denotes a whole that is composed of things connected to one another with contextual relationships. A thing captures its meaning through the relationships it has to the other things in that context. To recognize a proper set of contextual concepts and relationships, we drew upon relevant meaning theories. Based on the three topmost layers in the semiotic ladder (Stamper, 1975), we identified semantics (especially case grammar by Fillmore (1968)), pragmatics (Levinson, 1983), and the activity theory (Engeström, 1987) to be such theories. They concern sentence context, conversation context, and action context, correspondingly.

In the case grammar (Fillmore, 1968), the sentence in its basic structure consists of a verb and one or more noun phrases, each associated with the verb in a particular case relationship. The notion of case is a language element that is more stable than surface-level grammatical terms. Cases identify "certain types of judgments human beings are capable of making about the events which are going on around them, judgments about such matters as who did, who it happened to, and what got changed," (Fillmore, 1968, p. 24). Pragmatics is "the study of the ability of language users to pair sentences with the contexts in which they would be appropriate," (Levinson, 1983, p. 23). In such a study, one of the most essential issues deals with deixis. Deixis concern the ways in which "languages encode or grammaticalize features of the context of expressions or speech events," (Levinson, 1983, p. 54). Traditional categories of deixis are person, place, and time deixis. The activity theory presents highly general propositions of the nature of human activity, incorporating several psychological, educational, cultural, and developmental approaches (Leont'ev, 1978). According to the theory, there exists a fundamental type of context called activity. Activity is a minimal meaningful context for individual actions. The systemic structure of human activity (Engeström, 1987; Engeström, 1999), built upon the activity theory, is composed of seven fundamental concepts: subject, object, tool, rules, community, division of labor, and outcome from the activity. The concepts are interrelated in terms of mediating; for instance, the relationship between subject and object is mediated by tools.

Based on this groundwork, we define seven domains which serve concepts for specifying and interpreting contextual phenomena. These contextual domains are: purpose, actor, action, object, facility, location, and time (Figure 1). To structure the concepts within and between these domains, we specify the Seven S's scheme: *For **Some** purpose, **Somebody** does **Something** for **Someone**, with **Some** means, **Sometimes** and **Somewhere**.*

Implied from the above, we define the *contextual approach* to be the approach according to which individual things in reality are seen to play specific roles in a certain context, and/or to be contexts themselves. The contexts can be decomposed into more elementary ones and related to one another through inter-context relationships (see Figure 1). As far as we know, there is no approach or framework similar to our contextual framework. The closest is the so-called "5Ws and H" scheme, which is based on six interrogatives ("Why," "Who," "What," "Where," "When," and "How"). This scheme is used for many purposes (see Couger, Higgins, & McIntyre, 1993; Curtis, Kellner, & Over, 1992; Krogstie & Sölvberg, 1996; Short, 1991; Sowa & Zachman, 1992; Söderström, Anderson, Johannesson, Perjons, & Wangler, 2002; Zachman, 1987; Zultner, 1993). However, no theoretical grounds have been presented for the scheme, and it addresses only part of the contextual aspects that our framework does.

We have previously applied the contextual approach to enterprise ontologies (Leppänen, 2005b), method engineering (Leppänen, 2005c), and method integration (Leppänen, 2006). Here, we apply it to ISD. Based on the contextual approach, we see *information system development* as a context in which ISD actors carry out ISD actions to produce ISD deliverables contributing to a renewed or a new IS, by means of ISD facilities, in a certain organizational and spatio-temporal context, in order to satisfy ISD stakeholders' goals. The notion provides an extensive view on contextual aspects of ISD. ISD work is guided by ISD requirements and goals which, through elicitations and negotiations, become more complete, shared, and formal (Pohl, 1993). ISD work is carried out

Figure 1. Contextual framework

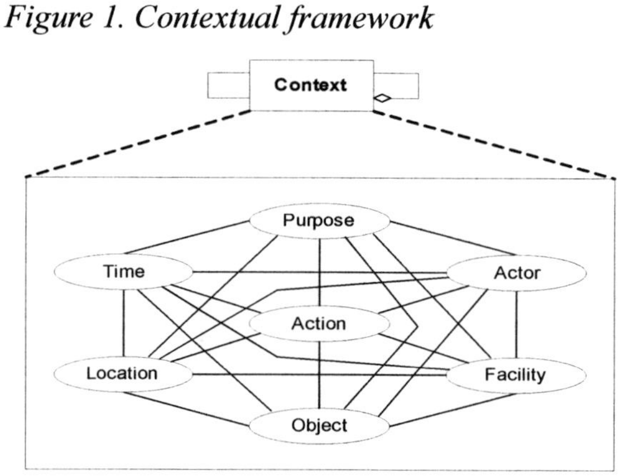

by ISD actors with different motives, skills, and expertise, acting in different roles in organizational units that are situationally established. ISD work is composed of various ISD actions, structured in concordance with the selected ISD approaches and ISD methods, and customized according to conventions in the organization. The final outcome of ISD is a new or improved information system composed of interacting social arrangements and technical components. ISD work consumes resources (e.g., money and time) and is supported by computer-aided tools (e.g., CASE tools). ISD actors, ISD deliverables, and ISD facilities are situated in certain locations, and are present in certain times.

Based on the aforementioned, we define the ISD ontology as follows: the *ISD ontology* provides concepts and constructs for conceiving, understanding, structuring, and representing contextual phenomena in ISD. The concepts and constructs in the ISD ontology have been defined in a deductive and inductive manner, as described below. Following an iterative procedure, derived from the works of Uschold and King (1995), Fernandez-Lopez, Gomez-Perez, Pazos-Sierra, and Pazos-Sierra (1999), and Staab, Schnurr, Studer, and Sure (2001), we first determined the purpose, domain, and scope of the ontology. Second, we searched for disciplines and theories that address social and organizational contexts and derived the basic categorization of concepts into contextual domains from them. Third, we analyzed current ISD artifacts to find out whether they include parts that could be reused and integrated, as such or refined, into our ontology. Fourth, we defined the basic concepts and constructs for each contextual domain, and when possible, adapted and integrated those concepts of other artifacts that were found suitable. We also closely examined empirical studies on ISD practice (e.g., Sabherwal & Robey, 1993) to test the relevance of our concepts. Our aim was to establish a common core from which concepts and constructs for specific ISD approaches could be specialized. Results from this gradually evolving conceptualization were presented in a graphical form. The last step of the ontology engineering procedure was evaluation. We applied a set of quality criteria for ontologies (e.g., Burton-Jones, Storey, Sugumaran, & Ahluwalia, 2005; Gruber, 1995; Uschold, 1996; Weinberger, Te'eni, & Frank, 2003) to evaluate the ISD ontology in several stages.

In the following, we define four of the ISD domains, namely the ISD purpose domain, the ISD actor domain, the ISD action domain, and the ISD object domain. The other three ISD domains are excluded due to the page limit. For each domain, we define basic concepts, relationships, and constraints. After that, we delineate relationships between the domains. A more profound discussion about the ISD domains and the inter-domain relationships is given in Leppänen (2005a).

ISD Purpose Domain

The *ISD purpose domain* embraces all those concepts and constructs that refer to goals, motives, or intentions of someone or something in the ISD context (Figure 2). The concepts show a direction in which to proceed, a state to be attained or avoided, and reasons for them. Reasons, expressed in terms of requirements, problems, and so forth, are used to indicate why certain goals have been or should be set up. The ISD purpose domain is highly important as, only through its concepts, it is possible to demonstrate "Why" an ISD effort, an ISD action, or an ISD deliverable is necessary.

An *ISD goal* expresses a desired state or event with qualities and quantities, related to the ISD context as a whole, or to some parts thereof. *Hard ISD goals* have pre-specified criteria for the assessment of the fulfillment of ISD goals, while *soft ISD goals* have not (Lin & Ho, 1999; Mylopoulos, Chung, Liao, & Wang, 2001). An *ISD requirement* is some quality or performance demanded in and for the ISD context. It is a statement about the future (NATURE Team, 1996). ISD requirements

Figure 2. Meta model of the ISD purpose domain

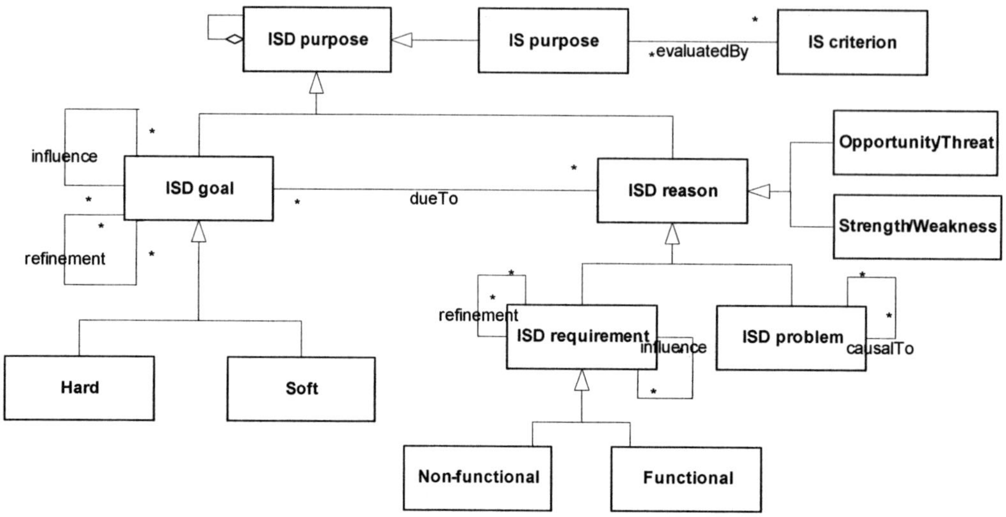

can be classified along three orthogonal dimensions (Pohl, 1993): specification, representation, and agreement. In the specification dimension, the requirements range from opaque to complete. The representation dimension categorizes requirements into informal, semi-formal, and formal requirements. The agreement dimension reflects the fact that ISD requirements are initially personal views which are negotiated and agreed on to achieve a shared view. ISD requirements become goals in the ISD context after agreement has been reached. All the requirements cannot be accepted as goals, since their fulfillment may, for instance, go beyond the resources available. An *ISD problem* is the distance or mismatch between the prevailing ISD state and the state reflected by the ISD goals (cf. Goldkuhl, & Röstling, 1988; Jayaratna, 1994). ISD problems can be structured, semi-structured, or non-structured.

Strength signifies something in which one is good, something that is regarded as an advantage and thus increases the possibility of gaining something better. *Weakness* means something in which one is poor, something that could or should be improved or avoided. The "one" can refer to any contextual element of the ISD, the current IS, the business system deploying the IS, or the environment. *Opportunity* is a situation or condition favorable for attainment of a goal (Webster, 1989). *Threat* is a situation or condition that is a risk for attainment of a goal.

Some of the ISD purposes directly concern an IS. They are called *IS purposes*, and they are sub-divided into IS goals and IS reasons, and further into IS requirements, IS opportunities/IS threats, and IS strengths/IS weaknesses. IS goals are specified to guide the ISD actors in the selection and implementation of IS requirements. A large variety of IS criteria are available for the evaluation and comparison of IS designs, implementation, and use. An *IS criterion* is a standard of judgment presented as an established rule or principle for evaluating some feature(s) of an IS in terms of IS purposes. Next, we consider the IS requirements more closely. An *IS requirement* stands for a condition or capability of the IS needed by an IS client or an IS worker to solve a problem or achieve a goal (cf. IEEE, 1990). The IS requirements are divided into functional requirements and non-functional requirements. A *functional IS requirement* specifies what the IS should do and for whom (cf. Pohl, 1993). A *non-functional*

IS requirement sets some quality attributes upon the services or functions offered by the IS (Cysneiros, Leite, & Neto, 2001; Pohl, 1994). It can be expressed in terms of performance, safety, quality, maintainability, portability, usability, reliability, confidentiality, security, accuracy, and so forth (Chung, Nixon, Yu, & Mylopoulos, 2000, Cysneiros et al., 2001).

The ISD goals, as well as the ISD requirements, are related to one another through refinement relationships and influence relationships. A *refinement relationship* means that an ISD goal can be reached when certain ISD goals, also known as satisfying or argumentation goals (Cysneiros et al., 2001), below it in the ISD goal hierarchy are fulfilled (Rolland, Souveyet, & Ben Achour, 1998). An *influence relationship* means that an ISD goal impacts the achievement of another ISD goal (Kavakli, & Loucopoulos, 1999; Loucopoulos et al. 1998,). The influence can be either positive or negative. The ISD goals with negative interrelationships are referred to as conflicting requirements (Chung et al., 2000, Lee, Xue, & Kuo, 2001). A *causalTo relationship* between two ISD problems means that the appearance of one ISD problem (e.g., lack of human resources) is at least a partial reason for the occurrence of another ISD problem (e.g., delays in the delivery of project outcomes).

ISD Actor Domain

The *ISD actor domain* consists of all those concepts and constructs that refer to the human and active part of the ISD context (Figure 3). Actors own, communicate, transform, design, interpret, and code objects in the ISD context. They are responsible for or responsive to triggering and causing changes in the states of objects. They are also aware of their own intentions and capable,

Figure 3. Meta model of the ISD actor domain

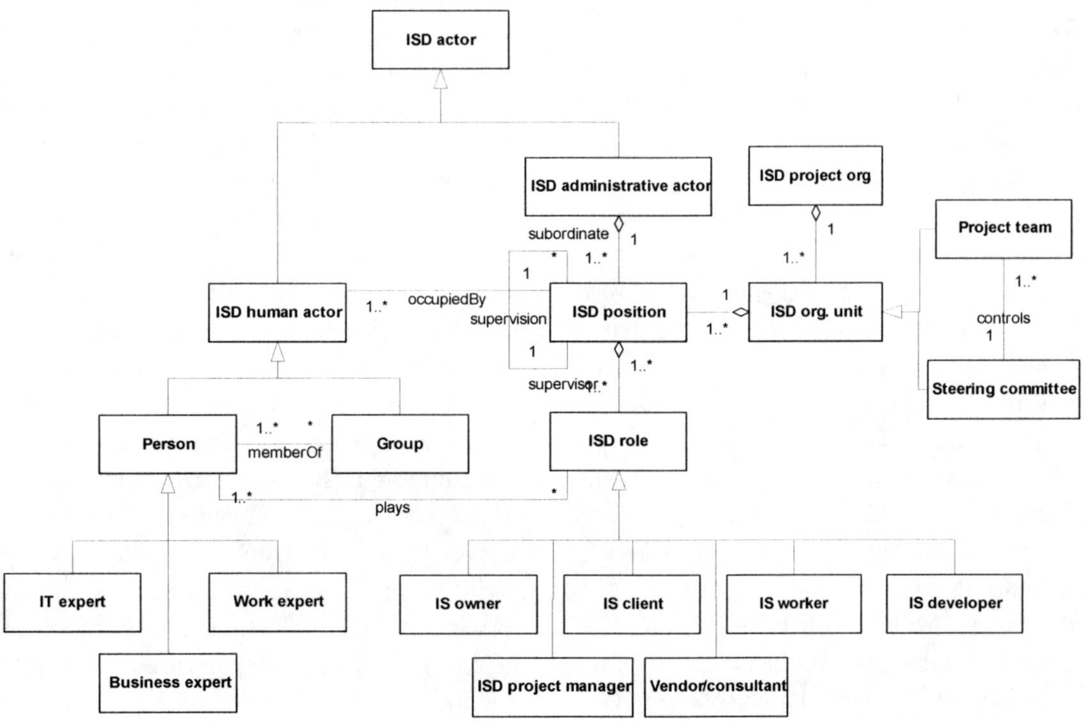

at least to some degree, of reacting to fulfill their goals.

An *ISD actor* is an ISD human actor or an ISD administrative actor who is, one way or another, involved in the ISD context. An *ISD human actor* means an individual person or a group of persons contributing to ISD work. An *ISD administrative actor* is an ISD position or a composition of ISD positions. An *ISD position* is a post of employment occupied by an ISD human actor in the ISD context (e.g., a database administrator). It is identified with a title, composed of the defined ISD roles, and equipped with a set of skill or capability characterizations (i.e., expertise profile). A capability denotes a skill or attribute of the personal behavior, according to which action-oriented behavior can be logically classified (Acuna & Juristo, 2004). An *ISD role* is a collection of ISD responsibilities and authorities, stipulated in terms of ISD actions (e.g., a member of a project team, a database expert). Some ISD roles may not be included in any ISD position but are nonetheless played by one or more persons.

In ISD literature, ISD roles are categorized in various ways, for instance, into social roles and technical roles (Constantine, 1991). Divisions among social ISD roles, in turn, have been derived from the views of seeing ISD as a problem solving process (a problem owner and a problem solver (Vessey & Conger, 1994)), as a change process (a facilitator or a change agent, and a change implementator (Rettig & Simons, 1993)), as a political process (self-interest agents employed to perform some services on behalf of the principals (Markus & Björn-Andersen, 1987; Robey, 1984)), or as a learning process (a mentor and a student or an apprentice). The divisions among technical ISD roles have resulted from applying, for instance, a stakeholder view (e.g., Macauley, 1993), a software business view (e.g., Franckson, 1994), or an organizational view.

In this work, we base our categorization of the ISD roles on the works of Checkland (1988), Baskerville (1989), Sabherwal and Robey (1995) and Mathiassen (1998). We distinguish between six major ISD roles that unify social and technical features of ISD work. The roles are: an IS owner, an IS client, an IS worker, an IS developer, an ISD project manager, and a vendor/consultant.

An *IS owner* has a financial interest in the IS and, thereby, the responsibility for and the authority of making decisions on the IS as though it were his/her property. An IS owner does not directly intervene in ISD project work, unless the project is so large and important that it has a major impact on the organization. An *IS client* is the ISD role player for whom the IS is to be developed. They are a beneficiary or a "victim" of the IS (Graham, Henderson-Sellers, & Younessi 1997). Therefore, they are expected to be active in specifying information requirements for the IS in terms of contents, form, time, and media. An IS client also acts as an informant for inquiries on business processes, and as an acceptor of the designs of ISD deliverables (cf. the so-called client tests) and plans of re-engineering business processes and work contents (cf. Brinkkemper, 1990). An *IS worker* works with the current IS and/or is going to work with the new IS. They collect, record, store, transmit, and processe data with or without the help of the computerized information system, in order to produce information needed by IS clients. An *IS developer* attempts to satisfy the needs and requirements put forward by ISD actors in the other roles. For that purpose, their analyses IS requirements and IS goals expressed and refines them into more elaborated specifications, searches for social and technical solutions, and implements those selected. An *ISD project manager* makes plans on how to organize the ISD effort. This includes making plans on ISD phases, schedules, milestones, base lines, resource allocations, and so forth. A *vendor/consultant* role is played by a person from outside the organization. With this role, more expertise on some specific organizational or technical issues is imported to the ISD project. Expertise may be related to technologies (e.g., J2EE platforms, Web services), methods (e.g., agile methods), techniques (e.g., TQM) or the like, that is something new to the organization.

The ISD work is mostly organized in the form of a project. An *ISD project* is a temporary effort with well-defined objectives and constraints, the established organization, a budget and a schedule, launched for the accomplishment of the ISD effort. An *ISD project organization* is a composition of ISD positions, ISD roles, and ISD teams, wherein the responsibility, authority, and communication relationships are defined (cf. Fife, 1987). A large project organization is composed of several *organizational units*. The most common units in the ISD project are a steering committee and a project team. A *steering committee* carries the responsibility for the overall management of the ISD project. A *project team* is collected for the execution of the ISD effort. If a project is large, there may be a need for several teams acknowledging their share in the common responsibility for developing the IS. The day-to-day management is delegated to the project manager, who directs and controls the actions of specialists in various disciplines.

Some of the positions and roles in the ISD project are full-time vacancies due to the amount of responsibilities and time they require. Some other positions and roles do not require full-time commitment. The most suitable person is sought for each ISD position. In order to be suitable, the person's skill and experience profile has to match with the expertise profile stated for the ISD position (cf. Acuna & Juristo, 2004). Sometimes, no person with the required qualifications can be found from inside the organization, and thus an expert (e.g., a consultant) from another organization is hired.

The persons involved in ISD can be categorized into IT experts, business experts, and work experts according to their expertise. *IT experts* are persons whose education, skills, experience, as well as their former positions, are related to information technology and/or ISD methods. *Business experts* are knowledgeable in business strategies, policies, markets, competition, trends, legislation, and so on, in other words, in matters relating to ways of doing business, in general or in the organization. *Work experts* master daily routines, for instance, in marketing, invoicing, production planning, and inventory control.

ISD Action Domain

The *ISD action domain* comprises all those concepts and constructs that refer to deeds in the ISD context (Figure 4). We use the general term *ISD action* to signify those deeds. ISD actions are carried out to manage and execute an ISD effort. By them, procedures, rules, and policies are selected, customized, incorporated, implemented, and applied to produce desirable ISD deliverables. To manage this extensive variety of ISD actions, several categorizations of ISD actions and ISD processes have been presented in the literature of the field (e.g., Curtis et al., 1992; Dowson, 1987). We recognize eight fundamental ISD action structures that are orthogonal to, and highly intertwined with, one another. They are categorized into two groups: generic action structures and ISD-specific action structures. The *generic action structures* include the decomposition structure, the control structure (i.e., sequence, selection, iteration), and the temporal structure (e.g., overlapping, parallel, disjoint). The *ISD-specific action structures* are the ISD management-execution structure, the ISD workflow structure, the ISD phase structure, and the IS modeling structure. The aforementioned ISD action structures provide a natural basis for specializing and decomposing ISD work into more specific ISD actions, if needed. Each ISD action is governed by one or more *ISD rules* with the ECAA structure (Herbst, 1995). In the following, we consider the ISD-specific action structures in more detail.

Figure 4. Meta model of the ISD action domain

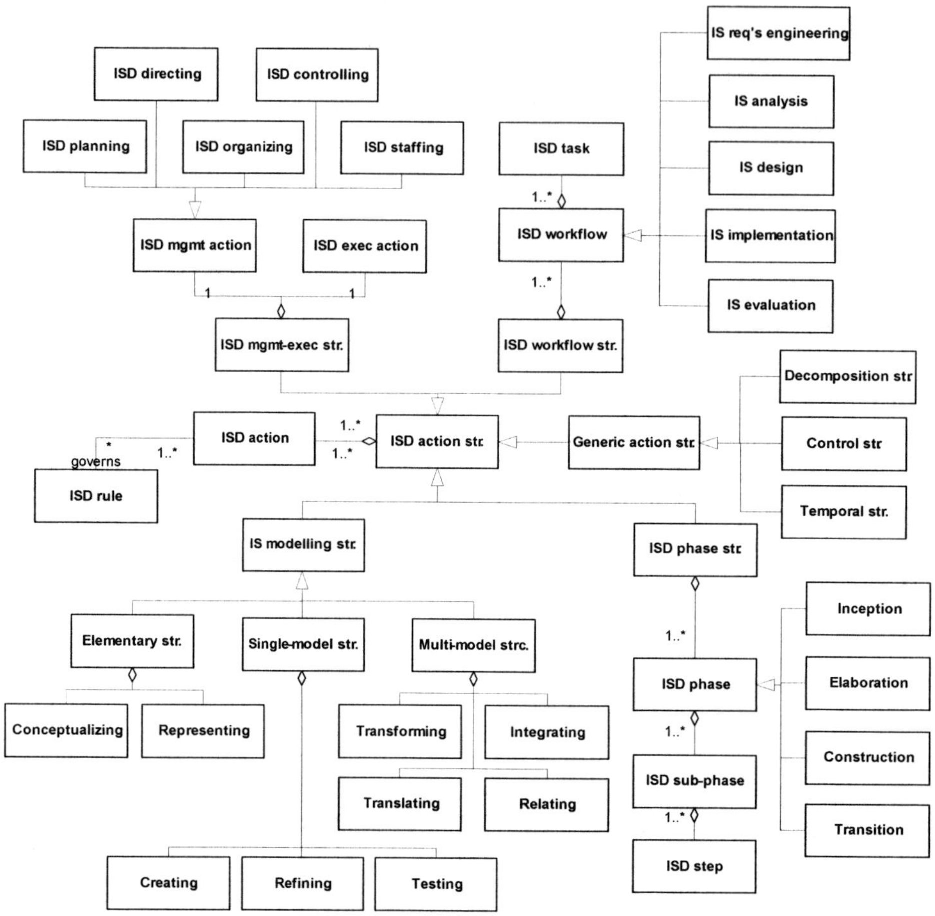

ISD Management-Execution Structure

An ISD can be seen as a functional and behavioral unity that is composed of two kinds of actions—ISD execution actions and ISD management actions. *ISD execution actions* aim to produce the required ISD deliverables under the guidance and control of ISD management. These actions include, for instance, knowledge acquisition about the current IS and problems encountered there, requirements specification for a new IS, and design and implementation of specifications into a working system. Besides the actions directly contributing to the deliverables, ISD execution actions comprise supporting actions, for instance, training and guidance of users, installation of computer-aided engineering environments, and so forth.

ISD management actions plan, organize, staff, direct, and control ISD work (Thayer, 1987). *ISD planning* refers to all those actions that specify the goals of an ISD project and the strategies, policies, programs, and procedures for achieving them. These actions involve partitioning managerial and technical requirements into measurable actions and tasks, determining milestones, priorities, and schedules, estimating necessary resources and figuring them as a budget. *ISD organizing* signifies all those actions that are needed to design an instance-level structure of ISD execution actions and authority relationships between them. These comprise aggregating actions into ISD roles and ISD positions, establishing organizational units, and specifying titles, duties, qualifications, and relationships of ISD positions. *ISD staffing* designates all those actions that are needed to fill the ISD positions and to keep them filled. These comprise, for instance, recruiting qualified people, orientating them into technical and social environment, and educating them in required methods, skills and equipment. *ISD directing* is needed for, among others, clarifying the assignments of ISD personnel, assigning actions to organizational units, teams and individuals, motivating and inspiring personnel, and resolving disagreements between personnel and between the ISD project and external stakeholders. *ISD controlling* aims to ensure that execution actions are carried out according to the plans. This includes developing standards of performance and methods for the assessments, establishing reporting and monitoring systems, measuring and auditing progress and status of a project and so on.

ISD Workflow Structure

ISD work is composed of various ISD workflows. An *ISD workflow* is a coherent composition of ISD actions, which are organized to accomplish some ISD process, share the same target of action, and produce valuable results for stakeholders. A part of an ISD workflow is called an *ISD task*. ISD workflows can be identified among the ISD management actions as well as among the ISD execution actions. In the following, we consider them in the context of the ISD execution actions. We distinguish between five core ISD workflows: IS requirements engineering, IS analysis, IS design, IS implementation, and IS evaluation (cf. Jacobson, Booch, & Rumbaugh, 1999). Besides the core workflows, there are supporting workflows, such as configuration and change management (cf. Kruchten, 2000), but these are not discussed here.

IS requirements engineering aims to identify and elicit IS clients' and IS workers' requirements for the IS, as well as to establish and maintain, at least to some extent, agreement on what the IS should do and why. IS requirements engineering is commonly decomposed into feasibility study, requirements analysis, requirements definition, and requirements specification (Sommerville, 1998). *IS analysis* means the ISD workflow which models the problem domain. The purpose is to represent the business system in a manner that is natural and concise enough, and to make an overall description of the information system that is easy to maintain. The workflow starts with looking at the system from outside. *IS design* means the ISD workflow that models the solution domain. It involves the elicitation, innovation, and evaluation of design options in the form of IS models on various levels of abstraction. IS design looks at the system from inside. A decision is also made on which part of the system will be automated and which part is to be implemented as a manual system. *IS implementation* fleshes out the architecture and the system as a whole by carrying IS models into effect. There are two kinds of implementation actions. Technical implementation, known as construction in Iivari (1991), involves all those actions that are necessary to construct/acquire and carry into effect technical components of the IS. Organizational implementation, referred to as institutionalisation in Iivari (1991), means actions that are necessary to create and change social norms, conventions, procedures and structures for information processing. *IS evaluation* aims at assessing the current system, as well as specifications, designs and implementations made for the new system. Evaluation is based on quality criteria derived from functional and non-functional requirements.

ISD Phase Structure

ISD work is commonly organized to be carried out in sequential phases. An *ISD phase* stands for a composition of ISD actions which are executed between two milestones, and by which a well-defined set of goals is met, ISD deliverables are completed, and decisions are made on whether or not to move into the next phase (cf. Kruchten, 2000). *Milestones* are synchronization points where ISD management makes important business decisions and ISD deliverables have to be at a certain level of completion (Heym & Österle, 1992). Major milestones are used to establish baselines (see the next section for the definition of a baseline).

A large variety of phases with different names are suggested in ISD methods. Without wanting to commit to any of them, we have selected, as an example of the ISD phase structure, the set of phases defined in Jacobson et al. (1999) and Kruchten (2000). It comprises four phases: IS inception, IS elaboration, IS construction, and IS transition. *IS inception* focuses on understanding overall requirements and determining the scope of the development endeavor. The scope is specified to understand what the architecture has to cover, what the critical risks are, and to determine the boundaries for costs and schedule. IS inception resolves the feasibility of the proposed system development. In *IS elaboration* the focus is on detailed requirements engineering, but some actions of systems design and implementation aimed at prototyping can also be carried out. Prototyping is deployed to better understand IS requirements, to test the established architecture and/or to learn how to use certain tools or techniques. The phase ends with the baseline for the next phase. *IS construction* focuses on design and implementation of the system. During this phase, a software product, which is ready for the initial operational release, is produced. Also, plans for organizational changes are "operationalized" for realization. *IS transition* is entered when at least some part of the ISD baseline is mature enough to be deployed. The phase comprises, for instance, beta testing, fixing bugs, adjusting features, conversion of operational databases, and training of users and maintainers. At the end of the phase, the final product has been delivered and the new organizational arrangements are fully in operation.

IS Modeling Structures

Modeling has a focal role in the full range of ISD actions. It is a necessary and frequently used means, equally utilized in the ISD management actions and in the ISD execution actions. Here, we focus on modeling in the latter, and refer to it as *IS modeling*. The target of IS modeling can be the existing IS, or the new IS. We refer to the structures of actions targeted at the IS models as the *IS modeling structures*. There are three kinds of IS modeling structures: the elementary modeling structure, the single-model action structure, and the multi-model action structure. The *elementary modeling structure* comprises actions that are always present in IS modeling. These are conceptualizing and representing. By *conceptualizing*, relevant perceptions of the existing reality and conceptions of the imagined reality are interpreted, abstracted, and structured according to some conceptual model (cf. Falkenberg et al., 1998). *Representing* is an ISD action through which conceptions are made "visible" and suitable for communication.

The *single-model action structure* comprises IS modeling actions that involve a single model at a time. These actions are creating, refining, and testing. *Creating* is an ISD action by which an IS model is conceptualized and represented for some specific use. After creation, some corrections, modifications, and extensions are often required. These IS modeling actions are called *refining* actions. *Testing* is an ISD action by which a model is verified and/or validated against the given quality criteria (cf. Krogstie, 1995). The *multi-model action structure* comprises IS modeling actions that involve, in some way or another, two or more IS models at the same time. These actions include transforming, translating, relating, and integrating. *Transforming* is an ISD action by which conceptions structured according to one IS model are transformed into conceptions structured according to another IS model. *Translating* is an ISD action through which conceptions represented in some language are translated into another language. Two or more IS models are *related*, or mapped, to one another by finding common concepts within the models, or by defining "bridging" relationships between the concepts of the models. *Integrating* means an ISD action by which a new model is crafted by assembling together concepts and constructs of two or more other IS models.

ISD Object Domain

The *ISD object domain* comprises all those concepts and constructs that refer to something to which ISD actions are directed (Figure 5). In the current ISD frameworks, these are commonly called deliverables (Cimitile & Visaggio, 1994; Glasson, 1989; Heym & Österle, 1992), artifacts (Hruby, 2000; Jacobson et al., 1999), decisions (Rose & Jarke, 1990; Wild, Maly, & Liu, 1991), products (Aoyama, 1993; Hazeyama & Komiya, 1993; Saeki et al., 1993), work products (Firesmith & Henderson-Sellers, 1999; Henderson-Sellers & Mellor, 1999; Hidding, 1997), and design products (Olle et al., 1988). To emphasize the linguistic nature of the ISD objects and our orientation to the ISD objects in the execution part of the ISD, we use the generic term *ISD deliverable.* An ISD deliverable can be, on the elementary level, an assertion, a prediction, a plan, a rule, or a command, concerning the ISD itself, the existing IS, the new IS, the object system (OS), or the utilizing system. We use the term '*OS_{ISD} construct*' to denote some part of the object systems of ISD. The *signifies relationship* expresses a semantic relationship between an ISD deliverable and an OS_{ISD} construct.

The *ISD management deliverables* mean plans for, decisions on, directives for, and assessments of goals, positions, actions, deliverables, locations, and so forth, in the ISD context. The *ISD execution deliverables* refer to descriptions about and prescriptions for why, what, and how information processing is carried out or is to be carried out in the current IS context or in a new IS context, respectively. The ISD execution deliverables comprise informal drafts and scenarios as well as more formal presentations. The former include instructions and guidelines, produced for IS actors, in the form of training materials, handbooks, and manuals. The latter are presented in *IS models* (e.g., ER schemes, DFDs, and program structure charts) or they are *IS implementations* of those models (e.g., software modules, prototypes, files, and databases).

Figure 5. Meta model of the ISD object domain

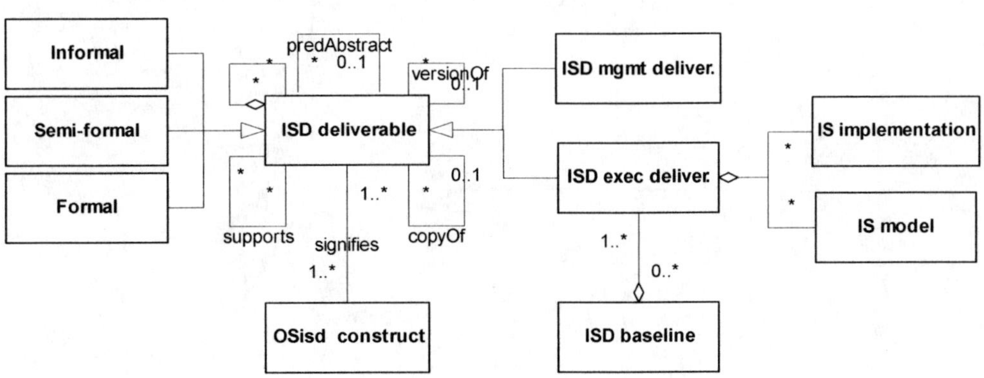

Some of the ISD execution deliverables are specified to be parts of the ISD baselines with milestones in the project plan. An *ISD baseline* is a set of reviewed and approved ISD deliverables that represents an agreed basis for further evolution and development, and can be changed only through a formal procedure such as configuration and change management (Jacobson et al., 1999). The ISD deliverables are presented in some language(s). Presentations may be informal, semi-formal, or formal, including texts, lists, matrices, program codes, diagrams, charts, maps, pictures, voices, and videos.

The ISD deliverables are related to one another through five kinds of relationships. An ISD deliverable can be a *part of* another ISD deliverable. An ISD deliverable can be used as input to, or as a prescription for, another ISD deliverable (e.g., the *supports relationship*). That is, an ER schema is a major input to a relational schema. An ISD deliverable can be the next *version of* or a *copy of* another ISD deliverable. Finally, an ISD deliverable may be more abstract than another ISD deliverable in terms of predicate abstraction (e.g., the *predAbstract relationship*).

ISD INTERDOMAIN RELATIONSHIPS

In the previous sections, the ISD concepts and constructs have been considered from the perspective of one ISD domain at a time. The ISD domains are, however, inter-related in many ways. Figure 6 presents, on a general level, the meta model, which illustrates essential *inter-domain relationships*. In the meta model, one or more main concepts from each of the ISD domains are depicted and related to concepts of the other domains. The multiplicities associated with the relationships are omitted to keep the model

Figure 6. Meta model of ISD inter-domain relationships

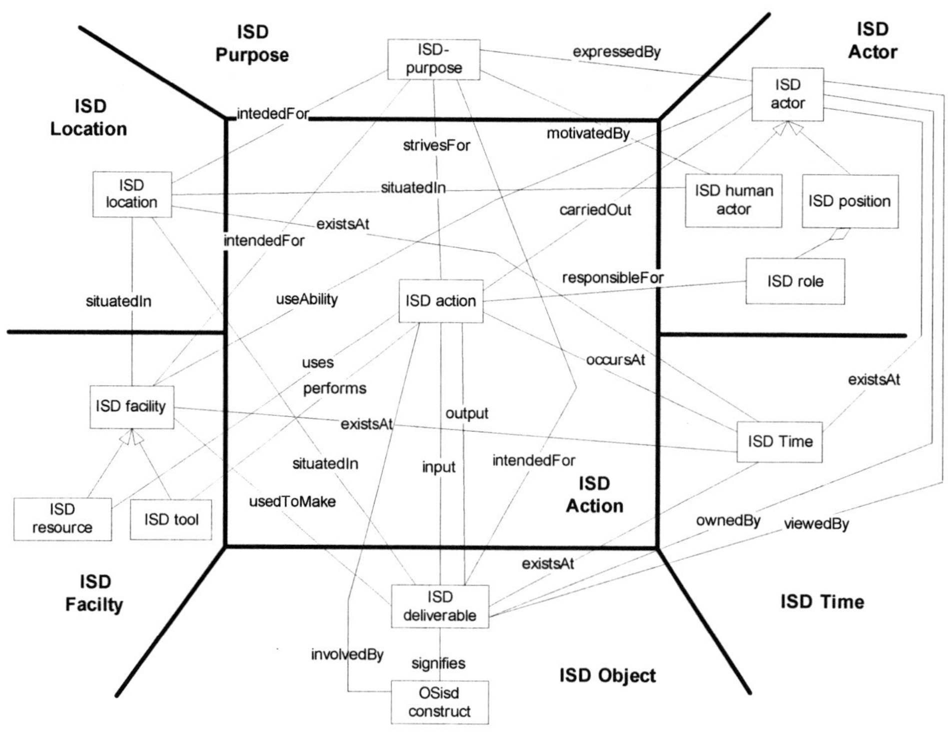

simple. It is not possible here to discuss all the inter-domain relationships. There are, however, two relationships, which are worth considering in more detail. These are the viewedBy relationship and the strivesFor relationship. Through these relationships, we can highlight the nature of ISD as an organizational context in which ISD actors have different views and opinions and ISD actions are guided by design rationale.

The *viewedBy relationship* between an ISD deliverable and an ISD actor means that an ISD deliverable represents views, insights, or opinions of a certain ISD actor. If associated with a person or a group of persons, an ISD deliverable represents a subjective or inter-subjective view whereas, if associated with an ISD position, an ISD deliverable reflects an organizational view or a so-called "official" view. According to Stamper (1992), there is no knowledge without an agent. With this relationship, an ISD deliverable can be tied to the person or organization concerned. Through this relationship, it is also possible to bring forth differences between, and conflicts among, the views. The significance of this relationship is acknowledged especially in requirements engineering literature. Lang and Duggan (2001) identify the "proposes" relationship between "Stakeholder" and "User requirement" in the meta model for RM-tool (requirements management tool). Lee et al. (2001) argue that the requirements should be incorporated into the stakeholders who have presented them. This is important because of traceability, conflict resolving, and prioritization. Nuseibeh, Finkelstein, and Kramer (1996) outline the ViewPoints framework, which acknowledges the existence of ISD actors "who hold multiple views on a system and its domain," (p. 267). The multiple views can be specified and managed by the use of the ViewPoint pattern (Finkelstein, Kramer, Nuseibeh, Finkelstein, & Goedicke, 1992) which is related to the ViewPoint owner. The owner acts as the domain knowledge provider.

The *strivesFor relationship* between an ISD action and an ISD purpose means that an ISD action is to be conducted, is conducted, or was conducted for satisfying a certain goal. The goal may be inferred from encountered problems, specified requirements, observed opportunities, or perceived threats. The strivesFor relationship, together with the input and output relationships between the ISD actions and the ISD deliverables, can be used to express design rationale (Goldkuhl, 1991; Ramesh & Jarke, 2001). Design rationale means a "record of reasons behind the decision taken, thus providing a kind of design/project memory and a common medium of communication among different people," (Louridas & Loucopoulos, 1996, p. 1). With this knowledge, it is possible to trace reasons for the decisions made and actions taken, which is especially beneficial in requirements engineering (e.g., Nguyen & Swatman, 2003; Pohl, Dömges, & Jarke, 1997).

COMPARATIVE ANALYSIS

The ISD literature suggests a large number of frameworks, meta models, and reference models, here called ISD artifacts, for ISD and ISD methods. In this section, we report on a comparative analysis of prominent ISD artifacts. By the analysis, we want first to find out what kinds of ISD artifacts exist, how comprehensive they are in terms of contextual features, and how they are focused on ISD domains. Second, we aim to test the usability of our ISD ontology as an analytical means for these kinds of exercises. In the following, we first categorize ISD artifacts and make the selection of artifacts for the analysis. Then, we give an overview of the selected ISD artifacts and describe the results from the overall analysis. Finally, we deepen the analysis through the four ISD domains of the ISD ontology.

Categorization and Selection of ISD Artifacts

ISD artifacts can be categorized into two main groups: those that describe and structure ISD, and those that have been developed to analyze, compare, and/or engineer ISD methods, or parts thereof. Artifacts in the first group characterize and structure ISD in terms of ISD paradigms (e.g., Hirschheim & Klein, 1989; Iivari, Hirschheim, & Klein, 1998), ISD approaches (e.g., Hirschheim, Klein, & Lyytinen, 1995; Iivari, Hirschheim & Klein, 2001; Wood-Harper & Fitzgerald, 1982), or ISD processes (e.g., Boehm, 1988; Iivari, 1990; NATURE Team, 1996). Most of the artifacts in this group have too narrow a scope or too general a view of ISD to be of interest to us. There are, however, some exceptions. For instance, Iivari (1990) presents the hierarchical spiral model, which provides an abstract explanatory model for IS/SW design process, containing strictly defined concepts and constructs in a large variety.

Another set of ISD artifacts, included in the first group, consists of meta models and ontologies for structuring specific aspects of ISD. For instance, NATURE Team (1996) proposes the process meta model, which views requirements engineering process as being composed of inter-linked contexts. OMG (2005) presents the Software Process Engineering Meta model (SPEM), which describes a concrete software development process or a family of related software development processes. Ontologies such as the Frisco framework (Falkenberg et al., 1998) and the Bunge-Wand-Weber model (e.g., Wand & Weber, 1990) cover elementary phenomena of the IS quite well, but they do not extend sufficiently to the ISD layer. There are also some ontologies that do concern systems engineering (Kishore, Zhang, & Ramesh, 2004; Kitchenham et al., 1999; Ruiz, Vizcaino, & Piattini, 2004), but their focus is on software maintenance and thus, they are too specific to serve as a generic and comprehensive basis for the conceptualization of ISD.

The ISD artifacts in the second group have been constructed for the analysis, comparison, and engineering of ISD methods. Some of them provide feature lists (e.g., Bodart et al., 1983; Karam & Casselman, 1993; Kelly, & Sherif, 1992; Maddison et al., 1984; Rzevski, 1983), taxonomies (e.g., Blum, 1994; Brandt, 1983), or frameworks (e.g., Iivari & Kerola, 1983; Jayaratna, 1994). Although these artifacts have been built with concepts referring to specific aspects of ISD, the concepts are not explicitly defined, nor are they properly structured. The same holds for contingency frameworks (e.g., Davis, 1982; Kettinger, Teng, & Guha, 1997; Lin & Ho, 1999; Punter & Lemmen, 1996; van Slooten & Brinkkemper, 1993; van Swede & van Vliet, 1993).

The second group also contains meta models that model notations and conceptual contents of ISD methods. Here, we are especially interested in those ISD artifacts that specify the conceptual contents of the ISD methods. These kinds of ISD artifacts are the "framework for understanding" of Olle et al. (1988), the framework and the reference model of Heym and Österle (1992), the meta model of Saeki et al. (1993), the framework of Song and Osterweil (1992), the framework of a situational method of Harmsen (1997), the views of ISD methods of Gupta and Prakash (2001), the conceptual model of the MMC (method for method configuration) Framework of Karlsson and Ågerfalk (2004), and the OPEN Process Framework (OPF) Meta model of Firesmith and Henderson-Sellers (2002).

We apply the following criteria in the selection of ISD artifacts for our analysis: (a) ISD artifacts describe, in a comprehensive and detailed manner, contextual phenomena of ISD, and (b) ISD artifacts are presented in an unambiguous and precise manner, preferably in a graphical notation. Based on these criteria, we decided to select the following seven ISD artifacts from the two groups (in alphabetical order): Firesmith and Henderson-Sellers (2002), Harmsen (1997), Heym and Österle (1992), Iivari (1990), NATURE Team (1996), Saeki et al. (1993), and Song and Osterweil (1992).

OVERALL ANALYSIS

Here, we first present a brief overview of the selected ISD artifacts and then analyze them in terms of five aspects: purpose of use, theoretical basis, ISD approach(es) applied, representation form, and acts for validation of the artifacts.

The OPEN Process Framework (OPF) meta model of Firesmith and Henderson-Sellers (2002) defines the core process concepts (e.g., Endeavor, Language, Producer, Stage, Work Product, and Work Unit) and their most important sub-concepts and associations, needed to specify a process component. Process components can be selected, combined, customized, and instantiated to form an actual process with the method. Harmsen (1997) proposes a framework, a language, and a procedure to assemble a situational method from building blocks, called method fragments. For defining the method fragments, Harmsen (1997) specifies an ontology and a process classification system. Heym and Österle (1992) present a framework and a reference model for describing, understanding, and comparing ISD methods. The framework categorizes the aspects of ISD methods into three perspectives: application type, life cycle, and model focus. In the reference model, the methodology knowledge is decomposed and structured by five meta models. Iivari (1990) presents the hierarchical spiral model for ISD and SE, based on the conceptual framework for IS/SW product (Iivari, 1989). The NATURE Project (NATURE Team, 1996; Grosz et al., 1997) suggests the process meta model based on the novel approaches to theories underlying requirements engineering (NATURE) approach, according to which requirements engineering is modeled as a set of related contexts in which a decision is made on how to process product parts and in which order. Saeki et al. (1993) present a meta model for representing software specification and design methods, with the purpose of covering "atomic concepts" that are common to all the methods. Song and Osterweil (1992) suggest the base framework for the identification of method components that are comparable in different methods. It is composed of two parts: the type framework and the function framework.

The summary of the overall analysis of the seven ISD artifacts is presented in Table 1. The table also includes the ISD ontology. As can be seen in the table, only two of the artifacts (e.g., Iivari, 1990; NATURE Team, 1996) have been established on some theoretical grounds. Most of the artifacts have been abstracted from existing ISD methods. For some artifacts, no grounds are mentioned. This situation is unsatisfactory for two reasons. First, only with a sound theoretical background can we be sure that phenomena of ISD become properly conceived, understood, and structured. Second, abstracting from existing methods in a way replicates properties of the methods and does not help recognize phenomena of ISD not addressed by the methods. We have built our ISD ontology by following the contextual approach, which has been established on several underlying theories, including semantics, pragmatics, and activity theory. In addition, we have utilized a large array of ISD literature on ISD theories and ISD methods.

In the ISD artifacts, divergent approaches are applied: a transformation approach (Iivari, 1990; Saeki et al., 1993; Song and Osterweil, 1992), a decision-oriented approach (Iivari, 1990; NATURE Team, 1996), and a learning approach (Iivari, 1990). Some of the artifacts give no preference for approaches. The ISD ontology is based on the contextual approach, thus enabling a comprehensive conceptualization of ISD. Most of the ISD artifacts have been validated by using them for intended purposes, for instance, for describing and/or integrating methods, and/or as a basis for prototypes of computer-aided method engineering (CAME) environments. The OPF meta model of Firesmith and Henderson-Sellers (2002) has been the most largely used. The ISD ontology has been used as a basis of a number of comparative analyses and in the construction

Table 1. Overview of the ISD artifacts

Reference	Artifact	Purpose	Theoretical basis	ISD approach	Representation	Validation
This study	ISD ontology	For understanding the ISD domain and for analyzing and constructing other ISD artifacts	Theories underlying the contextual approach, ISD theories, ISD methods	Contextual approach	Definitions in English, meta models in a graphical notation	Used as a framework in a number of comparative analyses and in the construction of methodical support for method engineering
Firesmith et al. (2002)	Process framework Meta model	For specifying process/method components	Not mentioned	Not recognizable	Definitions in English, the Meta model in a graphical notation	Used as a basis for the repository of more than 1000 open-source reusable process/ method components, and in a number of projects
Harmsen (1997)	Ontology (MDM), Process classification system	For assembling a situational method from method fragments	Literature on existing ISD methods	Not recognizable	Definitions in English, supported with the use of first order predicate calculus	Implemented as a prototype of the Method Base System that has been used in empirical studies
Heym and Österle (1992)	Framework, Reference model	For describing, understanding, and comparing ISD methods	Not mentioned	Not recognizable	Definitions in English, the reference model in a graphical notation	Used as the data model of the MERET tool, which has been deployed in several organizations
Iivari (1990)	Hierarchical spiral model	For providing an abstract explanatory model for the IS/SW design process	Socio-cybernetics, Information economics	Transformation, learning process, and decision-oriented approaches	Definitions in English	Not mentioned
NATURE Team (1996), Grosz et al. (1997)	Process meta model	For defining way-of-working in requirements engineering	Theory of plans	Decision-oriented approach	Definitions in English, partly in a graphical notation	Widely used in succeeding projects; Prototype
Saeki et al. (1993)	Meta model	For representing software specification and design methods	Not mentioned	Transformation approach	Definitions in English, partly in a graphical notation	Used to develop representations of ISD methods; Prototype
Song and Osterweil (1992)	Framework	For identifying method components	Abstracted from existing methods	Transformation approach	Definitions in English	Not mentioned

of methodical support for method engineering (Leppänen, 2005a). It still needs more acts for validation.

CONTEXTUAL ANALYSIS

For the second part of the analysis, called the contextual analysis, we categorized the concepts and constructs of the selected ISD artifacts to match them with the four ISD domains of the ISD ontology (see Appendix 1 for the categorization based on the ISD action domain). The following findings and conclusions can be made from the contextual analysis. Only two artifacts (Harmsen, 1997; NATURE Team, 1996) provide, even to some extent, concepts and constructs for the ISD purpose domain. This is unfortunate when taking into account that most of the artifacts have been constructed for describing, analyzing, and comparing the ISD methods. Concepts of the ISD purpose domain are important for presenting, for instance, motivations and design rationale (Ramesh and Jarke, 2001). Three of the artifacts (Firesmith and Henderson-Sellers, 2002; Harmsen, 1997; Heym and Österle, 1992) explicitly offer concepts and constructs for the ISD actor domain. Concepts of the ISD actor domain should be included in the ISD artifacts in order to bring out, for instance, who are responsible for ISD actions, and differences between viewpoints of ISD actors (Nuseibeh et al., 1996).

Emphasis in all the artifacts is on the ISD action domain, as expected when considering the ISD approaches they apply. From the ISD action structures, the ISD management-execution structure is included in Heym and Österle (1992) and, to some extent, in NATURE Team (1996). The ISD workflow structure can be recognized in Harmsen (1997) and Heym and Österle (1992). The ISD phase structure is included in Iivari (1990) and on a general level in Heym and Österle (1992). Parts of the IS modeling structures can be found in Heym and Österle (1992), Iivari (1990), NATURE Team (1996) and Song and Osterweil (1992). The control structures are embedded in every artifact, except in Song and Osterweil (1992). Firesmith and Henderson-Sellers (2002) define a number of sub-concepts, including phase and workflow, but do not suggest any specific action structures based on them. Only four artifacts (Harmsen, 1997; Heym and Österle, 1992; Iivari, 1990; Song and Osterweil, 1992) present categorizations of ISD deliverables grounded on some specific criteria (e.g., IS perspectives, IS domains). Firesmith and Henderson-Sellers (2002) present a large array of work product types, mostly technical ones, but without any explicit categorization.

From the seven artifacts, the ontology of Harmsen (1997) appeared to be the most comprehensive in terms of contextual aspects of ISD, although it has some shortcomings in the coverage of the ISD actor domain and the ISD action domain. The artifact can also be criticized for its incoherence and ill-structuredness. The second most comprehensive is the reference model of Heym and Österle (1992). Although it lacks the concepts of the ISD purpose domain, it provides basic concepts and constructs for the three other ISD domains. The OPF meta model by Firesmith and Henderson-Sellers (2002) also ignores the ISD purpose domain, but it defines some concepts and sub-concepts for the ISD actor domain, the ISD action domain and the ISD object domain. The hierarchical spiral model by Iivari (1990) mainly focuses on the ISD action domain. In addition, it defines some concepts for the ISD object domain. The process meta model by NATURE Team (1996) introduces the notion of intention for the ISD purpose domain, ignores the ISD actor domain, and provides a number of decision-based concepts for the ISD action domain as well as a few concepts for the ISD object domain. The meta model of Saeki et al. (1993) and the framework of Song and Osterweil (1992) were found to be insufficient in all the ISD domains, although they are aimed to provide a comprehensive basis for the description, analysis, and comparison of ISD methods. They address neither the ISD purpose domain, nor the ISD actor domain. Also, the other ISD domains are inadequately covered.

DISCUSSIONS AND IMPLICATIONS

In this chapter, we have presented a coherent and comprehensive conceptualization of ISD in the form of ISD ontology. The ISD ontology is based on the contextual approach grounded on fundamental theories with special interest in contextual phenomena (Engeström, 1987; Fillmore, 1968; Levinson, 1983). Implied from the contextual approach, ISD is seen as a context composed of concepts and constructs of seven contextual domains referring to purposes, actors, actions, objects, facilities, locations, and time. For four of these domains, we have defined a wide range of concepts and constructs and presented them in meta models.

The ISD ontology differs favorably from existing ISD artifacts as the comparative analysis in the previous section showed. The current artifacts mostly lack a theoretical background, and they have mainly been abstracted from existing ISD methods. They are also narrow-scoped as regards the contextual aspects of ISD. The ISD ontology provides a large array of concepts and constructs within four contextual domains, organized into a flexible and easy-to-adapt structure.

In the literature of ontology engineering (e.g. Burton-Jones et al., 2005; Gruber, 1993; Uschold, 1996), a large variety of quality criteria for ontologies are suggested. Most commonly, these criteria comprise clarity, consistency, coherence, comprehensiveness, extendibility, and applicability. It is not possible here to consider the quality of the ISD ontology in detail in terms of all of these criteria. We can, however, say that, through the application of the contextual approach, we have pursued achievement of a conceptualization of ISD that is natural and understandable (cf. face validity), thus advancing clarity. Semi-formal meta models have helped us evaluate consistency and coherency of our ontology. We have carefully checked that there are no contradictions between the definitions of concepts and constructs (consistency), and each concept is related, directly or indirectly, to every other concept (coherence). Comprehensiveness is relative to the needs for which the ontology is used. Extendibility has been furthered by the use of a modular structure of the ontology. Our aim has been that the ISD ontology can be extended with new and more specialized concepts without the revision of existing definitions.

The ultimate measure of the quality of an ontology is, naturally, its applicability. The ISD ontology has been intended for descriptive, analytical, and constructive use. In the previous sections, we deployed the ISD ontology to analyze and compare existing ISD artifacts. As far as we know, this kind of comparative analysis has not been made before. In this analytical task, the ISD ontology appeared to be a useful means to uncover the orientation, emphases, and limitations of the ISD artifacts as regards how they reflect contextual features of ISD. We have also deployed the ISD ontology as groundwork for engineering an ISD method ontology and a methodical skeleton for method engineering (MEMES) (Leppänen, 2005a). In this construction task, the ISD ontology offered a rich set of concepts and constructs for specifying and elaborating the semantic contents of an ISD method, and helped distinguish structure and relate approaches, actions, and deliverables for MEMES.

The ISD ontology is not without limitations. It should be enhanced with concepts and constructs of the ISD facility domain, the ISD location domain, and the ISD time domain. Second, many of the concepts included in the ontology should be further specialized to cover more specific phenomena of ISD. Third, the set of constraints expressed through multiplicities in the meta models should be supplemented with more ISD specific constraints. Fourth, to help the application of the ISD ontology in different kinds of situations, it is necessary to specify perspective-based sub-sets of the ISD ontology. For instance, to analyze and construct those parts of ISD methods that concern IS analysis, it is often sufficient to use only concepts and constructs in the ISD purpose domain, the ISD action domain, and the ISD object domain. These kinds of perspective-based sub-sets have already been outlined in Leppänen (2005a). Fifth, the ISD ontology should be employed in more kinds of situations to gain stronger evidence of its applicability. This is also necessary for validating the ontology.

In future research, our aim is, besides making the ISD ontology more complete, to apply it in the analysis of empirical ISD research and ISD approaches. For the former purpose, we have collected conceptual models underlying empirical studies on "how things are in ISD practice." These models are, typically, quite specific, which hinders building an integrated understanding of the results of the studies. The ISD ontology may serve as a coherent and comprehensive foundation to define, analyze, and integrate conceptual models, in the way an ontology for software maintenance (Kitchenham et al., 1999) is suggested to be used. For the latter purpose, we will examine ISD artifacts, applying specific ISD approaches more closely to find out how their commitments are visible in aggregates of concepts within each ISD domain and in inter-domain relationships.

REFERENCES

Acuna, S., & Juristo, N. (2004). Assigning people to roles in software projects. *Software—Practice and Experience*, *34*(7), 675-696.

Aoyama, M. (1993). Concurrent development process model. *IEEE Software*, *10*(4), 46-55.

Baskerville, R. (1989). Logical controls specification: An approach to information systems security. In H. Klein & K. Kumar (Eds.), *Proceedings of the IFIP Working Conference on Systems Development for Human Progress* (pp. 241-255). Amsterdam: Elsevier Science Publishers.

Blum, B. (1994). A taxonomy of software development methods. *Communications of the ACM*, *37*(11), 82-94.

Bodart, F., Flory, A., Leonard, M., Rochefeld, A., Rolland, C., & Tardieu, H. (1983). Evaluation of CRIS 1 I.S. development methods using a three cycles framework. In T. Olle, H. Sol, & C. Tully (Eds.), *Information systems design methodologies: A feature analysis* (pp. 191-206). Amsterdam: Elsevier Science Publishers.

Boehm, B. (1988). A spiral model of software development and enhancement. *IEEE Computer*, *21*(5), 61-72.

Brandt, I. (1983). A comparative study of information systems design methodologies. In T. Olle, H. Sol, & C. Tully (Eds.), *Information systems design methodologies—A feature analysis* (pp. 9-36). Amsterdam: Elsevier Science.

Brezillon, P., Pomerol, J.-Ch., & Saker I. (1998). Contextual and contextualized knowledge: An application in subway control. *International Journal of Human-Computer Studies*, *48*(3), 357-373.

Brinkkemper, S. (1990). *Formalization of information systems modeling*. Unpublished dissertation thesis, University of Nijmegen, Amsterdam.

Burton-Jones, A., Storey, V., Sugumaran, V., & Ahluwalia, P. (2005). A semiotic metric suite for assessing the quality of ontologies. *Data & Knowledge Engineering*, *55*(1), 84-102.

Chandrasekaran, B., Josephson, J., & Benjamins, R. (1999). What are ontologies, and why do we need them? *IEEE Intelligent Systems*, *14*(1), 20-26.

Checkland, P. (1988). Information systems and system thinking: Time to unite? *International Journal of Information Management*, *8*(4), 239-248.

Chung, L., Nixon, B., Yu, E., & Mylopoulos, J. (2000). *Non-functional requirements in software engineering.* Dordrecht: Kluwert.

Cimitile, A., & Visaggio, G. (1994). A formalism for structured planning of a software project. *International Journal of Software Engineering and Knowledge Engineering, 4*(2), 277-300.

Clark, H., & Carlson, T. (1981). Context for comprehension. In J. Long, & A. Baddeley (Eds.), *Attention and performance*, IX (pp. 313-330). Hillsdale, NJ: Erlbaum.

Constantine, L. (1991). Building structured open teams to work. In *Proceedings of Software Development '91.* San Francisco: Miller-Freeman.

Couger, D., Higgins, L., & McIntyre, S. (1993). (Un)structured creativity in information systems organizations. *MIS Quarterly, 17*(4), 375-397.

Curtis, B., & Kellner, M., & Over, J. (1992). Process modeling. *Comm. of the ACM, 35*(9), 75-90.

Cysneiros, L., Leite, J., & Neto, J. (2001). A framework for integrating non-functional requirements into conceptual models. *Requirements Eng.*, 6(2), 97-115.

Davis, G. (1982). Strategies for information requirements determination. *IBM Systems Journal, 21*(1), 4-30.

Dowson, M. (1987). Iteration in the software process. In *Proceedings of the 9th International Conference on Software Engineering* (pp. 36-39). New York: ACM Press.

Engeström, Y. (1987). *Learning by expanding: An activity theoretical approach to developmental research.* Helsinki: Orienta-Konsultit.

Engeström, Y. (1999). Activity theory and individual and social transformation. In Y. Engeström, R. Miettinen, & R. Punamäki (Eds.), *Perspectives on activity theory. Cambridge* (pp. 19-38). UK: Cambridge University Press.

Falkenberg, E., Hesse, W., Lindgreen, P., Nilsson, B., Oei, J., Rolland, C., Stamper, R., van Asche, F., Verrijn-Stuart, A., & Voss, K. (1998) Frameworkof information system concepts. *The Frisco Report* (*Web edition*), IFIP.

Falkenberg, E., Nijjsen, G., Adams, A., Bradley, L., Bugeia, P., Campbell, A., Carkeet, M., Lehman, G., & Shoesmith, A. (1983). Feature analysis of ACM/PCM, CIAM, ISAC and NIAM. In T. Olle, H. Sol, & C. Tully (Eds.), *Information systems design methodologies—A feature analysis* (pp. 169- 190). Amsterdam: Elsevier Science Publishers.

Fernandez-Lopez, M., Gomez-Perez, A., Pazos-Sierra, A., & Pazos-Sierra, J. (1999). Building a chemical ontology using METONTOLOGY and the ontology design environment. *IEEE Intelligent Systems & Theory Applications,* 4(1), 37-46.

Fife, D. (1987). How to know a well-organized software project when you find one. In R. Thayer (Ed.), *Tutorial: Software engineering project management* (pp. 268-276). Washington: IEEE Computer Society Press.

Fillmore, C. (1968). The case for case. In E. Bach, & R. T. Harms (Eds.), *Universals in linguistic theory* (pp. 1-88). New York: Holt, Rinehart, and Winston.

Finkelstein, A., Kramer, J., Nuseibeh, B., Finkelstein, L., & Goedicke, M. (1992). Viewpoints: A framework for integrating multiple perspectives in system development. *International Journal of Software Engineering and Knowledge Engineering, 1*(2), 31-58.

Firesmith, D., & Henderson-Sellers, B. (1999). Improvements to the OPEN process Meta model. *Journal of Object-Oriented Programming, 12*(7), 30-35.

Firesmith, D., & Henderson-Sellers, B. (2002). *The OPEN process framework. An introduction,* Harlow: Addison-Wesley.

Franckson, M. (1994). The Euromethod deliverable model and its contributions to the objectives of Euromethod. In A. Verrijn-Stuart & T. Olle (Eds.), *Methods and associated tools for the information systems life cycle* (pp. 131-150). Amsterdam: Elsevier Science Publishers.

Glasson, B. (1989). Model of system evolution. *Information and Software Technology,* 31(7), 351-356.

Goldkuhl, G. (1991). Information systems design as argumentation—An investigation into design rationale as a conceptualization of design. In K. Ivanov (Ed.), *Proceedings of the 14th Information Systems Research Seminar in Scandinavia (IRIS 1991),* Umeå, Sweden.

Goldkuhl, G., & Röstling, A. (1988). *Förändringsanalysi—arbetsmetodik och förhållningssätt för goda förändringsbelust.* Lund: Studentlitterature.

Graham, I., Henderson-Sellers, B. & Younessi, H. (1997). *The OPEN process specification.* Reading: Addison-Wesley.

Grosz, G., Rolland, C., Schwer, S., Souveyet, C., Plihon, V., Si-Said, S., Achour, C., & Gnaho, C. (1997). Modelling and engineering the requirements engineering process: An overview of the NATURE approach. *Requirements Engineering, 2*(2), 115-131.

Gruber, T. (1993). A translation approach to portable ontology specification. *Knowledge Acquisition, 5*(2), 119-220.

Gruber, T. (1995). Towards principles for the design of ontologies used for knowledge sharing. *International Journal of Human-Computer Studies, 43*(5/6), 907-928.

Gupta, D., & Prakash, N. (2001). Engineering methods from method requirements specifications. *Requirements Engineering, 6*(3), 135-160.

Halliday, M. (1978). *Language as social semiotic: The social interpretation of meaning.* London: Edwards Arnold.

Harmsen, F. (1997). *Situational method engineering.* Unpublished doctoral dissertation, University of Twente, Moret, Ernst, & Young Management Consultants, The Netherlands.

Hazeyama, A., & Komiya S. (1993). Software process management system supporting the cooperation between manager and developers. In S. Brinkkemper, & F. Harmsen (Eds.), *Proc. of the Fourth Workshop on the Next Generation of CASE Tools* (pp. 183-188). Memoranda Informatica 93-32, University of Twente, The Netherlands

Henderson-Sellers, B., & Mellor, S. (1999). Tailoring process-focused OO methods. *Journal of Object-Oriented Programming, 12*(4), 40-45.

Herbst, H. (1995). A meta model for business rules in systems analysis. In J. Iivari, K. Lyytinen, & M. Rossi (Eds.), *Advanced information systems engineering* (LNCS 932, pp. 186-199). Berlin: Springer.

Heym, M., & Österle, H. (1992). A reference model for information systems development. In K. Kendall, K. Lyytinen, & J. DeGross (Eds.), *Proceedings of the IFIP WG 8.2 Working Conference on the Impacts on Computer Supported Technologies on Information Systems Development* (pp. 215-240). Amsterdam: Elsevier Science Publishers.

Hidding, G. (1997). Reinventing methodology: Who reads it and why? *Comm. of the ACM, 40*(11), 102-109.

Hirschheim, R., & Klein, H. (1989). Four paradigms of information systems development. *Comm. of the ACM, 32*(10), 1199-1216.

Hirschheim, R., Klein, H., & Lyytinen, K. (1995). *Information systems development—Conceptual and philosophical foundations.* Cambridge: Cambridge University Press.

Hruby, P. (2000). Designing customizable methodologies. *Journal of Object-Oriented Programming, 13*(8), 22-31.

IEEE (1990). *Standard glossary of software engineering terminology.* IEEE Standard 610.12-1990.

Iivari, J. (1989). Levels of abstraction as a conceptual framework for an information system. In E. Falkenberg & P. Lindgren (Eds.), *Information system concepts: An in-depth analysis* (pp. 323-352). Amsterdam: Elsevier Science Publishers.

Iivari, J. (1990). Hierarchical spiral model for information system and software development. Part 2: Design process. *Information and Software Technology, 32*(7), 450-458.

Iivari, J. (1991). A paradigmatic analysis of contemporary schools of IS development. *European Journal of Information Systems, 1*(4), 249-272.

Iivari, J., Hirschheim, R., & Klein, H. (1998). A paradigmatic analysis of contrasting IS development approaches and methodologies. *Information Systems Research*, 9(2), 164-193.

Iivari, J., Hirschheim, R., & Klein, H. (2001). A dynamic framework for classifying information systems development methodologies and approaches. *Journal of Management Information Systems*, 17(3), 179-218.

Iivari, J., & Kerola, P. (1983). A sociocybernetic framework for the feature analysis of information systems design methodologies. In T. Olle, H. Sol, & C. Tully (Eds.), *Proceedings of the IFIP WG 8.1 Working Conference on Feature Analysis of Information Systems Development Methodologies* (pp. 87-139). Amsterdam: Elsevier Science Publishers.

Jacobson, I., Booch, G., & Rumbaugh, J. (1999). *The unified software development process.* Reading: Addison-Wesley.

Jarke, M., Jeusfeld, M., & Rose, T. (1990). A software process data model for knowledge engineering in information systems. *Information Systems, 15*(1), 85-116.

Jayaratna, N. (1994). *Understanding and evaluating methodologies: NIMSAD—A systemic framework.* London: McGraw-Hill.

Karam, G. & Casselman, R. (1993). A cataloging framework for software development methods. *IEEE Computer, 26*(2), 34-46.

Karlsson, F., & Ågerfalk, P. (2004). Method configuration: Adapting to situational characteristics while creating reusable assets. *Information and Software Technology, 46*(9), 619-633.

Kavakli, V., & Loucopoulos, P. (1999). Goal-driven business process analysis application in electricity deregulation. *Information Systems, 24*(3), 187-207.

Kelly, J., & Sherif, Y. (1992). Comparison of four design methods for real-time software development. *Information and Software Technology, 34*(2), 76-82.

Kettinger, W., Teng, J., & Guha S. (1997). Business process change: A study of methodologies, techniques, and tools. *MIS Quarterly, 21*(1), 55-80.

Kishore, R., Zhang, H., & Ramesh, R. (2004). A Helix-Spindel model for ontological engineering. *Comm. of the ACM, 47*(2), 69-75.

Kitchenham, B., Travassos, H., von Mayrhauser, A., Nielssink, F., Schneiderwind, N., Singer, J., Takada, S., Vehvilainen, R., & Yang, H. (1999). Towards an ontology of software maintenance. *Journal of Software Maintenance: Research and Practice, 11*(6), 365-389.

Krogstie, J. (1995). *Conceptual modeling for computerized information systems support in organizations.* Unpublished doctoral dissertation, University of Trondheim, Norway.

Krogstie, J., & Sölvberg, A. (1996). A classification of methodological frameworks for computerized information systems support in organizations. In B. Brinkkemper, K. Lyytinen, & R. Welke (Eds.), *Proceedings of the IFIP TC8 WG 8.1/8.2 Working Conference on Method Engineering: Principles of Method Construction and Tool Support* (pp. 278-295). London: Chapman & Hall.

Kruchten, P. (2000). *The rational unified process: An introduction*. Reading: Addison-Wesley.

Kyng, M., & Mathiassen, L. (Eds.). (1997). *Computers and design in context*. Cambridge, MA: MIT Press.

Lang, M., & Duggan, J. (2001). A tool to support collaborative software requirements management. *Requirements Engineering, 6*(3), 161-172.

Lee, J., Xue, N.-L., & Kuo, J.-Y. (2001). Structuring requirement specifications with goals. *Information and Software Technology, 43*(2), 121-135.

Leont'ev, A. (1978). *Activity, consciousness, and personality*. Englewood Cliffs, NJ: Prentice-Hall.

Leppänen, M. (2005a). *An ontological framework and a methodical skeleton for method engineering*. Unpublished doctoral dissertation, University of Jyväskylä, Finland.

Leppänen, M. (2005b). A context-based enterprise ontology. In G. Guizzardi & G. Wagner (Eds.), *Proceedings of the International Workshop on Vocabularies, Ontologies, and Rules for the Enterprise (VORTE'05)*, Enchede, The Netherlands (pp. 17-24).

Leppänen, M. (2005c). Conceptual analysis of current ME artifacts in terms of coverage: A contextual approach. In J. Ralyté, Per Ågerfalk, & N. Kraiem (Eds.), *Proceedings of the 1st International Workshop on Situational Requirements Engineering Processes (SREP'05)*, Paris (pp. 75-90).

Leppänen, M. (2006). Contextual method integration. In *Proceedings of the Conference on Information Systems Development (ISD 2006)*, Budapest, Hungary.

Levinson, S. (1983). *Pragmatics*. London: Cambridge University Press.

Lin, C.-Y., & Ho, C.-S. (1999). Generating domain-specific methodical knowledge for requirements analysis based on methodology ontology. *Information Sciences, 114*(1-4), 127-164.

Loucopoulos, P., Kavakli, V., Prekas, N., Rolland, C., Grosz, G., & Nurcan, S. (1998). *Using the EKD approach: The modelling component*. ELEKTRA—Project No. 22927, ESPRIT Programme 7.1.

Louridas, P., & Loucopoulos, P. (1996). A framework for evaluating design rationale methods. In K. Siau & Y. Wand (Eds.), *Proceedings of the Workshop on Evaluation of Modeling Methods in Systems Analysis and Design (EMMSAD'96)*.

Macauley, L. (1993). Requirements capture as a cooperative activity. In *Proceedings of the IEEE International Symposium on Requirements Engineering* (pp. 174-181). IEEE Computer Science Press.

Maddison, R., Baker, G., Bhabuta, L., Fitzgerald, G., Hindle, K., Song, J., Stokes, N., & Wood, J. (1984). Feature analysis of five information system methodologies. In T. Bemelmans (Ed.), *Beyond productivity: Information systems for organizational effectiveness* (pp.277-306). Amsterdam: Elsevier Science Publishers.

Markus, M., & Björn-Andersen, L. (1987). Power over users: Its exercise by system professionals. *Comm. of the ACM, 30*(6), 498-504.

Mathiassen, L. (1998). Reflective systems development. *Scandinavian Journal of Information Systems, 10*(1/2), 67-117.

Moynihan, T. (1993). Modelling the software process in terms of the system representations and transformation steps used. *Information and Software Technology, 35*(3), 181-188.

Mylopoulos, J., Chung, L., Liao, S., & Wang, H. (2001). Exploring alternatives during requirements analysis. *IEEE Software, 18*(1), 92-96.

NATURE Team (1996). Defining visions in context: Models, processes, and tools for requirements engineering. *Information Systems, 21*(6), 515-547.

Nguyen, L., & Swatman, P. (2003). Managing the requirements engineering process. *Requirements Engineering, 8*(1), 55-68.

Nuseibeh, B., Finkelstein, A., & Kramer, J. (1996). Method engineering for multi-perspective software development. *Information and Software Technology*, 38(4), 267-274.

Olle, T., Hagelstein, J., MacDonald, I., Rolland, C., Sol, H., van Assche, F., & Verrijn-Stuart, A. (1988). *Information systems methodologies—A framework for understanding* (2nd ed.). Reading: Addison-Wesley.

OMG. (2005). *Software process engineering Meta model specification* (Version 1.1). Object Management Group.

Pohl, K. (1993). The three dimensions of requirements engineering. In C. Rolland, F. Bodart, & C. Cauvet (Eds.), *Proc. of the 5th Int. Conf. on Advanced Info. Systems Engineering (CAiSE'93)* (LNCS 685, pp. 275-292). Berlin: Springer.

Pohl, K. (1994). The three dimensions of requirements engineering: A framework and its application. *Information Systems, 19*(3), 243-258.

Pohl, K., Dömges, R., & Jarke, M. (1997). Towards method-driven trace capture. In A. Olive & J. Pastor (Eds.), *Proceedings of the 9th International Conference on Advanced Information Systems Engineering (CAiSE'97)* (pp. 103-116). Berlin: Springer.

Punter, T., & Lemmen, K. (1996). The MEMA-model: Towards a new approach for methods engineering. *Journal of Information and Software Technology, 38*(4), 295-305.

Ramesh, B., & Jarke, M. (2001). Towards reference models for requirements traceability. *IEEE Trans. on Software Engineering, 27*(1), 58-93.

Rettig, M., & Simons, G. (1993). A project planning and development process for small teams. *Comm. of the ACM, 36*(10), 45-55.

Robey, D. (1984). Conflict models for implementation research. In R. Schultz (Ed.), *Management science implementation.* New York: American Elsevier.

Rolland, R., Souveyet, C., & Ben Achour, C. (1998). Guiding goal modeling using scenarios. *IEEE Trans. on Software Engineering, 24*(12), 1055-1071.

Rolland, C., Souveyet, C., & Moreno, M. (1995). An approach for defining ways-of-working. *Information Systems, 20*(4), 337-359.

Rose, T., & Jarke, M. (1990). A decision-based configuration process model. In *Proceedings of the 12th International Conference on Software Engineering* (pp. 316-325). Los Alamitos: IEEE Computer Society Press.

Ruiz, F., Vizcaino, A., Piattini, M., & Garcia, F. (2004). An ontology for the management of software maintenance projects. *International Journal of Software Engineering and Knowledge Engineering, 14*(3), 323-349.

Rzevski, G. (1983). On the comparison of design methodologies. In T. Olle, H. Sol, & C. Tully (Eds.), *Information systems design methodologies—A feature analysis* (pp. 259-266). Amsterdam: Elsevier Science Publishers.

Sabherwal, R., & Robey, D. (1993). An empirical taxonomy of implementation processes based on sequences of events in information system development. *Organization Science, 4*(4), 548-576.

Sabherwal, R., & Robey, D. (1995). Reconciling variance and process strategies for studying information system development. *Information Systems Research, 6*(4), 303-327

Saeki, M., Iguchi, K., Wen-yin, K., & Shinokara M. (1993). A meta model for representing software specification & design methods. In N. Prakash, C. Rolland, & B. Pernici (Eds.), *Proceedings of the IFIP WG8.1 Working Conference on Information Systems Development Process* (pp. 149-166). Amsterdam: Elsevier Science Publishers.

Short, K. (1991). Methodology integration: Evolution of information engineering. *Information and Software Technology, 33*(9), 720-732.

Slooten van, K., & Brinkkemper, S. (1993). A method engineering approach to information systems development. In N. Prakash, C. Rolland, & B. Pernici (Eds.), *Proceedings of the IFIP WG8.1 Working Conference on Information Systems Development Process* (pp. 167-188). Amsterdam: Elsevier Science Publishers.

Sol, H. (1992). Information systems development: A problem solving approach. In W. Cotterman & J. Senn (Eds.), *Challenges and strategies for research in systems development* (pp. 151-161). New York: John Wiley & Sons.

Sommerville, I. (1998). *Software engineering* (5th ed.). Reading: Addison-Wesley Longman.

Söderström, E., Andersson, B., Johannesson, P., Perjons, E., & Wangler, B. (2002). Towards a framework for comparing process modeling languages. In A. Banks Pidduck, J. Mylopoulos, C. Woo, & T. Ozsu (Eds.), *Proceedings of the 14th International Conference on Advanced Information Systems Engineering (CAiSE 2002)* (pp. 600-611). Berlin: Springer-Verlag.

Song, X., & Osterweil, L. (1992). Towards objective, systematic design-method comparison. *IEEE Software, 9*(3), 43-53.

Sowa, J. (2000). *Knowledge representation—Logical, philosophical, and computational foundations.* Pacific Grove, CA: Brooks/Cole.

Sowa, J., & Zachman J. (1992). Extending and formalizing the framework for information system architecture. *IBM Systems Journal, 31*(3), 590-616.

Staab, S., Schnurr, H.P., Studer, R., & Sure, Y. (2001). Knowledge processes and ontologies. *IEEE Intelligent Systems, 16*(1), 26-34.

Stamper, R. (1975). Information science for systems analysis. In E. Mumford & H. Sackman (Eds.), *Human choice and computers* (pp. 107-120). Amsterdam: Elsevier Science Publishers.

Stamper, R. (1992). Signs, organizations, norms and information systems. In *Proceedings of the 3rd Australian Conference on Information Systems* (pp. 21-65). Department of Business Systems, Univ. of Wollongong, Australia.

Swede van, V., & van Vliet, J. (1993). A flexible framework for contingent information systems modeling. *Information and Software Technology, 35*(9), 530-548.

Thayer, R. (1987). Software engineering project management—A top-down view. In R. Thayer (Ed.), *Tutorial: Software engineering project management* (pp. 15-56). IEEE Computer Society Press.

Uschold, M. (1996). Building ontologies: Towards a unified methodology. In *Proceedings of the 16th Annual Conference of the British Computer Society Specialist Group on Expert Systems*, Cambridge, UK.

Uschold, M., & King, M. (1995). Towards a methodology for building ontologies. In *Workshop on Basic Ontological Issues in Knowledge Sharing*, Montreal, Canada.

Vessey, I., & Conger, S. (1994). Requirements specification: Learning object, process, and data methodologies. *Comm. of the ACM, 37*(5), 102-113.

Wand, Y., & Weber, R. (1990). An ontological model of an information system. *IEEE Trans. on Software Engineering, 16*(11), 1282-1292.

Webster (1989). *Webster's encyclopedic unabridged dictionary of the English language.* New York: Gramercy Books.

Weick, K. E. (1995). *Sensemaking in organizations.* CA: Sage Publications.

Weinberger, H., Te'eni, D., & Frank, A. (2003). Ontologies of organizational memory as a basis for evaluation. In *Proceedings of the 11th European Conference of Information Systems*, Naples, Italy.

Wild, C., Maly, K., & Liu, L. (1991). Decision-based software development. *Software maintenance: Research and practice*, *3*(1), 17-43.

Wood-Harper, A., & Fitzgerald, G. (1982). A taxonomy of current approaches to systems analysis. *The Computer Journal*, 25(1), 12-16.

Zachman, J. (1987). A framework for information systems architecture. *IBM Systems Journal, 26*(3), 276-292.

Zultner, R. (1993). TQM for technical teams. *Comm. of the ACM*, *36*(10), 79-91.

APPENDIX

Table 2. Summary of the concepts and relationships of the ISD action domain in the ISD artifacts

References/ Concepts	ISD Ontology	Firesmith & Henderson-Sellers (2002)	Harmsen (1997)	Heym & Österle (1992)
Generic concept	ISD action	Work unit	Process fragment	Process
Sub-concepts	ISD workflow, ISD phase, ISD process	Activity, Task, Stage, Workflow, Phase	Process role, Basic action	Phase, Activity
ISD management-execution structure	Mgmt action: ISD planning, ISD organizing, ISD staffing, ISD directing, ISD controlling; Execution action			Decision, Planning, Control
ISD workflow structure	ISD worflow: IS req's engineering, IS analysis, IS design, IS implementation, IS evaluation	Workflow	Action type: Planning, Analysis, Synthesis, Evaluation, Implementation, Evolution	ISD stage: Analysis, Design, Construction design, Construction, Test and installation, Maintenance
ISD phase structure	ISD phase: Inception, Elaboration, Construction, Transition	Phase		Phase
IS modeling structure	Conceptualizing, Representing, Creating, Refining, Testing, Transforming, Translating, Integrating, Relating			Abstraction, Checking, Review, Form conversion
Control structures	sequence, selection, iteration	sequence iteration	precedence, choice	sequence, refinement jump, branching path, unifying path, iteration
Abstraction structures	partOf, isA, memberOf, instanceOf		contents	aggregation

continued on following page

Table 2. continued

References/ Concepts	Iivari (1990)	NATURE Team (1996)	Saeki et al. (1993)	Song & Osterweil (1992)
Generic concept	Design act	Action	Procedure	Action
Sub-concepts	Main phase, Subphase, Design act			Step
ISD management-execution structure		Plan Execution		
ISD workflow structure				
ISD phase structure	Phase structure: Org. design, Conceptual/ infological design, Data-logical/technical design, Implementation			
IS modeling structure	Diagnosis/ Design, Verification/Validation, Observation/Analysis, Manipulation/Refinement	Transformation		Create, Modify
Control structures	iteration	precedence, alternative	precede	
Abstraction structures	component of		has	part of, is a

Chapter XXI
Personalization Issues for Science Museum Web Sites and E-Learning

Silvia Filippini-Fantoni
The University of Paris I Sorbonne University, France

Jonathan P. Bowen
London South Bank University, UK

Teresa Numerico
London South Bank University, UK

ABSTRACT

E-learning has the potential to be a very personalized experience and can be tailored to the individual involved. So far, science museums have yet to tap into this potential to any great extent, partly due to the relative newness of the technology involved and partly due to the expense. This chapter covers some of the speculative efforts that may improve the situation for the future, including the SAGRES project and the Ingenious Web site, among other examples. It is hoped that this will be helpful to science museums and centers that are considering the addition of personalization features to their own Web site. Currently, Web site personalization should be used with caution, but larger organizations should be considering the potential if they have not already started to do so.

BACKGROUND

In the past few years, the number of people visiting museums' Web sites has gone up rapidly. As a consequence, museums have to face the significant challenge of creating virtual environments that are progressively more adapted towards the different needs, interests and expectations of their heterogeneous users. Increasingly, museums and science centers are using their Web sites to augment their learning facilities in potentially innovative ways (Tan et al., 2003). In particular, museums need to provide for differing online requirements such as teaching, e-learning and research (Hamma, 2004). One of the solutions available to help is the introduction of personalization techniques (Dolog & Sintek, 2004) that, by providing differentiated access to information and services according to the user's profile, make facilities and applications more relevant and useful for individual users, thus improving the overall visitor's experience. Science museums, by their very technological nature, ought to be at the vanguard of applying new techniques like personalization.

Developed in the early 1990s in an attempt to try to respond to the different needs and characteristics of an ever-growing number of Internet users, personalized or adaptive Web systems have since been exploited in different sectors such as commerce, tourism, education, finance, culture and health. What distinguishes these systems from the traditional static Web is the creation of a user model that represents the characteristics of the user, utilizing them in the creation of content and presentations adapted to different individuals (Brusilovsky & Maybury, 2002). By so doing, personalization becomes a useful tool in the selection and filtering of information for the user, facilitating navigation and increasing the speed of access as well as the likelihood that the user's search is successful.

The techniques available to collect information about users, as well as the methods used to process such information to create user profiles and to provide adapted information, are varied. A brief description of the different approaches will be presented here before moving on to illustrate different application examples within the science museum world.

PERSONALIZATION TECHNIQUES

A first important distinction concerning the amount of control the user has on the adaptation process can be made between customization and personalization. *Customization* or *adaptability* occurs when "the user can configure an interface and create a profile manually, adding and removing elements in the profile" (Bonnet, 2002). The control of the look and/or content of the site are explicit and user-driven; that is, the user is involved actively in the process and has direct control. In *personalization* or *adaptivity*, on the other hand, the user is seen as being passive, or at least somewhat less in control (Bonnet, 2002). Modifications concerning the content or even the structure of a Web site are performed automatically by the system based on information concerning the user stored in the so-called *user profile*. Such information about the user is provided either *explicitly*, by the user themselves, using online registration forms, questionnaires and reviewing (static profiles) or *implicitly* by recording the navigational behavior and/or preferences of each user through dynamic profiling Web technologies such as *cookies*[1] and *Web server log files*[2] (Eirinaki & Vazirgiannis, 2003).

Once the data concerning the users is collected either implicitly or explicitly, or even in both ways, as is often the case, appropriate information that matches the users' need is determined and delivered. This process usually follows one or more of the following techniques: content-based filtering, collaborative filtering, rule-based filtering and Web usage mining.

Content-based systems track user behavior and preferences, recommending items that are similar to those that users liked in the past (Eirinaki & Vazirgiannis, 2003). *Collaborative filtering* compares a user's tastes with those of others in order to develop a picture of like-minded people. The choice of material is then based on the assumption that this particular user will value information that like-minded people also enjoyed (Bonnet, 2002). The user's tastes are either inferred from their previous actions or else measured directly by asking the user to rate products. Another common technique is *rule-based filtering*, which allows Web site administrators to specify rules based on static or dynamic profiles that are then used to affect the information served to a particular user (Mobascher et al., 2000).

Last but not least, there is *Web usage mining*, which relies on the application of statistical and data-mining methods based on the Web server log data, resulting in a set of useful patterns that indicate users' navigational behaviors. The patterns discovered are then used to provide personalized information to users based on their navigational activity (Eirinaki & Vazirgiannis, 2003).

The information provided to the user through any of the above techniques can be adapted at three different levels: content, navigation and presentation (Brusilowsky & Nejdl, 2004). Adaptive content selection is based mostly on adaptive information retrieval techniques: "when the user searches for relevant information the system can adaptively select and prioritize the most relevant items" (Brusilowsky & Nejdl, 2004). By doing so, the user can obtain results that are more suitable for their knowledge capabilities. Adaptive navigation support is founded mainly on browsing-based access to information: "when the user navigates from one item to the other the system can manipulate the links to guide the user adaptively to most relevant information items" (Brusilowsky & Nejdl, 2004).

Finally, adaptive presentation is based on *adaptive explanation* and *adaptive presence,* which were largely developed in the context of intelligent systems: "when the user gets to a particular page the system can present its content adaptively" (Brusilowsky & Nejdl, 2004). The possibilities of content and presentation adaptability are a relevant element in the reuse of the same resources for different purpose, provided they have been correctly customized in advance. Considering the high cost of personalization, adaptability of resources can also offer an interesting byproduct in term of reuse of the same resources in different contexts, provided that their description is correctly defined through standard metadata applications to allow interoperability of the same service in different environments.

From the perspective of different platform services, adaptability becomes a strategic issue. It could be decided to personalize content for the relatively small screen of mobile devices, for example. Moreover, whereas personalization and adaptability on the Web is based only on the user, in the case of mobile support there is also the need for adaptation with regard to the user's environment (Brusilowsky & Nejdl, 2004).

In a museum visit, taking into account the environment where the service will be used can make a notable difference to the experience. For example, an explanation of the items kept in a single room of the exhibition can be offered while the visitor is in that room. There are some projects exploring these opportunities with special regard to mobile devices used by museum learning services (Oppermann & Specht, 1999).

WHY USE PERSONALIZATION IN MUSEUMS?

Even if some of the techniques described in the previous section, especially the more sophisticated ones, are employed mainly on commercial Web sites, such as Amazon.com, etc., there is already some awareness of the need for their use in cultural institutions, museums, science centers, etc. Personalized access to collections, alerts, agendas, tour proposals and audio guides are just a few examples of the different applications that have recently been developed by museums all over the world (Bowen & Filippini-Fantoni, 2004). The reasons for such an affirmation are numerous, as personalization can help museums respond to various and different needs.

First of all, personalization has the advantage of improving the *usability* of a Web site by facilitating its navigation and aiding people in finding the desired information. With some knowledge about the user, the system can give specific guidance in its navigation, limiting the visitation space appropriately. The system can supply, or even just suggest, the most important links or content that could be relevant for the user, something that can help prevent them from becoming lost in a Web site's potentially intricate hyperspace.

Accessibility for the disabled (Bowen, 2004), a specific aspect of usability that concentrates in widening the number of users, can gain from personalization techniques. The ability to select the text foreground or background color, size and font, can make interfaces more easily readable for the partially sighted. A text only view of a Web site may be easier for such users and also those who are completely blind. For example, the London Science Museum has an option from the home page for a text only version of the Web site (www.sciencemuseum.org.uk). The basic content is the same, but the presentation is different. Legislation in the UK, for example, now ensures that learning materials for students in educational establishments, including those provided by university science museums, must be covered by an accessibility strategy (HMSO, 2001).

Personalized systems help to recreate the *human element* that listens to the visitor with understanding by offering an individual touch; this is another important factor that contributes to the success of Web personalization in museums. It is a particularly important element, especially for audio guides, which must offer a certain level of flexibility in order to adapt the contents to the needs and interests of the users, just like a real museum guide would do. It also helps online, making the visitors feel comfortable and oriented in the virtual space, through virtual avatars for example. Studies indicate that the "social metaphor represented through the presence of personalized animated characters (similar to real life people) can reduce anxiety associated with the use of computers" (Bertoletti et al., 2001).

Personalization could also be a useful tool in the creation and development of *online communities* for museums (Beler et al., 2004). In fact, thanks to personalized applications such as alerts, thematic newsletters, customizable calendars and recommendation systems[3] providing tailored content to people with specific interests, museums can identify homogeneous communities of users with the same concerns and needs. Once these different online communities have been identified, it is in the museum's interest to foster them by developing tools and services that aid them in their functioning, especially by stimulating communication. This is when personalization can assist once again. In particular, online forums (Bowen et al., 2003) can benefit from the introduction of personalizing features such as notification of debates or issues that might be of interest to the user, information about other users with interests on specified topics (facilitating the networking between community users), personalized news generation based on personal interests, etc. These kinds of personalized services can increase the value of the underlying museum's "e-community" beyond a social networking environment: "the website becomes an attractive permanent home base for the individual rather than a detached place to go online to socialize or network, thus strengthening the relation between the user and the institution" (Case et al., 2003).

By providing targeted information to users with different profiles and interests, personalized systems are much more likely to satisfy the visitor, who, as a consequence, is stimulated to come back and reuse the system or to encourage other people to try it as well. This is why personalization is also a fundamental *marketing* tool for the development of visitor fidelity, as well as new audiences.

Personalization and Learning

Besides helping museums to respond to their usability, marketing and accessibility needs, personalization has much potential when it comes to stimulating learning, as underlined by Brusilovsky (1994) who, early in the development of the Web, pointed out how personalization techniques could be an important form of support in education. The reasons for this are varied. First of all, visitor studies seem to confirm that learning is encouraged when the information provided is described in terms that the visitor can understand. Using different terms and concepts, that take into consideration the level of knowledge, age, education of the user, etc., can therefore improve the overall didactic experience. This is precisely what happens with personalized applications where the information delivered to the visitors often changes according to whether they are a child, an adult, a neophyte or an expert.

Research also indicates that learning is facilitated when the information provided makes reference to visitors' "previous knowledge"; that is to say, to what people already know or to concepts already encountered during navigation or exploration (Falk & Dierking, 1992). This suggests that museums should focus on how to activate visitors' prior knowledge if possible. One of the means at their disposal is personalization, which could open new and effective means for long-term learning by providing adaptive descriptions of artifacts based on objects or concepts that the visitor has already visited or explored. This is, for example, the case in projects like ILEX, Hyperaudio, HIPS and the Marble Museum's Virtual Guide — see Filippini-Fantoni (2003) for descriptions — that, through dynamically generated text, provide personalized information taking into consideration the user's history. The description of the object being viewed or selected can make use of comparisons and contrasts to previously viewed objects or concepts. By providing such coherent and contextualized information, modeled on the user interaction with the exhibition space as well as with the system itself, such applications have enormous potential from the learning point of view.

Another mechanism that can be used to justify the use of personalization to stimulate learning is "subsequent experience" (Falk & Dierking, 1992). A number of researchers have hypothesized that repetition is the major mechanism for retaining memories over a long period of time (Brown & Kulick, 1997). This is why, by allowing the visitor to bookmark objects or concepts of interest during their navigation in the virtual or real environment and to explore them more in detail subsequently (see later for further information), personalization can make it possible to further deepen and continue the learning process from home by creating continuity between the visit and post-visit experiences.

Last but not least, learning is stimulated when a person can pursue their individual interests. Researchers distinguish between "situational interest" and "individual interest," the first being defined as "the stimulus that occurs when one encounters tasks or environments with a certain degree of uncertainty, challenge or novelty" (Csikszentmihalyi & Hermanson, 1995). This is, for example, the case for museums where the presence of incentives like surprise, complexity and ambiguity lead to motivational states that result in curiosity and exploratory behavior (Csikszentmihalyi & Hermanson, 1995).

However this is not enough to guarantee that the visitor is actually stimulated to learn. In order for this to happen, museums have to attempt to respond to their visitors' "individual interests," that is "their preference for certain topics, subject areas or activities" (Hidi, 1990), as the pursuit of individual interests is usually associated with increased knowledge, positive emotions and the intrinsic desire to learn more. Personalizing an educational activity in terms of themes, objects or characters of high prior interest to students should therefore enhance the overall learning experience. Take, for example, those personalized applications (see later for details) that provide tailor-made visitor plans with consideration of the individual interests of a single visitor or a group of visitors. By suggesting artifacts relating to the visitor's individual curiosity, the visit is more likely to result in fruitful learning activity.

In conclusion, by providing information at the right level of detail, stimulating subsequent experiences and taking into consideration individual interests as well as prior knowledge, personalization represents an excellent tool for all those educators wishing to stimulate and facilitate learning. This is why personalization techniques are often exploited in the creation of *formal* e-learning applications such as long-distance courses that are able to adapt to the student's level of knowledge, cognitive preferences and interests, etc. For example, see the AHA Project on *Adaptive Hypermedia for All* [aha.win.tue.nl] at the Technical University of Eindhoven, The Netherlands, and the European IST ELENA Project on *Enhanced Learning for Evolutive Neural Architectures* [www.elena-project.org].

However, personalization can be also applied to more *informal* e-learning solutions like the ones that are often available on museums' Web sites or interactive devices, which, although not being actual lessons, represent very useful educational experiences that contribute to increasing the visitor's knowledge and understanding about a specific issue.[4]

WEB PERSONALIZATION FOR SCIENCE MUSEUMS

Until now, we have discussed more general issues concerning the use of personalization techniques in museums, focusing in particular on its potential to stimulate and facilitate the learning experience. In this section we consider some examples of how science museums in particular are applying these principles online. In fact, even if science museums are not the only cultural institutions to have experimented with personalization both online and on-site in the past few years — for a more general description of personalized applications in museums see Bowen and Filippini-Fantoni (2004) — they are among the ones that have expressed the strongest interest in these techniques. This is because science museums and science centers, whose exhibits are designed to promote playful exploration and discovery of scientific phenomena, have always been relatively aggressive adopters of information technology and innovative approaches; as a consequence, they have also been more eager to experiment with personalization.

Some museums have been focusing more on the usability and marketing aspects of personalization privileging applications such as personalized agendas, alerts and newsletters, which, although having an intrinsic pedagogical value, seem to focus more on promotion. However, science museums have been among the first to understand the real value of personalization as a learning tool, concentrating particularly on stimulating "subsequent experience," "previous knowledge," and "individual interest" in such a way as to explicitly encourage the continuity between the pre-visit, visit and post-visit experiences.

The first examples of Web personalization in a museum context were developed in the late 1990s in strict relation with the affirmation of academic research on adaptive hypermedia. Among them (Bowen & Filippini-Fantoni, 2004) was the SAGRES system (sagres.mct.purcs.br), developed in 1999 by the Museum of Sciences and Technology of PUCRS (MCT), Porto Alegre, Brazil.

The SAGRES system (Bertoletti, 1999; Moraes, 1999) is an educational environment that presents the museum's content adapted to the user's characteristics (capacities and preferences). Based on information provided directly

Figure 1. The architecture of the SAGRES system

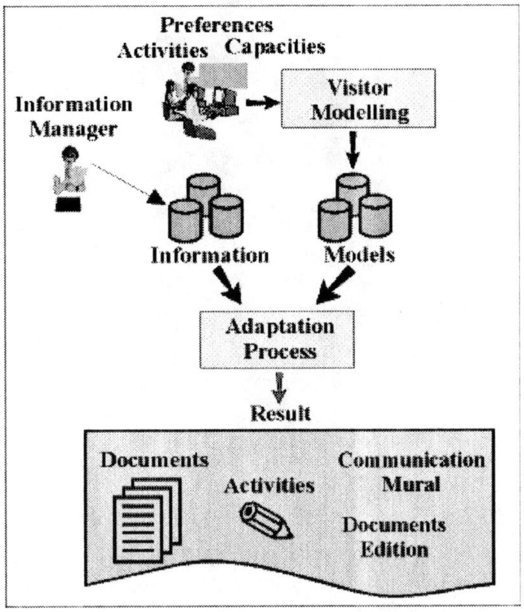

by the user or by the teacher (for students), the system determines the group of links appropriate to the user(s) and presents them in a personalized Web page.

The principle behind the project was an attempt to overcome the limitations implicit in the one fits all approach and to take the user's individual interests as well as their level of knowledge into consideration when delivering information, with the aim of improving the overall learning experience. This is possible through an adaptation process that first generates a user model, based on information provided by the user[5]. Once these data about the user have been collected, the adaptation process can select different types of documents conforming to the visitor's model. This results in a dynamically generated HTML page with links pointing to personalized information: the page is created dynamically during the interaction of the user with the system and presents links to the documents, as well as connections to the communication mural (where users can interact with each other), to the document edition, and to the activities the user should perform (in the case of a group visit).

As well as being designed for individual users, the system is particularly meant for use in an educational setting. Through SAGRES, teachers are given the opportunity to define and register their students' profiles, to accompany them and to evaluate their performance during the visit, using reports delivered by the system. At the same time, students are allowed to interchange ideas with colleagues in their groups and to work on the activities and subjects determined by the teacher.

PERSONALIZED VIRTUAL WEB SPACES

The main aim of the SAGRES project was to facilitate learning through the provision of information adapted to the level of knowledge and interest of the user. Since then, other methods have been adopted to guarantee a similar outcome. Various science museums, for example, provide users with tools that allow them to save images, articles, links, search results, forum discussion topics, as well as other types of information during navigation of the Web site. By doing so, the user creates a personal environment within the museum's Web site, where they can return, find specific information of interest, and to which new items can be continuously added. This environment can be further equipped with other personalized services such as individual agendas or the ability to send personal e-cards.

Once the page has been created, visitors can log in every time they access the Web site to find all the information they need. By doing so, the user has the chance not only to find information of interest more easily, but also and especially to strengthen the learning process through reuse and repetition. The learning value of these applications for certain categories of users such as students

Figure 2. Ingenious home page

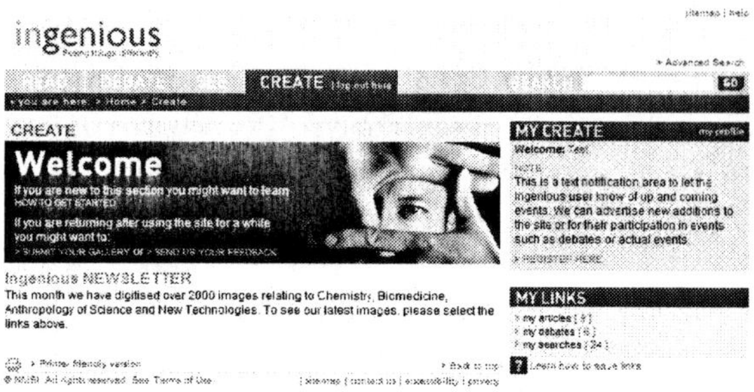

Figure 3. Ingenious electronic cards

Figure 4. Ingenious selected hyperlinks

Figure 5. Ingenious saved images

Figure 6. Ingenious Web galleries

and teachers is even greater. The personal space can offer teachers the possibility of suggesting of exhibits for their students to visit and questions that they would like the students to answer during the exploration. In response, the students can save links to the exhibits that most interest them, as well as making short notes both about questions they had at the beginning and about new questions that arise during the exploration.

One of the most interesting examples of this type of application is provided by the *Ingenious* project, undertaken by the *National Museum of Science and Industry* group in the United Kingdom and funded by the UK New Opportunities Fund (NOF) (www.nmsi.ac.uk/nmsipages/nofdigitise.asp). This project, online from mid-2004, aims at creating a learning environment for the public from the digitized collections of the Science Museum (London), the National Railway Museum (York) and the National Museum of Photography, Film and Television (Bradford) in the UK. Users of the Ingenious Web site (www.ingenious.org.uk) can explore and discover the rich collections of these museums through 50 narrative topics and over 30,000 images and other content-rich resources, such as library and object records. In addition visitors are provided with tools for entering a topical debate and personalizing their experience in the so called "CREATE" area, where registered users can save images and/or links from the debate areas, read sections and search queries. The users can also send personalized e-cards of images by e-mail and create a personal Web gallery from their bookmarked images, including the ability to incorporate personal comments that can be e-mailed to friends and colleagues.

Figure 2 shows a general shot of the Ingenious home page. The facilities include "My E-cards" to sent electronic cards (Figure 3), selected hyperlinks (Figure 4), saved images (Figure 5) and Web galleries (Figure 6).

Even if in the wider picture for *Ingenious* users, the umbrella group is lifelong learners, the application can be particularly suitable for older age school children, teachers, and researchers who could first explore a topic in the "read" or "see" sections of the site, then use the "save image" and e-card features and gradually progress to Web gallery tools for creating a personal resource. The Web gallery outcome would be used for a project, research, shared among a group of subject enthusiasts or a class (for instance). Community building could follow from this, through the usage of the debate features available on the site.

THE POST-VISIT EXPERIENCE

In some cases, personal virtual spaces can also include information about a visitor's actual visit to museums, thus creating a direct link between the visit and the post-visit experience. Personalization is an effective tool for stimulating visitors at home to follow up on what caught their attention during the exhibition through a museum's Web site. For example, the London Science Museum's "*In touch*" project allows a record of a visitor's interaction with various exhibits in the Wellcome Wing including an eye scan, voice, face and fingerprint recognition, photo editing, etc., to be recorded using their fingerprint as an identifier, thus avoiding the need for any physical ticket (www.sciencemuseumintouch.org.uk). The results are made available as part of a personal space within the museum's Web site that can be accessed via the visitor's first name and birth date.

Since 2000, when the project was originally implemented, Joe Cutting of the Science Museum reports that (as of January 2004) more than 400,000 Web pages have been created, of which around 8% have been accessed at least once. In order to simplify the system, reduce the operational problems that derive from such a large database, and increase the percentage of visitors using it, the museum has decided to replace the fingerprint method (which is not completely reliable in practice) by "an email it to me" option by the end of 2004. Every time a person wants to save one of the interactions, an e-mail address will have to be provided. By doing so, there will be no more automatically generated personal pages for the visitors. However, the museum is considering the inclusion of a link in the e-mail that would allow the visitors to set up a personal page if they wish. In this way only those who are really interested will set up a page and the museum will not have to maintain a huge and largely unused database. Figure 7 shows two screenshots from the exhibition itself and Figure 8 shows example pages from the associated Web site.

In a similar manner, the *Visite Plus* service offered by the *Cité des Sciences et de l'Industrie* (www.cite-sciences.fr) in Paris, which has been used on a number of successive temporary exhibitions, *"Le Cerveau Intime," "Le Canada Vraiment,"* and *"Opération Carbone,"* allows the visitor to configure a personal profile (with information on preferred language, disabilities, etc.) on an interactive kiosk placed at the beginning of the exhibition through a special bar-coded ticket or on a PDA (Personal Digital Assistant). This data can then be used to access adapted information from the different interactive devices and to play various games and quizzes in the exhibitions. The results of such interaction, as well as the path followed by the visitor, are automatically saved by the *Visite Plus* system on a personal Web page, accessible on the museum's

Figure 7. "In touch" exhibition screen shots

Figure 8. "In touch" Web pages

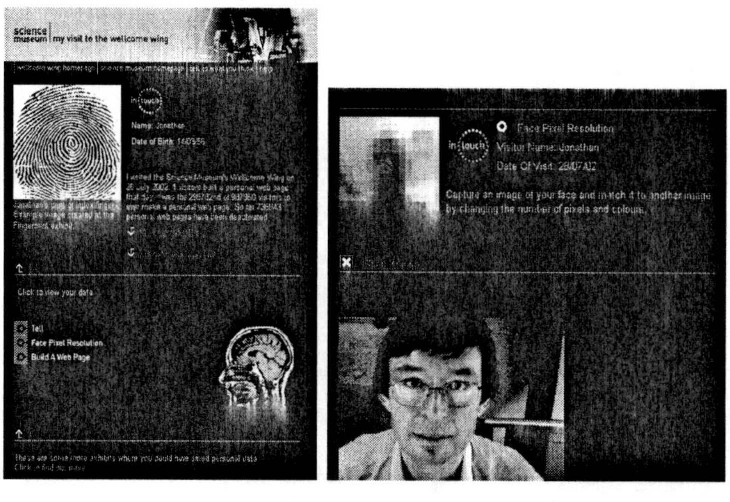

Web site after the visit through the number of the bar-coded ticket or PDA. In this way, the visitors are able to analyze in more depth the subjects that particularly interested them during the exhibition (through the provision of additional information) and to compare results of their interactions with those of other visitors.

The fact that an important part of the content concerning the exhibition is accessible after the actual visit, at home or in another context, allows the visitor to focus more on experimentation and discovery while in the museum and to leave the more traditional didactic aspects for later. The *Visite Plus* system also offers the possibility of subscribing to a personalized periodical newsletter that focuses on a series of themes selected by the visitor at the moment of the registration. Options include selecting from a list of available subjects or receiving a complete dossier of the exhibition. See Figure 9 for an example of the view of the exhibit from the personalized Web site. Each square corresponds to a content area in the exhibition. The squares that are in full color represent the ones that have been accessed during the visit to the exhibition while the white ones correspond to the ones that have not been visited.

Similar concepts have been introduced and tested in the framework of the *Electronic Guidebook Research Project* (www.exploratorium.edu/guidebook), which began in 1998 at the San Francisco *Exploratorium* in California, in partnership with Hewlett-Packard Laboratories and the Concord Consortium. This is aimed at developing a roving resource to enhance a visitor's experience at the museum (Hsi, 2003). In particular, the purpose of the project is to investigate how a mobile computing infrastructure enables museum visitors to create their own "guide" to the Exploratorium, using a personalized interactive system. This helps in better planning of their visit, getting the most out of it while they are in the museum and enabling reference back to it once they have returned to their home or classroom. The guidebook allows users to construct a record of their visit by bookmarking exhibit content, taking digital pictures from a camera near the exhibit, and accessing this information later on

Figure 9. Visite Plus personalized Web site

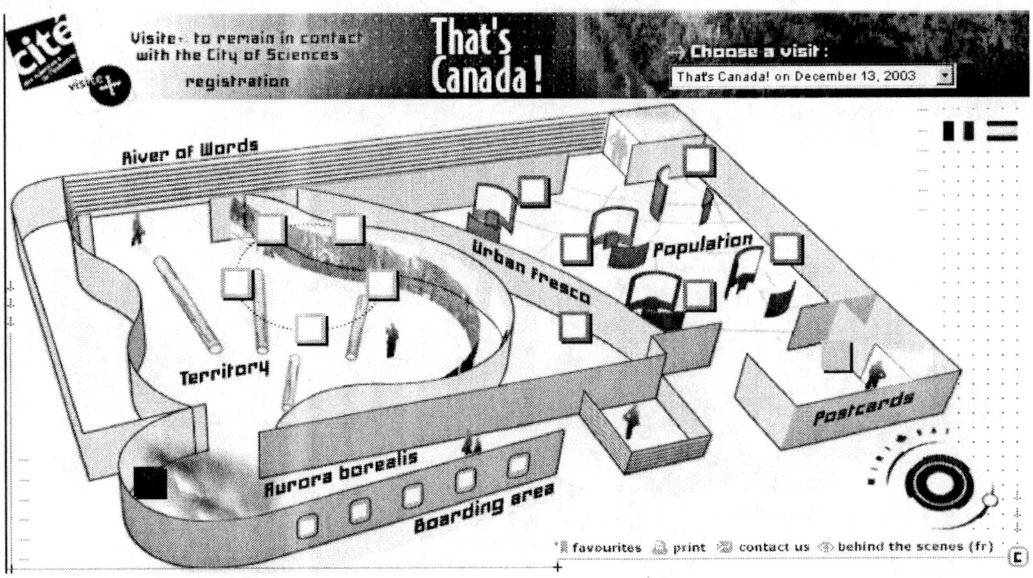

a personal "MyExploratorium" Web page in the museum or after their visit (Figure 10).

The project was designed as a proof of concept study to explore potential avenues for future research and development and therefore was not envisioned to support the implementation of a fully functional system. Nevertheless, the tests that have been run so far revealed interesting conclusions. Above all, the visitors liked the idea of being able to bookmark information for later reference. Both teachers and pupils thought this feature would allow the children to play more during their museum visit, completing related homework assignments after the visit (Semper & Spasojevic, 2002).

THE PRE-VISIT EXPERIENCE

The link between visit and post-visit experience can be also extended to the pre-visit phase through the implementation of systems that allow visitors to create personalized tours based on their interests and needs. Most museum visitors, even those who have not visited before, arrive with expectations about what will happen during the visit. Such hopes might concern specific subjects of interest that the person wants to explore, the physical characteristics of the museum, the types of activities that can be undertaken or the social context in which the exploration takes place (alone, as a family, within a larger organized group, etc.). All these factors merge to create a visitor's *personal agenda* (Falk & Dierking, 1992). The success of the museum experience is partially defined by how well it corresponds to the visitor's personal agenda.

Personalization is a useful tool to create such a correlation because it helps a visitor to find out what, within the museum, could fit better with their personal agenda or correspond more to their expectations. This can be done either from home on the museum's Web site or directly on-site through interactive devices available in the museum. Upon completing a profile, where the intending visitor must indicate different types of information such as how and when they are tentatively planning to visit, with whom, how long they plan to stay, what sort of interest(s) they have and which language they understand, the system will be able to provide a personalized plan for the visit that takes the submitted information into consideration. Personalized museum plans can be very useful, especially for large museums where visitors are likely to be overwhelmed by the number of objects or exhibits available for viewing during a single visit. In such a context, visitors are often disoriented and find it difficult

Figure 10. MyExploratorium set-up

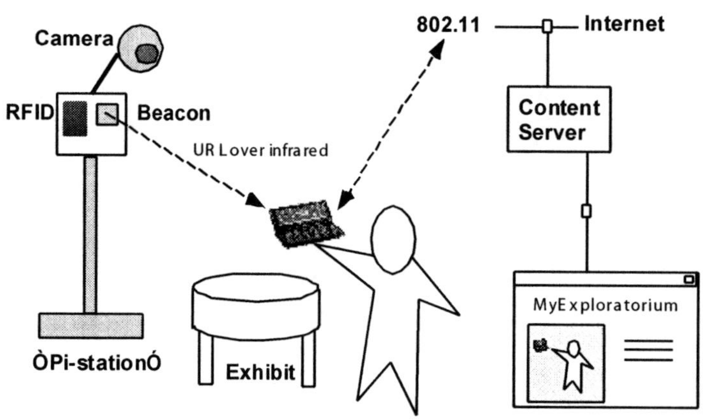

to decide what they want to see or do. Answering a few very simple questions, or defining a few criteria, can help them to overcome these limitations, enjoy the visit more fully and learn more easily.

A number of museums are working on developing online and onsite applications based on these principles. The *National Museum of Ethnology* in Leiden, the Netherlands (www.rmv.nl), for example, has developed an onsite facility called *"The tour of the world in 80 questions"* that allows children aged 7 to 13 to print out a personalized tour plan of the museum based on an individual choice of subjects and continents. The tour plan, which is colorful and easy to understand for children, includes a series of maps that help locate the objects, a brief description of the artifacts and a list of questions related to the subjects chosen, which the young visitors need to answer during their museum exploration.

The *Cité des Sciences et de L'Industrie* in Paris is undertaking a project called *"Navigateur"* (Navigator), which will allow visitors to create a personalized tour based on an individual choice amid a set of criteria which include the context of the visit (alone, family, group), the language spoken, the particular interests, the time available and the type of experience desired. Once the visitor has set the criteria that are most relevant for them and has checked the offerings on the museum interactive plan, the personalized proposal can be saved on the museum bar-coded ticket, which will be used during the actual visit, when using different interactive devices throughout the museum, to obtain further assistance in finding the recommended exhibits or to reset the criteria based on new interests that might have arisen during exploration. The system will be linked directly with Visit Plus, thus creating continuity between the pre-visit, actual visit and post-visit experience, through the use of personalization.

CONCLUSION

The examples provided here from different science museums all over the world help to prove the potential role that personalization could play in strengthening the overall learning process before, during and after the actual visit, in advance through activities that orient visitors and afterwards through opportunities to continue reflection and explore related ideas. However, despite the obvious potential benefits that these applications can bring to the visitor's experiences, there is still very little evidence that these systems work in the terms envisaged by their promoters, especially with respect to learning. This is because, due to their relatively recent nature, most of these projects have not yet been subjected to thorough evaluations that focus on establishing, among other things, the long-lasting effects of personalization on the learning process. Until now, the very few evaluations that have been carried out have focused mainly on whether people use the systems or not, why they do so, where they encounter most difficulties and on their usability in general. Despite the fact that further studies are needed in order to shed light on the effectiveness of personalization as a pedagogical tool, the first evaluations of these early examples, as well as other similar projects, have given initial help in indicating various pros and cons related to their use.

The overall feedback concerning the introduction of personalizing applications to audio guides and virtual environments seems to be reasonably positive: visitors are spending more time in the virtual and real museum, they access information at the level of detail desired and appreciate the idea of being able to bookmark information for reference later (Semper & Spasojevic, 2002). In particular, a study by Cordoba and Lepper (1996) has evaluated the consequences of personalization with respect to stimulating intrinsic motivation and learning in a computer-based educational environment. The findings provide strong evidence that the students for whom the learning contexts had been personalized, through the incorporation of incidental individualized information about their backgrounds and interests, displayed better gains in motivation, involvement and learning than their counterparts for whom the contexts had not been personalized.

However some drawbacks have also emerged[6]. First of all, there are the issues related to the difficulty and expense of implementation and also problems in practical use by visitors[7]. So far it seems that only a limited number of visitors take advantage of the benefits available through personalization, partly because the systems are not implemented in a clear and easy manner and partly because most visitors are either not ready for technology or not willing to invest time in it. Therefore it is important to remember that personalization should not be implemented for the sake of it but when and because it brings added value to the museum for, if not all, a good percentage of visitors. Only if this occurs can the costs for investment and development be justified.

Some experts have warned against the use of personalization. Nielson (1998) has argued that personalization is over-rated, saying that good basic Web navigation is much more important. For example, it is helpful to consider different classes of use in the main home page, such as physical visitors, the disabled, children, teachers, researchers, groups, etc., and to give each of these a relevant view of the resources that are available (Bowen & Bowen, 2000). Such usability issues are certainly important, and relatively cheap to address with good design, but even Nielson admits that there are special cases were personalization is useful.

More recently, there have been further questions about the effectiveness of personalization (Festa, 2003; McGovern, 2003), despite the enthusiasm of some. For example, the costs may be up to four times that of a normal Web site, around a quarter of users may actually avoid personalized Web sites due to privacy concerns and only 8% are encouraged to revisit because of personalized facilities (Jupiter Research, 2003). This compares with 54% who considered fast-loading pages and 52% who rate better navigation as being important. However, other surveys indicate that personalization can be effective, for example in the field of downloadable music (Tam & Ho, 2003).

Another issue that needs to be stressed in personalization is related to standardization procedures and applications. This process is central both for content description and user profile definition using metadata (Conlan et al., 2002). The description process can however be very time-consuming and expensive, but if it is pursued properly it allows the resources to be reused for different purposes and a visitor profile to be created using various different sources of information following evaluation criteria. Museums are sometimes not very quick in adopting new technologies but in some cases the slow perspective allows them to make the most of other institutions' initial mistakes and thus to avoid them. Involvement with standards provides a good opportunity to share such knowledge.

Thus it is recommended for museums to use personalization on Web sites judiciously at the moment, although science museums with good funding may wish to be more adventurous. There is a place for personalization in leading-edge Web sites and for certain innovative facilities like advanced Web support for specific exhibits. It is an area that museums should certainly consider, but the costs should be weighed against the benefits. Of course, the costs are likely to decrease as commercial and open source support improves in this area. At the moment, not insignificant development effort is needed for such facilities, but in the future they could be increasingly packaged with standard database-oriented Web support software, such as content management systems, as understanding of what is useful and not useful is gained from practical experience. This is certainly an interesting and fast-moving area that should be monitored by innovative science museums, especially at a national level.

REFERENCES

Beler, A., Borda, A., Bowen, J. P., & Filippini-Fantoni, S. (2004). The building of online communities: An approach for learning organizations, with a particular focus on the museum sector. In J. Hemsley, V. Cappellini, & G. Stanke (Eds.), *EVA 2004 London Conference Proceedings* (pp. 2.1-2.15). University College London, The Institute of Archaeology, UK.

Bertoletti, A.C., & Costa, A.C.R. (1999). Sagres – A virtual museum. In D. Bearman & J. Trant (Eds.), *Proceedings of Museums and the Web 1999.* Archives & Museum Informatics. Retrieved from www.archimuse.com/mw99/papers/bertoletti/bertoletti.html

Bertoletti, A.C. et al. (2001). Providing personal assistance in the SAGRES virtual museum. In D. Bearman & J. Trant (Eds.), *Proceedings of Museums and the Web 2001,* Seattle, Washington, March 14-16. Archives & Museum Informatics. Retrieved from www.archimuse.com/mw2001/papers/bertoletti/bertoletti.html

Bonnet, M. (2002, June). Personalization of Web services: Opportunities and challenges. *Ariadne,* (28). Retrieved from www.ariadne.ac.uk/issue28/personalization

Bowen, J.P. (2004, January). Cultural heritage online. *Ability,* 53, 12-14. Retrieved from www.abilitymagazine.org.uk/features/2004/01/A53_Cover_story.pdf

Bowen, J.P., & Bowen, J.S.M. (2000). The website of the UK Museum of the Year, 1999. In D. Bearman & J. Trant (Eds.), *Proceedings of Museums and the Web 2000.* Minneapolis, Minnesota, April 16-19. Pittsburgh, PA: Archives & Museum Informatics. Retrieved from www.archimuse.com/mw2000/papers/bowen/bowen.html

Bowen, J.P., & Filippini-Fantoni, S. (2004). Personalization and the Web from a museum perspective. In D. Bearman & J. Trant (Eds.), *Museums and the Web 2004: Selected Papers from an International Conference,* Arlington, Virginia, March 31-April 3, (pp. 63-78). Pittsburgh, PA: Archives & Museum Informatics. Retrieved from www.archimuse.com/mw2004/papers/bowen/bowen.html

Bowen, J.P., Houghton, M., & Bernier, R. (2003). Online museum discussion forums; What do we have? What do we need? In D. Bearman & J. Trant (Eds.), *Proceedings of MW2003: Museums and the Web 2003,* Charlotte, North Carolina, March 19-22. Pittsburgh, PA: Archives & Museum Informatics. Retrieved from www.archimuse.com/mw2003/papers/bowen/bowen.html

Brown, R., & Kulick, J. (1997). Flashbulb memories. *Cognition, 5,* 73-79.

Brusilovsky, P. (1994, August 17). *Adaptive hypermedia: An attempt to analyse and generalize.* Workshop held in conjunction with UM'94 4th International Conference on User Modeling, Hyannis, Cape Cod, Massachusetts. Retrieved from wwwis.win.tue.nl/ah94/Brusilovsky.html

Brusilovsky, P., & Maybury, M.T. (2002). From adaptive hypermedia to the adaptive Web. *Communications of the ACM, 45*(5), 30-33. Retrieved from doi.acm.org/10.1145/506218.506239

Brusilovsky, P., & Nejdl, W. (2004). Adaptive hypermedia and adaptive Web. In M. Singh (Ed.), *Practical handbook of Internet computing.* CRC Press. Retrieved from www.kbs.uni-hannover.de/Arbeiten/Publikationen/2003/brusilovsky-nejdl.pdf

Case, S., Thint, M., Othani, T., & Hare, S. (2003). Personalisation and Web communities. *BT Technology Journal, 21*(1), 91-97.

Conlan, O., Dagger, D., & Wade, V. (2002, September). Towards a standards-based approach to e-learning personalization using reusable learning objects. In *E-Learn 2002, World Conference on E-Learning in Corporate, Government, Healthcare and Higher Education*. Montreal, Canada. Retrieved from www.cs.tcd.ie/Owen.Conlan/publications/eLearn2002_v1.24_Conlan.pdf

Cordova, D.I., & Lepper, M.R. (1996). Intrinsic motivation and the process of learning: Beneficial effects of contextualisation, personalization and choice. *Journal of Educational Psychology, 88*(4), 715-730.

Csikszentmihalyi, M., & Hermanson, K. (1995). Intrinsic motivation in museums: What makes visitors want to learn? *Museum News, 74*(3), 34-37, 59-61.

Dolog, P., Henze, N., Nejdl, W., & Sintek, M. (2004). Personalization in distributed e-learning environments. In *Proceedings of 13th World Wide Web Conference* (pp. 170-179). New York City, IW3C2/ACM. Retrieved from www2004.org/proceedings/docs/2p170.pdf

Eirinaki, M., & Vazirgiannis, M. (2003). Web mining for Web personalization. *ACM Transactions on Internet Technology, 3*(1), 1-27. Retrieved from doi.acm.org/10.1145/643477.643478

Falk, L., & Dierking, L. (1992). *The museum experience*. Ann Arbor, MI: Whalesback Books.

Festa, P. (2003, October 14). Report slams web personalization. *CNETNews.com*. Retrieved from news.com.com/2100-1038_3-5090716.html

Filippini-Fantoni, S. (2003). Museums with a personal touch. In J. Hemsley, V. Cappellini, & G. Stanke (Eds.), *EVA 2003 London Conference Proceedings,* University College London, July 22-26, (pp. 25.1-25.10) (Cf. Beler et al. ref).

Hamma, K. (2004, May). The role of museums in online teaching, learning, and research. *First Monday, 9*(5). Retrieved from firstmonday.org/issues/issue9_5/hamma

Hidi, S. (1990). Interest and its contribution as a mental resource for learning. *Review of Educational Research, 60*, 549-571.

HMSO. (2001). *Special Educational Needs and Disability Act 2001.* UK Government, Her Majesty's Stationery Office. Retrieved from *www.hmso.gov.uk/acts/acts2001/20010010.htm*

Hsi, S. (2003). A study of user experiences mediated by nomadic web content in a museum. *Journal of Computer Assisted Learning, 19*(3), 308-319.

Jupiter Research. (2003, October 14). *Beyond the personalization myth: Cost effective alternatives to influence intent.* Jupiter Media. Retrieved from http://www.internet.com/corporate/releases/03.10.14-newjupresearch.html

McGovern, G. (2003, October 20). Why personalization hasn't worked. *New Thinking*. Retrieved from www.gerrymcgovern.com/nt/2003/nt_2003_10_20_ personal ization.htm

Mobascher, B., Cooley, R., & Srivastava, J. (2000). Automatic personalization based on web usage mining. *Communications of the ACM, 43*(8), 142-151. Retrieved from doi.acm.org/10.1145/345124.345169

Moraes, M.C., Bertoletti, A.C., & Costa, A.C.R. (1999). The SAGRES Virtual Museum with software agents to stimulate the visiting of museums. In P. De Bra & John J. Leggett (Eds.), *Proceedings of WebNet 99: World Conference on the WWW and Internet,* Honolulu, Hawaii, USA, October 24-30, (Vol. 1, pp. 770-775). Charlottesville, VA: Association for the Advancement of Computing in Education (AACE).

Nielsen, J. (1998, October 4). Personalization is over-rated. *Alertbox*. Retrieved from www.useit.com/alertbox/981004.html

Oppermann, R., & Specht, M. (1999). Adaptive information for nomadic activities a process oriented approach. In *Software Ergonomie '99* (pp. 255-264). Walldorf, Germany. Stuttgart: Teubner.

Semper, R., & Spasojevic, M. (2002). The electronic guidebook: Using portable devices and a wireless Web-based network to extend the museum experience. In D. Bearman & J. Trant (Eds.), *Proceedings of Museums and the Web 2001.* Boston, April 18-20. Pittsburgh, PA: Archives & Museum Informatics. Retrieved from www.archimuse.com/mw2002/papers/semper/semper.html

Tam, K.Y., & Ho, S.Y. (2003). Web personalization: Is it effective? *IT Professional*, *5*(5), 53-57. Retrieved from csdl.computer.org/comp/mags/it/2003/05/f5053abs.htm

Tan, W.L.H., Subramaniam, R., & Aggarwal, A.K. (2003). Virtual science centers: A new genre of learning in Web-based promotion of science education. In *Proceedings of the 36th Annual Hawaii International Conference on System Sciences (HICSS'03)* (Vol. 5, pp. 156-165). IEEE Computer Society.

ENDNOTES

1. A "cookie" is a small piece of data sent by a website and stored on the client-side (browser) computer that can be reused later on the server-side (the Web site that sent the cookie) as unique information concerning a user.
2. A Web server log is a record of each access to a Web server with information such as the name of the client computer, the date/time and the resource accessed.
3. These applications are currently available on a number of different museums' Web sites such as the Metropolitan Museum of Art, the Whitney Museum of American Art, etc. For a detailed description of these applications (see Bowen & Filippini-Fantoni, 2004).
4. Please note that the distinction between *formal* and *informal* education is used here in a rather loose sense. Usually, in the educational sector, classrooms are considered formal learning settings, while museums are considered informal learning settings. As an alternative, we propose here to use the term formal e-learning tools in relation to proper courses meant for students who cannot attend classes; while by informal e-learning tools we refer to online or onsite educational environments.
5. Note that the acquisition of knowledge about the visitor is done in an explicit way: information is directly extracted, through the filling of forms, with direct answers to questionnaires. SAGRES works with two kinds of models: individual model and group model. The group model is built by the teacher and used by students. The teacher is responsible for the definition of the students' characteristics, by the definition of the group stereotype (subject, knowledge level and language of the consultation), the activities stereotypes and the classes (name of the students presented in the group).
6. It is not the intention of this chapter to be negative towards the use of personalization techniques in museums, but to highlight constructively some of the questions that come to light when the social uses and design problems are considered.
7. For more detailed information on the problems related to the implementation and use of personalization techniques see Filippini-Fantoni (2003).

Chapter XXII
A Virtual Museum Where Students can Learn

Nicoletta Di Blas
Politecnico di Milano, Italy

Paolo Paolini
Politecnico di Milano, Italy

Caterina Poggi
Politecnico di Milano, Italy

ABSTRACT

SEE, Shrine Educational Experience, represents an example of how Internet and multimedia technologies can effectively be exploited to deliver complex scientific and cultural concepts to middle and high school students. SEE (a project by Politecnico di Milano and the Israel Museum, Jerusalem) is based on a shared online 3-D environment, where students from four possibly different countries meet together to learn, discuss and play, visiting the virtual Israel Museum with a guide. The educational experience combines online engagement and cooperation to "traditional" off-line learning activities, spread across six weeks. Data from an extensive two-year-long evaluation of the project, involving over 1,400 participants from Europe and Israel, prove the educational effectiveness of this innovative edutainment format.

INTRODUCTION

SEE—Shrine Educational Experience—is an e-learning project based on a shared online 3-D environment, where students from different countries meet to learn, play, and engage in a high-level scientific debate about the Dead Sea Scrolls, one of the major archaeological discoveries of the 20th Century. The Dead Sea Scrolls were written by a Hebrew community who lived in the archaeological site of Khirbet Qumran between 170 BC and 68 AD (Roitman 1997). They represent the earliest known version of books from the Bible, and a precious source to understand the roots of Western civilization.

SEE is the result of cooperation between the Politecnico di Milano and the Israel Museum, Jerusalem. As part of its educational mission, the Museum wished to make its large body of knowledge and artefacts upon the Dead Sea Scrolls accessible to the public at large, and to open issues of scientific research to a broader public, with respect to the small group of scholars to whom the discussion is usually restricted.

Thanks to Internet technologies, providing simultaneous access to users independently from their geographical location, (middle and high school) students from all over the world can visit the virtual Shrine of the Book (Figures 1-2), and take part in discussions, games, and debates with international experts, discussing state-of-the-art research about the Dead Sea Scrolls.

Each SEE experience involves four classes of students between 12 and 19 years of age, located in different geographical areas: they meet, in the online virtual world, four times (over a period of six to seven weeks). Through the online meetings students get acquainted with each other, discuss, play, answer quizzes, present their social and cultural environment, etc. Students, in addition, cooperate off-line, under their teacher's supervision, studying background material (based upon interviews with leading international experts) and carrying on their own homework.

This innovative learning experience aims at four major educational goals:

Figure 1. A screenshot of the virtual Shrine of the Book, reproducing the wing of the Israel Museum where the Scrolls are preserved

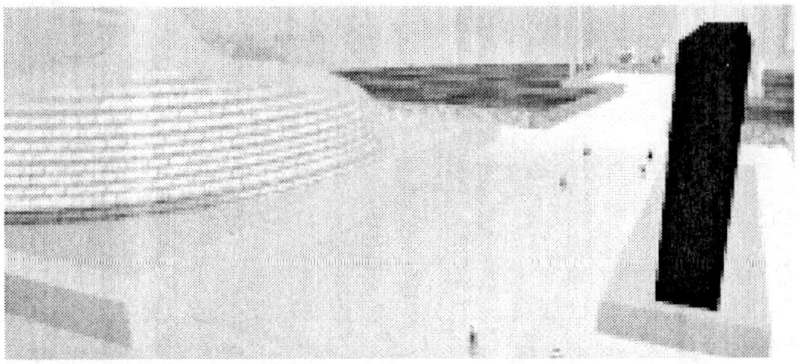

Figure 2. The real buildings of the Shrine of the Book at the Israel Museum, Jerusalem

1. Providing rich, in-depth knowledge about the Dead Sea Scrolls and related issues, including the scientific methods of philological/archaeological research.
2. Favouring a truly international, cross-cultural approach, where students of different countries can understand/compare their tradition, their background, their views and beliefs, etc. Developing a better understanding of differences and respect for the "other" is the underlying goal.
3. Fostering the use of information and communication technologies for educational purposes, with innovative teaching-learning paradigms.
4. Offering interaction, fun and engagement (i.e., powerful motivators, encouraging students' active participation, even in the context of a demanding learning activity).

A massive field-test evaluation, involving over 1,400 students and teachers between November 2002 and May 2004, has proved the effectiveness of SEE: the experience achieves all the main goals (above mentioned) and, in addition, it produces a wide range of beneficial side-effects and generates an overall strong educational impact.

HOW THE SEE EXPERIENCE WORKS

Activities

A SEE experience consists of 4 cooperative sessions (i.e., online meetings in a 3-D virtual world) spread across 6 weeks, and of several learning activities, that participating classes (four at a time) perform in the intervals between a session and the next one (Figure 3).

Cooperative sessions are not expressly meant to be a learning moment; they are devoted to social activities, such as students introducing themselves, discussions upon the themes of the experience, and games testing the students' knowledge of content. In order to be prepared for the sessions, students must study detailed material in advance. For this "traditional" learning activity, "old fashioned" methods remain the most effective: students download documents in printable

Figure 3. Schema of SEE learning activities

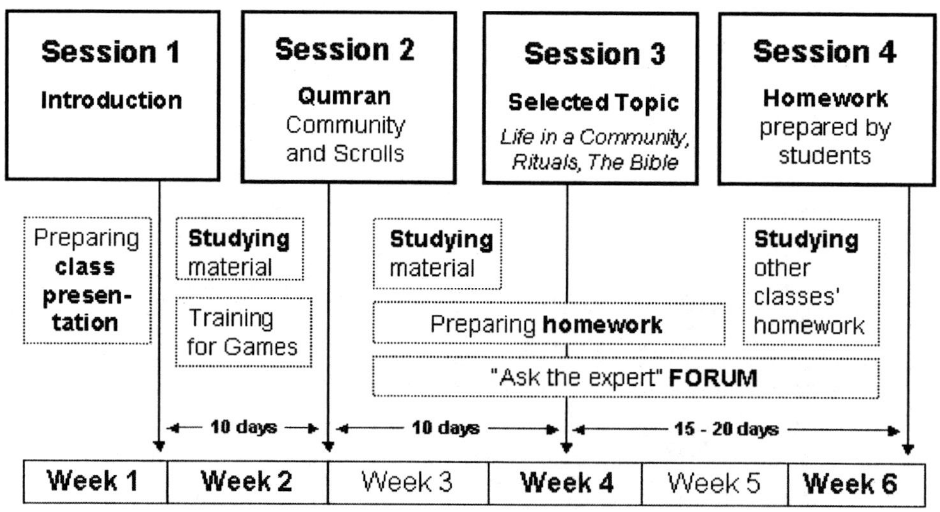

format from SEE Web site, and study them at home or in the classroom.

The four sessions are organized in order to bring pupils from a basic knowledge of the Dead Sea Scrolls to a more in-depth analysis of some particular topic of interest. At the moment of registration, teachers can select from a set of available topics the one they wish to study in depth. Sample topics are: "Life in a Community," "Rituals in Qumran," and "Canons and the Holy Bible." Students are then required to do further research on this topic, investigating its links with aspects of their own environment and searching through local sources. In the final session they will present in turn to each other the results of their research.

All the considerations that follow are the result of direct onsite observation of over 70 online cooperative sessions performed during SEE evaluation, between November 2002 and May 2004 (see the third section of this chapter for details). More than 1,400 students and teachers from over 30 schools in Europe and Israel were involved: in addition to making the project real, they have been an invaluable source of insights, anecdotes and information about the actual educational impact of the SEE experience.

What Happens Online

Users in SEE online environment are represented by avatars (Figure 4). Two students per class connect to the 3-D world, and therefore have an avatar to control: they move around, see other users, and communicate with them in real-time via chat. The rest of the class supports them in various ways, either grouped around the two computers or following the session with the help of a projector, connected to one of the monitors.

During the **first session** students introduce themselves, their school and their country to each other (Figures 4-5). Then they are briefly introduced by a "museum guide," that is, a member of the staff (also represented by an avatar), to the historical—geographical context of the experience. The goal of the first session is to stir the students' interest and motivate them to study the first set of documents. The evaluation tests in

Figure 4. Avatars introducing themselves in the Shrine virtual environment. The boards in the background, once clicked, activate a pop-up window showing classes' presentations

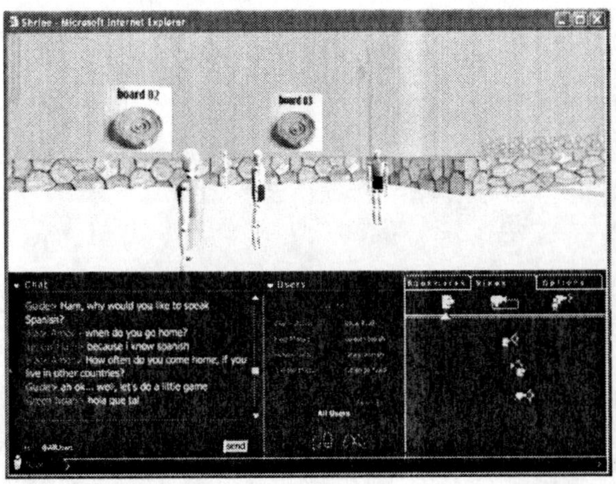

Figure 5. An example of class presentation. Before the first session, classes are asked to send a HTML page with a picture and a short self-presentation

schools showed that the engagement of exploring a new virtual world and the excitement of meeting peers from faraway countries are extremely powerful motivators, able to capture the students' interest.

During the **second session** students enter the museum (Figure 6), where they are shown pictures of archaeological findings and other historical evidences (Figure 7). Discussions start concerning both the background material and the most interesting issues surfaced in the session itself. The "museum guide" moderates the discussion, asks questions (also to test the students' knowledge) and encourages participants to think about their own experience related to the issues being raised.

The guide coordinates every cooperative session, directing the activities (Chang, 2002), stimulating the discussion, assisting students with technical problems, assigning scores for the games and even assigning penalties for improper behaviour. In order to avoid waste of time, disorientation, and ineffective interactions, each slot of time in a session is dedicated to a specific activity: the guide makes sure that everyone knows what to do and does it. This is crucial for keeping the experience fast-paced and educationally effective; the guide is also the ultimate referee for the games.

The guide awards scores to students depending on their contributions to the discussion. We could observe that assigning scores highly increases their participation and commitment to answer as correctly as possible. Classes are paired to form two teams: competition between them is strong from the very beginning. However, it touches its

Figure 6. Avatars in the corridor of the virtual Shrine of the Book; boards (once clicked) show significant images of objects preserved in the museum, or of the place where these were found.

Figure 7: a board showing rests of a pool for ritual baths at Qumran.

highest point in the games (Figures 8-9), where students demonstrate both their "physical" skill in controlling their avatar and their knowledge of the study material. Games in fact combine "movement" and "thinking:" despite their ability to move in the 3-D world, students earn no point if they cannot solve the riddles based on the content they should have studied.

The second session includes one game: a Treasure Hunt, where students are given clues to identify four particular museum objects among a set of 20 hidden in a labyrinth.

In the **third session**, the discussion about the topic of interest is followed by two games: a quiz, based on multiple-choice questions (Figures 8-9), and a matching pairs game, where students have to identify meaningful associations between couples of objects, again scattered in a labyrinth (Figure 10).

Finally, the **fourth session** is entirely devoted to the presentation of the students' homework: this is definitely, from a cultural point of view, the most intense moment of the experience. Students have the opportunity to explain their work, confront their views with the others', and answer to peers' critiques with passionate argumentations (Figure 11). The possibility of being confronted with different points of view is always interesting and valuable: when the discussion is about socio-cultural phenomena (such as aspects of the students' everyday life somehow related to the Scrolls' world), a cross-cultural approach bringing together people from very different backgrounds becomes intrinsically informative and enriching.

At the end of the fourth session, the guide announces the final scores—taking into consideration also the quality of the teams' homework—and proclaims the winner.

Figure 8. An avatar performs an ability game in the Quiz. If he reaches the top of the stairs before his opponent, he earns the right to answer the Quiz question first.

Figure 9. Avatars reflect on the answer to Quiz question 1. When their team member finishes the ability game, they must counsel him about the answer he should choose.

Figure 10. Matching Pairs Game. Avatars try to reconstruct meaningful pairs among the objects found in the labyrinth

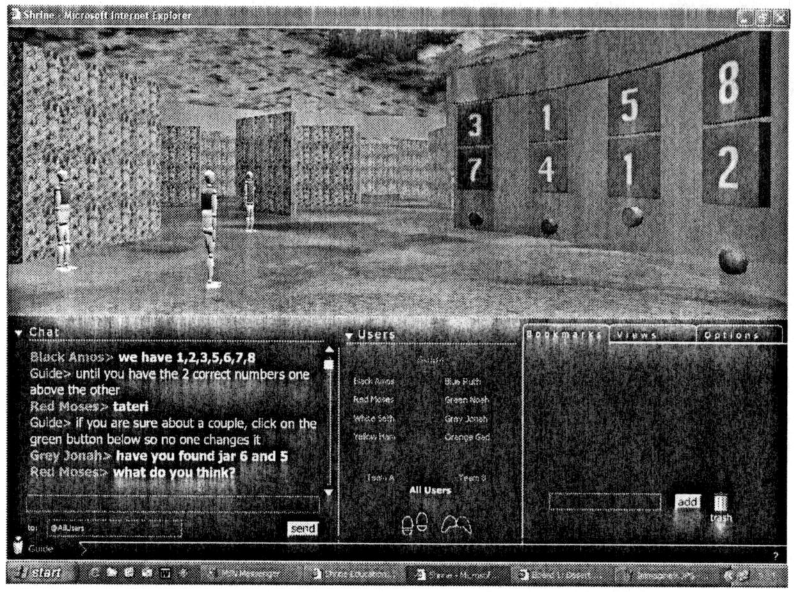

Figure 11. The vault space inside the Shrine of the Book white dome. Discussions of the third and fourth sessions take place here

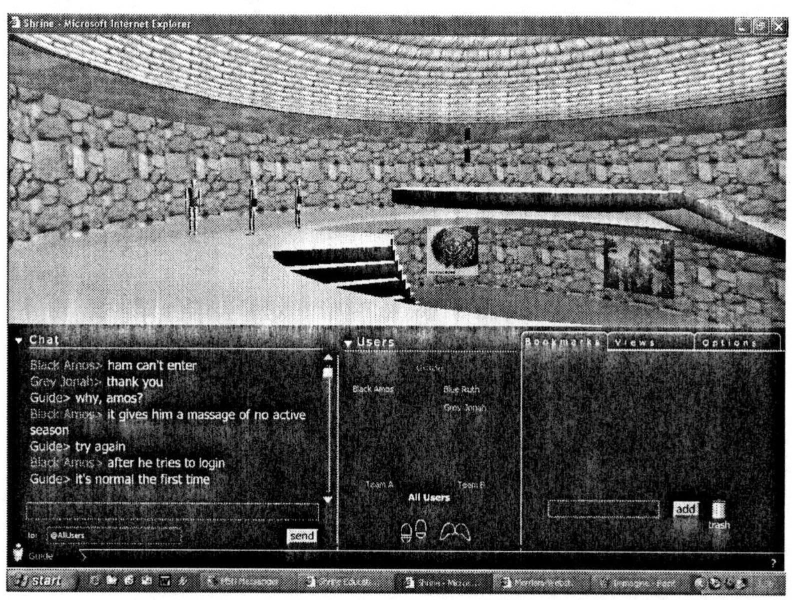

What Happens Off-Line

The effectiveness of a SEE experience from a learning point of view is determined, in large part, by the involvement of the teachers, especially in supervising the activities performed by each class in the intervals between a session and the next one.

Teachers are able to transmit their enthusiasm to the students, motivating them to study and do their homework accurately. When the teacher is not motivated (no matter how perfectly the technology works, how smart, responsible, hardworking the students are) the experience will probably be a failure. Well-motivated teachers, on the contrary, are able to make the best of a SEE experience, even with their most disaffected students.

Class work can be organized in different ways. While 4th year high school students are able to organize themselves quite autonomously, middle school kids need more directions and support from their teachers. In both cases, classes participate as a group, not as individuals: students split in sub-groups, divide the material among the sub-groups, and everyone takes charge of one particular task. They know that everyone's contribution is important for the team, and therefore they do their part with strong commitment for the team's success. Students, moreover, are implicitly taught how to collaborate in a group (Vygotsky, 1978): very important skills nowadays, when working environments frequently imply teamwork.

Teachers may decide to act only as supervisors, encouraging the students' initiative and personal responsibility; or they may exploit the interest stirred up by the project, either treating more in-depth the parts of the curricular program more related to the core theme, or basing lessons, class activities and exercises on the project's material, or taking advantage of its multidisciplinary character to involve as many colleagues as possible, and offering a multi-perspective approach to the subject matter.

Students, on their part, enjoy the game-like approach of the project and the use of technologies—which in some cases they know even better than their teachers. When they see the teacher at a loss with technical problems, they take the initiative and try to find a solution: their responsibility and resourcefulness are stimulated.

The project's offline activities include: downloading, printing and studying the contents, keeping in touch with remote team members, and collaborating with them to prepare the research homework.

The peculiar format of contents and the means for asynchronous communication with other participants are described in detail in the next sections.

WHAT IT'S ALL ABOUT

The Interviews: A Dialogic Approach

Detailed content is offered to students in the format of interviews to leading international experts on subjects like Dead Sea Scrolls, Holy Scriptures, Ancient Literature, Hebrew, Christian and Middle-East Culture in general. Unlike school textbooks, interviews provide a faceted, thought-provoking overview of the current state of research at academic levels, in a readable, straightforward style. Since debate over some issues is still open, students are startled to find (in the interviews), sometimes, totally conflicting assertions by different experts. They realize that historical and archaeological researches are not as linear and problem-free as they appear in history schoolbooks. They become curious of finding out which is the most convincing hypothesis. Teachers are thrilled to see how eagerly they engage in further research, investigating the criteria on which each hypothesis is based.

Interviews are integrated by a rich set of auxiliary material, including summaries, maps, anthological excerpts from the Scrolls, the Bible, or other sources quoted by the experts in the interviews, and editorial insets on relevant historical characters, peoples, or events. These also help integrating the backgrounds of students from different countries and of different ages.

The Experts' Forum: Debating with Researchers

If the dialogic format of the interviews gives the flavour of—as a teacher defined it—"a debate at academic level" reflecting "the state of the art of research," an even more exciting opportunity is offered to the students: one or more of the experts interviewed is available during the experience to answer the participants' questions about the issues presented in the interviews, or that emerged during online discussions. Experts communicate with the classes via a shared online message board provided on SEE Web site, allowing every user to see public messages and keep track of message threads.

This is a wonderful opportunity for middle and high school students, who would hardly ever have a chance to reach high-level scholars directly and ask them questions, not to speak of engaging in a serious discussion with them.

The message board is also the place where discussions started during cooperative sessions (and cut off at a certain point for lack of time) can be resumed and continued in a less hectic style. Although extremely stimulating, the chat is often frenetic and confusing: a sort of forum on the online message board allows users to post their contribution, somewhat lengthier and deeper than a chat message, possibly after having thought about it for a while. Even the experts might be involved in the discussions started online.

The Virtual Museum

Every cooperative session starts either outside or inside the virtual Shrine of the Book. A SEE experience is a totally new museum experience. Many factors influence a museum visit, the social aspect being not the least important (Falk & Dierking, 1992). Moreover, museum visits are far more significant from an educational point of view when preceded and followed by activities enhancing the comprehension of the objects exposed (Falk & Dierking, 2000). A SEE experience is a highly social activity, requiring participants to discuss together, play together, work and learn together. Additionally, all activities are aimed at enhancing the comprehension of the museum's content—which would appear rather enigmatic, even when seen for real, if not accompanied by explanations.

The virtual museum therefore reproduces only those aspects that, in the real Shrine, are meant to help visitors entering in the "Scrolls world", recreating the atmosphere of Qumran. For example, the members of the community who wrote the Scrolls referred to themselves as "the sons of light," and to their enemies as "the sons of darkness:" this opposition is symbolized by the contrast between the white dome and the black basalt wall, forming the architecture of the Shrine of the Book (Figures 12-14). The white dome emerges from a pool of water, representing the bathing pools (Figure 7) used by the inhabitants of Qumran for purification rituals. Furthermore, it is shaped like a lid of the jars inside which the Scrolls were stored. The

Figure 12. The Shrine buildings

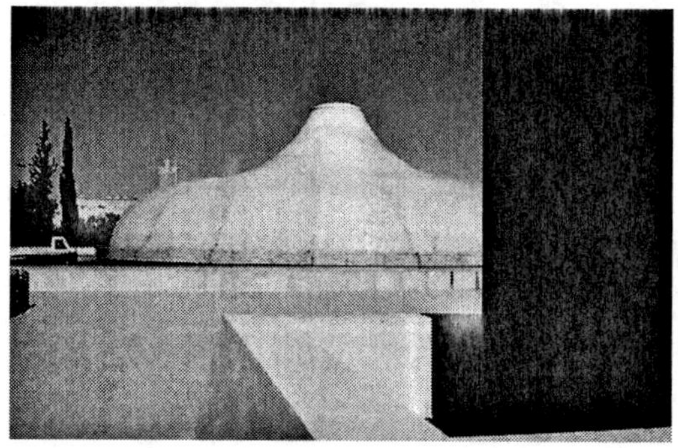

Figure 13. The virtual Shrine – external environment

Figure 14. Inside the white dome

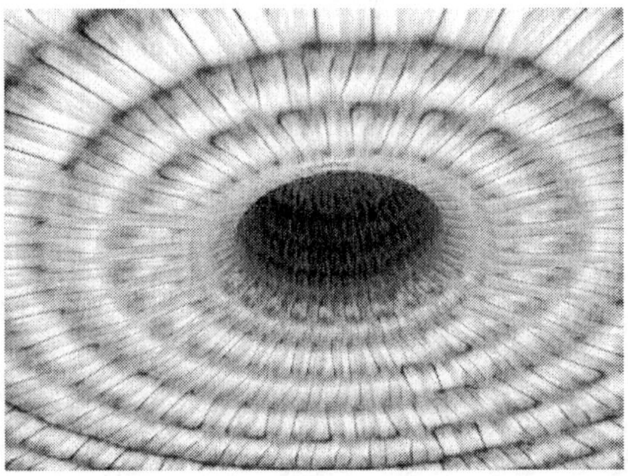

corridor (Figure 6) reminds of the caves where the jars were found, and so on…

Rather than striving to create a perfect virtual reproduction of the "real" museum, SEE aims at helping students to "get into the atmosphere:" they absorb a great deal of information almost effortlessly, by simply looking around and talking about what they see. The engagement of interaction, discussion, and competition stirs their interest in the subject matter: at the end of the experience, many students—who did not even know about the Scrolls' existence before—were fascinated by them, and wished to visit the real museum.

How We Know It Works

The educational effectiveness of the experience has been assessed through massive on-field experimentation (Table 1) started in November 2002 and continued through three different phases.

Phase 1 aimed at testing the effectiveness of the **technological platform** and **interaction dynamics**: a restricted number of schools simulated the sessions (with mock-up contents), first within a single class, and then with students of different schools logging in simultaneously, playing the games and chatting together. Observers in schools

Figure 15. Orientation of the schools involved

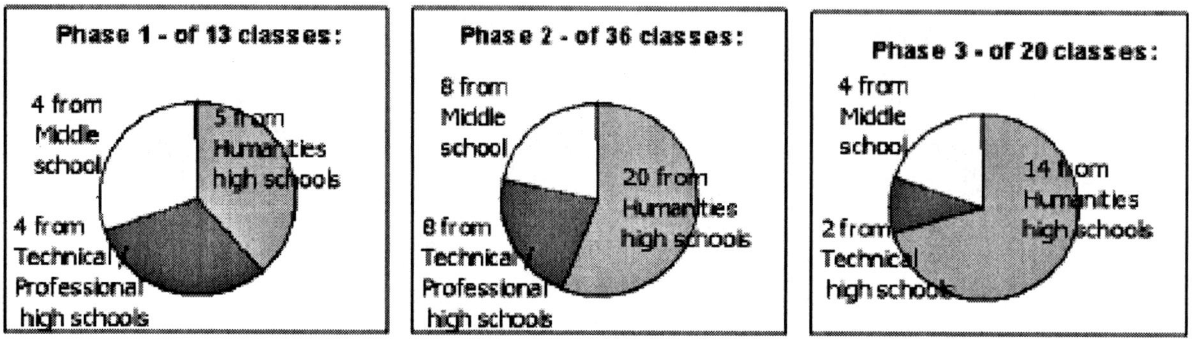

Table 1. Schools involved in SEE Experimentation. Students' ages ranged from 12 to 18. Computer expertise varied with the kind of schools; however, skilled computer-users were present in every class.

Phase 1: Nov. -Dec. 2002	Phase 2: Mar.-May 2003	Phase 3: Mar.-May 2004
7 schools in Italy	22 schools in Italy and Israel	9 schools in Europe and Israel
13 classes	36 classes	20 classes
15 teachers	44 teachers	21 teachers
Over 200 students	Over 700 students	Nearly 500 students
15 sessions performed	36 sessions performed (each one involving 4 classes)	20 sessions performed (each one involving 4 classes)

witnessed every session, detected problems, and collected comments and suggestions from students and teachers, on the basis of which several minor adjustments were introduced. On the whole, however, Phase 1 showed that the experience is definitely engaging: students enjoyed the interactive and competitive aspects very much, and wished that sessions were longer.

Phase 2 was an extensive, full-scope testing of the whole **educational experience**, assessing contents, subject-related discussions, off-line activities, games, homework, timing, organizational aspects and coordination with teachers. Observers monitored each cooperative session in every single school, registering notable aspects on written reports, and offering assistance to teachers if needed. Questionnaires were sent to students and teachers after the end of the experience, to evaluate its educational effectiveness and the users' satisfaction.

Phase 3 focused especially on the international, **cross-cultural value** of the experience: a larger proportion of participants outside Italy were involved, bringing fascinating multi-perspective contributions to online discussions. Scheduling, instructions for teachers and the workflow of activities were refined, enabling schools to manage all the complex organizational issues of the project without the assistance of a person from the staff physically present in the school. Again, feedback was collected through questionnaires before, during and after the experience, and an accurate analysis of chat flows disclosed many interesting insights about the educational value of online cross-cultural cooperation.

Direct Observation

Monitoring cooperative sessions in presence proved a rich and reliable source of information, necessary to understand and complete questionnaires results. Observers could easily assess the content's level of complexity, the effectiveness of interaction dynamics, and understand the nature of those problems, which caused a generic sense of frustration in students and teachers, without them being able to explain why.

After witnessing a session, observers had to write an overall evaluation on a report, with precise feedback concerning interaction, content, and technology.

Many refinements and improvements were made to the experience, basing on the experience thus accumulated and on the observers' reports. Their analysis revealed several interesting aspects; for example, even significant technical problems (such as users repeatedly disconnecting) did not hinder the students' enthusiasm if they were able to take part in the interaction and play at least part of the games. On the other hand, students get really upset when they are involved in some engaging activity (either game or discussion) and suddenly they have to stop. They are also disappointed when they do not get as high scores as they thought they deserve. Observing the users, we realized that what they really appreciate is the engagement of interaction, the excitement of competition, and the gratification for the guide's rewards (for their correct answers or contributions). Despite technical and organizational problems, when these elements are present the session is successful.

Students' Questionnaires

After the end of the second experimental phase, students were asked to fill in a questionnaire, sent to the teachers via e-mail and then distributed in the classes. 226 questionnaires were filled in and sent back. Some of the questions had a 4-scale predefined set of answers (such as "a lot, enough, not so much, not at all"); others were just open questions, to collect opinions and suggestions. We shall focus now on a few of them:

Q6: Would you be happy to repeat the SEE experience? 50% of the students declared themselves very keen on repeating the experience; another 40% said they would be glad to do it again. Only 1% answered that they wouldn't. The main reason to repeat the experience was the intercultural aspect, that is, the "possibility of meeting other students from different countries and cultures;" the second reason was the interest in the topic and the third one was the fun of the experience. Actually, as also the observers had reported, the most appreciated session turned out to be the fourth one, during which every group presented to the others a research and discussed it, comparing different cultural points of view.

Q11 and 12: Which game did you enjoy best? Do you have any suggestions or critiques about any game? The most appreciated game turned out to be the quiz, that is, the one in which the rules were the clearest and the "physical" and cultural part most clearly distinct (while the avatar was performing an ability game, the rest of the class tried to find the correct answer to the quiz). Students suggested making questions more difficult: they had studied hard and felt underestimated when questions were too easy.

Q17: Which of the 4 sessions did you like best? The outcomes (Figure 16), apart from confirming

Figure 16. Data from students' questionnaires

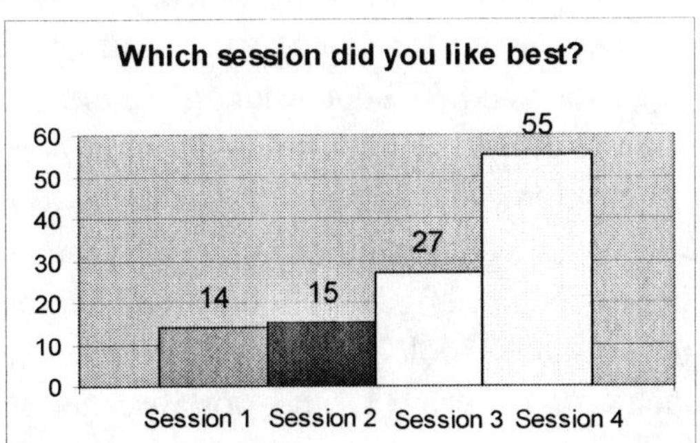

the fact that students liked discussing their homework in Session 4, also show an ever-increasing interest and involvement in the activity, with a climax in the last meeting that evidently left them, so to speak, with a "good flavour."

Data concerning the outcomes of the third experimental phase have been compared with the expectations collected before its beginning.

Expectations on the overall impact of the experience were actually a bit higher than the final outcomes, although the difference is very slight. This clearly proves that both students and teachers are eager and ready to exploit innovative educational tools; this outcome clearly shows that "traditional" e-learning is probably already outdated and encourages us to keep in this path.

Teachers' Questionnaires and Focus Groups

Teachers were involved in the design and assessment processes from the very first steps of the project. Five focus groups were held to choose the cultural topics, structure online activities, define the format of the background material and of the homework; three additional focus groups provided precious insights about the project's educational impact. Their contribution to the tuning of the project was invaluable.

At the end of the second experimental phase, questionnaires were distributed to all the teachers who had taken part in the project. 19 questionnaires were filled in and given back to us. On the whole, scores ranged from "good" to " very good," never scoring "very bad." About students' interaction (during the cultural discussions, the games and the preparation of the homework), teachers would have appreciated more communication outside online sessions among the schools involved; they suggested that schools should be helped to keep in touch after the project's end, possibly meeting in the "real" world. In the third experimental phase, more attention was devoted to encourage cooperation among schools.

Teachers found the interaction very engaging and a powerful stimulus for studying; moreover, the use of new technologies was a good opportunity to couple "diligent" students with those more apt at interacting in a virtual environment, thus emphasizing their different skills (Gardner, 1983). Particularly rewarding was the outcome of Question 3 (*How do you evaluate the educational impact of the experience?*): two teachers judged the educational impact of the experience "excellent," eight scored it as "very good," another eight as "good;" only one scored it as bad, and none as "very bad."

The outcomes of the focus groups will be discussed in detail in the next section.

IN WHICH SENSE IT WORKS

Teachers were constantly consulted before, during and after every experimental phase. Their contributions, collected through interviews, personal communications and focus groups, were illuminating—especially as far as the educational benefits and unexpected effects of the experience are concerned. A second valuable source of information were the chat flows, registering students' conversations, and showing how each one's remark stimulated the others' thoughts and provoked reactions, in a progressing discovery process.

SEE educational impact was observed on three fronts: (1) Content; (2) Students' motivation and attitude; (3) Learning methodologies.

Learning the Content

Teachers particularly appreciated the interview format, enhancing **critical thinking** and stimulating students to evaluate the experts' different contributions, possibly assuming an opinion of their own. They said: *"The interview approach is* *extremely interesting: it shows the state-of-the-art of the research, a debate at academic level."*

Quotes from teachers' statements collected during focus groups are reported in italics between quotation marks.

The strong **interdisciplinary** character of the experience was also appreciated. Students could see how many different disciplines, with their diverse criteria and methods, may converge on one single issue, each one bringing its special contribution. *"Among teachers, great emphasis was put on the interdisciplinary quality of the project. We discussed on how to involve as many subjects as possible: Italian Literature, English, and Religion. It was important for us to involve not only our students, but also our colleagues. If the class coordinator feels involved in the project, and works in collaboration with teachers of other subjects, this becomes a real strength. Students realize that the Experience is multidisciplinary."* In some humanistic high schools, teachers exploited the interest stirred by SEE introducing new topics related to the subject: *"I slightly modified the curricular program of History, Latin and Greek Literature, studying in depth the authors which had more to do with the project. We read Greek excerpts from the Genesis and Josephus Flavius [...]; students were very curious about him, because they knew he had to do with the project."*

Finally, the **cross-cultural** exchange is one of the most fascinating aspects of the experience. Students discuss in real-time with peers located in distant countries, discovering how different their perspectives can be. While Italian students, for instance, tend to regard the Dead Sea and Jerusalem as remote, almost fabulous places, Israeli pupils are much more concrete about them, because many have been there: they described the archaeological site of Qumran, the heat, the rocks, the bathing pools; they talked about Qumran religious feasts that are still celebrated today; when someone suggested that the inhabitants of Qumran used to eat fish, they immediately pointed out that "there is no fish in the Dead Sea." After studying the *Rituals in Qumran*, each class presented its research on a particular rite or feast celebrated in its local area: it was wonderful to observe the variety of uses and traditions, and to discover how all of them were originated by the same need for celebrating important events, that is shared by human communities of all times and places. *"The 'otherness' element, the meeting with other countries and cultures, is always stimulating. During the first session, it was exciting for the students to see themselves and the boys and girls of the other class. They are right there, and so faraway at the same time..."*

Enhancing Students' Motivation

SEE's unusual approach, dealing with complex and serious matters in a playful, engaging way, had strong effects on motivation and attitude:

Figure 17. Scenes from the experimental phases

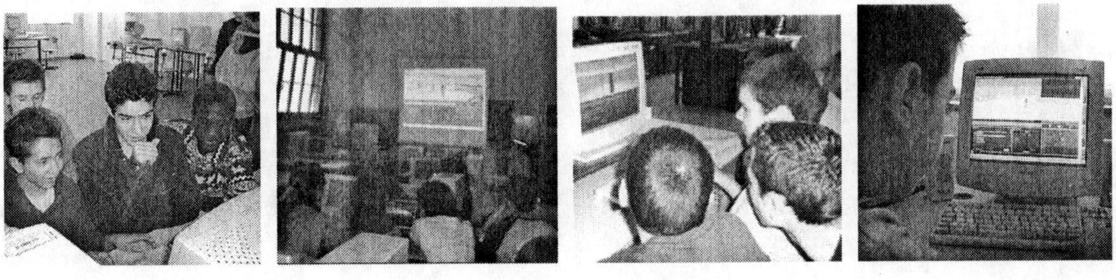

we observed a general increase in students' care and attentiveness, the occasion for "bringing out" problematic students and the improvement of discipline.

Competition, the desire of winning the games, and the engagement of communicating with peers of different countries, are powerful motivators for studying both the material and the language in which it is discussed during the sessions: *"They realized the importance of learning English."*

"They read the interviews at home, then we discussed them in class; we inquired on the historical perspective, doing further research on the different opinions of the experts. I never threatened examinations; nevertheless they studied with great care to be prepared for the Experience. They probably wouldn't have been so committed, without the games' spur." It was amazing to see how even very young students became deeply knowledgeable about "difficult" subjects, such as the history of Middle East, religious issues, etc. In SEE, interaction drives the content: the thrill of meeting peers from far away, the impression—given by the 3-D virtual world—of "being there" with them in a remote country, the desire to win the games, are crucial for arousing the students' interest.

Teachers typically chose for experimenting SEE their most motivated, hardworking students; some teachers instead made a different choice: *"We selected our least motivated students: we thought that, if something could "rescue" them, it would be a project like this. And we were right."* The innovative teaching-learning style proposed by SEE offered disaffected students an opportunity to show their **commitment**: *"All of them participated with enthusiasm. Even two kids with comprehension problems had studied well and knew everything."*

Of the many different skills pupils possess, only few are evaluated in "traditional" school activities. A different learning approach gives these '**hidden talents**' a chance to emerge, and such abilities are extremely appreciated by the class. Teachers, on their part, are glad to reward the kids' keen involvement and commitment: *"One of my students had never been outstanding in Greek; however, being good at using computers (and being the only guy in a class of girls), he was chosen to play all the games, and to supervise any activity involving the use of technologies. He worked very seriously and accurately. I gave him a good mark to reward his active participation in the project."*

Some **discipline** rules had to be followed during online meetings: no offence was tolerated, and scores were taken from teams for misbehaviour. Sometimes students, while cheering for their team, tended to address the opponents via chat in rather unfriendly terms; when necessary, the guide admonished and punished them, yet, most of the times, it was the students themselves who urged their classmates to be disciplined, and restrained each other from reacting to provocations. In classes with discipline problems, teachers regarded this fact as a huge improvement.

Learning How to Study

There are many ways to organize class activities related to the experience. Once agreed on few essential guidelines, necessary for coordinating work among different schools, much is left to the creativity and initiative of the teachers. Without their passionate and professional work, the SEE experience would never work, no matter how carefully prepared by the staff. On the whole, the project had two basic effects concerning learning methodology.

1. All the students of a class felt as a "team," understanding that they had to cooperate in order to successfully participate in the experience.
2. Students learnt how to work in groups, autonomously and responsibly (although with the fundamental supervision and support of the teacher).

The project has a sort of "**team spirit building**" effect: all the students felt "as one," knowing that *"each one's skills were resources for the class. They understood that, by playing their role well, the whole team would benefit." "I saw none of the usual jealousy for those who controlled mouse and keyboard: they stood together, united to win."*

In order to better organize their effort, they usually split in groups, each one taking charge of a specific part of the study material, sharing their knowledge with the others and answering the cultural questions during the online experience. While sometimes it was the teacher who formed the groups and assigned materials, in most cases the kids organized **autonomously** and **responsibly**. *"Students worked a lot by themselves. They really had the idea that this was* their *project.* "

They had to work in group for preparing the homework: they met together after school hours, doing research, interviewing local experts and even working at the teacher's house, who put his/her library at their disposal: *"They live in the same neighbourhood and met in the afternoons to study together, whereas usually they work alone."* Again, teachers' supervision played a crucial role: *"They worked hard, preparing schemas and conceptual maps. We worked on two fronts: knowledge and method; we wanted them to learn not only the contents, but also how to distinguish important information from secondary aspects."*

On the whole, they learnt how to **effectively collaborate** in view of a common goal – a very precious skill in today's society—and the experience left its mark: *"One of my pupils of last year, who now attends a senior high school with two other ex-students of mine, came to see me and told me about her new schoolmates. She said: 'we had to do some work in groups, and the others are* so *clumsy! You know, they didn't do the Scrolls'..."*

CONCLUSION

We are convinced today that the "format" of SEE is effective and applicable to a variety of subjects (including scientific and technological ones), but also we have derived a number of "lessons" about what to do and about what not to do. We do not claim that we have completely understood what happened during the experimentation, but we can provide the readers with a few (possibly) useful hints:

A. Trying to "reconstruct" a museum (and this was our starting point in 1999, when the project begun—see the works of Barbieri et al., Di Blas et al.) in 3-D is of little relevance. A 3-D virtual museum never conveys the magic of "being there" in the real place, and therefore it can't emotionally influence the students. 3-D can be used, however, for recreating the general "atmosphere" (e.g., Jerusalem, the main architectural features of the Israel Museum, etc.), but success or failure do not depend upon the quality or faithfulness of the reproduction.

B. Showing, in a virtual world, all the objects on display in the real museum is useless: a virtual museum cannot be "used" as a real museum (e.g., for a group visit). In order to emphasize the "objects" (always an important goal for a museum) a different approach is needed.

C. The "virtual visit" must be compelling, engaging, and fast-paced; we decided that its main purpose, in our case, was to meet other people "there," in the virtual museum.

D. Motivations and interaction dynamics typical of the real world do not always work properly in the virtual world. The social sense and warmth of being "in a group" in a real museum is not easily conveyed in a virtual one; the natural engagement of a guided tour (with a good guide) in a museum is hard to replicate in a virtual one. On this ground, we have used games and competition as a key factor for creating engagement, stimulating social interaction, and motivating the students. Moreover, the 3-D environment is not the place where substantial learning happens; yet, the activities in the virtual environment are tremendous "motivators" for the learning process, which mostly takes place off-line, in the classrooms.

E. Competition, involving the whole class, in cooperation with another class, acts as a global strong motivator both for teachers and students: they want to "win." Competition builds up a strong feeling of team-ship within the class and produces long lasting beneficial effects.
F. Games, within the sessions, involve two students per class only, and we were afraid that the rest of the class would not be involved. As a matter of fact, instead, classes followed their "champions" playing for them, cheering and trying to help.
G. Interviews have played an important role: their format, their natural way of exposing difficult problems, their "state-of-the-art" quality, and their mutual inconsistency (they often contradict each other) have captured the interest of the students and teachers and stimulated their critical thinking.
H. The discussions, in the 3-D environments, have been alive and vibrant: more than we expected. The fast pace and the action of the "guide" played a crucial role in this.
I. Homework was felt as very important: students showed their own specific traditions and cultural background, illustrating their discoveries—with great satisfaction—to the other classes during the homework's comparison.

We can ask now, to ourselves and to the readers, two fundamental questions:

A. Does an experience like SEE provide benefits of any kind for a museum?
B. Is SEE applicable to any kind of museum, and to scientific-technical ones in particular?

As far as the first question is concerned, the answer depends, of course, on what a museum perceives as its mission: if a museum conceives itself as "objects-holder" and "objects-displayer" for the public, then an activity such as the one described in this paper has little to do with it. Many museums, however, are meant to be "culture facilitators or mediators," that is, a means through which culture is popularised. The main difference with respect to universities or research centres is that museums are places where anybody can go, and interaction with the museum content is at the centre of the experience: "abstract" knowledge, unrelated to a sort of "physical experience," is not appropriate for a museum. Scientific museums in particular consider themselves as a place where visitors do learn something (rather than simply looking at objects). If the goal of a museum is to facilitate learning, then we can consider our "format" as a novel way to achieve its goal.

The second question requires a little bit of thought: gaming, competition, quizzes, etc., would certainly work with scientific and/or technological topics; nonetheless, two crucial factors would be missing: the display of local traditions and culture (we assume that science and technology are "the same" everywhere) and the consequent discussion, that create an atmosphere of cross-cultural environment.

Interviews again would work as content's format, but they should be carefully crafted: they should present state-of-the-art research, but with terminology and concepts acceptable to students and teachers. The attitude of teachers could be also a source of problems: our long experience (since 1996) in introducing technologies in public schools has shown that teachers of scientific-technological subjects are often afraid of state-of-the-art content, since they do not understand it, in most cases.

The above said, we are not afraid to take up a new challenge and try to adapt the SEE format for a science museum: candidates are welcome.

ACKNOWLEDGMENT

We wish to acknowledge the work of all the people who contributed to make SEE a successful experience (details can be found in www.seequmran.it).

REFERENCES

Barbieri, T. (2000). Networked virtual environments for the Web: The WebTalk-I and WebTalk-II Architectures. In *Proceedings of IEEE for Computer Multimedia & Expo 2000* (ICME). New York.

Barbieri, T., & Paolini, P. (2000). Cooperative visits to WWW museum sites a year later: Evaluating the effect. In D. Bearman & J. Trant (Eds.), *Museums and the Web 2000: Selected Papers*. Pittsburgh, PA: Archives and Museum Informatics.

Barbieri, T., & Paolini, P. (2001). Cooperation metaphors for virtual museums. In D. Bearman & J. Trant (Eds.), *Museums and the Web 2001: Selected Papers*. Pittsburgh, PA: Archives and Museum Informatics.

Barbieri, T. et al. (1999). Visiting a museum together: How to share a visit to a virtual world. In D. Bearman & J. Trant (Eds.), *Museums and the Web 99: Selected Papers* (pp. 27-32). Pittsburgh, PA: Archives and Museum Informatics.

Barbieri, T. et al. (2001). From dust to StardDust: A collaborative virtual computer science museum. In *International Cultural Heritage Informatics Meeting: Proceedings from ICHIM 2001*. Milano, Italy.

Bowman, D., Hodges, L., & Bolter, J. (1998). The virtual venue: User-computer interaction in an information-rich virtual environment. *Presence: Teleoperators and Virtual Environments, 7*(5), 478493.

Bowman, D., Kruijff, E., LaViola, J., & Poupyrev, I. (2001). An introduction to 3D user interface design. *Presence: Teleoperators and Virtual Environments, 10*(1), 96-108.

Bowman, D., Wineman, J., Hodges, L., & Allison, D. (1999). The educational value of an information-rich virtual environment. *Presence: Teleoperators and virtual environments, 8*(3), 317-331.

Chang, N. (2002). The roles of the instructor in an electronic classroom. In *Proceedings of ED-Media 2002*. Denver, CO: AACE.

Di Blas, N., Paolini, P., & Hazan, S. (2003a) Edutainment in 3D virtual worlds. The SEE experience. In D. Bearman & J. Trant (Eds.), *Museums and the Web 2003: Selected Papers*. Pittsburgh, PA: Archives and Museum Informatics.

Di Blas, N., Paolini, P., & Poggi, C. (2003b). SEE (Shrine Educational Experience): An online cooperative 3D environment supporting innovative educational activities. In D. Lassner & C. McNaught (Eds.), *Proceedings of ED-Media 2003*. Norfolk, VA: AACE.

Di Blas, N., Paolini, P., & Poggi, C. (2003c). Shared 3D Internet environments for education: usability, educational, psychological and cognitive issues. In J. Jacko & C. Stephanidis (Eds.), *Human-computer interaction: Theory and practice. Proceedings of HCI International 2003* (Vol. 1). Mahwah, NJ: Lawrence Erlbaum Associates.

Di Blas, N., Paolini, P., & Poggi, C. (2004). Learning by playing: An edutainment 3D environment for schools. In *Proceedings of ED-Media 2004*. Lugano, Switzerland.

Falk, J.H., & Dierking, L.D. (1992). *The museum experience.* Washington, DC: Whalesback Books.

Falk, J.H., & Dierking, L.D. (2000). *Learning from museums: Visitor experiences and the making of meaning.* Walnut Creek, CA: Altamira Press.

Gardner, H. (1983). *Frames of mind: The theory of multiple intelligences.* New York: Basic Books.

Roitman, A. (1997). *A day at Qumran: The Dead Sea sect and its scrolls.* Jerusalem: The Israel Museum

Vygotsky, L.S. (1978). *Mind in society.* Cambridge, MA: Harvard University Press.

This work was previously published in E-Learning and Virtual Science Centers, edited by R. Subramaniam & L. Tan, pp. 308-326, copyright 2005 by Information Science Publishing (an imprint of IGI Global).

Chapter XXIII
Enhancing Learning Through 3-D Virtual Environments

Erik Champion
School of ITEE, University of Queensland, Australia

ABSTRACT

We cannot begrudge students their envy in looking at popular films and computer games as major contenders for their spare time. While we as teachers could attempt to fight the popularity of games, I suggest a more useful endeavor would be to attempt to understand both the temptation of games, and to explore whether we could learn from them, in order to engage students and to educate them at the same time. There are still few applicable theories and successful case studies on how we could do this using virtual environments and associated technology (referred to by some as virtual reality, or VR). To help answer the question of "but what can we do about it," I will outline several simplified theories of cultural learning based on interaction, and the experience I gained from employing them in two different virtual environment projects.

INTRODUCTION

Today's computer games are vast, powerful, and engaging digital environments. Students buy them, play them, and modify them. With no prompting from teachers, they tear through tutorials and manuals, test new hardware and software, and spend thousands of hours engaged in "hard fun," as well as being immersed in creating characters, animation, sound, and 3-D environments.

Yet in academic research institutes, we see a huge outpouring on the advantages of virtual reality, but little significant educational content. While recent academic literature has criticized the content-poor output of traditional virtual reality research, it has so far been reticent in developing guidelines and practically applicable theories for creating virtual environments that succeed as an engaging medium for entertainment and education.

There are many difficult issues in creating virtual environments: not least is the problem of wrestling with cutting-edge technology. However, I propose the major problem that educators should concentrate on, and help virtual reality researchers with, is understanding how virtual environments, as digital media, relate to how people learn.

To explain that relationship, we need some history on the development of virtual environments, and why, despite being developed in research institutes, they do not immediately lend themselves to teaching. I am going to suggest that a major issue has not been technological constraint, but meaningful content. We lack extensive exploration in choosing and creating interaction that is meaningfully related to specific content, and, for various reasons, we lack impartial evaluation of the projects. Once we can understand that relationship, we can develop an appropriate strategy. That strategy must address the issue of how digital media simulates, augments, or replaces traditional learning through appropriate interaction with meaningful content.

Secondly, we need to ascertain whether entertainment technology, that is, games, offers us more accessible ways of developing virtual learning environments than commercial virtual reality packages. I will suggest that they often do, but that there are several major issues to consider when evaluating and using them. Thirdly, no matter what type of technology we choose, we must have a clear idea of the learning-based goals we hope the participants will reach. Fourthly, once we know the learning-based goals, we will need to scope a different type of interaction that through digital media, simulates, augments, or makes possible those goals. Finally, we need to know if, when, and how these goals are achieved; we have to have an evaluation plan in place.

MISSIONS AND CONCERNS

Until recently, virtual environments have been single-user, with limited ability to interact with the environment. In the rare case where they were multiuser, the interaction possible between participants was limited not just by technical constraints or the desktop personal computer (PC) interface, but also by a lack of thematic relationship between the content and the perceived learning experience. As noted by Johnson (1997), participants often feel they are looking at a computer screen, rather than existing in a real place. Weckström (2004) noted that even when there was a feeling of spatial immersion, of "3-D-ness," the environments were still empty and devoid of apparent purpose.

> *This thesis began from the fact that, when a group of students were exploring and researching other 'virtual worlds' in order to begin developing Marinetta, they reported that all the worlds seemed empty and hollow, like stage sets. There were neat buildings in these spaces but no sense that these buildings had been built for any real purpose. The students noted that these so called virtual worlds did not seem to be worlds at all, but just architectural spaces that did not give them any feeling of worldliness.* (Weckström, 2004, p. 9)

Why this separation of "world" from "architectural space?" In order to visualize spaces, architects have not been worried about social agency, about how participants can relate to each other in virtual environments. They have been concerned about presenting the environment in the best possible light, in order to create impressive fly-throughs.

Even though architecture is about the inhabitation of space, virtual reality, to architects, has been seen as a tool to sell the idea of inhabitation in order to be commissioned to build real buildings. Hence, we should not look to them for the best way on interacting with a virtual interactive world, for they are not interested in building them. I have spoken to several architectural visualization experts about this issue and they agree with me: architects see the technology as an extension of computer aided design and drafting software (CADD or CAD), as a way of presenting objects; they are not (yet) worried about interaction.

I have suggested in previous writings that the way we classify, define, and evaluate virtual environments, needs a major conceptual overhaul, and not just a waiting game for faster computer networks or rendering power (Champion, 2003; Champion & Sekiguchi, 2005). I suggest that why virtual environments have not lived up to their potential as learning environments is due to a variety of reasons, but I also suggest these issues can be addressed.

LEARNING VIA INTERACTIVE DIGITAL MEDIA

Teaching Issues

Hampered by the continual change and advancement of cutting edge technology, and motivated by the allure of predicting the future, the way people have written about and classified virtual learning environments has been misleading and often unhelpful for the design of learning environments. We do need to create guidelines for immersive learning environments, but citing science fiction, movies, and literature is a dangerous move. Meaningful learning comes from meaningful interaction, rather than from photo-realistic representation of fanciful futuristic situations.

> *A virtual world has to support the following factors: there has to be a feeling of presence, the environment has to be persistent, it has to support interaction, there has to be a representation of the user and it has to support a feeling of specific worldliness.* (Weckström, 2004, p. 38)

To sell books, especially on new and exciting technology, it is very tempting to make outrageous promises. Without mentioning the specific examples, (you can find them by looking for books with "cyberspace" or "virtual reality" in the title from the 1990s), these books trumpeted the paradigm shifting promise of virtual reality. The literature was spearheaded by famous academics who were inspired by science fiction television and films. Typically, these academics had not actually created their own virtual environments via the then available, and to my mind, highly unsuitable technology of proprietary CADD packages, and complex programming languages, such as C/C++, not something learnt overnight!

I would agree that virtual reality technology is often perceived as too expensive, complicated, or time-consuming for teachers. However, recent advances in home entertainment technology (such as in commercial computer games) actually brings the potential of immersive environments as a learning medium closer to the classroom, and to the learning "comfort zone" of today's students.

On the other hand, the actual barrier I have found amongst educationalists is not due to the technology, but to the concept of interactivity. Too many teachers view virtual environments as a digital depository of conventional media: they do not yet see that children can learn from these virtual environments, and that they learn not by reading and reciting, but by exploration and "trial and error" interaction.

Perhaps this has also been due to the success of marketing: attempting to find "virtual" products and case studies on the Web leads to a plethora of digital panoramas, and "virtual media" libraries of HTML and word documents. When I think of virtual reality, I think of 3-D space, and meaningful interaction, not merely two-dimensional pictures, and certainly not files that happen to be available over the Internet.

Designing Places for Learning

Virtual environments are often criticized for evoking "cyberspace" but not "place." In other words, they lack the richness of the associations and encounters that occur in real space (Benedikt, 1991; Coyne, 1999; Johnson, 1997). But what is place? How do we design it? How do we know if this design has worked? More specifically, how we can best create it digitally, in order to enhance learning through interaction, is still vague (Champion & Sekiguchi, 2005).

One would think that virtual heritage environments, being designed to educate us in how people from a previous or distant society saw their world, would encompass and transmit their way of living. Yet writers such as Mosaker (2001) and Gillings (2002) have stated that virtual environments lack meaningful content, and virtual heritage environments and virtual archaeology are a case in point. "VR systems do not offer an alternative 'reality'; they do, however, provide simulated worlds that seem 'realistic'" (Schroeder, 1996, p. 15).

Designers may use this conflation to persuade the viewer that high-resolution images imply a high degree of archaeological certainty, when this is not the case.

> *The distinctions between real and hypothetical are not simple but subtle, complex, and far-reaching .... As Mr. Emele pointed out in his article, a partially known site cannot be reconstructed satisfactorily .... Our reconstructions are also too clean and neat.* (Eiteljorg, 1998, p. 2)

Being designed for visualization, rather than for interaction, most virtual environments are single-user. Where they allow several people to see each other, sharing of information is usually restricted to chat, sending files or hyperlinks; control of social interaction is limited. People are, by nature, social creatures: they will almost certainly want to interact with and be recognizable to other participants. On the other hand, they might want some control over the quantity or even quality of social interaction.

In order to understand how we learn through interaction with the environment, I turned to the literature of cultural geography. Here I found the ideas of Relph, in his book *Place and Placelessness,* offered me a way of both *describing* and *prescribing* attributes of virtual environments.

> *The identity of a place is comprised of three interrelated components, each irreducible to the other, physical features or appearance, observable activities and functions, and meanings or symbols.* (Relph, 1976, p. 61)

Relph's book enabled me to see that virtual environments are typically designed to aid visualization, to foster activities (such as games), or (potentially) allow people to develop their own projected identities, and interpret that of others, either directly via social interaction, or indirectly through observing, investigating, and through playing with cultural practices and artifacts. And it is easiest to create the first type of environment, for it involves creating an interface that facilitates navigation around static objects, but no other *directed* form of interaction. The second type, the activity based virtual environment, requires the creation of goals, strategies, and, (typically), rewards.

Collaborative learning environments typically require the notion of an *owned* and *shared* space (or place). While the first two types of virtual environments do not require collaboration, the third type typically does. As Yi-Fu Tuan notes (1998), culture adds a nonvisible layer of interpretation to visible objects, yet virtual environments typically only attempt to simulate what is there.

The third type of virtual environment must somehow present the notion of the intangible; it is genuinely difficult to create. The third type of virtual environment requires the environment itself to be both modifiable and readable in a meaningful way. This third type of environment is the most desirable learning environment: rather than learn about objects (produced by people), or procedures (learnt via activity), the most powerful way of learning is to see how people identify, share, and commemorate what is important to them.

Hence, to foster this form of cultural learning, we require interaction. The approach suggested here is constructivist; learners construct their own meaning (Hein, 1991). In his article, Hein argued that interactivity in exhibits creates more engagement by allowing the user to apply the tool directly to their own life. I totally agree with him. In my own evaluations of people using virtual environments, the most popular requests have been for personalization of their avatars, and for modification of the environment.

For a learning environment, social agency allows students to motivate each other through competition or collaboration. It allows the teacher to "enter" the "world" of the user as a fellow participant rather than as an invigilator. Social agency can help structure and direct the learning experience. Coupled with personalization, social agency encourages the student to explore, take control, and express themselves to others (which requires they learn the skills to do so).

Secondly, the WIMP (windows, icons, menus and pointers) interface of typical workstation computers can be cheaply replaced, thanks again to the aggressive marketing and add-ons of gaming technology. There are force-field generators, exercise machines connected to console games as navigation and interface devices, "VR goggles," skateboards, haptic devices, and even low-cost biosensors that control navigation and selection of objects through monitoring the participants stress levels and heartbeat. In all these cases, the products are available for a few hundred American dollars, not the thousands of dollars of specialized commercial virtual reality solutions.

Nonconventional Learning Suitable for Virtual Environments

As a learning platform, the virtual environment, and its much-hyped sister, Internet-based distance learning, has been savagely attacked by philosophers such as Dreyfus (2001). Critics have argued that virtual environments cause disembodiment, disorientation, discomfort, and social alienation.

On the other hand, psychologists use virtual environments for curing phobias (especially spatial ones), distracting the attention of the participant during painful surgery, improving hand-eye coordination, for leadership simulation training, and even for improving cultural understanding of soldiers in foreign lands.

Virtual reality therapy already helps many patients overcome phobias: from fear of flying to fear of spiders. Jacobson (2000) notes similar systems are being tested to see if they can reduce bouts of anorexia and bulimia.

Virtual environments can help promote technology for the sake of technology, for example, in creating 3-D product showcases, available over the Internet. However, this does not help teachers create learning environments: being impressed by technology is not the same as being inspired by it.

More importantly for teachers, digital media can synergise learning by the use of various multimedia, for example, 3-D modelling packages can be used to create models of the human heart in action, or they can use graphic cutaways, 3-D models, and sound, to demonstrate how to service a car's engine. The same technology can also preserve cultural artefacts through a three- or even four-dimensional record of history.

The interactive possibilities include seeing a reconstruction, as well as an idea of how it was inhabited, along with artefacts used as they had been intended, and in context. Time-based media can present ideas, objects, or techniques that are difficult to visualise either in real life, or through conventional media. Yet imaginative digital visualisations and reconstructions are only part of the story. Even more importantly, through interactive digital media, we can learn by doing.

SOLUTIONS

Interaction for Meaningful Learning Experiences

In education circles, it is possible to find Websites with two-dimensional information labelled "virtual" or "digital" media. But to do so is to miss out on the magic of three-dimensional space, which is necessary to create a rich and atmospheric sense of spatial presence. Coupled with meaningful activity, space becomes place; it identifies, commemorates, and records the meeting of a group with a task.

"Yet, paradoxically, remote learning—one of the rapidly growing uses of Cyberspace—is little more than an organized way of distributing learning materials in an efficient, electronic way. All the participants in 'remote learning' (the teachers and the students), miss out on the rich, cultural and social phenomenon of the learning experience itself. While the method is efficient, it is hardly the type of experience most learners will remember fondly many years later, like remembering their place-specific high school or college years" (Kalay, 2004, p. 196).

Once we have three-dimensional space, students can more easily see what can take place inside the environment. They can learn about spatial proximity, they can personalise the environment in relation to others, and identify themselves to others through the creation of avatars and by the "marking" or annotation of the virtual environment.

For this process to be meaningful, and for there to be enough motivation for individuals to meet and collaborate, there needs to be activities and goals that allow the participants to explore, attempt, and to identify themselves with or against. We also need to have clear ideas as to how types of interaction affect the ways in which we learn, and how they can be approximated by the limited interaction typically available in virtual environments.

What Games have to Teach us about Interaction

Making content appealing to the end-learner may be the lesson that the e-learning industry needs to learn most of all. (Aldrich, 2004, p. 7)

A considerable amount of literature has argued that interactive engagement in a computer medium is best demonstrated by games (Aldrich, 2004; Champion, 2003; Laird, 2001; Manninen, 2004; Prensky, 2001; Schroeder, 1996).

Constructivism and constructionism are education theories that seem to directly support the use of games as learning environments (Brooks & Brooks, 1999; Wong, 2003). For example, Papert worked with Alan Kay on the cross-platform and open source project Croquet. Croquet is designed to allow participants to meet each other in 3-D spaces, which allowed them to collaborate on any files on any PC, even if some of the participants did not have the native applications to open them (Lombardi & Lombardi, 2005). Perhaps more radically, Prensky argues that students of today perceive and think differently to past generations (Prensky, 2001). He believes that by using their cultural artifacts to communicate to them, we are both acknowledging their cultural worth, and are more likely to impart learning that is both more accessible and more meaningful to them.

Some teachers use commercial game engines and online role-playing games as a catalyst to talk about social identities (Gee, 2003); others use games in class to teach students historical processes and how to examine counterfactual history (Squire, 2002). Games can also be developed to enhance and discuss collaboration and teamwork practices (Squire, Makinster, Barnett, Barab, & Barab, 2003). Designing an engaging virtual environment, which challenges, fosters skills, and inspires new learning, in order to develop successful strategies, can thus be helped by an understanding of game design. Games can have context (user-based tasks), navigation reminders, inventories, records of interaction history (i.e., damage to surroundings), and social agency. Games are a familiar medium to users, and help train us how to learn and how to use props as cultural tools. Games provide competition, and therefore challenge: a feature typically lacking in virtual environments. Further, just as the most popular games (excluding Tetris) require representations of opponents (social agents), so too do virtual environments. As in games, virtual environment users may prefer personalization. Engaging virtual environments also requires interaction geared towards a task, a goal. This is a crucial feature for learning environments: the virtual environment as game has to motivate the participant, not the teacher (Amory, Naicker, Vincent, & Adams, 1999).

As users become engaged in the tasks, it is easier to observe them without damaging their level of engagement, especially as games traditionally have built-in evaluation mechanisms. Furthermore, games cater to learning curves of new users by advancing in complexity over time, and this can be incorporated into virtual learning environments.

If we could only crack the issue of why the "hard fun" of games has not been seen in institutional learning, we may be able to create *educational* and *engaging* learning experiences, using the techniques of these highly immersive virtual environments, and matching them to meaningful learning goals.

So what is a game? Part of the attraction of games is certainly due to their interactive and engaging nature, as explained by the following definition by Aldrich (2004, p. 240). For him, a game is "An interactive and entertaining source of play, sometimes used to learn a lesson."

More helpful for designers is the definition by Salen and Zimmerman, as it attempts to explain what makes games entertaining. In their large tome on game design, they wrote the following, often-quoted definition of a game. "A game is a system in which players engage in an artificial conflict, defined by rules, that results in a quantifiable outcome" (Salen & Zimmerman, 2003, p. 572).

To my mind, one powerful feature of games has been downplayed in the above example. Games are systematic in that they are rules-based, but they are also characterised by inspirational difficulties. The harder the tasks in a game, the more people are inspired to try to solve them. With that in mind, here is my working definition of a computer game (different to Salen and Zimmerman); a game is a challenge that offers up the possibility of temporary or permanent tactical resolution without harmful outcomes to the real-world situation of the participant.

Games Culture and Learning

Many people may well object that games merely involve developing hand-eye coordination, that they do not have meaningful interaction, for people do not learn about other cultures and societies. In order to answer this important question, I wish to reconsider the nature of culture, and how we can develop a model of how culture is learnt.

"Culture consists of patterns, explicit and implicit, of and for behaviour acquired and transmitted by symbols, constituting the distinctive achievement of human groups, including their embodiment in artefacts; the essential core of culture consists of traditional (i.e. historically derived and selected) ideas and especially their attached values; culture systems may on the one hand, be considered as products of action, on the other as conditioning elements of further action" (Kroeber & Kluckhohn, 1952, p. 357).

Given the above definition of culture, we can see that cultural learning involves different modes of interaction. When we visit other cultures, we often learn new, and hitherto foreign, cultural perspectives through copying others' behaviour. We also learn through listening (to their language, to their myths and music), or through reading text and viewing media (as tourists and students).

However, we also learn by making hypotheses, by applying the right words in the wrong situations, and learning the correct phrase or protocol through social embarrassment and sometimes ridicule.

Consider, for a moment, the distinction between travellers and tourists. Ideally, we would also try to develop interactive scenarios for inhabitants. Unlike tourists and even travellers, inhabitants have certain roles, responsibilities, and powers (Gee, 2003; Weckström, 2004).

Travellers require more contextual interaction than tourists do: they have goals; places to see within a certain period of time, and without too much exertion; people to find or to avoid; items to seek out, purchase, or utilize. Inhabitants are more constrained, yet knowledgeable in different ways than visitors (travellers and tourists); they have certain place-related tasks to complete using local resources. Giving people goals (as travellers or inhabitants) may increase their engagement or sense of authenticity (Mosaker, 2001; for an alternative viewpoint, see Hedman, 2001).

Travellers and tourists learn about places by going there, observing events, and being instructed by signs, by guides, and by reading printed material. Such learning in games is typically before the start of the actual game, in the form of a textual introduction or voice-over. It is seldom part of the overall gameplay itself. Game tutorials, on the other hand, are procedural. Some games offer short walkthroughs, where users may practice learning to jump, sidestep, use weapons, and so forth. As contextually appropriate simulations, these games within games offer something real-world tourism seldom encompasses; learning by doing.

When we develop cultural knowledge, we do so through observation, through being told by others, or through trial and error. It is possible to classify game devices (to create challenge or provide information) according to these learning modes.

For example, gamers can learn about the background or potential dangers in the place by how old or worn it is. They also learn as spectators, watching other players, or observing other players strategies while competing with them. Observation-based learning is common to many types of games, and perhaps most evident in Tetris and Space Invaders (they do not require instruction to learn how to play or the outcomes).

Other ways of learning include social learning (by people telling you or instructing you). However, being told what to do is anathema to gamers, as they typically want to act rather than to listen. Games that offer ways of learning how to play without reading instruction manuals seem to be more popular than other games, however, strategy manuals seem popular for gamers to establish themselves as experts once they have mastered beginning gameplay. Ways of providing instructions in games include cut-scenes, dialogue by non-playing characters (NPC), notes found in the scene, the introduction, and strategically placed or timed voice-overs.

The third major way of learning appears to be by trial and error. We can learn about a place through task-based activity there (for example, we learn a swimming pool is suitable for swimming). Gamers learn how to use weapons by making mistakes and firing when too close to a wall. By making mistakes, gamers can learn what is forbidden or promoted by the game rules. For example, in some early shooter games, gamers discovered that shooting missiles at their own feet did not damage them, but allowed them to levitate over walls. This strategy was not foreseen by the game designers, but was later incorporated into the artificial intelligence of the computer-driven players.

I note here that in both computer games and in real life, we often learn through a hybrid of the above. We observe or read why or how people do things, we get some advice on what we are doing wrong, or we overhear how or why other people do it, then we try out different strategies in order to most enjoy it, or most successfully complete the task. Even simplistic 3-D shooter games often involve instruction (at the start), observation (where enemies are hiding or where "health" can be restored), and trial and error (learning how and when to use tools or weapons).

Once we have categorised types of learning, we notice a further separation, between learning by doing, and learning by being shown. Games incorporate both, but "gameplay," the innate and unique engagement created by the game as an interactive goal-directed experience, is built on learning by doing. And it is revealing that learning by doing is the main component of games, wherever possible: learning by being shown is relegated to the beginning of the game, to tutorials, and to online help documentation.

In other words, knowledge developed can be either procedural or prescriptive. The hugely successful market of computer games has shown us that unlike traditional media, interactive virtual environments can be highly useful for procedural learning.

Learning Content that Needs to be Incorporated

I have given several examples of virtual environments that matched content with learning aims and technology. I do not suggest commercial games are directly suitable for education, as they improve hand-eye coordination and spatial cognition: nor are they necessarily suitable for teamwork, or understanding different social perspectives. However, when modified, their cheap and accessible technology, along with the familiarity of their interface conventions to students, can provide for rich learning environments.

There is a developing hybrid game genre that may also prove advantageous to teachers. The new editors for online games and collaborative environments are powerful and inexpensive. The environments that they can support range from role-playing to strategy; some incorporate both. The interactivity can be geared towards collaboration and reconfiguration, rather than outright destruction and competition, depending on the interests of the builder.

Placing the Teacher in the Learning Experience

Where does the teacher stand in relation to the virtual environment experience? Does the teacher become a participant, a level designer, a teacher of the technology? Does the teacher stand back, and help fix things (a one-person help desk), engage with the others in the environment as a character, or evaluate, either remotely or in the classroom?

There are many possible answers, but here I would like to briefly outline a few advantages and disadvantages to each option. For exploring visualization-based archaeology type worlds, leading the class through a virtual environment by voice while allowing each person to navigate their own avatar on their own computer, is useful to the students, and requires less hands-on work However, it is more difficult to evaluate student learning, and ensure that each student is maximizing their learning experience.

For language learning, there still seems to be resistance to using spatial environments. While virtual environment technology can allow students from different cultures, who are learning each other's language, to learn directly from each other, generally, the environments are used as meet and greet 3-D add-ons to chat programs. There is much exciting work to be done in how the reconfiguration of avatar and designed worlds can allow students to identity and test out distinctive social, cultural, and linguistic purposes, but the immediate challenge is, perhaps, to show language teachers what could be done, and make the technology more robust, cross-platform, and modifiable for distance learning.

How We can Evaluate User Responses

Academic virtual environment evaluation usually involves requesting test users to fill out questionnaires indicating a level of presence against three, four, or five general criteria (a feeling of physical space, negative feelings, social agency, naturalism or realism, and engagement).

Questionnaires are prone to error according to Slater (1999). Evaluating people after their experience of the virtual environment may be prone to error, as it relies on memory recall, and on their noticing and communicating exactly what made their sense of engagement seem powerful, weak, or nonexistent.

If a virtual environment seems "natural" to viewers, they may not notice important features that a trained expert would consider distracting or ineffective. We need "passive" evaluation mechanisms to determine the level and type of engagement, without breaking that level of engagement.

Games are actually highly efficient evaluation mechanisms. Their speed and accuracy in evaluating success, or otherwise, is one of the important features of computer games. Game-style abstraction can be just as engaging to users as a sense of realism. Further, as users become engaged in the tasks, it is easier to observe them without damaging their level of engagement, especially as games traditionally have built-in evaluation mechanisms. However, there are issues in applying evaluation techniques to learning about culture. For learning environments, we are not normally interested in task performance: we are interested in understanding.

If we can define understanding to the point where we can test it, there are many ways that evaluation can be built into a virtual environment, with or without the direct participation of the student. If the environment is goal-based, we can evaluate the student's task performance. If the student can act as world builder, we may be able to incorporate peer feedback, especially if the virtual environment is amenable to annotation by visitors.

In the near future, it may also be possible to gauge the physiological state of the participants. I am not here referring to brain scanning, which is already used to evaluate a sense of virtual presence, but is expensive and inaccessible to most teachers. The introduction of biosensors to commercial games is opening up the market to future innate, automatic, and thematically related evaluation of user engagement.

How We can Interactively Augment the VE Content

There are several famous projects using augmented reality as learning experiences (Azuma, 1997). However, we can also incorporate real-time data into the game, especially if we are connected to the Internet, or if we are using certain types of game accessories. Why would we want to do that, and is it feasibly within the scope of teachers?

Firstly, I believe it is possible. Digital technology can integrate the real and the conjectural, as well as synchronous and asynchronous data, into conceptual, user-specific information. This capability suggests that virtual environments may augment, for example, real-world travel and tourism experiences, rather than merely emulate them.

It is possible to have various aspects of the environment dependent on real world data, connecting across the Internet. One virtual heritage project contained animated fireflies; their movement was directly dependent on real-time stock market movement delivered via the Internet (Refsland, Ojika, & Berry, 2000). Using a bit of imagination, and a Web-based data mining script, one could show people the effect of tourism, or how changing conditions affect environments.

For example, real-world places have changing conditions: rain, wind, heat, and so forth. Using real-time data that feeds into a virtual environment via a Web-connected database, visitors in a virtual world could see real-time weather conditions of a place on the other side of the planet. There are already games that, via the Internet, download your local weather conditions into the game itself.

Case Study

In this section, I wish to outline two learning environments recently undertaken.

The first project attempted to answer the following questions:

1. **Place vs. cyberspace.** What creates a sensation of place (as a cultural site) in a virtual environment, in contradistinction to a sensation of a virtual environment as a collection of objects and spaces?
2. **Cultural presence vs. social presence and presence.** Which factors help immerse people spatially and thematically into a cultural learning experience?
3. **Realism vs. interpretation.** Does an attempt to perfect fidelity to sources, and to realism, improve or hinder the cultural learning experience?
4. **Education vs. entertainment.** Does an attempt to make the experience engaging improve or hinder the cultural learning experience?

The prototype solution was the creation of an online reconstruction of an ancient Mayan city in Mexico, and by using techniques learnt from game-style interaction, to evaluate the effect of certain types of interaction on the cultural understanding and subjective preferences of the users.

I had identified certain devices that I believed aided cultural learning in terms of observation, trial and error, or by conversation. In order to test cultural understanding, I created a virtual reconstruction of a world heritage site (Figure 1). I split the reconstruction into three thematic parts, and then assigned each the three different types of interaction "modes," but with similar content to each other. These interaction modes were instruction (scripted chat agents), observation (finding and reading hidden inscriptions), and activity (having to identify and move objects around in order to navigate through to specific goals). The match of environment to interaction mode, I termed a "world." I then set up tasks, and five different types of evaluation. I also had three different audience groups: archaeology students, visualization and heritage experts, and employees of a major travel publication company.

From the observations of the participants, and by comparing their engagement in these archaeological worlds compared to more game-style environments that I designed for them, I found that when they were told something was a game, they automatically seemed more comfortable. And although the game-worlds did not score as well on their subjective preference rankings when answering a questionnaire, they were much more unwilling to leave these worlds than the archaeological ones!

With the archaeology students, rather than set them specific tasks, in one class I walked them through the world. That is, I talked about inter-

Figure 1. Case study 1

esting things on the site, and suggested which "view" button related to what I talked about. They controlled the navigation, appearance, and orientation of their avatar, and followed me quite happily through the site, at their own pace. While talking about the history of the site, I asked them how easy it was to navigate, what they wanted to do, and other simple questions. The most popular request was not for more detail and information, but for more ability to change their avatar, and destroy things!

The practical experience I gained from these experiments was invaluable, but not immediate. I say not immediate because the evaluations themselves were not conclusive. I found that gender, age, and computer experience (in descending order) were important factors, but that task performance could not be directly related to understanding (tested by asking general knowledge questions afterwards), as people were divided on wanting to explore or to compete.

After some more questioning, I came to the following conclusions. There were at least three types of participants: those that wanted to explore, those that wanted to chat, and those that wanted to compete. I later found that games researchers suggest there are actually four types of personality profiles (Bartle, 1999).

I also realized that my theoretical model of cultural learning was inaccurate: people do not just learn by observation, instruction, or by trial and error, they also learn through a combination of these methods. I also realized that traditional learning of historical sources is not procedural; it is not learnt by trial and error, but by books and dictation. Many students have difficulty in prescriptive learning, so perhaps procedural learning may offer specific advantages to them. This raises the issue of whether virtual environments should scope out the preferred learning style of the participant and cater to that style.

The game genre is both a powerful device for improving usability (the conventions for interaction, navigation, and defining goals are well known), and a dangerous one. When playing a game, people do not notice anything in the environment that they do not consider directly related to solving the game goals.

We also lack examples of digital interaction in games that are not destructive, and do not relate to user response times. While strategy games involve the learning of resources, they, along with other games, may confuse the participant as to what is real, and what is imaginative. That is, playing a historical strategy game may help one develop an idea of where to go to buy a catapult, or even what the catapults were called, but one can't say for certain if they were used, where they were used, or their symbolic and cultural value to the local inhabitants.

The second project used similar technology to create a learning environment for cross-cultural language learning, with social collaboration between language students in Japan and in Australia (Champion & Sekiguchi, 2005). This was a very interesting project, as many of the staff had initial reservations about why 3-D added to the learning experience. It was also a testbed for new ideas on how certain types of interaction in space can help our learning of such things as foreign languages.

The evaluation of this project is ongoing, but it raised interesting issues of evaluation without direct teacher input, as the students could participate in their own time, and wherever there was a suitable computer that was connected to the Internet. In the first stage, I scripted triggers that recorded who spoke and to whom, what rooms they went into, and for how long. For the second stage, I suggested a review of what learning was actually possible, and whether we could evaluate that directly, rather than merely record where students went, and so forth.

This ongoing collaboration helped me see the issues that nontechnology focused teachers may have in incorporating digital media. The students find it highly engaging, other staff members may fail to see pedagogical returns, and it can be difficult to scope out interactive scenarios that directly relate to learning outcomes. I believe that in this example, we can borrow from usability methods, particularly the "teaching out loud" method. Instead, we could develop the "speaking/chatting out loud" method, whereby students can teach each other their language through asking and answering questions, through trying to work out who is a native or non-native speaker, and so forth.

I have developed strategies for single-user learning through puzzle games, and through scripts that allow for exact, or near exact answers in different languages to open doors, change worlds, or change avatars. However, I believe that getting the students to build and invigilate the learning environments is the most powerful way of using interactive digital media. There should not be a blind push to use digital media as hoops: we should investigate whether world-building and other unique features of virtual environments offer greater educational advantages. We should also reexamine learning itself, in context. Would imaginative environments help real-world learning? Are particular forms of interaction more suitable than others? Can we develop alternatives to computer shooters that engage the students?

FUTURE TRENDS

In game design, there appears to be a trend towards online collaborative and mixed genre environments. The game level editor as a world builder phenomenon means that designing virtual environments is within the reach of classes. The proliferation of software that allows designers to change between different modelling and animation formats is also encouraging. However, and at the risk of sounding repetitive, there still needs to be more research on meaningful interaction.

The case studies I have mentioned have given me new learning models that encourage student participation: encourage them to separate fact from fiction, allow for innate behind-the-scenes evaluation, and provide for peer feedback, which I believe is an additional powerful form of learning. Unfortunately, I am still scoping out these projects, and final results are not currently available.

"There is a shortage of research integrating theory and practice on how best to augment or invoke the user-experience of place via digital media" (Gillings, 2002, p. 17). By concentrating on achieving photo-realism rather than on understanding the unique capabilities for digital media to enrich the user-experience, there are significant questions still to be answered.

Case studies of learning via game-style simulations exist (Aldrich, 2004), as well as descriptions of how we learn via video games (Gee, 2003), so it seems only a matter of time before performance evaluation can be conducted contextually and indirectly.

CONCLUSION

I don't believe that virtual learning environments are a waste of money, or an ineffective learning tool. I have taught games design by getting the students to build game levels using the applications discussed, and then getting them to mark each other's creations. Not only did they learn the difficulties of designing for others, but they also began to develop a critical vocabulary relevant to them and to their peer group.

Games are far more accessible, and in some cases, more powerful than specialist "virtual reality" environments, and they now offer editors that individuals can use at home on personal computers to extend or create digital environments that they can then explore and share with others. They also offer inbuilt evaluation mechanisms, and as they are typically goal-based, they offer a platform for creating learning tasks.

The many dedicated and hybrid game genres each afford different types of learning experiences, and we are only just beginning to understand which type of interface and interaction suits specific learning requirements. Briefly, these "worlds" can help augment learning in terms of placing historical studies and events, learning about cultural strategies and processes through trial and error, or through collaborating with students from different social and cultural backgrounds far away. The case studies mentioned also revealed how designing and evaluating cultural environments can, in turn, reveal to us new insights into cultural learning and understanding.

How to challenge students to learn meaningful content is a fundamental, pedagogical issue. Developing game-like interaction seems a promising way of achieving this, for games are challenging, in the sense of being difficult in a good *and* engaging way (Rieber, 1996). The trend in commercial games towards multiplayer, and highly customizable environments, is a positive move for education. For rather than try to get students to learn about static content, which needs to be somehow impressive and dynamic to keep their interest, the new games encourage them to create and communicate meaningful content, rather than just be passive consumers.

It is tempting to suggest virtual learning environments have failed because teachers have not understood the technology. Is the technology too difficult? Perhaps for some of us, but for students the technology is *challenging.* While the tools of creating new game "levels" and game "mods" may appear difficult to teachers, why then are there so many game levels built by students?

I would rather suggest that we, as educators, have not yet fully realized that learning itself, needs to be reexamined. If we see games as user-directed virtual environments, it may become clearer how difficult it is to teach prescriptive knowledge, rather than to allow students to learn procedurally.

The implications of digital media and immersive virtual places are not just novel and entertaining, they may be more suited to the ways in which today's students can learn and express themselves. We need to move past what students appear to be doing when they play games, and see what they are learning, and how they are learning, inside these games.

REFERENCES

Aldrich, C. (2004). *Simulations and the future of learning: An innovative (and perhaps revolutionary) approach to e-learning.* San Francisco: Jossey-Bass.

Amory, A., Naicker, K., Vincent, J., & Adams, C. (1999). The use of computer games as an educational tool: Identification of appropriate game types and game elements. *British Journal of Educational Technology, 30*(4), 311-321. Retrieved January 7, 2005, from http://www.nu.ac.za/biology/staff/amory/bjet30.rtf

Azuma, R. (1997). A survey of augmented reality. *Presence: Teleoperators and Virtual Environments, 6*(4), 355-385. Retrieved August 9, 2005, from http://www.cs.unc.edu/~azuma/ARpresence.pdf

Bartle, R. (1999). *Hearts, clubs, diamonds, spades: Players who suit Muds.* Retrieved August 5, 2005, from http://www.mud.co.uk/richard/hcds.htm

Benedikt, M. (1991). *Cyberspace: First steps.* Cambridge, MA: MIT Press.

Brooks, J. G., & Brooks, M. G. (1999). *In search of understanding: The case for constructivist classrooms.* Alexandria, VA, USA: ASCD - Association for Supervision and Curriculum Development.

Champion, E. (2003). Applying game design theory to virtual heritage environments. In S. Spencer (Ed.), *Proceedings of Graphite International Conference on Computer Graphics and Interactive Techniques in Australasia and South East Asia* (pp. 273-274). Melbourne, Australia: ACM SIGGRAPH.

Champion, E., & Sekiguchi, S. (2005). Suggestions for new features to support collaborative learning in virtual worlds. In T. Sakai, K. Tanaka, K. Rose, H. Kita, T. Jozen, & H. Takada (Eds.), *Proceedings of C5: The Third International Conference on Creating, Connecting and Collaborating through Computing* (pp. 129-136). Shiran Kaikan, Kyoto University, Japan: Kyoto University. Retrieved August 8, 2005, from http://doi.ieeecomputersociety.org/10.1109/C5.2005.25

Coyne, R. (1999). *Technoromanticism: Digital narrative, holism, and the romance of the real.* Cambridge, MA: The MIT Press.

Dreyfus, H. (2001). *On the Internet.* London: Routledge.

Eiteljorg, H. (1998). Photorealistic visualizations may be too good. *CSA Newsletter, XI*(2). Retrieved January 5, 2005, from http://www.csanet.org/newsletter/fall98/nlf9804.html

Gee, J. P. (2003). *What video games have to teach us about learning and literacy.* New York: Palgrave Macmillan.

Gillings, M. (2002). Virtual archaeologies and the hyper-real. In P. Fisher & D. Unwin (Eds.), *Virtual reality in geography* (pp. 17-32). London; New York: Taylor & Francis.

Hedman, A. (2001). *Visitor orientation: Human-computer interaction in digital places.* Unpublished master's thesis, The Royal Institute of Technology in Stockholm (KTH), Sweden. Retrieved January 7, 2005, from http://cid.nada.kth.se/pdf/cid_107.pdf

Hein, G. E. (1991, October). *Constructivist learning.* Theory, Institute for Enquiry. Presented at The Museum and the Needs of People CECA (International Committee of Museum Educators) Conference, Jerusalem, Israel. Retrieved January 7, 2005, from http://www.exploratorium.edu/IFI/resources/constructivistlearning.html

Jacobson, L. (2000, August 14). A virtual class act technology aims to help hyperactive students. *Washington Post.* Retrieved October 29, 2003, from http://www.washingtonpost.com/ac2/wp-dyn?pagename=article&node=&contentId=A21148-2000Aug13 &notFound=true

Johnson, S. (1997). *Interface culture: How new technology transforms the way we create and communicate.* San Francisco: Harper Edge, New York: Basic Books.

Jones, J. G. (2004). 3-D online distributed learning environments: An old concept with a new twist. *Proceedings of the Society for Information Technology and Teacher Education* (pp. 507-512). Atlanta, GA: SITE. Retrieved August 7, 2005, from http://courseweb.unt.edu/gjones/wp0304a.html

Kalay, Y. E. (2004). Virtual learning environments, *ITcon, Special Issue ICT Supported Learning in Architecture and Civil Engineering, 9*, 195-207. Retrieved August 5, 2005, from http://www.itcon.org/2004/13

Kroeber, A., & Kluckhohn, C. (1952). *Culture: A critical review of concepts and definitions.* New York: Vintage Books.

Laird, J. E. (2001). Using computer games to develop advanced AI. *Computer, 34*(7), 70-75. Retrieved January 7, 2005, from http://ai.eecs.umich.edu/people/laird/papers/Computer01.pdf

Lombardi, M. M., & Lombardi, J. (2005). Croquet learning environments: Extending the value of campus life into the online experience. In T. Sakai, K. Tanaka, K. Rose, H. Kita, T. Jozen, & H. Takada (Eds.), *Proceedings of C5: The Third International Conference on Creating, Connecting and Collaborating through Computing* (pp. 137-144). Shiran Kaikan, Kyoto University, Japan: Kyoto University. Retrieved August 8, 2005, from http://doi.ieeecomputersociety.org/10.1109/C5.2005.25

Manninen, T. (2004). *Rich interaction model for game and virtual environment design.* Unpublished doctoral dissertation, University of Oulu: Finland. Retrieved January 7, 2005, from http://herkules.oulu.fi/isbn9514272544/isbn9514272544.pdf

Mosaker, L. (2001). Visualizing historical knowledge using VR technology. *Digital Creativity S&Z, 12*(1), 15-26.

Prensky, M. (2001). *Digital game-based learning.* New York: McGraw-Hill.

Refsland, S., Ojika, T., & Berry, R. (2000). The living virtual Kinka Kuji Temple: A dynamic environment. *IEEE Multimedia, 7*(2), 65-67. Retrieved August 8, 2005, from http://portal.acm.org/citation.cfm?id=614975

Relph, E. C. (1976). *Place and placelessness.* London: Pion Ltd.

Rieber, L. P. (1996). Seriously considering play: Designing interactive learning environments based on the blending of microworlds, simulations, and games. *Educational Technology Research & Development, 44*(2), 43-58. Retrieved August 7, 2005, from http://it.coe.uga.edu/~lrieber/play.html

Salen, K., & Zimmerman, E. (2003). *Rules of play: Game design fundamentals.* Cambridge, MA: MIT Press.

Schroeder, R. (1996). *Possible worlds: The social dynamic of virtual reality technology.* London: Westview Press.

Slater, M. (1999). Measuring presence: A response to the Witmer and Singer presence questionnaire. *Presence: Teleoperators and Virtual Environments, 8*(5), 560-565. Retrieved August 7, 2005, from http://www.cs.ucl.ac.uk/staff/m.slater/Papers/pq.pdf

Squire, K. (2002). Cultural framing of computer/video games. *Game Studies, 2*(1). Retrieved August 8, 2005, from http://www.gamestudies.org/0102/squire/

Squire, K. D., Makinster, J., Barnett, M., Barab, A. L., & Barab, S. A. (2003). Designed curriculum and local culture: Acknowledging the primacy of classroom culture. *Science Education, 87,* 1-22.

Tuan, Y. (1998). *Escapism.* Baltimore: John Hopkins University Press.

Weckström, N. (2004). *Finding "reality" in virtual environments.* Unpublished master's thesis, Arcada Polytechnic: Helsingfors / Esbo, Finland.

Wong, D. (2003). *The heritage & legacy of thinking and computer games. Online course essay.* Retrieved August 8, 2005, from http://www.msu.edu/user/buchan56/coursework/cep911_intellectual_history/hl_thinking.htm

This work was previously published in Enhancing Learning Through Technology, edited by E. K. Sorensen and D. O. Murchu, pp. 103-124, copyright 2006 by IGI Publishing, formerly known as Idea Group Publishing (an imprint of IGI Global).

Compilation of References

Abbey, B. (Ed.). (2000). *Instructional and cognitive impacts of web-based education.* Hershey, PA: Idea Group.

Aberley, D. (1993). *Boundaries of home: Mapping for local empowerment.* Gabriola Island, British Columbia, Canada: New Society Publishers.

Abowd, G. (1999). Classroom 2000: An experiment with the instrumentation of a living educational environment. *IBM Systems Journal, 38*(4), 508-530.

Acevedo, D., Vote, E., Laidlaw, D.H., & Joukowsky, M.S. (2000). ARCHAVE: A virtual environment for archaeological research. *Work in Progress report presented at IEEE Visualization*, Salt Lake City, Utah.

Acuna, S., & Juristo, N. (2004). Assigning people to roles in software projects. *Software—Practice and Experience, 34*(7), 675-696.

Ahlberg, J. (2001). Candide-3 – an updated parameterized face, *Technical report no. lith-isy-r-2326.*

Aldrich, C. (2004). *Simulations and the future of learning: An innovative (and perhaps revolutionary) approach to e-learning.* San Francisco: Pfeiffer.

Aldrich, C. (2005). *Learning by doing: A comprehensive guide to simulations, computer games, and pedagogy in e-learning and other educational experiences.* San Francisco: Pfeiffer.

Alessi, S., & Trollip, S. (2001). *Multimedia for learning – methods and development.* Massachusetts: Allyn & Bacon.

Allen, I., & Seaman, J. (2004). *Entering the mainstream—The quality and extent of education in the United States, 2003 and 2004.* Needham, MA: Sloan-C. Retrieved September 10, 2005, from http://www.sloan-c.org/resources/entering_mainstream.pdf

ALPAC. (1966). *Language and machines: Computers in translation and linguistics* (ALPAC report). A report by the Automatic Language Processing Advisory Committee. Division of Behavioral Sciences, National Academy of Science. National Research Council. Washington D.C.

Amory, A., Naicker, K., Vincent, J., & Adams, C. (1999). The use of computer games as an educational tool: Identification of appropriate game types and game elements. *British Journal of Educational Technology, 30*(4), 311-321. Retrieved January 7, 2005, from http://www.nu.ac.za/biology/staff/amory/bjet30.rtf

Anderson, J. R. (1983). *The architecture of cognition.* Cambridge, MA: Harvard University.

Anderson, J. R. (1990). *The adaptive character of thought.* Hillsdale, NJ: Erlbaum.

Anderson, J. R. (1993). *Rules of the mind.* Hillsdale, NJ: Erlbaum.

Anderson, J. R., Reder, L. M., & Simon, H. A. (1998). Radical constructivism and cognitive psychology. In D. Ravitch (Ed.), *Brookings papers on educational policy: 1998* (pp. 227–255). Washington, DC: Brookings Institute.

Anderson, T., & Elloumi, F. (Eds.) (2004). *Theory and practice of online learning.* Athabasca, Canada: Athabasca University.

Andrefsky, B. (2003). Archaeological field methods. Retrieved October 25, 2007, from Department of Anthropology Washington State University, http://www.indiana.edu/~arch/saa/matrix/afm.html

Antelman, K. (2004). Do open-access articles have a greater research impact? *College & Research Libraries News, 65*(5), 372-382.

Antonnen, S., Onnela, T., & Terho, H. (2006). *E-learning history. Evaluating European experiences.* Turku.

Aoyama, M. (1993). Concurrent development process model. *IEEE Software, 10*(4), 46-55.

Applied Research Laboratory, the Pennsylvania State University (1996). Definitions of instructional design. Adapted from *Training and instructional design* at http://www.umich.edu/~ed626/define.html. University of Michigan. Retrieved October 25, 2007, from http://www.arl.psu.edu/

Armstrong, M. P. (1994). Requirements for the development of GIS-based group decision support systems. *Journal of the American Society for Information Science, 45*(9), 669-677.

Arnold, D. J., Balkan, L., Meijer, S., Humphreys, R.L., & Sadler, L. (1994). *Machine translation: An introductory guide* (PDF version of the book). London: Blackwells-NCC.ISBN: 1855542-17x. Retrieved October 27, 2007, from http://www.essex.ac.uk/linguistics/clmt/MTbook/PostScript/

Arnstein, S. R. (1969). A ladder of citizen participation. *Journal of the American Institute of Planners, 35*(4), 216-224.

Aronson, E., Blaney, N., Stephan, C., Sikes, J., & Snapp, M. (1978). *The jigsaw classroom.* Sage Publications.

Asher, R. E. (1994). Machine translation: History and general principles. *The encyclopedia of languages and linguistics.* Oxford: Pergamon Press.

Atarashi, R. S., Imai, M., Sunahara, H., Chihara, K., & Katana, T. (2004). Building archaeological photograph library. In *Proceedings of the Research and Advanced Technology for Digital Libraries: 4th European Conference*, Lisbon, Portugal, (Vol. 1923/2000). Berlin/Heidelberg: Springer-Verlag.

Atkinson, R. C., & Shiffrin, R. M. (1968). Human memory: A proposal system and its control processes. In K. W. Spence, & J. T. Spence (Eds.), *The psychology of learning and motivation: Advances in research and theory* (pp. 89–195). New York: Academic Press.

Atlantis - Fact, fiction or exaggeration? (1999). Retrieved October 27, 2007, from http://www.activemind.com

Attwell, G. (2007). The personal learning environments - the future of eLearning? *eLearning Papers, 2(1).* Retrieved October, 24, 2007, from http://www.elearningpapers.eu/index.php?page=doc&doc_id=8553&doclng=6

Avern, G. (2001). *Progress report on a new technique for recording archaeological sites and excavations.* Belgium: Université Libre de Bruxelles.

Azuma, R. (1997). A survey of augmented reality. *Presence: Teleoperators and Virtual Environments, 6*(4), 355-385. Retrieved August 9, 2005, from http://www.cs.unc.edu/~azuma/ARpresence.pdf

Babot, I. (2003). *E-learning, corporate learning.* Barcelona: Gestión 2000.

Baddeley, A. D. (1986). *Working memory.* Oxford: Oxford University Press.

Baddeley, A. D. (1999). *Essentials of human memory.* East Sussex, UK: Taylor and Francis.

Baddeley, A. D., & Hitch, G. J. (1974). Working memory. In G. H. Bower (Ed.), *Recent advances in learning and motivation.* New York: Academic Press.

Baddeley, A. D., & Logie, R. H. (1999). Working memory: The multiple-component model. In A. Miyake, & P. Shah (Eds.), *Models of working memory: Mechanisms of active maintenance and executive control* (pp. 28–61). Cambridge, UK: Cambridge University Press.

Badre, A., & Shneiderman, B. (Eds.). (1982). *Directions in human-computer interaction.* Norwood, NJ: Ablex Pub. Corp.

Bailey, D.W., & Panayotov, I. (Eds.). (1995). *Prehistoric Bulgaria.* Monogr. World Arch. 22. Madison, Wisconsin.

Balram, S. (2005). *Collaborative GIS process modelling using the Delphi method, systems theory and the unified modelling language (UML).* PhD Thesis, McGill University, Montreal, Canada.

Balram, S., Dragicevic, S., & Meredith, T. (2003). Achieving effectiveness in stakeholder participation using the GIS-based collaborative spatial Delphi methodology. *Journal of Environmental Assessment Policy and Management, 5*(3), 365-394.

Balram, S., Dragicevic, S., & Meredith, T. (2004). A collaborative GIS method for integrating local and technical knowledge in establishing biodiversity conservation priorities. *Biodiversity and Conservation, 13*(6), 1195-1208.

Bampton, M., & Mosher, R. (2001). A GIS driven regional database of archeological resources for research and CRM in Casco Bay, Maine. In Z. Stancic & T. Veljanovski (Eds.), *Computing archaeology for understanding the past, CAA 2000, BAR International Series 931, 28th Conference*, Ljubljana, Slovenia, (pp. 139-142).

Bannon, L. J., & Schmidt, K. (1989). CSCW: Four characteristics in search of a context. In J. Bowers & S. Benford (Eds.), *Studies in computer supported cooperative work: Theory, practice and design* (pp. 3-16). Amsterdam: North-Holland.

Banvard, R. (2002, September 29-October 3). The visible human project image data set: From interception to completion and beyond. In *18th International Conference CODATA 2002: Frontiers of Scientific and Technical Data,* Montréal, Canada.

Barberà, E. (2004). *La educación en la red. Actividades de enseñanza y aprendizaje.* Barcelona: Paidós.

Barbieri, T. (2000). Networked virtual environments for the Web: The WebTalk-I and WebTalk-II Architectures. In *Proceedings of IEEE for Computer Multimedia & Expo 2000* (ICME). New York.

Barbieri, T. et al. (1999). Visiting a museum together: How to share a visit to a virtual world. In D. Bearman & J. Trant (Eds.), *Museums and the Web 99: Selected Papers* (pp. 27-32). Pittsburgh, PA: Archives and Museum Informatics.

Barbieri, T. et al. (2001). From dust to StardDust: A collaborative virtual computer science museum. In *International Cultural Heritage Informatics Meeting: Proceedings from ICHIM 2001.* Milano, Italy.

Barbieri, T., & Paolini, P. (2000). Cooperative visits to WWW museum sites a year later: Evaluating the effect. In D. Bearman & J. Trant (Eds.), *Museums and the Web 2000: Selected Papers*. Pittsburgh, PA: Archives and Museum Informatics.

Barbieri, T., & Paolini, P. (2001). Cooperation metaphors for virtual museums. In D. Bearman & J. Trant (Eds.), *Museums and the Web 2001: Selected Papers.* Pittsburgh, PA: Archives and Museum Informatics.

Barbour, J. M. (1972). *Tuning and temperament: A historical survey.* New York: Da Capo Press.

Barcelo J. A. (2004). *The nature of archaeological problems.* Retrieved October 27, 2007, from http://seneca.uab.es/prehisto ria/Barcelo/

Barcelo, J. A. (2001). *Expert systems as cognitive emulation.* An archaeological viewpoint. Retrieved October 27, 2007, from http://seneca.uab.es/prehistoria/Barcelo/

Barcelo, J. A. (2004). *Notes about the use of neural networks for archaeological modelling.* Retrieved October 27, 2007, from http://seneca.uab.es/prehistoria/Barcelo/

Barker, A. (1989). *Greek musical writings II.* Cambridge.

Bartle, R. (1999). *Hearts, clubs, diamonds, spades: Players who suit Muds.* Retrieved August 5, 2005, from http://www.mud.co.uk/richard/hcds.htm

Baskerville, R. (1989). Logical controls specification: An approach to information systems security. In H. Klein & K. Kumar (Eds.), *Proceedings of the IFIP Working Conference on Systems Development for Human Progress* (pp. 241-255). Amsterdam: Elsevier Science Publishers.

Bates, A. W. (1995). *Technology, open learning and distance education*. London: Routledge.

Bates, A. W. (1999). *Managing technological change: Strategies for academic leaders*. San Francisco: Jossey Bass.

Bates, A.W. (2004). *Technology, e-learning and distance education*. San Francisco: Jossey-Bass.

Bates, A.W., & Escamilla, J.G. (1997). Crossing boundaries: Making global distance education a reality. *Journal of Distance Education, XII*(1/2), 49-66.

Bates, A.W., & Pool, G. (2003). *Effective teaching with technology in higher education: Foundations for success*. San Francisco: Jossey-Bass.

Bates, T. (2005). *Technology, e-learning and distance education*. London: Routledge.

Bathe, K. J. (1982). *Finite element procedures in engineering analysis*. Upper Saddle River, NJ: Prentice Hall.

Baum, H. S. (1999). Community organizations recruiting community participation: Predicaments in planning. *Journal of Planning and Education Research, 18*, 187-199.

Baumeister, H. -P., Williams, J., & Wilson, K. (Eds). (2000). *Teaching across the frontiers. A handbook for international online seminars*. Tübingen: Deusches Institut für Fernstudienforschung an der Universität Tübingen.

Bautista, G., Borges, F., & Forés, A. (2006). *Didáctica universitaria en entornos virtuales de Enseñanza-Aprendizaje*. Madrid: Narcea.

Baxter, M.J., & Freestone, I.C. (2006). Log-ratio compositional data analysis in archaeometry. *Archaeometry, 48*(3), 511-531.

Beale, R., McNab, R. J., & Witten, I. H. (1997). Visualising sequences of queries: A new tool for information retrieval. *Proceedings of the IEEE Conference on Information Visualisation,* London, August (pp. 57-62).

Beeching, A., & Brochier, J.L. (2003). Espace et temps de la Préhistoire: biaisage et problèmes de representation. In Gasco J., Gutherz X. et de Labriffe P.A. (dir.), *Temps et espaces culturels du 6° au 2° millénaire en France du Sud, Actes des quatrièmes rencontres méridionales de Préhistoire récente* (pp. 21-32), 28 et 29 octobre 2000, Nîmes.

Beler, A., Borda, A., Bowen, J. P., & Filippini-Fantoni, S. (2004). The building of online communities: An approach for learning organizations, with a particular focus on the museum sector. In J. Hemsley, V. Cappellini, & G. Stanke (Eds.), *EVA 2004 London Conference Proceedings* (pp. 2.1-2.15). University College London, The Institute of Archaeology, UK.

Benecke N., & Lichardus, J. (1999). Der „arme" Hund von Drama. Bemerkungen zu einem früheisenzeitlichen Hundeskelett aus Südost-Bulgarien. In C. Becker u. a. (Hrsg.), *Historia animalium ex ossibus. Festschrift für Angela von den Driesch*. Internat. Arch. Stud. Honoraria, 8, 67-77.

Benedikt, M. (1991). *Cyberspace: First steps*. Cambridge, MA: MIT Press.

Benett, S. (1993, May 19). Copyright and innovation in electronic publishing: A commentary. *The Journal of Academic Librarianship*, 87-91.

Benko, H., Ishak, E., & Feiner, S. (2003). Collaborative visualisation of an archaeological excavation. In *Proceedings of the Workshop on Collaborative Virtual Reality and Visualisation (CVRV 2003),* Lake Tahoe, CA.

Bennett, P. (1993). The *interaction of syntax and morphology in machine translation*. London: Pinter.

Bernard, M. (dir.) (2005). *Le E-learning: la distance en question dans la formation* . París: CIEF – L'Harmattan.

Bertemes, F. (1998). Der mittelbronzezeitliche Kultgraben von Drama und seine kulturhistorische Stellung in Südosteuropa. *Arch. Nachrbl.* 3, 322-330.

Bertemes, F. (2002). Heiligtum und Kultplatz in der thrakischen Ebene im 3. Jahrtausend v. Chr. *Ber. RGK* 83, 23-144.

Bertemes, F., & Krastev, I. (1998). Die bulgarisch-deutschen Ausgrabungen in Drama, Bez. Burgas - Katalog. In A. Fol & J. Lichardus (Hrsg.), Macht, *Herrschaft und Gold. Das Gräberfeld von Varna (Bulgarien) und die Anfänge einer neuen europäischen Zivilisation*, 241-266.

Bertoletti, A.C. et al. (2001). Providing personal assistance in the SAGRES virtual museum. In D. Bearman & J. Trant (Eds.), *Proceedings of Museums and the Web 2001,* Seattle, Washington, March 14-16. Archives & Museum Informatics. Retrieved from www.archimuse.com/mw2001/papers/bertoletti/bertoletti.html

Bertoletti, A.C., & Costa, A.C.R. (1999). Sagres – A virtual museum. In D. Bearman & J. Trant (Eds.), *Proceedings of Museums and the Web 1999.* Archives & Museum Informatics. Retrieved from www.archimuse.com/mw99/papers/bertoletti/bertoletti.html

Bider, M. (2003). Copyright and the network. *Learned Publishing, 16*(2), 103-109.

Birkenbihl, M. (1990). *Train the trainer: Arbeitsbuch für Ausbilder und Dozenten.* Darmstadt: Moderne Industrie Verlag.

Blake, C. L., & Merz, C. J. (1998). UCI repository of machine learning databases. *University of California, Irvine, Department of Computer Science.* Retrieved from http://www.ics.uci.edu/~mlearn/MLRepository.html

Bloom, B. (1956). Taxonomy of educational objectives. *Handbook I: The cognitive domain.* New York: David McKay.

Blum, B. (1994). A taxonomy of software development methods. *Communications of the ACM, 37*(11), 82-94.

Bodart, F., Flory, A., Leonard, M., Rochefeld, A., Rolland, C., & Tardieu, H. (1983). Evaluation of CRIS 1 I.S. development methods using a three cycles framework. In T. Olle, H. Sol, & C. Tully (Eds.), *Information systems design methodologies: A feature analysis* (pp. 191-206). Amsterdam: Elsevier Science Publishers.

Boehm, B. (1988). A spiral model of software development and enhancement. *IEEE Computer, 21*(5), 61-72.

Böhle, K., Riehm, U., & Wingert, B. (1997). Vom allmählichen Verfertigen elektronischer Bücher. Ein Erfahrungsbericht, Frankfurt am Main u. a.

Bonev, A. (1998). *Trakija i egejskijat vjat prez vtorata polovina na II chiljadoletie pr. n.e.* Razkopki i proučvanija 20. Sofija.

Bonnet, M. (2002, June). Personalization of Web services: Opportunities and challenges. *Ariadne*, (28). Retrieved from www.ariadne.ac.uk/issue28/personalization

Börner, W. (2000). Vienna archaeological GIS. In *Proceedings of the 28th CAA Conference*, op.cit., (pp. 149-152).

Borzacchini, L., & Minnuni, D. (2001). *A mathematica notebook about ancient Greek music and mathematics.* University of Bari.

Bouras, C., & Tsiatsos, T. (2005). *Educational virtual environments: Design rationale and architecture multimedia tools and applications journal.* Kluwer Academic Publishers (to appear).

Bowen, J.P. (2004, January). Cultural heritage online. *Ability*, 53, 12-14. Retrieved from www.abilitymagazine.org.uk/features/2004/01/A53_Cover_story.pdf

Bowen, J.P., & Bowen, J.S.M. (2000). The website of the UK Museum of the Year, 1999. In D. Bearman & J. Trant (Eds.), *Proceedings of Museums and the Web 2000.* Minneapolis, Minnesota, April 16-19. Pittsburgh, PA: Archives & Museum Informatics. Retrieved from www.archimuse.com/mw2000/papers/bowen/bowen.html

Bowen, J.P., & Filippini-Fantoni, S. (2004). Personalization and the Web from a museum perspective. In D. Bearman & J. Trant (Eds.), *Museums and the Web 2004: Selected Papers from an International Conference,* Arlington, Virginia, March 31-April 3, (pp. 63-78). Pittsburgh, PA: Archives & Museum Informatics.

Retrieved from www.archimuse.com/mw2004/papers/bowen/bowen.html

Bowen, J.P., Houghton, M., & Bernier, R. (2003). Online museum discussion forums; What do we have? What do we need? In D. Bearman & J. Trant (Eds.), *Proceedings of MW2003: Museums and the Web 2003,* Charlotte, North Carolina, March 19-22. Pittsburgh, PA: Archives & Museum Informatics. Retrieved from www.archimuse.com/mw2003/papers/bowen/bowen.html

Bowman, D., Hodges, L., & Bolter, J. (1998). The virtual venue: User-computer interaction in an information-rich virtual environment. *Presence: Teleoperators and Virtual Environments,* *7*(5), 478493.

Bowman, D., Kruijff, E., LaViola, J., & Poupyrev, I. (2001). An introduction to 3D user interface design. *Presence: Teleoperators and Virtual Environments,* *10*(1), 96-108.

Bowman, D., Wineman, J., Hodges, L., & Allison, D. (1999). The educational value of an information-rich virtual environment. *Presence: Teleoperators and virtual environments,* *8*(3), 317-331.

Boyadziev, Y. (1995). Chronology of prehistoric cultures in Bulgaria. In D.W. Bailey & I. Panayotov (Eds.), *Prehistoric Bulgaria.* Monogr. World Arch. 22. Madison, Wisconsin, 149-191.

Brace-Govan, J. (2003). *A method to track discusión forum activity: The moderator's assessment matrix.* The Internet and Higher Education 6.

Brandt, I. (1983). A comparative study of information systems design methodologies. In T. Olle, H. Sol, & C. Tully (Eds.), *Information systems design methodologies—A feature analysis* (pp. 9-36). Amsterdam: Elsevier Science.

Brandt, M. (1998). Public participation GIS - Barriers to implementation. *Cartography and Geographic Information Systems, 25*(2), 105-112.

Brezillon, P., Pomerol, J.-Ch., & Saker I. (1998). Contextual and contextualized knowledge: An application in subway control. *International Journal of Human-Computer Studies, 48*(3), 357-373.

Brinkkemper, S. (1990). *Formalization of information systems modeling.* Unpublished dissertation thesis, University of Nijmegen, Amsterdam.

Broadbent, D. E. (1958). *Perception and communication.* London: Pergamon.

Brochier, J.L. (1988). Les sédiments, documents archéologiques. *Nouvelles de l'Archéologie*, pp. 15-17.

Brochier, J.L. (1994). *Étude de la sédimentation anthropique. La stratégie des ethnofaciès sédimentaires en milieu de constructions en terre. Le site de Kovačevo* (pp 619-645) Bulletin de Correspondance Hellénique, n°118.

Brochier, J.L. (1999). Taphonomie de sites : fossilisation et conservation de l'espace habité, In Beeching A. et Vital J. (dir.), *Préhistoire de l'espace habité en France du Sud, Travaux du centre d'Archéologie préhistorique de Valence*, pp. 19-28.

Brooks, J. G., & Brooks, M. G. (1999). *In search of understanding: The case for constructivist classrooms.* Alexandria, VA, USA: ASCD - Association for Supervision and Curriculum Development.

Brown, A., & Perrin, N, K. (2000). A model for the description of archaeological archives. *English Heritage Centre for Archaeology.* Retrieved October 25, 2007, from http://www.english-heritage.org.uk

Brown, R., & Kulick, J. (1997). Flashbulb memories. *Cognition, 5,* 73-79.

Bruffee, K. A. (1995). Sharing our toys: Cooperative learning vs. collaborative learning. *Change,* (January/February), 12-18.

Brusilovsky, P. (1994, August 17). *Adaptive hypermedia: An attempt to analyse and generalize.* Workshop held in conjunction with UM'94 4th International Conference on User Modeling, Hyannis, Cape Cod, Massachusetts. Retrieved from wwwis.win.tue.nl/ah94/Brusilovsky.html

Brusilovsky, P., & Maybury, M.T. (2002). From adaptive hypermedia to the adaptive Web. *Communications of the ACM, 45*(5), 30-33. Retrieved from doi.acm.org/10.1145/506218.506239

Brusilovsky, P., & Nejdl, W. (2004). Adaptive hypermedia and adaptive Web. In M. Singh (Ed.), *Practical handbook of Internet computing.* CRC Press. Retrieved from www.kbs.uni-hannover.de/Arbeiten/Publikationen/2003/brusilovsky-nejdl.pdf

Burenhult, G. (2001). *Archaeological informatics: Pushing the envelope.* CAA 2001. Computer Applications and Quantitative Methods in Archaeology. BAR International Series. Oxford: Archaeopress.

Burkert, W. (1972). *Lore and science in Ancient Pythagoreanism.* Cambridge, MA: Harvard University Press.

Burrough, P. A. (1986). *Principles of GIS for land resources assessment.* Oxford: Clarendon Press.

Burton-Jones, A., Storey, V., Sugumaran, V., & Ahluwalia, P. (2005). A semiotic metric suite for assessing the quality of ontologies. *Data & Knowledge Engineering, 55*(1), 84-102.

Busquets, A., & Girona, C. (2006). Instructional design and quality: The two walk together. In *Paper presented at the ICDE Conference: The key factor of distance and ICT-based education: Quality*, Tianjin, China.

Carlson, C., Ternstrom, S., & Sundberg, J. (1991). A new digital system for singing synthesis allowing expressive control. In *Proceedings of ICMC 91, International Computer Music Conference*, Montreal.

Carver, S. (1991). Integrating multicriteria evaluations with geographical information systems. *International Journal of Geographical Information Systems, 5*(3), 321-339.

Case, S., Thint, M., Othani, T., & Hare, S. (2003). Personalisation and Web communities. *BT Technology Journal, 21*(1), 91-97.

Cassell, J., Bickmore, T., Campbell, L., Vilhjálmsson, H., & Yan, H. (2000). Human conversation as a system framework: Designing embodied conversational agents. In J. Cassell, J. W. Sullivan, S. Prevost, & E. F. Churchill (Eds.), *Embodied conversational agents* (pp. 29-63). Cambridge, MA: MIT Press.

Catherall, P. (2005). *Delivering e-learning for information services in higher education.* Oxford: Chandos Publishing.

Chalmers A. and Stoddart S.K.F. (1996). Photorealistic graphics for visualising archaeological site reconstructions. In A. Higgins, P. Main, and J. Lang (eds.), *Imaging the Past. Electronic imaging and computer graphics in museums and archaeology,* British Museum occasional paper 114, pp. 85-93. London: British Museum

Champion, E. (2003). Applying game design theory to virtual heritage environments. In S. Spencer (Ed.), *Proceedings of Graphite International Conference on Computer Graphics and Interactive Techniques in Australasia and South East Asia* (pp. 273-274). Melbourne, Australia: ACM SIGGRAPH.

Champion, E., & Sekiguchi, S. (2005). Suggestions for new features to support collaborative learning in virtual worlds. In T. Sakai, K. Tanaka, K. Rose, H. Kita, T. Jozen, & H. Takada (Eds.), *Proceedings of C5: The Third International Conference on Creating, Connecting and Collaborating through Computing* (pp. 129-136). Shiran Kaikan, Kyoto University, Japan: Kyoto University. Retrieved August 8, 2005, from http://doi.ieeecomputersociety.org/10.1109/C5.2005.25

Chandler, P., & Sweller, J. (1991). Cognitive load theory and the format of instruction. *Cognition and Instruction, 8*(4), 293–332.

Chandler, P., & Sweller, J. (1992). The split-attention effect as a factor in the design of instruction. *British Journal of Educational Psychology, 62*(2), 233–246.

Chandrasekaran, B., Josephson, J., & Benjamins, R. (1999). What are ontologies, and why do we need them? *IEEE Intelligent Systems, 14*(1), 20-26.

Chang, N. (2002). The roles of the instructor in an electronic classroom. In *Proceedings of ED-Media 2002.* Denver, CO: AACE.

Chase, M., Macfadyen, L., Reeder, K., & Röche, J. (2002). Intercultural challenges in networked learning: Hard technologies meet soft skills. *First Monday, 7*(8).

Retrieved September 10, 2005, from http://firstmonday.org/issues/issue7_8/chase/index.html

Checkland, P. (1988). Information systems and system thinking: Time to unite? *International Journal of Information Management, 8*(4), 239-248.

Chierchia, G., & McConnell-Ginet, S. (1990). *Meaning and grammar: An introduction to semantics*. Cambridge, MA: MIT Press.

Chowning, J. (1981). Computer synthesis of singing voice, ICMC 81. In *Proceedings of the International Computer Music Conference*, La Trobe University, Melbourne.

Chung, L., Nixon, B., Yu, E., & Mylopoulos, J. (2000). *Non-functional requirements in software engineering.* Dordrecht: Kluwert.

Čičikova, M. (1972). Nouvelles données sur la culture Thrace de l'époque du Hallstatt en Bulgarie du Sud. *Thracia* 1, 79-100.

Cimitile, A., & Visaggio, G. (1994). A formalism for structured planning of a software project. *International Journal of Software Engineering and Knowledge Engineering, 4*(2), 277-300.

Clark, H., & Carlson, T. (1981). Context for comprehension. In J. Long, & A. Baddeley (Eds.), *Attention and performance*, IX (pp. 313-330). Hillsdale, NJ: Erlbaum.

Clark, J. M., & Paivio, A. (1991). Dual coding theory and education. *Educational Psychology Review, 3*(3), 149–210.

Clark, R. C. (2003). *E-learning and the science of instruction: Proven guidelines for consumers and designers of multimedia learning.* San Francisco: Jossey-Bass/Pfeiffer.

Clark, R. E. (1983). Reconsidering research on learning from media. *Review of Educational Research, 53*(4), 445–459.

Clark, R. E. (1994). Media will never influence learning. *Educational Technology Research and Development, 42*(2), 21–29.

Clarke, J. (2001). Questions raised by electronic publication in archaeology. *Journal Bar International Series, 931*, 351-356.

CLIPS: A tool for building expert systems. Retrieved October 27, 2007, from http://www.ghg.net/clips/CLIPS.html

Codd, E.F. (1970). A relational model of data for large shared data banks. *Communications of the ACM, 13*(6), 377-387.

Collis, B. (1998). New didactics for university instruction: Why and how? *Computers & Education, 31*, 373-393.

Conlan, O., Dagger, D., & Wade, V. (2002, September). Towards a standards-based approach to e-learning personalization using reusable learning objects. In *E-Learn 2002, World Conference on E-Learning in Corporate, Government, Healthcare and Higher Education*. Montreal, Canada. Retrieved from www.cs.tcd.ie/Owen.Conlan/publications/eLearn2002_v1.24_Conlan.pdf

Conole, G., & Oliver, M. (Eds.). (2007). *Contemporary perspectives in e-learning research: Themes, methods and impact on practice*. New York: Routledge.

Conolly, J, & Lake, M. (2006). *Geographical information systems in archaeology.* Cambridge University Press.

Conrad, D.L. (2002). Engagement, excitement, anxiety, and fear: Learners' experiences of starting an online course. *The American Journal of Distance Education, 16*(4), 205-226.

Constantine, L. (1991). Building structured open teams to work. In *Proceedings of Software Development '91.* San Francisco: Miller-Freeman.

Conti, F., Barbagli, F., Morris, D., & Sewell, C. (2005). CHAI: An open-source library for the rapid development of haptic scenes demo. In *paper presented at IEEE World Haptics,* Pisa, Italy.

Cook, P. (1993). Spasm, a real-time vocal tract physical model controller, and singer the companion software synthesis system. *Computer Music Journal, 17*(1). Boston: MIT Press.

Cook, P. R., Kamarotos, D., Diamantopoulos, T., & Philippis, J. (1993). IGDIS: A modern Greek text to speech/singing program for the SPASM/Singer instrument, ICMC 93. In *Proceedings of the International Computer Music Conference*, Tokyo.

Coomey, M., & Stephenson, J. (2001). Online learning: It's all about dialogue, involvement, support and control according to research. In J. Stephenson (Ed.), *Teaching and learning online: Pedagogies for new technologies*. London: Bogan Page.

Cordova, D.I., & Lepper, M.R. (1996). Intrinsic motivation and the process of learning: Beneficial effects of contextualisation, personalization and choice. *Journal of Educational Psychology, 88*(4), 715-730.

Correia, A. (2003). *"When differences collide"—Lessons learnedfrom a cross-cultural team.* Retrieved September 10, 2005, from http://www.indiana.edu/~gist/conference2003/Documents/Correia.pdf

Couger, D., Higgins, L., & McIntyre, S. (1993). (Un)structured creativity in information systems organizations. *MIS Quarterly, 17*(4), 375-397.

Cowan, A. (1999). An embedded-process model of working memory. In A. Miyake, & P. Shah (Eds.), *Models of working memory: Mechanisms of active maintenance and executive control* (pp. 62–101). Cambridge, UK: Cambridge University Press.

Coyne, R. (1999). *Technoromanticism: Digital narrative, holism, and the romance of the real.* Cambridge, MA: The MIT Press.

Craig, W. J., Harris, T. M., & Weiner, D. (Eds.). (2002). *Community participation and geographic information science*. London: Taylor and Francis.

Csikszentmihalyi, M., & Hermanson, K. (1995). Intrinsic motivation in museums: What makes visitors want to learn? *Museum News, 74*(3), 34-37, 59-61.

Cuban, L. (1986). *Teachers and machines: The classroom use of technology since 1920.* New York: Teachers College Press.

Cuban, Larry. (1993). *How teachers taught: Constancy and change in american classrooms 1890-1990.* 2nd ed. New York: Teachers College Press.

Cunningham, S. J., Holmes, G., Littin, J., Beale, R., & Witten, I. H. (1998). Applying connectionist models to information retrieval. In S. –I. Amari & N. K. Kasabov (Eds.), *Brain-like computing and intelligent systems* (pp. 435-457). Berlin: Springer-Verlag.

Curtis, B., & Kellner, M., & Over, J. (1992). Process modeling. *Comm. of the ACM, 35*(9), 75-90.

Cysneiros, L., Leite, J., & Neto, J. (2001). A framework for integrating non-functional requirements into conceptual models. *Requirements Eng.*, 6(2), 97-115.

Damarin, S. (1993). Schooling and situated knowledge: Travel or tourism?. *Educational Technology, 33*(10).

Date, C. J. (2004). *Introduction to database systems* (8th ed.). Addison Wesley.

Davis, G. (1982). Strategies for information requirements determination. *IBM Systems Journal, 21*(1), 4-30.

Deloughry, T. J. (1995, September 15). Copyright in cyberspace. *The Chronicle of Higher Education*, A22, A24.

Demoule, J.P., & Lichardus-Itten, M. (1994). Fouilles franco-bulgares du site néolithique ancien de Kovačevo, Bulgarie du Sud-Ouest. In *rapport préliminaire (campagnes 1986-1993)*, Bulletin de Correspondance Hellénique, n°118, pp. 561-618.

Demoule, J.P., & Lichardus-Itten, M. (2001). Kovačevo (Bulgarie), un établissement du néolithique le plus ancien des Balkans. In Guilaine J. (dir.),*Communautés villageoises du Proche-Orient à l'Atlantique* (pp. 85-99) (8000-2000 avant notre ère), Séminaire du Collège de France.

Densham, P. J., & Rushton, G. (1996). Providing spatial decision support for rural public service facilities that require a minimum workload. *Environment and Planning B-Planning & Design, 23*(5), 553-574.

DeRouin, R. E., Fritzsche, B. A., & Salas, E. (2004). Optimizing e-learning: Research-based guidelines for learner-controlled training, *Human Resource Management, 43*, 147-162.

DeSanctis, G., & Gallupe, R. B. (1985). Group decision support systems: A new frontier. *Database, 16*(1), 377-387.

Desmarais, N. (2001). Copyright and fair use of multimedia resources. *The Acquisitions Librarian, 26*, 27-59.

Devine, A.M., & Stephens, L.D. (1994). *The prosody of Greek speech*. New York: Oxford.

Dewey, J. (1916). *Democracy and education*. New York: The Macmillan Company.

Dezhi, W., & Hiltx, R. (2004, April). Predicting learning from asynchronous online discussions. *Journal of Asynchronous Learning Networks, 8*(2).

Di Blas, N., Paolini, P., & Hazan, S. (2003) Edutainment in 3D virtual worlds. The SEE experience. In D. Bearman & J. Trant (Eds.), *Museums and the Web 2003: Selected Papers*. Pittsburgh, PA: Archives and Museum Informatics.

Di Blas, N., Paolini, P., & Poggi, C. (2003). SEE (Shrine Educational Experience): An online cooperative 3D environment supporting innovative educational activities. In D. Lassner & C. McNaught (Eds.), *Proceedings of ED-Media 2003*. Norfolk, VA: AACE.

Di Blas, N., Paolini, P., & Poggi, C. (2003). Shared 3D Internet environments for education: usability, educational, psychological and cognitive issues. In J. Jacko & C. Stephanidis (Eds.), *Human-computer interaction: Theory and practice. Proceedings of HCI International 2003* (Vol. 1). Mahwah, NJ: Lawrence Erlbaum Associates.

Di Blas, N., Paolini, P., & Poggi, C. (2004). Learning by playing: An edutainment 3D environment for schools. In *Proceedings of ED-Media 2004*. Lugano, Switzerland.

Dillenbourg, P. (1999). What do you mean by collaborative learning?. In Dillenbourg, P., (Ed.), *Collaborative-learning: Cognitive and computational approaches* (pp. 1-16). Amsterdam: Pergamon.

Djindjian, F. (1997). L'analyse spatiale de l'habitat pré-et protohistorique, perspectives et limites des méthodes actuelles. In Auxiette G., Hachem L et Robert B.(dir.), *Espaces physiques espaces sociaux dans l'analyse interne des sites du Néolithique à l'âge du fer, actes du 119ème Congrès national des sociétés historiques et scientifiques*, Amiens, 26-30 octobre 1994, pp. 13-21.

Dobson, R. (2002). *Programming Microsoft SQL Server 2000 with Microsoft Visual Basic .NET.* Microsoft Press.

Dolog, P., Henze, N., Nejdl, W., & Sintek, M. (2004). Personalization in distributed e-learning environments. In *Proceedings of 13th World Wide Web Conference* (pp. 170-179). New York City, IW3C2/ACM. Retrieved from www2004.org/proceedings/docs/2p170.pdf

Doolittle, P. E. (2001). The need to leverage theory in the development of guidelines for using technology in social studies teacher education. *Contemporary Issues in Technology and Teacher Education, 4*(1), 501–516.

Dourish, P., & Harrison, S. (1996). Re-placing space: The roles of place and space in collaborative systems. In *Proceedings of the ACM CSCW'96 Conference on Computer Supported Cooperative Work*, (pp. 68-85).

Dowson, M. (1987). Iteration in the software process. In *Proceedings of the 9th International Conference on Software Engineering* (pp. 36-39). New York: ACM Press.

Draves, W.A. (2002). *Teaching online*. River Falls: LERN Books.

Dreyfus, H. (2001). *On the Internet.* London: Routledge.

Duckham, M., Goodchild, M. F., & Worboys, M. F. (Eds.). (2003). *Foundations of geographic information science*. New York: Taylor & Francis.

Dumas, C., Saugis, G., Degrande, S., Plénacoste, P., Chaillou, C., & Viaud, M. (1999). Spin: A 3D interface for cooperative work. *Virtual reality*. London: Springer-Verlag. ISSN: 1359-4338 (Paper) 1434-9957 (Online).

Dymond, R. L., Regmi, B., Lohani, V. K., & Dietz, R. (2004). Interdisciplinary Web-enabled spatial decision support system for watershed management. *Journal of Water Resources Planning and Management, 130*(4), 290-300.

EAMT - European Association for Machine Translation. Retrieved October 27, 2007, from http://www.eamt.org/

Echt, R. (2001). Die eisenzeitliche Kultanlage von Drama-Kajrjaka - ein thrakisches Heiligtum im Wandel der Zeit. In *Thrace and the Aegean: Proceedings of the Eighth International Congress of Thracology*, Sofia - Yambol, 25-29 September 2000. Sofia, 187-205.

Eder, F.X., & Fuchs, E. (2004). Lernmodelle und neuen medien: Historisches lernen und lernen am beispiel Geschichte Online (GO). *Histoire et Informatique 15*, 263-181.

Edmundson, A. (2003). *Decreasing cultural disparity in educational ICTs: Tools and recommendations*. Retrieved November 10, 2005, from http://tojde.anadolu.edu.tr/tojde11/articles/edmundson.htm

Eirinaki, M., & Vazirgiannis, M. (2003). Web mining for Web personalization. *ACM Transactions on Internet Technology, 3*(1), 1-27. Retrieved from doi.acm.org/10.1145/643477.643478

Eiteljorg, H. (1998*)*. Photorealistic visualizations may be too good. *CSA Newsletter, XI*(2). Retrieved January 5, 2005, from http://www.csanet.org/newsletter/fall98/nlf9804.html

Elmes, G. A., Epstein, E. F., McMaster, R. E., Niemann, B. J., Poore, B., Sheppard, E., et al. (2005). GIS and Society: Interrelation, integration, and transformation. In R. B. McMaster & E. L. Usery (Eds.), *A research agenda for geographic information science* (pp. 287-312). Boca Raton, FL: CRC Press.

Engeström, Y. (1987). *Learning by expanding: An activity theoretical approach to developmental research.* Helsinki: Orienta-Konsultit.

Engeström, Y. (1999). Activity theory and individual and social transformation. In Y. Engeström, R. Miettinen, & R. Punamäki (Eds.), *Perspectives on activity theory. Cambridge* (pp. 19-38). UK: Cambridge University Press.

Epple, A., & Haber, P. (Eds.). (2004). *Geschichte und Informatik. Histoire et Informatique* 15. Bern.

Ericsson, K. A., & Kintsch, W. (1995). Long-term working memory. *Psychological Review, 102*, 211–245.

Faber, B. G., Watts, R., Hautaluoma, J. E., Knutson, J., Wallace, W. W., & Wallace, L. (1996). A groupware-enabled GIS. In M. Heit, H. D. Parker, & A. Shortreid (Eds.), *GIS applications in natural resources 2* (pp. 3-13). Fort Collins, CO: GIS World Inc.

Fakas, G.J., Lamprianou, I., Andreou, A., Pampaka, M., & Schizas, C. (2005). The evaluation of the cultural journeys in the information society environment as an educational aid. *Computers & Education*, (45), 123-139.

Falk, J.H., & Dierking, L.D. (2000). *Learning from museums: Visitor experiences and the making of meaning.* Walnut Creek, CA: Altamira Press.

Falk, L., & Dierking, L. (1992). *The museum experience*. Ann Arbor, MI: Whalesback Books.

Falkenberg, E., Hesse, W., Lindgreen, P., Nilsson, B., Oei, J., Rolland, C., Stamper, R., van Asche, F., Verrijn-Stuart, A., & Voss, K. (1998) Framework of information system concepts. *The Frisco Report* (*Web edition*), IFIP.

Falkenberg, E., Nijjsen, G., Adams, A., Bradley, L., Bugeia, P., Campbell, A., Carkeet, M., Lehman, G., & Shoesmith, A. (1983). Feature analysis of ACM/PCM, CIAM, ISAC and NIAM. In T. Olle, H. Sol, & C. Tully (Eds.), *Information systems design methodologies—A feature analysis* (pp. 169- 190). Amsterdam: Elsevier Science Publishers.

Fall, A., Daust, D., & Morgan, D. G. (2001). A framework and software tool to support collaborative landscape analysis: Fitting square pegs into square holes. *Transactions in GIS, 5*(1), 67-86.

Faust, N. L. (1995). The virtual reality of GIS. *Environment and Planning B: Planning and Design, 22*, 257-268.

Fecht, F. (2002). Die Karanovo V-zeitlichen Öfen in Drama-"Merdžumekja". In Lichardus-Itten, M., Lichardus, J., & Nikolov V. (Hrsg.) *Beiträge zu jungsteinzeitlichen*

Forschungen in Bulgarien. Saarbrücker Beitr. Altkde. 74. Bonn, 511-528.

Fecht, F. (2004). F. FECHT, Karanovo V-zeitliche Häuser von Drama-Merdžumekja. In V. Nikolov, K. Băčvarov, & P. Kalchev (Eds.), *Prehistoric Thrace. Proceedings of the International Symposium in Stara Zagora*, 30.09 - 04.10.2003. Sofia-Stara Zagora, 283-291.

Feick, R. D., & Hall, B. G. (1999). Consensus-building in a multiparticipant spatial decision support system. *URISA Journal, 11*(2), 17-23.

Fernandez-Lopez, M., Gomez-Perez, A., Pazos-Sierra, A., & Pazos-Sierra, J. (1999). Building a chemical ontology using METONTOLOGY and the ontology design environment. *IEEE Intelligent Systems & Theory Applications,* 4(1), 37-46.

Festa, P. (2003, October 14). Report slams web personalization. *CNET News.com.* Retrieved from news.com.com/2100-1038_3-5090716.html

Fiedler, H. (1991). Zukunftsperspektiven des Fachkommunikation. In H. Fiedler (Ed.), *Rechtsprobleme des elektronischen Publizierens.* Köln.

Fife, D. (1987). How to know a well-organized software project when you find one. In R. Thayer (Ed.), *Tutorial: Software engineering project management* (pp. 268-276). Washington: IEEE Computer Society Press.

Filippini-Fantoni, S. (2003). Museums with a personal touch. In J. Hemsley, V. Cappellini, & G. Stanke (Eds.), *EVA 2003 London Conference Proceedings,* University College London, July 22-26, (pp. 25.1-25.10) (Cf. Beler et al. ref).

Fillmore, C. (1968). The case for case. In E. Bach, & R. T. Harms (Eds.), *Universals in linguistic theory* (pp. 1-88). New York: Holt, Rinehart, and Winston.

Finkelstein, A., Kramer, J., Nuseibeh, B., Finkelstein, L., & Goedicke, M. (1992). Viewpoints: A framework for integrating multiple perspectives in system development. *International Journal of Software Engineering and Knowledge Engineering, 1*(2), 31-58.

Firesmith, D., & Henderson-Sellers, B. (1999). Improvements to the OPEN process Meta model. *Journal of Object-Oriented Programming, 12*(7), 30-35.

Firesmith, D., & Henderson-Sellers, B. (2002). *The OPEN process framework. An introduction*, Harlow: Addison-Wesley.

Fischer, F., & Forester, J. (Eds.). (1993). *The argumentative turn in policy analysis and planning.* Durham, NC: Duke University Press.

Flores, J. (2005). *How to become a proficient online learner.* EEUU: 1stBooks.

Fol, A. (Ed.). (2001, September 25-29). Thrace and the Aegean. In *Proceedings of the Eighth International Congress of Thracology. Sofia - Yambol, 25-29 September 2000.* Sofia

Fol, A., &. Lichardus, J. (Eds.). (1998). *Macht, Herrschaft und Gold. Das Gräberfeld von Varna (Bulgarien) und die Anfänge einer neuen europäischen Zivilisation.* Saarbrücken.

Fol, A., Katinčarov, R., Lichardus, J., Bertemes, & Iliev, I. (1989). Bericht über die bulgarisch-deutschen Ausgrabungen in Drama (1983-1988). Neolithikum - Kupferzeit - Bronzezeit. *Ber. RGK* 70, 1989, 5-127.

Forester, J. (1999). *The deliberative practitioner: Encouraging participatory planning processes.* Cambridge, MA: MIT Press.

Forte, M., & Siliotti, A. (1997). *Virtual archaeology: Great discoveries brought to life through virtual reality.* London: Thames and Hudson.

Franckson, M. (1994). The Euromethod deliverable model and its contributions to the objectives of Euromethod. In A. Verrijn-Stuart & T. Olle (Eds.), *Methods and associated tools for the information systems life cycle* (pp. 131-150). Amsterdam: Elsevier Science Publishers.

Frankfurt, H.P. (1992). Palamede: Application of expert systems to the archaeology of prehistoric urban civilizations. In K. Lockyear & S. P. Q. Rahtz, (Eds.), *Computer applications and quantitative methods in archaeology*

1990, (pp. 211-214), BAR International Series, No. 565. Oxford.

Franklin, J. C. (2005). Hearing Greek microtones. In S. Hagel & Ch. arrauer (Eds.), *Ancient Greek music in performance*. Vienna: Wiener Studien Beiheft 29.

Frazier, K. (1995, June 30). Protecting copyright and preserving fair use in the electronic future. *The Chronicle of Higher Education*, A40.

Friedman-Hill, E. (2003). *Jess in action, rule-based systems in Java*. Manning Publishing Company.

Frischer, B., Abernathy, D., Favro, D., Liverani, P., & De Blaauw, S. (2000). *Virtual reality and Ancient Rome: The UCLA cultural VR lab's Santa Maria Maggiore project* (pp. 155-162). Barcelo: Forte and Sanders.

Früschütz, J. (1997). *Dynamik des elektronischen Publizierens, Daten, Märkte, Strategien*. Frankfurt a.M. 1997.

Fuller, S. (2002). *Social epistemology* (2nd ed.). Bloomington, IN: University Press.

Gardin, J. C. (1988). *Artificial intelligence and expert systems: Case studies in the knowledge domain of archaeology*. Prentice Hall.

Gardner, H. (1983). *Frames of mind: The theory of multiple intelligences*. New York: Basic Books.

Gardner, J. (2006). *E-learning: Concepts and practice*. Thousand Oaks, CA: Sage Publications.

Garrison, D., & Anderson, T. (2003). *E-learning in the 21 century. A framework for research and practice*. London: Routledge.

Garson, G. (2005). *Participant observation (PA 765 research methodology)*. Retrieved November 10, 2005, from http://www2.chass.ncsu.edu/garson/pa765/index.htm

Gee, J. P. (2003). *What video games have to teach us about learning and literacy*. New York: Palgrave Macmillan.

Geertman, S. (2002). Participatory planning and GIS: A PSS to bridge the gap. *Environment and Planning B: Planning and Design, 29*(1), 21-35.

Georgaki, A. (2004). Virtual voices on hands: Prominent applications on the synthesis and control of the singing voice. In *Proceedings of SMC 2004, Sound and Music Computing 2004*, Paris, France.

Georgiev, G.I. (1961). Kulturgruppen der Jungstein- und der Kupferzeit in der Ebene von Thrazien (Südostbulgarien). In *L'Europe à la fin de l'âge de la pierre; actes du Symposium Consacré aux Problèmes du Néolithique Européen, Prague, Libice, Brno 5. - 12. oct. 1959*. Praha, 45-100.

Georgiev, G.I. (1967). Beiträge zur Erforschung des Neolithikums und der Bronzezeit. *Arch. Austriaca* 42, 90-144.

Gerjets, P., & Scheiter, K. (2003). Goal configurations and processing strategies as moderators between instructional design and cognitive load: Evidences from hypertext-based instruction. *Education Psychologist, 38*(1), 33–42.

Ghose, R. (2001). Use of information technology for community empowerment: Transforming geographic information systems into community information systems. *Transactions in GIS, 5*(2), 141-163.

Gillings, M. (2002). Virtual archaeologies and the hyper-real. In P. Fisher & D. Unwin (Eds.), *Virtual reality in geography* (pp. 17-32). London; New York: Taylor & Francis.

Gimblett, H. R. (Ed.). (2002). *Integrating geographic information systems and agent-based modeling techniques for simulating social and ecological processes*. New York: Oxford University Press.

Glasson, B. (1989). Model of system evolution. *Information and Software Technology*, 31(7), 351-356.

Godschalk, D. R., McMahon, G., Kaplan, A., & Qin, W. (1992). Using GIS for computer-assisted dispute resolution. *Photogrammetric Engineering & Remote Sensing, 58*(8), 1209-1212.

Gokhale, A. A. (2001). Environmental initiative prioritization with a Delphi approach: A case study. *Environmental Management, 28*(2), 187-193.

Goldkuhl, G. (1991). Information systems design as argumentation—An investigation into design rationale as a conceptualization of design. In K. Ivanov (Ed.), *Proceedings of the 14th Information Systems Research Seminar in Scandinavia (IRIS 1991)*, Umeå, Sweden.

Goldkuhl, G., & Röstling, A. (1988). *Förändrings-analysi—arbetsmetodik och förhållningssätt för goda förändringsbelust.* Lund: Studentlitterature.

Gombosi, O. (1944). *Johannes. New light on Ancient Greek music.* International Congress of Musicology, New York 1939, New York, p. 168.

Gómez-Pérez, A., Fernández-López, M., & Corcho, O. (2004). *Ontological engineering.* London; New York: Springer-Verlag.

Goodchild, M. F. (1992). Geographical information science. *International Journal of Geographical Information Systems, 6*(1), 31-45.

Goodlad, John I. (2004). *A place called school: Twentieth anniversary edition.* 2nd ed. New York: McGraw-Hill.

Goodyear, P., Salmon, G., Spector, J.M., & Tickner, S. (2001). Competentes for online teaching: A special report. *Educational Technology, Research and Development, 49*(1), 65-72.

Gorry, G. A., & Scott Morton, M. S. (1971). A framework for management information systems. *Sloan Management Review, 13*(1), 55-70.

Görsdorf, J., & Bojadžiev, J. (1996). Zur absoluten Chronologie der bulgarischen Urgeschichte. Berliner 14C-Datierungen von bulgarischen archäologischen Fundplätzen. *Eurasia Antiqua*, 2, 105-173.

Gould, P. R. (1966). *On mental maps.* Ann Arbor: University of Michigan.

Grace, R. (1996). Expert systems for Lithic analysis. Retrieved October 27, 2007, from http://www.hf.uio.no/iakk/roger/lithic/expsys.html

Gracia, F. (2001). Docència presencial v. docència virtual (UOC-UB). El ejemplo de la asignatura de Cultura Ibérica. In *Jornades d'Arqueologia I Tecnologies de la Informació i la Comunicació: Recerca, docència i difusió.* (pp 135-142). Barcelona.

Graham, I., Henderson-Sellers, B. & Younessi, H. (1997). *The OPEN process specification.* Reading: Addison-Wesley.

Grosz, G., Rolland, C., Schwer, S., Souveyet, C., Plihon, V., Si-Said, S., Achour, C., & Gnaho, C. (1997). Modelling and engineering the requirements engineering process: An overview of the NATURE approach. *Requirements Engineering, 2*(2), 115-131.

Gruber, T. (1993). A translation approach to portable ontology specification. *Knowledge Acquisition, 5*(2), 119-220.

Gruber, T. (1995). Towards principles for the design of ontologies used for knowledge sharing. *International Journal of Human-Computer Studies, 43*(5/6), 907-928.

Guardia, L. (1999). El disseny formatiu: un nou enfocament del disseny perdagògic dels materials didàctics en suport digital. In Sangrà, A. Et al. *Aprenentatge i virtualitat.* Disseny pedagògic de materials didàctics per al www. Editorial UOC i Pòrtic. Barcelona.

Guertler, L. (2003). Conference note: Third workshop "Qualitative psychology: Research questions and matching methods of analysis" (34 paragraphs). *Forum qualitative sozialforschung / forum: Qualitative Social Research (online journal), 4*(1). Retrieved September 10, 2005, from http://www.qualitative-research.net/fqs-texte/1-03/1-03tagung-guertler-e.htm

Guilbert, L., & Ouellet, L. (2002). *Étude de cas. Apprentissage par problèmes.* Québec:PUQ.

Guo-Yuan, C. (1998). *3D reconstruction modelling from varied data sources.* Doctoral dissertation, University of Glasgow.

Gupta, D., & Prakash, N. (2001). Engineering methods from method requirements specifications. *Requirements Engineering, 6*(3), 135-160.

Habermas, J. (1971). *Knowledge and human interests* (J. J. Shapiro, Trans.). Boston: Beacon Press.

Hachmann, R. (Ed.). (1969). *Vademecum der Grabung Kāmid el-Lōz.* Saarbrücker Beitr. Altkde. Bonn.

Halaris, C. *Music of Ancient Greece, booklet and CD.* Halaris has reconstructed Ancient Greek Music instruments. He has exhibited them and his ensemble performs with them.

Hall, E. (2000). *Monochronic and polychronic time.* In L. A. Samovar & R. E. Porter (Eds.), *Intercultural communication: A reader* (9th ed.). Belmont.

Hall, E., & Hall, M. (1989). *Understanding cultural differences.* Yarmouth, ME: Intercultural Press.

Halliday, M. (1978). *Language as social semiotic: The social interpretation of meaning.* London: Edwards Arnold.

Hamdorf, D. (2003). Towards managing diversity: Cultural aspects of conflict management in organizations. *Conflict & Communication Online, 2*(2).

Hamma, K. (2004, May). The role of museums in online teaching, learning, and research. *First Monday, 9*(5). Retrieved from firstmonday.org/issues/issue9_5/hamma

Hänsel, B. (1976). *Beiträge zur regionalen und chronologischen Gliederung der älteren Hallstattzeit an der unteren Donau. Teil 1 Text; Teil 2 Tafeln, Karten und Beilagen mit Erläuterungen.* Beitr. ur- u. frühgesch. Arch. Mittelmeer-Kulturraum. Bonn, 16-17.

Hänsel, B. (Ed.). (1982). *Südosteuropa zwischen 1600 und 1000 v. Chr.* Prähist. Arch. Südosteuropa, 1. Berlin.

Hare, M., Gilbert, N., Medugno, D., Asakawa, T., Heeb, J., & Pahl-Wostl, C. (2001). The development of an Internet forum for long-term participatory group learning about problems and solutions to sustainable urban water supply management. In L.M. Hilty & P.W. Gilgen (Eds.), *Sustainability in the Information Society, 15th International Symposium Informatics for Environmental Protection, Part 2: Methods/Workshop Papers*, (pp. 743-750). Marburg: Metropolis Verlag.

Harmonia, M. (1979). *Musique de la Grece Antique*, booklet and CD, HMA 1951015, France.

Harmsen, F. (1997). *Situational method engineering.* Unpublished doctoral dissertation, University of Twente, Moret, Ernst, & Young Management Consultants, The Netherlands.

Harris, B. (1960). Plan or projection: An examination of the use of models in planning. *Journal of the American Institute of Planners, 26*, 265-272.

Harris, T., & Weiner, D. (1998). Empowerment, marginalization and community-integrated GIS. *Cartography and Geographic Information Systems, 25*(2), 67-76.

Harton, L., & Ingram, A. (2002). Cooperation and collaboration using computer mediated communication. *Journal of Educational Computing Research, 26*(3), 325-347.

Haupt, S. (2002). *Electronic Publishing*, München.

Hay, K. E., Elliot, D., & Kim, B. (2002). Collaborative network-based virtual reality: The past, the present, and the future of the virtual solar system. In *Paper presented at the CSCL Conference*, Boulder, CO. Retrieved October 24, 2007, from http://newmedia.colorado.edu/cscl/151.pdf

Hazeyama, A., & Komiya S. (1993). Software process management system supporting the cooperation between manager and developers. In S. Brinkkemper, & F. Harmsen (Eds.), *Proc. of the Fourth Workshop on the Next Generation of CASE Tools* (pp. 183-188). Memoranda Informatica 93-32, University of Twente, The Netherlands

Healey, P. (1992). Planning through debate: The communicative turn in planning theory. *Town Planning Review, 63*(2), 143-162.

Healey, P. (1993). Planning through debate: The communicative turn in planning theory. In F. Fischer & J. Forester (Eds.), *The argumentative turn in policy analysis and planning* (pp. 233-253). Durham, NC: Duke University Press.

Healey, P. (1997). *Collaborative planning: Shaping places in fragmented societies.* Vancouver, BC: UBC Press.

Heckerman, D. *(1996). Advances in knowledge discovery and data mining* (pp. 273-305). Cambridge, MA: MIT Press.

Hedman, A. (2001). *Visitor orientation: Human-computer interaction in digital places.* Unpublished master's thesis, The Royal Institute of Technology in Stockholm (KTH), Sweden. Retrieved January 7, 2005, from http://cid.nada.kth.se/pdf/cid_107.pdf

Hein, E. (1991, October 15-22). Constructivist learning theory (The museum and the needs of people). *CECA (International Committee of Museum Educators) Conference*, Jerusalem. Retrieved September 10, 2005, from http://www.exploratorium.edu/IFI/resources/constructivistlearning.html

Hein, G. E. (1991, October). *Constructivist learning.* Theory, Institute for Enquiry. Presented at The Museum and the Needs of People CECA (International Committee of Museum Educators) Conference, Jerusalem, Israel. Retrieved January 7, 2005, from http://www.exploratorium.edu/IFI/resources/constructivistlearning.html

Henderson-Sellers, B., & Mellor, S. (1999). Tailoring process-focused OO methods. *Journal of Object-Oriented Programming, 12*(4), 40-45.

Hendley, R. J., Drew, N., Beale, R., & Wood, A. M. (1999). Narcissus: Visualising information. In S. Card, J. Mackinlay, & B. Shneiderman (Eds.), *Readings in information visualization* (pp. 503-511). San Mateo, CA: Morgan Kaufmann.

Herbst, H. (1995). A meta model for business rules in systems analysis. In J. Iivari, K. Lyytinen, & M. Rossi (Eds.), *Advanced information systems engineering* (LNCS 932, pp. 186-199). Berlin: Springer.

Hess, G. R., & King, T. J. (2002). Planning open spaces for wildlife I: Selecting focal species using a Delphi survey approach. *Landscape and Urban Planning, 58*, 25-40.

Heym, M., & Österle, H. (1992). A reference model for information systems development. In K. Kendall, K. Lyytinen, & J. DeGross (Eds.), *Proceedings of the IFIP WG 8.2 Working Conference on the Impacts on Computer Supported Technologies on Information Systems Development* (pp. 215-240). Amsterdam: Elsevier Science Publishers.

Hidding, G. (1997). Reinventing methodology: Who reads it and why? *Comm. of the ACM, 40*(11), 102-109.

Hidi, S. (1990). Interest and its contribution as a mental resource for learning. *Review of Educational Research, 60*, 549-571.

Hiller, S., & Nikolov, V. (Ed.). (2000). *Karanovo 3: Beiträge zum Neolithikum in Südosteuropa.* Wien.

Hiller, S., & Nikolov, V. (Eds.). (1970). *Karanovo 1: Die Ausgrabungen im Südsektor 1984-1992.* Salzburg: Sofia.

Hirschheim, R., & Klein, H. (1989). Four paradigms of information systems development. *Comm. of the ACM, 32*(10), 1199-1216.

Hirschheim, R., Klein, H., & Lyytinen, K. (1995). *Information systems development—Conceptual and philosophical foundations.* Cambridge: Cambridge University Press.

HMSO. (2001). *Special Educational Needs and Disability Act 2001.* UK Government, Her Majesty's Stationery Office. Retrieved from *www.hmso.gov.uk/acts/acts2001/20010010.htm*

Hofstede, G. (1986). Cultural differences in teaching and learning. *International Journal of Intercultural Relations, 10*(3), 301-320.

Hofstede, G. (2001). *Culture's consequences: Comparing values, behaviors, institutions, and organizations across nations* (2nd ed.). Thousand Oaks, CA: Sage Publications.

Holmberg, B. (1995). *Theory and practice of distance education.* New York: Routledge.

Horita, M. (2000). Mapping policy discourse with CRANES: Spatial understanding support systems as a medium for community conflict resolution. *Environment and Planning B: Planning and Design, 27*, 801-814.

Hruby, P. (2000). Designing customizable methodologies. *Journal of Object-Oriented Programming, 13*(8), 22-31.

Hsi, S. (2003). A study of user experiences mediated by nomadic web content in a museum. *Journal of Computer Assisted Learning, 19*(3), 308-319.

Hugenholtz, P. B. (2006). The new database right: Early case law from Europe. Retrieved October 26, 2007, from http://www.ivir.nl

Huggett, J. (1985). Expert systems in archaeology. In J. Richards & M. Cooper (Eds.), *Current issues in archaeological computing* (pp. 123-142). Oxford: British Archaeological Reports.

Huggett, J. (1985). Expert systems in archaeology. In J. Richards & M. Cooper (Eds.), *Current issues in archaeological computing* (pp. 123-142). Oxford: British Archaeological Reports.

Huggett, J., & Ross, S. (Eds.). (2004). Archaeological informatics: Beyond technology. *Special Issue, Internet Archaeology, 15.*

Huggett, J., & Ryan, N. (Eds.). (1994). *Computer applications and quantitative methods in Archaeology.* British Archaeological Reports Int. Ser. 600.

Hutchins, J. (2006). Computer-based translation in Europe and North America, and its future prospects. *JAPIO 2006 Yearbook* (Tokyo: Japan Patent Information Organization, 2006) (pp. 170-174). Retrieved October 27, 2007, from http://www.hutchinsweb.me.uk/JAPIO-2006.pdf

Hynst, S., Gervautz, M., Grabner, M., & Schindler, K. (2001). A work-flow and data model for reconstruction, management, and visualization of archaeological sites. In *Proceedings of the 2001 Conference on Virtual Reality, Archeology, and Cultural Heritage*, Glyfada, Greece, (pp. 43-52). ACM Press.

IEEE (1990). *Standard glossary of software engineering terminology.* IEEE Standard 610.12-1990.

Iivari, J. (1989). Levels of abstraction as a conceptual framework for an information system. In E. Falkenberg & P. Lindgren (Eds.), *Information system concepts: An in-depth analysis* (pp. 323-352). Amsterdam: Elsevier Science Publishers.

Iivari, J. (1990). Hierarchical spiral model for information system and software development. Part 2: Design process. *Information and Software Technology, 32*(7), 450-458.

Iivari, J. (1991). A paradigmatic analysis of contemporary schools of IS development. *European Journal of Information Systems, 1*(4), 249-272.

Iivari, J., & Kerola, P. (1983). A sociocybernetic framework for the feature analysis of information systems design methodologies. In T. Olle, H. Sol, & C. Tully (Eds.), *Proceedings of the IFIP WG 8.1 Working Conference on Feature Analysis of Information Systems Development Methodologies* (pp. 87-139). Amsterdam: Elsevier Science Publishers.

Iivari, J., Hirschheim, R., & Klein, H. (1998). A paradigmatic analysis of contrasting IS development approaches and methodologies. *Information Systems Research*, 9(2), 164-193.

Iivari, J., Hirschheim, R., & Klein, H. (2001). A dynamic framework for classifying information systems development methodologies and approaches. *Journal of Management Information Systems*, 17(3), 179-218.

Jackson, P. (1999). *Introduction to expert systems* (3rd ed.). Addison-Wesley.

Jackson, R. L., & Winn, W. (1999). Collaboration and learning in immersive virtual environments. In C. Hoadley & J. Roschelle (Eds.), *Proceedings of the Computer Support for Collaborative Learning (CSCL)* Conference. Mahwah, NJ: Lawrence Erlbaum.

Jacobson, I., Booch, G., & Rumbaugh, J. (1999). *The unified software development process.* Reading: Addison-Wesley.

Jacobson, L. (2000, August 14). A virtual class act technology aims to help hyperactive students. *Washington Post.* Retrieved October 29, 2003, from http://www.washingtonpost.com/ac2/wp-dyn?pagename=article&node=&contentId=A21148-2000Aug13 &notFound=true

James, W. (1958). *Talks with teachers.* New York: Norton. (Originally published in 1899.)

Jankowski, P. (1989). Mixed-data multicriteria evaluation for regional planning: A systematic approach to the decision-making process. *Environment and Planning A, 21*, 349-362.

Jankowski, P. (1995). Integrating geographical information systems and multiple criteria decision-making methods. *International Journal of Geographical Information Systems, 9*(3), 251-273.

Jankowski, P., & Nyerges, T. (2001). *Geographic information systems for group decision making: Towards a participatory geographic information science*. New York: Taylor and Francis.

Jankowski, P., & Nyerges, T. (2001). GIS-supported collaborative decision making: Results of an experiment. *Annals of the Association of American Geographers, 91*(1), 48-70.

Jankowski, P., Nyerges, T., Smith, A., Moore, T. J., & Horvath, E. (1997). Spatial group choice: An SDSS tool for collaborative spatial decision-making. *International Journal of Geographical Information Science, 11*(6), 577-602.

Jarke, M., Jeusfeld, M., & Rose, T. (1990). A software process data model for knowledge engineering in information systems. *Information Systems, 15*(1), 85-116.

Jayaratna, N. (1994). *Understanding and evaluating methodologies: NIMSAD—A systemic framework*. London: McGraw-Hill.

Jensen, M. B. (1992). Making copyright work in electronic publishing models. *Serials Review,* 18, 1-2, 62-65.

Jiang, J., & Chen, J. (2002). A GIS-based computer-supported collaborative work (CSCW) system for urban planning and land management. *Photogrammetric Engineering & Remote Sensing, 68*(4), 353-359.

Jin, Z., Mason, R., & Yim, P. (1998). *Bridging USA-China cross-cultural differences using Internet and groupware technologies.* Retrieved September 10, 2005, from http://www.cim-oem.com/bridge_8c18c.html

Johnson, D. W., Johnson, R. T., & Smith, K. A. (1998). *Active learning: Cooperation in the college classroom*. Edina, MN: Interaction Book Company.

Johnson, S. (1997). *Interface culture: How new technology transforms the way we create and communicate.* San Francisco: Harper Edge, New York: Basic Books.

Jones, J. G. (2004). 3-D online distributed learning environments: An old concept with a new twist. *Proceedings of the Society for Information Technology and Teacher Education* (pp. 507-512). Atlanta, GA: SITE. Retrieved August 7, 2005, from http://courseweb.unt.edu/gjones/wp0304a.html

Jupiter Research. (2003, October 14). *Beyond the personalization myth: Cost effective alternatives to influence intent.* Jupiter Media. Retrieved from http://www.internet.com/corporate/releases/03.10.14-newjupresearch.html

Kaestner, J. (Ed.). (1999). *Legal aspects of intellectual property rights in electronic commerce*. München.

Kahin, B., & Varian, H. (Eds.). (2000). *Internet publishing and beyond: The economics of digital information and intellectual property.* Cambridge, MA: MIT Press.

Kalawsky, R. S. *Exploiting virtual reality techniques in education and training: Technological issues.* A report prepared for AGOCG. Retrieved October 24, 2007, from http://www.agocg.ac.uk/reports/virtual/vrtech/title.htm

Kalay, Y. E. (2004). Virtual learning environments, *ITcon, Special Issue ICT Supported Learning in Architecture and Civil Engineering, 9*, 195-207. Retrieved August 5, 2005, from http://www.itcon.org/2004/13

Kallinikou, D. (2005). *Copyright and related rights* (in Greek) (p. 84).

Karagkiozidis, A., Mpampouklis, K., Triantafyllou, V., Loli, M., Grivas, I., & Printziou, E. (2006). Virtual museums: A flash presentation about rendering. In D. Politis (Ed.), *The e-learning dimension of computer applications in archaeology* (pp. 111-122). The SEEArchWeb project. Athens: Kleidarithmos.

Karam, G. & Casselman, R. (1993). A cataloging framework for software development methods. *IEEE Computer, 26*(2), 34-46.

Karlsson, F., & Ågerfalk, P. (2004). Method configuration: Adapting to situational characteristics while creating reusable assets. *Information and Software Technology, 46*(9), 619-633.

Katzenberger, P. (1996). *Elektronische Printmedien Und Urheberrecht: Urheberrechtliche Und Urhebervertragsrechtliche Fragen Der Elektronischen Nutzung Von Zeitungen Und Zeitschriften*. Verlag: Schäffer-Poeschel.

Kauffman, J., Ferrachiati, F. C., Matsik, B., Mintz, E. N., Narkiewicz, J. D., Tegels, K., et al. (2002). *Beginning ASP.NET Databases Using VB.NET.* Wrox.

Kavakli, V., & Loucopoulos, P. (1999). Goal-driven business process analysis application in electricity deregulation. *Information Systems, 24*(3), 187-207.

Kearsley, G. (2000). *Online education: Learning and teaching in cyberspace*. Belmont, CA: Wadsworth.

Keegan, D. (1996). *Foundations of distance education* (3rd ed.). New York: Routledge

Kelly, J., & Sherif, Y. (1992). Comparison of four design methods for real-time software development. *Information and Software Technology, 34*(2), 76-82.

Kerres, M. (2001). *Multimediale und telemediale Lernunggebungen. Konzeption und Entwicklung.* Viena.

Kettinger, W., Teng, J., & Guha S. (1997). Business process change: A study of methodologies, techniques, and tools. *MIS Quarterly, 21*(1), 55-80.

Khan, B. H. (2005). *Managing e-learning strategies: Design, delivery, implementation and evaluation.* Hershey, PA: Information Science Publishing.

Khan, B.H. (2005). *E-learning QUICK checklist*. Hershey, PA: Information Science Publishing.

Kindler, P. (2000). „Leistungsschutz für Datenbanken ohne Werkcharakter – Eine Zwischenbilanz.“ *Kommunikation & Recht 2000*, 265-272.

Kirkpatrick, D.L. (1998). *Another look at evaluating training programs.* Alexandria, VA: American Society for Training & Development.

Kishore, R., Zhang, H., & Ramesh, R. (2004). A Helix-Spindel model for ontological engineering. *Comm. of the ACM, 47*(2), 69-75.

Kitchenham, B., Travassos, H., von Mayrhauser, A., Nielssink, F., Schneiderwind, N., Singer, J., Takada, S., Vehvilainen, R., & Yang, H. (1999). Towards an ontology of software maintenance. *Journal of Software Maintenance: Research and Practice, 11*(6), 365-389.

Klass, G. (2000). Plato as distance education pioneer: Status and quality threats of Internet education. *First Monday, 5*(7). Retrieved October, 24, 2007, from http://www.firstmonday.org/issues/issue5_7/klass/index.html

Kleimann, B., & Wannemacher, K. (2005). E-learning-strategien deutscher Universitäten. *Fallbeispiele aus der Hochschulpraxis.* Hannoer (http://his.de/Service/Publikationen/Kib/pdf/kib200504.pdf)

Kleimann, B., & Wannemacher, K. (2006). Es geht nicho mehr ohne: E-Learning als element der Hochschulentwicklung. *Forschung & Lehre,* 7, 372-374.

Kling, R., & Covi, L. (1995). Electronic journals and legitimate media in the systems of scholarly communication. *The Information Society, Special Issue on Electronic Journals and Scholarly Publishing, 11*(4), 261-271.

Klosterman, R. E. (1999). The What if? Collaborative planning support system. *Environment and Planning B: Planning and Design, 26*(3), 393-408.

Klosterman, R. E. (2001). Planning support systems: A new perspective on computer-aided planning. In R. K. Brail & R. E. Klosterman (Eds.), *Planning support systems: Integrating geographic systems, models, and visualization tools* (pp. 1-23). Redlands, CA: ESRI Press.

Kozma, R. (1994). Will media influence learning: Reframing the debate. *Educational Technology Research and Development, 42*(2), 7–19.

Krauss, R. (2006). *Die prähistorische Besiedlung am Unterlauf der Jantra vor dem Hintergrund der Kulturgeschichte Nordbulgariens.* Prähist. Arch. Südosteuropa 20. Rahden/Westfalen.

Kroeber, A., & Kluckhohn, C. (1952). *Culture: A critical review of concepts and definitions.* New York: Vintage Books.

Krogstie, J. (1995). *Conceptual modeling for computerized information systems support in organizations.* Unpublished doctoral dissertation, University of Trondheim, Norway.

Krogstie, J., & Sölvberg, A. (1996). A classification of methodological frameworks for computerized information systems support in organizations. In B. Brinkkemper, K. Lyytinen, & R. Welke (Eds.), *Proceedings of the IFIP TC8 WG 8.1/8.2 Working Conference on Method Engineering: Principles of Method Construction and Tool Support* (pp. 278-295). London: Chapman & Hall.

Kruchten, P. (2000). *The rational unified process: An introduction.* Reading: Addison-Wesley.

Kwok, C.N. (2007). Replacing face-to-face tutorials by synchronous online technologies: Challenges and pedagogical implications. *The International Review of Research in Open and Distance Learning, 8*(1).

Kyem, P. K. (2000). Embedding GIS applications into resource management and planning activities of local and indigenous communities: A desirable innovation or a destabilizing enterprise? *Journal of Planning Education and Research, 20*, 176-186.

Kyem, P. K. (2004). On intractable conflicts and participatory GIS applications: The search for consensus amidst competing claims and institutional demands. *Annals of the Association of American Geographers, 94*(1), 37-57.

Kyng, M., & Mathiassen, L. (Eds.). (1997). *Computers and design in context.* Cambridge, MA: MIT Press.

Laird, J. E. (2001). Using computer games to develop advanced AI. *Computer, 34*(7), 70-75. Retrieved January 7, 2005, from http://ai.eecs.umich.edu/people/laird/papers/Computer01.pdf

Lane, N.E. (1986). Global issues in evaluation of expert systems. In *Proceedings of the IEEE International Conference on Systems, Man, and Cybernetics IEEE,* (pp. 121-125). Piscataway, NJ: Computer Society Press.

Lane, N.E. (1986). Global issues in evaluation of expert systems. In *Proceedings of the IEEE International Conference on Systems, Man, and Cybernetics IEEE,* (pp. 121-125). Piscataway, NJ: Computer Society Press.

Lang, M., & Duggan, J. (2001). A tool to support collaborative software requirements management. *Requirements Engineering, 6*(3), 161-172.

Latreille, A. (2000). The legal classification of multimedia creations in French law. In I. Stamatoudi & P. Torremans, *Copyright in the new digital environment* (p. 58). London: Sweet & Maxwell.

Laurillard, D. (1993). *Rethinking university teaching.* London: Routledge

Laurini, R., & Milleret-Raffort, F. (1990, July 23-27). Principles of geomatic hypermaps. In K. Brassel (Ed.), *Proceedings of the 4th International Symposium on Spatial Data Handling* (pp. 642-651). Zurich.

League for Innovation in the Community College. (1999). *League connections and leadership* abstracts.

Lee, J., Xue, N.-L., & Kuo, J.-Y. (2001). Structuring requirement specifications with goals. *Information and Software Technology, 43*(2), 121-135.

Lehmann, M. (2000). Digitisation and copyright agreements. In I. Stamatoudi, & P. Torremans. *Copyright in the new digital environment* (p. 195; Zahrt, op. cit, pp. 1674-1675).

Lejano, R. P., & Davos, C. A. (1999). Cooperative solutions for sustainable resource management. *Environmental Management, 24*(2), 167-175.

Leont'ev, A. (1978). *Activity, consciousness, and personality.* Englewood Cliffs, NJ: Prentice-Hall.

Leppänen, M. (2005). *An ontological framework and a methodical skeleton for method engineering.* Unpublished doctoral dissertation, University of Jyväskylä, Finland.

Leppänen, M. (2005). A context-based enterprise ontology. In G. Guizzardi & G. Wagner (Eds.), *Proceedings of the International Workshop on Vocabularies, Ontologies, and Rules for the Enterprise (VORTE'05)*, Enchede, The Netherlands (pp. 17-24).

Leppänen, M. (2005). Conceptual analysis of current ME artifacts in terms of coverage: A contextual approach. In J. Ralyté, Per Ågerfalk, & N. Kraiem (Eds.), *Proceedings of the 1st International Workshop on Situational Requirements Engineering Processes (SREP'05)*, Paris (pp. 75-90).

Leppänen, M. (2006). Contextual method integration. In *Proceedings of the Conference on Information Systems Development (ISD 2006)*, Budapest, Hungary.

Leroi-Gourhan, A., & Brézillon, M. (1972). *Fouilles de Pincevent: essai d'analyse d'un habitat magdalénien: la section 36*, Gallia-Préhistoire, suppl. 7.

Levinson, S. (1983). *Pragmatics*. London: Cambridge University Press.

Liaw, S. S. (2002). An Internet survey for perceptions of computers and the World Wide Web: Relationship, prediction and difference. *Computers in Human Behavior, 18*, 17-35.

Lichardus, J. (Ed.). (1991). *Die Kupferzeit als historische Epoche. Symposium Saarbrücken und Otzenhausen 6-13.11.1988.* Saarbrücker Beitr. Altkde. 55. Bonn.

Lichardus, J., & Iliev, I. (2004). Die relative Chronologie des Neolithikums und der Kupferzeit in der Mikroregion von Drama und die Verbindungen zu Zentralthrakien. In Nikolov, V., Băčvarov, K., Kalchev, P. (Eds.) *Prehistoric Thrace. Proceedings of the International Symposium in Stara Zagora*. 30.09 - 04.10.2003. Sofia-Stara Zagora, 34-45.

Lichardus, J., & Iliev, I. K. (1994). Frühe Vorgeschichte auf dem Gebiet der heutigen Stadt Jambol in Zusammenhang mit der Entwicklung an der unteren Tundža. In Draganov, D. (Ed.) *Studies on Settlement Life in Ancient Thrace*. Jambol, 13-20.

Lichardus, J., & Iliev, I. K. (2000). Das frühe und mittlere Neolithikum an der unteren Tundža (Südostbulgarien); ein Beitrag zu den chronologischen und kulturellen Beziehungen. In Hiller, S., & Nikolov, V. (Hrsg.) *Österreichisch-bulgarische Ausgrabungen und Forschungen in Karanovo 3: Beiträge zum Neolithikum in Südosteuropa*. Wien, 75-108.

Lichardus, J., & Iliev, I. K. (2001). Die Cernavoda-III-Siedlung von Drama-Merdžumekja in Südostbulgarien und ihre Bedeutung für Südosteuropa. In *Symposium Cernavodă III - Boleráz - ein vorgeschichtliches Phänomen zwischen dem Oberrhein und der Unteren Donau Mangalia, Neptun 18. - 24. Oktober 1999.* Stud. Danubiana Pars romaniae Ser. symposia 2.Bucureşti, 166-198.

Lichardus, J., & Iliev, I.K. (1993). Tonamulette aus Drama und das Problem der nordöstlichen Einflüsse in der Kupferzeit an der unteren Tundža. In Nikolov, V. (Hrsg.) *Praistoričeski nachodki i iszledvanija. Sbornik v pamet na prof. Georgi I. Georgiev*. Sofia, 141-149.

Lichardus, J., Echt, R., Iliev, I.K., Christov, Ch. J., Becker, J.S., & Thiele, W.- R. (2002). Die Spätbronzezeit an der unteren Tundža und die ostägäischen Verbindungen in Südostbulgarien. *Eurasia Antiqua*, 8, 133-182

Lichardus, J., Fol, A., Getov, L., Bertemes, F., Echt, R., Katinčarov, R., & Iliev, I.K. (1997). Bericht über die bulgarisch-deutschen Ausgrabungen in Drama (1989-1995). *Ber. RGK* 77, 1996 (1997), 5-106 Taf. 1-30 Beil. 1-8.

Lichardus, J., Fol, A., Getov, L., Bertemes, F., Echt, R., Katinčarov, R., & Iliev, I.K. (2000). 18 Jahre bulgarisch-deutsche Forschungen in Drama, obština Tundža (Kurzer Bericht). 18 godini bălgarsko-germanski archeologičeski izsledovanija kraj s. Drama, obština Tundža. *Vesti na Jambolskija muzej* 3, 3-14.

Lichardus, J., Fol, A., Getov, L., Bertemes, F., Echt, R., Katinčarov, R., & Iliev, I.K. (2000). *Forschungen in der Mikroregin von Drama (Südostbulgarien). Zusammenfassung der Hauptergebnisse der bulgarisch-deutschen Grabungen in den Jahren 1983-1999*. Bonn.

Lichardus, J., Fol, A., Getov, L., Bertemes, F., Echt, R., Katinčarov, R., & Iliev, I.K. (2001). *Izsledvanija v mikroregiona na s. Drama (Jugoiztočna Bălgarija). Obobštenie na osnovnite rezultati na Bălgaro-germanskite razkopki ot 1983 do 1999 g.* Sofia.

Lichardus, J., Fol, A., Getov, L., Bertemes, F., Echt, R., Kubiniok, J., & Iliev, I.K. (2004). Die bulgarisch-deutschen Forschungen in der Mikroregion von Drama (1983-2003). In *Die Thraker. Das goldene Reich des Orpheus [Katalog der Ausstellung vom 23. Juli bis 28. November 2004 in der Kunst- und Ausstellungshalle der Bundesrepublik Deutschland in Bonn].* Mainz, 37-60.

Lichardus, J., Fol, A., Getov, L., Echt, R., Gleser, R., Katinčarov, R., et al. (2003). Bericht über die bulgarisch-deutschen Ausgrabungen in Drama (1996-2002). Neolithikum - Kupferzeit - Bronzezeit - Eisenzeit - Römerzeit. *Ber. RGK.* 84, 155-221.

Lichardus, J., Gatsov, I., Gurova, M., & Iliev, I. K. (2000). Geometric Microliths from the Middle Neolithic Site Drama-Gerena (South Bulgaria) and the Problem of Mesolithic Tradition in South Eastern Europe. *Eurasia Antiqua.* 6, 1-12.

Lichardus, J., Iliev, I.K., & Christov, Ch. J. (2002). Die Karanovo I-IV-Perioden an der unteren Tundža und ihre chronologische Stellung zu den benachbarten Gebieten. In Lichardus-Itten, M., Lichardus, J., & Nikolov, V. (Hrsg.) *Beiträge zu jungsteinzeitlichen Forschungen in Bulgarien.* Saarbrücker Beitr. Altkde. 74. Bonn: Habelt, 325-410.

Lichardus-Itten, M., Demoule, J.P., Perničeva, L., Grebska-Kulova, M., & Kulov, I. (2002). The Site of Kovačevo and the Beginnings of the Neolithic Period in South-Eastern Bulgaria, the French-Bulgarian excavation 1986-2000. In Licharchus-Itten M., Lichardus J. & Nikolov V. (dir.), *Beiträge zu Jungsteinzeitlichen Forschungen in Bulgarien, Saarbrücker Beiträge zur Altertumskunde*, Bonn, pp. 99-158.

Lichardus-Itten, M., Lichardus, J., & Nikolov, V. (Eds.). (2002). *Beiträge zu jungsteinzeit-lichen Forschungen in Bulgarien.* Saarbrücker Beitr. Altkde. 74. Bonn.

Liebowitz, J. (1997). *Handbook of applied expert systems.* Boca Raton, FL: CRC Press.

Lin, C.-Y., & Ho, C.-S. (1999). Generating domain-specific methodical knowledge for requirements analysis based on methodology ontology. *Information Sciences, 114*(1-4), 127-164.

Linstone, H. A., & Turoff, M. (1975). *The Delphi method: Techniques and applications.* Reading, MA: Addision-Wesley.

Litman, J. (2001). *Digital copyright.* Amherst, NY: Prometheus Books.

Lock, G. (2003). *Using computers in archaeology: Towards virtual pasts.* New York: Routledge.

Loewenheim. (1999). In Schricker (Ed.), *Urheber Gesetz*, § 2, 1999, nr. 1.

Lombardi, M. M., & Lombardi, J. (2005). Croquet learning environments: Extending the value of campus life into the online experience. In T. Sakai, K. Tanaka, K. Rose, H. Kita, T. Jozen, & H. Takada (Eds.), *Proceedings of C5: The Third International Conference on Creating, Connecting and Collaborating through Computing* (pp. 137-144). Shiran Kaikan, Kyoto University, Japan: Kyoto University. Retrieved August 8, 2005, from http://doi.ieeecomputersociety.org/10.1109/C5.2005.25

Loucopoulos, P., Kavakli, V., Prekas, N., Rolland, C., Grosz, G., & Nurcan, S. (1998). *Using the EKD approach: The modelling component.* ELEKTRA—Project No. 22927, ESPRIT Programme 7.1.

Louridas, P., & Loucopoulos, P. (1996). A framework for evaluating design rationale methods. In K. Siau & Y. Wand (Eds.), *Proceedings of the Workshop on Evaluation of Modeling Methods in Systems Analysis and Design (EMMSAD'96).*

Luscombe, B. W., & Peucker, T. K. (1975). *The Strabo technique.* Burnaby, Canada: Simon Fraser University, Department of Geography Discussion Paper Series.

Lutzker, A. (2002). *Content rights for creative professionals: Copyrights & trademarks in a digital age.* Burlington, MA: Elsevier Science.

Lymna, F. (1981). The responsive classroom discussion. In A. S. Anderson (Ed.), *Mainstreaming digest.* College Park, MD: University of Maryland College of Education.

Macauley, L. (1993). Requirements capture as a cooperative activity. In *Proceedings of the IEEE International*

Symposium on Requirements Engineering (pp. 174-181). IEEE Computer Science Press.

Macdonald, J. (2003). Assessing online collaborative learning: Process and product. *Computers & Education, 40*(4), 377-391.

MacEachren, A. M., & Kraak, M. (2001). Research challenges in geovisualization. *Cartography and Geographic Information Science, 28*(1), 3-12.

MacEachren, A., Brewer, I., Cai, G., & Chen, C. (2003, August 10-16). Visually enabled geocollaboration to support data exploration and decision-making. Paper presented at the *Proceedings of the 21st International Cartographic Conference*, Durban, South Africa.

Macedonia, M. R., Zyda, M. J., Pratt, D., Brutzman, R., Donald, P., & Barham, P.T. (1995). Exploiting reality with multicast groups: A network architecture for large-scale virtual environments. In *Proceedings of the IEEE Virtual Reality Annual International Symposium (VRAIS'95)*, North Carolina.

Macfadyen, L., Chase, M., Reeder, K., & Roche, J. (2003). Matches and mismatches in intercultural learning: Designing and moderating an online intercultural course. In *Proceedings of the UNESCO Conference on International and Intercultural Education,* Jyvaskyla, Finland.

Maddison, R., Baker, G., Bhabuta, L., Fitzgerald, G., Hindle, K., Song, J., Stokes, N., & Wood, J. (1984). Feature analysis of five information system methodologies. In T. Bemelmans (Ed.), *Beyond productivity: Information systems for organizational effectiveness* (pp.277-306). Amsterdam: Elsevier Science Publishers.

Malczewski, J. (1996). A GIS-based approach to multiple criteria group decision-making. *International Journal of Geographical Information Systems, 10*(8), 955-971.

Manninen, T. (2004). *Rich interaction model for game and virtual environment design.* Unpublished doctoral dissertation, University of Oulu: Finland. Retrieved January 7, 2005, from http://herkules.oulu.fi/isbn9514272544/isbn9514272544.pdf

Maragliano, R. (2004). *Pedagogie dell'e-learning.* Roma: Laterza.

Marble, D. F. (1990). The potential methodological impact of geographic information systems on the social science. In K.M.S. Allen, S.W. Green, & E.B.W. Zubrow (Eds.), *Interpreting space: GIS and archaeology, applications of geographic information systems.* London: Taylor & Francis.

Marchionini, G. (1990). Evaluating hypermedia-based learning. In Jonassen, D. H., & Mandl, H. (Eds.). (1990). *Designing Hypermedia for Learning* (pp. 355-376). London. Springer-Verlag.

Margounakis, D. (2006, September 29-30). ARION – the Ancient Greek singer. In *Proceedings of the 1st SEEArch-Web Conference E-Learning and Computer Applications in Archaeology,* Thessaloniki, Greece.

Marinetti, A., & Dunn, P. (2002). *Cultural adaptation—A necessity for e-learning.* Retrieved September 10, 2005, from http://www.linezine.com/7.2/articles/pdamca.htm

Marinos, M. T. (2004). *Copyright law* (in Greek) (p. 105).

Markus, M., & Björn-Andersen, L. (1987). Power over users: Its exercise by system professionals. *Comm. of the ACM, 30*(6), 498-504.

Maschner, D. G. (Ed.). (1996). *New methods, old problems: Geographic information systems in modern archaeological research.* Southern Illinois University.

Mathiassen, L. (1998). Reflective systems development. *Scandinavian Journal of Information Systems, 10*(1/2), 67-117.

Matthew, A., Hutchins, L., Duncan, R., Stevenson, Gunn, C., Krumpholz, A., et al. (2005). Communication in a networked haptic virtual environment for temporal bone surgery training. *Virtual reality.* London: Springer-Verlag. ISSN: 1359-4338 (Paper) 1434-9957 (Online).

Mautone, P. D., & Mayer, R. E. (2001). Signaling as a cognitive guide in multimedia learning. *Journal of Educational Psychology, 93*(2), 377–389.

Mayer, R. E. (1997). Multimedia learning: Are we asking the right questions? *Educational Psychologist, 32*(1), 1–19.

Mayer, R. E. (2001). *Multimedia learning.* Cambridge, UK: Cambridge University Press.

Mayer, R. E., & Anderson, R. B. (1991). Animations need narrations: An experimental test of a dual-coding hypothesis. *Journal of Educational Psychology, 83*(4), 484–490.

Mayer, R. E., & Anderson, R. B. (1992). The instructive animation: Helping students build connections between words and pictures in multimedia learning. *Journal of Educational Psychology, 84*(4), 444–452.

Mayer, R. E., & Chandler, P. (2001). When learning is just a click away: Does simple user interaction foster deeper understanding of multimedia messages? *Journal of Educational Psychology, 93*(2), 390–397.

Mayer, R. E., & Moreno, R. (1998). A split-attention effect in multimedia learning: Evidence for dual processing systems in working memory. *Journal of Educational Psychology, 90*(2), 312–320.

Mayer, R. E., & Moreno, R. (1998). Nine ways to reduce cognitive load in multimedia learning. *Educational Psychologist, 38*(1), 43–52.

Mayer, R. E., Heiser, J., & Lonn, S. (2001). Cognitive constraints on multimedia learning: When presenting more material results in less understanding. *Journal of Educational Psychology, 93*(1), 187–198.

McConnell, D. (2006). *E-learning groups and communities.* The Society for Research into Higher Education. Berkshire: Open University Press.

McGovern, G. (2003, October 20). Why personalization hasn't worked. *New Thinking.* Retrieved from www.gerrymcgovern.com/nt/2003/nt_2003_10_20_personalization.htm

McGrath, J.E. (1990). Time matters in groups. In J. Galegher, R. E. Kraut, & C. Egido (Eds.), *Intellectual team work: Social and technological foundations of cooperative work.* Mahwah, NJ: Lawrence Erlbaum Associates, Inc.

McHarg, I. L. (1969). *Design with nature.* Garden City, NY: Natural History Press.

McMaster, R. B., & Usery, E. L. (Eds.). (2005). *A research agenda for geographic information science.* Boca Raton, FL: CRC Press.

McNaught, C. (2006). *Are learning repositories likely to become mainstream in education?* WEBIST 2006, Sétubal.

McVay Linch, M. (2002). *The online educator. A guide to creating the virtual classroom.* London: Routledge.

Mehrer, M. W., & Wescott, K.L. (Eds.). (2006). *GIS and archaeological site location modeling.* Boca Raton: CRC Press.

Mehrotra, C., Hollister, D., & McGahey, L. (2001). *Distance learning: Principle for effective design, delivery, and evaluation.* London; New Delhi: Sage Publications.

Merkyte, I. (2005). Lîga. Copper Age Strategies in Bulgaria. *Acta Arch. København* 76, 1, 1-194 = Centre World Arch. Publ. 2. København.

Meyer, G. J. F. (1975). *The organization of prose and its effects on memory.* New York: Elsevier.

Meyer, K.A. (2004, April). Evaluating online discussions: Four different frames of analysis. *Journal of Asynchronous Learning Networks, 8*(2).

Microsoft Research on MT. Retrieved October 27, 2007, from http://research.microsoft.com/nlp/Projects/MTproj.aspx

Millis, B. J., & Cottell, P. G. (1998). Cooperative learning for higher education faculty. *American Council on Education: Series on higher education.* Phoenix: The Oryx Press.

Mitcham, C. (1997). Justifying public participation in technical decision making. *IEEE Technology and Society, 16*(1), 40-46.

Mitkov, R. (2003). Machine translation: General overview. *The Oxford handbook of computational linguistics.* Oxford: University Press.

Miyake, A., & Shah, P. (Eds.). (1999). *Models of working memory: Mechanisms of active maintenance and executive control.* Cambridge, UK: Cambridge University Press.

Mizrachi, D., & Shoham, S. (2004). Computer attitudes and library anxiety among undergraduates: A study of Israeli B.Ed students. *The International Information & Library Review, 36*(1), 29-38.

Mobascher, B., Cooley, R., & Srivastava, J. (2000). Automatic personalization based on web usage mining. *Communications of the ACM, 43*(8), 142-151. Retrieved from doi.acm.org/10.1145/345124.345169

Moller T., & Haines, E. (2002). *Real–time rendering.* London: AK Peters.

Montani, R., Scateni, & Scopigno, R. (1994). Discretized marching cubes. In *Proceedings of Visualization 94,* (pp. 281-287). Washington: IEEE Computer Society Press.

Moore, D. M., Burton, J. K., & Myers, R. J. (1996). Multiple-channel communication: The theoretical and research foundations of multimedia. In D. H. Jonassen (Ed.), *Handbook of research for educational communications and technology* (pp. 851–875). Mahwah, NJ: Lawrence Erlbaum Associates.

Moore, M. G. (2001, June 6). *Distance education in the United States.* In *Proceedings of the Conference given at UOC.* Retrieved October 25, 2007, from http://www.uoc.es/web/esp/art/uoc/moore/moore.html

Moore, M. G., & Anderson, W. G. (2003). *Handbook of distance education.* Lawrence Erlbaum & Associates.

Moote, M. A., McClaran, M. P., & Chickering, D. K. (1997). Theory in practice: Applying participatory democracy theory to public land planning. *Environmental Management, 21*(6), 877-889.

Moraes, M.C., Bertoletti, A.C., & Costa, A.C.R. (1999). The SAGRES Virtual Museum with software agents to stimulate the visiting of museums. In P. De Bra & John J. Leggett (Eds.), *Proceedings of WebNet 99: World Conference on the WWW and Internet,* Honolulu, Hawaii, USA, October 24-30, (Vol. 1, pp. 770-775). Charlottesville, VA: Association for the Advancement of Computing in Education (AACE).

Moreno, R., & Mayer, R. E. (1999). Cognitive principles of multimedia learning: The role of modality and contiguity. *Journal of Educational Psychology, 91*(2), 358–368.

Moreno, R., & Mayer, R. E. (2000). A coherence effect in multimedia learning: The case for minimizing irrelevant sounds in the design of multimedia instructional messages. *Journal of Educational Psychology, 92*(1), 117–125.

Moreno, R., & Mayer, R. E. (2002). Verbal redundancy in multimedia learning: When reading helps listening. *Journal of Educational Psychology, 94*(1), 156–163.

Morgan, C., & O'Reilly, M. (1999). *Assessing open and distance learners.* London: Bogan Page.

Mosaker, L. (2001). Visualizing historical knowledge using VR technology. *Digital Creativity S&Z, 12*(1), 15-26.

Moschos, G., Nikolaidis, N., & Pitas, I. (2004). Anatomically-based 3D face and oral cavity model for creating virtual medical patients. In *Proceedings of IEEE ICME 2004*, Taipei, Taiwan, (pp. 867-870).

Moshman, D. (1982). Exogenous, endogenous and dialectical constructivism. *Developmental Review, 2,* 371-384.

Motiwalla, L. F. (2007). Mobile learning: A framework and evaluation. *Computers & Education, 49,* 581-596.

Mousavi, S. Y., Low, R., & Sweller, J. (1995). Reducing cognitive load by mixing auditory and visual presentation modes. *Journal of Educational Psychology, 87*(2), 319–334.

Moynihan, T. (1993). Modelling the software process in terms of the system representations and transformation steps used. *Information and Software Technology, 35*(3), 181-188.

Munro, K. (2002). *Conflict in cyberspace: How to resolve conflict online.* Retrieved September 10, 2005, from http://www.kalimunro.com/article_conflict_online.html

Mylopoulos, J., Chung, L., Liao, S., & Wang, H. (2001). Exploring alternatives during requirements analysis. *IEEE Software, 18*(1), 92-96.

NATURE Team (1996). Defining visions in context: Models, processes, and tools for requirements engineering. *Information Systems, 21*(6), 515-547.

New Media Consortium. (2007). The Horizon Report: 2007 Edition. Retrieved October 24, 2007, from http://www.nmc.org/horizon/2007/report

Nguyen, L., & Swatman, P. (2003). Managing the requirements engineering process. *Requirements Engineering, 8*(1), 55-68.

Nielsen, J. (1998, October 4). Personalization is overrated. *Alertbox*. Retrieved from www.useit.com/alertbox/981004.html

Nikolov, V. (1998). *Proučvanija vărchu neolitnata keramika v Trakija. Keramičnite kompleksi Karanovo II-III, III i III-IV v konteksta na Severozapadna Anatolija i Jugoistočna Evropa.* Sofia.

Nikolov, V. (Ed.). (2000). *Trakija i săsednite rajoni prez neolita i chalkolita.* Sofia.

Nikolov, V., Băčvarov, K., & Kalchev, P. (Eds.). (2004). Prehistoric Thrace. *Proceedings of the International Symposium in Stara Zagora, 30.09 - 04.10.2003.* Sofia - Stara Zagora.

Nikolova, L. (1999). *The Balkans in later prehistory. Periodization, chronology and cultural development in the Final Copper and Early Bronze Age (Fourth and third millenia BC).* BAR Internat. Ser. 791. Oxford.

Nikolova, L. (Ed.). (1995-1997). *Early Bronze Age settlement patterns in the Balkans (ca. 3500-2000 BC, Calibrated Dates)* vol 1-3. Sofia.

Nikopoulos, N., & Pitas, I. (1997). An efficient algorithm for 3D binary morphological transformations with 3D structuring elements of arbitrary size and shape. In *Proceedings of the 1997 IEEE Workshop on Nonlinear Signal and Image Processing* (NSIP'97).

Nirenburg, S. (1993). *Progress in machine translation.* Amsterdam: IOS Press.

Nuseibeh, B., Finkelstein, A., & Kramer, J. (1996). Method engineering for multi-perspective software development. *Information and Software Technology,* 38(4), 267-274.

Nyerges, T. L., & Jankowski, P. (1997). Enhanced adaptive structuration theory: A theory of GIS-supported collaborative decision making. *Geographical Systems, 4*(3), 225-257.

Nyerges, T., Jankowski, P., & Drew, C. (2002). Data-gathering strategies for social-behavioural research about participatory geographical information system use. *International Journal of Geographical Information Science, 16*(1), 1-22.

O'Neill, K., Singh, G., & O'Donoghue, J. (2004). Implementing e-learning programmes for higher education: A review of the literature. *Journal of Information Technology Education, 3*, 313-323.

Oakeshott, M. (1975). *On human conduct.* Oxford, UK: Oxford University Press.

Oberlandesgericht. (1999). (Court of Appeal) Düsseldorf 29 June 1999 (baumarkt.de).

Olle, T., Hagelstein, J., MacDonald, I., Rolland, C., Sol, H., van Assche, F., & Verrijn-Stuart, A. (1988). *Information systems methodologies—A framework for understanding* (2nd ed.). Reading: Addison-Wesley.

OMG. (2005). *Software process engineering Meta model specification* (Version 1.1). Object Management Group.

Oppermann, R., & Specht, M. (1999). Adaptive information for nomadic activities a process oriented approach. In *Software Ergonomie '99* (pp. 255-264). Walldorf, Germany. Stuttgart: Teubner.

Organisation for Economic Co-operation and Development. (2005). *E-learning in tertiary education. Where do we stand*? OECD: OECD Publishing.

Osborne, A. (1963). *Applied imagination.* New York: Scribner's.

Paas, F., & van Merrienboer, J. J. G. (1994). Instructional control of cognitive load in the training of complex cognitive tasks. *Educational Psychology Review, 6*(4), 351–371.

Paas, F., Renkl, A., & Sweller, J. (2003). Cognitive load theory and instructional design: Recent developments. *Educational Psychology, 38*(1), 1–4.

Paivio, A. (1971). *Imagery and verbal processes.* New York: Holt, Rinehart, and Winston.

Paivio, A. (1975). Coding distinctions and repetition effects in memory. In G. H. Bower (Ed.), *The psychology of learning and motivation* (Vol. 9, pp. 179–214). New York: Academic Press.

Paivio, A. (1990). *Mental representations: A dual coding approach.* New York, NY: Oxford University Press.

Palaigeorgiou, G. E., Siozos, P. D., & Konstantakis, N. I. (2006). CEAF: A measure for deconstructing students' prior computer experience. *Journal of Information Systems Education, 17*(4), 459-468.

Palloff, R.M., & Pratt, K. (2003). *The virtual student: A profile and guide to working with online learners.* San Francisco: Jossey-Bass.

Palo Alto Research Center. (1994). *Xerox PARC map viewer.* Retrieved November 11, 2005, from http://www2.parc.com/istl/projects/mapdocs/

Panajotov, I. (1989). Zur Chronologie und Periodisierung der Bronzezeit in den heutigen bulgarischen Gebieten. *Thracia* 9, 74-103.

Parzinger, H. (1993). *Studien zur Chronologie und Kulturgeschichte der Jungstein-, Kupfer- und Frühbronzezeit zwischen Karpaten und mittlerem Taurus.* Röm.-Germ. Forsch. 52. Mainz.

Patel, C., & Patel, T. (2006). Exploring a joint model of conventional and online learning systems. *E-service Journal, 4*(2), 27-46.

Patel, J., & Stutt, A. (1998). *KIVA: An archaeological interpreter Human Cognition* (Research Laboratory Tech. Rep. No. 35). Milton Keynes: The Open University.

Pelgrum, W. (2001). Obstacles to the integration of ICT in education: Results from a worldwide educational assessment. *Computers & Education, 37*(2), 163-178.

Peterson, L. R., & Peterson, M. J. (1959). Short-term retention of individual verbal items. *Journal of Experimental Psychology, 58*, 193–198.

Plato. (1986). *Phaedrus* (C. J. Rowe, Trans.). Warminster, UK: Aries & Phillips.

Pohl, K. (1993). The three dimensions of requirements engineering. In C. Rolland, F. Bodart, & C. Cauvet (Eds.), *Proc. of the 5th Int. Conf. on Advanced Info. Systems Engineering (CAiSE'93)* (LNCS 685, pp. 275-292). Berlin: Springer.

Pohl, K. (1994). The three dimensions of requirements engineering: A framework and its application. *Information Systems, 19*(3), 243-258.

Pohl, K., Dömges, R., & Jarke, M. (1997). Towards method-driven trace capture. In A. Olive & J. Pastor (Eds.), *Proceedings of the 9th International Conference on Advanced Information Systems Engineering (CAiSE'97)* (pp. 103-116). Berlin: Springer.

Pöhlmann, E., & West, M. L. (2001). *Documents of ancient Greek music.* USA: Oxford University Press.

Politis, D. (2006). Introduction: E-learning trends in archaeology. In C. Carreras (Ed.), *Open and distance learning (ODL) strategies.* Athens: Klidarithmos Publications.

Politis, D. (Ed.) (2006). *The e-learning dimension of computer applications in archaeology.* Athens: Klidarithmos Publications.

Politis, D., & Margounakis, D. (2003). Determining the chromatic index of music. In *Proceedings of WEDELMUSIC 2003, 3rd International Conference on the Web Delivering of Music*, Leeds, UK.

Politis, D., Gkatzogias, M., Karamalis, A., & Pyrinis, K. (2005). GIS driven Internet multimedia databases for multiple archaeological excavations in Greece and the region of South-Eastern Europe: The SEEArchWeb project. *WSEAS Transactions on Advances in Engineering Education, 2*(2), 54-61.

Politis, D., Margounakis, D., & Mokos, K. (2004). Vizualizing the chromatic index of music. In *Proceedings of WEDELMUSIC 2004, 4th International Conference on the Web Delivering of Music*, Barcelona, Spain.

Porter, L. (1997). *Creating the virtual classroom (distance learning with the Internet).* Wiley: Computer Publishing.

Prensky, M. (2001). *Digital game-based learning.* New York: McGraw-Hill.

Price, T.D., & Gebauer, A.B. (2002). *Adventures in Fugawiland. A computerized simulation in Archaeology.* London: McGraw-Hill.

Pryke, A. N. (1999). *Data mining using genetic algorithms and interactive visualisation.* PhD thesis, Department of Computer Science, University of Birmingham, UK.

Pryke, A. N., & Beale, R. (2005). Interactive comprehensible data mining. In C. Yang (Ed.), *Ambient intelligence for scientific discovery: Foundations, theories, and systems* (pp. 48-65). Berlin: Springer-Verlag.

Punter, T., & Lemmen, K. (1996). The MEMA-model: Towards a new approach for methods engineering. *Journal of Information and Software Technology, 38*(4), 295-305.

Quinlan, J. R. (1987). Simplifying decision trees. *International Journal of Man-Machine Studies, 27*, 221-234.

Quinlan, J. R. (1992). *C4.5: Programs for machine learning.* San Mateo, CA: Morgan Kaufmann.

Quinlan, J. R. (1993). Combining instance-based and model-based learning. *Proceedings of the 10th International Conference of Machine Learning, University of Massachusetts, Amherst* (pp. 236-243). San Mateo, CA: Morgan Kaufmann.

Ragan, L. C., & Terheggen, S. L. (2003). Effective workload management strategies for the online environment. Report: *Findings of a research.* The Alfred P. Sloan Foundation. Pennsylvania State University U.Ed. OCE 03–1818. Retrieved October 25, 2007, from http://www.worldcampus.psu.edu/pdf/fac/workload_strat.pdf

Ramaiah, C., Foo, S., & Choo, H.P. (2006). Trends in electronic publishing. In H. S. Ching, P. Poon, & C. McNaught (Eds.), *E-learning and digital publishing* (p. 111). Dordrecht: Springer.

Ramesh, B., & Jarke, M. (2001). Towards reference models for requirements traceability. *IEEE Trans. on Software Engineering, 27*(1), 58-93.

Ranta, J. F., & Aviles, W. A. (1999). The virtual reality dental training system—simulating dental procedures for the purpose of training dental students using haptics. In *Proceedings of the 4th PHANTOM Users Group Workshop.*

Redfern, S., & Galway, N. (2002). Collaborative virtual environments to support communication and community in Internet-based distance education. *Journal of Information Technology Education (JITE), 1*(3), 201-211.

Reeder, K., Macfadyen, L., Roche, J., & Chase, M. (2004, May). Negotiating cultures in cyberspace: Participation patterns and problematic. *Language Learning and Technology, 8*(2) 88-105. Retrieved September 10, 2005, from http://llt.msu.edu/vol8num2/reeder/default.html

Reeves, T. (1997). *Evaluating what really matters in computer-based education.* Retrieved September 10, 2005, from http://www.educationau.edu.au/archives/cp/reeves.htm

Reeves, T.C., & Hedberg, J.G. (2003). *Interactive learning systems evaluation.* Englewood Cliffs, NJ: Educational Technology Publications.

Refsland, S., Ojika, T., & Berry, R. (2000). The living virtual Kinka Kuji Temple: A dynamic environment. *IEEE Multimedia, 7*(2), 65-67. Retrieved August 8, 2005, from http://portal.acm.org/citation.cfm?id=614975

Reilly, P. (1989). Data visualization in archaeology. *IBM Systems Journal, 28*(4), 569-579.

Relan, T.I., & Gillani, B.B. (1997). Web page-based instruction and the traditional classroom: Similarities and differences. In B. H. Khan (Ed.), *Web page-based instruction*. New Jersey: Educational Technology Publications.

Relph, E. C. (1976). *Place and placelessness*. London: Pion Ltd.

Rescher, N. (2003). *Epistemology: An introduction to the theory of knowledge*. Albany: State University of New York Press.

Resnick, M. (2002). Rethinking learning in the digital age. In G. Kirkman (Ed.), *The Global Information Technology Report: Readiness for the networked world*. Oxford University Press.

Rettig, M., & Simons, G. (1993). A project planning and development process for small teams. *Comm. of the ACM, 36*(10), 45-55.

Rheingold, H. (1996). *La comunidad virtual. Una sociedad sin fronteras*. Barcelona.

Richards, J.D. (1998). Recent trends in computer applications in Archaeology. *Journal of Archaeological Research, 6*(4), 331-382. Springer-Verlag.

Rieber, L. P. (1996). Seriously considering play: Designing interactive learning environments based on the blending of microworlds, simulations, and games. *Educational Technology Research & Development, 44*(2), 43-58. Retrieved August 7, 2005, from http://it.coe.uga.edu/~lrieber/play.html

Rieger, M. (1996). *Music before and after Solesmes*. Penn State University: STS Working-Papers.

Riehm, U., Böhle, K., & Wingert, B. (2004). Elektronisches Publizieren. In R. Kuhlen, T. Seeger, & D. Strauch (Hg.), *Grundlagen der praktischen Information und Dokumentation*. München: Band 1.

Riehm, U., Böhle, K., Gabel-Becker, I., & Wingert, B. (1992). *Elektronisches Publizieren. Eine kritische Bestandsaufnahme*. Berlin u. a.

Rittel, H., & Webber, M. (1973). Dilemmas in a general theory of planning. *Policy Sciences, 4*, 155-169.

Robey, D. (1984). Conflict models for implementation research. In R. Schultz (Ed.), *Management science implementation*. New York: American Elsevier.

Robinson, M., Pekkola, S., Korhonen, J., Hujala, S., Toivonen, T., & Saarinen, M-J. (2001). Extending the limits of collaborative virtual environments. In E. Churchill, D. Snowdon, & A. Munro (Eds.), *Collaborative virtual environments: Digital places and spaces for interaction*, (10), London Berlin Heidelberg, Germany: Springer-Verlag.

Rocha, E. M. (1997). A ladder of empowerment. *Journal of Planning and Education Research, 17*(1), 31-44.

Roffe, I. (2002). E-learning: Engagement, enhancement and execution. *Quality assurance in education, 10*(1), 40-50.

Roitman, A. (1997). *A day at Qumran: The Dead Sea sect and its scrolls*. Jerusalem: The Israel Museum

Rolland, C., Souveyet, C., & Moreno, M. (1995). An approach for defining ways-of-working. *Information Systems, 20*(4), 337-359.

Rolland, R., Souveyet, C., & Ben Achour, C. (1998). Guiding goal modeling using scenarios. *IEEE Trans. on Software Engineering, 24*(12), 1055-1071.

Roman, P. (Ed.). (1997). The Thracian World at the Crossroads of Civilizations. *Proceedings of the Seventh International Congress of Thracology Constanţa, Mangalia, Tulcea, 20 - 26 May 1996.* Bucureşti.

Roman, P. (Ed.). (2001). *Symposium Cernavodă III-Boleráz - ein Vorgeschichtliches Phanomen zwischen dem Oberrhein und der Unteren Donau: Mangalia, Neptun (18.-24. Oktober 1999).* Stud. Danubiana / Pars romaniae / Ser. symposia 2. Bucureşti.

Romiszowski, A. (1997). Web-page based distance learning and teaching: Revolutionary invention or reaction to necessity. In B. H. Khan (Ed.), *Web page-based instruction*. New Jersey: Educational Technology Publications.

Rösch, O., Loew, R., & Pfeifer, A. (2003). Interkulturelle Kompetenz—heute eine unerlässliche Schlüsselqualifikation. Zwischenbericht zu einem Forschungsprojekt an der TFH Wildau. In: *Wissenschaftliche Beiträge der Technischen Fachhochschule Wildau.*

Rose, J. T., Buchanan, J., & Sarrett, D. C. (1999). Software reviews – the DentSim system. *Journal of Dental Education, 63*, 421-423.

Rose, T., & Jarke, M. (1990). A decision-based configuration process model. In *Proceedings of the 12th International Conference on Software Engineering* (pp. 316-325). Los Alamitos: IEEE Computer Society Press.

Rouet, J., Levonen, J., & Biardeau, A. (Eds.). (2001). *Multimedia learning: Cognitive and instructional issues*. London: Pergamon.

Rowe, J., & Razdan, A. (2003). A prototype digital library for 3D collections: Tools to capture, model, analyze, and query complex 3D data. *In Museums and the Web 2003: Selected Papers from 7th International Conference*, Charlotte, NC.

Rowntree, D. (1997). *Making materials-based learning work*. London: Routledge

Ruiz, F., Vizcaino, A., Piattini, M., & Garcia, F. (2004). An ontology for the management of software maintenance projects. *International Journal of Software Engineering and Knowledge Engineering, 14*(3), 323-349.

Ryan, N. (1996). Computer based visualisation of the past: Technical "realism" and historical credibility. In P. Main, T. Higgins, & J. Lang (Eds.), *Imaging the past: Electronic imaging and computer graphics in museums and archaeology* (pp. 95-108). London: The British Museum.

Ryan, S., Scott, B., Freeman, H., & Patel, D. (2000). *The virtual university: The Internet and resource based learning*. London: Kogan Page.

Rzevski, G. (1983). On the comparison of design methodologies. In T. Olle, H. Sol, & C. Tully (Eds.), *Information systems design methodologies—A feature analysis* (pp. 259-266). Amsterdam: Elsevier Science Publishers.

Sabherwal, R., & Robey, D. (1993). An empirical taxonomy of implementation processes based on sequences of events in information system development. *Organization Science, 4*(4), 548-576.

Sabherwal, R., & Robey, D. (1995). Reconciling variance and process strategies for studying information system development. *Information Systems Research, 6*(4), 303-327

Sadoski, M., & Paivio, A. (2001). Imagery and text: A dual coding theory of reading and writing. Mahwah, NJ: Erlbaum.

Saeki, M., Iguchi, K., Wen-yin, K., & Shinokara M. (1993). A meta model for representing software specification & design methods. In N. Prakash, C. Rolland, & B. Pernici (Eds.), *Proceedings of the IFIP WG8.1 Working Conference on Information Systems Development Process* (pp. 149-166). Amsterdam: Elsevier Science Publishers.

Sager, J. C. (Ed.). (2000). *Essays on definition*. Amsterdam; Philadelphia: J. Benjamins Publishers.

Salen, K., & Zimmerman, E. (2003). *Rules of play: Game design fundamentals*. Cambridge, MA: MIT Press.

Salmon, G. (2000). *E-moderating: The key of teaching and learning online*. London: Kogan Page.

Salmon, G. (2001). *E-tivities: The key to active online learning*. London: Kogan Page.

San Francisco Performances. Guitar trek: Ancient origins. Retrieved October 27, 2007, from www.performances.org

Sangrà, A., Cabrera, N., & Girona, C. (2005). *El Quadre de comandament: una eina per a la millora metodològica en l'àmbit de l'ensenyament universitar* (http://www.upf.edu/bolonya/butlletins/200/marc1/quadre.pdf).

Sangra, A., Guardia, L., Gonzalez Sanmamed, M. (2007). Educational design as a key issue in planning for quality improvement. *Making the transition to e-learning: Strategies and issues*. Hershey, PA: Idea Group.

Scavone, G., & Cook, P. (2004). Synthesis toolkit in C++ (STK). In K. Greenebaum & R. Barzel (Eds.), *Audio anecdotes* (Vol. 2). Natick, MA: A.K. Peters Press.

Schafer, W. A., Ganoe, C. H., Xiao, L., Coch, G., & Carroll, J. M. (2005). Designing the next generation of distributed, geocollaborative tools. *Cartography and Geographic Information Science, 32*(2), 81-100.

Schloen, J. D. (2004). Archaeological data models and Web publication using XML. *Computers and the Humanities, 35*(5), 123-152. Springer Netherlands.

Schmidt, D., Gruhler, G., & Fearns, A. (Hrsg.) (2003). *E-Learning Experimente und Laborübungen zur Automatisierungstechnik über das Internet: Nutzungsmöglichkeiten, Beispiele und die Simulation am Bildungsmarkt*: Europa-Lernmittel Verlag.

Schnotz, W. (2001). Sign systems, technologies, and the acquisition of knowledge. In J. Rouet, J. JU. Levonen, and A. Biardeau (Eds.), *Multimedia learning: Cognitive and instructional issues* (pp. 9–30). New York: Pergamon.

Schrage, M. (1991). *Shared minds: The new technologies of collaboration*. Random House.

Schroeder, R. (1996). *Possible worlds: The social dynamic of virtual reality technology.* London: Westview Press.

Selwyn, N. (1999). Students' attitudes towards computers in sixteen to nineteen education. *Education and Information Technologies, 4*(2), 129-141.

Semper, R., & Spasojevic, M. (2002). The electronic guidebook: Using portable devices and a wireless Web-based network to extend the museum experience. In D. Bearman & J. Trant (Eds.), *Proceedings of Museums and the Web 2001*. Boston, April 18-20. Pittsburgh, PA: Archives & Museum Informatics. Retrieved from www.archimuse.com/mw2002/papers/semper/semper.html

Shaper, R., & Ashmore, W. (1993). *Archaeology: Discovering our past.* California: Mayfield Publishing Company.

Shiffer, M. J. (1992). Towards a collaborative planning system. *Environment and Planning B: Planning and Design, 19*(6), 709-722.

Short, K. (1991). Methodology integration: Evolution of information engineering. *Information and Software Technology, 33*(9), 720-732.

Sideris, A. (2006). A virtual cradle for democracy: Reconstructing the ancient agora of Athens. In *E-learning and computer applications in archaeology, Proceedings of 1st SEEArchWeb Conference*, Thessaloniki, Greece.

Sideris, A., & Roussou, M. (2002). Making a new world out of an old one: In search of a common language for archaeological immersive VR representation. In *CREATIVE Digital Culture, Proceedings of 8th International Conference on Virtual Systems and Multimedia*, Gyeongju, Korea.

Sideris, A., Roussou, M., & Gaitatzis, A. (2004). The virtual reconstruction of the Hellenistic Asklepieion of Messene. *Imeros, 4*, 208-216.

Sidiropoulos, G., & Sideris, A. (2002). Requirements and assumptions in visualization process of urban and surrounding areas (The case of Greek city in time). In *Proceedings of the CAA 2002 The Digital Heritage of Archaeology, Computer Applications and Quantitative Methods in Archaeology Conference*, Heraclion, Crete, Greece.

Sieber, R. E. (2000). GIS implementation in the grassroots. *URISA Journal, 12*(1), 15-29.

Singhal, S., & Zyda, M. (1999). *Networked virtual environments: Design and implementation.* ACM Press.

Slater, M. (1999). Measuring presence: A response to the Witmer and Singer presence questionnaire. *Presence: Teleoperators and Virtual Environments, 8*(5), 560-565. Retrieved August 7, 2005, from http://www.cs.ucl.ac.uk/staff/m.slater/Papers/pq.pdf

Sloniowski, L. (1993). *Report of findings: Distance education working group student survey project.* Retrieved September 10, 2005, from http://artemis.uwindsor.ca/kits/gailj/99009a/vck13materials.nsf/0/875ef62fa9e00a5185256e01005aa78a/$FILE/dereport_of_findings.doc

Slooten van, K., & Brinkkemper, S. (1993). A method engineering approach to information systems development. In N. Prakash, C. Rolland, & B. Pernici (Eds.), *Proceedings of the IFIP WG8.1 Working Conference on*

Information Systems Development Process (pp. 167-188). Amsterdam: Elsevier Science Publishers.

Smith, J. B. (1994). *Collective intelligence in computer-based collaboration.* Hillsdale, NJ: Lawrence Erlbaum and Associates.

Smith, J. W., Everhart, J. E., Dickson, W. C., Knowler, W. C., & Johannes, R. S. (1988). Using the ADAP learning algorithm to forecast the onset of diabetes mellitus. *Proceedings of the Symposium on Computer Applications and Medical Care* (pp. 261-265). Piscataway, NJ: IEEE Computer Society Press.

Smith, M. (2005). Fair use and distance learning in the digital age. *The Journal of Electronic Publishing.* Retrieved October 26, 2007, from http://www.press.umich.edu/jep/05-04/smith.html

Smith, S., & Kandel, A. (1993). *Verification and validation of rule-based expert systems.* Boca Raton, FL: CRC Press.

Söderström, E., Andersson, B., Johannesson, P., Perjons, E., & Wangler, B. (2002). Towards a framework for comparing process modeling languages. In A. Banks Pidduck, J. Mylopoulos, C. Woo, & T. Ozsu (Eds.), *Proceedings of the 14th International Conference on Advanced Information Systems Engineering (CAiSE 2002)* (pp. 600-611). Berlin: Springer-Verlag.

Sol, H. (1992). Information systems development: A problem solving approach. In W. Cotterman & J. Senn (Eds.), *Challenges and strategies for research in systems development* (pp. 151-161). New York: John Wiley & Sons.

Sommerville, I. (1998). *Software engineering* (5th ed.). Reading: Addison-Wesley Longman.

Song, X., & Osterweil, L. (1992). Towards objective, systematic design-method comparison. *IEEE Software, 9*(3), 43-53.

Sowa, J. (2000). *Knowledge representation—Logical, philosophical, and computational foundations.* Pacific Grove, CA: Brooks/Cole.

Sowa, J., & Zachman J. (1992). Extending and formalizing the framework for information system architecture. *IBM Systems Journal, 31*(3), 590-616.

Spellmann, P., Mosier, P., Deus, L., & Carlson, J. (1997). Collaborative virtual workspace. In *Proceedings of GROUP'97,* Phoenix, AZ, (pp. 197-203). ACM.

Squire, K. (2002). Cultural framing of computer/video games. *Game Studies, 2*(1). Retrieved August 8, 2005, from http://www.gamestudies.org/0102/squire/

Squire, K. D., Makinster, J., Barnett, M., Barab, A. L., & Barab, S. A. (2003). Designed curriculum and local culture: Acknowledging the primacy of classroom culture. *Science Education, 87,* 1-22.

Staab, S., Schnurr, H.P., Studer, R., & Sure, Y. (2001). Knowledge processes and ontologies. *IEEE Intelligent Systems, 16*(1), 26-34.

Stamatoudi, I. (2000). *To what extend are multimedia products databases.* In I. Stamatoudi, & P. Torremans (Eds.), *Copyright in the new digital environment* (pp. Op. cit, pp. 21-22).

Stamper, R. (1975). Information science for systems analysis. In E. Mumford & H. Sackman (Eds.), *Human choice and computers* (pp. 107-120). Amsterdam: Elsevier Science Publishers.

Stamper, R. (1992). Signs, organizations, norms and information systems. In *Proceedings of the 3rd Australian Conference on Information Systems* (pp. 21-65). Department of Business Systems, Univ. of Wollongong, Australia.

Star, J., & Estes, J. (1990). *Geographic information systems.* New Jersey: Prentice Hall.

Stefanovich, M., Todorova, H., & Hauptmann, H. (Eds.). (1998). *In the steps of James Harvey Gaul* (Vol. 1). Sofia.

Stephenson, J. (2001). *Teaching and learning online: Pedagogies for new technologies.* London: Kogan Page.

Strauch, A.B. (2001). (Ed.). *Publishing and the law: Current legal issues.* New York: Hawork Information Press.

Suler, J. (2002). The online disinhibition effect. In *The psychology of cyberspace.* Retrieved September 10, 2005, from http://www.rider.edu/~suler/psycyber/dis inhibit.html

Sutherland, R. (2004). Designs for learning: ICT and knowledge in the classroom. *Computers and Education, 43*(1-2), 5-16.

Swede van, V., & van Vliet, J. (1993). A flexible framework for contingent information systems modeling. *Information and Software Technology, 35*(9), 530-548.

Sweller, J. (1994). Cognitive load theory, learning difficulty, and instructional design. *Learning and Instruction, 4*, 295–312.

Sweller, J., van Merrienboer, J. J. G., & Paas, F. G. W. C. (1998). Cognitive architecture and instructional design. *Educational Psychology Review, 10*(3), 251–296.

SYSTRAN SA. Corporate site and free Web translation services. Retrieved October 27, 2007, from http://www.systransoft.com

Talen, E. (1999). Constructing neighborhoods from the bottom up: The case for resident-generated GIS. *Environment and Planning B: Planning and Design, 26*(4), 533-554.

Talen, E. (2000). Bottom-up GIS: A new tool for individual and group expression in participatory planning. *Journal of the American Planning Association, 66*(3), 279-294.

Tam, K.Y., & Ho, S.Y. (2003). Web personalization: Is it effective? *IT Professional, 5*(5), 53-57. Retrieved from csdl.computer.org/comp/mags/it/2003/05/f5053abs.htm

Tan, W.L.H., Subramaniam, R., & Aggarwal, A.K. (2003). Virtual science centers: A new genre of learning in Web-based promotion of science education. In *Proceedings of the 36th Annual Hawaii International Conference on System Sciences (HICSS'03)* (Vol. 5, pp. 156-165). IEEE Computer Society.

Thayer, R. (1987). Software engineering project management—A top-down view. In R. Thayer (Ed.), *Tutorial: Software engineering project management* (pp. 15-56). IEEE Computer Society Press.

The eLearning Guild Research. (2006). Future Directions in e-Learning Research Report 2006. Retrieved June, 10, 2007 from http://www.elearningguild.com/pdf/1/apr06-futuredirections.pdf

Tindall-Ford, S., Chandler, P., & Sweller, J. (1997). When two sensory modes are better than one. *Journal of Experimental Psychology: Applied, 3*(4), 257–287.

Ting-Toomey, S., & Oetzel, J. (2001). *Managing intercultural conflict effectively.* Thousand Oaks, CA: Sage.

Todorova, H. (1981). Das Chronologiesystem von Karanovo im Lichte der neuen Forschungsergebnisse in Bulgarien. *Slovenská Arch.* 29, 203-216.

Todorova, H. (1982). *Kupferzeitliche Siedlungen in Nordostbulgarien.* Mat. Allg. Vergl. Arch. 13. München.

Todorova, H. (1986). *Kamenno-mednata epocha v Bălgarija.* Sofia.

Todorova, H. (1989). *Durankulak 1.* Sofia.

Todorova, H. (2002). *Durankulak 2. Die prähistorischen Gräberfelder.* Sofia.

Tomlinson, R. F. (1967). *An introduction to the geographic information system of the Canada Land Inventory.* Ottawa, Canada: Department of Forestry and Rural Development.

Torkzadeh G., & Van Dyke T.P. (2002). Effects of training on Internet self-efficacy and computer user attitudes. *Computers in Human Behavior, 18*, 479-494.

Torres-Fonseca, F., & Egenhofer, M. (2000). Ontology-driven geographic information systems. *Computers, Environment and Urban Systems, 24*(3), 251-271.

Toulmin, S. E. (1958). *The uses of argument.* Cambridge, UK; New York: Cambridge Press.

Trompenaars, F. (1998). *Riding the waves of culture: Understanding the waves of cultural diversity in global business.* New York: McGraw-Hill.

Tsahalinas, K. et al. (1997). Physical modeling simulation of the Ancient Grek Auloi. In *ICMC 97: International Computer Music Conference,* Thessaloniki.

Tuan, Y. (1998). *Escapism.* Baltimore: John Hopkins University Press.

Uschold, M. (1996). Building ontologies: Towards a unified methodology. In *Proceedings of the 16th Annual Conference of the British Computer Society Specialist Group on Expert Systems*, Cambridge, UK.

Uschold, M., & King, M. (1995). Towards a methodology for building ontologies. In *Workshop on Basic Ontological Issues in Knowledge Sharing,* Montreal, Canada.

Vasseur, L., LaFrance, L., Ansseau, C., Renaud, D., Morin, D., & Audet, T. (1997). Advisory committee: A powerful tool for helping decision makers in environmental issues. *Environmental Management, 21*(3), 359-365.

Vessey, I., & Conger, S. (1994). Requirements specification: Learning object, process, and data methodologies. *Comm. of the ACM, 37*(5), 102-113.

Vitiello, G. (2001). A European policy for electronic publishing. *Journal of Electronic Publishing, 6*(3). Retrieved October 26, 2007, from http://www.press.umich.edu/jep/06-03/vitiello.html

Vlachos, A., Peters, J., Boyd, C., & Mitchell, J. L. (2001). Curved PN triangles. In *Proceedings of the ACM Symposium on Interactive 3D Graphics.*

Vollmann, D. (2004). Die neolithischen Häuser von Drama-"Gerena". In: Nikolov, V., Băčvarov, K., Kalchev, P. (Eds.) *Prehistoric Thrace. Proceedings of the International Symposium in Stara Zagora, 30.09 - 04.10.2003.* Sofia-Stara Zagora, 269-277.

von Wodtke, M. (1993). *Mind over media: Creative thinking skills for electronic media.* New York: McGraw-Hill.

Vygotsky, L.S. (1978). *Mind in society.* Cambridge, MA: Harvard University Press.

Wand, Y., & Weber, R. (1990). An ontological model of an information system. *IEEE Trans. on Software Engineering, 16*(11), 1282-1292.

Wang, D., Zhang, Y., Wang, Y., Lee, Y.-S., Peijun, L., & Yong, W. (2005). Cutting on triangle mesh: Local model-based haptic display for dental preparation surgery simulation, *IEEE Transactions on Visualization and Computer* Graphics, *11*(6), 671-683.

Waterman, D. A. (1986). *A guide to expert systems.* Reading, MA: Addison-Wesley.

Watkins, R. (2005). *75 e-learning activities: Making online learning interactive.* San Francisco: Pfeiffer.

Webler, T., Tuler, S., & Krueger, R. (2001). What is a good public participation process? Five perspectives from the public. *Environmental Management, 27*(3), 435-450.

Webster (1989). *Webster's encyclopedic unabridged dictionary of the English language.* New York: Gramercy Books.

Weckström, N. (2004). *Finding "reality" in virtual environments.* Unpublished master's thesis, Arcada Polytechnic: Helsingfors / Esbo, Finland.

Weick, K. E. (1995). *Sensemaking in organizations.* CA: Sage Publications.

Weil, S., Hussain, T., Brunye, T., Sidman, J., & Spahr, L. (2005). The use of massive multi-player gaming technology for military training: A preliminary evaluation. In *Proceedings of the 49th Annual Meeting of the Human Factors and Ergonomics Society*, Orlando, FL.

Weinberger, H., Te'eni, D., & Frank, A. (2003). Ontologies of organizational memory as a basis for evaluation. In *Proceedings of the 11th European Conference of Information Systems*, Naples, Italy.

Weller, M. (2002). *Delivering learning on the net. The why, what and how of online education.* London: Routledge.

Weller, M. (2007). *Virtual Leaning Environments: Using, choosing and developing your VLE.* Routledge; 1st edition (April 12, 2007). ISBN-10: 0415414318.

West, M. L. (1992). *Ancient Greek music.* Oxford: Clarendon Press.

Wheatley, D., & Gillings, M. (2002). *Spatial technology and archaeology: The archaeological applications of GIS*. London: Taylor & Francis.

Whitman, P. (1994). Experts and their interventions: A model of the field of urban improvement. *Environment and Planning B: Planning and Design, 21*(6), 759-768.

Wilcock, J. D. (1985). A review of expert systems, their shortcomings, and their possible applications in Archaeology. *Computer applications in Archaeology* (pp. 139-144). University of London.

Wilcock, J. D. (1990). A critique of expert systems, and their past and present use in archaeology. In R. Ennals, & J. C. Gardin (Eds.), *Interpretation in the humanities: Perspectives from artificial intelligence* (pp. 130-142). LIR Rep. 71. London: British Library Board.

Wild, C., Maly, K., & Liu, L. (1991). Decision-based software development. *Software maintenance: Research and practice*, *3*(1), 17-43.

Wilson, B. G. (2005). Broadening our foundation for instructional design: Four pillars of practice. In E. Rose (Ed.), *Educational Technology, 45*(2), 10-15. Special issue on cultural studies.

Wilson, B.G. (Ed.). (1996). *Constructivist learning environments: Case studies in instructional design.* Englewood Cliffs, NJ: Educational Technology Publications.

Wilson, M. A., & Howarth, R. B. (2002). Discourse-based valuation of ecosystem services: Establishing fair outcomes through group deliberations. *Ecological Economics, 41*, 431-443.

Winnington-Ingram, R.P. (1932). Aristoxenos and the intervals of Greek music. *The Classical Quarterly, 26*(3-4), 195-208.

Wolff, S. J. (2003). *Design features of the physical learning environment for collaborative, project-based learning at the community college level.* St. Paul, MN: National Research Center for Career and Technical Education. (http://www.nccte.org)

Wong, D. (2003). *The heritage & legacy of thinking and computer games. Online course essay.* Retrieved August 8, 2005, from http://www.msu.edu/user/buchan56/coursework/cep911_intellectual_history/hl_thinking.htm

Wood, A. M., Drew, N. S., Beale, R., & Hendley, R. J. (1995). HyperSpace: Web browsing with visualisation. *Proceedings of the 3rd International World-Wide Web Conference*, Darmstadt, Germany, April (pp. 21-25).

Wood-Harper, A., & Fitzgerald, G. (1982). A taxonomy of current approaches to systems analysis. *The Computer Journal*, 25(1), 12-16.

Wright, D. J., Goodchild, M. F., & Proctor, J. D. (1997). Demystifying the persistent ambiguity of GIS as "tool" vs. "science." *Annals of the Association of American Geographers, 87*(2), 346-362.

Xydas, G., & Kouroupetroglou, G. (2001). The DEMOSTHENES speech composer. In *Proceedings of the 4th ISCA Tutorial and Research Workshop on Speech Synthesis*, Perthshire, Scotland, (pp. 167-172).

Young, A. (1997). Mentoring, modeling, monitoring, motivating: Response to students' ungraded writing as academic conversation. In M. D. Sorcinelli & P. Elbow (Eds.), *Writing to learn: Strategies for assigning and responding to writing across the disciplines*. New Directions for Teaching and Learning, No. 69.

Zachman, J. (1987). A framework for information systems architecture. *IBM Systems Journal, 26*(3), 276-292.

Zahrt, M. (2003). Elektronisches Publizieren. In G. Gounalakis (Ed.), *Rechtshandbuch Elektronic Business* (pp. 1663 et seq.). München: Beck Juristischer Verlag.

Zaltsman, R. (2004). *Conflict paradigm in distance learning cross-cultural online settings.* Doctoral dissertation, Academy of Personnel Management, Kiev: IAPM.

Zaltsman, R. (2005, August). The challenge of intercultural electronic learning: English as lingua franca. *Cybercultures: Exploring Critical Issues, 3rd Global Conference,* Prague, (under review). Retrieved September 10, 2005, from http://www.inter-disciplinary.net/ci/cybercultures/c3/prog.htm

Zaltsman, R., & Belous, A. (2004, June). Considerations to the applications possibilities of E-learning in TRIZ. *QFD-/TRIZ-Kongress,* Kassel, Germany.

Zongmin, M. (Ed.). (2006). *Web-based intelligent e-learning systems: Technologies and applications.* Hershey, PA: Information Science Publishing.

Zultner, R. (1993). TQM for technical teams. *Comm. of the ACM*, *36*(10), 79-91.

Zurita, G., & Nussbaum, M. (2004). Computer supported collaborative learning using wirelessly interconnected handheld computers. *Computers & Education, 42*(3), 215-317.

About the Contributors

Dionysios Politis is a lecturer of the multimedia lab, in the Department of Informatics, Aristotle University of Thessaloniki. He has earned his BS in physics (1987), MSc in radio engineering and electronics (1990), and PhD in computer science (1998) from the same university. He is a holder of a Graduate Diploma in Computing Studies (1991) from RMIT University as a scholar of the Australian government. He has served as coordinator of the EU funded multinational project "SEEArchWeb – South Eastern Europe Archaeology Web" (2004-2006). He has been a collaborator of the Centre of International and European Economic Law (1992-2002) and has participated in various computer law projects, mainly focusing on the preaccession route of southeastern Europe countries to EU integration. His research interests focus on multimedia reconstructions and visualizations, mainly with an e-learning orientation. He has edited, published or presented more than 50 books, chapters in books, journals, magazines, newspapers, radio-television emissions and international conferences.

* * *

Joan Campàs is a lecturer in humanities at the Universitat Oberta de Catalunya (UOC- Barcelona, Spain). Her research interests focus on how the various disciplinary spheres are being reshaped in the digital world, and on the use of digital resources within network learning.

Cèsar Carreras is currently junior lecturer in the Department of Humanities of the Universitat Oberta de Catalunya (UOC, Spain) since 1997. He holds a PhD in ancient history (1995) from the University of Barcelona (Spain), another PhD in archaeology (1994) from the University of Southampton (UK), and MSc in archaeological computing (1991) from the University of Southampton (UK). Nowadays, he is lecturing computer applications in humanities and ancient history in the university. Besides, he is director of the research group Òliba (http://oliba.uoc.edu), whose main aim is the evaluation of applications of IT to cultural heritage. He is coordinating and taking part in different European projects such as COINE (Cultural Objects in Networked Environments), **SEEArchWeb** (An interactive Web-based presentation of Southeastern European Archaeology) and national projects such as **ARACNE** (Evaluation of ICT applications). He has produced different books and papers related to Roman archaeology and information technologies applications in cultural heritage.

Rudolf Echt is head of the Institute of Pre- and Protohistory at the University of Saarland (Saarbrücken, Germany) since 2004. He holds a PhD in art history (1979) and habilitated in pre- and protohistory (1992). As a field surveyer, he took part in R. Hachmann's excavation in Kamid el-Loz (Lebanon) and was vice-field director in J. Lichardus excavation in Drama (Bulgaria). Since 2004, he manages the Drama research project, funded by the German Research Foundation (Deutsche Forschungsgemeinschaft).

Eleftheria Giannaka obtained her diploma from the Department of Informatics, Aristotle University of Thessaloniki, Greece, and her MSc from the Computer Engineering and Informatics Department, University of Patras. Greece. She is currently a PhD candidate of the aforementioned department of the Patras University. Furthermore, she is working as an R&D computer engineer at the Research Unit 6 of the Computer Technology Institute in Patras (Greece). Her interests include computer networks, system architecture, internet application, electronic commerce, database implementation and administration, virtual reality applications, performance evaluation, programming and distributed virtual envoronments.

Cristina Girona is a researcher of the Internet Interdisciplinary Institute (IN3) in the Universitat Oberta de Catalunya (UOC, Spain). Her research interests focus on e-learning methodologies.

Alexandros S. Gouniotis (born in Heraklion, Greece, 1983) is a postgraduate student at the Department of Informatics, Aristotle University of Thessaloniki (Greece) in the sector of "Information and Communication Technologies in Education." He concluded his basic studies in the same department, in 2005. He has worked as a network supporter in the region of Central Macedonia. Currently, he works for a technical company. He specializes in Web design, multimedia applications development and software engineering.

Ioannis Iglezakis is currently visiting lecturer in the faculty of law of the University of Thessaloniki since 2004. He holds a PhD in legal informatics from the University of Thessaloniki, a Master's in information law from the University of Hannover, Germany, and a Master's in philosophy, sociology and history of law from the University of Thessaloniki. He became a member of the Legal Bar of the Thessaloniki in 1990. He specializes in computer law, legal informatives, economic and administrative law. He has five monographs and a contribution in the book "Cyberlaw in Hellas," published in Kluwer Law. He has published widely in Greek law journals and also in Computer Law Review International (CRi) and Computer Law and Security Report.

Cynthia Jaulneau is currently a researcher and PhD candidate of the Department of Archaeology at the Université Panthéon Sorbonne (Paris I), France. Along with professor Marion Lichardus, she has excavated in the Neolithic settlement of Kovačevo, in Bulgaria.

Athanasios Karamalis was born 1983 in Munich, Germany. After finishing his secondary education in Germany he studied computer science in Greece and earned his Bachelor's degree from the Aristotle University of Thessaloniki. His BS thesis focused on databases for multiple archaeological excavations and Internet applications. Currently, he studies informatics in the MSc program of the Technische Universität München, Germany. His research interests are databases and information systems, software engineering and computer graphics.

Konstantinos Kechagias was born in Thessaloniki, Greece, in 1966. He received the BS degree in physics in 1989, the diploma of postgraduate studies in radio engineering and electronics in 1994 and the PhD in telecommunications in 1998, all from Aristotle University of Thessaloniki, Greece. Since then, he has been a research assistant in the Radio Communications Laboratory at the Department of Physics, Aristotle University of Thessaloniki. He has worked as assistant professor at the Department of Electronics, Technological Educational Institute of Thessaloniki, Greece, until 2004. He is currently a professor of physical sciences and technology in the Second Chance School of Giannitsa, Greece, a school that offers adult education.

Theofanis G. Korlos (born in Athens, Greece, 1984) is a postgraduate student at the School of Informatics, Aristotle University of Thessaloniki, in the sector of "Information and Communication Technologies in Education." He is also member of the Greek Computer Society (2006). He concluded his basic studies at the school of Applied Informatics of University of Macedonia (Greece) in 2006. He specializes in machine translation systems, multimedia applications development and in CSCL and constructivist environments.

Panagiotis Linardis is an associate professor at the Department of Informatics, Aristotle University of Thessaloniki. His research interests focus on computer architecture, digital systems, design automation and parallel systems. Apart from his scientific interests, he is member of various ministerial committees focusing on the implementation of information and communication technologies on a nationwide level in Greece.

Dimitrios G. Margounakis (born in Athens, Greece, 1982) is a computer tutor and a scientific researcher in the field of computer music. He concluded his basic studies in informatics at the Aristotle University of Thessaloniki, Greece, in 2003. He holds a Master's certificate in business informatics at the Aristotle University of Thessaloniki (2005) and is also an owner of a music diploma in piano (2004). He is currently a PhD candidate at the Computer Science Department of the Aristotle University. He specializes in "Languages and Interfaces for Computer Music" and is also the editor of the column "Music & Technology" of the Greek magazine "Paradosi." His published research about music visualization, ancient Greek music and Internet business models in the music industry have been presented in several conferences worldwide.

Ionnis Marras is a PhD student and researcher in the field of digital signal processing. He focuses his research on projects of computer vision and image processing, working for the Artificial Intelligence and Information Analysis Laboratory (AIIA) of the Department of Informatics, Aristotle University of Thessaloniki, Greece.

George E. Palaigeorgiou holds a PhD in students-computers interactions from the Computer Science Department of the Aristotle University of Thessaloniki. He has several publications in scientific journals, such as the Journal of Computer Assisted Learning and Computers & Education, and he has participated in many funded research projects. His research interests include computer experience and attitudes, cognitive tools, participatory design and Computer ethics.

Panagiotis D. Siozos is a postgraduate student at the multimedia lab of the Computer Science Department, at the Aristotle University of Thessaloniki, holding a BS from the same department. He has extensive work experience, both as a secondary education computer science teacher and as a software developer, having taken part in several EU-funded research projects. He is currently working on a research project designing the "future classroom." His research interests include computer assisted assessment, intelligent tutoring systems, educational metadata and computer ethics.

Charilaos Thomos, was born in 1984 in Ioannina, Greece. He concluded his BSc studies in the Department of Informatics Artistotle University of Thessaloniki in 2007. During this span, he took part in many research projects, concerning the World Wide Web and its supportive use in the everyday life. Moreover, he had been the project manager, and programmer of the Microsoft Imagine Cup awarded software *.Pigeon* (ranked 2nd in Greece). His research led to various papers, journals and publications international conferences and magazines. Currently, he is a MSc student in "Web Technologies" in Southampton University. He specializes in Web user interfaces and Web application development. He maintains a popular blog concerning Web technologies and usability, "The last Web stand."

Athanasios M. Tryferidis (born in Thessaloniki, Greece, 1978) is an electrical and computer engineer, member of the Technical Chamber of Thessaloniki. He holds a position of project manager and computer software engineer in the R&D Department of MLS Multimedia S.A. – Greece, since 2002. He concluded his basic studies at the electrical and computer engineering of Aristotle University of Thessaloniki (Greece) in 2000. He holds an MSc in information systems of the University of Macedonia (Greece) since 2005. He specializes in linguistic technologies (machine translation systems, speech dictation and synthesis), software engineering and multimedia applications development.

Thrasyvoulos Tsiatsos obtained his diploma, his Master's degree and his PhD from the Computer Engineering and Informatics Department of Patras University (Greece). He is currently lecturer in the Department of Informatics of Aristotle University of Thessaloniki, as well as research member at the Research Unit 6 of Research Academic Computer Technology Institute. His research interests include computer networks, telematics, networked virtual environments, multimedia and hypermedia. More particular, he is engaged in distant education with the use of computer networks, real time protocols and networked virtual environments. He has published more than 40 papers in journals and in well known refereed conferences and he is coauthor of two books. He has participated in R&D projects such as OSYDD, RTS-GUNET, ODL-UP, VES, ODL-OTE, INVITE, EdComNet and VirRAD and he is currently involved in the projects SAPSAT (Vocational Education and Training program) and promotion of broadband in western region of Greece.

Ioannis Tsoukalas is currently the secretary general for research and technology of the Greek government. He was born in Thessaloniki in 1941. He has studied physics in the Aristotle University of Thessaloniki. He has received his PhD in solid state physics from the same university. He has committed post graduate studies in the UK (Liverpool University), Germany (Braunschweig Polytechnic University), France (Grenoble) and USA (MIT). He has published more than 100 papers and articles in books, highly ranked journals, newspapers and international conferences. He has lectured in various universities as visiting professor (England, France, Germany, USA, and Japan), and was head of the Department of Physics (1984-1989) and of the Department of Informatics (1990-1997). He has directed or participated as a member in various committees, boards and research projects, which include, among others, the EU funded project VALUE (1990-1993), "Information Society SA" (2001-2004), the Data Protection Authority in Greece (2003-2004), and the Senate of the Aristotle University in Thessaloniki (1984-1997, 2003-2004). He has served as first coordinator of the EU funded multinational project "SEEArchWeb – South Eastern Europe Archaeology Web" (2003-2004).

Index

A

active-processing assumption 300
activity theory 344
adaptability 373
adaptive content 374
AHA project 377
analytical hill shading 152
ArcGIS 131–146
ArchES 201–210
ArcIMS 132, 134–137
ArcXML 137
ARION 149, 175, 177–183, 185–199
associative processing 295
asynchronous communication 60
avatar 392, 413

B

balkanization 256
biosensors 417
blog 261–263

C

C4.5 319
cognitive architecture 295
cognitive load theory 291, 295
cognitive theory of multimedia learning 300
cognitive walkthrough method 169–170
coherence principle 304
collaborative filtering 373
collaborative geographic information systems (CGIS) 326
collaborative learning 411
collaborative spatial decision making (CSDM) 333
collaborative virtual environments (CVEs) 20, 27, 31
computer aided design (CAD) 131
concept of interactivity 410
constructionism 413
constructivism 413
constructivist 279
content-based filtering 373
content management systems 263–269
contextual approach 344–345
contiguity principle 306
cookies 373
cooperation distinction 328
copyright protection 223–225
cross-cultural e-learning 277
cross-cultural language learning 419
CSound 180

D

dandelion head 317
data mining 319, 321
delphi method 334
digital elevation model (DEM) 152
distance education 3
Drama-Merdžumekja 230–254
dual-channel assumption 300
dual-coding theory 291, 293
dual-store model 291
Dynamic Virtual Museum 158–174

E

e-journal 255

e-learning 2.0 8
e-publishing 223–229
eclectic integration 327
electronic forums, posting in 255–276
electronic guidebook research project 382
electronic publishing, legal issues 222–229
elementary modeling structure 353
ELENA project 377
epistemology 329
evaluation mechanisms 417
EVE Training Area 19, 24–27, 29
excavation terms 108
excavation units (U.F.) 88–89
expert systems (ES) 200–211
exploratorium 382
extraneous cognitive load 296

F

foreign key (FK) 112
formal e-learning 377
functional ACT-R model 291

G

genetic algorithm (GA) 319
genetic algorithm techniques 312
geographical information systems (GIS) 80–81, 129–146, 151
germane cognitive load 297
GIScience 335

H

Haiku 312, 314, 319, 322
hypermedia 58
hypertext 60, 74

I

immersive learning environments 410
influence relationship 348
informal e-learning 377
Ingenious project 380
Instructional Design 41–45
interactive digital media 420
interdependence 293
internet map server (IMS) 133–134
In Touch project 380
Intrinsic cognitive load 295

J

Java Expert System Shell (Jess) 205

K

Kithara 175
knowledge discovery 312, 314, 319
knowledge domain 329
Kovačevo 84–104

L

learner-centered approach 299
learning platform 143–145
limited-capacity assumption 300

M

machine translation (MT) 212–221
memory load 295
metacognitive strategy 298
methodical skeleton for method engineering (MEMES) 361
methodological resources assistant (MRA) 44
microthemes 30
mixed genre environments 420
mobile computer supported collaborative learning (mCSCL) 9
modality principle 303
morphology 213–214
multidimensional construct 295
Multimedia Educational Resource for Learning and Online Teaching (MERLOT) 8
multimedia pedagogy 295
multimedia principle 302
multimodel action structure 353
MySQL 158–159

N

National Center of Geographic Information and Analysis 333
Newtonian space 316
nonconventional learning 412
nonverbal system 294

O

ontology 328
OPEN process framework (OPF) 358
Open University of Catalonia (UOC) 36–48, 65–79
ORPHEUS 149, 175, 183–185

P

p-journal 255
parthenogenesis 4
passive evaluation mechanisms 417
pragmatic theory 344
prescriptive learning 419
preventive excavation 82
procedural learning 416

R

radiosity 154
rasterization 154
ray casting 154
ray tracing 154
reconstruction 147
redundancy principle 304
referential processing 294
refinement relationship 348
remote learning 413
representational processing 294
rescue excavation 82
research excavation 82
Romc Rcborn projcct 13
rule-based filtering 374

S

SAGRES system 377
sea navigation 49–50
SEEArchWeb 129, 138, 201, 212, 216–219, 255, 269–274
segmentation principle 307
semantic theory 344
Seven S's scheme 345
Shrine Educational Experience (SEE) 389–407
signaling principle 305
single-model action structure 353
smart environments 10
social modeler 200–211
solid modeling 150
spatial analysis 80
spatial decision process 327
spatially contiguous 307
spatial map 334
stratigraphy 83–84
surface modeling 150

T

taphonomy 85–86
triangulated irregular networks (TINs) 152

U

ubiquitous computing 10

V

verbal system 294
VirRAD European project 22
virtual classroom 389
Virtual Conference 19, 22–23, 26–27
virtual environments 408
virtual exhibition 257–258
virtual learning communities 50–56
virtual learning environment (VLE) 37, 39, 40
virtual museums 149
virtual reality (VR) 147
virtual reality modeling language (VRML) 159–160
virtual reconstructions 147–157
virtual settings 281
virtual worlds 12–13
Visite Plus service 381
visual interaction tool for archaeology (VITA) 155
visualisation 314, 317

W

Web-based instruction (WBI) 57–58
Web-based learning 389
Web 2.0 10–11
Web usage mining 374
working memory model 291
World Open Material project 8